# SINGER
# sewing book

# SINGER
# sewing book

Revised Edition

Jessie Hutton
Gladys Cunningham

Book design, art direction and
production supervision
Claire F. Valentine

Published by THE SINGER COMPANY

Portions of the section entitled
*The Many Faces of Knits* were
first published in a slightly different
form as chapters in the book entitled
"Singer Sewing Series for Home and Fashion."

LIBRARY OF CONGRESS CATALOG CARD NUMBER: 72-5728
ISBN 0-394-48067-8

PRINTED IN THE UNITED STATES OF AMERICA
PUBLISHED SIMULTANEOUSLY IN CANADA

SECOND EDITION

FIRST PRINTING

**You** are about to begin an adventure in creativity: you are going to sew. And you are going to sew well. You may open this book as a beginner, eager to make an absolutely smashing dress; or you may open it as an experienced sewer, determined to master tailoring. Whatever your reason, we believe the book will satisfy you, for it aims to teach the novice basic sewing skills and help the advanced seamstress perfect her ability.

Sewing today is an exciting and rewarding pastime. Whether you sew for economy or fashion, you have at your disposal superb fabrics in brilliant colors and interesting textures and weaves; you have patterns by famous designers; and you have a versatile and compliant helpmeet—your sewing machine.

Begin your adventure with a simple dress, and follow the rules explicitly. When you have mastered them, decide where you can cut corners without sacrificing good workmanship. (Many of the basic principles of sewing must never be omitted.) Each time you make a dress, select a design that is a little more difficult. Gradually work up to bound buttonholes, set-in pockets, and finally suits and coats. Follow the same principle when sewing for your home. Start with a simple curtain or bedspread and advance to draperies, slipcovers, and designs featuring decorative detail. If you are skilled in sewing, use this book to broaden your knowledge — to acquaint yourself with the new construction methods that today's fabrics and fashions demand.

Sewing is an art and, as such, demands the discipline of an art. Bring to it desire, enthusiasm, and imagination, and it will give you in return a satisfaction that is unique: the joy of creating something that is truly yours.

# Acknowledgments

Many talented persons have applied their skills and abilities
to making this book informative, useful, and attractive.

*Jacket Design*—Ralph Castenir

*Editorial*
Editorial supervision—Elna Wallace

Special thanks are due to Mary Skemp Perkins, who provided
creative editorial assistance to Miss Cunningham in the
preparation of the first edition of the SINGER Sewing Book.
Kathleen Fredrick contributed helpful editorial review.
Kathleen Coyle edited a substantial portion of *The Many
Faces of Knits.*
Proofreading—Kathleen Coyle, Mary Littell, Christine Scanlon Tracey,
Jean Crawford Weir.

*Text Illustration*
Drawings for the text were made by A. Bernasconi, Sr., Helen Disbrow,
Ralph Castenir and Derek Moore. Valerie Allen and Harold Skelton
did most of the color-separation overlays. Anthony Schmidt was most
cooperative in supplying sewing machine drawings.
Edward Hauser did most of the illustrations for *The Many
Faces of Knits,* and the color-separation overlays were
made by Myron and Joel Goetz.

*Color Photographs*
Design and execution of sewing projects—Ruth Kirkpatrick, June King,
Marjory Firrantello, Edith Paul, Barbara Ann Swenson, Maybelle Bronca,
Luci Ciancia.
Photographic and mechanical supervision—Sherman Deutsch
Photography—Rudy Muller Studio
Line drawings—Ester Larsen, Robert Flinn, Helen Disbrow.
Color-wheel mechanical—Charles Palmer
Permission to reproduce the beautiful interior photographs in the
four-color pages is gratefully acknowledged. The source is given
under each illustration.

Our appreciation is extended to the following for their generous
assistance in providing material and information—
Margaret Brindle—F. Schumacher & Company; Conso Products, Inc.;
Kirsch Company, Inc. and Man-made Fiber Products Association.

THE SINGER COMPANY

# Contents

# Color Plates

# A Place To Sew

To FIND IN SEWING the pleasure that is waiting there, you need a cheerful, comfortable, neatly organized sewing area where you can keep your sewing machine and sewing supplies. The ideal place, of course, is a room where you can leave the machine open, the pressing board up, and the work spread out when you have to stop. But most women have to compromise and sequester a corner where they can.

Much, of course, depends on the space available and the time you spend in sewing. If you sew in the evening, you may be able to find a place in the family room where you can work while the rest of the household is busy with television, a record player, homework, reading, or a hobby. A large closet might be outfitted with your sewing and pressing supplies and the dining-room table might double as your cutting table. Or, if you have a light and modern laundry area that is large enough for all your sewing equipment, you might make that your sewing studio.

Study the layout of your own house. You are sure to come up with several good ideas. If you cannot have a room of your own for sewing, make the best compromise—one that offers the most convenience to you with the least disruption to family life. Remember, if you have only a short time to sew, you do not want to spend most of it getting out your sewing and putting it away. And the pleasure possible in sewing will certainly be diminished if you have to sew in one room, press in another, and store your sewing supplies in still another.

## ARRANGING YOUR SEWING AREA

Wherever the space you have found for your sewing nook, you can, with skillful planning, arrange your sewing equipment and tools for long sewing sessions. The success with which you do this will be apparent in your sewing results.

### Sewing and Pressing Area

Place your sewing machine near a window if possible so that you may have the benefit of natural daylight. Use a stool or straight chair without arms so that you can move your own arms and body freely as you work.

Since pressing as you sew is essential, place the pressing board and other pressing equipment close to the machine. Be sure the section is well lighted. The light on your machine is focused on the stitching area; to illuminate the section for both sewing and pressing, place a floor lamp or table lamp nearby.

Keep a wastebasket handy for scraps and threads. If you keep your working area neat as you go along, you will find that you can quickly clean up when you have finished sewing.

If you have a dress form, place it near the sewing unit so that it is handy for fitting and assembling your garments. (Store it in the closet when you have finished.)

### Pattern Layout and Cutting Area

You will need a smooth surface. A bedboard, which can be supported with two bridge tables, or a ping-pong table is quite satisfactory since both are about 60 inches long. The bedboard can be stored between the mattress and box spring and the ping-pong table can be folded when not in use.

Locate the table so that you can walk around at least two sides. Use it not only when laying out the pattern and cutting but also when marking the cutout garment and when basting the sections together.

If you have to use the dining-room table, be sure to protect it with heavy brown paper or a stiff table pad. (And don't let sewing interfere with family meals.)

For fitting you will need a full-length mirror (a three-way mirror is better) so that you can inspect the fit of your garments as you try them on during various stages of construction. A mirror on a closet door solves this nicely. Other members of the family will probably appreciate it too when they are dressing.

## Storage Area

The storage area should be near the sewing area if possible. The amount of space needed will depend on your sewing supplies and tools and the kind of sewing you do. You may need two or three drawers in a chest or linen closet to store fabrics, interfacings, trimmings, patterns, and related items. A sewing basket or sewing box is ideal for the smaller items such as scissors, needles, pins, bobbins, thread, thimbles, pin cushion, snaps, tape measure, and the like. You can keep the basket on a closet shelf.

All your pressing equipment should be stored together so that it is readily accessible when you are sewing.

You should have closet space for hanging dresses, coats, and suits that are under construction and for hanging lengths of fabric that you may buy ahead and make up later. You should also keep on hand several padded hangers. As soon as darts are basted, pin the seam edges of the dress together and hang the dress on the padded hanger instead of folding or laying it on the table or bed. This will keep the fabric free of wrinkles and save you time later because you will not have to press the dress before you start working on it again.

Store sewing books on the closet shelf or in a bookcase; store fashion magazines on a shelf or in a magazine rack.

When storage space is limited, you might consider a storage wall. Secure a pegboard with hooks inside a closet door and use it for small tools such as a yardstick, tape measures, scissors, and the like.

# EQUIPMENT AND SUPPLIES

Besides a good sewing machine, your place to sew should be outfitted with many small tools and sewing supplies. They will facilitate your sewing and help you attain a professional look in your finished product. Purchase quality tools and supplies, take care of them properly, and store them so that you can quickly locate what you need when you start to sew. You will be repaid with good service, convenience, and praiseworthy sewing results.

The following are essential for good sewing:

**Thread.** Have on hand silk, mercerized, and synthetic thread in an assortment of colors for sewing, basting, and making tailor's tacks. Also have a large spool of white basting thread as well as thread that matches the color of the fabric you are sewing. (Leftover spools of thread may be used for tailor's tacks.)

**Hand-sewing needles.** Buy good-quality steel needles to be sure of perfect sewing performance. Keep them in the package to prevent rust. Needles are available in sizes from 3 to 10; the selection depends on the weight and character of the fabric. There are also many types of needles to choose from; here the selection depends on the kind of stitching you expect to do. The following will guide you:

*Straw* and *Milliner's* needles are long and slender with round eyes. Because of their length, slender shaping, and flexibility, they produce good results when multiple stitches are woven onto the needle as in basting, hand shirring, overcasting, and similar stitching.

The *Betweens* are the very short, round-eyed needles. Use them, as tailors do, to make the fine, short, sturdy, invisible stitches that are a mark of good tailoring.

The all-purpose *Sharps* are medium-length, round-eyed needles. Use them for general sewing.

*Crewel* needles are similar to the Sharps in length but have a long, oval eye for easy threading and for carrying multiple strands as in hand embroidery.

*Darners* are long needles with long, oval eyes that are designed to carry multiple strands of thread. Because of their length, many stitches can be woven onto the needle with a single stroke.

*Upholstery* needles are curved and are made for stitching into a cushioned surface. The curved needle rises out of the cushion with each stitch, thus facilitating stitching that would be difficult with a straight needle.

**Machine needles.** Keep an assortment of sizes from 9 to 18. Select the size that is suited to the weight and character of your fabric. *Fabric, Thread, Needle, and Stitch Length Chart,* page 24, gives complete information on selecting the proper needle for the fabric used. A machine needle should be changed after it has been used to stitch two or three garments since it becomes bent and burred from use.

**Pins.** Select fine, slender dressmaking pins with needlelike points and smooth blades. Always keep them separate from household pins since they will become bent and burred if used for purposes other than sewing.

**Tape measure.** Select a tape measure with metal tips, 60 inches in length, reversible, and numbered to read from each end. Linen, plastic, and plastic-coated tape measures are best because they will not stretch.

**Gauges.** Keep several 6-inch sewing and knitting gauges for measuring short distances.

**Rulers.** Have one *18-inch ruler* and a *yardstick* for measuring fabric grain line on pattern layout, and a *folding ruler* or *steel tape* for measuring windows for curtains and draperies.

**Thimbles.** Be sure that thimbles fit well, and use one in all hand sewing and basting.

**Scissors.** You will use three kinds; (1) *Bent-handle dressmaker's shears* with 6- or 7-inch blades for cutting. These shears have a small ring handle for the thumb and a large ring for two or three fingers. (2) *Light trimmers* for trimming seams and for small jobs. These have a small ring handle for the thumb and a large ring for two or three fingers. (3) *Small embroidery scissors* for cutting threads and buttonholes. Left-handed sewers should use *left-handed shears* for greater ease and accuracy in cutting.

**Pinking shears.** Use them only for finishing seam edges.

**Pressing equipment.** You will need a steam iron, sleeveboard, seamboard, ironing board, press-mitt and tailor's ham, three kinds of press cloths, sponge, paintbrush, clothes brush, and pressing pad. *Pressing as You Sew*, on page 64, explains how you will use this equipment.

**Pin cushion.** Use for needles and a few pins.

**Emery cushion.** Use it to sharpen needles and remove rust.

**Extra bobbins.** Keep a good supply on hand for your machine. Always have one bobbin wound with black thread and one with white for ready use in mending.

**Awl or stiletto.** Use it to punch holes for eyelets.

**Tweezers.** They are handy for removing tailor's tacks and short basting threads.

**Bodkin.** Have one for inserting cord in casing. It is also useful when you are forming a thread shank while sewing buttons.

**Scalloped rulers.** Get an assortment of sizes to simplify marking scallops.

**Skirt marker.** It is a must for marking hemlines.

**Embroidery hoops.** Keep two or more, 6 inches and smaller, for darning and embroidery.

**Tailor's chalk or chalk pencil.** You will need this for transferring pattern markings to some fabrics, for marking adjustments in garments, and for marking the width of hems.

**Tracing wheel and dressmaker's tracing paper.** These are useful for transferring pattern markings on interfacing, underlining, and some fabrics.

**Beeswax.** Keep a piece on hand for waxing thread before you sew buttons on coats, jackets, waistbands, and tough fabrics. It strengthens the thread and prevents snarling and snagging. Use it also for smoothing the surface of the iron.

**Staple notions.** Keep an assortment of snaps, hooks and eyes, elastic, straight seam binding, bias seam binding, and zippers.

**Buttons.** It is wise to have several cards of pearl buttons of various sizes, which can be used for blouses and children's clothes and for many mending jobs. Also, keep a box for buttons that you have removed from discarded garments; they may be used again.

Besides these supplies, a small "reference" library is strongly recommended. It should contain: 1. The instruction book for your machine. 2. This sewing book. 3. A scrap book or folder of fashion clippings and interiors from newspapers and magazines for ideas that you would love to copy or use for inspiration. Also, watch for new sewing aids to appear on notion counters from time to time. You may find some item that can help you save time and make your sewing more professional.

# Your Sewing Machine

IF YOU ARE AN EXPERIENCED SEWER, you know how valuable and essential a good sewing machine is to a well-run home. You also know how important it is to keep your machine in first-class condition. (Information on caring for your machine appears at the end of this chapter.)

In addition, you should realize that advances in fabrics have caused many changes in your stitching needs. To the familiar fabrics loomed of natural fibers—cotton, silk, wool, and linen—have been added many man-made or synthetic fibers. The blending of natural and synthetic fibers and new finishing methods have revolutionized the appearance and properties of fabrics. Double-knit, stretch, bonded, permanent press, and many other fabrics have increased the stitching range you will require from your machine.

Added to all these fabric developments are the ever fickle whims of fashion, which have changed sewing methods.

Fashion emphasis on simple, straight seams places emphasis, in turn, on the quality of stitching that holds the seam. Knit and stretch fabrics, for example, require greater seam strength and flexibility. In loosely woven and textured fabrics, the seam should be finished by machine to prevent raveling and eliminate bulk. (Machine finishing will also save time.) Underlining and lining, which are now widely used to help retain the shape of the fabric and give added body, require stitching through several layers of unlike fabrics. This makes the feeding qualities of your machine more important.

Your sewing is simplified if your machine is easy to thread and if you can adjust the needle-thread tension, pressure, and stitch length with a minimum of effort. You should be able, with minor adjustments of one or more of these, to stitch the newest fabrics without puckered seams or skipped stitches.

Sewing machine manufacturers have kept pace with fabrics, fashion sewing, and modern living. And sewing machines today offer many features that facilitate your sewing tasks.

Deluxe zig-zag machines offer finger-tip switch from straight stitching to zig-zag stitching for finishing seams, buttonholing, blindstitching hems, sewing buttons, and mending as well as doing decorative stitching. Simple zig-zag machines have limited zig-zag features and are less expensive. Straight stitch machines are designed to do excellent straight stitching and detailed sewing and to make buttonholes with the aid of a Buttonholer.

Some machines have other features that make sewing more pleasant—for example, a slant needle for maximum vision, a horizontal spool pin that permits the thread to unwind without drag from the spool, and a push-button bobbin that lets you fill the bobbin directly from the needle. Some machines will even chain stitch for easy-to-remove temporary stitching. In fact, modern sewing machines do more practical stitching jobs than you can imagine.

Many machines are light enough to carry as portables; or they can be placed in attractive cabinets that match or blend with your furniture.

The type of machine you need will depend on the extent to which you use a machine and the kind of sewing you do. Remember that your sewing machine is the main equipment in your place to sew. Arrange all sewing tools and supplies around it.

## Caring for Your Machine

Just as a good craftsman is meticulous about the care of his tools, so should you be about the care of your sewing machine. By accustoming yourself early to removing dust and lint regularly, to oiling the machine frequently, and to having it cleaned at reasonable intervals, you will be assured of a faithful sewing companion—one that will give you pleasure, satisfaction, and service. Suggestions on dusting and oiling the machine are given below; as for cleaning, your Singer Center can render this service whenever you wish.

### Removing Dust and Lint

Many fabrics, when sewed, drop lint and particles of fiber or filling. These, mixed with dust and moisture from the air, collect around the bobbin case and feed dog. Lint and dust also collect around the moving parts of the machine.

Expose the working parts by removing the throat plate and face plate (on some machines the slide plate should be removed), and brush away the dust and lint. A special lint brush and a piece of cheesecloth are ideal for this job.

### Oiling the Machine

Oiling keeps the machine running freely and prevents friction and wear. If the machine is used all day and every day, it should be oiled daily. If it is used moderately, it should be oiled every week or two. *Always remove the dust and lint before oiling the machine.* If the machine has not been used for some time, oil it the day before you start to sew to be sure that no oil will soil the fabric.

To locate the oiling points, refer to the diagram in the instruction book. Use just a drop or two of oil at each point; never drench the machine

with oil. After the machine has been thoroughly oiled, run it slowly for several minutes to allow the oil to work into the moving parts. Then remove the excess oil from the thread-handling parts with clean cheesecloth or any other lintless fabric. Polish the take-up lever, the thread guides, and the area around the needle and presser foot. Pass the cloth between the tension discs, being careful to avoid catching the take-up spring.

If you are going to give the machine an extended rest, remove the lint and oil the machine before placing it in storage. Lint absorbs moisture from the air and holds it against the metal parts, increasing the risk of rust damage in humid climates or over a long period of nonuse.

Some machines have gears that are lubricated instead of oiled; motors equipped for gear drive should be lubricated only once a year. Motors with grease tubes require lubrication every six months, however. On many machines, the motor is sealed and requires no lubrication.

Read carefully the instruction book accompanying your machine. It will tell you exactly how to care for it—whether to oil or lubricate it, where to apply the lubricant, and how often. A word of caution: always buy a high-quality oil or lubricant made specifically for sewing machines.

# What You Should Know About Color and Fabric

EAGER AS YOU MAY BE to get started on sewing, you should sit back for a moment and consider where you are going. Essential to planning a wardrobe is a knowledge of color and fabrics. This chapter will acquaint you with the fundamentals. Then you are on your own.

## ABOUT COLOR

Color can be exciting. Used wisely—and imaginatively—it will give your wardrobe a lift, contribute to the smartness of your costume, and enhance your appearance by flattering your eyes and adding a glow to your skin tone and a radiance to your hair.

Since color has a strong influence on everyday life, you should know a few facts about it before you begin. Then you can be your own watchdog. Simply explained, color has three attributes: hue, shade, and tint. Hue denotes the pure or "true" color, which may be described as red, yellow, or blue, or intermediates between two of these, as orange, green, and violet. If you add varying degrees of grey or black to the true color, you get a *shade* or a color value darker than the true color; if you add varying degrees of white, you get a *tint* or a color value lighter than the true color. The color wheel, plate 17 opposite page 340, illustrates the principle, and the text on page 338 tells you many of the rules of color.

### Selecting the Right Color

One season's fashions may be a splash of color, another's may be subdued. Although it is easy to be carried away by a vivid, brilliant, or new shade, you should resist the temptation until you have satisfied yourself that the color is right for you. Put personal preferences aside for a moment. Here are some tests you can apply in selecting a color:

*Is the color becoming to you?* It should compliment your skin tone and bring out the beauty of your hair and eyes. Let your mirror be the judge. At the fabric counter, drape the fabric over one shoulder; study yourself in both natural and artificial light to see what the color does for you. Or, buy a package of assorted colors of construction paper. Round out a section to fit your neckline and try different colors against your face to determine which are the most becoming. Make a memo of those colors in your sewing notebook, or on the color bibs.

*Is the color flattering to your figure?* Light, bright, or vivid shades of almost any color tend to make the figure appear larger or heavier; on the other hand, darker, subdued tones of the same color have a slenderizing effect. This does not mean that if you are stocky or overweight, you must always choose dull colors. Rather, you should select fashion lines that minimize your figure.

Remember, too, that the chic black dress is always in fashion and certainly is a must for almost every woman's wardrobe. It can be worn all year round and changed or accented with colorful jewelry or a scarf.

### Achieving Color Harmony

Color harmony is important to the attractiveness of your costume and the rules for achieving it are explicit.

Of the many types of color harmony, the best known is perhaps the monochromatic, which is the use of various shades and tints of one color.

You can also obtain interesting effects by combining different textures, weaves, and fibers of the same color. Before combining them, however, be sure that they look well together and are comparable in weight. Never mix two prints, two plaids, or a print and plaid. Also make sure that your repetition of one color does not produce a monotonous effect. If it does, try adding a slight or decided contrast.

Combining contrasting colors is another way of achieving a richness in your ensemble. But watch out! Two colors may give a pleasing contrast; three or more may introduce complications that destroy the harmony you are seeking. A sharp contrast in color is usually effective; however, use the strong, contrasting color sparingly. Complementary colors lie opposite each other in the color wheel, Plate 17. Combining two of these colors produces a striking effect with proper balance of color, and a negative effect with improper balance.

These, then, are the rules. But like all rules, fashion occasionally breaks them and combines clashing colors and prints. In this she is being true to her role of shocking the eye once in a while and thus jolting her followers into a new awareness of the beauty and possibilities of color.

To use such shocks skillfully, however, first learn the rules. Then you are at liberty to break them just as the modern painter does when he splashes color on a canvas, seemingly heedless of line and form.

### A Word about Accessories and Cosmetics

Accessories play a major role in color harmony. Rather than have all your accessories of a contrasting color, choose shoes and handbag to match, or hat and gloves to match, or hat, shoes, and handbag to match. Vivid colors are often more dramatic when worn with conventional black accessories.

If a limited budget prevents you from having several sets of accessories, the wise thing is to choose a color for your coat and accessories which will blend with the other colors you are apt to choose for dresses and suits. This basic color will enable you to achieve color harmony without exceeding your budget. It will also give continuity to your wardrobe.

About cosmetics: Train yourself to select them as carefully as the colors you wear, for they can kill an otherwise harmonious appearance. As skin tone and fashion colors change, so should make-up. Manufacturers of cosmetics keep pace with fashion colors; beauty consultants at cosmetic counters know how to match shades of cosmetics with skin tone and colors. Do not hesitate to seek their advice at regular intervals.

Always remember this: If you learn to use color to your best advantage in every way, friends will compliment you and not the dress.

## ABOUT FABRICS

You cannot sew successfully without a knowledge of fabrics, for fashion is found in fabrics as surely as it is found in pattern designs. Fabrics are available in a variety of weaves, textures, and colors. Often they are so exciting that you must choose a simple pattern design that will not detract from their beauty.

Unlike choosing a color, however, choosing a fabric calls for more than your eye or common sense to guide you. You must know whether the fabric is suitable for your use, whether its durability justifies your expenditure of time and money, whether its upkeep is practical for your situation.

Without being overly technical, this section will give you some fabric facts that will help you select the fabric best suited to your requirements.

### Fibers

Fabric is made up of either *natural fibers* or *man-made fibers* that are spun into yarns and woven together on various types of looms. The natural fibers are *cotton, linen, silk,* and *wool.* Cotton fiber is made from the cotton plant, linen fiber from the flax plant, silk fiber from the cocoon of the silkworm, and wool fiber from the fleece of sheep or lamb or the hair of certain goats or camels.

*Man-made fibers* are those synthetic or manufactured fibers that are produced through chemistry. Their list is long and, since new types appear on the market almost every year, never quite complete. The chart that follows gives the generic classification, the trade-mark name, and the manufacturer of some of the more familiar fibers or yarns. (The manufacturers listed produce only the basic fibers; they do not make the fabric containing these fibers.)

It is wise to make a note of the fiber content of the fabrics you buy and file it for future reference. You should know what special qualities or service you may expect from the fabric and whether it is sunfast, tubfast, or preshrunk. Look for this information on the label or hang-tag. It is important in the care and handling of the fabric, particularly in dry cleaning or washing and in pressing. Also, stitching techniques and the type of thread used depend to a large extent on the fabric—and the behavior of the fabric depends on the fibers and the finish.

# MAN-MADE FIBERS OR YARNS
## (Synthetics)

| Generic Classification | Trademark Name | Manufacturer or Source |
|---|---|---|
| **ACETATE** | ACELE | E. I. duPont de Nemours & Co., Inc. |
| | ARNEL | Celanese Fiber Company, Division of Celanese Corporation |
| | AVISCO | FMC Corporation, American Viscose Division |
| | CELANESE | Celanese Fiber Company, Division of Celanese Corporation |
| | CELAPERM | Celanese Fiber Company, Division of Celanese Corporation |
| | CHROMSPUN | Eastman Kodak Company, Tennessee Eastman Company Division |
| | ESTRON | Eastman Kodak Company, Tennessee Eastman Company Division |
| **ACRYLIC** | ACRILAN | Monsanto Company, Textiles Division |
| | CRESLAN | American Cyanamid Company, Fibers Division |
| | ORLON | E. I. duPont de Nemours & Co., Inc. |
| | ZEFKROME | Dow Badische Company |
| | ZEFRAN | Dow Badische Company |
| **GLASS FIBER** | BETA | Owens-Corning Fiberglas Corporation |
| | FIBERGLAS | Owens-Corning Fiberglas Corporation |
| | PPG FIBER GLASS | PPG Industries, Inc. Fiber Glass Division |
| | UNIFAB | Ferro Corporation Fiber Glass Division |
| **METALLIC YARNS** | CHROMEFLEX | Metal Film Company, Inc. |
| | FAIRTEX | Fairtex Corporation |
| | LUREX | Dow Badische Company |
| | MALORA | Malina Company, Inc. |
| | METLON | Metlon Corporation |
| | MYLAR | E. I. duPont de Nemours & Co., Inc. |
| **MODACRYLIC** | DYNEL | Union Carbide Corporation Fibers and Fabric Division |
| | VEREL | Eastman Kodak Company, Tennessee Eastman Company Division |
| **NYLON** | ANTRON | E. I. duPont de Nemours & Co., Inc. |
| | CELANESE | Fiber Industries, Inc., Marketed by Celanese Fibers Company, Division of Celanese Corporation |
| | CHEMSTRAND | Monsanto Company, Textiles Division |
| | BLUE C NYLON | Monsanto Company, Textiles Division |
| | CAPROLAN | Allied Chemical Corporation, Fibers Division |
| | ENKA | American Enka Corporation |
| | QIANA | E. I. duPont de Nemours & Co., Inc. |

| Generic Classification | Trademark Name | Manufacturer or Source |
|---|---|---|
| **OLEFIN** | DPL | Dawbarn Division, W. R. Grace & Company |
| | HERCULAN | Hercules Incorporated, Fibers & Film Department |
| | VECTRA | Vectra Company, Division of The National Plastic Products Company, Inc. |
| **POLYESTER** | AVLIN | FMC Corporation, American Viscose Division |
| | BLUE C | Monsanto Company, Textiles Division |
| | DACRON | E. I. duPont de Nemours & Co., Inc. |
| | FORTREL | Fiber Industries, Inc., Marketed by Celanese Fibers Company, Division of Celanese Corporation |
| | KODEL | Eastman Kodak Company, Tennessee Eastman Company Division |
| | VYCRON | Beaunit Corporation, Beaunit Fibers Division |
| | IRC | Midland-Ross Corporation, IRC Fabrics Division |
| **RAYON** | AVISCO | FMC Corporation, American Viscose Division |
| | AVRIL | FMC Corporation, American Viscose Division |
| | AVRON | FMC Corporation, American Viscose Division |
| | BEMBERG | Beaunit Corporation, Beaunit Fibers Division |
| | COLORAY | Courtaulds North America, Inc. |
| | CUPIONI | Beaunit Corporation, Beaunit Fibers Division |
| | ENGLO | American Enka Corporation |
| | ENKA | American Enka Corporation |
| | ENKROME | American Enka Corporation |
| | FIBRO | Courtaulds North America, Inc. |
| | FORTISAN | Celanese Fiber Company, Division of Celanese Corporation |
| | JETSPUN | American Enka Corporation |
| | NUB-LITE | Beaunit Corporation, Beaunit Fibers Division |
| | PURILON | FMC Corporation, American Viscose Division |
| | RAYFLEX | FMC Corporation, American Viscose Division |
| | STRAWN | Midland-Ross Corporation, IRC Fibers Division |
| | ZANTREL | American Enka Corporation |
| **SARAN** | ROVANA | Dow Badische Company |
| | VECTRA | Vectra Company, Division of The National Plastic Products Company, Inc. |
| | LUS-TRUS | Southern Lus-Trus Corporation |
| **SPANDEX** | LYCRA | E. I. duPont de Nemours & Co., Inc. |
| | VYRENE | UniRoyal Fiber and Textile Division of UniRoyal, Inc. |
| **VINYON** | AVISCO | FMC Corporation, American Viscose Division |

## Yarns

Next, fibers are spun into yarns. Yarns may be made from short or "staple" fibers or from long or "filament" fibers, and the construction may be simple or complex. One of the natural fibers or one of the man-made fibers may be used alone; or two or more fibers may be blended or mixed to give durability and beauty to the fabric or to facilitate the manufacturing process. The number and size of the fibers, the tightness of the twist, the roughness or smoothness of the yarn are some of the many factors that determine the characteristics of the fabric made from the yarn.

Processing techniques can be varied to produce novelty yarns such as bouclé, ratiné, nub, seed, slub, spiral or corkscrew, or looped, which are unusual in texture or appearance or both. Textured yarns may be formed from man-made fibers. Through certain processing techniques the filaments are coiled, crimped, curled, or looped. These yarns are called textured, bulk, or stretch yarns.

## Woven Fabrics

Each fabric begins with the yarn threaded lengthwise on the weaving loom. Next, the filler yarn is woven crosswise, over and under the lengthwise threads. The lengthwise yarn is called the "warp," and the crosswise or filler yarn is called the "weft" (old term "woof"). The extreme outside finished edges, which are parallel to the lengthwise yarns, are called "selvage." These woven threads form the true lengthwise and crosswise grains of the fabric.

By varying the number of yarns on a loom, it is possible to produce many different weaves and achieve interesting textures and effects. It is often difficult to distinguish one man-made fiber from another or from the natural fibers because the weaves are so much alike. Rayon may look like silk, cotton may look like wool tweed. The weave of the fabric plays a greater part in determining the appearance of the final product than fiber or finish.

### Familiar Types of Weaves

Here is a description of the common types of weaves that you may be using in your sewing. These standard weaves can be varied to produce many interesting effects.

*Plain weave.* In this, the simplest and most common of all weaves, the horizontal threads (weft or filler) pass alternately over and under successive vertical threads (warp). Muslin and taffeta are examples. Variations are the basket weave and the rib weave.

*Twill weave.* This is more closely woven than a plain weave. In it, the warp and filler threads are interlaced to form a diagonal ridge or rib on the face of the fabric. Gabardine is an example. Fancy designs can also be produced; the herringbone is a common variation.

*Satin weave.* Threads are interlaced at irregular intervals, with one set of threads floating over the opposite set of threads. The floats lie parallel to each other thus forming a smooth, lustrous finish. Cotton sateen and damask are examples.

*Leno weave.* This is a porous, open-looking weave used to produce lightweight, gauzy fabrics—for example, marquisette.

**Jacquard weave.** This is an intricate, figured weave made on a Jacquard loom. Examples are damasks, brocades, and tapestries.

**Dobby weave.** This weave is produced by placing a dobby attachment on the loom. It is simpler and less expensive than the Jacquard weave and consists of small, geometric designs that are repeated frequently throughout the fabric.

**Double-cloth weave.** More than one set of warp and filler yarns are used in weaving to produce a fabric with two distinct faces—for example, double damask.

**Pile weave.** Three sets of yarns are interlaced in such a manner that the third set forms cut loops that stand up densely on the surface. Examples are velvet, velveteen, corduroy, and plush. An exception is terry cloth, which has uncut loops, usually on both sides of the fabric.

## Finishes

Many fabrics are given a "finish" after they are woven to increase their body, to prevent shrinkage (sanforized) or wrinkling (pre-cured or permanent-press type), to impart crispness to the surface, or to make them wash-and-wear, water repellent, stain resistant, mothproof, drip-dry, or crease resistant. It is unnecessary—and almost impossible—to list the many finishes manufacturers are able to produce; however, they can be described as dull, shiny, stretch, rough, soft, smooth, coarse, fine, lustrous, hard, laminated, or napped.

**Napped fabrics** (such as wool broadcloth, duvetyn, doeskin, and flannel) have fuzzy or hairlike fibers lying in one direction. This effect is achieved in the finishing process by a revolving brush that is used to raise the fibers of the cloth to the surface.

## Stretch Fabrics

Stretch fabrics are woven fabrics that have been made to "give" with the body and then recover their normal dimensions. Do not confuse them with knit fabrics.

Stretch characteristic can be given to classic fabrics such as denim, tweed, gabardine, twill, corduroy, seersucker, batiste, and broadcloth, as well as to many of the newer fabrics. It can also be given to all-cotton fabrics; to blends with natural fibers, rayon, or acetate; or to all wool.

The amount of stretch a fabric will deliver varies; so do the processes of achieving stretch.

There are three kinds of stretch fabrics:

*Lengthwise* (warp) stretch, which is recommended for pants and slacks.

*Crosswise* (filling) stretch, which is used for blouses, shirts, jackets, coats, sport dresses, skirts, and shorts.

*Lengthwise and crosswise, or two-way stretch,* which is used mostly in swimsuits.

Some of the stretch fabrics are woven to look the same lengthwise as crosswise even though they stretch only in one direction. They can be used in any garment. Always examine the fabric carefully before purchasing it to be sure that the stretch goes in the direction you want. See page 218.

Stretch fabrics can be given wash-and-wear or water-repellent qualities.

## Knit Fabrics

Knit fabrics are made of interlocking loops of yarn. There are two types of knit construction, warp and weft knits.

**Warp knits,** which are made on flat-bed machines, are generally tighter, flatter, and less elastic than weft knits. In warp knitting, multiple yarns (all part of a single system of yarns) run vertically and parallel to each other. The fabric is constructed by manipulating all of these warp yarns at the same time into loops that are interconnected. Tricot and raschel are common types.

**Weft knits,** which are made on either circular or flat-bed knitting machines, are constructed in much the same way as hand knits, with one yarn at a time running in a horizontal direction. The most familiar types are jersey, rib knits, double knits, and jacquards. See *The Many Faces of Knits,* page 417.

## Blends and Combinations

Techniques of blending and combining fibers have revolutionized the fabric world and simplified in many ways the homemaker's life. Although most consumers apply the term "blend" to any fabric containing more than one kind of fiber or yarn, there is a difference between blends and combinations. *Blended fabrics* are made of yarns in which

11

two or more fibers have been mixed before spinning; the yarns may be used either as warp or filler or as both. *Combination fabrics* are made by combining different yarns, each of a single fiber, in the weaving process. In other words, the warp yarn may be of one fiber and the filler of another. Examples are silk/wool; silk/cotton/linen (two or more natural fibers); cotton/Dacron polyester (natural and man-made fibers); or Orlon acrylic/rayon/nylon (two or more man-made fibers).

## Bonded and Laminated Fabrics

Like blends and combinations, the terms "bonded" and "laminated" are often used interchangeably by the shopper. And they are similar in one respect—both describe fabrics that are made of two layers.

In *bonded* fabrics, two layers of fabric are permanently joined either by an adhesive or by a thin layer of urethane foam, which is heat-set to form a bond.

Although almost any fabrics can be bonded, the most common bonds are of lining and face fabric. Acetate tricot seems to be favored for the lining; the face fabric may be wool, synthetic, a blend of wool and man-made fibers, loopy tweed with a mohair look, and knits. Bonding makes lace suitable for a tailored costume; the bonded lining adds stability to the fabric and prevents stretching.

Bonded fabrics are appropriate for dresses, coats, suits, and sportswear. See page 220.

In *laminated* fabrics a backing of synthetic *foam* is bonded, or heat-set, to adhere permanently to a *face fabric*. Laminates have warmth without weight and require no interfacing; however, they should be lined to protect the foam backing. You will find laminated wool, jersey, cotton, and synthetic fabrics that are appropriate for jackets, coats, sportswear, rainwear, children's wear, and coat linings. Most of them can be washed or dry-cleaned. See page 221.

## Nonwoven Fabrics

Nonwoven fabrics have no grain. They are made by pressing fibers together. Examples are felt, plastic film, Pellon, Keyback, and Interlon.

## Selecting Fabric

The judgment and taste you exercise in coordinating the fabric with the pattern can determine the success of your finished product. On the back of the pattern envelope you will find a list of fabrics appropriate for the design. This is a good guide if you are in doubt.

Suits and tailored dresses require firm fabrics with body. Dresses with shirring, draping, or gathers require soft fabrics.

Remember too that a print, plaid, or design should be in proportion to your figure. A small figure should not wear large stripes, plaids, or prints. A large figure may wear large prints; however, a large plaid will emphasize figure proportions. Narrow stripes will make the figure appear taller, broad stripes will make it appear shorter. Large prints and plaids on the tall, thin figure will break the height.

The finish of the fabric also affects the appearance of your figure. For slimness, choose fabrics with a smooth, dull finish. The bulk of heavyweight or rough-finished fabrics makes the figure look larger. If handled with too much fullness, such fabrics may overpower a small figure and add weight to a full figure; simply handled they may be very flattering.

The following list will help you select suitable fabrics for various garments.

| Daytime and Tailored Dresses | |
|---|---|
| Jersey | Corduroy |
| Silk | Velveteen |
| Gingham | Linen |
| Broadcloth | Surah |
| Dotted Swiss | Barathea |
| Crepe—Silk or Rayon | Shantung |
| Wool Crepe | Cotton |
| Pima Cotton | Honan |
| Raw Silk | Piqué |
| Heavy Sheers | Tie Silk |
| Cotton and Dacron | Faille |
| Blend | Double Knit |

| Soft, Draped Dresses | |
|---|---|
| Sheer Woolens | Chiffon |
| Soft Silk | Surah |
| Jersey | Barathea |
| Voile | Lace |
| Nylon | Velvet |
| Blends or Combinations | |
| of Natural and Synthetic Fibers | |

Flannel

Denim

Chintz

Sailcloth

Cottons

Woolens

Corduroy

Velveteen

Gingham

Seersucker

Polished Cotton

Stretch Fabrics

Bonded Fabrics

Madras

Blends or Combinations
of Natural and Synthetic Fibers

| *Suits* | *Dresses* |
|---|---|
| Moiré | Taffeta |
| Peau de Soie | Brocade |
| Satin | Faille Taffeta |
| Taffeta | Peau de Soie |
| Ottoman | Heavy or Firm Lace |
| Brocade | Velvet |
| Bengaline | Velveteen |
| Velvet | Matelassé |
| Velveteen | Metallic |
| Metallic | Surah |
| Matelassé | Chiffon |
| Wild or Raw Silk | Moiré |

| | |
|---|---|
| Lace | Peau de Soie |
| Chiffon | Dotted Swiss |
| Taffeta | Organdy |
| Velvet | Net |
| Velveteen | Brocade |
| Piqué | Metallic |
| Cottons | Surah |
| Sheers | Moiré |
| Silks | Satin |

| | |
|---|---|
| Linen | Tussah |
| Faille | Heavy Cottons |
| Silk and Wool Blends | Corduroy |
| or Combinations | Duvetyn |
| Silk and Cotton Blends | Seersucker |
| or Combinations | Double Knit |
| Lightweight Wool | |

Woolens—
    Medium or Heavyweight

| | |
|---|---|
| Tweed | Ottoman |
| Wool Broadcloth | Douppioni |
| Twill | Wild or Raw Silk |
| Flannel | Gabardine |
| Linen | Glen Checks |
| Heavy Cottons | Tussah |
| Silk and Wool Blends | Bengaline |
| or Combinations | Double Knit |

| | |
|---|---|
| Coating | Corduroy |
| Wool Broadcloth | Velveteen |
| Flannel | Suede Cloth |
| Camel's Hair | Fur Fabric |
| Vicuna | Brocade |
| Cashmere | Jersey Coating |
| Silk Faille | Worsted |
| Ottoman | Tweed |
| Nubbed Wool | Douppioni |

## Fabric Width

Fabric widths vary greatly, and before buying a fabric you should refer to the back of the pattern envelope to see how many yards you will need of the fabric width you have chosen. Linens, velveteens, and corduroys are 36 inches wide; cottons, 36 to 39 inches; silks and synthetics usually 39 to 42 inches; wools, 54 to 60 inches; and felts, 36 to 70 inches. Jersey is usually circular and about 56 inches all around; double knit is a flat knit about 54 inches wide. Imported silks are often only 27 inches wide and imported cottons may be 50 inches wide. Most interfacings are from 25 to 50 inches wide.

## Know the Right Side of the Fabric

Simple as it may seem, knowing the right side of the fabric can be tricky.

In satins and polished cottons, the lustrous face is on the right side; in pile and napped fabrics, the longer threads or pile is on the right side. Cottons and linens are usually folded right side out. The weave of many fabrics will help you identify the right side; so will the selvage, which is smoother on the right side than on the wrong. Often you must examine the selvage closely, however, to detect the "smoother" side. Many cottons, plaids, and solid colors can be used on both sides.

## Grain Lines

In any sewing you do, you must consider the grain lines of the fabric because they have a direct influence on the way the garment fits and hangs.

The *lengthwise grain* of the fabric is the thread parallel to the selvage and is known as the "warp" thread in weaving. It is marked on all pattern sections and must be observed when laying and cutting any garment or article.

The *crosswise grain* is at a right angle to the lengthwise grain; it runs from selvage to selvage and is known as the "weft" thread in weaving. In most fabrics there is some "give" in the crosswise grain, but very little in the lengthwise grain.

The *true bias* of the fabric is the diagonal line formed by folding the lengthwise grain parallel to the crosswise grain. The maximum amount of "give" in any fabric is found in the true bias.

## Preparing the Fabric for Cutting

Here you are concerned with three questions:
1. Are the fabric ends (crosswise grain) straight?
2. Does the lengthwise grain need straightening?
3. Has the fabric been shrunk?

### Straightening Fabric Grain

In the manufacturing process—perhaps during finishing, printing, or rolling—some fabrics are pulled "off grain," and you must straighten them before cutting the garment so that the grain lines are correct; otherwise your garment will not fit and hang as it should.

*To straighten the fabric ends,* find the crosswise grain of the fabric as follows:

—Snip through the selvage edge with scissors.

—With the fingers, grasp one thread that runs across the weave.

—Pull it gently, allowing the fabric to gather on the thread.

—Cut carefully along this pulled thread only as far as you can follow it clearly.

—Grasp it again (or the one next to it) in your fingers and repeat the pulling and cutting until you have reached the other selvage.

Some fabrics will tear easily and you can clip the selvage and tear quickly across from selvage to selvage to straighten the ends. However, drawing a thread is preferred because tearing sometimes pulls the fabric "off grain."

*To determine whether the fabric grain needs straightening,* place the fabric on a flat surface and fold it with the selvages together. Pin the edges together along the straightened end. If the fabric lies flat when the selvages are together, the two grains are at a right angle and need no further attention. If not, the fabric must be straightened.

*To straighten the fabric grain is simple.*

—First, straighten the ends as explained above.

—Then, gently pull the fabric on the true bias (as illustrated at the top of opposite page) and gradually work down the full length of the fabric.

—Repeat along the length, if necessary.

Pressing with steam is helpful in straightening some fabrics; or you may have to dampen the fabric and then straighten it.

wearing, hanging, or pressing.

If a print or plaid is finished "off grain," the design will not match at the seamline when the garment is cut on the true grain. Examine the fabric closely before making a purchase. If it is printed "off grain," do not buy it.

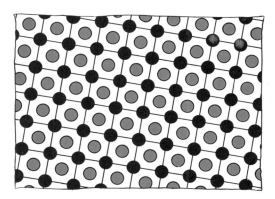

*If dampening is necessary,* proceed as follows:

*On cottons and linens,* use a damp sponge to moisten the fabric, then pull gently.

*On wools,* place a wet sheet over the fabric and leave it long enough to moisten the wool (about two or three hours). Be sure that the fabric lies flat and that there are no wrinkles in either the fabric or the sheet. Pull gently to straighten the fabric.

*If fabrics such as chintz, polished cotton, and those with crush-resistant finish cannot be straightened because of their finish,* square off the crosswise grain with a ruler. Place the fabric flat on a table with the selvage parallel to the side of the table. Lay a ruler across the cut end of the fabric so that it forms a right angle with the selvage, and draw a line with chalk from selvage to selvage; then cut on this line. Use only the lengthwise grain as a guide when cutting the garment. These fabrics are quite satisfactory as they will not lose their shape in

### Checking the Fabric for Shrinkage

Most fabrics are preshrunk and information to that effect usually appears on the descriptive hangtag or on the selvage. Look for the labels "preshrunk," "Sanforized," or, in the case of fine wools, "ready for the needle" or "sponged."

If one of them is used, it means that the fabric will not shrink more than 1 inch per yard; if you fail to find any information, ask the saleswoman. Fabrics that have not been preshrunk must be shrunk before cutting except wool crepe and silk crepe.

*To shrink a fabric,* clip the edge every 2 or 3 inches along each selvage. If the selvage is not cut, it will draw up in the shrinking process.

For *cottons, linens,* and other *washable fabrics,* open the fabric its full width and form deep folds (about 18 inches) on the crosswise grain. Place the fabric in the bathtub, cover it with lukewarm water, and leave it immersed for an hour. At the end of an hour, drain the water from the tub. Then press the water out of the fabric with your hands. (Do not wring or wrinkle the fabric.) Hang the fabric lengthwise over the shower rod or the clothesline. Be sure that it is straight and smooth. Remove as much water as you can with a towel. Before the fabric is completely dry, press it on the wrong side. Glide the iron with the lengthwise grain. Press out the center fold.

If you are uncertain about the necessity of shrinking washable fabrics, make a test: Cut a swatch on the true lengthwise and crosswise grains and make a note of its length and width. Shrink the swatch as instructed above. After pressing, measure again. If the swatch is smaller than the original size, you will have to shrink the fabric.

For *woolens,* fold the fabric lengthwise on the straight grain and place it between the folds of a wet sheet. Fold on the crosswise grain in deep folds. Avoid wrinkles in the fabric and wet sheet. Cover the folded sheet with a towel so that the top section will not dry, and leave for eight or ten hours. Then remove the sheet and spread the fabric

on a flat surface to dry. Be sure that the grains are straight. When dry, press on the wrong side with a press cloth or cheesecloth between the fabric and iron. Press out the center fold.

(Woolens can also be shrunk by a dry cleaner if they are not "ready for the needle."

Be sure to shrink *woven interfacings* that are not preshrunk as well as *belting* and *grosgrain* ribbon that will be used in washable garments. Follow the immersion method described above.

## Interfacings

Interfacing is a third thickness of a carefully selected fabric that is cut in the same shape as the section interfaced and placed between the facing and garment section.

An interfacing adds body to the collars, cuffs, facings and peplums of dresses, blouses, suits, and coats, and it adds strength to the areas around buttonholes and buttons. It is also used to mold and hold the shape in certain sections of the garment. It gives a professional look to anything that is well made.

Pattern envelopes usually include a separate pattern for the interfacing or instruct you to cut it the same as the garment section. Woven interfacing, which has a lengthwise and crosswise grain, must be cut with the same grain as the garment; non-woven interfacing has no grain and can be cut with the pattern laid in any direction.

Interfacing is available in a variety of textures and weights and should be selected with care. Consider the firmness and weight of the fabric to be interfaced as well as the style of the garment. Lay the interfacing between two layers of your fabric and manipulate the materials so that you can judge the final effect. Before buying interfacing, make sure that:

—It can be washed or dry-cleaned as the rest of the garment.

—The weight is appropriate for the fabric.

—The quality of the interfacing equals the quality of the garment fabric.

The following table shows you the variety of interfacing fabrics that are on the market. Use it as a guide only in shopping; you should examine the interfacing carefully before you buy, for several types may be correct for your garment, depending on the effect desired. Note that one fabric is missing from the list—that is self fabric, which is frequently used as interfacing, especially if the garment fabric is sheer.

# FABRICS FOR INTERFACINGS

| FABRIC | TYPE | DESCRIPTION | COLORS | WEIGHT | USE | CARE |
|---|---|---|---|---|---|---|
| Armo[1]† "Acro" | Woven | Hair canvas | Ecru | Medium | Washable dresses, suits, and coats | Machine wash-and-wear; dry-cleanable |
| Armo[1] P-27 | Woven | Hair canvas | Natural | Light | Tailored dresses and lightweight suits | Dry-clean only |
| Armo[1] P-17 | Woven | Hair canvas | Natural | Medium | Suits and medium-weight coats | Dry-clean only |
| Armo[1] P-20 | Woven | Hair canvas | Natural | Heavy | Heavy suits and coats; also under-lining for bouffant jackets and coats | Dry-clean only |
| Armo[1] "Fino" | Woven | High-quality worsted hair canvas | Natural | Medium | Light- and medium-weight suits and coats | Dry-clean only |
| Armo[1] "Finolight" | Woven | High-quality hair canvas | Sand | Light | Silk and lightweight wool suits | Dry-clean only |
| Instant Armo[1] P-93 | Woven | Hair canvas iron-on | Natural | Heavy | Heavy suits and coats | Dry-clean only |
| Instant Armo[1] P-94 | Woven | Worsted hair canvas iron-on | Natural | Medium | Medium- and heavy-weight suits and coats | Dry-clean only |
| Batiste | Woven | Fine cotton | All colors | Light | Soft silk, cotton, and linen dresses and blouses | Washable; shrink before using |
| Bravo[2] | Woven | Canvas | Natural, white | Medium | Silk and light- to-medium-weight wool suits and coats | Dry-clean only |
| Bravo-Set[2] | Woven | Canvas | Eggshell | Light | Suits and coats made of silk, light- and medium-weight wools, and blends | Washable; dry-cleanable |
| Capri[3] | Woven | Closely woven | Black, white | Light—soft finish; Light—crisp finish | Soft silk and cotton dresses and blouses. Medium-weight fabric for firm shapes | Washable; dry-cleanable |
| Everflex[3] | Woven | Mesh | Black, white, natural | Medium | Silk and medium-weight wool suits | Washable; dry-cleanable |
| Formite [Z] [1] | Woven | Sheer canvas | Black, white, natural | Medium | Dress-weight fabrics, knits, and sportswear | Washable; dry-cleanable |

†Numbers indicate owners of trademark names, as shown on page 19.

(continued on following page)

| FABRIC | TYPE | DESCRIPTION | COLORS | WEIGHT | USE | CARE |
|---|---|---|---|---|---|---|
| Hymo[2]† "Regular" | Woven | Hair canvas | Natural | Medium | Suits and medium-weight wool coats | Dry-clean only |
| Hymo[2] "Special" | Woven | Hair canvas | Natural | Heavy | Medium-to-heavy wool suits and coats | Dry-clean only |
| Interlon[2] | Non-woven | Has no grain line | Black, white | Light | Soft, fluid shapes | Washable; dry-cleanable |
| | | | | Regular | Soft, yet firm shapes | |
| | | | | Heavy | Heavy fabrics—firmly molded shapes | |
| Keybak[3] | Non-woven | Visibly porous | Black, white | Light | Soft, fluid shapes | Washable; dry-cleanable |
| | | | | Medium | Soft, yet firm shapes | |
| | | | | Heavy | Heavy fabrics—firmly molded shapes | |
| Keybak[3] Hot Iron | Non-woven | Visibly porous | Black, white | Medium | To reinforce small areas | Washable; dry-cleanable |
| Kyrel[4] | Non-woven | Has no grain line | Black, white | Light | Lightweight dresses and blouses | Drip-dry; dry-cleanable |
| Adheron Kyrel[4] | Non-woven | Iron-on | Black, white | Light | To reinforce small areas | Drip-dry; dry-cleanable |
| All Bias Kyrel[4] | Non-woven | Has "give" in any direction | Black, white | Very light | Loosely woven or stretch fabrics where shape is needed | Drip-dry; dry-cleanable |
| Lawn | Woven | Semi-sheer | All colors | Light | Soft, lightweight dresses and blouses | Washable; shrink before using |
| Marquisette | Woven | Mesh | All colors | Very light | To add body to delicate fabrics | Washable; dry-cleanable; shrink before using |
| Muslin | Woven | Medium; heavy | White or unbleached | Medium | Cotton dresses and blouses, as well as sleeve hems and bottom hems of suits and coats | Washable; dry-cleanable; shrink before using |
| Organza | Woven | Sheer silk | All colors | Very light | To add body to delicate chiffons and other sheer fabrics | Dry-cleanable |
| Pelomite[5] | Non-woven | Iron-on | Black, white | Light | To reinforce small areas | Washable; dry-cleanable |

†Numbers indicate owners of trademark names, as shown on page 19.

(continued on following page)

| FABRIC | TYPE | DESCRIPTION | COLORS | WEIGHT | USE | CARE |
|---|---|---|---|---|---|---|
| Regular Pellon[5] | Non-woven | Has no grain line | Black, white | Light | Light, soft shapes | Machine wash-and-wear; dry-cleanable |
| | | | | Medium | Light, yet firm shapes | |
| | | | | Heavy | Firmly woven shapes | |
| "All Bias" Pellon[5] | Non-woven | Has "give" in any direction | Black, white | Light, Medium | Loosely woven or stretch fabrics where shape is needed | Wash-and-wear; dry-cleanable |
| Poplin | Woven | Dress fabric | All colors | Medium | Soft, yet firm shapes for cottons and linens | Washable; shrink before using |
| Steflex[2] "All-Purpose" | Woven | Iron-on | Black, white | Medium | To reinforce small areas | Washable; dry-cleanable |
| Staflex-[2] for-Wools | Woven | Canvas iron-on | Natural, white | Medium | Medium- and heavy-weight wool suits and coats | Dry-clean only |
| Sta-Shape[2] SS/50 | Woven | Tailor's canvas | Black, white, natural | Light | Medium-weight suits and coats; also underlining for bouffant jackets and coats | Washable; dry-cleanable |
| Sta-Shape[2] SS/65 | Woven | Canvas | Natural | Medium | Medium-weight suits, coats, and tailored dresses | Dry-clean only |
| Sta-Shape[2] SS/77 | Woven | Hair canvas | Natural | Medium | Medium- and heavy-weight suits and coats | Dry-clean only |
| Super Siri[1] | Woven | Closely woven | Black, white | Super soft | Cotton dresses and blouses; also used for underlining | Machine wash-and-wear; dry-cleanable |
| | | | | Soft | Soft, yet firm shapes | |
| | | | | Firm | Lightweight suits and sportswear | |
| Taffeta | Woven | Silk or rayon | All colors | Light | Soft silks and woolens; also used as underlining for lace and chiffon as well as woolens | Dry-clean only |
| Veriform[2] "Basic Liner" | Woven | Mesh | Black, white, natural | Medium | Heavy cottons, silks, and soft woolens; also used as underlining in suits and separate skirts | Washable; dry-cleanable |

[1] David B. Carmel & Company
[2] Stacy Fabrics Corp.
[3] Chicopee Mills, Inc.
[4] Kimberly-Stevens Corporation
[5] Pellon Corporation

## Underlining and Lining

Underlining and lining are a second thickness of fabric that supports the garment fabric and gives it extra resistance to strain. Both help to hold the shape of dresses, suits, coats, shorts, and at-home wear. *Underlining and Lining*, beginning on page 95, describes how to underline or line dresses of various styles and of various fabrics.

Underlining and lining should be selected with care. The fiber content need not be the same as that in the dress fabric, except in sheer fabrics; however, the colors should match.

Fabrics that are appropriate for underlining and lining—or are made expressly for them—are: silk organza, China silk, taffeta (silk or rayon), batiste, voile, peau de soie, silk crepe, silk and acetate underlining, acetate sheath lining, UnderCurrent, and SiBonne (synthetic underlining), all of which are available in colors. Silk and acetate underlining and acetate sheath lining resemble China silk but are less expensive. SiBonne is available in a soft or crisp finish. Veriform, an underlining with a soft or crisp finish, is available in black and white and is suitable for underlining or lining many opaque fabrics.

The table below suggests types of fabrics that can be used for underlining and lining different dress and suit fabrics.

| DRESS OR SUIT FABRICS | SUGGESTED UNDERLINING AND LINING FABRICS |
|---|---|
| Soft silks and lightweight rayons that will be dry-cleaned | Silk organza, China silk, UnderCurrent[1], SiBonne[2], silk and acetate underlining, acetate sheath lining — all available in colors. |
| Heavy and medium-weight silks, wools, and rayons | Silk organza, China silk, UnderCurrent, SiBonne, taffeta, silk and acetate underlining, acetate sheath lining — all available in colors. |
| Cottons that will be dry-cleaned | Batiste, voile, China silk, UnderCurrent, SiBonne, organza — all available in colors. (Shrink batiste and voile.) |
| Sheer wools and chiffons | Taffeta, peau de soie, silk crepe, satin — all available in colors. |
| Lightweight wools | China silk, organza, silk and acetate underlining, UnderCurrent, SiBonne, acetate sheath lining — all available in colors. |
| Jersey and loosely woven fabrics | China silk, silk and acetate underlining, UnderCurrent, SiBonne, acetate sheath lining, voile, batiste — all available in colors. (Shrink batiste and voile.) If skirt is full, use taffeta. |
| Wool suit skirts | China silk, silk and acetate underlining, UnderCurrent, acetate sheath lining, SiBonne, crepe with which jacket is lined — all available in colors. |
| Linens that will be dry-cleaned | Voile, batiste, SiBonne, UnderCurrent, China silk, silk and acetate underlining — all available in colors. (Shrink voile and batiste.) |
| Lace | Taffeta, satin, peau de soie, polished cotton, silk organza, net, marquisette, chiffon — all available in colors. |

Some of the fabrics suggested for interfacing are also used for underlining and lining, particularly for gored and circular skirts and suits and coats that are bouffant—for example, hair canvas, Siri, Pellon, or Veriform "Basic Liner."

[1] UnderCurrent — Trademark of David B. Carmel & Company
[2] SiBonne — Trademark of Stacy Fabrics Corp.

# Beginning To Sew

IF YOU ARE A BEGINNING SEAMSTRESS, you may sometimes think that your sewing machine was built only to outwit you. But be patient. This carefully constructed piece of equipment requires some understanding. Those of you who have sewn for a while know that if you take a little time to master your machine, you will have a versatile and willing partner in creativity.

## GETTING TO KNOW YOUR MACHINE

The operation of any sewing machine is simple if you understand the function of the principal parts and know how to thread the machine and regulate the three elementary controls: tension, pressure, and stitch length. Your instruction book contains information on these essential points. Do not hesitate to refer to it frequently.

The principal parts of the *Touch & Sew°* sewing machine by Singer are illustrated below. Although your machine may be of a different model or make, it has many features in common with all machines, and the explanations that follow will be applicable to it.

**PRINCIPAL PARTS AND FEATURES**
**GOLDEN *Touch & Sew***
**SEWING MACHINE / 750**

Spool Holder

Stitch-Pattern Discs

Disc Holder
Stitch-Pattern Dial
Tension Dial
Tension Discs
Take-up Lever
Pressure Dial
Threading Chart
Built-in Needle Threader
Thread Cutter
Presser Foot
Soft-Touch Feed
Throat Plate
Slide Plate

Presser-Foot Lifter
Bobbin
Bobbin Latch
Bobbin Push Button

Built-in Stitch Chart
Disc-Release Lever
Stitch-Balance Dial
Pattern-Start Indicator
Hand Wheel
Power and Light Switch
Needle-Position Dial
Stitch-Width Dial
Stitch-Control Dial
Reverse-Stitch Lever
Buttonhole Dial
Sewing Light
Needle Clamp

## Threading the Machine

In threading the machine, you are concerned with four operations: (1) winding the bobbin, (2) threading the bobbin case, (3) threading the needle (or upper threading), and (4) raising the bobbin thread. Always follow the diagram shown in the instruction book given with your machine.

**Winding the bobbin.** Many machines have the conventional bobbin winder on the right hand side as in the illustration above. The *Touch & Sew* machine, which is illustrated on page 21, has push-button bobbin winding—that is, you wind the bobbin with the needle thread without removing it from the machine. Refer to your instruction book.

Here are the basic rules:

1. Start with an empty bobbin so that the new thread can pass through the eyelet on the side. *Never wind one color over another.*

2. Select a thread identical to the one used for upper threading.

3. Wind it evenly in level layers across the bobbin.

4. Do not wind the bobbin so full that it will be tight in the bobbin case; it should fit in easily.

If you observe these rules, you will find that the bobbin thread will feed evenly to the very end of your stitching. This is important because it influences the quality and regularity of your stitch.

**Threading the bobbin case.** On some machines the bobbin thread leads off in a clockwise direction; in others it is counterclockwise. Refer to your instruction book and follow the directions carefully. If you thread the bobbin case improperly, the thread will usually slip out of the threading notches and from under the tension spring.

**Threading the needle.** Upper threading is simple if you follow this sequence:

1. Raise the take-up lever to its highest point.

2. Lead the thread from the spool pin through the threading points as shown in diagram—(1) thread guide, (2) needle-thread tension discs, (3) thread guide, (4) take-up lever, (5) thread guides, and (6) needle. The direction for threading the needle varies. Some machines are threaded from left to right, others from right to left, and others from front to back.

3. Draw enough thread through the eye of the needle to start sewing.

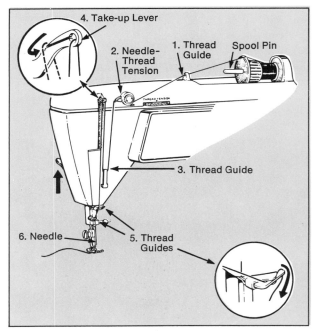

**Raising the bobbin thread.** You must now draw the bobbin thread through the needle hole in the throat plate. To do that:

1. Hold the needle thread lightly with the left hand.

2. Turn the hand wheel toward you until the needle goes down and up again and the take-up lever returns to its highest point.

3. Pull the needle thread; the bobbin thread will follow and form a large loop.

4. Undo the loop with your finger.

5. Place both needle and bobbin threads under the presser foot and lay them diagonally to the right.

You are now ready to sew. If you want to begin at once, turn to page 27, which starts you off with a simple seam.

## Regulating Stitch Length

The length of your stitch depends on the weight and texture of the fabric you are sewing as well as the type of sewing you are doing. Form the habit of testing the stitch length on a swatch of the fabric.

*Delicate* fabrics require a *short, fine stitch*.

*Heavy* fabrics require a *long, heavy stitch*.

*For topstitching*, the stitch length should be shorter than inside stitching when fine thread is used, longer when heavy thread is used.

*Curved seams* require a shorter stitch than that used for straight stitching. If you are using a 12 stitch length for straight stitching, you will need a 15 stitch for curves to give the seams greater elasticity and strength.

*Bias* and *semi-bias cut seams* also require a short stitch since they must have more elasticity than seams following the lengthwise or crosswise grain of the fabric.

*Scallops* require a shorter stitch than curves to maintain a smooth, rounded contour and permit close blending of seams.

*Bound buttonholes* and *pockets* are made with a short stitch to ensure strength and durability—generally a 20 stitch length.

When stitching is used to *control fullness* at the sleeve cap, at the elbow of long sleeves, at the top of a hem, or at a point where one seam edge is eased to another, a slightly longer stitch is required than the one used for straight stitching.

The three types of *temporary stitching* require different stitch lengths. For regular machine basting, use a 6-to-8 stitch length. For chainstitching, which is available on some sewing machines, use a 10-to-12 stitch length. For speed basting, which is also available on some models, you have a wide choice. You can choose any length from 6 to "fine" and produce a basting stitch up to 2 inches long.

In some *zig-zag sewing*, such as decorative satin stitching and buttonholes, use a "fine" stitch setting. For other zig-zag sewing, use longer stitches.

If you compare different grades of clothing, you will notice that quality garments are stitched with a short stitch and appropriate weights and types of thread and that economy clothing is often stitched with a longer stitch and less durable thread.

To determine the stitch length appropriate for your fabric, test the stitch on a swatch of fabric.

For directions on setting the stitch length selector on your machine, check your machine instruction book as well as the diagram shown here. A stitch length selector that is clearly marked is easy to set.

## Selecting the Thread

The rules that guide thread selection are easy to observe:

*Select a thread two shades darker than the fabric.* Since thread on the spool appears to be darker than it actually is, draw a strand over the fabric to make sure you have the right color.

*Select the proper thread for your fabric.* There are three types of general-purpose thread: polyester core with mercerized cotton wrap, mercerized, and spun polyester. When fine thread is appropriate, choose silk, nylon twist, or fine spun polyester for lingerie.

When stitched, the thread must set into the weave of the fabric. A thread that is too heavy will remain on the surface and give shorter serv-

## FABRIC, THREAD AND NEEDLE CHART†

| FABRIC | THREAD | NEEDLES | |
|---|---|---|---|
| | | TYPE | SIZE |
| DELICATE — tulle, chiffon, fine lace, organza | Fine mercerized cotton<br>Fine synthetic thread | Catalog 2020<br>(15x1) | 9†† |
| LIGHTWEIGHT — batiste, organdy, jersey, voile, taffeta, crepe, chiffon velvet, plastic film | 50 mercerized cotton<br>"A" silk<br>Synthetic thread<br>Polyester core/cotton | Catalog 2020<br>(15x1) | 11 |
| MEDIUM WEIGHT — gingham, percale, pique, linen, chintz, faille, satin, fine corduroy, velvet, suiting, knits, deep-pile fabrics, vinyl | 50 mercerized cotton<br>60 cotton<br>"A" silk<br>Synthetic thread<br>Polyester core/cotton | Catalog 2020<br>(15x1) | 14 |
| MEDIUM HEAVY — gabardine, tweed, sailcloth, denim, coatings, drapery fabrics, vinyl, deep-pile fabrics | Heavy-duty<br>mercerized cotton<br>40 to 60 cotton<br>Synthetic thread | Catalog 2020<br>(15x1) | 16 |
| HEAVY — overcoatings, dungaree, upholstery fabrics, canvas | Heavy-duty<br>mercerized cotton<br>24 to 40 cotton<br>Synthetic thread | Catalog 2020<br>(15x1) | 18 |
| ALL WEIGHTS — decorative top stitching | "D" silk†††<br>(Buttonhole twist) | Catalog 2020<br>(15x1) | 18 |
| ALL WEIGHTS — decorative hemstitching | 50 mercerized cotton<br>"A" silk<br>Synthetic thread | Catalog 2020<br>(15x1) | 18 |
| SYNTHETIC KNITS AND STRETCH FABRICS — polyester double knit, nylon tricot, jersey, spandex, ciré tricot, panné velvet | "A" nylon<br>50 mercerized cotton<br>"A" silk<br>Polyester core/cotton | Catalog 2045<br>Ball Point (Yellow Band)<br>Catalog 2021<br>Ball Point | 14<br><br>11 |
| LEATHER — suede, kidskin, capeskin, lambskin, lined leathers | 50 mercerized cotton<br>Synthetic thread<br>"A" silk<br>Polyester core/cotton | Catalog 2032<br>(15x2) | 11<br>14<br>16 |
| LIGHT AND MEDIUM WEIGHTS — decorative twin-needle stitching | 50 mercerized cotton | Catalog 2028<br>(twin) | 14 |

†Does not apply to chainstitching. ††Size 9 needle recommended for sewing only. For bobbin winding, use larger size needle. †††Use with 50 mercerized cotton or "A" silk in bobbin.

ice and less strength than a fine thread that imbeds itself in the texture of the fabric.

Consult the chart above for further suggestions on thread selection.

## Selecting the Sewing Machine Needle

In selecting the needle, remember that: (1) You must consider both the thread and the fabric. (2) The eye of the needle must be large enough for the thread to pass through freely; a needle too fine for the thread will cause the thread to fray. (3) The needle blade must be fine enough to enter the fabric without marring it with a large puncture, yet heavy enough to pierce the fabric without being bent or deflected. (4) A needle too fine for the fabric may break.

Regular, general-purpose needles are available in sizes 9, 11, 14, 16, and 18. Ball-point needles, which separate the yarns rather than piercing them when penetrating the fabric, are recommended for knits. A special wedge-point needle is available for sewing real and fake leather fabric.

Always have a supply of all sizes on hand to meet your needs. A bent needle causes the fabric to draw to one side, feeding in a curve rather than a straight line. A blunt needle can cause pulls in the fabric.

Also take care to position the needle properly in the needle clamp. If you do not, your machine will skip stitches or not stitch at all.

Refer again to the chart above for further information on needle selection.

## Regulating the Pressure

Pressure is the force the presser foot exerts on the fabric when it is being stitched. Pressure is important because it influences the straightness of your seams, the uniformity of stitch length, and the even handling of both layers of fabric. The pressure should be heavy enough to prevent side creepage and light enough to carry the fabric without marking it. *Too light a pressure* will cause irregular feeding, which affects the quality of the stitch and evenness of seams. *Too heavy a pressure* will affect the stitch length and seam quality and mar a smooth surface or pile fabric.

*Regulate the pressure according to the fabric.* Generally, heavy fabrics require heavy pressure; medium-weight fabrics require pressure midway between light and heavy; and lightweight fabrics require light pressure. Surface finish and texture must also be considered; soft fabrics, for example, require less pressure than crisp.

**To test for pressure,** take two layers of fabric cut on the lengthwise grain and stitch without thread. If all seam edges are handled evenly, the pressure is correct; if they are not, turn the pressure dial or thumb screw until they are and until the fabric moves easily under the presser foot without showing feed marks.

*To decrease pressure,* turn the thumb screw counterclockwise.

*To increase pressure,* turn the thumb screw clockwise.

If you have a Singer machine with a pressure dial inside:

*To decrease pressure,* turn the dial to a lower number.

*To increase pressure,* turn the dial to a higher number.

PRESSURE DIAL

INCREASE          DECREASE          DARNING

LIGHT          MEDIUM          HEAVY

## Regulating the Tension

Tension controls the threads as they interlock to form a stitch on the sewing machine. There are two tensions—the upper, which controls the needle thread, and the lower, which controls the thread from the bobbin case or shuttle. A perfectly locked stitch can be formed only when the two tensions are in balance and the two threads are drawn into the fabric to the same degree. The tensions should be heavy enough to pull the threads to the center of the fabric and form a good stitch.

Both tensions correct

To determine whether your tension adjustment is correct, test the stitch on a scrap of your fabric with the needle and thread you are going to use. You will find that a seam stitched with balanced tensions is twice as strong as one stitched with unbalanced tensions. It is easy to verify this by making the following **strength-of-seam test:**

—Use a size 14 needle.

—Thread the machine with size 50 mercerized thread, using a light color for the upper threading and another color for the bobbin.

—Set a stitch length at 10 or 12.

—On a square of fine muslin or the equivalent, stitch on the bias and on both the lengthwise and crosswise grains.

—Inspect the lines of stitching. They should not pucker and the stitch formation should appear well set on the top and underside of the muslin. If the lines of stitching pucker, you are likely to find also that they are not equally set on the top and underside and look like this:

Loose upper tension
Tight lower tension

Tight upper tension
Loose lower tension

—*To determine whether the upper tension is too tight or too loose,* use the following test. Grasp the bias line of stitching between the thumb and index finger. Space the hands about 3 inches apart and pull with an even, quick force until one thread breaks. If the broken thread is the color of the needle thread, you know that the upper tension is too tight. If the broken thread is the color of the bobbin thread, you know that the upper tension is too loose. If both threads break together and require more force to break, you know the tensions are balanced.

*To decrease tension,* turn the thumb nut counter-clockwise. Each lower number denotes less tension.

*To increase tension,* turn the thumb nut clockwise. Each higher number denotes increased tension.

**TENSION DIAL**

**INCREASE**          **DECREASE**

—Repeat the test until both threads break together.

*Bobbin-thread tension.* The tension on the bobbin thread is regulated by the small screw on the bobbin case or shuttle. It is seldom necessary for you to change it since you can usually obtain a balanced stitch by varying the tension on the needle thread.

TO INCREASE TENSION TURN SCREW TO RIGHT

TO DECREASE TENSION TURN SCREW TO LEFT

Here are some simple rules to guide you in adjusting the upper tension for different types of threads and fabrics:

*To sew with silk thread.* Set the upper tension from one to two points lower than when stitching with mercerized thread. The bobbin tension remains the same.

*To sew with heavy cotton or linen thread.* In general, increase the upper tension when sewing with this weight of thread on dense fabrics. The bobbin tension remains the same.

*To sew with certain sewing machine accessories.* Follow the instructions given in this book for the specific accessory. Sometimes an adjustment of the upper tension is necessary.

*To sew on zig-zag machines.* Loosen the upper tension when doing decorative, closely spaced satin stitches. Wide, closed stitching requires a lighter needle-thread tension than narrow stitching. See page 266.

*To stitch special fabrics.* Nylons, dense fabrics, polished cottons, some resin-treated wash-and-wear fabrics, and others of similar close weave usually require tension adjustment. Always test your stitch on a scrap of your fabric.

# YOUR FIRST STEPS IN SEWING

Your machine is threaded and ready to go. If this is your first venture into serious, creative sewing, you should allow yourself a period of practice before you try a pattern.

First, familiarize yourself with simple stitching. Work carefully and correctly from the start. The good habits you form now will make all your later work easier and more professional looking. Proof of your efficient handling of the sewing machine will be found not only in an evenly controlled acceleration of the machine and a perfectly formed and positioned first stitch in a seam, but in the exact assembling of seams, collars, facings, and pockets, and a competence in all the intricate details of sewing.

Begin your practice period with the "exercises" described here.

## Posture and Speed Control

Correct posture at the machine enables you to work comfortably and well. Follow these rules:

1. Sit back on the chair or stool squarely in front of the needle. Do not lean against the chair back; instead, bring your body forward slightly.

2. Place both feet flat on the floor, with one foot forward. If your machine has a knee control, place the left foot forward and press the right knee against the control. If your machine has a foot control, place the right foot forward and press on the control.

3. Position the bulk of the fabric to the left of the needle and the seam edge to the right.

4. Place the left hand lightly on top of the fabric so that your fingers can control it. Make sure that the weight of your left arm is not resting on the fabric since this will cause uneven feeding.

5. Place the right hand 3 or 4 inches in front of the needle so that your fingers can guide the edge.

6. Gradually press on the foot or knee control until you reach a slow, even speed. Never try to sew too fast. Skillful machine operation depends on your ability to sew easily, rhythmically. You

can work up to a high speed later when you are stitching long, straight seams.

## How to Start and End a Seam

To start and end a seam, take these steps in sequence:

1. Raise the take-up lever to its highest point by turning the hand wheel toward you.

2. Place both needle and bobbin threads under the presser foot and lay them diagonally to the right.

3. Place the fabric under the presser foot with the bulk of the fabric to the left and the seam edge to the right.

4. Lower the needle into the fabric where the first stitch is to begin. Hold the thread ends and lower the presser foot.

5. Stitch with a slow, rhythmic speed.

6. When you reach the end of the seam, turn the hand wheel to raise the take-up lever to its highest point.

7. Raise the presser foot and removed the fabric by drawing it to the back and left.

8. Clip the thread ends on the thread cutter.

The Seam Guide and throat plate guidelines will help you keep the stitching parallel to the seam edge. See page 81.

## How to Reinforce a Seam with Backstitching

Follow the procedure described on previous page. At step 4, lower the needle into the fabric about ½ inch from the seam end and backstitch to the end of the fabric. Then stitch forward to end of the seam and finish with backstitching to reinforce the end.

## How to Guide and Support the Fabric

Most fabrics need to be guided only in front of the presser foot. Exceptions are fabrics of unusual

texture and weave, filmy sheers, crepes, knits, tricots, and the like. For them, gently apply tension

to the seam by holding the fabric in front and in back of the presser foot as illustrated at bottom of previous column. Never pull the fabric when sewing. If you are sewing fabric of unusual texture on a zig-zag machine, use the straight-stitch throat plate and presser foot for close control.

## How to Pivot

You need to "pivot" when stitching corners on collars, lapels, shaped necklines, bound buttonholes, and pockets. Here is what you do:

1. Stitch to the interesecting seamline at the corner.

2. With the needle in the fabric, turn the hand wheel forward to bring the needle to its upward stroke. Just before the needle leaves the fabric, raise the presser foot and turn the fabric, pivoting on the needle.

3. Lower the presser foot and stitch.

4. To avoid bulk at the point of a collar or lapel, take from one to three stitches diagonally between the intersecting lines of stitching. See page 91. Practice pivoting a few times. You will find that it is easy.

## How to Stitch Curved Seams

Curved seams should be stitched slowly. To guide the fabric on small curves, such as scallops, stop the machine with the needle in the fabric, lift the presser foot slightly, and turn the fabric just enough to follow the seamline.

Practice stitching and guiding straight seams, curved seams, and corners until you have mastered them.

The chapter beginning on page 81 tells you how to make many different kinds of seams.

Some hand sewing is required in almost all the work you will be doing. If you already know how to sew by hand, check yourself against the guides given here. You may find some suggestions that will improve your technique or your deftness.

## Threading the Hand Needle

1. With sharp scissors, cut the thread end on an angle. Avoid breaking, biting, or tearing the thread, for then you will have trouble threading it through the needle eye.

2. Hold the needle in the left hand and the thread end tightly in the right hand between the thumb and index finger. Then pass the thread through the needle eye, and with the same motion, transfer the needle into the grip of the right thumb and index finger. With the left hand, draw the thread end from the eye about halfway down the remaining supply of thread.

3. Always sew with a short thread. For finishing stitches, use less than a 24-inch length; for basting, use a slightly longer thread. A thread that is too long will tangle and weaken from being pulled through the fabric repeatedly; also, it requires tiring arm motions to draw each stitch in place. With the exception of sewing on buttons, snaps, and hooks and eyes, you will seldom need to use a double thread in hand sewing. Some prefer a single thread for all operations.

## Tying a Knot

To prevent the longer thread end from pulling through at the beginning of the stitching, form a secure knot as follows:

1. Hold the thread end between the thumb and first finger of the left hand.

2. Use the right hand to bring the thread over and around the finger tip of the left hand, crossing it over the thread end.

3. Hold the longer thread taut while pushing the thumb toward the finger tip. This causes the thread to roll around the loop.

4. Slip the loop off the finger tip and at the same time pull against the longer thread held in the right hand to set the knot.

## Using a Thimble

Do not allow yourself to develop the habit of sewing without a thimble. A thimble will prevent your finger from being roughened and sore and will enable you to sew better and faster.

Thimbles are available in sizes 5 to 12 in both metal and plastic. It is easy to select an inexpensive one that fits your finger snugly.

The thimble is worn on the second finger of the right hand and is used to direct and force the needle through the fabric. At first it may seem to be awkward and uncomfortable. If so, make hand stitches on a heavy, dense fabric such as drill cloth. You immediately will feel the need for the protection a thimble gives. If you continue to find sewing with a thimble awkward, make sure you are using a needle of appropriate length for the work you are doing. In general, use a long needle for long stitches or running stitches and a short needle for short, single stitches. Check the description of needles on page 2 to determine the best size and style for your work.

## Fastening Stitches

The fastening stitch is used at the end of a line of basting to hold the stitches in place. To fasten a line of basting, take one short backstitch. This is easy to remove when the permanent stitching has been completed.

To fasten a line of fine hand stitching, bring the needle through to the underside. Take one backstitch, catching only a single thread in the fabric;

pull the needle through, leaving a small loop in the thread. Take another small backstitch, then pass the needle through the thread loop of the first stitch and set the knot close to the fabric. Repeat if greater security is needed.

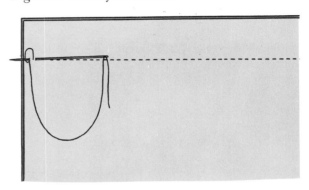

## Removing Kinks and Twists

The simple process of pulling thread through fabric often causes the remaining supply of thread to twist. Some threads twist more readily than others —for example, buttonhole twist. And some hand sewing operations, such as fine overstitching, tend to cause greater twisting and kinking than straight running stitches.

To remove the excessive twist without unthreading the needle, merely hold the thread end in the left hand while sliding the needle down against the fabric. Then without holding the thread end, slide the needle upward on the thread to a sewing position. This motion pushes the extra twist to the end of the thread and the remaining work can be completed without troublesome knotting and kinking.

# Pattern Preliminaries

BUYING THE RIGHT PATTERN is a challenge, for it requires that you reconcile the often conflicting demands of fashion, figure, practicability, and purse. Selecting the correct size may pose a problem too, especially if you are buying a pattern for the first time.

Read carefully the suggestions given here. They offer practical guides to keep you out of trouble.

## SELECTING A PATTERN STYLE

Whatever you make should reflect current style and fashion. With that in mind:

Study the fashions in magazines, newspapers, and store windows as well as in the pattern catalogs. Choose a pattern from the latest fashions *but do not follow fashion blindly.* The extremes in high fashion are attention getting but quickly outdated.

Look for lines and styles that dramatize your best points. Do not be misled by an attractive style modeled by a 20 year old if you are twice that age, or by a style that emphasizes all the wrong proportions of your figure. Remember that vertical lines give an illusion of tallness, a full skirt draws attention to large hips, a bloused bodice makes a full bust look larger, and a "V" neckline makes a pointed chin more pronounced.

Consider wearability, practicability, and purpose. Can the garment be worn year-round? Will it be fashionable for more than one season? Will it require special accessories? Does it suit the occasion?

If you already have the fabric, be careful to choose a pattern that suits its texture and weight.

## DETERMINING THE CORRECT PATTERN SIZE

Clothes that look well, fit well. And proper fit begins with the selection of the correct pattern size. To determine that, take body measurements accurately. Wear a good foundation garment, the lingerie you normally wear, and the same style of shoes you will wear with the finished garment.

### Taking Your Measurements

Measurements must be taken with the correct location of these seams in mind:

The *shoulder seam* begins at the neckline, 1 inch behind the ear lobe, and extends across the top of the shoulder to the arm joint.

*Side seams* are perpendicular to the floor, hanging straight from underarm to lower edge. Locating this seam is known as "forming a plumb line" from the underarm.

*The natural armhole, or armscye, seam* falls straight down from the arm joint for 2½ to 3 inches, depending on size, then curves under the arm about 1 inch below the armpit.

*The natural neckline or beadline* hugs the base of the neck closely, crossing just above the pit of the throat and the prominent vertebra at the back of the neck.

*The waistline* is the smallest part of the torso. To locate it readily when taking your measurements, pin a ¼-inch tape or elastic around your waist before you start. Always measure *to* the bottom of this tape for bodice length and *from* the bottom for skirt length.

*The bustline measurement* is taken across the fullest part of the bust and from the back, with the tape very slightly raised.

*The bodice length* is measured from the shoulder seam at the neckline, over the fullest part of the bust, to the waistline.

*The hipline measurement* is taken over the fullest part of the hips and from the front. If the distance from waistline to hipline (measure at side seam) varies from the standard 7 inches, show the correct figure on your measurement chart.

# Recording Your Measurements

The illustrations below show you exactly where to take the measurement for each part of your body. *Measure from the right side, unless otherwise indicated,* and enter each measurement in the space provided on the Measurement Chart. As your figure changes with time, correct the recorded measurements.

# MEASUREMENT CHART

| | YOUR OWN MEASUREMENT (INCHES) | USUAL ALLOWANCE FOR EASE (INCHES) | PATTERN MEASUREMENT† (INCHES) |
|---|---|---|---|
| **1. CHEST** — Tape straight across back ............. | _____ | _____ | _____ |
| **2. BUST** — Fullest part; tape slightly higher in back .... | _____ | 3 | _____ |
| **3. WAISTLINE** — | | | |
| **a**—Locate natural waistline. Place tape or elastic band around waist .................. | _____ | 1 | _____ |
| **b**—Across front, side seam to side seam ...... | _____ | _____ | _____ |
| **4. HIPLINE** — | | | |
| **a**—3″ below waist; mark with pins .......... | _____ | | _____ |
| **b**—7″ below waist .......... | _____ | 2 | _____ |
| **c**—9″ below waist .......... | _____ | 2 | _____ |
| **5. SHOULDER LENGTH** — | | | |
| Neck to seam line — Right ................ | _____ | _____ | _____ |
| Neck to seam line — Left ................ | _____ | _____ | _____ |
| **6. SLEEVE LENGTH** — | | | |
| **a**—Shoulder to elbow ............... | _____ | _____ | _____ |
| **b**—Elbow to wrist ............... | _____ | _____ | _____ |
| **c**—Inside from underarm seam to wrist ...... | _____ | _____ | _____ |
| **7. SLEEVE WIDTH** — | | | |
| **a**—Upper arm ............... | _____ | 2 to 3 | _____ |
| **b**—Lower arm (below elbow) ............ | _____ | _____ | _____ |
| **c**—Wrist ............... | _____ | _____ | _____ |
| **8. UNDERARM TO WAISTLINE** — | | | |
| 1″ below armpit — Right ................ | _____ | _____ | _____ |
| 1″ below armpit — Left ................ | _____ | _____ | _____ |
| **9. SHOULDER TO WAISTLINE** — H.P.†† ......... | _____ | ½ to 1 | _____ |
| **10. CENTER FRONT** — Neck to waistline ............. | _____ | _____ | _____ |
| **11. SHOULDER TO BUSTLINE** — H.P.†† ......... | _____ | _____ | _____ |
| **12. CENTER FRONT TO BUSTLINE** | _____ | _____ | _____ |
| **13. BACK LENGTH** — | | | |
| **a**—Neckline to waistline ........... | _____ | ½ to 1 | _____ |
| **b**—Shoulder (H.P.††) to waistline—Right ..... | _____ | _____ | _____ |
| **c**—Shoulder (H.P.††) to waistline—Left ..... | _____ | _____ | _____ |
| **14. SHOULDER TO SHOULDER** ................ | _____ | _____ | _____ |
| **15. BACK WIDTH** — 4″ below neckline with arms forward and raised slightly .................. | _____ | ½ to 1 | _____ |
| **16. FULL LENGTH** — Waistline to floor | | | |
| **a**—Center front ............ | _____ | _____ | _____ |
| **b**—Center back ............ | _____ | _____ | _____ |
| **c**—Left side ............ | _____ | _____ | _____ |
| **d**—Right side ............ | _____ | _____ | _____ |
| **17. SKIRT LENGTH PLUS HEM ALLOWANCE** .......... | _____ | _____ | _____ |

†Consider seam allowance in checking with pattern
††Highest point

## Basic Rules for Pattern Size

Pattern sizes are based on actual body measurements and allow enough ease for comfort and proper fit. The amount of ease will vary with the style and with the manufacturer. Some pattern companies may allow more ease than others; however, this does not mean that you cannot use all makes of patterns.

Pattern sizing has recently been changed to correspond more closely to standard ready-to-wear sizing. However, patterns with former sizing may be available for some time. All patterns using the new sizing will be clearly indicated on the envelope.

Generally, you will take one or two sizes larger in a pattern than in ready-to-wear. Check your measurements with those on the back of the pattern envelope, and *select your pattern by bust measurement* and make any needed adjustments in other places. It is easier to adjust the waist and hip than the shoulder and bust. (Remember that an "up-lift" bra will very often raise the bustline enough to measure a size larger.)

If, however, the bust is larger in proportion to the other measurements, take a chest measurement. If the difference between bust and chest is 4 inches or more, buy your pattern one size smaller than the bust measurement and enlarge it through the bust. The smaller size is recommended for this reason: It is important that your pattern fit well through the shoulders and armholes; therefore, to retain shape and fit, that area should be changed as little as possible. If you buy a pattern by the larger (bust) measurement, you will also have to cope with a longer shoulder line and deeper armholes than you may need. The smaller size pattern, however, will probably match your measurements more closley.

If only the bust is large in proportion to the rest of your body, and if you prefer not to alter the bustline, buy two patterns, one by bust measurement, the other a size smaller. Use only the front bodice of the larger pattern and all other pattern pieces of the smaller pattern. Increase the darts at underarm, shoulders, and waistline so that the front and back sections are equal at the seams.

*For skirts.* In general, select the pattern by waist measurement. However, if hips are full, buy the pattern according to hip measurement since it is easier to adjust the waistline than the hipline.

*For pants.* Buy the pattern according to hip measurement.

Always purchase the same pattern size for dresses, suits, and coats.

### TYPES OF PATTERNS AVAILABLE TO YOU

| | | |
|---|---|---|
| **Girls'** | **Size 7 to 14** | Designed for underdeveloped figure. **Not an age.** |
| **Young Junior/Teen** | **Size 5/6 to 15/16** | Designed for the developed pre-teen and teen figures; about 5'1" to 5'3" without shoes. |
| **Junior Petite** | **Size 3JP to 13JP** | Designed for the well-proportioned, petite figure with shorter waist and larger bust than the Junior pattern; about 5' to 5'1" without shoes. |
| **Junior** | **Size 5 to 15** | Designed for the well-proportioned, short-waisted figure; about 5'4" to 5'5" without shoes. |
| **Misses'** | **Size 6 to 18** | Designed for the well-proportioned, developed figure with normal waist length; about 5'5" to 5'6" without shoes. |
| **Women's** | **Size 38 to 46 (sometimes to 48 and 50)** | Designed for the larger, more fully mature figure; about 5'5" to 5'6" without shoes. |
| **Half-Size** | **Size 10½ to 20½ (sometimes to 24½)** | Designed for the shorter woman with fully developed figure and a short backwaist length. Waist and hips are larger in proportion to bust than the "Misses'" and "Women's" patterns. About 5'2" to 5'3" without shoes. |

## Types of Patterns Available to You

To lessen the need for pattern adjustment, pattern companies have designed patterns *proportioned to conform with many figure types.*

The table on the opposite page, which was made up from information found on the last pages of pattern catalogs, calls your attention to what is available. This is a general summary; not all companies show these exact proportions for each figure type. The illustration below shows the difference in pattern proportion.

Pattern companies have also developed *patterns that combine two sizes in one pattern.* This should make it easier for certain figure types to obtain the right fit. Two of these improvements are discussed here.

*The standard size pattern with cutting guidelines for two sizes of patterns (your size and the size smaller or larger).* If you measurements require the smaller size bodice and the larger size waistline and hipline, you can use the cutting guidelines that agree with your figure proportions. This is only one example of the possible combinations you may select for the two sizes.

*The standard size pattern with additional cutting guidelines for a smaller and a larger size at waistline and hipline.* You can use the cutting guidelines that conform to your measurements.

Each of these pattern innovations also has complete instructions for other combinations of bust, waist, and hip measurements.

The difference in pattern proportions is illustrated below in five front-bodice patterns for different figure types. Size 12 is used for each except the "Junior," which is size 11, and the "Half-Size," which is size 12½.

## Recognizing Your Figure Type

It is important that you recognize your figure type before selecting your pattern size. Each figure illustrated in the two groups here measures the same in the bustline; however, height, width of shoulders, hips, and height of bustline differ. It can readily be seen that certain pattern adjustments will be necessary. If the proper pattern is selected, however, those adjustments can be kept to a minimum.

Study the illustrations and find the figure type that most closely approaches yours. Use the size and adjustment suggestions as a guide.

In the first group shown, each figure type is Size 12, but figure proportions are quite dissimilar.

*Average figure* should select Size 12 "Misses'" pattern since she has no figure problem.

*Short figure* with small waistline and high bust should select the "Junior" pattern, Size 11.

*Tall figure* should select Size 12 "Misses'" pattern and lengthen both bodice and skirt.

*Figure with wide shoulders and narrow hips* should select Size 12 "Misses'" pattern and widen the bodice through the shoulders and narrow the skirt through the hips.

*Figure with large hips and narrow shoulders* will probably obtain a better fit by selecting Size 10 "Misses'" pattern and enlarging through the hips.

*Figure with narrow hips and average shoulders* should select Size 12 "Misses'" pattern and narrow the skirt through the hips.

Each figure type illustrated in the group at the bottom of the page is Size 40. The pattern size is proportioned for the more mature figure.

*Average figure* should select Size 40 "Women's" pattern since she has no figure problem.

*Short figure with narrow shoulders and large waistline* should consider the "Half-Size" pattern, Size 20½.

*Tall figure* should select Size 40 "Women's" pattern and lengthen both bodice and skirt.

*Figure with a high, large bust* should select Size 38 "Women's" pattern and adjust the bustline in both width and length.

*Figure with a low bust and large waistline and hips* should select Size 40 "Women's" pattern and lower the dart at underarm and enlarge through waistline and hips.

*Figure with narrow hips and broad shoulders* should select Size 40 "Women's" pattern and widen the bodice through the shoulders and narrow the skirt through the hips.

**Plate 1**
**Decorative bands and borders**
add individuality to simple clothes.

*Left:* Three decorative stitch patterns accent a child's linen dress.

*Right:* A combination of stitch patterns turns a simple faille top into a Russian peasant blouse.

*Above:* Satin zig-zag stitch and an open stitch pattern form a leaf design on double organdy hem.

*Left:* Black velveteen diamonds appliquéd on wool in the style of Chanel.

*Right:* A combination of stitch patterns used both to apply and to decorate metallic braid on chiffon.

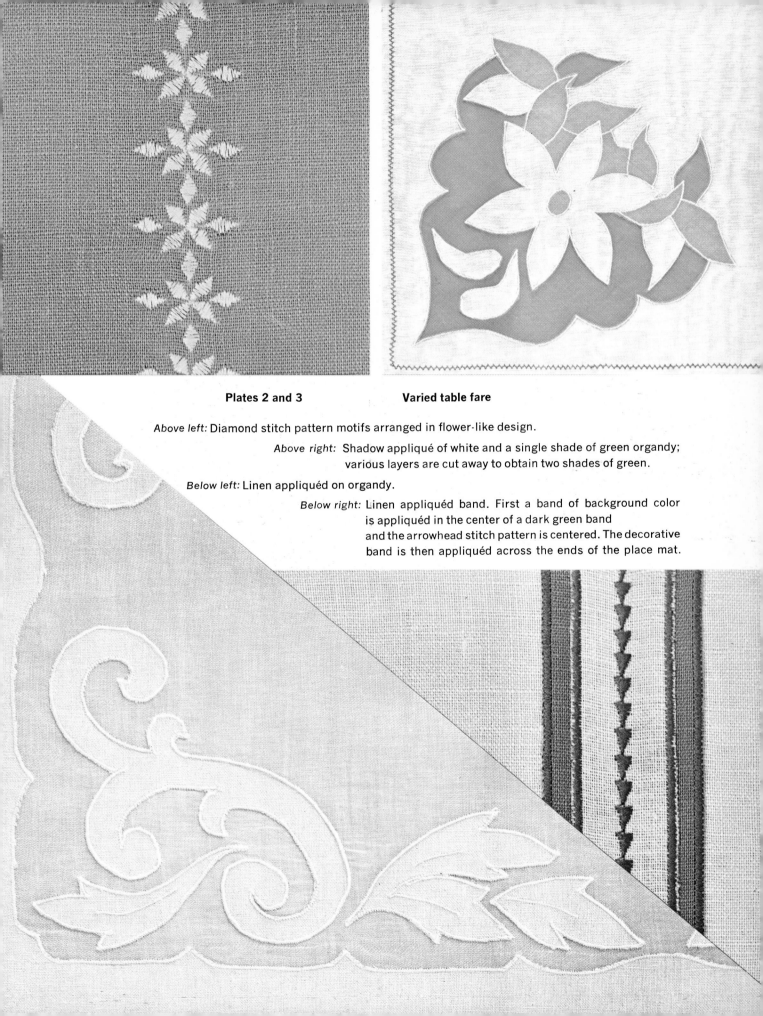

**Plates 2 and 3**     **Varied table fare**

*Above left:* Diamond stitch pattern motifs arranged in flower-like design.

*Above right:* Shadow appliqué of white and a single shade of green organdy; various layers are cut away to obtain two shades of green.

*Below left:* Linen appliquéd on organdy.

*Below right:* Linen appliquéd band. First a band of background color is appliquéd in the center of a dark green band and the arrowhead stitch pattern is centered. The decorative band is then appliquéd across the ends of the place mat.

**Plate 4**

**Decorative ways with wool**

*Left:* Machine-worked buttonholes used as design element in border of various decorative stitches on wool coat.

*Below Left:* Tweed triangles appliquéd on suede band form an interesting texture contrast.

*Below Right:* Suede pocket with corded wool edge is enhanced by appliquéd wool motif.

This technique would also be suitable for an initial.

# Fitting the Pattern to Your Figure

ALL THE WORK you have done so far has been a build-up to the steps you are about to take. For now you are ready to open the pattern envelope and begin.

To bring the pattern into complete conformity with your figure, proceed as follows:

1 Check the pattern against the measurements you recorded on your chart

2 Try on the tissue pattern

3 Adjust the pattern where necessary.

## CHECKING THE PATTERN AGAINST YOUR MEASUREMENTS

The pattern envelope shows different versions of the pattern. Choose the one you prefer, and then read carefully the pattern guide inside the envelope. Select the pattern pieces you need for the version you have chosen and replace the others in the envelope.

Press all pattern pieces with a lukewarm iron

to remove the creases. Be careful not to use too hot an iron, for it will cause tissue patterns to curl.

Measure the pattern from seam allowance to seam allowance in the same places that body measurements were taken. When there is no center seam or opening, measure from seam allowance to center line. *Never include seam allowances in pattern measurements.*

When comparing the pattern measurements with your body measurements, do not expect them all to match exactly. All pattern companies allow ease for comfort and body movement, and some allow more than others. In addition, some styles call for more ease than others. To make sure that you retain the style of the design, as well as the necessary ease, *do not overfit.*

The check list below indicates where pattern measurements should be the same as body measurements and where you should allow for ease. Compare the pattern measurements with your own—allowing for ease where required—and note any necessary adjustments on the pattern. In noting your adjustments, remember that only half the pattern in given. Therefore, in all girth measurements, make *one-fourth* the amount of the adjustment in the front section and *one-fourth* in the back section. If only the front or back section requires changing, make *one-half* the amount of the adjustment in the one pattern section.

*Shoulder length* must be identical to your body measurement. Measure length of shoulders on the pattern front, not on the back, since the back shoulder seam has ease or a dart.

*Across the back, from armhole to armhole,* allow ease for freedom of arm movement.

*In the bustline,* allow between 2 and 3 inches for ease, depending on the style of the pattern. A smoothly fitted garment will require 3 inches of ease; a loosely fitted one, a little more. For a strapless evening dress or sun dress, where you need just enough ease to breathe freely, 2 inches should be sufficient. In such dresses, additional darts are usually provided at the upper edge for ample freedom across the bustline and a snug fit at the upper edge.

*The waistline* should fit snugly. Add about 1 inch to your total measurement. However, this may be adjusted according to individual preference.

*The length of the pattern from shoulder to waistline* must be from ½ to ¾ inch longer than the body measurement. Some pattern styles require as much as 2 inches for ease.

*Darts* must conform with the contour of your figure. If they are poorly fitted, your dress will be uncomfortable and will not look well. For specific instructions on the correct position of darts, see page 100.

*Buttons and buttonholes* should be spaced in harmony with the individual figure. If you lengthen or shorten the pattern, or change the bustline, change the spacing of buttonholes. If you plan to use buttons larger than the size designated on the pattern, make the proper allowance in the measurement between the center line and the finished edge. This is fully explained under *Position of Buttonhole,* page 107.

*The high hipline measurement,* which falls about 3 inches below the waistline, requires a minimum ease of 1 inch in girth.

*The regular hipline measurement,* which usually falls about 7 inches below the waistline, requires between 2 and 4 inches for ease. Allow enough ease so that you can sit down without straining the seams. A skirt that fits too tightly will rip at the seam or cause the woven threads in the fabric to separate. When you are sitting, it will wrinkle across the front; when you are standing, it will

cup under the buttocks.

*The length of the skirt pattern* should be the measurement from waistline to hemline plus sufficient allowance for the hem.

## TRYING ON THE TISSUE PATTERN

Although a tissue pattern fits a little differently from the fabric, this fitting will enable you to prove that the pattern adjustments you noted are necessary. It will also help you determine whether the style is suitable for your figure type.

In every step of fitting, wear a good foundation garment, the lingerie you normally wear, and shoes with the correct heel height.

To prepare the tissue pattern for fitting, trim the pattern margins from the armhole and neckline seams. Pin in darts, tucks, and ease allowance. Pin shoulder seams, side seams, and seams within the bodice or skirt sections by placing pattern sections, wrong sides together, with seam edges even. Place the pins parallel to the seamline, taking the seam allowance indicated on the pattern (usually ⅝ inch). Pin bodice and skirt sections together.

Try the pattern on the right side of the figure. If shoulder pads or shapes will be worn in the garment, slip them in place under the tissue pattern.

Check the fit. The shoulder seam should be directly on top of the shoulder, and side seams should hang straight from armpit to lower edge. If the pattern has a set-in sleeve, the underarm seam of the armhole should fall at least 1 inch below the armpit. If this seam is fitted too high, it is uncomfortable; if fitted too low, it causes strain across the sleeve. A round, high neckline should fit snugly. The pattern has an extended seam allowance, which makes the neckline seem smaller than it will be in the finished dress.

## ADJUSTING THE PATTERN

### Rules to Remember

1. When you need to lengthen or widen a pattern, use tissue paper for the adjustment. Cut it 1 inch wider than the adjustment so that the pattern will overlap the tissue ½ inch on each side of the adjustment.

2. Pin the pattern to the tissue, placing the pins parallel to the adjustment. If the pattern is one you may use more than once, machine-baste after pinning.

3. When making a pattern piece smaller with the use of tucks or darts, remember that the width of the tuck or dart should be just half the amount to be removed.

4. When making pattern pieces wider or narrower, and only half the pattern is given, divide the amount of the adjustment into fourths, and add or subtract one-fourth in both the front and the back of the pattern. If only a front or back section requires adjustment, add or subtract one-half the amount of the adjustment in the section that needs it.

5. Always measure the pattern again after making adjustments.

### To Lengthen the Pattern

Slash across the pattern on the printed lengthening line. Place a piece of tissue underneath. Spread the pattern the necessary amount and pin it to the tissue. Keep the grain line straight. If the grain line does not extend as far as the lengthening line, extend it the full length of the pattern before slashing. Adjust the facing the same amount.

## To Shorten the Pattern

Fold the pattern on the printed shortening line and pin in a tuck, even in width, of the necessary amount. Remember that the width of the tuck should be just half the amount to be removed. For example, to shorten a pattern ½-inch, make a ¼-inch tuck. Keep the grain line straight. Adjust the facing the same amount.

## Full Bust

When a pattern fits everywhere except over a very full bust, buy the pattern by chest measurement and adjust the bustline. You will need extra length and width. Two methods are shown:

***Method 1: With shoulder dart*** (Below left)
Draw a line from the center of the waistline dart to the fullest part of the bust and another from the shoulder to the fullest part of the bust. Then draw a horizontal line across the fullest part of the bust. Place a large piece of tissue underneath and slash the pattern on these lines. Pin the upper center section to the tissue and spread the pattern, using the point where the lines cross as a pivot. Add the necessary amount on the horizontal line and one-half the amount needed on the vertical line. Pin the remaining three sections in position. Keep the grain line straight and the pattern flat. Adjust the facing the same amount on the horizontal line.

To take up excess width, add a dart at the shoulder as indicated by the dotted lines. The dart should point toward the fullest part of the bust. Increase the underarm dart so that the front and back bodice are the same length; keep waistline darts the same length but increase the width (note the dotted lines). Trim the outer edge of the tissue.

***Method 2: Without shoulder dart*** (Above right)
Draw a line over the fullest part of the bust from the shoulder to the center of the waistline dart. Then draw a horizontal line across the fullest part of the bust. Place a large piece of tissue underneath and slash the pattern on these lines. Pin the upper center front section to the edge of the tissue. Then pin the lower center front section, allowing the additional length necessary. Bring the shoulder edges of the two upper sections together and spread

the pattern at the bustline, adding one-half the width necessary. Pin to tissue. Spread the lower side section and pin to tissue. Keep the grain line straight and the pattern flat. Adjust the facing the same amount on the horizontal line.

Keep underarm and waistline darts the same length but increase them the necessary amount in width, as shown by the dotted lines. Straighten the shoulder line. Trim off the outer edges of the tissue.

## Flat Bust

Adjust the necessary amount by folding a tuck across the chest, decreasing in width at the armhole. Pin in place. Make a corresponding dart in front of the sleeve so that the armhole and sleeve will fit correctly. Remember, the width of the dart is just half the amount to be removed.

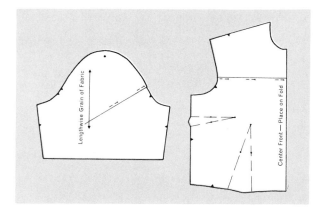

## Hollow Chest

Fold a dart across the chest, tapering toward the armhole. Pin in place. Remember, the width of the dart is just half the amount to be removed. Straighten the center front as shown by the dotted lines. No sleeve adjustment is necessary since the point of the dart ends at the armhole.

## Low Bust

A low bust requires lowering the dart at the underarm. Slash across the pattern the length of the dart, about 1 inch below the armhole; then slash down toward the waistline. Place the tissue underneath and pin it to the pattern at the upper edge of the slash. Slide the dart section down until the point of the dart is aligned with the fullest part of the bust. Pin to tissue. Form a tuck in the pattern below the dart so that the pattern will lie flat.

## Erect Back (Above)

Slash across the pattern just above the waistline. Lap and pin the slashed edges the necessary amount, tapering to a point at the side seam. Straighten the center back and dart as illustrated by the dotted lines.

*(Continued)*

41

If the pattern is too long from shoulder to arm-pit, pin a tuck across the shoulder. Dart the back of the sleeve to correspond with the bodice so that the sleeve and armhole will fit correctly. Straighten the grain line on the sleeve as indicated by the dotted lines.

## Square Shoulders

Slash across the pattern front and back, from the armhole toward the center, just below the shoulder line. Place a piece of tissue underneath and raise the shoulder line the necessary amount. Pin the pattern to the tissue. Raise the armhole at the underarm the same amount to retain size. Straighten the dart at the shoulder as illustrated by the dotted lines.

## Round Shoulders

Slash across the pattern from the center to the armhole at the fullest part of the back. Place the tissue underneath and raise the pattern at the neck to add the necessary amount across the shoulders. Add the amount required at center back to keep it straight. Pin the pattern to the tissue. Fold a dart at the neckline to take up the amount added and to retain size.

## Sloping Shoulders

Slash across the pattern front and back, from the armhole toward the center, just below the shoulder line. Lap and pin the slashed edges the necessary amount at the armhole, tapering to a point. Lower the armhole the same amount at underarm to retain the shape and size of the armhole as illustrated by the dotted lines. Straighten the shoulder dart.

## Broad Shoulders

Slash the pattern front and back, from the center shoulder down as far as the armhole notches. Then slash across almost to the armhole edge. Place the tissue underneath and spread the outer edge of the shoulder the necessary width. Pin the pattern to the tissue. Straighten the shoulder line as illustrated by the dotted lines.

**For kimono sleeves,** place a large piece of tissue under pattern front and back, and cut it the same shape as the shoulder and sleeve of the pattern. Slash the pattern from shoulder to waistline. Spread the pattern and add the necessary amount at the shoulder. Bring the slashed edges together at the waistline. Pin the pattern to the tissue. Adjust the sleeve edges as illustrated by the dotted lines and the tissue to retain the original contour.

## Narrow Shoulders

Slash the pattern front and back from the center shoulder line diagonally to the notches in the armhole. Lap and pin the slashed edges the necessary amount at the shoulder. Adjust the shoulder seam as illustrated.

**For kimono sleeves,** place the tissue under the pattern front and back and cut it the same shape as the shoulder and sleeve of the pattern. Fold and pin a dart at the shoulder to take up the necessary amount. Adjust the edges to retain the original shape, as illustrated by the dotted lines.

## To Lengthen Back Bodice (Right)

If you need extra length in the back and under-arm but not in the front below the bust, slash across the back bodice on the lengthening line. Place the tissue underneath and spread the pattern the necessary amount. Pin it to the tissue. Slash across the front bodice almost to the center line. Place the tissue underneath and spread the pattern at the underarm seam the same amount as the back bodice, tapering to a point at the center front. Pin the pattern to the tissue. Straighten the center front, front darts, and side seams, as illustrated by the dotted lines.

## Large Waistline

For this you must adjust both the bodice and the skirt. To adjust the bodice, slash the pattern front and back from the waistline toward the shoulder. Place the tissue underneath. Spread both front and back bodices to add the necessary width. Divide the required amount into fourths and add one-fourth to each section. Pin the pattern to the tissue.

To adjust the skirt, slash the pattern front and back from the waistline down toward the hipline. Place the tissue underneath and spread the pattern to correspond with the bodice section. Pin the pattern to the tissue.

When the fullness is only at the front or back,

add one-half the amount of the adjustment to only the one pattern section.

## Small Waistline

Take up the same amount in both the bodice and the skirt in the front and back of the pattern by increasing the depth of each waistline dart or tuck. To decrease the waistline 1 inch, for example, increase the two darts in the front and the two in the back ⅛ inch in depth.

If you need to decrease still more, take up at the side seams. Either make the side seams deeper or slash the pattern, bodice and skirt, from the waistline and lap the slashed edges the necessary amount. A seam allowance ¼ inch deeper at the sides, or a ¼-inch lapped slash will decrease the waistline 1 inch.

## Large Arm

On each side of the sleeve, draw a horizontal line about 3 inches long, beginning at the underarm; from this, draw a vertical line to the lower edge on each side. (If the sleeve is short, carry the vertical slash to the end of the sleeve.) Slash on these lines and place the tissue underneath. Spread the pattern, adding one-half the necessary amount on each side. Pin the pattern to the tissue.

To adjust the armhole seam, slash from the armhole almost to the waistline on the front and back bodice. Place the tissue underneath and spread the pattern sections to correspond with the sleeve adjustment. Adjust the armhole seam as illustrated.

## Large Upper Arm

To enlarge the upper part of the sleeve, use either of these methods:

*Method 1:* Place the sleeve over tissue of the same size and trim the tissue to match the cap of the sleeve. Slash the pattern from the shoulder line to the lower edge. Then spread each side of the pattern to add the additional width. Pin the lower sections of the pattern to the tissue. Bring the slashed edges of the cap together at the top and fold a dart on each side so that the pattern will lie flat. Pin the pattern to the tissue. Keep the grain line straight. Lower the armhole in the bodice at the underarm to fit the adjusted sleeve.

*Method 2:* Slash the sleeve from the shoulder line to the lower edge. Place the tissue underneath and spread the pattern to add the necessary width. Pin the pattern to the tissue. Lower the armhole in the bodice at the underarm to fit the adjusted sleeve.

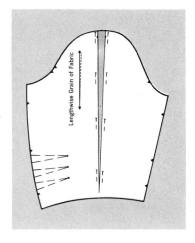

## Small Arm (Below left)

Fold a small tuck, lengthwise, through the center of the sleeve and increase the underarm seam the necessary amount. Raise the armhole at the underarm the same amount so that the sleeve and armhole will fit correctly, as illustrated for "Square Shoulders," but omit the slash to raise the shoulder line.

## Fullness at Elbow (Above right)

Extend the grain line the full length of the sleeve. Slash the sleeve across the elbow to the center; then slash up to the top of the sleeve. Place the tissue underneath and spread the pattern the necessary width. Pin the pattern to the tissue. Increase each dart by dividing the number of darts into the amount of the increase.

Straighten the grain line by drawing a straight line between the two ends as illustrated by the dotted lines. Increase the outer edge at the elbow as shown.

## Full Hips (top of next column)

Slash the front and back skirt, near the side seams, from the lower edge to the waistline. Keep the grain line straight. Place the tissue underneath and pin it to the inside edge of the slash. Spread the outer edge of the pattern to add the necessary width at the hipline. Add one-fourth the amount needed to both the front and the back of the skirt. Pin the other slashed edge of the pattern to the tissue from the waistline to the hipline. Form a dart in the pattern below the hip, tapering to the

side seam, as illustrated, to remove excess fullness at the lower edge. Pin the edge to the tissue below the dart. Add the necessary length to the lower outside edge to compensate for the dart.

## Narrow Hips

Remove excess width from the skirt front and back and divide the amount into fourths. At the hipline, form a lengthwise tuck in the skirt front and back to take up one-fourth the amount in each section. Taper the tuck to a point at the waistline but keep it the same width from hipline to lower edge. Make the adjustment near the side seam to avoid crossing darts and grain line.

## Large Derrière

Extend the grain line the full length of the pattern. To add width across the hips and length at the center back, draw a line through the center of the waistline dart to the hemline. Draw another line from the center back to the side seam at the fullest part of the hips. Place the tissue underneath. Slash the pattern on the drawn lines. Spread the upper sections of the pattern to add one-half the necessary width across the hips. Pin the edges to the tissue.

Spread the lower center section to add the necessary length to the center back. Pin it to the tissue. Spread the lower outside section to add length and width; join the upper and lower sections at the seam edge. Pin to the tissue. Form a dart below the hipline to avoid excess fullness at the hem edge. Pin lower section to tissue. Add length to the lower outside edge, as illustrated, to keep the pattern even.

Adjust darts to fit the waistline, and straighten the seamline at the point of adjustment, as illustrated by the dotted lines.

## Swayback

Use either of these methods:

*Method 1:* Slash across the skirt from the center back to the seam edge about 2 inches below the waistline. Lap and pin the slashed edges at the center back (usually about ½ inch), tapering to a point at the seamline. Use cellophane tape to hole the point in place. Add, as illustrated, to the center back to keep it straight. Straighten darts as shown by the dotted lines.

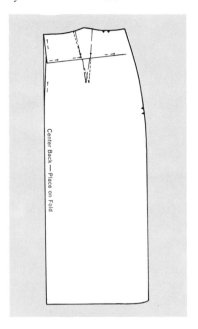

*Method 2:* You may also adjust for a swayback after you have cut the skirt. To do that, measure ½ inch down from the waistline edge of the fabric at the center back and place a pin. Then form a line with pins, gradually tapering to the seam edge at each side, as illustrated. Baste along this line. Do not trim off the edge at this time. In fitting and joining the skirt to the bodice, form a seam ⅝ inch below the basted line. Trim off the excess seam allowance after you have made the permanent line of stitching.

## Gored or Flared Skirt

*To lengthen.* Extend the grain line of the front and back skirt the full length of the pattern. Draw a line across the pattern at a right angle to the grain line and slash on this line. Place tissue underneath and spread the pattern far enough to add the necessary length. Keep the grain line straight. Pin the pattern to the tissue.

*To shorten.* Follow the same instructions for lengthening, but fold a tuck across the pattern to take up the necessary length. Remember that the width of the tuck is just half the amount to be removed.

*To enlarge waistline.* Slash the front and back pattern sections lengthwise, from the waistline to the lower edge. Place tissue underneath. Spread the pattern and add one-fourth the necessary width to both the front and the back. (When extra width is needed at the waistline, it is usually needed the entire length of the skirt to retain the grain line and contour of the pattern.)

If the skirt has a matching bodice, make corresponding adjustments in the bodice. See *Large Waistline*, page 44.

## Shorts and Slacks

Buy the pattern by the hip measurement and make adjustments in the crotch and waist as illustrated below.

**Method 1, Model seated:** Measure at the side seam from the waistline to the chair seat. (Chair seat should be firm). Add ½ inch for ease on small sizes and 1 inch on large sizes. *Recommended for the average figure.*

*To measure the pattern,* extend the grain line on the front and back sections the full length of the pattern. Draw a line at a right angle to the grain line, from the point where the seams join at the crotch to the side seam, as illustrated. Measure the pattern from the waistline to the drawn line as shown. If there is a difference in pattern and body measurements, adjust both the front and the back pieces. Pin the pattern pieces together and try on.

**Method 2, Model standing:** Measure the crotch from the front waistline, between the legs, to the back waistline. Add 3 inches for ease. *Recommended for the rounded figure.*

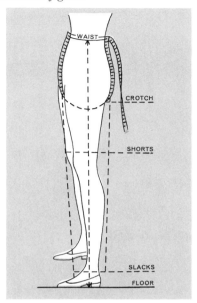

*To measure the pattern,* pin the front and back sections together at the crotch. (Fold under the seam allowance on one side and lap over the seam allowance on the other). Measure around the crotch from the back waistline to the front waistline *at the seamline* not the seam edge. (Stand the tape on edge to get an accurate measurement of the curve of the crotch.) If there is a difference between body measurement and pattern measurement, adjust as follows:

If the figure is equally proportioned, adjust both front and back. If the figure is large in the back, add only to the back section. Pin the pattern pieces together and try on. Lengthen or shorten the pattern as illustrated.

For length of slacks, measure from waistline to floor at front and side seams. Then measure the number of inches desired from the floor and subtract from the total length. Add the necessary amount for hem or cuff. The belt is not included in full-length measurements.

# Laying Out the Pattern and Cutting

BEFORE LAYING THE PATTERN PIECES on the fabric, be sure that you have completed the following steps;

1) Pressed your pattern and made all necessary pattern adjustments. See page 37.

2) Shrunk the fabric, if necessary, and straightened the fabric ends. See page 14.

3) Pressed out all creases and wrinkles in the fabric. See pressing instructions, page 64.

The guides given here cover the three steps you will take now:

1  Working with your pattern layout
2  Cutting the fabric
3  Transferring notches and markings to the fabric sections.

## PATTERN LAYOUT

### Rules to Remember

1. Clear a large, flat surface to accommodate your work. A dining-room table (protected with brown paper), a cutting board, a bedboard placed on the bed, or a ping-pong table, makes an excellent cutting surface.

2. Study the cutting layouts shown in the instruction guide included with your pattern. Select and circle the layout for the view you have chosen

45" fabric without nap sizes 14-16-18

as well as for your pattern size and for the width and type of fabric you are using.

3. Consider the type of fabric you will be working with. Some plaids and florals have an "up" and "down" to the design and must be matched. Napped and pile fabrics have the nap or pile running in one direction and therefore must be cut with all pattern pieces laid in the same direction. Satin, wool broadcloth, and similar weaves often show a varied degree of sheen in different directions; when in doubt, stay on the safe side by laying all pattern pieces in one direction.

4. Lay the pattern pieces printed side up unless otherwise instructed.

### Solid Colors or Small Prints

When the cutting layout shows a *double thickness*, fold the fabric right sides together. Pin edges together along the ends and selvages. Slash the selvage edges if they draw.

When the cutting layout shows a *single thickness*, lay the fabric right side up and the pattern printed side up. When right and left sides are cut separately, be sure *to turn the pattern pieces over to cut the second half of the garment*; otherwise you will have two bodice or skirt sections for the same side, or two sleeves for one arm.

When the layout shows a combination of *single and double layers of fabric*, make sure that you lay the correct pattern pieces on the single or double layer and that they face the direction shown in the layout.

Some layouts show the fabric opened to its full width and folded on the crosswise grain, right sides together. Napped, pile, plaid, and floral fabrics cannot be cut by this layout. See page 53.

The lengthwise grain line printed on the pattern must always parallel the fabric selvage. Place each pattern piece accurately on the fabric, and

## Rules to Remember

1. Use bent-handle dressmaker's shears with 6- or 7-inch blades. *Do not use pinking shears;* they are for seam finishing only.

2. Keep the fabric flat on the table and cut along the "cutting line" or edge of the pattern. Cut with long smooth strokes but do not close the shears to the point. Doing that will produce irregular edges. Leave pattern pieces pinned to the fabric until all markings have been made.

3. Cut the notches after cutting each garment section except when they are cut outward. See *Notches*, page 56.

4. Cut out the entire garment at one time. Also, cut the interfacing and underlining before beginning to sew. The underlining is usually cut by the same pattern as the garment after all markings have been made on the fabric.

pin at one end of the grain line marking. Use a tape measure or yardstick to measure, and adjust the pattern position so that the distance from grain line marking to selvage is the same at both ends. Then complete pinning along the grain line.

For pattern pieces designated "place on lengthwise fold of fabric," place the fold line *exactly* on the lengthwise fold of the fabric, and pin along the fold. (This designation appears when there is no center or back seam or opening in a bodice or skirt section.)

After you have accurately located the grain line, smooth out the pattern so that it will lie flat on the fabric. Pin pattern sections to the fabric along the edges, using plenty of fine, sharp pins to keep the fabric from slipping. Pin with the grain of the fabric and within the seam allowance. Re-check each grain line placement.

Lay and pin all pattern pieces before you start cutting.

## Plaids

If the pattern is appropriate for plaids, the pattern envelope will usually indicate how many yards of fabric you need. If it does not, buy an extra ¼ to ½ yard of fabric, depending on the size of the plaid.

A word about your pattern: To work successfully with plaids, avoid selecting a pattern with diagonal bustline darts, shoulder darts, or shaped joinings within a bodice or skirt. Too many seam joinings will break the continuity of the plaid. If the pattern shows darts at the waistline, convert them to tucks or gathers so that the plaids will match.

The plaid must match exactly in color and stripe at side seams, center seams or openings, shoulder seams, waistline, armholes, and sleeves. Therefore, during dress construction, slip-baste all seams following the instructions on page 62. This will enable you to match the plaids successfully and will prevent the fabric from slipping during the stitching.

EVEN PLAID

Plaids may be *even* or *uneven*. Your pattern layout will depend on the type of plaid you have selected.

### Even Plaids

Even plaids repeat their design on *both the lengthwise and the crosswise stripes*. They are identical in color, right and left and up and down. To work with them, follow these rules:

1. Fold the fabric, right sides together, so that the center of the plaid or the center of a bold lengthwise stripe falls on the center back and center front of the bodice and skirt. The upper and lower layers of the folded fabric must match exactly in color and stripe; pin them together along the stripe lines to prevent slipping during cutting.

2. Lay the pattern pieces on the fabric in either direction. Notches that will be joined together must be placed on the same color stripe. Matching notches occur at side seams, shoulder seams, armholes, sleeves, and waistline. Be careful to match at the *seamline*, not the seam edge. Match crosswise stripes of the sleeves and bodice.

### Uneven Plaids

Plaids may be *uneven* in *lengthwise* or *crosswise* directions or in *both*.

When *only the crosswise stripes* of the plaid are *uneven*, follow these rules:

1. Fold the fabric lengthwise, right sides together, so that the center of the plaid or the center of a bold lengthwise stripe falls on the center back and center front of the bodice and skirt. The upper and lower layers of the folded fabric must match exactly in color and stripe; pin them together along the stripe lines to prevent slipping during cutting.

2. Lay all pattern pieces on the fabric in *one direction*. Notches that will be joined together must

be placed on the same color stripe. Match at the *seamline,* not the seam edge. Match crosswise stripes of the sleeves and bodice.

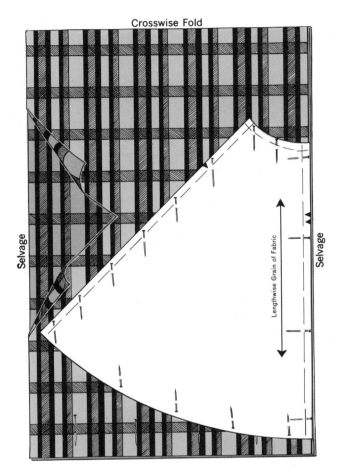

Crosswise Fold

Selvage

Lengthwise Grain of Fabric

Selvage

When *only the lengthwise stripes* of the plaid are *uneven,* they can be matched only when the pattern has a center seam or opening in the front and back of both bodice and skirt.

1. Open the fabric its full width and fold on the crosswise grain, right sides together. Match the identical stripes in the upper and lower layers of the folded fabric and pin them together along the stripe lines to prevent slipping during cutting.

2. Lay the pattern pieces on the fabric in *one direction* with the center of the plaid or the center of a bold lengthwise stripe falling on the center back and center front of the bodice and skirt. Notches that will be joined together must be placed on the same color stripe. Match the *seamline,* not the seam edge. Match the crosswise stripes of the sleeves and bodice.

When both *lengthwise and crosswise stripes* are *uneven,* they can be matched only when the fabric

has no right or wrong side and when the pattern has a center seam or opening in the front and back of both bodice and skirt.

1. Use the pattern layout "with nap"; lay the fabric right side up.

2. Lay all pattern pieces in *one direction* on *a single thickness of fabric,* with the center seam on a prominent lengthwise stripe. Notches that will be joined together must be placed on the same color stripe. Match at the *seamline,* not the seam edge. Match the crosswise stripes of the sleeves and bodice. Cut this half of the garment.

3. For the second half, lay the pattern on the fabric with the first half still pinned to it, matching identical lengthwise and crosswise stripes. Cut the second half of the garment. Cut notches and make markings through the two layers of fabric.

4. Reverse one side of each garment section when joining seams because there is no right or wrong side to the fabric.

UNEVEN PLAID

Selvage

## Stripes

Stripes may be *even* or *uneven.* They are cut the same as plaids. In placing the pattern on the fabric, be sure that notches that will be joined together fall on the same stripe.

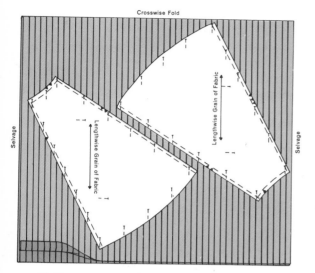

If the garment is cut on the bias, select a pattern with a center seam or opening in the front and back and follow these rules:

1. Fold the full width of the fabric on the crosswise grain, right sides together.

2. Lay the pattern with the grain line parallel to the selvage. Notches that are to be joined together must be on the same stripe. Stripes must be matched at side seams and center seams or center openings. Match at the *seamline,* not the seam edge.

3. During dress construction, slip-baste all seams.

When the stripes are *uneven,* lay the pattern pieces on the fabric in *one direction.*

Incorrect    Correct

## Checks

Checks ¼ inch or more in size *must* be matched; smaller checks are more attractive when matched. Follow instructions for cutting plaids.

## Florals, Prints, and Jacquards

Many floral fabrics have an "up" and "down" to the motif, and when they do, you must lay all pattern pieces in *one direction.*

To achieve a pleasing effect with medium or large motifs, make sure that they fall above the bustline instead of directly over it, approximately in the same position in the front as in the back, and in the same place on each sleeve. Match at the seamline whenever possible.

As with plaids, avoid patterns that require many seams within the bodice and skirt. Simple lines are more appropriate for prints, both large and small.

Incorrect    Correct

## Pile Fabrics

Pile fabrics such as velvet, velveteen, and corduroy should be cut with the pile standing up to emphasize the rich, dark tone. To determine the direction of the pile, brush the fabric with the fingers. If the surface is smooth, you are brushing with the pile; if rough, you are brushing against the pile. Use the "rough" direction for the top of your pattern layout; and lay all pieces in the *same direction,* following the "with nap" instruction guide with the pattern. Use fine needles to pin the pattern to the fabric.

## Napped Fabrics

Napped fabrics such as wool broadcloth, duvetyn, vicuna, and cashmere, have fuzzy fibers running in *one direction*. Often the direction is visible to the eye. If it is not, brush the fabric with your fingers as for velvet.

Cut napped fabrics with the *nap running down*. Lay all pattern pieces in *one direction*. Use fine needles to pin the pattern to the fabric.

# TRANSFERRING NOTCHES AND MARKINGS

The notches and markings on the pattern are your key to successful dress construction. Each has a special meaning and each must be transferred to the fabric while it is still pinned to the pattern.

## Notches

Notches are guides for joining the garment sections. They indicate which edges are seamed together and where the ease is located. On some patterns they are numbered to indicate the sequence in which the seams are sewn. Like notches are always joined.

Notches may be cut *inward* or *outward*, depending on the fabric you are using and your personal preference. Fabrics that fray readily or seam formations requiring an untrimmed, smooth seam edge, such as a French seam or a flat felled seam, should be cut with notches outward. Some beginners prefer to cut notches outward as a precaution against cutting too deeply into the seam allowance. Patterns designate both inward and outward methods.

### To Cut Notches Inward

After cutting the pattern piece, lift the fabric and fold it in the center of the notch. With the scissor points toward the outer edge, as illustrated, cut the notch only ⅛ inch deep. Be careful not to

cut too deeply because this will weaken the seam allowance.

### To Cut Notches Outward

Notches are cut outward as the garment is cut, following the markings that project beyond the seam edge. Cut them the exact shape of the pattern or you will not get an accurate joining. Use outward notches on chiffons and other sheer fabrics.

### Other Methods for Marking Notches

If the fabric ravels easily, make a tailor's tack (see below) at the point of each notch. Or, if you are an experienced sewer, clip in ⅛ inch from the edge of the fabric at the point of each notch, using scissors that cut sharply at the point. This is a timesaving method. However, watch closely for these clipped edges when assembling the garment.

## Markings

Dots, squares, triangles, or crosses on the pattern indicate the position for darts, buttonholes, tucks and pleats, seam allowances, joining points for gussets and yokes, and other construction details. To transfer these markings from the pattern to the fabric, use tailor's tacks, chalk, chalked thread, tracing wheel and tracing paper, or pins. The safest of these is tailor's tacks, which are preferred for fine fabrics. The other methods are quicker and can be safely used on many fabrics if you observe the precautions noted here.

Since all markings must be accurately made, transfer them while each pattern piece is pinned in position.

### Tailor's Tacks

Tailor's tacks are markings that will not rub off, press off, or mar the fabric. To make them, use a double thread about 24 inches in length and in a contrasting color to the fabric. Do not knot the end. Use a different color for each symbol, then it is simple to join like colors. Although regular mercerized thread is suitable, some sewers prefer embroidery or darning thread because it is soft and clings to the fabric. Follow these rules:

1. At the point to be marked, take a small stitch through the pattern and double thickness of fabric, leaving about a ¾-inch thread end.

2. Take a backstitch in the same place, and leave a loop a little shorter than the thread end. Clip the thread, leaving a ¾-inch thread end.

Continue in this manner until all markings have been finished.

If a group of tailor's tacks are made together, such as in darts, move from one marking to another without clipping the thread between the marks.

Before removing the pattern, clip the threads between the tacks. Remove pins, and carefully remove the pattern by pulling the threads through the tissue so that the tailor's tacks are not disturbed.

3. Raise the upper layer of fabric slightly, and clip the threads between it and the bottom layer, leaving thread tufts in both layers of fabric.

### Chalk

Tailor's chalk may be used when there is no danger of marring the fabric. Since it rubs off easily, use it only when the construction will be done immediately. (Always mark the wrong side of the fabric.) Chalk is available in several colors, with or without a wax base.

1. Place a pin through the pattern and double thickness of fabric at the point of the marking. Carefully slip the tissue pattern over the heads, then the points of the pins.

2. With tailor's chalk, mark the fabric over the pins on one side. Turn the section over and chalk the other side in the same place.

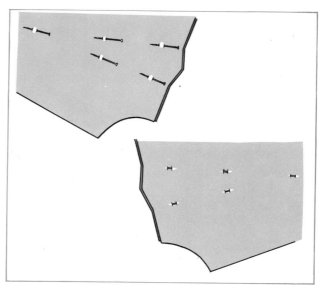

### Chalked Thread

Chalked thread is thread that has been coated with tailor's chalk. Use it as you would tailor's chalk above.

Thread a needle, using a double thread about 12 inches long. Do not knot the end.

1. Pull the thread around the square of tailor's chalk several times until it is well coated, even to the end.

2. Take a stitch in each marking through the pattern and double thickness of fabric. As the chalked thread is pulled out, it leaves a tiny chalked marking in each thickness of fabric. Rechalk the thread frequently.

### Tracing Wheel and Tracing Paper

Dressmaker's tracing paper is available in white, blue, red, yellow, and orange. Several colors are combined in one package. If you plan to use it, observe these cautions:

1. Use white tracing paper whenever possible. If you need a color, choose one near the color of the fabric but sufficient in contrast to make visible marks.

2. *Always mark the wrong side of the fabric* since the marks remain on the fabric until it is washed or cleaned. Although they can be removed from almost any fabric with a household dry cleaner such as carbon tetrachloride, energine, or benzine, on·many delicate fabrics good judgment dictates that you choose a safer method of marking.

3. Work on a flat surface. If you use a table, cover it with heavy cardboard so that it will not be marred by the tracing wheel.

4. Mark lightly with the tracing wheel. Do not press down too hard because the points of the wheel will mar the fabric.

5. Use small pieces of tracing paper and move them from one section to another as you are marking.

Practice using the tracing wheel and tracing paper on a swatch of the same fabric before marking the garment.

**To mark a double thickness of fabric,** which you will have when you cut with the fabric folded right sides together, use two pieces of tracing paper. Place one, right side up, under the botton layer of fabric. Remove enough pins to slip the second piece of tracing paper, right side down, between the pattern and top layer of fabric. (See illustration above.)

Use a ruler to keep the lines straight as you mark with the tracing wheel. Move the tracing wheel along the exact line of the darts or other details with one smooth, even stroke so that you do not change their shape. *Do not "saw" back and forth.*

If the fabric is heavy, you may have to mark one layer at a time.

**To mark the right side of the fabric,** as you must for pockets, buttonholes, and similar details, mark the wrong side with the tracing wheel and tracing paper and then baste along the marked line to transfer the markings to the right side.

**To mark a single thickness of fabric,** which you will have when you cut with the right side of the fabric up, place a piece of tracing paper, right side up, under the fabric and mark.

### Marking with Pins

Pin markings are not suitable for fine fabrics or patterns with intricate details. Use this method only when the darts, tucks, or other details will be basted immediately after each section is marked. Do not pin and set aside and later expect to find the pins in place.

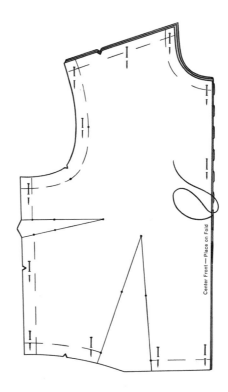

From the pattern side, plunge a pin through the pattern markings and two layers of fabric. Push the pins down so that the heads are tightly against the pattern.

Turn the section over and place a second pin through in the same point as the first pin.

Remove the pattern, carefully pulling the pinhead through the pattern.

When the two layers are separated, the fabric is pin-marked on both the left and the right sides.

### Center Line Markings

The center line of both front and back sections of the skirt and bodice is a guide for fitting as well as for joining facings and collars at the neck, lapping two sections when there is an opening, positioning buttonholes, joining the bodice and skirt, and folding the hem smoothly. Mark the center line after you have completed *all* other markings. Use a thread of contrasting color to the fabric and the other markings.

**On folds,** make long basting stitches in the fold, using a single thread. Knot the end of the thread at the beginning and take one backstitch at the end. (See top right.)

**For openings,** baste through the pattern and two layers of fabric along the center line, using a double thread. Make the stitches small and about 2 inches apart, leaving a loop between the stitches. Clip the looped thread between the stitches and carefully lift the pattern from the fabric, leaving the thread markings in the fabric.

Raise the upper layer of fabric and clip the thread between the two layers. Fold on the line of thread tacks, and pin. Make long basting stitches in the fold, following the instructions above. Remove the thread tacks.

# Assembling Your Work

With the fabric sections before you, with pins handy, and with a threaded needle and a threaded machine waiting to be used, the moment has come to put your creation together. Your work will proceed in this sequence:

1 Stay stitching
2 Basting.

## STAY STITCHING

Stay stitching is a line of machine stitching, placed through a single thickness of the seam allowance, ½ inch from the seam edge. It is used to hold the original shape of necklines, shoulder lines, waistline, and hiplines, and to prevent them from stretching when fitting and handling the garment. Stay stitching is not always a necessary step in dress construction. Some sewers like to stay-stitch fabrics that stretch easily or that will be pin-basted.

For your stitching, use matching thread and the appropriate stitch length for stitching seams in your fabric. Chain stitching can also be used to stay-stitch seams. See page 63.

### Direction of Stay Stitching

**Neckline**—from shoulder to center
**Shoulder line**—from neckline to armhole
**Waistline** (skirt and blouse)—from side seams to center
**Hipline** and bias skirt seams—from lower edge to waistline
**"V" neckline**—from point of "V" to shoulder line

## BASTING

Basting is a temporary stitch made to hold two or more pieces of fabric together before final stitching. It facilitates seaming and fitting and contributes to the appearance of good workmanship in the finished product. Basting may be done by hand, by machine, or by pins. In all cases, it is removed after each seam is completed.

### Hand Basting

Use a long, slender needle and a single strand of thread not more than 30 inches in length and contrasting in color so that it can easily be seen in the fabric. You may use regular "basting" thread, which is soft and lightly twisted, or mercerized thread. Use silk thread for fine fabrics when basting on the top side to hold two or more layers in position during final pressing—for example, along the finished edge of a facing, the fold for a hem, and similar details. In these cases silk is preferred because it does not leave a mark after pressing and will not mar fine fabrics at the needle puncture.

When basting sections of a garment, work on a flat surface such as a table or lap board. Place the seam edges together; pin at each end, at notches, and at the center. Then distribute the pins at equal intervals, working toward the seam ends. Place the pins at right angles to the seamline, with heads to the seam edge. Do not ease or stretch the seam.

Knot the longer end of the thread at the beginning of the basting line and fasten the line with a short backstitch at the end. Hand-baste, using one of the methods illustrated.

### Uneven Basting

Uneven basting may be used to baste regular seams on all fabric and *should* be used to mark the stitching line for top-stitching zippers, seams, facings, and the like.

Working from right to left, make a short stitch on the underside of the fabric and a long stitch on the top side. To remove, clip every 3 to 5 inches and pull out.

### Even Basting

Even basting may also be used to join side seams on any fabric. It is the preferred basting method for fabrics with a smooth finish and for areas that require close control—for example, set-in sleeves.

Working from right to left, take several long running stitches on the needle before pulling it through. To remove, clip every 3 to 5 inches and pull out.

### Diagonal Basting

After the facing edges of collars, lapels, cuffs, scallops, and similar construction details have been stitched, blended, and turned, they are held in place for pressing with *diagonal basting*. This is usually done with silk thread. Diagonal basting is not used to indicate a stitching line or to hold a seam when fitting.

Working from right to left and with the needle pointed toward you, take a short stitch at a right angle to the edge through all layers of fabric. The stitch length should be from ¼ to ⅜ inch, depending on the thickness of fabric. Place succeeding stitches in the same way, spacing them ⅛ to ¼ inch apart. A diagonal stitch will appear on the upper side and a straight stitch, at a right angle to the edge, on the underside.

Diagonal basting is also used to hold interfacings and underlinings firmly against the fabric during assembly steps. In this application, the spacing between the short stitches may be as much as an inch.

To remove diagonal basting, clip the diagonal thread every three or four stitches, and pull out.

### Slip Basting

Use slip basting to match stripes or plaids and to join intricate curved sections.

Work from the right side of the garment; fold under the seam allowance on one edge and pin. (Baste if necessary.) Lap the folded edge over the seam allowance of the joining section, being careful to match each stripe or plaid. Place pins at right angles to the folded edge, with heads toward the seam edge. Space the pins about ½ inch apart, depending on the size of the stripe or plaid.

Insert the needle, from the wrong side, up through the three thicknesses of fabric near the folded edge, and pull through. Then from the top side, directly opposite the previous stitch, insert the needle through the single thickness and bring it up through the three thicknesses and near the folded edge. A long stitch appears on the underside and a short stitch appears under the folded edge. The long stitch is usually from ¼ to ⅝ inch in length but may vary with the shape of the joining, the pattern of the stripe or plaid, or the texture of the fabric.

If you used a basting thread to retain the fold, remove it before stitching. Machine-stitch the seam from the wrong side through the center of the short basting stitches.

To remove the basting, clip the longer basting threads every two or three stitches and pull out. Use tweezers if your fingers cannot grasp the threads.

## Machine Basting

Machine basting is quick and easy, but it should be used only on fabrics where the needle puncture will not show.

Pin the seam edges together as instructed for hand basting. Adjust the stitch length selector on the machine for a 6 to 8 stitch length and stitch on the seamline. To remove, clip the top thread at intervals of four or five stitches, then pull the bottom thread.

## Pin Basting

Pin basting may be used on straight seams in fabrics that are easy to handle.

Place pins at right angles to the seamline, with the heads toward the edge; if you are going to use the Seam Guide, place the points toward the seam edge. The pins should just nip into the fabric at the stitching line; they should not extend under both sides of the presser foot and should never be placed on the underside of the fabric in contact with the feed of your machine. Machine-stitch on the seamline, using a hinged presser foot.

## Chain Stitching

The chain stitch is made by the needle thread alone. On top it looks like regular stitching, on the underside you can see that it is a series of interlocking loops that can be removed with just a pull on the thread end. This makes chain stitching a convenient method of basting seams for fitting, marking construction guidelines, inserting

"growth tucks" in children's clothes, and applying removable trimming.

Chain Stitch accessories are provided with some machines by Singer. Check your instruction book for the many sewing jobs you can do with chain stitching.

# Pressing
## as You Sew

PRESSING OFTEN SEEMS TO BE an unnecessary interruption in your work. This is far from the truth, however, and you should disabuse yourself of that notion now, for *pressing is an integral part of sewing*.

After stitching seams, darts, tucks, facings, and hems, you must press them. You must also press garment sections before joining them. If you do this faithfully as you sew, a touch-up here and there is all you will need when you have finished your work.

Form the habit of pressing correctly and at the proper time, as instructed in this chapter, and you will attain a perfection in finish and fit in your sewing which equals that of custom-made clothes.

The instructions that follow explain what you should know about:

1 Pressing equipment
2 Fundamentals of pressing
3 Pressing different kinds of fabrics
4 Pressing various construction details.

## PRESSING EQUIPMENT

Begin with proper pressing equipment conveniently arranged near the sewing machine. This will encourage you to use the methods professionals use. Once you have established a routine, you will find these methods valuable timesavers. They produce good results immediately and eliminate the "doing-over" that is discouraging to the experienced sewer as well as to the beginner.

The following equipment is basic and essential for good pressing:

*Iron.* The undisputed "first" of good pressing tools is your iron. Select one with a dependable fabric dial so that you are always sure of using the degree of heat appropriate for your fabric.

A steam iron is a good investment and may be used for both pressing and ironing. On some fabrics and in some areas of pressing, steam from the iron may supply enough moisture; generally, however, you will need additional moisture for an expert pressing job.

*Ironing board.* A sturdy board that you can easily adjust to several heights is the next requirement. Make sure that your board has a smooth, padded surface.

*Sleeveboard.* This small ironing board, which is used on your regular ironing board, is required for pressing sleeves, seams, and all fine details. The ironing board supports the weight of the garment and prevents unfinished areas from stretching or wrinkling.

*Seamboard.* This board, which is also placed on the ironing board, is used for pressing seams open on facings and especially at points. It is excellent for worsteds and other fabrics with a hard finish which must be pressed on a firm surface if you want to get a flat, sharply pressed seam.

*Press mitt.* This is essential for pressing darts, the top of set-in sleeves, and curved seams where the contour and fit of the garment must be preserved. Place the press mitt on the small end of the sleeveboard.

**Tailor's ham.** The tailor's ham is used on the ironing board for pressing and shaping curved seams, darts, collars, and lapels on suits, coats, and other tailored garments. It may be purchased at a notions counter and where tailors' supplies are sold.

You can also make one quickly, easily, and inexpensively. Purchase about ½ yard of drill cloth and shrink it before cutting. Make a paper pattern, egg-shaped, about 14 inches long and 10 inches in width at the wide end. Then cut two pieces of drill cloth by the pattern. Pin them together and stitch ½ inch from the edge, leaving a 5-inch opening. Backstitch at each end of the stitching. Press, then turn to the right side. Fill with clean, sifted sand or sawdust, packing the filling firmly into the cover. Turn the raw edge under on one side and lap the folded edge over the opposite edge; close the opening with hand stitching.

**Press cloths.** You will need three kinds of press cloths to properly press the range of fabrics used by most women who sew: (a) a chemically treated press cloth for pressing heavy fabrics; (b) a double thickness of cheesecloth as a thin, starch-free press cloth, for pressing medium and lightweight fabrics; and (c) wool woven interlining fabric for top pressing on all fabrics.

You will also need a yard length of good quality cheesecloth. Use it, moistened, when pressing cottons and linens; place it over the dry press cloth to provide uniform moisture when pressing silks, woolens, and many construction details. To moisten the cheesecloth, dip it in water, then wring as dry as possible.

**Wooden pounding block.** Use this to flatten the edges of faced lapels and collars, hems, facings, and pleats on tailored garments made of heavy or bulky fabrics. Steam the area first, then quickly apply the pounding block. After a little practice you will be able to determine the amount of pressure needed.

**Sponge and small camel's hair paintbrush.** Use these to moisten the seams of woolens.

**Clothesbrush.** Use this for brushing napped fabrics after pressing.

**Pressing pad.** You will need a pressing pad when pressing monograms, lace, and construction details such as zippers, corded buttonholes, and pockets in napped fabrics.

To make a pad, take three or four thicknesses of wool interlining about 20 inches long and 14 inches wide, and stitch them to a backing of drill cloth. Place the pressing pad on the ironing board with the layers of wool interlining right side up.

## FUNDAMENTALS OF PRESSING

Pressing demands a different technique from ironing. In pressing there is little motion of the iron when it is in contact with the fabric. In ironing, you glide the iron over the fabric in the direction of the fabric grain to remove wrinkles and to restore the shape of a garment or fabric that has been laundered. The amount of heat, moisture, and pressure required will vary with the fiber content. Here are the rules to follow in pressing:

1. Always test the fabric for pressing. If necessary, make a seam or dart in a swatch of the same fabric and press it to determine how much heat and moisture the fabric requires. Labels are not always at hand and some fabrics are difficult to classify.

2. Place the garment in position for pressing, making sure that the fabric is straight and smooth. Lift the fabric with both hands when it is necessary to move it.

3. Always press on the wrong side to guard against shine.

4. Use a press cloth on all fabrics, except cottons and linens; place it between the iron and the fabric. The kind of press cloth to use and the amount of moisture required will depend on the fabric.

5. Place the iron lightly over the section to be pressed and allow the steam to enter the fabric. Use minimum pressure on the iron and press in the direction of the fabric grain. This helps to retain the shape. Lift the iron to move to another section.

*Do not overpress.* It will take the life out of the fabric and cause shine. Overpressing results when you use too hot an iron, leave the iron in one place too long, use an inadequate press cloth, apply too much moisture, or press too frequently.

## HOW TO PRESS
## DIFFERENT KINDS OF FABRICS

Fiber, texture, and thickness determine how a fabric is pressed. Fiber content dictates the temperature of the iron, texture dictates the method of handling the fabric.

**Nylon, Dacron, and similar fabrics** require little heat. Set the heat control to the lowest temperature. Press the fabric on the wrong side, using a thin press cloth. The iron will not steam at this low setting. If moisture is required, place a single thickness of a moist cheesecloth over the dry press cloth.

**Rayon** requires a low heat, slightly more than nylon. Set the heat control on "Rayon." Press the fabric on the wrong side using a thin press cloth. Generally, steam from the iron will supply sufficient moisture. For heavy seams on which you will need more moisture, place a single thickness of a moist cheesecloth over the thin, dry press cloth.

**Silk** requires slightly more heat than rayon. But guard against too hot an iron, for it will weaken the fiber and discolor pastels and white. Set the heat control on "Silk." Press the fabric on the wrong side. For lightweight silk, use a thin press cloth. The steam iron should give sufficient moisture. For added moisture on thick seams, place a single thickness of a moist cheesecloth over the thin dry press cloth. On medium and heavyweight silks, use a double thickness of moist cheesecloth over the thin, dry press cloth for extra moisture.

**Lightweight cotton** requires slightly more heat than silk. Set the heat control on "Cotton." Press on the wrong side. You may place the iron directly on the fabric unless you are using a dark color. To provide uniform moisture on seams, facings, and similar construction, cover with a moist cheesecloth; press dry.

**Wool** requires more heat than lightweight cotton. Turn the heat control to "Wool." Press on the wrong side using a heavy press cloth or a double thickness of cheesecloth, covered with a moist cheesecloth. *Do not press entirely dry.* (Overdrying will produce a shine.) If you are working with a napped fabric, brush it with a clothesbrush, while there is still a moist steam, to raise the nap after pressing.

**Linen and heavy cotton** require a very hot iron. Set the heat control on "Linen." Press on the wrong side. You may place the iron directly on linen except when the fabric is of a dark color. To prevent shine on thick seams and dark colors, use a thin press cloth covered with damp cheesecloth for added moisture. Press dry.

**Velvet and velveteen** are steamed. *Do not bring the iron in contact with the fabric or you will flatten the pile.* Stand the iron on its heel and place a damp turkish towel over the soleplate. Hold the wrong side of the velvet close to the towel and move it back and forth to allow the steam to penetrate the fabric.

You can also steam velvet and velveteen on a velvet pressboard, which has fine fiber needles, or you can use a wool-faced pressing pad for steaming. Place the velvet face down over the pressboard or pressing pad. Hold the steam iron close to the fabric—not on it—and brush the fabric lightly to distribute the steam. Press the seam open with the finger tips, and steam it by holding the iron close to it. Keep your fingers dry; to avoid finger marks, lift the velvet only when it is dry.

**Blends** require varying degrees of heat, depending on the fiber content. The fiber requiring the lowest heat determines the proper temperature for the fabric. Press blends on the wrong side, using a thin press cloth. For a blend of Dacron and cotton, steam from the iron should supply sufficient moisture. For a blend of Dacron and silk, you will need additional moisture; use a single thickness of a moist cheesecloth over a thin press cloth. For a blend of silk and wool, which requires more steam than silk and Dacron, use a heavy press cloth covered with a moist cheesecloth.

**Crepe weaves** may present a problem since they tend to draw in when damp and stretch when under pressure. Place the pressing pad *under* the crepe, and the cheesecloth or wool press cloth *over* the fabric to retain the crinkle in pressing. The iron temperature is governed by the fiber content.

## HOW TO PRESS VARIOUS CONSTRUCTION DETAILS

### Rules to Remember

1. Remove pins and basting stitches before pressing. Pins mar the fabric and the soleplate of the iron; basting stitches leave an imprint. If you need a basting to hold two or more layers of fabric together during pressing (for example, facings), use silk thread and diagonal basting as instructed on page 61.

2. When pressing the first detail of a garment, press the entire section and not merely the area around the seam or dart. In many cases, there is a slight shrinkage of the fabric even though it has been preshrunk.

### Seams

Always use a sleeveboard when pressing seams or a seamboard if you have one.

#### Plain Seam

A plain seam should be pressed as follows:

*Step 1:* Press the seam in the same position as it was stitched. This will give you a smooth seam and imbed the stitching. To prevent shine, place the proper press cloth over all fabrics except light-colored cottons, which need no protection.

*Step 2:* Place the seam over the sleeveboard so that you can see the detail clearly and the bulk of the garment can rest on the ironing board. Use the fingers and the *point of the iron* to open the seam. The fingers should work about 2 inches ahead of the iron. Use a moist sponge or camel's hair paintbrush to apply moisture in seams of woolens before pressing them open.

*Step 3:* Press the seam open, using a press cloth between the iron and fabric. See page 66, *How to Press Different Kinds of Fabrics,* for the amount of moisture and the weight of press cloth you need. For heavy fabrics, place a strip of brown paper under the seam allowance to prevent the imprint of the seam edge from appearing on the right side of the fabric.

### Curved Seam

A curved seam must be blended before it is pressed. See *Seam Blending*, page 89. For the first pressing, follow Step 1 above. Then place the curved seam over the curve of a press mitt (which has been placed on the end of a sleeveboard) or over the curve of a tailor's ham. Follow the pressing instructions in the second and third steps for the *Plain Seam*.

ing and press again. The final pressing occurs after you have made the second line of stitching; press the same as in the first step. Use a press cloth and moisture required by the fabric.

### Flat Felled Seam

The flat felled seam is usually formed on the right side of the fabric and must be pressed with a press cloth between the iron and fabric. Trim

### French Seam

The French seam is first pressed in the same position as it was stitched, then pressed open with the *point of an iron*. Remember, this seam is on the right side of the fabric and must be protected with a press cloth to guard against shine. After trimming the seam allowance and turning to the wrong side, fold sharply on the first line of stitch-off the edge of one seam allowance, then press the seam open the same as the French seam. Fold on the seamline and press both seam edges in the same direction, with the longer edge on top. After turning the edge under and stitching a second time, press again from the wrong side, covering with a press cloth. (See the two illustrations at bottom of previous page.)

### Lapped Seam

A lapped seam is pressed on the wrong side after the edge on one side has been folded under and basted. Press only the very edge on curved seams. Cover the fabric with the proper press

cloth and use moisture. Press again on the wrong side after the seam is lapped and stitched. If top pressing is required, place the wool press cloth over the fabric.

## Darts

Darts should be pressed with care, for pressing further molds the dart to bring shape and roundness to the garment.

1. Press the dart flat, as it was stitched, *carrying the crease only as far as the stitching.* Protect the fabric with the proper press cloth and use the sleeveboard.

2. Place the dart over the curve of a press mitt, which has been placed on the small end of a sleeveboard, or over the curve of a tailor's ham. Darts are pressed *toward the center* of skirt front and back, blouse front and back, and shoulders; they are pressed *downward* at the underarm and elbow. Turn your dart in the proper direction and if the fabric is heavy, slip a strip of brown paper under the dart to prevent the imprint of the dart from appearing on the right side of the fabric. Cover the dart with the appropriate press cloth and use the amount of moisture required by the fabric. Press toward the point of the dart. Then press the entire section of the garment, using a press cloth.

### Darts in Heavy Fabrics

Darts in heavy fabrics are slashed and pressed open. After pressing the dart flat, as stitched, place the dart over the curve of a press mitt or tailor's ham. Open the dart with the *point of the iron.*

Place a strip of brown paper under each side of the dart, cover with the appropriate press cloth, and use the proper amount of moisture. Press the dart open.

### Contour Darts

Contour darts are slashed at the waistline to within ¼ inch of the stitching to relieve strain.

Press them in two operations: (1) press one-half the dart over the curve of a press mitt or tailor's ham the same as the conventional dart above; (2) reverse the garment and press the other half. Protect the fabric with a press cloth and use the moisture required by the fabric.

## Tucks and Gathers

### Tucks

Tucks are first pressed in the same position as they were stitched. Do not allow the point of the iron to go beyond the stitching. Then press the tucks in the proper direction, which is usually toward the center. When tucks are formed on the outside, the pattern may show them pressed either toward or away from center. Protect the fabric with the correct press cloth and use the proper moisture for the fabric.

### Gathers

Gathers are pressed by moving the point of the iron upward to the stitching. Lift the iron and repeat. The pressing can be done best with the iron directly against the wrong side of the fabric; for that reason, control of the iron's heat is very important. Since gathers are customarily made in soft fabrics, steam from the iron should give sufficient moisture.

## Buttonholes and Pockets

To achieve professional-looking buttonholes and pockets, you must not only follow scrupulously the sewing instructions but press at every step of construction. There are several excellent methods of making bound buttonholes and pockets. (Refer to *"Buttonholes"* or *"Pockets."*) The pressing technique illustrated here is one you should master since it is basic to most buttonholes and can be applied as well to pockets, which follow a construction sequence closely related to that of buttonholes.

The first pressing is done after the fabric patch is stitched in place for the buttonhole or pocket. Place the work, wrong side up, over the sleeveboard. Cover with the proper press cloth and press, using moisture appropriate for the fabric.

After slashing through the center and to each corner, turn the facing to the wrong side. Place the work, wrong side up, over the sleeveboard. Fold back the facing and pull the triangular ends away from the opening to square the corners. Apply moisture with a moist cheesecloth, and press away from the opening with the *point of the iron.* If the corners are slashed deeply enough, they will be square.

On each side of the buttonhole, fold the patch back, apply moisture with a moist cheesecloth, and press the seam allowances away from the opening, with the point of the iron touching the stitching. Press the entire length of the patch to crease the fold beyond each end of the stitching.

After basting the folds in place to fill the opening, press on the wrong side, using the proper press cloth and the appropriate amount of steam. Slip brown paper between the buttonhole seam allowances and garment to prevent the imprint of the

seam allowance from appearing on the right side of the fabric.

Follow the same pressing rules after the final

stitching and after the garment facing has been hemmed to the buttonhole as illustrated above.

For the final pressing of corded buttonholes, corded pockets, patch pockets, and pockets with a flap, place the wool-faced pressing pad on the ironing board. (See above right.) Slip brown paper between the garment and pocket pouch and between the garment and pocket flap as shown at right. If it is necessary to do any pressing on the right side, cover the garment with a wool press cloth.

## Neckline Facing Seams

Press the seam in the same position as stitched after you have trimmed and slashed the seam allowances. Use the proper press cloth and moisture required by the fabric.

Place the seam over the seamboard and open it with the *point of the iron*. Apply moisture with a moist sponge or paintbrush. Carefully control the heat of the iron so that you can press without a press cloth in this step.

On the curve of the neckline, press just a small portion at a time. Lift the garment with both hands to move it.

Outside curved seams as in collars and cuffs are pressed open over the heel of the seamboard.

Turn the facing to the underside, then ease it under slightly at the stitching line and baste. Use silk thread and diagonal basting to hold the facing securely in place on silks and woolens. Silk thread will not leave an imprint on the fabric. Press on the underside; cover with a wool press cloth and use the amount of moisture appropriate for the fabric.

*To press faced lapels and collars* on tailored suits and coats that are made of heavy or bulky fabrics, steam the area until you have plenty of live steam, then quickly pound the finished edge of the garment with a wooden pounding block. This will force out the steam and leave a flat edge without shine. (See above.)

## Sleeves

Correct pressing makes the difference between a homemade and a professional-looking sleeve. The underarm seam is pressed as it was stitched, the same as a plain seam; then the sleeve is placed over a sleeveboard, and the seam is pressed open.

Your first pressing of a set-in sleeve comes after pin-fitting the sleeve in the armhole. See page 159 for instructions on setting the sleeve into the armhole. Follow these rules:

**1.** Remove the sleeve from the armhole. Use a press mitt on the small end of the sleeveboard. Place the sleeve cap over the press mitt and secure it with pins. Cover the seamline with a dry press cloth and moist cheesecloth. Move the *point of the iron over the seam allowance* to shrink out the fullness. Be careful not to press beyond the stitching and overflatten the sleeve.

**2.** After you have stitched the sleeve into the armhole, press the armhole seam allowances over the small end of the·sleeveboard. Use the *point of*

*the iron* and press into the sleeve *only as far as the stitching*, never beyond it. Turn the seam allowance into the sleeve without further pressing.

In heavy fabrics, such as coating, press the seam open. In a puffed sleeve, as in children's clothes, the seam should be turned into the sleeve.

## Plackets

The universally accepted placket closing is the zipper. See page 176 for instructions on various types of zipper insertions. Your first pressing comes after closing the opening with machine basting. Press

the curved seam open in the machine-basted area; place it over the curve of a press mitt, which has been placed on the small end of the sleeveboard or over the curve of a tailor's ham.

Your second pressing step comes after the final hand or machine stitching. Place the wool-faced pressing pad on the ironing board with the wool interlining upward. Lay the garment, right side down, on the pad. Place a dry press cloth, then a moist cheesecloth, on the wrong side of the garment and press along the stitching line. Do not press over the metal chain or synthetic coil of the zipper, for you may mar the fabric, zipper, and soleplate of the iron.

After you have removed the machine basting, you may need a touch-up pressing. Place a strip of brown paper between the placket opening and the metal chain or synthetic coil of the zipper. Protect the fabric with a wool press cloth and press only the stitching line.

## Hems

Hems should not be visible in the finished garment. To achieve this, you must not only mark, fold, and finish the hem properly (see page 187), but *press* it carefully.

The first pressing step occurs after you have folded the hem and basted ¼ inch from the fold. Place the garment, wrong side up, over the end of the ironing board; cover with the proper press cloth and apply the moisture required by the fabric. Do not glide the iron; lift it from one section

to the other, pressing lightly and forcing steam through the press cloth to form a sharp crease at the fold.

If the fabric is heavy or bulky, steam the hem edge; then use the wooden pounding block, following the directions for *Faced Lapels and Collars*, on page 73.

Fashion may dictate a **soft hem fold** for fabrics such as double knits, loosely woven woolens, raw silks, and bonded fabrics. In such cases, press the hem *very lightly* so that you do not flatten the fold.

### Hems in Gored and Flared Skirts

Gored and flared skirts have fullness at the top of the hem which is controlled with machine stitching. To shrink out any excess fullness before applying seam binding, place the free edge of the hem over the curve of a press mitt (which has been placed over the small end of the sleeveboard) or over the curve of a tailor's ham. Cover with the same press cloth and use the same amount of moisture required in the first step. Press to shrink out the fullness.

After you have stitched the seam binding in place or completed the appropriate finish, press the hem on the wrong side in the position it will be hand-stitched, using a press cloth. Move the iron upward from the bottom of the hem to the top of the seam binding.

When the garment is of a heavy fabric, slip a strip of brown paper between the skirt and hem before pressing. This prevents the imprint of the hem edge from appearing on the right side of the garment.

Press napped fabrics over the wool-faced pressing pad.

After the final hand stitching, cover with a press cloth, use moisture for steam, and press lightly on the wrong side.

### Hem Across Pleat

When the skirt has a pleat, press the seam open in the area of the hem. See page 191 for instructions on slashing the seam allowance before pressing it open.

After you have finished the hem, turn the skirt to the wrong side, turn the pleat away from the skirt and press.

*To sharpen the edge of a pleat,* turn the garment to the right side. Place the pleat section over the sleeveboard with the underfold of the pleat up. Cover with the wool press cloth and press the length of the pleat. For instructions on pressing pleated skirts, see page 211.

# Fitting as You Sew

FITTINGS ARE PLEASANT STEPS in sewing that show you how your work is progressing. Even though you adjusted the tissue pattern to your measurements before cutting the fabric, you are apt to find that minor changes are required when you fit the fabric.

*Be critical.* The success of your garment depends as much on its fit as on the suitability of the pattern design and fabric. Fashions can be copied, but the garment becomes individually yours when it fits your figure properly. For a good fit, the fabric grain lines must fall correctly in the proper places on your figure. This is explained below in *Understanding Balance Lines.*

In addition to acquainting you with balance lines, this chapter also takes you through the basic fittings. A word of advice: Do not feel bound to fit your dress only at the intervals given here. You may want to fit it more often—especially if the pattern is intricate or you are not sure of an adjustment or are a beginner. Sometimes it is necessary to try on only the bodice or skirt section to test the fit. Fit as often as you feel you should before making the permanent line of stitching. Remember, changes made at the proper time are easier and quicker, and your dress is sure to be a success.

## UNDERSTANDING BALANCE LINES

The lengthwise and crosswise grains of the fabric must be in proper relation to the individual figure for any garment to fit well. The positions of the key grain lines are known as "balance lines."

The grain lines are in the correct positions on the tissue pattern. However, if your figure does not conform to standard measurements, adjustments are necessary. In adjusting the pattern and in fitting your dress, you must retain the correct position of the balance grain lines on your figure so that your dress will fit as it should.

The illustrations and text here point out the correct position of balance lines on a sheath dress.

### Bodice Front

**Chest**—about 4 inches below the base of the neck, on the *crosswise grain.*

**Bust**—across the fullest part of the bust, on the *crosswise grain.*

**Waist**—about 1½ inches above the waistline, on the *crosswise grain.*

**Center Front**—center of body, from base of neck to waistline, on the *lengthwise grain.*

### Bodice Back

**Shoulder**—about 4 inches below the prominent vertebra, on the *crosswise grain.* (This corresponds with the chest on the bodice front.)

**Underarm**—about 1½ inches below the armhole, across the shoulder blades, corresponding with the bustline, on the *crosswise grain.*

**Waist**—about 1½ inches above the waistline, corresponding with the front grain line, on the *crosswise grain.*

**Center Back**—center of body, from prominent vertebra at neck to waistline, on the *lengthwise grain.*

*(Continued on next page)*

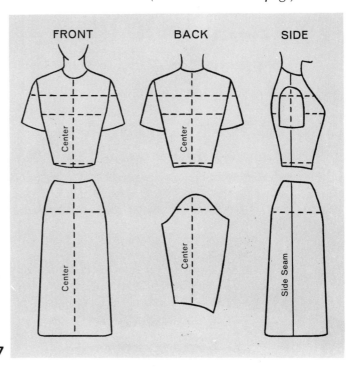

77

## Sleeves

**Center**—from shoulder line marking to center of wrist, on the *lengthwise grain.*

**Sleeve Cap**—about 3 inches below the shoulder line, across the sleeve cap at a right angle to the lengthwise grain. This line is on the *crosswise grain* and corresponds with the chest and shoulder grain line of the bodice.

## Skirt—Front and Back

**Center Front and Back**—center of body from waistline to hemline, on the *lengthwise grain.*

**Hips**—across the fullest part of the hips, usually about 7 inches below the waistline, parallel to the floor, on the *crosswise grain.*

The *side seams* of bodice and skirt must hang perpendicular to the floor although they are seldom cut on the straight grain of the fabric. In full skirts, the center front and back seams may be bias and the side seams may be straight grain, with a slight curve from the waistline about 4 inches down. All four seams must hang straight from waistline to hemline.

Always mark the center line on the fabric with hand basting. It is wise to baste the horizontal balance lines when sewing on fine fabrics, and it is especially important if you are a beginner in sewing.

When a muslin shell is made for use in fitting, draw the balance lines on the muslin before constructing the shell. In this way, you can easily determine whether the balance lines are in the correct position. If adjustments are necessary, make them in the muslin shell. Then make the same adjustments in the tissue pattern before cutting into the garment fabric. See *Muslin Shell,* page 315.

As you and your dress proceed through the basic fittings described below, keep an eye on the balance lines and make sure that they are in the correct position on your figure.

## PIN FITTING

### Assembling Your Dress

Before pin-fitting your dress, you should have completed these steps:

1) Transferred all markings from pattern to fabric.

2) Stay-stitched if necessary.

3) Basted darts and tucks.

4) Machine-stitched where needed to control any gathered fullness.

5) Basted sectional seams together so that you have four pieces: upper front, upper back, skirt front, and skirt back.

Work on a flat surface. Pin bodice sections together at the shoulder line and underarm seams, and skirt sections together at the side seams. Place pins parallel to the seamline with the fabric right side out and seam edges extended. Leave an opening on the left side of both bodice and skirt for the zipper. Turn under the waistline seam allowance of the skirt and pin.

## Fitting Your Dress

Try on the garment, right side out, in front of a full-length mirror if possible. Wear the lingerie and shoes you will wear with the finished garment. And don't forget make-up. It will help you visualize how the dress will look on you. If you plan to wear shoulder pads or shapes, insert them (and be sure to use them in every step of fitting).

If there is a center opening, lap the opening (with center lines coinciding) and pin together at buttonhole markings. Pin seams together in the opening for the zipper. Pin the bodice and skirt together at waistline, with the skirt seam allowance overlapping the bodice seam allowance; be sure to match center lines, darts, and side seams. Adjust the shoulder line to your figure and be certain that the basted center lines of the garment coincide with the center of your figure.

If you are a newcomer to dressmaking, you will probably be carried away by the fact that "it" actually looks like a dress. But let your eye roam critically over the several parts of the work. You will observe that the fabric fits a little differently from the tissue pattern. The need for minor adjustments, which you could not easily detect in fitting the tissue pattern, will become apparent now. As you make them, note them for future reference, for you will want to incorporate them in patterns you use later.

In studying your pin-fitted garment in front of the mirror, remember these points and consider them in your fitting:

1. The neckline has an extended seam allowance, which makes it seem smaller than it will be when the neckline is finished.

2. All ease allowances must be correct as outlined in checking and fitting the pattern. See page 37. Do not overfit the garment. The amount of fullness allowed in the pattern will differ with the style.

Fit the fabric for right- and left-figure differences, which occur most frequently at shoulders, waistline, and hipline. The paragraphs below explain how to make some of the usually needed adjustments.

### Bodice Adjustments

Observe and change when necessary the position of the waistline, placement of side seams and shoulder line, and alignment of buttonholes.

Check the length of the shoulder seam. Bring the arms forward to test the ease across the back, from armhole to armhole.

*Sloping shoulders* will cause the balance line to drop at the armholes and form wrinkles. To correct, re-pin the shoulder seams, making them slightly deeper as you approach the shoulder tips. This means lowering the armhole so that the sleeve will fit as it should. Baste the position of the new seamline. Lay the pattern on the fabric with the shoulder seamline of the pattern on the basted line of the fabric, and recut the armhole. Both shoulders are seldom identical and it may be necessary to change only one.

*If square shoulders* are the problem, the balance line swings up at the armholes and causes wrinkles to form diagonally toward the bustline and below the back neckline. Re-pin the shoulder seams, making them deeper at the neckline and tapering to a shallow seam allowance at the shoulder tips.

*Bustline darts* may need adjustment. Check the length and location of the darts. If there is full-ness below the bustline and the balance line seems to drop below the fullest part of the bust, raise the underarm darts enough to bring the points in line with the fullest part of the bust; if there is fullness above the bustline and the balance line is above the fullest part of the bust, lower the underarm darts.

*A small, flat bust* will cause the balance line to sag at the center front. Decrease the underarm darts enough to correct the balance line position and achieve a smooth effect. Now the bodice front will be longer than the bodice back at the underarm seams. *It is a common mistake for a beginner to make the bodice too short;* therefore, try on the dress again to prove the adjustment is correct. Then make a tuck across the tissue pattern, decreasing the length of the bodice front the same amount as you decreased the darts. Lay the pattern on the bodice front, and recut the lower edge of the fabric.

### Skirt Adjustments

*Difference in hips.* It is not unusual for the side seams to fit differently on the right and left sides of the skirt because one hip is higher or larger than the other. Be sure that the side seams hang straight from waistline to lower edge. The skirt should have enough ease at the hipline for you to sit comfortably and enough ease below the hipline so that the skirt will not cup.

*A swayback* will make the grain line sag at the center back and cause wrinkles below the waistline. To correct, raise the waistline of the skirt in the center back from ½ to ⅝ inch. Mark the adjusted seamline with basting, gradually tapering to the regular waistline seam allowance as you approach the side seams. Sometimes it is necessary to lift the skirt on only one side at the waistline.

*If the skirt hikes* in the front and the side seams jut forward, raise the back and sides of the skirt at the waistline just enough to bring the balance line in correct position and the side seams in a straight line to achieve a smooth effect.

*Skirt darts* should extend to the fullest part of the hips. It may be necessary to lengthen or shorten the darts to conform with the contour of your figure.

*Observe the length of the skirt* and the amount allowed for the hem.

Pin-mark any adjustments. Remove the garment and mark the adjustments with bastings.

You are now ready for some serious seaming. Before you begin, it may be wise to read over the pressing advice given in *Pressing As You Sew,* page 64.

## Garment Construction to Be Completed

The steps in construction to complete before this fitting are as follows:

1) Stitch and press all darts.

2) Make bound buttonholes if your pattern calls for them.

3) Baste, stitch, and press seams that occur within front and back sections.

4) If underlining is used, stitch and press the darts, then baste the underlining to the wrong sides of the garment sections.

5) Stitch and press shoulder seams.

6) Apply the interfacing, and finish the neckline and front or back opening.

7) If your dress has sleeves, baste the darts or control any fullness at the elbow. Baste the sleeve underarm seam.

8) Try the sleeve on the right arm, right side out, with the arm flexed to allow for muscle expansion. If there is a marked difference between the right and left arms, fit both sleeves.

9) Baste any adjustments and refit the sleeve. Stitch and press sleeve underarm seams.

10) Baste the side seams in the bodice and in the skirt, right sides together, observing the adjustments made in the pin fitting.

11) Pin and baste the sleeves into the armholes.

12) Baste bodice and skirt together at the waistline, right sides together, observing any changes made in the pin fitting.

## Fitting Your Dress

Try on the dress, right side out, to verify the adjustments noted in the pin fitting before stitching the side seams.

1. Lap and pin the opening. Position the seams and center lines correctly on your figure.

2. Tie a tape measure or a strip of fabric, about 1 inch wide, around your waist to locate the normal waistline. The seam should fall beneath the tape. Check the waist length, the ease allowances in all girth measurements, the placement of side seams and shoulder line, and the hang and true fit of the sleeves. The balance lines in the sleeves and bodice should correspond.

3. Bring the arm forward to test the ease across the back, from armhole to armhole, for freedom of arm movement. Insufficient ease will cause strain across the sleeve and be uncomfortable, and the sleeves will pull out at the seamline after you have worn the garment a few times. If shoulder seams are too long, the sleeves will drop off the shoulders and be uncomfortable. Bend the arms to be sure you have allowed enough ease in the sleeves for comfort. Pin-mark any adjustments. Baste the new adjustments and try on the garment again to prove them.

# SUBSEQUENT FITTINGS

## Fitting to Check Sleeve and Waistline

Before this fitting, remove the waistline and sleeve bastings. Stitch and press the side seams in the bodice and skirt. Baste sleeves into the armholes again and baste bodice to skirt, right sides together, observing any changes made in the preceding fitting.

Now, try on the dress; lap and pin the opening. Observe the bodice length, the fit in the waistline, the placement of the ease in the sleeves; determine the sleeve length. If you are satisfied, proceed with the final stitching.

## Your Final Fitting

Before the final fitting, sew sleeves into armholes, join skirt and bodice at the waistline, and sew in the zipper.

Try on the dress and test the fit. If you are satisfied, mark the hemline.

# Seams, Seams, Seams

SEAMS DO MORE than hold your dress together. Plain seams can express the lines of your dress through subtle shaping. Properly formed, they are almost invisible. Decorative seams can emphasize line in the dress design.

This chapter explains what you should know about seams to achieve the effect you want. The material is grouped in five sections:

1 General rules and helps in seaming
2 Different kinds of seams
3 Seam blending, beveling, or grading
4 Seam finishes
5 Understitching.

## GENERAL RULES AND HELPS IN SEAMING

A seam results when one or more lines of stitching are used to join two or more pieces of fabric. The steps in forming a seam are these:

1. Pin the seam edges together at ends, at notches, and at center, finally working between center and ends.

2. Hand-baste the seam. If your fabric is easy to handle and if you are sufficiently skilled in stitching, you can use pin basting instead of hand basting.

3. Stitch the seam with thread the exact color of the fabric. Set the stitch selector for the stitch length appropriate for your fabric (refer to the *Fabric, Thread, Needle, and Stitch Length Chart* on page 24) and then test the stitch on a swatch of the fabric. Stitch along one side of the basting thread, close to it but not through it. Backstitch at each end of the seam to secure the threads and to prevent the seam from raveling. Remove the basting thread.

4. Finish the seam edges. See page 91.

5. Press the seam in the same position as it was stitched and then press it open unless the pattern instructs otherwise.

## Seam Guidelines

The Seam Guide and throat-plate guidelines help you guide the stitching straight and parallel to the seam edge. The Seam Guide is adjustable for spacing stitching at any distance between ⅛ and 1¼ inches from the edge of the fabric. The throat-plate markings progress at ⅛-inch intervals, starting at ⅜ inch and extending to ¾ inch from the needle at the right. Since most patterns have a ⅝-inch seam allowance, the ⅝-inch line is more prominent than the other markings on the throat plate.

## Directional Stitching

There are also rules on the direction you should follow in stitching seams. In general, shoulder seams are stitched from the neckline to the arm-hole; bodice seams from underarm to waistline; sleeve seams from underarm to wrist; skirt seams from hem to waistline. There are exceptions, however; for example: pile fabrics such as velvet, velveteen, and corduroy are cut with the pile standing up, and all seams should be stitched upward with the pile (from lower edge to top edge).

Your pattern will indicate the types of seams you are to use, and below you will find instructions for forming them. Unless otherwise stated, all seams are stitched from the wrong side of the fabric.

## Plain Seam—Straight

The plain seam is formed with the right sides of fabric together. Place the seam under the needle, with the edges to the right. Position the needle about ½ inch from the back edge and lower the presser foot. Backstitch to the edge of the fabric for reinforcement; then stitch forward to the end of the seam and backstitch to reinforce it. Raise the presser foot and remove the fabric. Form the habit of using the Thread Cutter located at the back of the presser bar assembly and just above the presser foot.

## Plain Seam—Curved *(Top right)*

Curved seams require special attention in handling and shaping. Use a shorter stitch than for a straight seam. If you used a 12 stitch length for straight seams, use a 15 stitch length for curved seams to ensure extra elasticity and strength and to prevent seam failure under strain. Position the Seam Guide at an angle so that you get a uniform seam edge.

Curved seams must be blended so that they will lie flat. See instructions on page 89.

## Bias Seam

Hand-baste bias seams, leaving the threads loose at the ends. Allow your work to hang overnight before stitching. Always use a shorter stitch length for a bias seam. Fabric requiring a 12 stitch length on a straight seam requires a 15 stitch length on a bias seam to increase the elasticity of the seam. Stitch with the grain.

## Seam with Bias Edge and Straight Edge

To join a bias edge to a straight edge, pin and baste with the bias section on top. Stitch with the bias edge against the feed to ensure a smooth, even joining. *(See illustration at top of next page.)*

## Double-Stitched Seam

Use this seam in sheer fabrics and lace for curved as well as straight seams.

Place the first row of stitching on the seamline. Press. Place the second row of stitching within the seam allowance, about ¼ inch from the first row, using a fine multiple-stitch zig-zag. Straight stitching may also be used. Trim the seam allowance close to the outside row of stitching.

## Lapped Seam

Use lapped seams when joining sections of interfacing and interlining to eliminate bulk.

Lap one edge over the other, with the seamlines meeting in the center. Stitch through the center, using a multiple-stitch zig-zag or straight stitching. If the seam edges are too wide, trim after stitching.

## Abutted Seam

Use abutted seam in nonwoven interfacings and interfacings of hair canvas, muslin, and similar fabrics.

Trim away the seam allowance on both sections. Bring the two edges together and pin over an underlay of a lightweight fabric. The underlay should be 1 inch wide and slightly longer than the seam. Stitch from the right side, using the multiple-stitch zig-zag, widest stitch width, and 20 stitch length. Backstitch at each end. Be sure the abutted line is aligned with the center of the presser foot. Straight stitching may also be used on each side of the abutment.

## Ease in a Seam

A seam with slight ease often occurs at the shoulder or elbow where a long seam edge joins a shorter one.

Working from the long side, pin the edges together, matching at the ends of the seam and at the notches. Between the notches, ease the long side to the short side by inserting pins at frequent intervals, distributing the fullness evenly. Hand-baste, then stitch with the full side against the feed.

## Seams that Cross

Seams that cross occur at the shoulder line, waist-line, and underarm, and where darts join a seam or tuck.

Press the seams open and finish the edges as required by the fabric. To ensure accurately matched seams that cross, pin with a fine needle, with only the point nipped into the fabric at the stitching line; then pin on each side on the seamline. The

needle prevents one seam from slipping beyond the other during stitching and will not mar delicate fabrics. Blend away the excess seam allowance at the point where the seams cross.

## Top-Stitched Seam

Top stitching is used as a styling point along the finished edge of a garment or along the seam within a garment.

When preparing a curved, top-stitched seam, stay-stitch near the seamline on both the overlap and the underlap. Fold under the seam allowance on the overlap and pin, baste, blend, and press. Lap the folded edge a full seam's width over the underlap, then pin and baste. Remove the first basting. Top-stitch from the right side, close to the folded edge. If the stitching is ¼ inch or more from the edge, mark the stitching line with basting as instructed for *Top Stitching,* page 335.

## Tucked Seam

Use tucked seams as a styling accent in blouses, dresses, skirts, and other apparel.

Working from the right side, fold under the seam allowance on one side and pin; baste, if necessary. Lay the folded edge on the seamline of the second section and pin, keeping the raw edges even on the underside. Baste the tuck, maintaining an even distance from the folded edge to the basting line. Then stitch, following the even basted line. Trim off the seam edge on the undersection. The Quilter is an aid when stitching this seam because the guide keeps your stitching straight and parallel to the folded edge.

## Self-Bound Seam

Use self-bound seams in sheer curtains, children's clothes, blouses, and the like.

Make a plain seam and press it as stitched. Trim one edge to within ⅛ inch of the stitching. Turn under the other edge and pin it to the seam at the line of stitching, enclosing the first edge. Stitch near the folded edge.

## Hemmed Seam

A hemmed seam is appropriate when a fine, narrow seam is required, such as in sheer curtains and children's clothes.

When using this seam in a garment, the fitting must be done first and seam edges trimmed to ¼ inch. Attach the Hemmer Foot to the machine in place of the regular presser foot. With right sides of the fabric together, place the upper layer ⅛ inch to the left of the lower layer. Insert the edge into the scroll of the Hemmer and stitch so that the wide edge is hemmed over the narrow edge. See Hemmer Foot, page 283.

## Lingerie Seam

With zig-zag stitching, you can make dainty lingerie seams durable and rip-proof. This method is particularly good where flat bias seams are desired.

After straight-stitching the bias seam on the wrong side, press as stitched. Pink, and then press both seam allowances in the same direction. From the right side, stitch with a fine zig-zag stitch, allowing the needle to enter the seamline, then the seam thickness.

## Catch-Stitched Seam *(Right)*

A catch-stitched seam is used where the garment is interfaced or underlined. This is an excellent means of preventing seam edges from rolling when the garment is dry-cleaned. Use it in shoulder seams and notched collars, and where collar and facings join.

Trim the interfacing or underlining seam allowance close to the stitching. Press the plain seam open, then catch-stitch the seam edges by hand. Working from left to right, with the needle pointed to the left, catch only one or two threads in the seam allowance, then only a single thread outside the seam allowance and in the interfacing or underlining. Alternate the stitches along the seamline. The stitches are not visible from the top side.

## French Seam

Use a French seam in sheer fabrics, blouses, children's clothes, and lingerie. It is not appropriate for curved seams.

A French seam is a seam within a seam and, when finished, is usually ¼ inch or less in width. Place the wrong sides of the fabric together and stitch about ¼ inch from the seamline. Press as stitched. Trim seam allowances to within ⅛ inch of stitching and press the seam open. Turn the

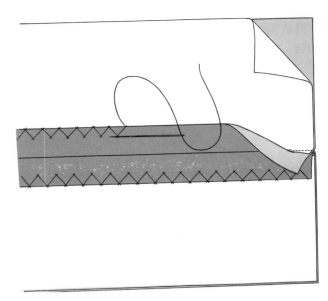

right sides of the fabric together; fold on the stitching line, and press. Then stitch on the seamline.

The Edge Stitcher may be used in making a French seam. The slot in the accessory assures a straight line of stitching. See page 284 for instructions on using the *Edge Stitcher*.

## Mock French Seam

Use this seam in sheer and lightweight fabrics, children's clothes, and blouses, in place of the conventional French seam. Both straight and curved seams may be finished in this way.

Stitch along the seamline with right sides of the fabric together. Press as stitched. Trim the seam edges slightly if they are too wide. Fold both seam edges to the inside and stitch them together.

## Flat Felled Seam

Men's and boys' wear usually calls for flat felled seams. They are also used in give a tailored appearance to women's sportswear. It is a matter of preference which side of the seam is made on the right side. One side reveals an inside seam paralleled by stitching, and the reverse side reveals a top-stitched seam paralleled by a row of stitching.

With right sides of the fabric outward, take the full seam allowance with the first row of stitching. Press the seam open, then press both seam allowances to one side, keeping the right side of the stitching on top. Trim the under seam allowance to one-half its width. Turn the upper seam allowance edge evenly over the trimmed edge; then top-stitch.

Opinions differ on the handling of flat felled seams. On men's wear, the seam edges that are blended are usually (1) the back seams on side seams and sleeve seams, (2) the sleeve seam edge on shoulder seams, (3) the garment section on yoke

seams, and (4) the front seam on shoulder seams.

Zig-zag stitching gives strength and durability to flat felled seams. You can substitute it for straight stitching, following the directions given above. Use a 15 stitch length and a medium-width zig-zag stitch.

## Slot Seam

Slot seams are used as fashion seams in skirts, blouses, dresses, suits, coats, and children's clothes made of heavy or medium-weight fabrics.

Pin and machine-baste on the seamline, leaving one long thread at each end. Press as stitched, then press the seam open. Clip the machine basting on one side at four- to five-stitch intervals. Cut an underlay of the same or contrasting fabric 1 inch wider than the two seam edges. Working from the wrong side, center the underlay over the seam and pin in position. Baste from the right side. Then from the right side, stitch along each side an equal distance from the seam depression. The distance may be from ¼ to ½ inch, depending on the fabric. If less than ¼ inch, gauge the distance with the presser foot; if more than ¼ inch, mark both stitching lines with basting as instructed for *Top Stitching,* page 335. Remove the machine basting by pulling the long thread, and remove any short threads that are visible.

The Quilter is convenient for top stitching. The space guide on the Quilter is guided into the depression of the machine-basted seam, ensuring an accurate stitching line parallel to the fold. See the instructions below for *Welt Seam.*

## Welt Seam

Welt seams are style seams that are often found in suits and coats made of firm fabrics.

Form a plain seam on the wrong side, using the stitch length appropriate for the fabric. Press first as stitched; then press the seam open. Trim 3/16 inch from one seam edge, and press both seam edges to one side so that the wide edge covers the narrow edge. Baste flat. From the right side, stitch an even distance from the seam depression. If the distance is greater than ¼ inch, mark the stitching line with basting as instructed for *Top Stitching,* page 335.

The Quilter is excellent for this top stitching since it gauges the stitching, keeping it straight and parallel to the seam depression. Insert the removable space guide from the right side of the Quilter and adjust it for the desired distance. If the fabric is heavy, tilt the space guide so that its wall will accommodate the layers of fabric. As you sew, guide the seam depression against the space guide.

## Hairline Seam

A dainty hairline finish is desirable for enclosed seams of sheer collars and facings.

Set your zig-zag machine for a short stitch length and a narrow stitch width, and use a filler cord of either heavy-duty thread or buttonhole twist. Unwind a sufficient amount of the filler cord to prevent strain or tension on the cord. Lead the end of the cord through the right eyelet on the Special Purpose Foot. Draw the cord under and in back of the foot. Stitch on the seamline, covering the filler cord. Press, and trim away the seam

allowance close to the stitching. Turn to the right side and press. Seam allowances that would ordinarily show through are eliminated.

## Seams in Chiffon

Carefully hand-baste seams in chiffon. Using a 15 to 20 stitch length, test the stitching on a swatch of the chiffon. The quality of the stitching depends on the machine and the softness of the fabric. Stitch slowly, and apply gentle tension on the seam by holding it both in front and in back of the presser foot.

If your machine does not stitch chiffon satisfactorily with the above method, place tissue paper under the seam before stitching. Remove the tissue paper by gently pulling it away from one side of the stitching, then from the other.

## Seams in Knit Fabrics

Because of their loop construction, knit fabrics are not always seamed and finished in the same way as woven fabrics. The kind of seam that is most appropriate for a specific knitted fabric will depend on the amount of stretch in the fabric, the weight or thickness of the fabric, the kind of garment it will be used for, and the position of the seam within the garment. The technique for easing one seam to another is quite different from that appropriate for woven fabrics. Also, the kind of seam finish, if one is required, and the seam width will vary from those appropriate for woven fabrics. See *Knits,* beginning on page 417.

## Seams in Kimono Sleeves

To make seams in kimono sleeves, see *Kimono Sleeve—without Gusset,* page 162; or *Kimono Sleeve —with Gusset,* page 164.

## SEAM BLENDING, BEVELING, OR GRADING

To blend, bevel, or grade a seam means to remove the bulk so that the seam will lie flat. The procedure varies depending on whether the seam is enclosed or fitted and whether it is an inside curve, an outside curve, a straight seam, or square corner or point. Seams that require blending are stitched and then blended according to the methods described here.

### Fitted Seams

Fitted seams are found at the shoulder line where the neck is built up, in a princess-line bodice, at the waistline in suit jackets, in yokes, and in seams extending over the bust and hipline. These seams are usually pressed open and the edges are finished as required by the fabric.

Fitted seams may be inside or outside curves. Do not trim them, but blend them as follows:

*Inside curves.* Slash into the seam allowance far enough to relieve the strain imposed by the seam edge so that it will lie flat. The depth of the slash and the number of slashes will vary with the degree of the curve and texture of the fabric; however, the slashes usually extend to within ¼ inch of the stitching and are made at evenly spaced intervals. There are times, however, when only one slash is necessary.

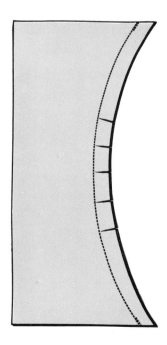

*Outside curves.* Cut narrow notches or wedges out of the seam allowance, sufficient in depth to remove only the portion of the seam edge that may overlap when the seam is pressed open. Avoid cutting out a wedge so large that it will produce a saw-tooth effect in the seam edge that will press through and mark the right side of the fabric. Cut the notches at evenly space intervals. The frequency and spacing depend on the degree of the curve and the texture of the fabric. When the curve is slight and the fabric flexible, it may not be necessary to blend the seam.

Often an inside curve is seamed to an outside curve. This requires slashing the inside curved edge and notching the outside curved edge.

## Enclosed Seams

Enclosed seams are found in facings. They may be straight, as in front and back facings of blouses, dresses, jackets, and coats; or curved or shaped as in necklines, collars, cuffs, shaped yokes, pockets, and similar construction. Blend them as follows:

*Straight seams.* Trim the interfacing close to the stitching if it is included in the seam. Blend the facing seam allowance to ⅛ inch and the garment seam allowance to ¼ inch. Press, then press the seam open. Turn to the right side; ease the facing under slightly at the seamline and baste. Use diagonal basting and silk thread. Press flat. *(See illustration at top of next column).*

*Inside curves.* If interfacing is included in the seam, trim it close to the stitching. Blend the facing seam allowance to ⅛ inch and the garment seam allowance to ¼ inch. Slash these blended seam edges to within ⅛ inch of the seamline at evenly spaced intervals. This relieves the strain imposed by the seam edge and prevents pulling. Press the seam open. Then, turn to the right side; ease the facing under slightly at the seamline and baste. Use silk thread and diagonal basting. Press flat.

*Outside curves.* If interfacing is included in the seam, trim it close to the stitching. Blend the facing seam allowance to ⅛ inch and the garment seam allowance to ¼ inch. Cut notches in the seam allowance at evenly spaced intervals to remove the bulk. Cut away only enough to permit the seam to lie flat so that you do not have a saw-tooth effect in the seam edge. Press, then press the seam open over the curved edge of a seamboard, a press mitt, or the finger. Turn to the right side;

ease the facing under slightly at the seamline and baste. Use silk thread and diagonal basting. Press flat.

**Square corners and points.** Square corners and points require diagonal stitching across the point to allow enough space to smoothly enclose the seam edge that turns to the inside. The number of diagonal stitches varies with the weight of the fabric. Lightweight, crisp fabrics may require only one stitch across the point and heavy fabrics may require as many as three.

Stitch to within one or two stitches of the intersecting seamline. Pivot with the needle in the

fabric, but on its upward stroke, and turn the fabric so the stitching is directed diagonally across the corner; then take one, two, or three stitches. Pivot again, turn the fabric, and stitch, following the seamline.

If interfacing is included in the seam, trim it close to the stiching. Blend the seam allowance on the facing to ⅛ inch and on the garment to ¼ inch. Trim away the seam allowance diagonally across the point and very close to the stitching; then trim away the seam allowance diagonally at the sides of the point. Press the seam open before turning to the right side. Ease the facing under slightly at the seamline and baste. Use silk thread and diagonal basting. Press.

## SEAM FINISHES

Seam edges are "finished" to prevent them from raveling during use and in washing or dry cleaning; to improve the appearance of the inside of your garment; and to strengthen the seam itself.

Seams in a garment should be finished during the assembly process and before being crossed by another seam. The seam finish must be without bulk so that it is not visible when the garment is worn and does not form a ridge on the right side when the garment is pressed.

You should know a variety of seam-finishing methods so that it will be easy for you to select the one best suited to your needs. When in doubt, try several different methods on test seams before making up your mind.

## Pinked Seam

Use a pinked seam on fabrics that will not fray or ravel.

After stitching a plain seam, pink the seam edges with pinking shears. Remove only the seam edge. Cut with a medium stroke; do not fully open the shears or cut entirely to the point. Press the seam in the same position as it was stitched, and then press it open.

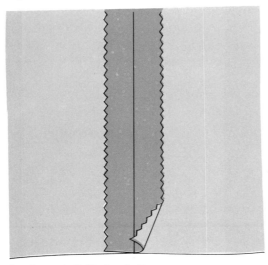

## Pinked and Stitched Seam

This seam finish may be used on almost any fabric that will ravel.

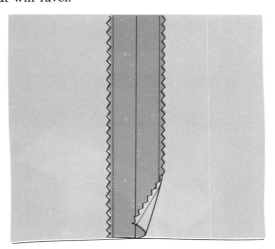

Form a plain seam. Place a line of stitching about ¼ inch from the seam edge, using a 20 stitch length. Pink the edges. The stitching will prevent the seam from raveling and curling.

## Edgestitched Seam *(Above)*

Use this finish on lightweight and medium-weight fabrics as well as on unlined jackets and boleros.

Stitch a plain seam. Press the seam flat, then press it open. Pink the edges; then fold them under ⅛ to ¼ inch and stitch on the folded edge. The Edge Stitcher will help you keep this stitching straight and parallel to the edge. For instructions on using it, see page 284.

## Open Bound Seam *(Below)*

Binding is an excellent finish for fabrics that tend to fray, such as tweed and heavy, coarse weaves, as well as for unlined jackets and coats. Instructions for using the *Binder* may be found on page 282.

Form a plain seam. Press the seam, then press it open. With the Binder on the machine and silk bias seam binding, bind each seam edge, using either straight stitching or an open zig-zag stitch. To prevent seam edges from stretching or fraying in loosely woven fabrics, place a row of stitching ⅛ inch from the seam edge before applying the binding.

## Net Bound Seam

Delicate fabrics that fray easily, such as chiffon velvet, and sheer metallic, may have seam edges bound with nylon net, which prevents fraying without adding bulk.

Cut the net into ½-inch strips and insert, unfolded, into the Binder. Feed seam edges into the Binder with napped or right side up. Stitch, using a medium-width zig-zag stitch.

## Plain Bound Seam *(Bottom, previous column)*

This seam is practical for household items such as cushions, simple slipcovers, and articles made of plastic.

After stitching a plain seam, trim the seam edges to a scant ¼ inch. Press. Insert both edges into the Binder and stitch, keeping the seam edges well into the scroll as you sew.

## Machine Overedged Seam

The blindstitch zig-zag provides an excellent finish for tweed, raw silk, double knit, and heavy woolens.

Form a plain seam. Press the seam as stitched, then press it open. Use the blindstitch zig-zag, and form the stitches over the edge of the seam. Both the stitch length and the stitch width settings vary with the fabric.

*When both seam edges are turned in the same direction* as in a sleeve armhole and pocket pouch, press the plain seam as stitched. Trim the seam allowance to about ¼ inch. Then stitch the edges together, using the blindstitch zig-zag.

## Zig-Zag Seam

Zig-zag stitching is an ideal seam finish for jersey, double knit, and other fabrics with "give" because the stitch is as flexible as the fabric. Either the plain or multiple-stitch zig-zag may be used.

After forming a plain seam, press it open. Select a plain zig-zag stitch, medium stitch width, and between 15 and 20 stitch length. Stitch near the seam edge but not over it. Press. Trim off the seam edge close to the stitching.

For the multiple-stitch zig-zag, select a wide stitch width and a short stitch length (in the "fine" area), and stitch close to the seam edge. Press.

## Seams Overcast by Hand

If the fabric has a tendency to ravel and a machine finish would be too harsh, finish the seam edge by hand.

Form a plain seam and press it open. By hand, make slanting stitches over the seam edge, about ¼ inch apart and about ⅛ inch in depth, depending on the weight of the fabric. Do not pull the threads too tightly.

When the seam is pressed open, overcast the edges separately. When both seam edges are turned in the seam direction (sleeve and waistline seams are examples), overcast the two edges together.

## UNDERSTITCHING

To prevent a facing edge from rolling beyond the garment edge, you must stitch the seam allowances to the facing on the underside.

Before doing this you will have completed a certain amount of garment construction—namely: the facing will be stitched in place and the seam blended and pressed; then the facing will be turned to the underside and eased under slightly at the seamline before pressing again.

To understitch, turn facing and seam allowances away from the garment and stitch from the right side, through facing and seam allowances, close to the seamline. Since this stitching is not on the right side of the garment, it is invisible in the finished work.

# Underlining and Lining

ADDING AN UNDERLINING OR LINING to your dress is one way of achieving a custom-made look in your clothes. Many fabrics and fashion styles require either one or the other to retain the shape and add body to the garment.

Simply defined, underlining and lining are a *second thickness* of carefully selected fabric that is used to support the garment fabric and add resistance to strain. *Underlining* is sewed into the seams with the garment fabric. Hand stitches that hold down facings and hems are made in the underlining instead of the garment fabric. *Lining* is constructed separately and attached to the skirt at the waistline seam or to the dress at the neckline, armhole, and waistline seams.

Do not confuse underlining and lining with interfacing. See page 134. When a garment is underlined or lined, interfacing is included in such areas as facings, collars and cuffs, lapels, and the like.

Whether or not you underline or line a gar-ment is a decision you should make when you are planning your dress and selecting a pattern. The type of underlining or lining you select depends on the fabric you are using as well as the effect you wish to achieve. For example, a sheer fabric such as organza makes an ideal underlining for soft silks and woolens, peau de soie, and imported cottons that will be dry-cleaned. It allows them to retain their naturally soft, luxurious feeling, which would be lost if a bulky or heavy underlining were used. For a closely woven wool or raw silk, a heavier fabric such as China silk or SiBonne may be a good choice—and lining rather than underlining may be preferable. Lay your dress fabric over the underlining or lining fabric so that you can judge the final effect.

Almost any fabric may be underlined; generally, however, only firm and opaque fabrics are lined. For guides on fabrics to use as underlining or lining, see page 20.

## HOW TO UNDERLINE DRESSES AND SKIRTS

You may underline the entire dress or just a section of it. The underlining in skirts may extend to the fold of the hem, to the top of the hem, or to about 12 inches below the hipline.

### Underlining a Dress

Cut the underlining by the same pattern pieces and on the same grain as the garment. Notch and mark each section the same as the dress fabric, and place the corresponding pieces together.

Stitch the darts and seams within the bodice and skirt sections separately in the dress fabric and underlining unless the fabric is sheer. See page 97. Finish seam edges, and press.

Place the fabric, wrong side up, on a flat surface; lay the underlining over it. Both pieces must be smooth and wrinkle-free. Pin them together along the center line, side seams, and waistline. Place several rows of diagonal basting within each section, as illustrated below and on the following page, to hold the two layers of fabric together.

Use silk thread and make the stitches from ⅜ to ½ inch in length and about 2 inches apart. Do not draw the thread tightly. *Do not remove these bastings until the hem is finished.* (If the two fabrics are of different lengths, the skirt will not hang evenly.) Hand-baste a scant ⅝ inch from all seam edges in the bodice and side seams of the skirt.

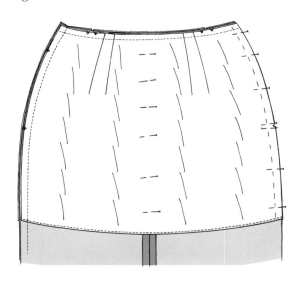

At the waistline of the skirt and bodice, machine-stitch the underlining to the dress fabric ½ inch from the seam edge. Handle the fabric and underlining as one piece of fabric in assembling the garment.

## Hemming Underlined Garments

*When the underlining extends to the top of the hem,* pink the lower edge of the underlining; then fold it under ¼ inch and stitch near the folded edge, using the multiple-stitch zig-zag.

*When the underlining extends to the fold of the hem,* fold the hem over the underlining and hand-stitch in place, making the stitches through only the underlining and hem.

Hem the skirt, using the method suitable for the fabric. See *Hems and Hem Finishes* page 187.

## Underlining a Skirt with a Pleat

When there is a pleat in the skirt, you should extend the underlining to the top of the hem.

*In the skirt fabric,* stitch the darts and seam for the pleat, following the instructions accompanying the pattern.

*In the underlining,* stitch the seam above the pleat from the waistline to the top of the pleat, leaving a slit in the pleat area. Trim off excess fabric, allowing a ⅝-inch seam allowance. Pink the seam edges and lower edge of the underlining

back and front. Fold the pinked edges under ⅝ inch and stitch around the lower edge and both sides of the slit, using the multiple-stitch zig-zag for added strength. Stitch the darts. Baste the fabric and underlining together, following the instructions for *Underlining a Dress,* above, and handle as one in assembling the garment.

## Underlining Sheer Fabrics

Fabrics such as chiffon and lace should be under-lined with a smooth, firm, opaque fabric, similar in fiber content to the sheer. Colors should match or complement each other to create an illusion of color intensity or variation. Two underlining methods are given here; select the one appropriate for the style of your dress and the effect you wish to achieve.

*Method 1:* A complete underlining, stitched as one with the garment fabric, permits you to treat a sheer as a heavier fabric and to use patterns with darts and styling seams since the underlining conceals them in the finished dress.

Place underlining sections, right side up, on a flat surface and the sheer dress fabric, right side up, over them. Baste together, following the directions for *Underlining a Dress*, page 95. Hand-baste through the center of darts to hold the two layers of fabric together. Pin, baste, and stitch the darts through the two layers. Handle the fabric and underlining as one in assembling the garment.

To create the illusion of a sheer yoke and sleeves or of strapless, bare shoulders, underline the upper part of the bodice with net or chiffon and the lower part of the bodice with a firm, opaque fabric. Join the two fabrics above the bustline.

*Method 2:* If the dress has a full skirt, the bodice section may be underlined and the skirt section lined—that is, the two fabrics in the skirt can be seamed and hemmed separately and joined only at the waistline.

Treat the bodice section as instructed above. For the skirt, follow the instructions given on page 99, *Lining a Sheer Skirt.*

## HOW TO LINE DRESSES AND SKIRTS

When dresses or skirts are lined, they are finished as nicely on the underside as on the top side. The top fabric and lining are constructed separately and are placed wrong sides together so that the seam allowances are hidden. In dresses, the lining is joined to the top fabric at the neckline, arm-hole, or waistline seams; in skirts it is joined to the top fabric at the waistline. Do not confuse these linings with those used in tailored coats and suits which are covered in *Graduate to Tailoring,* pages 325 and 329.

## Lining a Dress

In a blouse or sheath dress that is collarless and sleeveless, the lining can serve as a one-piece neck-line and armhole finish. In a collarless garment

97

with set-in sleeves, it can serve as a neckline finish. In both cases you eliminate the regular facing, which would only add unnecessary bulk.

**If the dress is collarless and sleeveless,** cut the lining by the dress pattern. Stitch the underarm seams separately in the dress and in the lining. Finish the seam edges and press the seams open. *Leave the shoulder seams open.* Apply the lining to the dress, following the instructions for the *One-piece Neckline and Armhole Facing,* page 141. But substitute the full-length lining for the facing in the instructions.

Hem the lining and dress separately, making the lining 1 inch shorter than the dress. To add a decorative touch, you can make a narrow hem in the lining and sew lace edging to the hemmed edge.

**If the dress has sleeves,** cut the lining by the dress pattern. Stitch the shoulder and underarm seams separately in the dress and in the lining. Finish seam edges. Press the seams, then press them open.

Turn the dress wrong side out and the lining right side out. Place the lining inside the dress, right sides together. Pin and baste the lining to the dress around the neckline, matching center lines, notches, and shoulder seams. Stitch.

Trim the lining seam allowance to ⅛ inch and the dress seam allowance to ¼ inch. Slash the seam allowances on curves and clip off corners where seams cross at the underarm. Press.

Turn the lining through the neck opening and over the wrong side of the dress; then turn the dress to the right side. Ease the lining under slightly at the seamline and baste. Press, then remove bastings. Understitch the seam to prevent the lining from rolling out of place (see page 94). Press. Arrange the lining smoothly against the underside of the garment fabric, then baste around the armholes. Handle as one fabric when you sew in the sleeves.

Hem the lining and dress separately, making the lining 1 inch shorter than the dress.

## Lining a Skirt

The skirt and lining are constructed separately and joined only at the waistline seam. This is an excellent treatment for heavy woolens and firmly woven cottons that will be dry-cleaned.

Cut the lining by the same pattern pieces and on the same grain as the skirt. Notch and mark each section the same as the skirt fabric.

Stitch and press the darts and all seams in the

skirt and sew in the zipper. Then stitch and press the darts and all seams in the lining. Make the opening for the zipper the same length in the lining as in the skirt fabric.

Place the lining inside the skirt, wrong sides together, and pin together at the waistline, matching seams, darts, and markings. Turn the skirt to the wrong side with the lining on the top side. At the end of the placket opening in the lining,

slash diagonally on each side, ¼ inch beyond the seamline. Fold under the edges and pin them to the zipper tape, as illustrated. Slip-stitch in place. Stitch the skirt and lining together at the waistline, ½ inch from the seam edge. Apply the waistband.

Hem the skirt and lining separately, making the lining 1 inch shorter than the skirt.

## Lining a Slit Skirt

In the method explained here, the slits in the lining do not correspond with those in the skirt. If the skirt is slit in the back, as in the illustration, the lining is slit at each side seam; if the skirt is slit at the side seams, the lining is slit in the center front or center back. Then a facing is stitched to the lining, directly under the slits of the skirt, which leaves a pleasing finish.

Cut the lining by the same pattern pieces and on the same grain as the skirt. Notch and mark each section the same as the skirt fabric.

Construct the skirt, leaving the seams open the depth of the slits plus hem. Reinforce with backstitching. Machine-baste the seams together in the slits.

Construct the lining so that the seams will face the seams in the skirt. Stitch darts and the full length of the seams that correspond with the slits in the skirt.

Cut a facing of the skirt fabric 5 inches longer than the slit plus hem and seam allowance, and 8 inches wide so that it will extend 4 inches on each side of the slit. (The skirt illustrated has two slits in the back and required only one piece of the fabric for the facing. It was cut 8 inches wider than the distance between the two slits.) Fold under the seam allowance at the top and each side of the facing. Press.

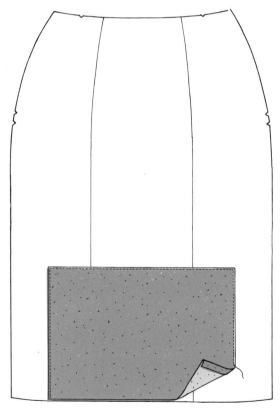

Center the facing right side up on the top side of the lining, keeping the lower edges even; pin. Baste, then stitch near the folded edges. (If the slits in the skirt are at the side seams, center the facings over the side seams of the lining.)

Pin the front and back lining sections together at the side seams. Stitch, leaving the seams open the depth of the slits. Reinforce with backstitching. Machine-baste the seams together in the slits. Finish the seam edges. Press, then press the seams open.

Turn the lining to the right side. Place it inside the skirt, with the faced side of the lining to wrong side of the skirt. Pin together at the waistline, matching seams and markings. Finish, following the instructions above under *Lining a Skirt*.

Hem the skirt and lining separately, keeping them the same length. See *Hem in Slit Skirt*, page 191.

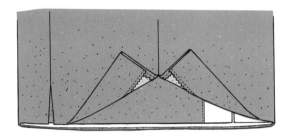

## Lining a Sheer Skirt

To create an interesting variation, the lining is sometimes fitted closely to the figure and the sheer top skirt is billowy or flowing, which creates a misty effect. Such treatment requires careful handling and finishing of all seams.

Seam the sheer fabric and lining separately; use a fine French seam in the sheer fabric. Place the lining inside the sheer skirt, with the right side of lining next to the wrong side of the skirt. Join them at the waistline (see page 98), then join the skirt to the underlined bodice. Hem the two fabrics separately. A narrow hem is essential for the sheer full skirt—make either a hand-rolled hem or a hem with horsehair briad. See pages 197 and 192. Make a 2-or 3-inch hem in the closely fitted lining.

If both the sheer and the lining are circular or flared, they must also be hemmed separately to keep the sheer from sagging and blousing over the lining. Make a narrow hem in each.

# Darts, Tucks, and Gathers

Darts, tucks, and gathers are three friends you will meet often in apparel construction. Darts are preferred in firm fabrics; tucks in smooth, drapable fabrics; and gathers in soft, sheer fabrics. All three have a functional and decorative use in sewing; each in its own way gives fit and contour to a garment. For purely decorative applications of tucks and shirring, see pages 235 and 243.

## DARTS

### Beginning Tips on Darts

Darts provide fullness at the bust, hip, shoulder, and elbow. They must point toward the fullest curve of the figure but must not extend as far as the curve.

It may be necessary to change the position of darts to conform with the contour of your figure. Darts extending from waistline to bustline are sometimes moved closer to the center or farther apart to bring them directly under the fullest part of the bustline. To accommodate a lower bustline, darts extending from underarm toward the bustline should be placed lower than indicated on the pattern.

The length of darts in a skirt may also have to be adjusted for better fit. A short figure may require shorter darts, and a very tall figure longer darts. If darts in the bodice are moved closer to the center or farther apart, then the darts in the skirt must be moved to correspond with them.

Darts are usually formed on the wrong side of the garment. They are stitched on the right side only when they are styling points and the continuous-thread dart is used. See page 101.

### Stitching a Dart

How you handle the fabric when forming and stitching a dart has a direct influence on the result. Since darts should be barely visible when completed, they must be tapered gradually to the point so that there is no bulge where the dart ends.

Fold the dart and match markings; start pinning at the seam edge, then at the point, and at intervals between. Place the pins at right angles to the seamline, with the heads toward the folded

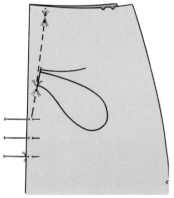

edge. Baste from the seam edge to the point. Remove the tailor's tacks. Start stitching near the seam edge and reinforce with backstitching, tapering gradually to the point where the last three or four stitches parallel the fold in the dart, *just a thread's width from the fold.* Continue stitching off the fabric to form a chain about ½ inch beyond the point. Clip the thread ends about 2 inches from the point. Tie the thread chain into a single knot, using a pin to set the knot close to the fabric.

*(Illustrated at top of next column)*

In heavy fabrics such as tweed and flannel, darts are frequently slashed and pressed open. If the fabric is one that ravels or frays easily, overcast the slashed edges. On firm fabrics that do not fray easily, finish with pinking shears.

## Pressing Darts

Pressing further shapes and molds the dart after stitching. Darts are pressed toward the center in skirt back, blouse front and back, and shoulder; and downward at the underarm and elbow. Use the curved surface of a press mitt or tailor's ham.

First press the dart flat as it was stitched, carrying the crease only as far as the stitching. Protect the fabric with a press cloth. Then place the dart over the tailor's ham or press mitt. Turn the dart in the proper direction. Cover it with a press cloth, and use the amount of steam required by the fabric. Press toward the point of the dart.

## Continuous-Thread Darts

The continuous-thread dart is used (1) on "outside" darts, that is, when the fold of the dart is on the outside of the garment; and (2) on inside darts when the fabric is sheer. The stitching begins *at the point* rather than the seam edge as in the conventional dart, and no thread ends are left to be tied in a knot at the point.

Thread the bobbin thread through the needle in the opposite direction from the usual threading, and tie it to the upper thread in a single knot. Rewind the spool until the knot has passed all threading points and is a sufficient distance from the last thread guide nearest the spool to provide enough thread to stitch the full length of the dart.

Position the tip of the needle into the point

KNOT DRAWN BACK

of the dart, *just a thread's width from the fold.* Pull the slack out of the thread by turning the spool. Lower the presser foot and stitch, carefully shaping the point while stitching toward the seam edge. Reinforce the seam edges with backstitching. Rethread the machine for each dart.

The *Touch & Sew* machine has push-button bobbin winding, which simplifies threading for continuous-thread darts. The bobbin stays in the machine and is wound with thread directly from the needle, which gives a continuous thread. If you have a *Touch & Sew* machine, wind an empty bobbin with enough thread to make a single dart (usually about one yard). Stitch as instructed above. Wind an empty bobbin for each dart.

## Skirt Darts

Darts in the back skirt extend to the fullest part of the hips and are pressed toward the center. Darts in the front skirt are smaller and may be in groups of two. Skirt and bodice darts must meet at the waistline.

## Underarm Darts

Underarm darts point to the fullest part of the bustline and may be on a horizontal or diagonal line. They are formed in the same manner as the conventional dart. Press flat as stitched; then press downward over a press mitt.

## Shoulder Darts

Shoulder darts are usually narrow and about 4 inches in length, depending on the size of the pattern. They are stitched in the same manner as the conventional dart and pressed toward the center over a press mitt.

## Elbow Darts

Close-fitting sleeves that extend below the elbow are usually darted for ease at the elbow. The darts are stitched in the same manner as the conventional dart. Press flat as stitched; then press downward over a press mitt.

## Contour Darts

Darts that fit the waistline and taper to a point at each end are known as "contour" darts. They are used in suits, princess-line coats and dresses, and overblouses.

To form the dart, fold the fabric and match markings; pin at the waistline, at each point, and at intervals between. Baste.

Stitch the dart in two steps, beginning at the waistline and stitching to the point each time. Overlap the stitching about ¾ inch at the waistline. Tie the thread ends at each point. Slash to within ¼ inch of the stitching at the waistline to relieve the strain. Press flat as stitched; then press each end over a press mitt.

*The continuous-thread method* may be used when stitching the contour dart. Follow the instructions for *Continuous-Thread Darts*. Start stitching from one of the points to ⅜ inch beyond the waistline. Rethread the machine (or, on a *Touch & Sew* machine, rewind the bobbin). Repeat the operation from the other point, overlapping the stitch about ¾ inch at the waistline. Slash and press the same as above.

## Diagonal Bust Darts

Diagonal darts may originate at the underarm seam or at the waistline, and they always point diagonally toward the fullest part of the bust. They may have the conventional fold or a cutout section where seam edges are joined.

To make the diagonal dart, begin at the waistline or underarm seam and place the seam edges of the dart together, matching markings. Pin at the wide end, at the point, and at intervals between, easing the seam on the long side. Baste. Begin stitching from the wide end; reinforce with backstitching, and gradually taper the stitching to the point where the last three or four stitches parallel the fold *and are just a thread's width from it.* Then tie the thread ends into a single knot, using a pin to set the knot close to the fabric.

Press flat as stitched; then press both edges toward the center over a press mitt. The seam in the dart may be pressed open if the fabric is heavy.

## Interfacing Darts

To shape darts in interfacing and eliminate bulk, cut out the dart allowance on the stitching line. Bring the two cut edges together and pin over an underlay of a lightweight fabric such as organza. Cut the underlay 1 inch wide and slightly longer than the dart. Stitch from the right side.

When using a zig-zag machine, select the multiple-stitch zig-zag, widest stitch width, and 20 stitch length. Align the abutted line with the center of the presser foot.

If you use straight stitching, stitch on each side of the abutted line. Reinforce with backstitching at each end. Press over the curved surface of a press mitt.

# TUCKS

## Tucks for Contour

Contour tucks are found at the front shoulder line, front and back waistline of the bodice, and the front section of the skirt. They are used to provide fullness and are usually formed on the wrong side of the garment. (They may, however, be formed on the right side as a styling point. See *Continuous-Thread Tucks* below.)

Tucks extending down from the shoulder seam

and up from the front waistline should be directly in line with the fullest part of the bust. Tucks in the front skirt section should match the tucks in the bodice section when joined.

Fold the tuck, match the markings, and keep the seam edges even. Pin and baste.

Start stitching at the seam edge and reinforce with backstitching. Continue stitching to the end of the tuck, then backstitch again for reinforcement.

## Continuous-Thread Tucks

When the fold of the tuck is formed on the right side of the garment to provide a style accent, the continuous-thread tuck is used so that no backstitching shows. (Threads may be drawn to the underside and tied, but the continuous-thread method is more durable and attractive.)

Pin and baste the tuck, keeping the seam edges even. Begin the continuous-thread stitching at the end of the tuck farthest from the seam edge (below the bustline) and finish it at the seam edge with backstitching.

Position the tuck under the needle and lower the presser foot. Hold the needle thread loosely with the left hand while turning the hand wheel with the right hand to form a stitch. Draw the bobbin thread up through the fabric. Thread the bobbin thread through the needle in the opposite direction, following the instructions for *Continuous-Thread Darts* on page 101. Then, position the point of the needle in the fabric and pull the slack out of the thread by turning the spool. Stitch slowly to the seam edge and reinforce with backstitching.

For instructions on pressing tucks, see page 70.

# GATHERS

## Gathering to Control Fullness

Patterns for soft or sheer fabrics may indicate gathering to control fullness at the shoulder, at the waistline of the bodice or skirt, at yoke joinings in a bodice or skirt, at the shoulder or cuff of sleeves, and at other styling points. The pattern should indicate the number of rows of stitching.

Use an 8 to 10 stitch length in medium-weight fabrics and a 12 to 15 stitch length in soft or filmy fabrics. Loosen the upper tension enough to draw the bobbin thread. (Do not forget to return the tension to its previous setting.)

Place the first row of stitching in the seam allowance a scant ⅝ inch from the seam edge; place the second row in the seam allowance about ½ inch from the seam edge. Neither of these rows will be visible in the finished garment. Additional lines of gathering, which will be visible in the finished garment, may be placed ⅛ to ¼ inch apart. Space the first additional row the selected distance from the first row of stitching at the ⅝-inch position.

At one end, draw the threads through to the underside. Tie by forming a single knot in the two strands of thread and set the knot tightly against

the fabric. Hold these thread ends and fold the fabric at the end of the rows of stitching. Stitch close to the fold, forming a pin tuck across the end, extending it from the seam edge to the last row of stitching. Cut off the ends of the gathering threads ½ inch from the stitching.

At the other end of the stitching, anchor the threads on the right side of the garment by forming a figure eight around a pin. One thread for each row of stitching remains on the wrong side of the garment. Tightly twist these threads together and pull, and at the same time ease the fabric back on the stitches to form uniform gathers. Finish the second end by drawing threads to the underside and tying. Cross with a pin tuck.

## Gathered Skirts

In gathered skirts, use heavy-duty mercerized or nylon thread on the bobbin because it will not break while you are easing the fullness across the width of the skirt.

First stitch the side seams and put in the zipper. Pin-mark the waistline at the zipper opening and at the right side seam. Then place the stitching for the gathers as instructed above; however, stitch the front and back sections separately. Extend the stitching from the right side seam to the zipper opening in each section, and leave 3-inch thread ends. (The pin tuck is eliminated in this method.)

Match markings on the skirt with those on the waistband or bodice, and pin. To gather each skirt section between the markings, pull the bobbin thread at each end of a section and ease the fullness toward the center. Pull threads to the underside and join the broken lines of stitching by tying the four threads together into a single knot close to the stitching. See illustration on page 306. Pin the skirt to the waistband or bodice at close intervals, then stitch.

# Buttonholes without Tears

THE THOUGHT OF MAKING BUTTONHOLES has been known to throw the budding seamstress into a panic. It need not. What may seem like the bane of dressmaking will soon become a pleasant routine if you approach the task cautiously but courageously.

Remember first that buttonholes may be decorative as well as functional. Properly positioned, they contribute to the fit and comfort of your garment.

This chapter tells you about the preparatory steps and explains how to make the several kinds of buttonholes—fabric bound, corded, machine-worked (using either the zig-zag machine or the Buttonholer), and hand-worked. The type of buttonhole you make depends on the fabric, the style of the garment, and your preference and skill. Corded and bound buttonholes are usually preferred in women's dresses, suits, and coats; machine-worked buttonholes are used in sportswear and children's clothes as well as men's and boys' wear; hand-worked buttonholes are found in babies' clothes and blouses of soft, fine silk, linen, or cotton.

## PREPARATORY STEPS

### Position of Buttonhole

The rules for positioning buttons and buttonholes apply to all types of buttonholes:

—Buttonholes in women's and girls' clothes are placed on the right side of the garment; in men's and boys' wear, on the left side.

—*Horizontal* buttonholes are placed to extend ⅛ inch beyond the center line basting; *vertical* buttonholes are placed so that the center line basting falls in the center of the buttonhole.

—Buttons are sewed on the opposite side of the garment with the center of the button positioned exactly on the center line basting. When the garment is buttoned, the center lines on the right and left sides coincide. If a closing overlaps more or less than the pattern indicates, the fit of the garment is altered.

—The pattern usually designates the button size the garment is designed to carry. The space from the center line basting to the finished facing edge must be from three-quarters to once the diameter of the button. With this spacing, the button will not extend beyond the facing edge when the garment is buttoned. If you plan to use a button size different from that indicated on the pattern, take this into account when cutting the garment so that you allow the proper distance between the center line and finished edge. Adjust facing width the same amount.

—Spaces between buttonholes should generally be equal, although fashion may show a different arrangement, especially in loosely fitted garments. Your pattern will designate the spacing required. However, if you have had to adjust the pattern—that is, lengthen or shorten the bodice or skirt, or alter the bustline—or if you use a button larger or smaller than the size indicated on the pattern, you will have to modify the buttonhole spaces accordingly.

Normally, buttonholes should be spaced in harmony with the figure. When they are incorrectly spaced, the closing gaps, giving the appearance of a poorly fitted garment.

—*The three key points for positioning buttonholes* are at the fullest part of the bust, the neckline, and the waistline.

Mark the position of the buttonhole at the fullest part of the bust, then at the neckline (and then at the waistline if you are making a coat, jacket, overblouse, or princess-line dress).

After locating these key points, space additional buttonholes evenly between them.

If the pattern has buttons all the way down the front, place the last buttonhole about 4 inches from the hem edge.

*—Determine the positions of the buttonholes and mark the fabric while the pattern is still pinned to it.* During the first fitting, check the positions to prove that they are accurate.

## Length of Buttonhole

Since the length of the buttonhole depends on the size of the button, *select buttons before making buttonholes.* To determine the length, measure the diameter plus the thickness of the button. To test the length, cut a slash in a double thickness of fabric swatch. If the button slips through the slash easily, the size is correct.

Always make a test buttonhole in a swatch of the fabric you are working with. Fold the fabric, duplicating a facing, and include the same type of interfacing you will use in the garment. Buttonholes should be long enough so that the button slips through easily, yet snug enough so that the garment stays buttoned.

## BOUND AND CORDED BUTTONHOLES

In making bound buttonholes, you have a range of methods from which to choose: the patch, one-piece, two-piece piped, and corded. All produce attractive durable buttonholes. The two-piece piped method is recommended for loosely woven fabrics; for all other fabrics, the selection is up to you.

Bound buttonholes are not difficult when you follow the directions given here. They are made through the garment fabric and either a stay or lightweight interfacing before the facing is attached.

Use a stay of a lightweight fabric such as batiste lawn, or silk organza to reinforce the stitching around the buttonhole when you are using a *heavy-weight* interfacing. *Never make bound buttonholes through hair canvas or heavy interfacing.*

When the interfacing is of a *lightweight* fabric such as batiste, lawn, organdy, it may serve as a stay as well as an interfacing.

Position the stay or lightweight interfacing on the wrong side of the garment, and pin. Then baste guidelines for the position and size of the buttonholes as instructed below.

*When making a series of bound buttonholes,* always carry through the same step for each buttonhole before proceeding to the next step. Press carefully after completing each step.

Always make a test buttonhole in a swatch of the same fabric you are using in the garment regardless of how many buttonholes you have made previously.

## Guidelines for Bound Buttonholes

Study the lines **A, B,** and **C** on the diagram. These lines of basting are made on the true grain of the fabric and are your guidelines for stitching the buttonholes. For basting, use thread contrasting in color to that of the fabric so that it can be easily seen and removed.

On the right side of the garment, place a vertical line of machine basting ⅛ inch outside the center line basting—as at **A.** (The center line should have been hand-basted before the pattern was removed from the fabric.) Measure the length of the buttonholes and place the second vertical line of machine basting the measured distance from **A**—as at **B.** Machine-baste the position of each buttonhole on a horizontal line, extending each end of the stitching about ¾ inch beyond the vertical markings—as at **C.** Use hand basting if machine basting will mar the fabric.

## Patch Method

The patch method requires additional markings for accurately stitched buttonholes. First, machine-baste the vertical and horizontal guidelines, **A, B,** and **C,** as instructed above. Then on the stay or

patch over each buttonhole marking, right sides
together. Pin in position; baste if necessary. See
bottom of previous column.

**3.** On the wrong side, stitch around the buttonhole, following the markings. Use a 20 stitch length.
Begin at the center of one side and stitch to the
end; leave the needle in the fabric, raise the presser
bar, and turn the fabric on the needle. Lower the
presser bar and stitch across the end, taking four
or five stitches. Continue stitching around the
buttonhole, turning each corner in the same way;
make the same number of stitches at each end and
overlap about four stitches at the starting point.
Press.

If you have a Singer Buttonholer for your zig-
zag machine, it will perform this basic stitching.
It controls the buttonhole length and width and
eliminates turning the fabric.

**4.** Remove basting threads across each end of
the buttonhole. Carefully cut through the center
of the buttonhole to within ¼ inch of each end; then
cut diagonally to each corner. Do not clip through
the stitching.

**5.** Draw the patch through the opening to the
underside.

lightweight interfacing on the underside, draw a
pencil line on each side of and ⅛ inch from the
horizontal basting—as at **D**. This is the stitching
line. If the fabric is bulky, draw the lines farther
from the basting but not more than ¼ inch.

**1.** For each buttonhole, cut a patch of fabric
on the crosswise grain or on the true bias, 2 inches
wide and 1 inch longer than the finished buttonhole. Crease lightly through the center, following
the crosswise grain (or true bias) of the fabric.

**2.** On the right side of the garment, center a

**6.** Carefully pull out the triangular ends to square the corners. If the slashes are made deep enough into the corners, the opening will be smooth. Press the triangular ends and side seam allowances away from the opening. See *Pressing as You Sew,* page 71.

**7.** Fold each side of the patch to form pleats that meet at the center of the buttonhole and cover the opening. Carry the folds to the edge of the

patch. From the right side, baste along the center of each fold, then overcast the folds together. Remove machine-basted guidelines. Press.

**8.** Place the garment right side up on the machine, fold it back, and stitch the pleats to the seam allowances. First stitch across the triangular ends on the original stitching line, beginning and

ending the stitching at the raw edge of the patch. Then stitch along the seams on each side, *just a hair's width from the original stitching line,* beginning and ending at the raw edge of the patch. The side stitching crosses the end stitching and squares the corners. The stitching is not visible on the right side.

**9.** Remove all hand bastings except the overcasting holding the pleats together. Press. Trim the patch to within ¼ inch of the stitching.

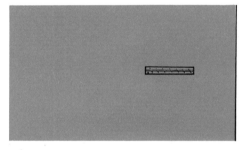

### Treating Heavy Interfacing

If the garment is interfaced with fabric such as Armo or any other hair canvas, use a stay of lightweight fabric under the buttonholes. Attach the interfacing to the garment after the buttonholes have been made. Be sure the interfacing lies smoothly against the fabric. Pin around each button-hole. From the right side, insert pins straight through each of the four corners to mark the position of the buttonhole on the interfacing. Using the pins as a guide, cut out a piece from the inter-facing, barely outside the pin mark, which is slight-ly longer and wider than the buttonhole. Pull the seam edges of the buttonhole through the opening in the interfacing.

### Finishing the Back of Buttonholes

Finish the back of buttonholes *after you have attached the facing* to the garment. Baste the fac-ing to the garment around each buttonhole, then finish it using one of the three methods illustrated below.

**Method 1:** Use this method if the fabric does not ravel easily and if the facing side of the but-tonhole will not be visible when the garment is open. From the right side, insert pins straight through each of the four corners to mark the posi-tion of the buttonhole on the facing. On the under-side, cut the facing between the pins to within ¼ inch of the ends; then cut diagonally to the cor-ners. Use the point of the needle to turn under the edges, and slip-stitch the facing in place. The facing side has the same rectangular shape as the front of the buttonhole.

**Method 2:** This method is preferred for tweeds and fabrics that ravel easily. From the right side, insert a pin straight through each end of the but-tonhole. Cut the facing between the pins. Turn under the edges with the point of the needle and slip-stitch the facing in place, forming an oval shape.

**Method 3:** If the facing side of the buttonhole will be visible at times (as in coats or suits that may be worn closed at the neckline or open with lapels), it must be as neat as the garment side.

After you have attached the facing (see pages 134 and 135), pin it in place around the button-hole. Mark the buttonhole position on it by in-serting pins straight through the four corners from the right side of the garment. Then from the fac-ing side, insert pins straight through the facing in the same places. Remove pins on the top side and around the buttonhole. Carefully separate the fac-ing from the garment, leaving the facing pin-marked. Hand-baste the outline of the buttonhole, using the pins as a guide.

Finish with a faced rectangular opening. Se-lect organza the exact color of the garment fabric. To cut, stitch, and turn the organza patch to form the opening, follow *Steps 2 through 5* on page 113 for the *Two-Piece Piped Method*. Then trim off the edges of the organza ⅜ inch from the opening.

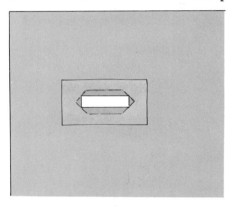

Pin, then baste, the facing in place again. The opening in the facing should be the exact size of the finished buttonhole in the garment, and the buttonhole stitching should not be visible. Be sure the organza does not show on the right side of the facing. Slip-stitch in place, making invisible stitches.

## One-Piece Method

Position the stay or lightweight interfacing on the underside, then baste guidelines to mark buttonhole positions as described on page 108.

**1.** For each buttonhole, cut a strip of fabric on the crosswise grain, 1 inch wide and 1 inch longer than the finished buttonhole.

**2.** Form the buttonhole strip by accurately folding the cut edges to the center, wrong side together, and baste along each fold. This will form a folded strip ½ inch in width. Cover with a press cloth, and press. Remove basting.

**3.** On the right side of the garment, center a buttonhole strip over each buttonhole marking, and pin at each end. Hand-baste through the center of each fold to hold the strip in place.

**4.** Stitch on each side of the buttonhole, using a short stitch. Position the stitching in the exact center between the fold and the cut edge on each side. Begin and end the stitching exactly on the basted lines designating the buttonhole length. Remove hand basting. Draw the threads through to the underside and tie. Press. See *Pressing as You Sew*, page 71.

**5.** Remove the horizontal basting designating the buttonhole position. Cut through the center of the *buttonhole strip only*.

**6.** Working from the underside, carefully cut between the two lines of stitching, through the garment and stay, to within ¼ inch of the ends of the buttonhole; then cut diagonally to each corner. The basted guidelines across the ends will prevent fraying at the corners until the ends are stitched to the strip.

**7.** Draw the strip through the opening to the underside, with the folded edges meeting at the center of the opening. Carefully pull the triangular ends away from the opening to square the corners. Press. Overcast the folded edges together.

**8.** Place the garment right side up on the machine; fold it back and stitch the triangular ends to the strip at each end of the buttonhole. Remove the vertical basted guidelines. Trim ends of the buttonhole strip to within ¼ inch of the stitching. Press.

Treat the interfacing as described on page 110. Finish the back of the buttonhole after the facing is attached, as instructed on page 111.

**A corded effect** may be given to buttonholes by cutting the strip on the true bias. Follow the same procedure given above for the *One-Piece Method* up to *Step 8*. From the underside, draw wool yarn through the pleats; a single or double strand may be used. Then stitch across the ends.

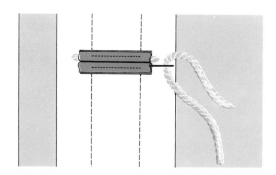

## Two-Piece Piped Method

Use this method when the fabric is heavy, bulky, or loosely woven. Since such fabrics require heavy interfacing, always apply the interfacing *after* making the buttonholes to eliminate bulk.

**1.** Position a stay of lightweight fabric on the underside, and baste guidelines to mark buttonhole positions as described on page 108. Then on the stay on the underside, draw a pencil line on each side of and about 3/16 inch from the horizontal basted line. This marks the stitching line.

**2.** Cut a patch of organza 2 inches wide and 1 inch longer than the finished buttonhole. (The organza must match the fabric exactly in color.) Center the patch over the buttonhole marking on the right side of the fabric. Pin; baste if necessary.

**3.** Turn the garment to the wrong side and stitch around the buttonhole, following the markings and using a 20 stitch length. Begin the stitching at the center of one side; at the corners, pivot the fabric on the needle; make the same number of stitches (four or five) across the ends; and overlap about four stitches at the starting point. Press. Carefully remove the basted guidelines through the center and across the ends of the buttonhole.

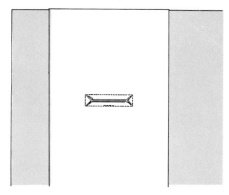

**4.** Cut through the center of the buttonhole to within ¼ inch of each end; then cut diagonally to each corner.

**5.** Turn the organza patch through the opening to the underside. Carefully pull out the triangular ends to square the corners and press them away from the opening. Turn the seam allowances and organza patch away from the opening along the sides, fold on the stitching line, and press flat against the fabric. You now have a faced rectangular opening.

**6.** *For the piping,* cut two strips of garment fabric on the crosswise grain, 1½ inches wider and 1 inch longer than the finished buttonhole. Place them right sides together and machine-baste through the center, following the fabric grain line. Leave threads at each end so the basting can be easily removed.

**7.** Press, then press the basted seam open. Be sure to place a press cloth between the fabric and iron because you are pressing on the right side of the fabric. (You should now have each strip folded, wrong sides together, and the two strips temporarily basted together along the folds.)

**8.** With the garment right side up, place the strip over the wrong side of the opening with the basted seam centered and the ends extending ½ inch beyond the opening. Pin the strip in place with fine needles close to the ends of the opening.

**9.** Place the garment right side up on the machine; turn back the edge and stitch the seam allowances and organza patch to the strip. Use a 20 stitch length and place the stitching barely beyond the previous stitching so that the organza patch will not be visible on the top side of the garment. First pin the triangular ends to the strip

with fine needles and stitch across the ends; then, just before stitching along each side, remove the needles on the top side and pin the seam allowances

and organza to the strip on the underside to prevent them from slipping during the stitching. Trim the ends of the strip to within ¼ inch of stitching; along the sides, trim the seam allowance on the top layer of the strip to ¼ inch and on the bottom layer to ⅜ inch. Before pressing, slip brown paper between the garment and seam allowance to prevent the outline of the seam allowance from pressing onto the fabric.

Treat the interfacing as described on page 110. Finish the back of the buttonhole after the facing is attached, following the directions on page 111. Remove the basting joining the buttonhole strips.

# Corded Buttonholes

Additional markings are required for accurate corded buttonholes. First, machine-baste the vertical and horizontal guidelines, as instructed on page 108. Then on the stay or lightweight interfacing on the underside, draw a pencil line on each side and 3/16 or 1/4 inch from the buttonhole marking.

Machine-baste on these lines to transfer the markings to the right side. The spacing of these lines from the buttonhole marking will vary, depending upon the size of the cord and the weight of the fabric used.

Prepare the corded strips from a true bias cut 1 inch wide and sufficient in length for all the buttonholes to be made. To determine the length of the corded strip needed, allow twice the length plus 2 inches for each buttonhole.

Use No. 9 cable cord or twine string for the cording. Replace the presser foot with the Zipper Foot. Fold the bias strip, right side out, around the cording. Stitch close to the cording, but do not crowd. Press.

**1.** For each buttonhole, cut two corded strips 1 inch longer than the buttonhole. Position two

strips over each buttonhole marking, aligning the corded edges with the outside markings and keeping the raw edges toward the center. Hand-baste in position.

**2.** Stitch on each side of the buttonhole, placing the stitching between the cord and previous line of stitching. Use a short stitch, and adjust the Zipper Foot to the left of the needle. Begin and end the stitching exactly on the guidelines designating the buttonhole length. Remove hand bastings. Pull the threads through to the underside and tie. Remove all horizontal basting lines. Press See *Pressing as You Sew,* page 71.

**3.** From the underside, carefully cut between the two lines of stitching, through the garment and stay, to within 1/4 inch of the ends of the buttonhole; then cut diagonally to each corner. The basted guidelines across the ends will prevent fraying at the corners until the ends are stitched in place.

**4.** Draw the strip through the opening to the underside, with the corded edges meeting at the center of the opening. Carefully pull the triangular ends away from the opening to square the corners. Press. Overcast the corded edges together.

**5.** Place the garment right side up on the machine; fold it back and stitch the traingular ends to the corded strip at each end of the buttonhole. Replace the Zipper Foot with the presser foot for this operation. Remove the vertical guidelines. Trim the ends and sides of the corded strip to within 1/4 inch of the stitching. Press. Treat the interfacing as described on page 110. Finish the back of the buttonhole after the facing is attached as described on page 111.

## Buttonholes in a Seam

Buttonholes in a seam are often found on a horizontal line at the waistline of a jacket, where the peplum joins the bodice, and in yoke seams across the bodice; and on a vertical line where a binding or an extended facing is used. Where there is no seam, additional buttonholes are made, using one of the conventional methods shown earlier in this chapter.

**1.** Carefully mark the position of the buttonhole in the seam. With right sides of fabric together, pin and baste a ⅝-inch seam in the garment.

**2.** Cut two stays for each buttonhole 1 inch longer than the buttonhole and 1¼ inches wide for reinforcement. Use batiste, organza, or a similar fabric, and cut the stays on the same grain as the garment. Place one on each side of the seam over the buttonhole marking, keeping seam edges even. Pin.

**3.** Beginning at the end of the seam, stitch to the buttonhole marking. Leave thread ends long enough to tie. Then from the opposite end of the buttonhole, stitch the entire length of the seam or

to the marking for the next buttonhole. At each end of the buttonhole, pull the threads to one side and tie. Remove tailor's tacks, if used, and basting, except across the buttonhole opening.

**4.** Press the seam, then press it open. Trim the stay on each side of the buttonhole to within ⅜ inch of opening.

**5.** Treat the interfacing as instructed on page 110. Finish the back of the buttonhole *after the facing is attached,* as described on page 111.

# WORKED BUTTONHOLES

Machine-worked and hand-worked buttonholes are made after the garment is finished. For machine-worked buttonholes you may use either the zig-zag machine or a straight stitch machine with a Buttonholer.

Use interfacing in the buttonhole area for reinforcement. It is essential if the fabric is loosely woven or is one that stretches easily (for example, a knit), for it holds the fabric firmly so that you can make a neat buttonhole; it also keeps the finished buttonhole in shape.

Determine the buttonhole position and length as described on pages 107 and 108.

## With Zig-Zag Machine

Worked buttonholes of any length and varying widths can be made quickly and easily on a zig-zag machine.

To determine the length of the cutting space (the opening through which the button passes), refer to page 108. The length of the finished buttonhole is the cutting space plus ⅛ inch at each

| MARKING LINES | LENGTH OF CUTTING SPACE | BAR TACKS AND SIDE STITCHING |
|---|---|---|

Center Line Basting

end for bar tacks. After determining the size of the buttonhole, mark the buttonhole size with either chalk or hand basting along the thread of the fabric.

Set the selectors on the machine for a plain zig-zag stitch, and set the stitch length selector for satin stitching. Work a sample buttonhole in a scrap of the same fabric used in the garment. Fold the fabric, duplicating the facing, and include the same type of interfacing used in the garment. Follow the instructions for making buttonholes in the instruction book accompanying the machine.

Finished edge of garment

Center line

**Corded buttonholes.** Both size 8 pearl cotton and buttonhole twist make suitable filler cords for corded buttonholes.

Unwind a sufficient amount of the filler cord to prevent tension or strain on the cord. Lead the end of the cord through the left eyelet of the Special Purpose Foot. Draw the cord under and in

back of the foot. Proceed with stitching as for regular buttonholes. The zig-zag stitches are made over the filler cord.

## With the Buttonholer

Mark the end position as well as the line of the buttonhole along the thread of the fabric. Use chalk or hand-baste. To determine the buttonhole position and length, see pages 107 and 108.

Select the size template required for the buttonhole and insert it in the Buttonholer. Regulate the stitch width and cutting space required according to the fabric.

Center line

Then make a test buttonhole in a swatch of the same fabric used in the garment. Fold the fabric, duplicating the facing, and include the same type of interfacing used in the garment. Follow the directions given in the instruction book accompanying the Buttonholer. See also *Buttonholer,* page 287.

## Hand-Worked Buttonholes

Hand-worked buttonholes may be made on a horizontal or vertical line. If horizontal, they have a fan at the outside end near the edge of the garment, which carries the strain, and a bar tack at the inside end. If vertical, they have a bar tack at each end.

Use the buttonhole stitch and thread that matches the fabric exactly in color. Work with a thread about 18 inches in length and rethread the needle for each buttonhole because the thread will wear when repeatedly pulled through the fabric.

Determine the buttonhole position and length as described on pages 107 and 108. Then follow the instructions below, beginning with a practice buttonhole in a swatch of your fabric.

### Horizontal Buttonhole

**1.** Carefully mark the length and line of the buttonhole with chalk or hand basting along the true grain of the fabric. Pin the layers of fabric together to prevent them from slipping.

**2.** Machine-stitch around the buttonhole for reinforcement. Use a 20 stitch length and place the stitching 1/16 inch from the buttonhole marking; take two or three stitches across the ends. In heavy fabrics, place the stitching about ⅛ inch from the marking. Take care that the stitching is straight and evenly spaced because it is a guide for the depth of the hand stitches (however, this stitching is not visible in the finished buttonhole). A fine hand running stitch, although not so firm, may be substituted for machine stitching. Press. If the fabric is one that will fray, overcast the edges.

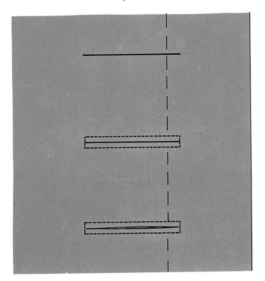

**3.** Cut the buttonhole between the two lines of stitching, using sharp, pointed scissors.

**4.** *Work from right to left.* Hold the fabric, needle, and thread in the position shown in the illustrations. With the right side of the garment up, *start working at the inside end.* Bring the cut buttonhole over the first finger of the left hand.

Do not knot the end of the thread. Take two small backstitches at the end to fasten the thread. Clip off the thread end after several stitches have been made. Bring the thread to the left, then to the right, to form a loop around the point where

the stitch will be made. Insert the point of the needle through the opening and up through the fabric just below the machine stitching. Keep the thread in back of both the point and the eye of the needle. Hold the lower edge of the loop with the left thumb until you draw up the thread for the stitch. Pull the needle through the fabric, then away from you, to place the purl of the stitch on the cut edge of the buttonhole. Pull the thread gently yet firmly enough to make smooth, flat stitches. Continue making buttonhole stitches until you reach the outside end. Keep the spacing between the stitches uniform and the depth as even as possible.

**5.** Fan the stitches at the outside end. Place about five or seven stitches in the fan and make them slightly longer than the side stitches so that they will appear to be the same length.

Work down the opposite side to the inside end. Turn the buttonhole to the right as you work around it.

**6.** Make a bar tack across the inside end by taking two straight stitches through the fabric.

**7.** Complete the bar by working over the stitches, using a blanket stitch. Make the stitches through the fabric and under the bar. Fasten the thread on the underside with two backstitches.

### Vertical Buttonhole

Vertical buttonholes are set so that the center line basting falls in the center of the buttonhole.

**1.** Mark the length and line of the buttonhole on the true lengthwise grain of the fabric.

**2.** Machine-stitch around the buttonhole for reinforcement. Use a 20 stitch length and place the stitching 1/16 inch from the buttonhole marking; take two or three stitches across the ends.

**3.** Cut the buttonhole between the two lines of stitching.

**4.** Place the garment right side up. Start working at the lower end, using the buttonhole stitch as described in *Step 4*, page 118. Make a bar tack across the upper end by taking two straight stitches through the fabric. Complete the bar by working across the stitches, using the blanket stitch. Make the stitches through the fabric and under the bar.

**5.** Work down the opposite side and finish the lower end with a bar tack. Fasten the thread on the underside with two backstitches.

### Tailored Buttonhole

Tailored buttonholes have an eyelet at the outside end near the edge of the garment. The shank of the button fits into the eyelet opening. This prevents the overlap from bulging when the garment is buttoned.

**1.** Mark the position of the buttonhole with hand basting, chalk, or pencil on the crosswise grain of the fabric.

**2.** Cut the buttonhole on the marked line. At the outside end, near the edge of the garment, make two small slashes about ⅛ inch in depth or punch a small hole, using a stiletto.

**3.** Overcast around the cut edges to keep them from fraying and to hold the layers of fabric together. Make the stitches about ⅛ inch in depth.

**4.** Start at the inside end, and place a strand of buttonhole twist along the edges of the buttonhole. Fasten the ends by forming a figure eight around a pin. Use buttonhole twist in the needle. Take one backstitch at the inside end to tie the thread. Follow the instructions on page 118 for *Steps 4 and 5,* and make buttonhole stitches over the twist. Fan the stitches at the eyelet end.

**5.** Make a bar tack across the inside end by taking two straight stitches through the fabric. Complete the bar by working over the stitches, using a blanket stitch. Make the stitches through the fabric and under the bar. Fasten the thread on the underside with two backstitches.

# Pick a
# Pretty Pocket

THE FASHION INTEREST in pocket styles fluctuates from the subtle set-in pocket to the bold patch pocket. Whatever the style, the secret of pocket making lies in accurately marking and stitching your pocket and pressing each step as it is completed. Pockets are not difficult if you remember that.

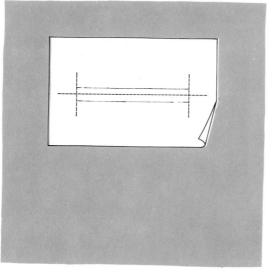

The pattern usually designates the position of pockets in a garment; however, if you decide to add them, do so in the planning stage so that you can measure and mark their position on the pattern. Make the pockets after the pin fitting, before assembling the garment pieces.

Always make a practice pocket in a swatch of the garment fabric before proceeding to work on the garment itself. For instructions on pressing, see page 71.

## SET-IN POCKETS

### Guidelines for Pockets

Mark the position of the pocket with tailor's tacks before removing the pattern from the garment section.

Place an underlay of batiste, muslin, lawn, or similar fabric under the stitching line to reinforce the opening and retain the shape of the pocket. Cut the underlay 1½ inches wider than the pocket opening and about 3 inches long. Center it over the markings on the wrong side of the garment, and pin.

From the right side, machine-baste across the ends of the pocket to mark the width. Then machine-baste through the center, extending the stitching about ¾ inch beyond the ends, to form guidelines. Follow the grain of the fabric unless the pocket is on a diagonal line. Use thread contrasting in color so that it can easily be seen and removed. Hand-baste if machine basting will mar the fabric.

On the wrong side, draw pencil lines on each side of and ¼ inch from the center basting to designate the stitching line. This distance may vary depending on the style of the pocket.

(Additional markings are required for a *corded pocket* and are illustrated under the instructions for making the pocket.)

120

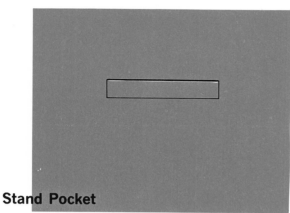

## Stand Pocket

Mark the guidelines of the pocket as instructed on opposite page.

Cut a piece of fabric on the lengthwise grain twice the pocket depth plus twice the depth of the stand, and 1 inch wider than the opening. Crease the pocket section crosswise, 1 inch above the center.

**1.** On the right side of the garment, place the pocket section, right sides together. Align the crease with the marking on the garment, extending the long end of the pocket below the marking. Pin. Baste, if necessary.

**2.** On the wrong side, stitch around the pocket, following the guidelines. Use a short stitch and begin the stitching at the center of one side; pivot the fabric on the needle at the corners and take the same number of stitches across each end. Overlap about six stitches at the starting point. Do not stitch on the bastings. Remove the basted guidelines, and press.

**3.** Cut between the two lines of stitching, through all thicknesses, to within ½ inch of the ends; then cut diagonally to each of the four corners. Do not clip through the stitching.

**4.** Draw the pocket through the opening to the wrong side. Pull out the triangles at the ends to square the corners. Press the triangular ends and seam allowances along the side away from the opening.

**5.** Fold the lower section of the pocket to form a pleat to cover the opening. Check both the right and wrong sides to be sure that the pleat is even and covers the opening. Hand-baste on the folded edge, carrying the basting to each end of the pocket. Press the folded edge. Overcast the fold to the top edge of the opening. (Pin the upper section of the pocket to the garment to keep it out of the way for the next step.)

121

**6.** Place the garment right side up on the machine; fold back the edge and stitch the seam allowances to the lower pocket section to hold the pleat in place.

**7.** Turn down the upper section of the pocket and pin it to the lower section. Press the top seam open.

**8.** Place the garment right side up on the machine; fold back the edge and stitch the two-pocket sections together. Stitch across the triangle at one end, around the pocket, and across the triangle at the opposite end. Stitch the triangular ends on the original line of stitching. Tie thread ends.

Trim seam allowances evenly and finish the

edges according to the fabric. Remove all bastings and press. Trim underlay to within ½ inch of stitching.

## Bound Pocket—Two-Piece

The bound pocket is often called a buttonhole pocket because it is made exactly like a buttonhole.

Mark the guidelines of the pocket as instructed on page 120.

Cut one pocket section the depth of the pocket plus 2 inches, and 1 inch wider than the opening. Cut another section the depth of the pocket plus the seam allowance, and 1 inch wider than the opening. (To avoid bulk in suits, coats, and garments of heavy fabric, you may cut the lower section [the short one] from the lining fabric or a lightweight fabric matching in color.)

**1.** On the right side of the garment, place the long section of the pocket, right side down, extending the edge 1½ inches below the marking. Pin. Baste, if necessary.

**2.** On the wrong side, stitch around the pocket, following the guidelines. Use a short stitch and begin stitching at the center of one side; pivot the fabric on the needle at the corners and take the

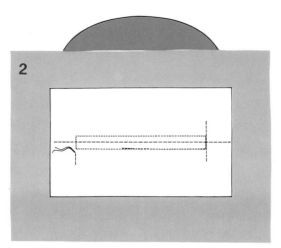

same number of stitches across each end. Overlap about six stitches at the starting point. Remove the basted guidelines at the ends, and press.

**3.** Cut between the two lines of stitching, through all thicknesses, to within ½ inch of the ends; then cut diagonally to each of the four corners. Do not clip through the stitching.

**4.** Draw the pocket through the opening to the underside. Pull out the triangular ends to square the corners. Press the triangular ends and seam allowances along the sides away from the opening.

**5.** Fold the pocket section to form a pleat on each side that meets at the center and covers the opening. Check both the right and wrong sides to be sure that the pleats are even in width. Baste along the center of each fold, then overcast the folded edges together. Carry the basting to the raw edge of the pocket section. Remove the center basted guideline, and press.

**6.** Place the garment right side up on the machine; fold back the edge and stitch the seam allowances to the pleats. First stitch across the triangular ends on the original stitching line; then stitch across the seam at the top, *just a hair's width from the original stitching line.* The side stitching crosses the end stitching and squares the corners.

**7.** Place the second pocket section under the bottom seam, right side up; then stitch the seam allowance to the pleat and lower pocket section in one operation.

**8.** Turn down the lower pocket section. The underside of the pocket is illustrated. Stitching is not visible on the right side. Remove all bastings except the overcasting holding the pleats together. Press.

**9.** Turn down the upper section of the pocket and pin it to the lower section. Place the garment right side up on the machine. Fold back the edge of the garment and stitch the two pocket sections together. Stitch across the triangle at one end, around the pocket, and across the triangle at the opposite end. Stitch the triangular ends on the original line of stitching. Tie thread ends.

Trim seam allowances evenly and finish the edges according to the fabric. Remove all bastings and press. Trim underlay to within ½ inch of the stitching.

## Welt Pocket

Mark the guidelines of the pocket as instructed on page 120.

*Welt.* If a pattern for the welt is not included, cut one on the crosswise grain the width of the pocket opening plus seam allowances, and twice the depth of the finished welt plus seam allowances. (Allow ¼ inch for each seam.)

If the fabric is not firmly woven, interface the welt to give added body. Two methods may be used, depending on the fabric.

*Method 1:* In cottons and lightweight fabrics, use a double thickness of muslin, batiste, or lawn for the interfacing. Shrink it; then cut it the same as the welt. Fold through the center and crease with the iron. Turn the welt wrong side up and place the fold of the interfacing along the center of the welt. Stitch close to the interfacing fold.

*Method 2:* In coats, suits, and garments of heavy fabric, interface with hair canvas. Shrink the interfacing; then cut it the width of the welt and one-half the depth. Trim off the seam allowance on each end and along the lower edge. On the wrong side of the welt, place the edge of the interfacing along the center of the welt. Pin and baste. Catch-stitch in place.

*For Methods 1 and 2,* fold the welt in half on the crosswise grain, right sides together. Stitch across the ends. Backstitch at each end for reinforcement. Cut diagonally across corners at the top edge. Trim the facing seam allowance to ⅛ inch. If Method 1 is used, trim the interfacing seam allowance close to the stitching. Press.

Turn the welt right side out. Fold on the stitching line; pull out the corners and press. Machine-stitch a scant ¼ inch from the lower edge to hold the layers of fabric together.

**Pocket.** Cut one pocket section the depth of the pocket plus 2 inches, and 1 inch wider than the opening. Cut another section the depth of pocket plus seam allowance, and 1 inch wider than the opening. (To avoid bulk in suits, coats, and garments of heavy fabric, you may cut the lower section [the short one] from the lining fabric or a lightweight fabric matching in color.)

To make the welt pocket, proceed as follows:

**1.** Turn garment right side up. Place the welt below the pocket marking, right side down, with the raw edge on the center basting line. (The ends must be even with the guidelines. Adjust if necessary.) Pin and hand-baste. On the underside, pin at each corner, using fine needles to prevent the welt from slipping as you stitch in *Step 3.*

**2.** On the right side of the garment, place the upper pocket section (the long one) over the marking, right sides together, extending the edge 1 inch below the center marking. Pin. Baste, if necessary.

**3.** From the wrong side of the garment, stitch around the pocket opening, following the guidelines. Use a short stitch and begin stitching at the center of the upper side; pivot the fabric on the needle at the corners and take the same number of stitches across each end. Overlap about six stitches at the starting point. Check the right side to be sure the end stitching does not extend beyond the welt. Remove all bastings, and press.

**4.** From the underside, cut between the two lines of stitching, through all thicknesses, to within ½ inch of the ends. Cut diagonally to each of the four corners. Do no clip through the stitching.

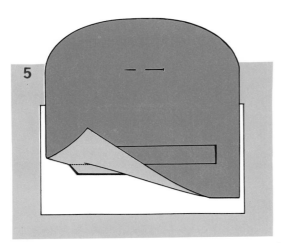

**5.** Turn the pocket through the opening to the underside. Pull out the triangular ends to square the corners, and turn the welt up on the right side to cover the opening. Press the triangular ends and seam allowances along the sides away from the opening. Turn the extended lower edge of the pocket away from the opening and press. (Pin the upper pocket section to the garment to avoid catching it in the stitching of the next step.)

**6.** Place the garment right side up and fold back the lower edge. Place the lower pocket section under the opening, right side up, keeping the cut edges even along the lower edge of the opening. Turn back the seam allowances, and stitch the pocket section together close to the previous stitching. Begin and end the stitching at the outer edges of the fabric. Press; then turn down the lower pocket section and press again.

**7.** Turn down the upper pocket section and pin the two sections together. Trim both sections to the same length. Place the garment right side up on the machine. Fold back the edge and stitch the pocket sections together. Stitch across the triangle at one end, around the pocket, and across

the triangle at the opposite end. Stitch the triangular ends on the original line of stitching. Tie the threads. Remove all bastings and press.

Finish seams as required by the fabric. Trim underlay to within ½ inch of the stitching.

**8.** On the right side, slip-stitch the ends of the welt to the garment.

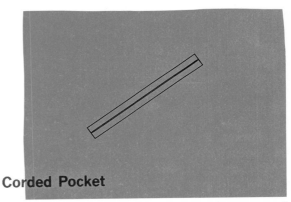

## Corded Pocket

Mark the guidelines of the pocket as instructed on page 120. Then mark additional lines for the position of the cording. The position of these lines is determined by the size of the cord; take twice the width of the cord plus 1/16 inch. (Size 40 cord, for example, will require a distance of 5/16 to ⅜ inch, depending on the thickness of the fabric.) On the underside, draw a pencil line on each side of and 5/16 inch (or the necessary distance) from the center basting. This designates the position of the corded strip. Machine-baste on these lines to transfer the markings to the right side.

**Cording.** Refer to *Cording*, page 244, for instructions on cutting the bias strip and covering the cord. For each pocket, cut two corded strips the width of the pocket plus 1 inch; avoid seams within the strips.

**Pocket.** Cut two pocket sections the depth of the pocket plus 1 inch, and 1 inch wider than the opening. (You will use them in *Steps 6 and 8.*)

To make the corded pocket, proceed as follows:

**1.** On the right side of the garment, place a corded strip on each side of the pocket markings. Align the corded edges with the outside markings, keeping the cut edges toward the center. Pin close to the cord. Check the underside to be sure that the pins are midway between the outside and center markings. (Use fine needles to pin heavy fabric.) Hand-baste, close to the cord, the entire length of the corded strip.

**2.** Using a short stitch, stitch the cording in place, placing the stitching between the cord and previous line of basting. Begin and end the stitching exactly on the end guidelines. Adjust the Zipper Foot to the left of the needle for this operation.

Check the underside to be sure the line of stitching on each side is midway between the center and outer guidelines. Pull the threads through to the underside and tie. Remove all bastings except those across the ends. Press.

**3.** From the underside, cut between the two lines of stitching through the garment and underlay, to within ½ inch of the ends; then cut diagonally to each of the four corners. Do not clip through the stitching, and hold the corded strips out of the way to avoid cutting into them.

**4.** Turn the cut edges of the corded strips through the opening to the underside, with the corded edges meeting at the center to cover the opening. Pull out the triangular ends to square the corners. Press the triangular ends and seam allowances along the sides away from the opening. Overcast the corded edges together.

**5.** Place the garment right side up on the machine; fold back the edge and stitch the triangular ends to the cording. Remove machine basting across the ends, and press.

127

**6.** On the underside, place one pocket section, wrong side up, over the pocket as illustrated. Pin to the lower seam allowance. (To avoid bulk in suits, coats, and garments of heavy fabric, you may cut this section from the lining fabric or a lightweight fabric matching in color.)

**7.** With the garment right side up, fold back the edge and stitch the seam allowances to the pocket section. Press. Fold the pocket section down, and press.

**8.** Stitch the other pocket section to the top seam allowances in the same way. Press. Fold this section down; then pin the two sections together.

**9.** Place the garment right side up on the machine; fold back the edge and stitch the two pocket sections together. Begin stitching at the edge above

the triangular point, around the pocket, and across the triangle at the opposite end. Stitch the triangular ends on the original line of stitching. Press.

Finish the seam edges according to the fabric. Trim the underlay to within ½ inch of the stitching. Remove the overcasting holding the two corded edges together.

## Pocket with Flap

Mark guidelines of the pocket as instructed on page 120.

*Flap.* Cut the flap and the facing the width of the opening plus seam allowances, and the depth desired plus seam allowances (¼-inch seam allowances are sufficient in most fabrics). Round the lower corners, if desired.

Interface the flap to give the added body necessary. Two methods are given below. Select the one most suitable for your fabric.

*Method 1:* In cottons and lightweight fabrics, interface with muslin, batiste, or lawn. Shrink, then cut a double thickness of interfacing the same size as the flap. Pin the interfacing to the wrong side of the flap. Baste, if necessary.

**Method 2:** Interface woolens, heavy silks, and similar fabrics with preshrunk hair canvas. Cut the interfacing the same size as the flap. Trim off the seam allowance plus ⅛ inch. Center the interfacing over the wrong side of the flap and baste. Catch-stitch in place around the edges. Press.

**For Methods 1 and 2,** pin the facing to the flap, right sides together. Stitch on the seamline, leaving the upper edge open. Backstitch at each end. Clip off corners at the lower edge. Trim the facing seam allowance to ⅛ inch and the flap seam allowance to ¼ inch. If *Method 1* is used, trim the interfacing seam allowance close to the stitching. Turn the flap right side out. Pull out the corners. Ease the facing under slightly at the seamline and baste. Press. Top-stitch if desired. Stitch across the cut edges a scant ¼ inch from the edge to hold the layers of fabric together. Remove bastings.

**Pocket.** Cut one pocket section the depth of the pocket plus 2 inches, and 1 inch wider than the opening. Cut another section the depth of the pocket plus seam allowance, and 1 inch wider than the opening. (To avoid bulk in suits, coats, and garments of heavy fabric, you may cut the lower section [the short one] from the lining fabric or a lightweight fabric matching in color.)

To make the pocket, proceed as follows:

**1.** Turn the garment right side up. Place the flap above the pocket marking, right side down, with the raw edge on the center basting line. The flap ends should just touch the end bastings. Baste. On the underside, use fine needles to pin each corner to prevent the flap from slipping as you stitch in *Step 3.*

**2.** On the right side, place the long pocket section, right sides together, over the opening, extending the lower edge 2 inches below the center basting. Pin in place.

**3.** From the wrong side, stitch around the pocket opening; use a short stitch and follow the guidelines. Start stitching at the center of the lower side; pivot the fabric on the needle at the corners and make the same number of stitches at each end. Overlap about six stitches at the starting point. Check to be sure the end stitching does not extend beyond the ends of the flap. Remove all bastings and press.

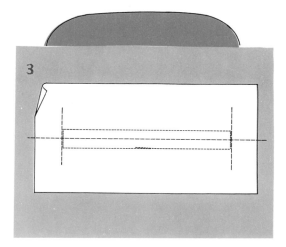

**4.** From the underside, cut between the two lines of stitching, through all thicknesses, to within ½ inch of the ends; then cut diagonally to each of the four corners. Do not clip through the stitching.

**5.** Turn the pocket through the opening to the underside. Pull out triangles at the ends to square the corners. Press triangular ends and seam allowances along the sides away from the opening. Turn

down the flap before pressing the seam across the top. Pin the upper pocket section to the garment to avoid catching it while stitching *Step 7.*

**6.** Fold the pocket extension, which is below the opening, to form a pleat that covers the opening. Hand-baste on the fold. Press.

**7.** Place the garment right side up; fold back the lower edge and pin the free edge of the pleat to the seam allowance. Place the lower pocket section underneath, right side up, and pin. Stitch the pleat and pocket section to the seam allowance at the same time. Press the seam; then turn down the lower pocket section and press. Trim the seam allowances to different widths to avoid forming a ridge on the right side when pressing.

**8.** Turn the upper pocket section down and pin the two sections together. Trim both sections to the same length. Place the garment right side up; fold back the edge and stitch the two pocket sections together. Stitch across the triangle at one end, around the pocket, and across the triangle at the opposite end. Stitch the triangular ends on the original line of stitching. Tie thread ends and press.

Finish seam edges as required by the fabric. Trim underlay to within ½ inch of the stitching.

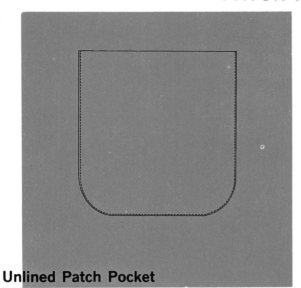

## Unlined Patch Pocket

Mark the position of the pocket with tailor's tacks before removing the pattern from the garment. If the addition of pockets is your idea, mark their position on the pattern; then mark the garment. Follow the fabric grain unless the pocket is on a diagonal line.

Cut the pocket the width and depth desired plus seam allowances and a hem at the top. Round the lower corners, if desired.

**1.** Fold under the top edge of the pocket ¼ inch and stitch near the fold. Press. Fold the top hem to the right side. Pin and stitch across the ends on the seamline. Backstitch at each end. Press. Stitch around the curve of the pocket, ½ inch from the edge, to control the fullness of the seam allowance. Leave thread ends long enough to draw. (Loosen the upper tension, if necessary. Do not forget to return the tension to its previous setting.)

**2.** Trim the seam allowance to within ¼ inch of the stitching and cut diagonally across corners at the top of the hem.

**3.** Turn the hem to the wrong side. Fold on the

stitching line, pull out corners, and press. Draw bobbin thread, easing the fabric back on the stitches around the curved edge. Adjust the fullness for a smooth curve.

**4.** Turn the edges under on the seamline and baste. Notch the seam allowance on the curve to remove bulk so that the seam will lie flat. Press. Pin the hem in place at the top and slip-stitch.

**5.** Pin and baste the pocket over the markings on the right side of the garment. Stitch close to the edge or slip-stitch in place. Pull threads to the underside and tie. Remove bastings and press.

## Lined Patch Pocket with Flap

Blend lining seam allowance to ⅛ inch and pocket seam allowance to ¼ inch. Cut diagonally across the corners, close to the stitching. Press.

**2.** Turn the pocket through the opening to the right side. Pull out the corners. Ease the lining under slightly at the stitching line and baste. Slipstitch the open edges together. Press.

Mark the position of the pocket the same as above.

*Pocket.* Cut the pocket and lining the depth and width desired, plus seam allowances. Use a lining of the same fabric or, if the fabric is heavy, use a lighter weight lining, matching in color.

**1.** Pin the lining to the pocket, right sides together. Stitch around the pocket, leaving a 2½-inch opening for turning. Backstitch at the beginning and ending of the seam and take one stitch across each corner for a smooth turning. Press.

**3.** Pin and hand-baste the pocket over the markings on the right side of the garment. Place a second basting exactly ⅜ inch from the edge to mark the stitching line. Use a gauge to measure and to keep the line even. The Quilter may also be used to gauge the stitching line. See *Top Stitching*, page 335, and *Welt Seam*, page 88.

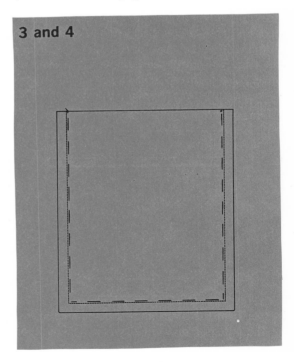

**4.** Stitch the pocket to the garment along the ⅜-inch line; pivot the fabric on the needle at the corners. Draw threads to the underside and tie. Remove bastings, and press.

If top stitching is not used, slip-stitch the pocket to the garment.

*Flap.* Cut the flap and facing the width of the pocket and depth required, plus seam allowances. Round the lower corners, if desired.

**5.** Interface the flap to give the added body necessary. See *Pocket with a Flap,* page 128, and use either *Method 1 or 2,* depending on the weight of the interfacing and the fabric used.

5

**For Methods 1 and 2,** pin the facing to the flap, right sides together. Stitch on the seamline, leaving the upper edge open. Backstitch at each end. Press.

Trim the lining seam allowance to ⅛ inch and the flap seam allowance to ¼ inch. If Method 1 is used, trim the interfacing seam allowance close to the stitching. Notch the curved edges. Press.

**6.** Turn the flap to the right side. Ease the lining under slightly at the stitching line and baste. Press. Pin the cut edges together and baste ⅝ inch from the edge. Top-stitch the flap ⅜ inch from the edge, following the direction for the pocket.

6

**7.** Pin and baste the flap to the garment, right sides together, placing the seamline ½ inch above the pocket. Stitch. Pull threads to the underside and tie. Press the seam. Turn under the cut edge and slip-stitch in place. Turn the flap down over the pocket.

7

# Neckline Finishes

How to finish a neckline depends on several things—pattern design, fabric, and in some instances even personal preference. Many different types of finishes are possible. You may, for example, face the neckline (and the front opening, too, if you have one); you may bind or cord it; or you may add a collar.

## Interfacing

For almost all the work you will be doing in neckline finishing, you will need to interface. Interfacing is a third layer of fabric placed between the facing and garment section. It gives added body to the neckline and front or back opening and to

collars and around buttonholes. In selecting interfacing be sure to choose one appropriate in type and weight for your fabric and style. Also, *shrink before cutting.* See page 16 for specific guides on the kind of interfacing to use.

Before you begin to work on the neckline, be sure that darts are stitched and pressed, shoulder seams stitched, seam edges finished, and seams pressed open.

Leave the underarm seams open because it is easier to finish the neckline when these seams are not joined and the work is flat.

## FACED NECKLINE FINISHES

### Faced Neckline and Front Opening

The type of interfacing you are using—whether lightweight or heavyweight—governs the method you should follow in attaching the interfacing to the neckline and front opening. If separate pieces for the interfacing are not included in the pattern, use the facing patterns as a guide. Cut the preshrunk interfacing and follow the appropriate instructions below.

#### *Facing with Lightweight Interfacing*

*Interfacing.* Join the interfacing pieces for the back and front sections at the shoulder line with a lapped seam, using the multiple-stitch zig-zag to eliminate bulk. See *Lapped Seam,* page 83.

Pin and baste the interfacing to the wrong side of the garment, keeping the seam edges even. (Bound buttonholes may be made through the garment and lightweight interfacing before the facing is stitched in place.)

*Facing.* Join facings for the back and front sections at the shoulder seams. Stitch, then press. Finish seam edges and press seams open.

Pin and baste the facing to the garment, right sides together, matching markings and shoulder seams. Stitch on the seamline, taking one stitch diagonally across the corners for a smooth turning.

Trim the interfacing seam allowance close to the stitching; then trim the facing seam allowance to ⅛ inch and the garment seam allowance to ¼ inch. Cut diagonally across the corners close to the stitching. Slash the seam allowance on the neckline curve at even intervals and clip off corners where seams cross at the shoulder line. Press, then press seams open.

Turn the facing to the underside. Pull out the corners to square them; ease the facing under slightly at the seamline and baste with silk thread. Use diagonal basting on woolens and silks. Press.

**Finish the free edge of the facing.** For lightweight fabrics, pink the edge, then fold under ¼ inch and edgestitch. For heavy fabrics, pink the edge, then stitch ⅛ inch from the edge, or stitch seam binding over the right side of the edge. The multiple-stitch zig-zag is ideal for finishing jersey, double knit, and similar fabrics. If bound buttonholes are used, you must finish the back of the buttonholes. See page 111. Tack the facing to the garment shoulder seam allowances.

**When the front facing and .bodice are cut-in-one,** turn the facing to the underside and press. Then turn the facing away from the garment. Trim off the front seam allowance on the interfacing.

Pin the interfacing to the wrong side of the garment, aligning the front edge with the crease for the facing. Baste the interfacing in place at the neckline and front opening; catch-stitch it in place along the front opening, and machine-stitch it to the waistline ½ inch from the seam edge.

On washable blouses and children's clothes you may eliminate the catch stitch. Buttons and buttonholes will hold the interfacing in place along the front opening; however, be sure to remove the bastings holding the interfacing after sewing on the buttons and making the buttonholes.

Finish the neckline, following the instructions given above.

**Facing with Heavyweight Interfacing**

**Interfacing.** Heavy interfacing such as hair canvas, Siri, Formite, or Pellon is used in dresses of heavy fabric and in suits and coats to give extra body to certain areas. Bound buttonholes are made *before* the heavy interfacing is attached to the garment.

To eliminate bulk, do not sew the interfacing in with the seam but attach it by one of the following methods:

**Method 1:** Mark the seam allowance at the shoulder line of the back and front pieces of the interfacing; mark the neckline and front sections a measured ¾ inch from the edge (⅝-inch seam al-allowance plus ⅛ inch). Trim off along the marked line. Clip off corners to avoid bulk when turned.

Join the interfacing pieces for the back neckline and front sections at the shoulder line with an abutted seam, and stitch, using the multiple-stitch zig-zag. See *Abutted Seam,* page 83.

Cut a strip of organza or a similar lightweight fabric 1½ inches wide on the lengthwise grain, using the pattern to shape the front and neckline edges.

Pin the organza strip over the interfacing, extending the edge ¾ inch beyond the interfacing. Then stitch in place, using the multiple-stitch zig-zag or two lines of straight stitching. Press.

Pin, then baste, the interfacing to the wrong side of the garment, keeping the organza strip and garment edges even. *(Illustrated lower left)*

This method ensures a thin seam since the organza, instead of the interfacing, is included in the seam.

**Method 2:** Mark the seam allowance at the shoulder line of the front and back pieces of the interfacing; mark the neckline and front sections a measured ¾ inch from the edge (⅝-inch seam allowance plus ⅛ inch). Trim off along the marked line; clip off the corners. Join at the shoulder line with an abutted seam, using the multiple-stitch zig-zag. See *Abutted Seam,* page 83.

Pin the interfacing to the wrong side of the garment, ¾ inch from the edge. Baste. Catch-stitch the interfacing to the garment, using matching thread. As the stitches are made, catch one thread in the fabric barely outside the seam line and only through the interfacing on the opposite side.

(For instructions on cutting the interfacing and slipping buttonholes through the cut opening, refer to page 110.)

Stitch, taking one stitch diagonally across the corners for a smooth turning.

Trim the facing seam allowance to ⅛ inch and the garment seam allowance (and organza in *Method 1*) to ¼ inch. Cut diagonally across the corners close to the stitching. Slash the seam allowance on the neckline curve at even intervals and clip off the corners where seams cross at the shoulder line. Press, then press the seam open. On soft woolens and fabrics that fray easily, press before blending the seam.

Turn the facing to the underside. Pull out the corners to square them; ease the facing under slightly at the seamline and baste with silk thread. Use diagonal basting on woolens and silks. Press.

Finish the free edge of the facing, following the directions on page 135.

If your garment is lined, you will not need to finish the facing edge. If bound buttonholes are used, you must finish the back of the buttonholes. See page 111.

## Slip-Stitched Facing

When a narrow facing is turned to the right side of the garment, use a slip stitch rather than top stitching to hold it in place.

For added body, place the interfacing between the top facing and garment. Use self fabric or a lightweight fabric such as organza or batiste, depending on the fabric in the garment. Cut the interfacing by the facing pattern.

*Self-fabric interfacing.* Place the facing and interfacing, wrong sides together, and pin along the inside edge as illustrated. Baste if necessary. Stitch on the seamline; pivot the fabric on the needle at the inside corners.

Trim the interfacing seam allowance to ⅛ inch and the facing seam allowance to ¼ inch. Clip into the corner almost to the stitching and notch the seam on the outside curve. Press, then press seam open.

Turn the facing and interfacing to the right side of the garment. Ease the facing under slightly at the seamline and baste, using diagonal basting and silk thread. Press.

*Facing.* For Methods 1 and 2, join the facing for the back neckline and front sections at the shoulder line. Stitch. Finish the seam edges, then press the seam open.

Pin and baste the facing to the garment, right sides together; match markings and shoulder seams.

On the wrong side, position the facing with the right side next to the garment and pin *only* the outside edge of the facing in place. Stitch on the seamline, taking one or two stitches diagonally across the point for a smooth turning.

Trim the interfacing edge to a generous ⅛ inch beyond the stitching of the facing seam. Carefully baste the interfacing to the facing. Leave this basting until the facing is finished on the top side.

baste the free edge of the facing to the garment. Slip-stitch in place. Remove all bastings and press.

**Lightweight interfacing.** Pin the interfacing to the wrong side of the facing. Stitch a scant ⅝ inch from the edge of the facing, as illustrated. Press.

On the wrong side of the garment, position the facing, to which the interfacing is attached, with the right side next to the garment, and pin along the outside edge. Baste, then stitch on the seamline.

Trim the interfacing seam allowance close to the stitching. Trim the garment seam allowance to ⅛ inch and the facing seam allowance to ¼ inch. Clip diagonally across the corners close to the stitching, and slash the seam on the inside curve. Press, then press the seam open.

On the free edge of the facing, trim the interfacing edge close to the stitching and trim the facing edge to within ¼ inch of the stitching. Clip

Trim the garment seam allowance to ⅛ inch and the facing seam allowance to ¼ inch. Clip diagonally across the corners close to the stitching. Slash the neckline seam allowance on the inside curve. Press, then press the seam open.

Turn the facing to the top side of the garment. Ease the garment side under slightly at the stitching line and baste. Pin and

into the corner almost to the stitching. Turn free edge to the wrong side, barely beyond the stitching and baste. Notch the seam allowances on the outside curve so that they will lie flat. Press.

Turn the facing to the top side of the garment and finish, following the procedure given for self-fabric interfacing.

## Faced Scallops

You may use scalloped facings in both heavy and lightweight fabrics, but avoid them in sheers because of the distracting shadow effect in the seams. Faced scallops accent the edges of front and back openings, sleeves, and hemlines of jackets and skirts. When handled correctly, they give a feminine look to your ensemble.

Interface shaped and bias edges with a lightweight fabric. Baste the interfacing to the wrong side of the fabric.

Lightly draw the scallops on the wrong side of the facing, using the scalloped ruler as a guide. Don't forget a seam allowance. (Plastic scalloped rulers are available in various sizes and simplify the marking when scallops are not shown on the pattern.) *Do not cut the scallops.* Pin and baste the facing to the garment, right sides together.

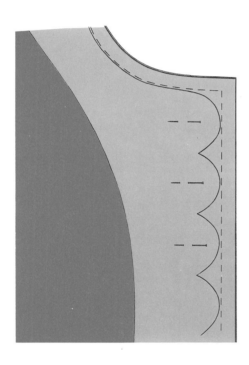

Use a short stitch and a lighter than regular pressure adjustment so that you can turn the fabric freely. Stitch on the traced outline of the scallops, taking one stitch across the point between each scallop. This space provides width when you are cutting and prevents the point between the scallops from pulling in the finished work. Remember that exactness in stitching assures a well-shaped scallop. The Quilter greatly facilitates stitching small scallops because of its open, short toe.

If the interfacing is included in the seam, trim it close to the stitching. Blend the garment and facing seam allowances to a scant ⅛ inch on small scallops and to a generous ⅛ inch on large scallops. Blend one edge shorter than the other except on small scallops. Slash at the point, almost to the stitching. Cut notches from the seam allowances at evenly space intervals. Press.

Turn the facing to the underside, gently working the seam edges between the thumb and finger to bring the stitching line to the very edge. Baste the edges with silk thread to retain the shape of the scallops until after pressing.

If you have a zig-zag machine, you will find that it greatly simplifies the stitching of small scallops. Set the selectors for the scallop pattern and adjust the stitch length and stitch width, which vary the length and depth of the scallop. Always start stitching at the beginning of a scallop unit. See page 266. As you sew, the fabric passes straight under the presser foot and the needle follows a scallop pattern. Press, blend the seams, and turn the facing as instructed on previous page.

## Round Neckline with Fitted Facing

Cut the facing and preshrunk interfacing to match the edge to be faced.

Join the interfacing at the shoulder seams, using a lapped seam. See *Lapped Seam*, page 83. Baste the interfacing to the wrong side of the garment.

Join front and back facings at the shoulder seams. Finish the seam edges and press the seams open.

Turn the garment to the right side. Pin the facing to the neckline, right sides together, matching markings, center lines, and shoulder seams. Stitch, using a short stitch around the curved neckline.

Trim the interfacing seam allowance close to the stitching; trim the facing seam allowance to ⅛ inch and the garment seam allowance to ¼ inch. Slash into seam allowances on the curve and cut off corners where seams cross at the shoulder line. Press.

Turn facing to the underside, ease it under slightly at the seamline, and baste. Press, then remove bastings. Understitch the seam to prevent the facing from rolling out of place.

Finish the free edge of the facing, following the directions on page 135. Tack the facing to the garment shoulder seam allowances.

## Square and V-Neckline with Fitted Facings

Follow the instructions for a round neckline, but pivot the fabric on the needle at the corners to square them, and clip diagonally into the seam allowances at the corners so that the facing will turn smoothly.

## One-Piece Neckline and Armhole Facing

If a one-piece facing is not included with your pattern, cut one using the blouse pattern as a guide. Lay the front and the back pattern pieces over a paper as wide as the pattern and long enough to extend 4 inches below the armhole at the underarm seam. Cut around the neckline, shoulder, armhole, and underarm to 4 inches below the armhole. Remove the pattern pieces. Trim off the lower edge of the facing pattern about 4 inches from the armhole and neckline edges. Cut the facing by this pattern.

Stay-stitch the neckline and armholes if you are not using interfacing. If you are using interfacing, you can omit stay stitching because the interfacing, which is cut the same shape as the neckline and armholes, is sufficient support.

Cut the interfacing by the facing pattern, and baste it to the underside of the garment with the cut edges even at the neckline and armholes. Stitch the underarm seams of the garment, right sides together, and include the interfacing. Finish the seam edges and press the seams open. *Leave shoulder seams open.*

Pin and stitch the underarm seams of the facing, right sides together. Trim the seam allowances to one-half their width and press the seams open. *Leave shoulder seams open.* Trim ⅛ inch off the armhole edges from the shoulder to the notches of the facing only. This will permit the neckline and armhole edges to roll under slightly at the seamline after the facing is turned. The result will be a neat, smooth finish because the facing will not be visible along the edges. To finish the free edge of the facing, pink it, then turn it under ¼ inch and edgestitch. For heavy fabrics, pink, then stitch near the edge, using a short stitch.

Two methods of applying a one-piece facing are illustrated. Select the one you prefer and feel competent to do. *Use the same method when underlining a collarless and sleeveless blouse or dress.*

**Method 1:** Fold under the seam allowance on the shoulder seam of the facing; baste.

Turn the garment to the right side. Pin the facing to the front and back neckline and each armhole, right sides together. Match notches, center lines, and underarm seams, and keep the cut edges even. Baste if necessary. Turn garment to the wrong side and stitch from the facing side.

Begin and end the stitching ⅝ inch (seam allowance) from the shoulder edge and backstitch at each end. Compare front and back shoulders to be sure that the distance between the neckline and armhole stitching is the same. Remove bastings.

Trim the interfacing seam allowance close to the stitching. Trim the facing seam allowance to ⅛ inch and the garment seam allowance to ¼ inch. Slash the seam allowances on curves and cut off corners diagonally where seams cross at the underarm. Press.

Turn the facing to the wrong side, ease it under slightly at the seamline, and baste. Press. Remove bastings.

Understitch the neckline and armhole seams to prevent the facing from rolling out of place. Begin and end the stitching about 2½ inches from the shoulder line.

Turn the garment to the wrong side. Pin the shoulder seams of the front and back bodice together. Stitch on the seamline and backstitch at each end. Press the seams open, then slip them under the open facing seam. Slip-stitch the folded edges of the facing together. Tack the outer edges of the facing to the underarm seam allowances.

**Method 2:** Prepare the dress and facing, following the directions beginning on page 141. If there is a neckline opening, sew in the zipper before applying the facing.

Turn the dress to the right side. Place the facing over the dress, right sides together, and pin along the seamline of the neck and each armhole. Match center lines, underarm seams, and notches; keep the cut edges even. Baste if necessary.

Turn the dress to the wrong side. Stitch around the front and back neckline and armholes from the facing side, beginning and ending the stitching 1½ inches from the shoulder edge. Backstitch at each end. Compare front and back shoulders to be sure that the distance between the neckline and armhole stitching is the same.

Trim the interfacing seam allowance close to the stitching. Trim the facing seam allowance to

⅛ inch and the garment seam allowance to ¼ inch where stitched. (Leave the full seam allowance above the stitching until you have stitched the shoulder openings.) Slash the seam allowances almost to the stitching and at frequent intervals. Clip diagonally across corners where seams cross at the underarm. Press seams.

Turn the facing to the underside. Ease it under slightly at the seamline and baste. Press, then remove the basting.

Turn the dress to the wrong side so that right sides of the dress are together. Pin the front and back shoulder seams of the dress together. (They are the two inside edges.) With the front of the dress toward you, slip your fingers up between the facing and the garment. Grasp the shoulder seam edges of both facing and garment (four of them); pull down on the edges and at the same time turn the front facing back to bring the shoulder seam into view. This procedure turns the front shoulder of the garment and facing right sides together and pulls the back shoulder and facing into the front one. The two shoulder seam edges that were previously pinned together are on the bottom, and the two facing edges are above, right sides together.

Stitch the shoulder seam of the garment, taking the regular ⅝-inch seam allowance. Then, pin and stitch the facing shoulder seam. Press seams.

Pull the back part of the shoulder seam farther into the front one so that the shoulder seam allowances are in full view and the unstitched portion of the neckline and armhole seams can be stitched. Press the shoulder seams open. Use a seamboard, and slip the pointed end through the open seam on each side of the garment; press.

Pin the neckline edges together and the armhole edges together; then stitch across the openings, overlapping the previous stitching on each side of the shoulder seam. Blend seam allowances, and press.

Turn the front facing to the wrong side of the dress, then pull the back shoulder into position. Press. Stitch the opposite shoulder.

Understitch the neckline and armhole, following the directions given for Method 1. Tack the outer edges of the facing to the underarm seam allowances.

## Faced Slash Opening

Mark the position of the slash. *Do not cut.* Stitch around the opening for the slash, using a short stitch. Begin at the neckline, a scant ¼ inch from the center, and gradually taper to 1/16 inch at the point; take one stitch across the point. Continue stitching up the opposite side, gradually tapering to a scant ¼ inch from the center at the neckline. This stitching is not visible in the finished work.

Cut the facing the same as the edge to be faced and about 2 inches longer than the front opening. Join the seams at the shoulder line. Finish the seams and press them open.

Turn the garment to the right side. Pin and baste the facing to the neckline, right sides together. Match markings, shoulder seams, and center lines.

Place the work under the needle with the facing next to the feed. Stitch the neckline seam from one shoulder line to within ¼ inch of the center front marking. Take one stitch diagonally, then stitch down one side of the center front marking, gradually tapering to 1/16 inch at the point. Take one stitch across the point, then continue up the opposite side in the same manner and around the neckline, overlapping a few stitches at the starting point. The width at the point provides space for cutting and prevents pulling at the point in the finished work.

Blend the facing seam allowance to ⅛ inch and the garment seam allowance to ¼ inch. Clip into the seam allowance on the curve and cut off corners where seams cross at the shoulder line. Cut between the two rows of stitching, almost to the point of the slash, then cut off corners at the top of the slash, close to the stitching.

Turn facing to the wrong side. Pull out the corners to square them. Fold on the seamline and baste. Press. Remove bastings.

Understitch the neckline seam to prevent the facing from rolling out of place. Do not understitch around the slash.

*(Continued)*

**To stay the point of the slash,** fold a 1½-inch length of straight seam binding through the center and press. Pin it to the underside of the facing with the upper edge exactly at the point of the slash. Stitch near the top edge of the seam binding.

## BOUND AND CORDED NECKLINE FINISHES

### Double-Fold Bias Binding

A double-fold bias binding is used as a neckline finish on blouses, dresses, and children's clothes. It is also applied to the edge of sleeves and at the waistline of a garment. The bias binding may be of self or contrasting fabric. The finished width is usually about ¼ inch.

If binding is not specified on the pattern, trim off the neckline seam allowance. Stay-stitch 3/16 inch from the edge. (This stitching is not visible in the finished work.)

Cut a strip on the true bias, six times the width of the finished binding. See *Cutting Bias Strips*, page 244. Fold it through the center, wrong sides together, and finger-press lightly.

On the right side of the garment, pin the double bias strip around the neckline, matching seam edges. Stretch the binding slightly on this inside curve. Join the bias on the lengthwise grain at the shoulder line. See *Joining Bias Strips*, page 244. Baste. Stitch a scant ¼ inch from the edge, using a short stitch, and overlap a few stitches at the starting point. Press the seam only.

Fold the binding over the seam edge to the stitching line on the underside, enclosing the cut edges. Pin. Finish by hand, using a slip stitch.

**When there is an opening at the neckline,** fold the facing for the opening to the underside and press. Pin and baste it to the neckline of the garment.

Turn under the end of the binding ¼ inch before folding it through the center. Align the folded end with the folded edge of the opening. Treat the neckline and facing as one, and pin the double bias strip around the neckline, matching seam

edges. Fold the binding under ¼ inch at the opposite end. Then finish, following the procedure given above. Slip-stitch the folded edges of the binding together at each end.

## Single-Fold Bias Binding

The single-fold bias binding may be used in place of the double-fold. The finished width is usually about ¼ inch.

Trim off the neckline seam allowance if binding is not specified on the pattern. Stay-stitch 3/16 inch from the edge. (This stitching is not visible in the finished work.)

Cut a strip on the true bias four times the finished width. See *Cutting Bias Strips*, page 244.

On the right side of the garment, pin one edge of the bias strip to the neckline, right sides together. Match the seam edges, and stretch the binding slightly along the edge when the seam is on inside curve. Join the bias on the lengthwise grain at the shoulder line. Baste. Stitch a scant ¼ inch from the edge, using a short stitch, and overlap a few stitches at the starting point. Press.

Turn under the cut edge of the binding ¼ inch and finger-press. Fold the binding over the seam edge to the stitching line on the underside, enclosing the cut edges. Pin. Finish by hand, using a slip stitch.

*When there is an opening at the neckline,* follow instructions given under *Double-Fold Bias Binding* on page 145.

## Corded Neckline

A fine, dainty, corded neckline in a smart finish for blouses, dresses, and children's clothes. It is a detail that is often found on expensive ready-to-wear garments. The covered cord may be made of self or contrasting fabric.

Follow instructions on page 245 for preparing the cording.

Pin the cording to the right side of the neckline, keeping the stitching of the cording on the seamline. The seam allowance on the cording is full and requires easing so that the cord will lie smoothly along the curve. Allow ⅝ inch at each end of the cording for joining at the shoulder line. Pull out the cord from its bias cover and clip off ⅝ inch at each end so the cord will just meet at the joining. Ease the two ends of the bias slightly toward the seam as illustrated. Adjust the Zipper Foot to the right of the needle. Stitch, using a stitch shorter than for straight stitching. *Do not crowd the stitching against the cord.* Press the seam.

Pin and baste the facing over the neckline, right sides together, matching the shoulder seams and center lines. Place the work under the needle with the first stitching uppermost so that you can use it as a guide. Stitch, crowding the stitching between the cord and the previous stitching; overlap a few stitches at the starting point.

Trim the corded seam allowance to ⅛ inch and the garment and facing seam allowances to ¼ inch. Clip into the seam edge on the inside curves at even intervals. Clip off corners where seams cross at the shoulder line. Press.

Turn the facing to the underside. Fold on the seamline and press. Finish free edge of the facing and tack it to the shoulder seam allowance.

**To eliminate bulk, the facing is often omitted,** especially if the fabric is double knit or heavy, and the garment is underlined. As the cording is stitched to the neckline, crowd the stitching between the cord and previous line of stitching. Trim the neckline seam allowance to ¼ inch and slash it at even intervals. Trim the cording seam allowance that will be next to the garment to ⅛ inch. Press, then turn the seam allowances to the underside and press. Pin the wide seam allowance to the garment; then catch-stitch, making stitches through the seam allowance and the underlining. (These stitches are not visible on the top side.)

---

**When there is an opening at the neckline,** stitch the facing to the opening, blend the seams, and press. Pin cording to the neckline, extending the end ⅝ inch beyond the facing seam on each side. Start stitching at the facing seam and continue around the neckline to the opposite facing seam. Tie the threads. (Below left).

Pull out the cord at each end and clip off ⅝ inch. Then fold the bias ends diagonally toward the neckline seam and stitch in place, as illustrated. Press.

Pin and baste the facing to the neckline, right sides together. Stitch, blend the seams, and press, following the procedure given above.

147

Before attaching a collar, make sure that you have:
1) stay-stitched the neckline of the garment; 2) stitched, finished, and pressed the shoulder seams and darts; 3) attached the facing and interfacing to the front opening, leaving the neckline edge free. Refer to *Faced Neckline and Front Opening,* page 134. Leave the underarm seams open for convenience in finishing the neckline.

Several methods of constructing and attaching a collar are described below. Choose the one that best suits your garment and fabric.

## Collar with Bias Facing

This method may be used for cotton fabrics and children's clothes.

Cut preshrunk interfacing by the same pattern as the undercollar, and baste it to the wrong side of the undercollar, matching markings.

Pin and baste the top collar to the undercollar, right sides together, matching markings. Stitch on the seamline, leaving the neckline edge open.

Trim interfacing seam allowance close to the stitching. Trim seam allowance on the undercollar to ⅛ inch and on the top collar to ¼ inch. Notch the outside curved edges. Press.

Turn the collar to the right side. Work the seam edges between the thumb and finger and ease the undercollar slightly to the underside at the seamline; then baste. Press. Top-stitch if desired.

### Attaching the Collar

Turn the garment to the right side. Pin and hand-baste the collar and the interfacing to the neckline edge, matching markings, shoulder line, and center lines. Roll the collar as it will be worn, allowing sufficient ease in the top collar for it to fit smoothly over the roll. Fold the front facing back over the right side of the collar and pin.

Cut a true bias strip 1¼ inches wide and long enough to extend around the neckline. Pin it over the collar at the neckline, allowing ¼-inch seam on the bias and extending the ends of bias strip ⅜ inch over the front facings. Stitch around the neckline in one continuous line from one front edge to the other. Backstitch at each end for reinforcement.

Trim the interfacing seam allowance close to the stitching. Trim collar and garment seam allowances to ¼ inch. Slash the seam allowance on the neckline curve at even intervals and cut diagonally across the corners close to the stitching. Cut off corners where seams cross at the shoulder line. Press.

Turn the front facings and the bias strip to the underside. Fold the bias under ¼ inch and pin it to the garment across the back of the neckline. Finish by hand, using a hemming stitch. Tack the front facings to the shoulder seam allowance. Press.

## Notched Collar with Back Facing

Use this method for a better finish and for fabrics that will require dry cleaning.

The notched collar may be cut in one or two pieces.

*One-piece collar.* Crease the collar crosswise through the center. Cut preshrunk interfacing one-half the width of the collar; clip off the corners. Pin the interfacing to the wrong side of the collar just below the crease. Fold the collar in half, right sides together, and stitch across the ends. Trim the interfacing seam allowance close to the stitching. Trim the seam allowance on the undercollar to ⅛ inch and on the top collar to ¼ inch. Cut diagonally across the corners close to the stitching.

Turn collar to the right side. Pull out the corners and ease the undercollar slightly to the underside at the seamline; baste. Press.

*Two-piece collar.* Cut preshrunk interfacing the same as the collar. Pin and baste it to the wrong side of the undercollar. Clip off the corners of the interfacing to avoid bulk when the collar is turned.

Lay the top collar over the undercollar, right sides together, matching markings. Pin and baste. Stitch on the seamline, leaving the neckline edge free. Take one stitch diagonally across the corners to allow for a smooth turning. Trim the interfacing seam allowance close to the stitching. Trim the seam allowance on the undercollar to ⅛ inch and on the top collar to ¼ inch. Cut diagonally across the corners close to the stitching. Turn the collar to the right side. Pull out corners and ease the undercollar slightly to the underside at the seamline. Baste and press.

### Attaching the Collar

After joining the front and back facings at the shoulder seams, stitch the facing to the garment, right sides together, along the front seams, leaving the neckline edges free. Press. Blend the seams and press them open. Slash into the neckline seam allowance almost to the stay stitching.

Pin and baste the undercollar and the interfacing to the neckline, matching markings, shoulder line, and center lines. Stitch in a continuous line, beginning ⅛ inch from one collar edge and stitching to within ⅛ inch of the opposite collar edge.

Turn the facing over the right side of the garment and pin it to the neckline from the front edge to the collar edge. Pin and baste the neckline facing to the top collar, matching markings and center lines. Stitch in a continuous line, beginning ⅛ inch from one collar edge and stitching to within ⅛ inch of the opposite collar edge.

Stitch the facing to the neckline from the front edge into the collar ⅛ inch, joining the previous line of stitching. Trim the interfacing seam allowance close to the stitching. Trim the facing seam allowance to ⅛ inch and the garment and the collar seam allowances to ¼ inch. Slash the seam allowances on the neckline curve at even intervals and cut diagonally across the corners close to the stitching. Cut off corners where seams cross at the shoulder line. Press, then press seams open.

Roll the collar over the left hand, shaping it as it will be worn, and pin through all thicknesses at the roll line. Allow sufficient ease for the top collar to fit smoothly over the undercollar. Bring the top and undercollar seams together, matching shoulder seams and center lines. Pin, then staystitch together by hand.

Turn the facing to the underside. Finish the free edge of the facing and tack it to the shoulder seam allowances.

## Notched Collar without Back Facing

Clip into the garment neckline seam allowance almost to the stay stitching.

Construct the notched collar as directed on page 149.

Pin the undercollar and the interfacing to the

150

neckline across the back from shoulder seam to shoulder seam, leaving the top collar free. Match markings and center lines. Then pin the undercollar, top collar, and interfacing to the neckline from shoulder to center front on each side, matching markings.

Turn the front facing over the collar, right sides together, and pin, matching markings. Baste from front edge to shoulder seam. Slash the top collar the depth of the seam allowance at each shoulder line, then baste the undercollar and interfacing to the neckline across the back. Continue basting to the opposite edge.

the neckline curve at even intervals and cut diagonally across the corners close to the stitching. Cut off corners where seam cross at the shoulder line. Press. Turn the facing to the underside.

Turn the seam allowance into the collar across the back neckline. Roll the collar over the left hand, shaping it as it will be worn, and pin through all thicknesses at the roll line. Allow sufficient ease for the top collar to fit smoothly over the undercollar. Turn under the free edge of the top collar and pin it to the stitching line across the back. Slip-stitch in place. Tack the front facings to the shoulder seam edges.

Stitch in a continuous line from one front edge to the other, leaving the top collar free across the back. Trim the interfacing seam allowance close to the stitching. Trim the garment and collar seam allowances to ¼ inch. Slash the seam allowance on

## Velvet Overcollar

An overcollar of velvet or velveteen will complement coats, suits, and sometimes dresses for women and children.

A velvet collar covers the finished collar and the entire garment should be completed before applying it.

Follow *Method 1* when the edge of the collar

151

forms a border around the velveteen as in the Peter Pan collar; follow *Method 2* when the velveteen covers the collar completely as in the illustration of the notched collar.

**Method 1:** Cut the velvet collar by the garment collar pattern, then trim off ¼ inch on the outer edge. Stay-stitch around the neckline and outer edge of the collar ½ inch from the edge. Fold under the ⅝-inch seam allowance and baste ¼ inch

from the folded edge. Notch the seam allowance on the outside curve and slash it on the neckline curve so that the seams will lie flat.

Place the velvet collar over the finished collar on the garment, matching center lines, shoulder line, and neckline seams. Pin at the neckline. Roll both collars over the left hand, shaping them as they will be worn, and pin through all thicknesses at the roll line. Allow sufficient ease for the velvet to fit smoothly over the finished collar. Then pin the outer edge of the velvet collar in place—a generous ¼ inch from the edge of the finished collar. Pin at the center back, front edges, then at intervals between. Slip-stitch velvet collar in place, catching only the upper layer of the finished collar.

**Method 2:** Cut the velvet collar by the pattern used for the garment collar. Stay-stitch around the neckline, ½ inch from the edge. Fold under the ⅝-inch seam allowance and baste ¼ inch from the

folded edge. Slash the seam allowance on the inside curve of the neckline and notch it on the outside curve so that the seams will lie flat.

Place the velvet collar over the finished collar on the garment, matching center lines, shoulder line, and neckline seams. Pin at the neckline. Roll both collars over the left hand, shaping them as they will be worn, and pin through all thicknesses at the roll line. Allow sufficient ease for the velvet to fit smoothly over the finished collar. Then pin the collars together near the outer edge.

Fold the velvet collar over the collar edge and pin it in place on the underside. Pin at the center back, front edges, then at intervals between. Miter corners. Baste.

Catch-stitch the velvet collar in place on the underside, then slip-stitch it in place at neckline on the right side.

# Waistline Joinings and Waistbands

BEFORE YOU JOIN THE BODICE AND SKIRT, you should have completed these steps:

1) Stay-stitched the waistline of both the bodice and the skirt.

2) Stitched the bodice underarm seams and the skirt side seams, finished the seam edges, and pressed the seams open.

The opening for the placket may be on the left side, as illustrated, or in the center back.

## To Join Bodice to Plain or Gored Skirt

Turn the skirt to the wrong side and the bodice to the right side. Place bodice inside the skirt, right sides together, and pin at the waistline, matching center lines, seams, darts, and notches. Baste.

Stitch around the waistline from one edge of the placket opening to the other. Reinforce with backstitching at each end. Press.

Turn the seam allowances away from the garment. On the bodice side, stitch preshrunk straight seam binding to the seam allowance barely below the first line of stitching. Begin and end the stitching about 1¼ inches from each side of the opening. Press. (The seam binding prevents the seam from stretching.) Clip off corners where seams

cross on the right side and at darts. Press. Turn the seam allowance down toward the skirt.

After the zipper is inserted, turn under the ends of the seam binding and tack them to the zipper tape.

## To Join Bodice to Gathered Skirt

Turn the skirt to the wrong side and the bodice to the right side. Place the bodice inside the skirt,

153

right sides together. Pin the bodice and skirt together at the waistline, matching center lines, side seams, and markings. Adjust the gathers to fit the waistline and pin. Baste. Turn to page 106 for instructions on *Gathered Skirts*.

Stitch the seam with the bodice next to the feed. Place a second row of stitching in the seam allowance ¼ inch from the first line of stitching. Pink the edges.

If the fabric is loosely woven, overcast the edges either by hand or by machine, using the blindstitch zig-zag. Turn seam allowance up against the bodice.

## To Stay the Waistline

To prevent stretching and to allow for ease in fitting, stay the waistline of a skirt with seam binding.

Cut preshrunk straight seam binding to the

waistline measurement plus seam allowances. Pin it to the wrong side of the skirt waistline, keeping edges even and the seam binding within the seam allowance so that the stitching will not be visible in the finished garment. Evenly distribute the slight ease in the skirt. Stitch the binding to the skirt. Press.

## To Attach Waistband to Skirt

Before attaching a waistband to the skirt, the waistline of the skirt should be stay-stitched; darts and seams stitched, finished, and pressed; and the zipper inserted in the placket on the left side or center back. See *Skirt Placket Zipper in Lapped Seam*, page 179.

The method used in joining a waistband to a skirt will vary, depending on the style of the garment, weight of the fabric, and personal preference. The band should be interfaced for added body. The band extension may either overlap on the front side, underlap on the back side, or lap on both sides. The width of the finished band is usually 1 inch to 1¼ inches.

*Method 1:* Cut the fabric for the waistband on the lengthwise grain as follows: twice the *finished width* plus seam allowances, and *the length* of the waistline measurement plus 2 inches for seam allowance and overlap on the front side of the closing and 2½ inches for seam allowance and underlap on the back side of the closing.

Fold the waistband lengthwise through the center, wrong sides together, and crease.

Cut the interfacing of nurses cloth or muslin twice the width of the finished waistband, less ¼ inch, and the same length. Fold it lengthwise through the center and press. Cut one end to a point.

Stitch the interfacing to the wrong side of the waistband back section barely below the crease and then along the opposite edge, leaving a seam allowance in the band at the pointed end.

Mark the wrong side of the waistband 2 inches from the pointed edge for the overlap, and 2½ inches from the opposite end for the underlap. The length between the two markings should be the waistline measurement.

Open the zipper. Place the waistband over the waistline of the skirt, right sides together, extending the pointed end 2 inches beyond the front edge of the placket, and pin. Extend the opposite end 2½ inches beyond the back seam of the placket opening, and pin. (This end should extend the width of the zipper underlay.) Pin waistband to waistline at the right side seam, allowing the same amount of ease in the front and back of the skirt.

Match the front seamline of the placket opening with the right side seam, and pin. Fold the front section of the waistband and pin-mark the center. Match the back seamline of the opening with the right side seam, and pin. Pin-mark the center back of the waistband in the same way as the front. Pin the band to the skirt at center front and back. Evenly distribute the ease in the skirt between the markings, and pin. Baste. Stitch on the seamline, and backstitch at each end. Clip off corners where seams cross at the right side and at darts. On firmly woven fabrics, trim the waistline seam allowance to ¼ inch.

Remove bastings, and press. Turn the waistband away from the skirt and press the seam allowances toward the waistband.

Fold the pointed end of the waistband in half, right sides together, and pin across the end and along the lower edge as far as the placket opening. Stitch barely outside the interfacing, taking one stitch across the point for a smooth turning. Reinforce each end of the seam with backstitching. Fold the opposite end, right sides together and pin; stitch across the end. Trim the seam allowances to ¼ inch and press. Turn the waistband to the right side and press the ends.

Fold the waistband in half and pin along the fold. Turn under the seam allowance on the free edge of the waistband and pin to the seam at the waistline, enclosing the seam allowances. Finish by hand, using a hemming stitch. Make the stitching through the waistband and seam allowance only so that it will not be visible on the top side. Press. If top stitching is desired, stitch around the waistband from the top side.

Sew on hooks and eyes, as illustrated. Make the stitches through the underside of the waistband and interfacing. If you want a button instead of hooks and eyes for the waistband closing, work a buttonhole near the point and sew the button in position at the opposite end. If a bound buttonhole is used, make it before attaching the interfacing to the waistband. However, sew on hooks and eyes at the end of the underlap to hold it in position on the underside.

**Method 2:** When there is no overlap on the front seam, cut the waistband on the lengthwise grain as follows: twice the *finished width* plus seam allowances, and the *length* of the waistline measurement plus 1 inch for depth of the point and seam allowance on the front side and 2½ inches for underlap and seam allowance on the back side.

Mark the waistband at these intervals. The length between the two markings should be the waistline measurement.

Open the zipper. Place the waistband (without interfacing) over the waistline of the skirt, right sides together, extending the end 1 inch beyond the front edge of the placket opening, and pin. Extend the opposite end 2½ inches beyond the back edge of the placket opening, and pin. (This end should extend the width of the zipper underlay.)

Finish pinning the waistband in place as instructed in *Method 1*. Baste.

For the interfacing, use a heavy grosgrain ribbon 1 inch in width or a fine quality of belting. Cut it the same length as the waistband and cut one end to a point.

Lap the grosgrain or other interfacing over the waistband side of the seam allowances, keeping the edge even with the seamline. Pin. Stitch on the edge of the interfacing with the skirt next to the feed. Backstitch at each end. Remove bastings and press.

Turn the waistband away from the skirt and press the seam allowances and interfacing toward the waistband. Trim seam allowances under the interfacing to ¼ inch and clip off corners where seams cross at the right side and at darts.

Pink the free edge of the waistband, then stitch ¼ inch from the edge, using a 20 stitch.

Fold the pointed end of the waistband, right sides together, and pin across the end. Stitch barely outside the interfacing. Take one stitch across the point for a smooth turning. Reinforce the ends with backstitching. Fold the opposite end, right sides together, and pin. Trim the end of the interfacing to the seamline of the waistband. Stitch across the end of the waistband. Trim the seam allowances to ¼ inch and press. Turn the ends to the right side, ease out the corners, and press.

Turn the free edge of the waistband over the interfacing and pin to the seam at the stitching line on the underside, enclosing the seam allowances. At the front seam, fold under the raw edges of the waistband as far as the zipper tape. Finish by hand with a backstitch, catching only into the seam allowance and waistband so that the stitches will not be visible on the top side. Sew on hooks and eyes as illustrated in *Method 1*.

## To Attach Waistband on Knit Fabric

To assure a snug fit in knit fabrics and still allow as much "give" in the waistband as in the fabric, use 1-inch elastic inside the waistband instead of grosgrain or fine belting. Use zig-zag stitching for flexibility.

Follow the instructions in *Method 2* on cutting the waistband and pinning it to the skirt.

Cut the elastic 1 inch shorter than the waistband and cut one end to a point. Lap the elastic over the waistband side of the waistline seam allowance, keeping the edge even with the seamline, and pin. Distribute the ease evenly in the front and back skirt section. Stitch near the edge of the elastic, stretching the elastic between the pins as you sew. Use a medium-width plain zig-zag stitch and 12 stitch length. Backstitch at each end for reinforcement.

Trim the seam allowance under the elastic to ¼ inch and clip off corners where seams cross at darts and at the right side seam. Turn the waistband away from the garment and press the seam allowance and elastic toward the waistband. Finish the free edge of the waistband with the multiple-stitch zig-zag.

Fold the pointed end of the waistband, right sides together, and pin. Stitch across the point, barely outside the elastic. Fold the opposite end, right sides together, and pin. Trim elastic end even with the seamline of the waistband. Stitch across the end of the band barely outside the elastic. Trim seam allowances to ¼ inch and press. Turn ends to the right side and press.

Fold the waistband smoothly over the elastic and pin to the seam at the stitching line on the underside, enclosing the seam allowances. Baste. Stitch from the top side, stretching the elastic as you stitch so that it will remain stretchable after the stitching is finished. Use a medium-width plain zig-zag stitch and a 12 stitch length. Sew on hooks and eyes as illustrated in *Method 1*. Make the stitches through the underside of the waistband and elastic. Or, work a buttonhole and sew on a button.

## To Attach Elastic at the Waistline

Your pattern design may show the bodice and skirt of a dress, or the bodice and peplum of a jacket, cut-in-one and belted at the waistline to form soft gathers. To ensure that the gathers are evenly distributed, stitch narrow elastic to the underside of the waistline.

Mark the waistline of the garment. Fit the elastic for the desired snugness at the waistline, allowing 1 inch for finishing at the opening.

Divide the garment waistline and elastic into quarters, allowing ½ inch at each end of the elastic for finishing.

Pin the elastic to the underside of the garment waistline at the quartered intervals; fold ends of the elastic under ½ inch and pin to facing or zipper tape on each side of the opening. Stretch the elastic between the pins as you stitch so that it will remain stretchable after the stitching is finished. A narrow multiple-stitch zig-zag or two rows of straight stitching may be used. Fasten the ends of the elastic securely with hand stitches.

# Sleeve Styles and Finishes

LOOK TO THE SLEEVE FOR FASHION. Construct it with care. It signals the difference between a homemade and a professional-looking garment.

Your pattern design specifies the style and finish of your sleeve and gives you explicit directions to follow. The paragraphs below will help you work carefully and confidently.

## CONSTRUCTING DIFFERENT SLEEVE STYLES

### Guidelines and Cautions

—Transfer accurately from pattern to fabric all *markings in the sleeve and armhole.*

—Never omit pinning and basting.

—The shoulder length of the bodice is important to the fit of the sleeve, especially the plain, set-in sleeve.

The fashion of the pattern may show the garment shoulder line extending beyond the natural shoulder line. Do not fit the fashion out of this sleeve. If the natural shoulder line is the fashion of your pattern, however, be sure that it is the correct length for your figure. If it is too wide, the sleeve will hang off the shoulder, giving the garment a homemade appearance; if it is too narrow, the sleeve will draw and may rip at the seam. There should always be sufficient ease for movement.

—If your pattern calls for shoulder pads or shapes, the allowance for them has been made in the pattern.

—Do not overlook proper pressing of the sleeve during construction.

Sleeve styles are numerous and almost every one is illustrated here. Variations should be constructed along the same lines as those described below.

### Set-in Sleeve

Carefully check and match notches in the sleeve cap with those in the armhole to avoid constructing two sleeves for the same arm.

Three-quarter and full-length sleeves have fullness at the elbow, which is controlled with darts or gathers. Stitch darts and press them downward over a press mitt. See *Elbow Darts,* page 103.

If gathers are indicated, control the fullness with a row of stitching between the notches, barely outside the seamline. Fold the sleeve, right sides together, and pin on the seamline, matching markings. Draw the thread to ease in the fullness at the elbow; distribute the fullness evenly between the notches. Baste, then stitch underarm seams and finish seam edges. Press the seam; then slip the sleeve over a sleeveboard, and press the seam open.

The two-piece sleeve is generally used in suits and coats. There is a slight ease in the upper sleeve section at the elbow. When joining sleeve sections, control the ease by pinning the seam at ¼-inch intervals between the notches. After the seam is basted and stitched, shrink the fullness by pressing.

### Setting Sleeve into Armhole (Above)

Turn the sleeve to the wrong side and, from the inside, place one or two lines of stitching around the cap of the sleeve between the notches to control the ease. Place the first line barely outside the seamline, in the seam allowance. Use the same length stitch as used in stitching the garment and leave thread ends long enough to draw. (Loosen the upper tension just enough to draw the bobbin thread to ease the fullness. Do not forget to return the tension to its previous setting.) If two lines of stitching are used, place the second line in the seam allowance, 3/16 inch from the first line of stitching.

Turn the sleeve to the right side. With the wrong side of the garment toward you, slip the sleeve into the armhole, right sides together. Pin, matching underarm seams, notches, and shoulder line. Working with the sleeve toward you, draw the bobbin threads at each end of the stitching, easing in the fullness from the notches to within ½ inch of the shoulder line. Draw the threads enough to fit the sleeve cap to the armhole. (The ½ inch at the shoulder line is on the straight grain of the fabric and should not be eased.) *Roll the seamline of the sleeve and armhole over the fingers and distribute the sleeve ease evenly.* Pin the sleeve

in the armhole at close intervals, taking only a small nip at the seamline.

Turn the garment to the right side and lay the shoulder over the hand to check the "hang" of the sleeve. Be sure the ease is in the correct place. The center lengthwise grain of the sleeve should fall in a straight line and the crosswise grain should fall at right angles to it. See *Understanding Balance Lines,* page 77.

With the sleeve toward you, baste, using a short stitch.

If you are working with wool, it may be necessary to shrink out the fullness at the sleeve cap before basting. See *Pressing*, page 74. Re-pin the sleeve in the armhole the same as before, then baste.

Try on the garment before sewing in the sleeve. Pin the bodice and skirt sections together so that the bodice will not slip out of place. Check the true fit of the sleeve. Make any necessary adjustments.

Stitch from the sleeve side, barely beyond the stitching used to control the ease. Begin the stitching at the underarm seam and continue around the sleeve, overlapping stitches about 1 inch at the underarm seam. Remove basting. Trim the seam allowance to one-half its width. Clip off the corners where seams cross at the underarm and shoulder. The first row of stitching, used to control the fullness, may be removed if desired. See *Sleeves*, page 323 for additional information.

Press into the sleeve as far as the stitching. Turn the seam allowance into the sleeve. In heavy coat fabric, use only one line of stitching to control the ease. Press the seam, then press it open. See *Pressing*, page 74.

## Raglan Sleeve

Pin, baste, and stitch the dart at the shoulder, matching markings. A dart in this position is usually slashed and pressed open. See *Darts*, page 101.

Stitch the underarm seams of the sleeve and bodice. Finish the seam edges and press the seam open. Turn the sleeve to the right side. Pin to the front and back bodice, right sides together, matching markings and underarm seams. Baste. Stitch in one continuous line from one neckline edge to the other. Remove bastings.

Slash the seam allowances on the inside curve and notch them on the outside curve. Clip off corners where seams cross at the underarm. Finish seam edges as required by the fabric. Press the seam open from the neckline to the curve at the underarm. Turn seam allowances toward the sleeve at the underarm.

## Epaulet Sleeve

The epaulet sleeve has a yoke extending over the shoulder from the top of the sleeve cap to the neckline.

At the cap of the sleeve, where the epaulet begins, stay-stitch the point where the seam allowance will be slashed. Use a short stitch and take one stitch across the point. Press. Stitch the underarm seams of the sleeve and bodice. Finish the seam edges and press the seam open.

Turn the sleeve to the right side. With the wrong side of the bodice toward you, place the sleeve into the armhole, right sides together. Pin, matching underarm seams, shoulder markings, and notches. Then with the sleeve toward you, pin at close intervals. Baste in one continuous line from one side of the shoulder to the other.

At the shoulder line of the sleeve, slash almost to the stay-stitched point. Pin the epaulet to the shoulder line of the bodice on each side, matching markings. Be sure that the corners do not pucker. Baste with a short stitch. Check the right side to be sure that the corners are square.

Stitch from the sleeve side in a continuous line from one neckline edge to the other. Pivot the fabric on the needle at the corners; take one stitch across the point; pivot again and continue stitching. Smooth out the fabric at the point so that a pleat is not formed. Remove bastings. Clip off the corners where seams cross at the underarm. Press the seam as stitched, then press the seam edges toward the epaulet. In the sleeve section, turn seam allowances toward the sleeve.

## Puffed Sleeve

Puffed sleeves are found in children's clothes, blouses, many shirtwaist dresses, and lingerie.

Stitch underarm seams. (A French seam is frequently used in children's clothes and garments made of sheer fabric.)

Turn the sleeve to the wrong side and, from the inside, place two lines of stitching around the cap of the sleeve between the notches. Place the first line of stitching barely outside the seamline in the seam allowance and the second line in the seam allowance, about 3/16 inch from the first.

At the lower edge of the sleeve, place a line of stitching between the markings. Gather and finish the lower edge.

Turn the sleeve to the right side. With the wrong side of the garment toward you, slip the sleeve into the armhole, right sides together. Pin, matching underarm seams, notches, and shoulder lines. With the sleeve toward you, draw the threads for both rows of stitching at the same time, and gather the sleeve between the notches to fit the armhole. Distribute the fullness evenly, and pin. Baste, using a short stitch.

Stitch from the sleeve side, barely beyond the first line of gathering stitches and overlap the stitching about 1 inch at the underarm. Stitch again on the second line of gathering stitches. Trim the seam allowance close to the second line of stitching. Press. Finish the seam edges with binding or overcast them together, using the blind-stitch zig-zag. Turn the seam allowances toward the sleeve.

In sheer fabrics, place the second line of stitching around the cap of the sleeve, ⅛ inch from the first line, and use only one line of stitching to sew in the sleeve. Trim the seam allowance on the sleeve side to ¼ inch. Turn the cut edge under ⅛ inch

on the bodice side; fold this seam allowance over the sleeve seam allowance to the stitching line, enclosing the cut edge. Pin. Slip-stitch to the sleeve seam barely above the stitching. This seam finish is barely visible through sheer fabric.

## Kimono Sleeve—without Gusset

To prevent the seam from breaking under strain, use a stay, following one of the methods given here.

*Method 1:* Pin, baste, and stitch the seam, using a shorter stitch on the curved section. Slash the seam allowances almost to the stitching line on the curve to relieve the strain. Press the seam, then press it open.

Use straight seam binding over the open seam from the hem fold in the sleeve to the lower edge of the bodice. Turn the seam allowance away from the garment and stitch the binding to each side of the seam allowance. Stitch again through the curve on one side, close to the seamline. The binding is stitched only to the single seam allowance and is not visible from the right side. Press seam open.

**Method 3:** Pin and baste the seam. Fold a 6-inch strip of straight seam binding lengthwise, and pin it over the seamline at the curve. Stitch the seam through the binding. Slash seam allowances at the curve to relieve the strain. Press the seam, then press it open.

**Method 4:** On **knit fabrics,** after stitching the underarm seam, baste straight seam binding over the curved section of the open seam. Then, from the right side, stitch the binding to the curved section of the seam, using a narrow zig-zag stitch (generally, a 12 to 15 stitch length and medium stitch width).

**Method 2:** Pin and baste the seam. Place straight seam binding over the basting line, with one edge extending over the seam allowance ⅛ inch, and pin. Stitch the seam through the seam binding. Slash seam allowances at the curve to relieve the strain. Press the seam, then press it open.

## Kimono Sleeve—with Underarm Gusset

Gussets in sleeves may be one-piece or two-piece. Reinforce the point of the slash with a facing of the seam fabric cut 2 inches wide and 2½ inches long. If the fabric is heavy, use straight seam binding of the same color as the fabric.

Mark the position of the gusset at the underarm seam. On the right side, pin the facing right side down over the point of the slash, extending the top edge ½ inch beyond the point. From the wrong side, stitch the facing to the garment, following the seamline and using a short stitch. At the point, pivot the fabric on the needle and take one stitch across; then pivot again and stitch down the other side. Press.

Slash halfway between the stitching lines to within a few threads of the point. Turn the facing on the stitching line to the wrong side. Press. The reinforcement forms a wider seam allowance at the point.

*One-piece gusset.* Stitch the underarm seams of the sleeve and bodice. Finish the seam edges as required by the fabric. Press the seams, then press them open.

Pin and baste the gusset to the slashed edges, matching markings at the point and at the seamline. Stitch with the gusset next to the feed. On one side, stitch from the underarm seam to the sleeve seam; take one stitch across the point; pivot again and stitch down the other side. On the other

Stitch with the gusset next to the feed. Follow the seamline to the point; pivot the fabric on the needle and take one stitch across the point; then pivot again and stitch down the other side. Press the seams, then press the seam allowance away from the gusset. Stitch the underarm seam in a continuous line from the sleeve edge to the waistline. Backstitch at both ends. Finish the seam edges as required by the fabric. Press the seam, then press it open.

***To prevent pulling.*** To prevent the gusset from being pulled out at the point of the slash, which can happen with frequent wearings, use straight seam binding over the shoulder from one point of the gusset to the other.

Turn one end of the straight seam binding under ¼ inch and pin it to the gusset seam allowance and reinforced facing, near the stitching line.

side, stitch from the sleeve seam to the underarm seam. Pull threads through to the underside and tie. Press seam allowances away from the gusset.

***Two-piece gusset.*** Pin and baste one gusset section to the slashed edges of the front bodice and the second gusset section to the back bodice, matching markings at the point and at the seamline.

Bring the binding over the shoulder and down to the same point on the opposite side, and pin. Pin a 1/16-inch tuck, under the binding, in both the front and the back of the bodice. Then adjust the length of the binding to fit smoothly over the shoulder line. Pin the binding to the shoulder seam allowance, then tack it in place at each point and at each side of the shoulder seam allowance. Remove the pin tucks, which will allow just enough slack in the garment to prevent pulling.

## Armhole with Fitted Facing

Cut the facing the same as the edge to be faced. Join seams at the shoulder and at the underarm. Finish seam edges, and press seams open.

Turn the garment to the right side. Pin the facing to the armhole, right sides together, matching notches and seams at the shoulder and underarm. Baste. Stitch around the armhole on the seamline, overlapping a few stitches at the starting point. Press.

Trim the facing seam allowance to ⅛ inch and the garment seam allowance to ¼ inch. Slash the seam allowance on inside curves and cut off corners where seams cross.

Turn the facing to the underside and ease it under slightly at the seamline. Baste, then press.

Understitch the seam to prevent the facing from rolling out of place. Press.

Finish the free edge of the facing by pinking; then turn it under ¼ inch and edgestitch. Press. Turn the facing into the armhole and press. Tack the facing to the seam allowances at the shoulder seam and the underarm seam.

To ensure a correct sleeve length, long sleeves or those varying in length between the elbow and wrist are finished at the lower edge after the sleeve is sewed into the armhole. Short sleeves may be finished before they are sewed into the armhole.

## Hemmed Edge—Short Sleeve

Fold the hem evenly to the underside and baste ¼ inch from the fold. Press. Pin, then stitch seam binding ¼ inch from the free edge of the hem. Join the binding by folding the end under ¼ inch and overlapping ½ inch at the seam. Press.

Pin the free edge of the binding to the sleeve. Baste. Slip-stitch in place, catching only a single thread of the fabric. Remove bastings, and press.

## Wrist Closing

Turn the sleeve to the wrong side. Pin, then stitch, straight seam binding to the front edge of the wrist opening ⅛ inch from the *seamline*, extending it ½ inch above the opening.

Pin, then stitch binding to the back edge of the wrist opening, ⅛ inch from the *seam edge*, extending it ½ inch above opening. Clip diagonally into this seam allowance from the top of the binding to the opening. Press.

At the back edge of the opening, fold the binding to the underside and pin the free edge to the sleeve. Finish by hand, using a hemming stitch. At the top of the opening, stitch the front and back seam edges together the depth of the seam allowance.

At the front edge of the opening, fold the binding to the underside and pin the free edge to the sleeve. Finish by hand, using a hemming stitch.

At the lower edge of the sleeve, pin, then stitch, binding ¼ inch from edge, extending the ends ¼ inch beyond the edges of the opening. Press. Cut diagonally across corners of the sleeve seam al-

lowance close to the stitching. Fold the binding to the underside, miter the corners, and baste the free edge to the sleeve. Press. Finish by hand, using a hemming stitch. Remove bastings and press. Sew on small snaps.

## Zipper Closing

Select a fine neckline zipper, about 4 to 6 inches long, for a wrist closing. Apply the zipper following the instructions for the *Neckline or Sleeve Zipper in Slot Seam,* on page 181. Then open the zipper and finish the lower edge of the sleeve with straight seam binding, following the method described above.

## Vent Closing

The vent closing is frequently used in the back seam of two-piece tailored sleeves. It is also used in jackets at center back or side seams.

### Sleeve Seams

Mark the line of the fold for the vent closing and for the hem at the lower edge of the sleeve. If a bound buttonhole is used in a three-quarter length sleeve, make the buttonhole before seaming the sleeve.

Join the seams of the upper and lower sleeve sections, leaving the back seam open below the marking for the vent. Reinforce seam ends with backstitching. Clip diagonally into the seam allowance of the under section from the cut edge to the top of the opening. (This wide seam allowance in the opening will extend under the front seam allowance when the vent is finished.) Press seams, then press them open, carrying the crease in the back seam of the upper section to the lower edge of the opening. Fold the bottom hem to the underside, and press.

### The Interfacing

Cut preshrunk muslin interfacing on the true bias, ½ inch wider than the hem and long enough to extend around the sleeve; extend one end the depth of the opening. Place the interfacing on the wrong side of the sleeve with the lower edge along the hem fold and the extended edge along the lengthwise fold of the opening on the upper section. Pin, then baste. Catch-stitch each edge of the interfacing along the hem; make a tiny stitch barely outside the interfacing, catching only a single thread in the fabric; then make a stitch on the opposite side through the interfacing only. Space the stitches about ⅝ inch apart. Do not pull the threads too tightly. Remove bastings. The interfacing along the fold of the opening will be held in place when the buttons are sewed on; you may catch-stitch it if you wish, however, and you should catch-stitch it if you do not plan to use buttons on the opening.

interfacing. Catch-stitch in place from the back edge to the lengthwise fold in the opening on the upper section, making the stitches through the hem and interfacing only. The stitches are not visible on the right side, and the interfacing above the hem will not be visible when the lining is in place.

*Side hem and opening.* On the upper section, trim the bottom hem to ¼ inch from the cut edge to the lengthwise fold in the opening. Miter the corner to the point where the lining will overlap the hem. Press. Fold the seam allowance in the opening to the underside and pin in place. Slip-stitch the mitered corner in place, then catch-stitch the free edge of the seam allowance to the interfacing the depth of the opening.

### The Hems

*Bottom hem.* Fold the bottom hem over the interfacing and baste ¼ inch from the fold. Press. Pin, then baste the free edge of the hem to the

Turn the sleeve to the right side. Lap the upper section over the under section the depth of the seam allowance in the opening and pin. Be sure the lower edges are even.

Work from the wrong side and catch-stitch the edge of the back seam allowance in place from the lower edge to the top of the interfacing.

Make fine stitches through the seam allowance and interfacing only. Tack the seam edges to the interfacing at the top of the opening. Remove all bastings and press.

Turn the sleeve to the right side and sew on buttons through all thicknesses of fabric. The interfacing above the hem will not be visible when the lining is hand-sewed in place.

## Hemmed Cuff

The hemmed cuff is an excellent finish for blouses and children's clothes. The cuff and sleeve are cut-in-one, with the cuff section shaped to turn back smoothly over the sleeve.

After you have stitched the underarm seam, fold the cuff hem to the underside and press. Baste before pressing if necessary. Fold the free edge of the hem under ¼ inch, and finger-press. Pin the free edge to the sleeve, matching seams. Stitch near edge. (In the illustration the sleeve is turned to the wrong side so that the work may be easily seen.)

Turn the sleeve to the right side. Turn the cuff back over the sleeve, ½ inch below the stitching.

## Turn-Back Cuff

The ends of the cuff may be stitched together, as illustrated here, or left open. When the ends are left open, construct the cuff in the same manner as a collar and attach it to the sleeve, following the instructions given below.

Stitch the ends of the cuff together on the undercuff and on the upper cuff. Reinforce with back-stitching. Press, then press seam open.

Cut preshrunk interfacing by the cuff pattern. The sewing and handling instructions for attaching it to the cuff vary, depending on the weight of the interfacing and the fabric in the garment. Follow the appropriate method below.

*With lightweight interfacing.* Join interfacing

ends with a lapped seam, using the multiple-stitch zig-zag to eliminate bulk. See *Lapped Seam*, page 83.

Turn the undercuff to the wrong side and slip interfacing over it, matching seams. The interfacing should fit smoothly over the cuff. Pin, then baste each edge of the interfacing to the cuff.

Turn the undercuff right side out with the interfacing to the inside. Slip the upper cuff over the undercuff, right sides together, matching markings and seams. Pin along the top edge, easing the upper cuff between the markings. Baste, then stitch, overlapping a few stitches at the starting point.

Trim the interfacing seam edge close to the stitching; then trim the seam allowance of the undercuff to ⅛ inch and of the upper cuff to ¼ inch. Notch the seam edges on the outside curve and clip off corners where seams cross. Press.

Turn the cuff to the right side with the upper cuff to the top. Ease the undercuff slightly to the underside at the seamline and baste. Press.

**With heavyweight interfacing.** Trim off the seam allowance plus ⅛ inch on the upper and lower

edges of the interfacing, and trim off the seam allowance at each end.

Cut two strips of organza 1½ inches wide—one the shape of the top of the cuff and the other the shape of the bottom. Lay the organza strip over the upper edge of the interfacing, extending it ¾ inch beyond the interfacing edge. Pin. Follow the same procedure at the lower edge. Then stitch, using the multiple-stitch zig-zag. Press. Join ends with an abutted seam. See *Abutted Seam,* page 83.

Turn the undercuff to the wrong side and slip the interfacing over it, matching seams. The interfacing should fit smoothly over the cuff. Pin, then baste each edge of the interfacing to the cuff.

Turn the undercuff right side out with the interfacing to the inside. Slip the upper cuff over the undercuff, right sides together, matching markings and seams. Pin along the top edge, easing the upper cuff between the markings. Baste, then stitch, overlapping a few stitches at the starting point.

Trim the undercuff seam allowance and organza strip to ⅛ inch and the upper cuff seam allowance to ¼ inch. Notch seam allowance on the curve and clip off corners where seams cross. Press.

Turn the cuff to the right side with the upper cuff to the top. Ease the undercuff slightly to the underside at the seamline, and baste, using diagonal basting and silk thread. Press.

### Attaching Cuff to the Sleeve

Turn the sleeve and cuff to the right side. Slip the cuff over the sleeve. Pin, then baste the undercuff and interfacing to the lower edge of the sleeve, matching markings and seams. (Fold back the upper cuff about 1 inch to keep it out of the way for the next step.) Stitch from the sleeve side, overlapping a few stitches at the starting point.

Trim the interfacing seam allowance close to the stitching; trim the undercuff seam allowance to ⅛ inch and the sleeve seam allowance to ¼ inch. Clip off corners where seams cross and slash the curved seam allowance of the cuff. Press, then press the seam open.

If a sleeve facing is not shown with the pattern, cut one about 3 inches deep, using the sleeve pattern as a guide. (The facing must not be deeper than the cuff.) Stitch the ends together, then press the seam open. Pin and baste the facing to the free edge of the upper cuff, matching markings and

seams. Stitch, overlapping a few stitches at the starting point.

Trim seam allowance to ¼ inch. Clip off corners where seams cross and slash the curved seam allowance at evenly spaced intervals. Press, then press the seam open.

Slip the fingers of the left hand between the sleeve and cuff and pin the cuff sections together about ½ inch above the lower edge. Stay the open seams of the two cuffs together, allowing sufficient ease in the upper cuff for it to fit smoothly over the fold of the interfacing and undercuff. This prevents the undercuff from wrinkling and slipping out of place at the top.

If the garment is unlined, finish the free edge of the facing, then turn the facing into the sleeve, and pin the free edge to the sleeve. Finish by hand, spacing the stitches about 1 inch apart.

**When a facing is not used,** follow the above method up to instructions for cutting the facing. Turn the cuff away from the sleeve and press the seam allowances toward the cuff. Turn the cuff back over the sleeve. Slip the fingers of the left hand between the sleeve and cuff and pin the cuff sections together about ½ inch above the lower edge. Fold under the seam edge on the upper cuff and pin it to the sleeve at the stitching line, enclosing the seam allowances inside the cuff. Allow sufficient ease in the upper cuff for it to fit smoothly over the fold for the interfacing and undercuff. Finish by hand, using a hemming stitch. (Work inside the sleeve.)

## French Cuff

The French cuff is a popular sleeve finish for tailored dresses, blouses, and shirts. It is cut twice the finished width and is folded crosswise through the center to form a double cuff that is open at the ends. It requires four buttonholes for cuff links or for buttons joined with French tacks.

If bound buttonholes are used, make them before stitching the cuff.

**Cuff.** Cut preshrunk interfacing by the cuff pattern. Baste it to the wrong side of the upper-cuff. Clip off the four corners of the interfacing to eliminate bulk when the cuff is turned.

Pin the upper cuff over the undercuff, right sides together, matching markings. Baste if necessary. Stitch around three sides, leaving open the edge that will join the sleeve. Take one stitch across the corners for a smooth turning and backstitch at each end of the seam. Remember to construct one cuff for the left sleeve and one for the right. Remove all bastings and press.

Trim the interfacing seam edge close to the stitching. Trim the undercuff seam edge to ⅛ inch

and the upper cuff seam edge to ¼ inch. Cut diagonally across corners, close to the stitching. Press. Turn the cuff to the right side. Pull out corners to square them. Ease the undercuff slightly to the underside at the seamline and baste. Press.

**Sleeve.** Mark the position for the opening in the sleeve and finish it with a continuous bound placket before stitching the underarm seams. See page 185.

Turn the sleeve to the wrong side and, from the inside, place two lines of stitching around the lower edge to gather the fullness. Place the first line of stitching a scant ⅝ inch from the seam edge and the second line in the seam allowance, ¼ inch from the first line. Use the same stitch length you used in stitching the garment and loosen the upper tension slightly. (Do not forget to return the tension to its previous setting). Leave thread ends long enough to draw.

### Attaching Cuff to Sleeve

Turn the sleeve to the right side. On the right side, wind the thread ends around a pin, forming a figure eight at each end of the stitching. Place the cuff over the sleeve, with the upper cuff and right side of the sleeve together. Pin the upper cuff and interfacing to the sleeve, matching markings and extending the placket binding beyond each end of the cuff.

Working with the wrong side of the sleeve toward you, draw both threads at the same time and gather the sleeve to fit the cuff. Distribute the fullness evenly, then pin the sleeve to the cuff at close intervals. Pull the gathering threads to the underside and tie.

Fold the placket binding back over the gathers, and pin. Baste the cuff to the sleeve. Stitch from the sleeve side, barely beyond the first line of and machine-worked buttonholes in fine cottons or woolens. Cut buttonholes and insert cuff links.

gathering stitches. Backstitch at each end. (Do not catch the undercuff on the stitching).

Trim the interfacing seam edge close to the stitching. Trim the cuff seam edge to ⅛ inch and the sleeve seam edge to ¼ inch. Press the seam, then turn the cuff away from the sleeve and press the seam edges toward the cuff.

Fold the cuff smoothly through the center. Slip the fingers of the left hand between the fold to be certain there is enough ease in the upper cuff for it to fit smoothly over the fold of the interfacing and undercuff. Pin through all thicknesses, about ½ inch above the fold. Fold the free edge of the cuff under ¼ inch and pin it to the sleeve at the stitching line, enclosing the gathered seam allowance inside the cuff. Slip-stitch in place.

## Cuff Cut-in-One with the Sleeve

The cuff cut-in-one with the two-piece sleeve is generally found in suits and coats. Since it is most often a soft cuff, it requires a light or medium-weight interfacing. The cuff opening is in the back seam of the sleeve.

Mark the sleeve for the turn of the cuff.

Join the upper and lower sleeve sections at the front seam, right sides together. Press the seam open.

Cut preshrunk interfacing by the cuff pattern. Trim off the seam allowance plus ⅛ inch on the top edge and at each end. Cut a strip of organza 1½ inches wide to fit across the top edge and the ends of the cuff, using the pattern to shape the outer edges. Pin the organza strip over the interfacing, extending the edges ¾ inch beyond the interfacing. Clip off the corners of the interfacing to eliminate bulk when the cuff is turned. Stitch, using the multiple-stitch zig-zag. Press.

Pin the interfacing over the wrong side of the undercuff, which is cut-in-one with the sleeve. Baste in place along the lower edge and each end of the cuff.

Check the position of buttonholes on both cuff layers to be sure that they coincide and then work a buttonhole at each end of both the cuff sections, using hand-worked buttonholes in soft, silk fabrics

Join the upper and lower sleeve sections at the back seam, leaving the seam open below the marking for the cuff. Backstitch at each end of the seam. Press, then press the seam open.

Turn the sleeve to the right side. Place the upper cuff over the undercuff, right sides together. Pin in place along the edge and ends, matching markings. Pin at the points and markings, then at intervals between, easing the upper cuff between the markings.

Stitch from the interfacing side, beginning at one end of the cuff opening and continuing around the cuff to the opposite end. Take one stitch across the corners for a smooth turning. Pull the threads to the underside and tie. Remove basting.

Pin the upper cuff seams together above the opening, then stitch. Press the seam open. Trim

the undercuff seam edge and organza strip to ⅛ inch and the upper cuff seam edge to ¼ inch. Cut diagonally across corners, close to the stitching. Press.

Turn the cuff to the right side. Pull out the corners to square them. Ease the undercuff to the underside slightly at the seamline, and baste, using diagonal basting and silk thread. Press.

With the sleeve right side out, turn the cuff back over the sleeve. Slip the fingers of the left hand between the sleeve and cuff and pin through all thicknesses, ½ inch above fold. Turn the free edge of the cuff into the sleeve, allowing sufficient ease in the upper cuff for it to fit smoothly over the fold of the interfacing and undercuff. Tack the free edge to the sleeve seam allowances. Remove all bastings. The lining, when it is attached, will hold the cut edge of the cuff in place.

## Double-Fold Bias Binding

A double-fold bias is used as a sleeve finish in blouses, dresses, and children's clothes. The same type of finish is also used at the neckline. The finished width of the binding is usually ¼ inch; the sleeve edge may be straight or gathered as in the puffed sleeve.

Trim the seam allowance on the lower edge of the sleeve to a scant ¼ inch. Gather the lower edge of the sleeve as indicated on the pattern.

Cut a strip on the true bias six times the width of the finished binding. See *Cutting Bias Strips*, page 244.

Join the bias strip on the lengthwise grain to fit the sleeve edge, taking a ¼-inch seam. Press the seam open.

Fold the bias through the center, wrong sides together, and finger-press lightly. Pin the double bias over the right side of the sleeve, keeping the cut edges even. Baste. Stitch from the sleeve side a scant ¼ inch from the edge, using a short stitch and overlapping a few stitches at the starting point. Press.

Turn the sleeve to the wrong side. Fold binding over the seam edge to the stitching line on the underside, enclosing the cut edges. Pin. Finish by hand, using a slip stitch.

# Homeward Bound:

## Zippers, Hems,
## Belts, and Buttons

YOUR DRESS at last looks almost ready to wear. The adjustments and fittings and the basting and stitching are over. All that is lacking now are the final details—a zipper, a hem, maybe a belt, and some buttons.

## ZIPPERS AND PLACKETS

There are several ways of inserting zippers; the one you select depends on the location of the zipper in the garment and the type of garment. Generally zippers are either concealed in a lapped seam with only one line of stitching visible or centered under a slot seam with two lines of stitching visible. The lapped seam application is used

in side seam closings for dresses, skirts, and shorts. It is also popular for center back closings when long zippers are used. The slot seam application is used in neckline, sleeve, and center back or front closings. It is sometimes used for side closings instead of a lapped seam.

The pattern envelope will designate the length and type of zipper to buy. To ensure a neat, professional zipper application, follow the step-by-step methods given below.

## Dress Placket Zipper in Lapped Seam

Before you put in the zipper, the bodice and skirt sections should be joined at the waistline. The left side seam should be open above and below the waistline. The placket opening should be ½ inch longer than the metal or synthetic portion of the zipper. Check the ends of the permanent stitching on both the skirt and bodice to be certain that they are reinforced with backstitching.

Inspect the fit of the dress; the side seams should hang straight from underarm to hemline.

If the waistline is small and the hips rounded, the seam below the waistline will be curved and applying the zipper will require a little extra care. If the waistline is comparatively large and the hips flat, the seam will be fairly straight, and the zipper application will require less caution. Compare the front and back seams of the opening to make sure they are the same length. Chalk or hand-baste exactly on the seamline on each side of the opening. Select a dress placket zipper of the correct length (9, 10, or 12 inches).

**1.** Turn the dress to the wrong side. Pin the

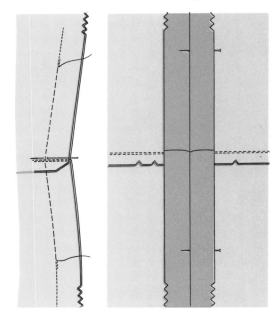

seams together, carefully matching the waistline seams. Machine-baste on the seamline the exact length of the opening. Clip off corners where seams cross at the waistline.

If the placket seam allowance is less than ¾ inch, stitch seam binding to the seam edge on the front side.

**2.** Press the seam open over the curve of a press mitt to retain the shape of the hipline. Press the zipper tape.

Mark the ends of the permanent stitching by placing pins across the seam but not through the dress.

**3.** Fold under the back seam allowance ⅛ inch from the machine-basted seam and place the fold over the right side of the zipper tape, with the bridge-top stop ⅛ inch below the top of the opening; pin. Roll the zipper and folded edge over the fingers of the left hand to ease the seam, then pin the folded edge to the zipper tape. The bottom stop should fall ⅛ inch above the opening in the skirt. This allows ¼ inch for ease throughout the length of the zipper. Pin the seam allowance to the tape above and below the opening. Hand-baste.

**4.** Replace the presser foot with the Zipper Foot and adjust the foot to the left of the needle.

*Turn the pull-tab up* to lessen bulk in stitching. Stitch from the bottom to the top near the edge of the fold. *Remove hand basting* and *turn the pull-tab down.*

**5.** Turn the dress to the right side. Turn the zipper and back seam allowance flat against front seam allowance. Place the fingers of the left hand under the zipper; press the zipper in position. Work from the right side and roll the zipper and seam over the fingers of the left hand to ease the fabric. Pin through all thicknesses, placing pins at right angles to the seam, through the fabric, and under the chain portion of the zipper. Alternate the direction of the pins to distribute the slight ease evenly.

Hand-baste a measured distance of ⅜ to ½ inch from the machine-basted seam, using a long and short basting stitch. Use the basting as a guide in stitching.

**6.** Adjust the Zipper Foot to the right of the needle. From the right side of the garment, stitch across the lower end, up along the zipper, following the even line of basting, and across the top end. Pull the thread ends to the underside and tie.

**7.** Remove the hand basting. Turn the dress to the wrong side and remove the machine basting under the back seam allowance by clipping every four or five stitches, then pulling the long thread. Press the work over the curve of a press mitt to retain the shape of the hipline. Cover it with a wool press cloth to protect the fabric from shine.

A dress placket handled in this way is almost invisible because the front seam overlaps the zipper ⅛ inch and the placket has been shaped to fit the curve of the hip.

### Hand-Finished Zipper Application

To add a professional touch, you can hand-sew the zipper with backstitches at the final step instead of top-stitching by machine. If you are working with chiffons, sheers, velvets, or any other delicate fabrics, you *must* hand-sew because machine stitching is too harsh.

**1.** To finish with hand sewing, follow the instructions given above up to Step 6, which is top stitching.

**2.** With a fine needle and matching thread, start working at the bottom of the zipper. Fasten the thread end with two backstitches on the underside of the zipper tape. Bring the needle through from the underside at the seamline. Take a backstitch

seam allowance to the zipper tape for added support.

Remove the hand basting and the machine basting under the back seam allowance. Press.

### Blindstitched Zipper Application

Blindstitching the final step of a zipper application gives a fine finish that is almost invisible. The placket seam allowance should be ⅞ inch and may be made wider when the garment is cut.

**1.** Follow the instructions beginning on page 176, up to *Step 6,* which is top stitching.

Select the blindstitch zig-zag on the zig-zag machine, 15 stitch length, and narrow stitch width. Adjust the Zipper Foot to the right of the needle.

**2.** Turn the dress to the wrong side. Place the lower end of the zipper tape over the feed of the machine and turn back the front section of the dress to the basting line, creating a soft fold. Position the work so that the straight line of stitching

across only one or two fabric threads; then bring the needle up through all thicknesses a scant ⅛ inch from the backstitch. Begin each additional backstitch just outside the preceding stitch. The stitches on the underside will be twice as long as those on the top side. Continue the stitches across the bottom end, up the side along the basted line, then across the top end. Push the needle through to the underside, and fasten the thread with two backstitches in the tape.

**3.** Turn the dress to the wrong side and machine-stitch the edge of the front

is made through the seam allowance and zipper tape, and the sideward stitch pierces only a few threads of the soft fold. Stitch slowly. Pull the thread ends to the underside and tie.

Hand-sew the front seam allowance to the zipper tape below the bottom stop and above the bridge-top stop. Remove both machine and hand bastings. Press.

### No-Pin, No-Baste Method

To use this method of applying a zipper, follow the rules below:

**1.** Turn the dress to the wrong side. Pin, then machine-baste the side seams together the exact length of the opening. Press the seam open over the curve of a press mitt to retain the shape of the hipline. Stay-stitch ⅜ inch from the seam edge on each side of the placket opening. Mark the length of the opening with pins.

**2.** Adjust the Zipper Foot to the right of the needle. Open the zipper and place it face down over the back seam allowance, with the edge of the teeth at the seamline and the bottom stop at the end of the opening. Stitch the tape to the seam allowance from bottom to top alongside the zipper.

**3.** Adjust the Zipper Foot to the left of the needle. Close the zipper and turn it face up.

Smooth back the seam allowance at the edge of the zipper and stitch it to the tape.

**4.** Turn the dress to the right side and work on the underside. Turn the zipper face down, flat over the front seam allowance. Stitch across the lower end, up the front along the zipper tape guideline, then across the top end. Pull the thread ends to the underside and tie. Remove machine basting under the back seam allowance. Press.

### Skirt Placket Zipper in Lapped Seam

A skirt placket zipper is used in shorts and slacks as well as skirts. It is a heavy zipper designed to withstand strain and is applied before the waistband.

A skirt must be fitted in the same careful way as a dress. The opening in the left seam should be 1 inch longer than the metal or synthetic part of the zipper. Compare the front and back seams of the opening to be sure they are the same length. Check the end of the permanent stitching to make certain that it is reinforced with backstitching. Chalk or hand-baste exactly on the seamline on each side of the opening.

**1.** Turn the skirt to the wrong side. Pin the seams together and machine-baste on the seamline the exact length of the opening.

**2.** Press the seam open over a press mitt to retain the shape of the hipline. Mark the bottom of the opening by placing a pin through the seam only.

**3.** Fold under the back seam allowance ⅛ inch from the machine-basted seam and place the folded edge over the right side of the zipper tape with the pull-tab ¾ inch (⅝-inch seam allowance plus ⅛ inch) below the seam edge at the top, and the

bottom stop ⅛ inch above the lower end of the opening; pin. This allows ⅛ inch for ease throughout the length of the zipper. Roll the zipper and folded edge over the fingers of the left hand and pin the folded edge to the zipper tape. Hand-baste.

**4.** Replace the presser foot with the Zipper Foot, and adjust the Zipper Foot to the left of the needle. *Turn the pull-tab up to lessen bulk when stitching.* Stitch from the bottom to the top near the edge of the fold. Remove *hand basting.*

**5.** Turn the skirt to the right side. Turn the zipper and back seam allowance flat against the front seam allowance with the *pull-tab still turned toward the top.* From the right side, roll the zipper and seam over the fingers of the left hand to ease the fabric. Pin through all thicknesses, placing pins at right angles to the seam, through the fabric, and under the chain portion of the zipper. Alternate the direction of the pins to distribute the slight ease evenly. See illustration on page 177, *Step 5.*

Hand-baste a measured ½ inch from the machine-basted seam, using a long and short basting stitch. Use the basting as a stitching guide.

**6.** Adjust the Zipper Foot to the right of the needle. Stitch across the lower end, then up along the zipper, following the even line of basting, to the waistline. Pull the thread ends to the underside and tie. (If hand sewing is used instead of machine stitching, follow the directions on page 178.)

**7.** Remove the hand basting. Then, turn the skirt to the wrong side and remove the machine basting under the back seam allowance. Press the work over a press mitt to retain the curve of the hipline. Cover it with a wool press cloth to protect the fabric from shine. Trim the tape even with the waistline seam edge.

### To Attach Underlay

An underlay is usually placed under the zipper to improve the fit of the skirt. It gives support to the underlap of the waistband and also helps prevent the zipper from clogging.

The underlay may be either a double or a single lengthwise strip of the same fabric cut the length of the zipper tape. If single, cut it 2½ inches wide, using the selvage of the fabric for the finished edge. If double, cut it 5 inches wide, and fold it lengthwise through the center; stitch near the fold and cut edge. Pink the edge.

Turn the skirt to the wrong side. Place the underlay over the zipper tape, keeping the cut edges even with the back seam edge. Pin only to the seam allowance. Turn the seam allowance and underlay away from the skirt and stitch the underlay to the seam allowance. Tack the lower end of the underlay to the front seam allowance. The skirt is now ready for the waistband.

## Neckline or Sleeve Zipper in Slot Seam

A neckline zipper is usually inserted in a center front or back seam at the neckline of a dress, hostess robe, or blouse or in a sleeve seam at the wrist. An extra fine neckline zipper is available for the closure.

Apply a neckline zipper before joining the front and back bodice at the shoulders and underarms since it is easier to work on a flat section than a partially assembled garment.

The length of the opening should be 1 inch longer than the metal or synthetic part of the zipper. (The seam allowance at the neckline is ⅝ inch, and ⅜ inch provides space for crosswise stitching at the bottom and top of the zipper.) You will not have to allow for ease since the zipper is usually set into a straight grain seam. The seam below the opening should be permanently stitched and the end reinforced with backstitching.

**1.** Turn the garment to the wrong side. Pin the seams together and machine-baste the exact length of the opening.

**2.** Press the seam, then press it open. Mark the end of the opening with a pin on the right side.

**3.** Turn the garment to the right side. Turn the zipper *pull-tab up to lessen bulk when stitching.* Pin the zipper in position, with the machine-basted seam centered directly over the chain portion. Place the pull-tab at the top, ¼ inch below the ⅝-inch seam allowance at the neckline, and the bottom stop ⅛ inch above the lower end of the opening. Place pins at right angles to the seam, through all thicknesses, and under the chain portion of the zipper. Alternate the direction of the pins. Hand-baste, on each side, a measured ¼ inch from the center seam. Use the basting as a guide in stitching.

**4.** Replace the presser foot with the Zipper Foot, and adjust the foot to the left of the needle. On the right side of the garment, stitch around the zipper ¼ inch to the left of the center seam, using the measured basting as a guide. Pivot the fabric on the needle at the corners and take the same number of stitches on either side of the center seam.

If the final step is hand-sewed instead of machine-stitched, follow the directions on page 178; however, machine-stitch the edge of the seam allowance to the zipper tape on each side for added support.

**5.** Remove both hand and machine bastings. Press carefully. Trim the zipper tape even with the neckline seam edge. The garment is ready for the neckline finish.

## Zipper in Center Back Lapped Seam

Before applying the zipper in a center back closing, join the dress sections at the shoulder line, underarm, and waistline seams.

Leave an opening 1 inch longer than the metal or synthetic part of the zipper. (The neckline seam allowance is ⅝ inch, and ⅜ inch provides space above and below the zipper.) You will not need to allow for ease since a center seam is usually on the straight grain of the fabric. Check the end of the permanent stitching in the skirt to make

sure that it is reinforced with backstitching. Compare the right and left seams of the opening; they must be the same length.

### To Finish Neckline

Before inserting the zipper, finish the neckline as instructed here to eliminate bulk across the top of the zipper.

**1.** Pin the facing to the neckline. Start stitching ¾ inch from the seam edge that is on the right-hand side when the dress is worn, and continue to within 1¼ inches of the seam edge on the left-hand side, taking a ⅝-inch seam.

**2.** Trim the facing seam allowance to ⅛ inch and the garment seam allowance to ¼ inch; then clip into the curved seam allowance. Press; then press the seam open. Turn the facing to the underside, ease it under slightly at the seamline, and baste. Press. Understitch the seam to prevent the facing from rolling out of place. Fold and press the garment and facing on the seamline, from the stitching to the center opening.

### To Insert the Zipper

Trim the waistline seam allowance that is on the right-hand side when the dress is worn, to ¼ inch from the center seam edge to a depth of ¾ inch, and trim the seam allowance on the opposite side to ¼ inch from the center seam edge to a depth of 1¼ inches. This removes bulk under the zipper seam.

**1.** Turn the dress to the wrong side. Turn the neckline facing away from the garment. Pin the center seams together, carefully matching waistline seams and folded seams at the neckline. (Be sure the seam edges of the opening are the same length.) Machine-baste the exact length of the opening. If the seam allowance that is on the left-hand side when the dress is worn is less than ⅝ inch, stitch seam binding to the edge.

**2.** Press, then press the seam open. Mark the bottom of the opening by placing a pin through the seamline only.

**3.** On the right-hand side when the dress is worn, fold the seam allowance under ⅛ inch from the machine-basted seam. Pin the folded edge over the right side of the zipper tape, with the pull-tab at the top, ¼ inch below the folded neckline

seam, and the bottom stop ⅛ inch above the end of the opening. Pin the seam allowance to the zipper tape below the opening. Hand-baste.

**4.** Adjust the Zipper Foot to the left of the needle. *Turn the pull-tab up* to lessen bulk when stitching. Stitch from the bottom of the zipper up to the neckline, close to the folded edge. Tie thread ends at the neckline. Remove hand basting.

**5.** Clip into the zipper tape on each side of the neckline, almost to the cord; then trim close to the cord up to the end of the tape.

Turn the ends of the tape away from the pull-tab and tack them to the seam allowance, using matching thread. Clip off the ends of the tape to ½ inch. This eliminates bulk at the neckline.

*(Continued)*

**6.** Turn the dress to the right side. With the *pull-tab still turned up,* turn the zipper and seam allowance flat against the left-hand side of the seam allowance. Press the zipper against the seam with the left hand. Working from the right side, place pins at right angles to the seam, through all thicknesses, and under the chain portion of the zipper. Alternate the direction of the pins.

Hand-baste a measured ½ inch from the machine-basted seam, using a long and short basting stitch. Use the basting as a guide in stitching.

**7.** Adjust the Zipper Foot to the right of the needle. On the right side of the dress, stitch across the lower end and up the side to the neckline, following the evenly basted line. Pull threads to the underside and tie. (When hand sewing is used instead of machine stitching, follow the directions on page 178.) Remove hand basting, then turn the dress to the wrong side and remove the machine basting under the seam allowance.

**8.** Fold under the center ends of the neckline facing, and trim the seam allowances to ½ inch. Pin the folded edges to the zipper tape and finish by hand, using a hemming stitch. Slip-stitch the edges together at the neckline where the fabric fold covers the zipper. Press.

Sew a hook to the underside of the fold covering the zipper at the neckline and make a thread eye on the opposite side. See *Thread Eye,* page 207.

## Continuous Bound Placket

The continuous bound placket may be in a seam or slash. It is found in sleeve openings where a cuff or band is used and in children's dresses.

### Placket in a Slash

**1.** Mark the position for the slash, and stay-stitch around the point, using a 20 stitch length. Take one stitch across the point to allow space for a smooth turning. Press. Slash the opening to within about two threads of the point.

**2.** Cut a strip of fabric on the lengthwise grain, 1¼ inches wide and twice the length of the opening. If the fabric is heavy, cut the strip 1½ inches wide.

At one end, pin the strip to the opening, right sides together, keeping the cut edges even. *Draw the point of the slash back 3/16 inch from the edge of the strip* and pin at the point; then pin at the opposite end, keeping the cut edges even. Pin at intervals between. Baste.

**3.** From the garment side, stitch ¼ inch from the *edge of the strip*, beginning at the end and stitching to the point. With the needle in the fabric, raise the presser foot and fold the garment back, forming a "V" at the point; then lower the foot and stitch to the opposite end of the opening. Reinforce the ends with backstitching. Press, then

turn the strip away from the garment and press the seam allowance over the strip.

**4.** Fold under the free edge of the strip ¼ inch and crease. Then fold the strip over the seam edge to the stitching line on the underside, enclosing the seam allowances. Pin. Either machine-stitch or finish by hand, using a short hemming stitch. Press. *(Continued)*

Fold the strip under on the side that will overlap, as illustrated. Press. The fabric strip is not visible in the closing.

### Placket in a Seam

**1.** Stitch the seam below the opening. Reinforce the end with backstitching. Clip into the seam allowances at the end of the opening, then trim the seam allowances to ¼ inch from this point to the end of the opening. Press the seam open below the placket opening.

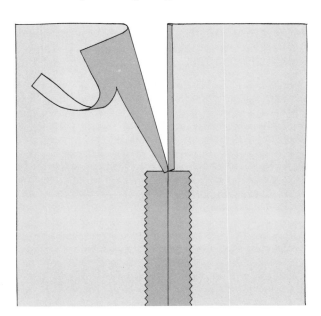

**2.** Cut a strip of fabric on the lengthwise grain 1½ inches wide and twice the length of the opening. Pin the strip to the opening, right sides together, keeping cut edges even. Pin at one end, at the point of the opening, then at the opposite end. Pin at intervals between.

**3.** Stitch from the garment side, taking a ¼-inch seam. Reinforce the ends with backstitching. Press, then turn the strip away from the garment and press the seam allowance over the strip.

**4.** Fold under the free edge of the strip ¼ inch and crease. Then turn the strip over the seam edge to the stitching line on the underside, enclosing the seam allowances. Pin. Either machine-stitch or finish by hand, using a short hemming stitch.

Fold the strip under on the side that will overlap, as illustrated in the slash above. Press. The fabric strip is not visible in the closing.

# HEMS AND HEM FINISHES

The hem is your last step in finishing the garment. It is usually finished by hand and the stitches should be invisible on the right side. However, a narrow hem, which is preferred for ruffles and sashes, may be finished either by machine or by hand. Proper pressing is essential in making a smooth hem; do not overlook it.

The hem in a skirt should never be obvious but should be wide enough to hang in smooth, graceful lines. A slim skirt usually requires a hem of greater width than a full skirt. The hem width designated on the pattern is generally the width you should use since it is appropriate for the style of the garment and the fabric recommended. If you want a wider hem than that shown on the pattern—for example, to create a shadow effect in a full-skirted dress made of sheer fabric—allow for the extra width when cutting the garment.

Although fashion dictates to some extent the length of skirts, do not follow it blindly but consider your figure proportions as well.

## Checking the Fit of the Dress

Try on the dress for the final inspection, wearing the foundation garment, slip, and shoes you will wear with the dress. Review the general fitting. Be certain that the front and back center line bastings are in place and hang perpendicular to the floor; that the waistline joining is comfortably positioned. If any adjustment in fit is necessary, make it before marking the skirt length. A skirt that hangs well is the result of correct pattern adjustments, careful cutting with the grain of the fabric, and proper pressing.

If your dress has a bias or semi-bias skirt, always allow it to hang overnight with the side seams hand-basted, threads loose at the ends, before stitching any seams. Then, after the skirt is assembled, hang it again overnight before taking the skirt length so that all the sag is evident at the points where the true bias occurs.

## Preparing the Hem

To ensure a smooth and inconspicuous hemline, follow closely the steps given below. They are basic for all hems. Step 4, however, will vary with the fabric, the style of the skirt, and individual preference.

### Step 1: Mark the Hemline

Mark the skirt an even distance from the floor. Use either a pin- or chalk-type skirt marker. To avoid any unnecessary shifting of posture or position, have the person taking the skirt length move around the model. If the lining is attached to the waistline only, mark the hemline in the skirt and in the lining separately.

For full-length evening dresses, have the model stand on a stool or platform that will allow the dress to hang freely over the edge.

### Step 2: Fold the Hem

Turn the hem on the chalk or pin line and place pins at right angles to the folded edge. The fold of the hem should follow an even line. Should slight irregularities occur, owing to the sway of the body or the unevenness of the floor, adjust the hem fold accordingly. However, *do not make radical adjustments*. Ease the hem down slightly at the seams to allow for the fold over the seam allowances.

Baste with silk thread ¼ inch from the folded edge. Press to sharpen the crease, gliding the iron along the lengthwise grain of the fabric. See *Hems*, page 75.

### Step 3: Even the Hem Width

Lay the skirt against a flat surface with the right side down and work from the hem side. Measure and chalk-mark the desired hem width. Then cut away the excess width. Trim all seam allowances to one-half their width from fold to hem edge.

### Step 4: Finish the Hem

A variety of methods for finishing hems are given below. Choose the one you prefer, keeping in mind the fabric you are working with and the shape of the skirt at the hemline.

## Finishes for Skirt Hems

### Edgestitched Hem

Edgestitching provides a sturdy hem finish for cottons that must withstand repeated laundering and for linings and underlinings that are hemmed separately from the skirt.

**1.** Prepare the hem for the finish, following the three steps outlined above.

**2.** Fold the free edge of the hem under ¼ inch and stitch near the edge of the fold. Press. Pin the hem to the skirt, matching seams and center lines. Hand-baste. Finish by hand, using a slip stitch. See page 228. Remove bastings, and press.

### Pinked Hem—Blind Catch Stitch

The pinked hem is suitable for fabrics that do not fray readily and are likely to show a line on the outside of the skirt if other hem finishes are used—for example, silk, crepe, jersey, double knit, and firmly woven woolens. The blind catch stitch is invisible and holds the hem securely without strain. This is also known as a *French hem.*

**1.** Prepare the hem for the finish, following the three steps outlined on page 187.

**2.** Pink the free edge of the hem, then stitch ¼ inch from the edge, using a 20 stitch length.

**3.** Pin, then hand-baste the hem to the skirt just below the stitching line, matching seams and center lines. With the left hand, fold back the pinked edge along the basting and blind catch-stitch below the hem edge and between the hem and skirt. Work from left to right with the needle pointed to the left. Hold the hem edge between the thumb and index finger. Make a stitch in the underside of the hem edge, then make a stitch in the skirt, catching only a single thread of the fabric. Alternate the stitches in a zig-zag fashion. Do not tighten this hand stitch, but knot the stitches frequently. Remove bastings, and press.

### Bound Hem

Hems in heavy or napped woolens and fabrics that fray easily are often finished with a bound edge of rayon or silk bias binding. They are not noticeable when the garment is worn.

1. Prepare the hem for the finish, following the three steps outlined on page 187.

2. Bind the free edge of the hem, using the Binder and a medium-width open zig-zag stitch. Press.

3. Pin the free edge of the hem to the skirt, matching center lines and seams; then, hand-baste just below the binding. Blind catch-stitch between the hem and skirt, as instructed for a *Pinked Hem —Blind Catch Stitch*, above. Knot the stitch at frequent intervals. Never pull the thread tight enough to dent the right side of the fabric. Remove bastings, and press over a pressing pad.

### Blindstitched Hem

Blindstitching provides a durable hem finish that is almost invisible on the right side of the garment. It is especially suited to children's clothes, straight and full skirts, and curtains. Taped, bound, edgestitched, or unfinished hem edges may be blindstitched by machine with equal ease.

1. Prepare the hem for the finish, following the three steps outlined on page 187.

2. When straight or bias seam binding is used, pin the binding to the hem ¼ inch from the free edge. Stitch, using a narrow zig-zag stitch and 12 to 15 stitch length. Press.

3. Hand-baste the hem to the skirt ¼ inch from the free edge.

4. Use the blindstitch zig-zag; select a narrow to medium stitch width and 12 to 20 stitch length. (The selection is determined by the weight and texture of your fabric.) The blindstitch zig-zag produces four straight stitches separated by a single sideward stitch to the left.

Place the hem edge over the feed of the machine; turn back the bulk of the fabric to the bast-

ing line, creating a soft fold. Position the work so that the straight stitches are made on the hem edge and the sideward stitches pierce only one or two threads of the soft fold.

Attach the Seam Guide to the machine and adjust it over the right toe of the presser foot so that it rests next to the soft fold. When stitching, feed the fold against the edge of the guide. After you have finished, swing the Seam Guide out of position before raising the presser foot. Remove bastings, and press.

### Catch-Stitched Hem

The catch-stitched hem is suitable for loosely woven woolens and raw silk. The hem edge may be finished with pinking as described on page 188 or with straight or bias seam binding and then catch-stitched in place.

**1.** Prepare the hem for the finish, following the steps outlined on page 187.

**2.** Finish the free edge of the hem.

**3.** Pin, then hand-baste the hem to the skirt ⅛ inch from the finished edge, matching center lines and seams. Catch-stitch in place. Work from left to right with the needle pointed to the left. Take a stitch in the binding, then one in the skirt over the edge of the hem, catching only a single thread in the fabric. Continue alternating the stitches. Press.

### Zig-Zag Hem—Double-Knit Fabric

The zig-zag hem finish is ideal for skirts made of double knits because it prevents fraying and the stitching has as much "give" as the fabric.

**1.** Prepare the hem for the finish, following the three steps outlined on page 187.

**2.** Finish the free edge of the hem with a row of multiple-stitch zig-zag, blindstitch zig-zag, or plain zig-zag stitch placed near the edge. Use a fine stitch length and the widest stitch width. Press. Trim the edge close to the stitching.

**3.** Pin, then hand-baste the free edge of hem to the skirt just below the zig-zag stitching, matching seams and center lines. Finish with a blind catch stitch between the hem and skirt, as instructed for the *Pink Hem—Blind Catch Stitch*, page 188.

### Gored and Semiflared Skirts

**1.** Prepare the hem for the finish, following the three steps outlined on page 187.

**2.** Control the fullness that exists with a line of stitching placed exactly ¼ inch from the free edge of the hem and extending from seam to seam. Pin the hem to the skirt, matching seams and center lines. Draw the bobbin thread and ease the fullness between the seams. Be careful not to draw in the top of the hem too much. The hem must conform exactly to the body of the skirt.

**3.** Place the hem over the curve of a press mitt and shrink out the fullness by pressing with steam.

**4.** Bias seam binding is often used on a hem with fullness. For silk and synthetic fabrics, use rayon or silk bias binding. Preshape the seam binding by steam pressing; pin, then stitch it to the hem edge, barely covering the control line of stitching. At the joining, fold under the end and overlap the binding about ⅜ inch. Press. (Binding may be applied as an inside seam, as illustrated, or it may be top-stitched.)

**5.** Pin the free edge of the hem to the skirt, matching seams and center lines. Hand-baste ⅛ inch from the edge. Finish by hand, using a blind hemming stitch. See page 228. When finished, fasten the threads with two tiny backstitches in the hem edge. Remove bastings and press.

### Hem across Pleat in Skirt (Upper right)

Seams on the inside fold of a pleat must be blended and pressed open in the hem area to eliminate bulk.

**1.** After you have marked the hem, press the seam open to the point where the hem will be sewed to the skirt. Blend the seam edges within the hem area to one-half their width. Slash seam allowances to within a few threads of the stitching at the top of the hem.

**2.** Proceed to form the hem, and finish according to the method best suited to the fabric.

### Hem in Slit Skirt

The pencil-slim skirt, without a pleat, is often slit at the seams to allow for greater freedom of movement. (For instructions on lining the skirt, see page 98.) To hem the skirt, proceed as follows:

**1.** Check the end of the seam above the slit to be certain that it is reinforced with backstitching. Pin, then machine-baste the seams together in the slit, beginning exactly at the top of the slit.

Stay-stitch ½ inch from the seam edge on each side of the slit. Press, then press the seam open.

*(Continued on following page)*

**2.** Cut a strip of preshrunk straight seam binding to fit the width of the open seam allowance. Fold through the center and press. Pin the binding to the seam allowance, keeping the lower edge even with the top edge of the machine-basted opening. Turn the seam allowance away from the skirt, and stitch the binding to one side of the seam allowance, as illustrated; then stitch the opposite side the same way. Follow this procedure for slits in the lining. The stays reinforce the ends in the slits and prevent ripping.

**3.** Prepare the hem for the finish, following the steps outlined on page 187.

**4.** Remove the machine basting in the slit. Finish the hems in the skirt and lining separately, following the method best suited to the fabric. Ease the hem under slightly on each side of the slit, and pin. Slip-stitch in place.

### Hem in Circular Skirt

To ensure a smooth hemline, the hem in a circular skirt should be narrow. A wide hem is bulky. Use rayon or silk bias binding for the finish. Before marking the hem, hang the skirt for 24 hours to allow for any "stretching" of the fabric.

**1.** Mark the hem as instructed in *Step 1*, page 187. Trim away the excess fabric ⅜ inch below the marking.

**2.** Pin bias seam binding ¼ inch from the edge of the skirt, right sides together. Apply seam binding as an inside seam, as illustrated. Stitch, guiding the fabric in both the front and the back of the needle to prevent puckering or stretching. Clip off corners where seams cross. Press.

**3.** Turn the binding to the underside, then fold the skirt ⅛ inch beyond the binding and hand-baste. Press.

**4.** Hand-baste the hem to the skirt near the edge of the binding. Finish by hand, using a blind hemming stitch or slip stitch. Remove bastings and press.

***Horsehair braid*** is often used to give stiffness to circular hems in evening, cocktail, and wedding dresses. Prepare the hem the same as above.

**1.** Baste 1-inch horsehair braid to the right side of the hem, edges even. Stitch ⅛ inch from the edge. Press. *(Illustrated at top of next page)*

**2.** Turn the horsehair braid to the underside; fold the hem ⅛ inch beyond the stitching line, and pin. The lower edge of the horsehair will extend to the hem fold. *(Continued)*

**3.** Work on the right side, and hand-sew the horsehair to the skirt, barely above the ⅛-inch hem, using a fine backstitch. See page 230.

### Spliced Hem

Heavy woolens sometimes resist the shaping and easing required to assure a smooth circular hem. Should this be the case, use the following method. (This type of skirt usually has a lining that extends to within an inch of the hem fold.)

**1.** Prepare the hem for the finish, following the three steps outlined on page 187.

**2.** Cut narrow wedges in the hem at regular intervals, several inches apart. Do not cut deeper than 1 inch from the hem fold.

Bring the cut edges together with a line of machine stitching ¼ inch from the free edge. Darn the slashes together with matching silk thread or a thread drawn from the weave of the fabric.

**3.** Pink the free edge. Finish with a blind catch stitch between the hem and skirt as instructed on page 188.

### Double-Stitched Hem

Wide hems, or hems in heavy fabrics, sometimes tend to sag because one line of stitching is insufficient for the weight of the hem. To prevent this, stitch the hem twice—once through the center and again at the free edge. The two rows of stitches distribute the weight of the hem, and the hem is not visible in the finished skirt.

**1.** Prepare the hem for the finish, following the three steps outlined on page 187.

**2.** Finish the hem edge, using the method best suited to the fabric. Pin, then hand-baste the center of the hem to the skirt, matching center lines and seams. Fold back the hem on the basting line, and blind catch-stitch between the hem and the skirt as instructed for a *Pinked Hem—Blind Catch Stitch,* page 188. Be careful not to pull the stitches too tight or they will dent the right side of the garment.

**3.** Pin, then hand-baste the free edge of the hem to the skirt, matching center lines and seams. Finish by hand, using a blind catch stitch between the hem and the skirt.

### Soft Hemline

Interface the hem if you want it to have a soft or slightly padded look. Use a fabric that does not crease easily—either hair canvas or lamb's wool. For additional softness in the hem fold, the garment should be underlined and the underlining should extend to the hem edge.

**1.** Prepare the hem as described under *Step 1*, page 187. Hand-baste the line of the hem but do

not fold or crease it. Mark the hem width as described under *Step 3*, page 188, and finish the free edge as required by the fabric.

**2.** Cut the interfacing on the true bias 2 inches wider than the hem and the length required plus 1 inch for seam allowances. Allow enough extra length so you can join the bias on straight grain. See *Joining Bias Strips*, page 244. Turn the interfacing up 1 inch along one edge, creating a soft fold. (Do not crease.) Pin, then hand-baste ¾ inch from the soft fold. Make small stitches, spacing them about ¼ inch apart; secure the thread ends because this is permanent basting that will prevent the interfacing from wadding at the hemline.

Place the interfacing over the underside of the garment and align the soft fold with hemline basting. Join ends on straight grain by lapping 1 inch and basting together. Pin the interfacing in place along top edge and catch-stitch. Make a stitch through interfacing and underlining, then a stitch in only the underlining over the interfacing edge so that stitches will not be visible on the top side. Continue alternating the stitches. Press.

**3.** Turn the hem over the interfacing and hand-baste in place, using silk thread. (The interfacing is 1 inch wider than the hem.) Finish by hand, using the blind catch stitch. Make the stitches through only the hem and interfacing. To keep the hem fold soft, do not press it, but do press along the line of the hand stitches. Remove all bastings.

A garment with this type of hem is generally lined, and the lining extends to within an inch or two of the hem fold, covering the interfacing.

### Hem at Corners

When the skirt of a garment is open all the way down the front or back, the opening is faced and you have a corner to deal with.

**1.** Prepare the hem for the finish, following the three steps outlined on page 187. However, extend the hem across the facing at the opening.

**2.** Finish the hem, using the method best suited to the fabric. (The edgestitched finish is shown in the illustration.) Remove bastings and press.

**3.** Fold the facing to the underside and press. Pin through the center of the facing, catching the hem beneath. Place the pins parallel to the facing edge. Fold the facing back on the pinned line and stay it to the hem by hand to prevent it from slipping out of place. Turn the free edge against the hem and pin; then catch-stitch it to the hem.

Since the hem is not cut out under the facing, the skirt can be lengthened later if necessary.

### Hem with Mitered Corner

Hems in linens are usually mitered at the corners to remove bulk.

**1.** Fold the hem along all edges, measuring the width evenly. Press. Fold under ¼ inch on the free edge and press.

**2.** Turn the hem away from the fabric. Turn the corner toward the inside, folding the lengthwise grain to the crosswise grain with the diagonal fold crossing exactly at the junction of the lengthwise and crosswise folds of the hem. Press. The diagonal fold indicates the exact position for stitching the miter.

**3.** Fold the lengthwise hem over the crosswise hem, right sides together, matching the crease on the diagonal line. Pin, then stitch, extending the stitching as far as the first fold of the hem. Backstitch at each end.

**4.** Blend the seam to ¼ inch and clip off the corner at the hem fold. Press, then press the seam open over the pointed end of a seamboard.

**5.** Turn the hem to the underside and carefully hand-baste the free edge in place. Linens may be finished with hemstitching, a decorative zig-zag stitch, machine stitching, or hand stitching.

## Narrow Hem Finishes

A narrow hem is used on ruffles, ties, scarves, lingerie, aprons, blouses, sashes in children's clothes, and circular skirts of evening and cocktail dresses. The hem may be finished by hand or by machine, depending on where it is used and the type of fabric.

### Machine-Stitched Hem

A machine-stitched hem is used to finish the edges of lingerie, ruffles and sashes in children's clothes and aprons, and ruffles in curtains. The Hemmer Foot is a must for this, for it forms a perfectly turned narrow hem without requiring any basting or pressing on your part. See *Hemmer Foot*, page 283.

Cut the edge of the fabric evenly on the lengthwise or crosswise grain or on a true bias. To prevent the fabric from stretching when it is cut on the bias, place a row of stitching near the edge, using a short stitch. Press, then trim as close to the stitching as possible before placing the fabric in the Hemmer Foot.

You can apply lace, if you are using it, over or under the hem in one operation.

You can also turn and decorate hems in one operation on a zig-zag machine. Select patterns that will form on the fold of the hem and adjust

the machine for the appropriate stitch length and stitch width; then hem from the right side of the fabric.

A **soft shell edge** makes an attractive finish for lingerie and many delicate fabrics. To obtain this effect, set the selectors on the machine for either the blindstitch or the multiple-stitch zig-zag; then hem with the fabric right side up.

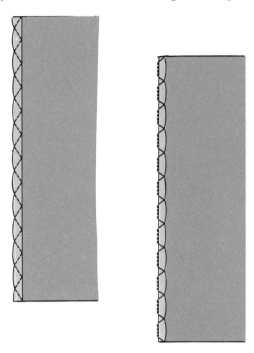

**To make a ¼-inch hem or one slightly wider,** use the presser foot and turn the fabric by hand the entire length of the hem. The edge of the fabric must be cut evenly. Make a double-fold hem so that the cut edge will not be visible through the fabric. *(Illustrated at top of next page)*

You can turn the hem easily if you work on an ironing board. As you turn and measure each fold, pin through the fabric into the ironing board pad, then press.

**1.** Turn a measured scant ¼ inch to the underside and pin along the cut edge. Press the fold. Then make the second turn a measured ¼ inch from the fold and pin along the first fold; press the second fold.

**2.** Stitch near the folded edge, using a shorter stitch than that used to stitch the garment. If the hem is slightly wider than ¼ inch, baste before stitching.

If you plan to finish the hem with decorative zig-zag stitching, baste the hemline to form a guide for the top stitching (except on sheer fabrics where the hem edge is visible through the fabric). Select the stitch pattern desired, set the stitch length selector for satin stitching, and stitch from the right side of the fabric.

### Hand-Rolled Hem

A hand-rolled hem is a delicate finish, suitable for chiffon, crepe, velvet, lace, wool, and many other fabrics. It is the preferred hem finish for scarves and full-skirted evening, cocktail, and wedding dresses.

**1.** Mark the hem as instructed under *Step 1* on page 187.

**2.** Machine-stitch ⅛ inch below the marking for the hem, using a short stitch. Trim off the seam allowance a scant ⅛ inch below the stitching. Press.

**3.** Fold the edge to the wrong side, barely beyond the stitching. Use a fine needle and matching thread. Working from right to left, or toward you, take a stitch through the fold; then, ⅛ inch from the fold, take a stitch diagonally in the garment, catching only a single thread. Continue, alternating the stitches and spacing them about ⅛ inch apart. After making about six stitches, pull the thread to draw the fold down and form a neatly rolled hem.

### Blouse Hems

A tuck-in blouse requires a tidy, unobtrusive finish at the lower edge so that it will lie smooth under the skirt. Two excellent methods are suggested.

**1.** For fabrics that are lightweight or that will fray easily, pink the lower edge of the blouse and fold it under ¼ inch. Stitch near the fold; then stitch again ⅛ inch from the hem fold.

**2.** For fabrics that will not fray, pink the edge and stitch ⅛ inch from the pinked edge, using a 20 stitch length.

Overblouses should be finished with a hem ½ inch to 2 inches wide. Either machine or hand stitching may be used.

Belts can be a special point of interest in your costume, providing a decided contrast in color or texture, or they can be a demure and utilitarian addition, blending in with the whole. Often you can alter the appearance of your dress by merely changing the belt.

The paragraphs below explain how to make several different kinds of belts and the carriers that hold your belt in place.

## Belt with Stiffening

If your pattern or preference demands a stiff belt, you must use a stiffening called "belting" inside your belt.

**1.** Cut the belting 4 inches longer than the waist measurement, and shape one end. Cut the fabric on the lengthwise grain, 1 inch longer than the belting and twice the width plus seam allowances. Fasten a safety pin on the right side of the fabric about 1½ inches from the shaped end. This will be used later to turn the belt to the right side.

**2.** Use the Zipper Foot in place of the presser foot on the machine. Adjust the toe to the right of the needle. Fold the fabric around the belting, wrong side out; turn the end with the safety pin toward the point. Stitch along the side, close to the belting. Press seam.

**3.** Move the fabric around the belting, bringing the seam to the center. Press the seam open, then trim the seam allowances to ¼ inch. Stitch the point barely outside the edge of the belting. Backstitch at each end. Trim the seam edges to ¼ inch. Withdraw the belting.

**4.** Turn the belt fabric to the right side by pushing the safety pin toward the open end and working the belt back over it. Work the end of the belt between the thumb and finger to bring the stitching to the very edge for a smooth point. Center the seam and press the entire belt.

**5.** Insert the belting, cupping the edges slightly between the thumb and forefinger to facilitate your work. Press. If top stitching is desired, stitch around the right side of belt, close to the edge. Sew on the buckle.

## Lined Soft Belt

**1.** Cut the fabric on the lengthwise grain 4 inches longer than the waist measurement and twice the width of the finished belt plus seam allowances. Fold lengthwise, wrong sides together, and crease.

Cut the interlining of lawn, nurses cloth, or organdy on the lengthwise grain, the length of the fabric and twice the finished width. Crease lengthwise through the center. Shape one end to a point, then cut off the end of the point to eliminate bulk when turned.

**2.** Place the folded edge of the interlining along the crease on the wrong side of the belt, with the point ¼ inch from the end. Stitch in place along each side and around the point. Press. Fasten a safety pin through the lining and fabric near the shaped end. This will be used later to turn the belt to the right side.

**3.** Fold the belt, right sides together, and pin

the seam edges together. Stitch just outside the edge of the interlining along the side and shaped end, taking one stitch across the point. Backstitch at each end. Trim seam edges. Press seam.

**4.** Turn the belt to the right side by pushing the safety pin toward the open end and working the belt back over it.

Carefully fold on the stitching line and press. If top stitching is desired, stitch around the right side of belt, close to the edge.

## Contour Belt

Maintaining the contour of the belt is your primary concern here. If you need to adjust the length of the belt, measure your waistline and add 5 inches. Measure the pattern and note the difference between the measurements. **To shorten,** take half the amount to be shortened from each end. **To lengthen,** add half the amount to be lengthened to each end. Construct the belt as follows:

**1.** Cut the belt and lining of the same fabric, using the pattern as a guide. Stay-stitch the top section of the belt ¼ inch from the seamline, in the seam allowance. Stay-stitch the lining barely outside the seamline in the seam allowance.

**2.** Use a double thickness of heavy Pellon for the interfacing. Pin the pattern over the Pellon and trace the outline of the pattern along the *seamline.* Place several lines of stitching across the two layers of Pellon to hold them together, using

the multiple-stitch zig-zag or straight stitching. Press. Cut out the Pellon interfacing, following the drawn lines.

**3.** Work on a flat surface with the wrong side of the top belt fabric up, and the pointed end to the left. Center the interfacing over the belt fabric and pin through the center. Fold the seam edge of the fabric over the interfacing and pin, working from the center to the outer edges. Clip into the seam edges on the inside curve almost to the stay stitching, and cut notches in the seam edges on the outside curve so that the seams will lie flat. Miter the corners at the pointed end. Baste.

**4.** Catch-stitch the fabric seam allowance to the interfacing, making the stitches through the seam allowance and interfacing only so that they are not visible on the right side. Press.

*(Continued on following page)*

**5.** Trim the seam allowance to ⅜ inch on all edges of the belt lining except the straight end that will be sewed to the buckle. Clip into the seam allowance on the inside curve and notch the seam allowance on the outside curve. Center the lining over the belt, wrong sides together, and pin through the center the length of the belt. Fold under the cut edge of the lining and pin barely below the belt edge. Slip-stitch in place.

If top stitching is desired, stitch around the right side of the belt, close to the edge.

## Narrow Tie Belt

The narrow tie belt may be from 1 inch to 1½ inches in finished width when cut on the lengthwise grain and about ½ inch when cut on the true bias. The ends should be long enough to lap or tie in a knot or bow. A wide seam allowance is used as an interlining in the instructions below.

**1.** Cut the belt on the lengthwise grain or on the true bias, the length of the waistline measurement plus the length desired for the tie, and four times the finished width.

**2.** Fold the fabric lengthwise through the center, right sides together, and pin. Baste through the center of the folded belt. Stitch 1/16 inch from the basting toward the cut edge. The seam allowance (from stitching line to cut edge) is ⅛ inch less than the width of the finished belt (from stitching line to folded edge); this difference will allow the seam allowances to fit smoothly inside the fin-

ished belt. (The Seam Guide adjusted the desired distance from the needle will help you guide and stitch the fabric evenly.)

**3.** Press, then fold one cut edge back on the stitching line and press the seam open. Clip off the corners diagonally from stitching to cut edge. If you are working with a lightweight fabric, leave both edges of the wide seam allowance for the interlining; however, if less thickness is required for the interlining, trim one edge of the seam allowance to ¼ inch.

**4.** Fasten a safety pin on the inside of one end, near the fold. Turn the belt to the right side by pushing the pin toward the open end and working the fabric back over it.

**5.** Carefully fold on the stitching line, and baste. Press. Turn the open ends into the belt ¼ inch, and pin. Slip-stitch the folded edges together.

## Sash Belt

The illustrated sash belt fits around the waistline, is crossed in the back and tied in the front. It is an attractive treatment for taffeta, satin, and many cottons. The sash is made of a double thickness of fabric that is cut on the true bias. Though the width may vary, a 9-inch finished sash is most becoming. The sash requires 1⅛ yards of 40-inch fabric so that only one joining is necessary.

**1.** Cut the sash on the true bias twice the length of the waistline measurement plus the length for the tie, and twice the finished width plus seam allowances. See *Cutting Bias Strips*, page 244.

**2.** Fold the sash through the center, right sides together, and pin. Shape the ends, and pin. Baste. Stitch, leaving a 4-inch opening near the center for turning the belt to the right side. Take one stitch across the points and backstitch at each end of the seam. Trim one seam edge to ⅛ inch and the other to ¼ inch. Clip off the corners at the points, close to the stitching.

**3.** Turn the sash to the right side through the opening in the seam. Fold on the stitching line, and baste. Press. Slip-stitch the edges of the opening together. Remove bastings.

## Corded Belt

Cording of various sizes may be used in belts. A single large cord or a braid of several cords is equally attractive. The cord is covered with a bias strip of soft satin or crepe. See *Tubular Cording,* page 247.

**1.** When braiding the cords, leave an unbraided length at each end for a tassel effect. At the end of the braiding, tie one tubular cord in a knot around the remaining cords. Tack the knot in place on the underside to prevent it from coming loose.

**2.** Trim the ends evenly. Pull out ½ inch of the cord and clip it off. Turn the ends of the fabric to the inside and slip-stitch them together, or knot

each end. Ease the knot down to within ½ inch of the end. Tuck the cut fabric ends under the knot with a heavy needle, and tack in place, taking care that the stitches are not visible.

## Cummerbund with Featherboning

**1.** Cut the fabric for the cummerbund on the true bias the length of the waistline measurement plus 2 inches for seam allowances and overlap, and about 9 inches in width. See *Cutting Bias Strips,* page 244. Cut the lining of the same fabric, the length and width of the cummerbund. If the fabric is heavy, cut the lining of soft silk of the same color.

**2.** Fold the cummerbund, extending the front section 1 inch beyond the back section (the front of the waistline is always larger than the back); and pin near the fold. Baste along the fold to mark the position of the seam on the right side.

**3.** Place the lining over the top fabric, right sides together, and pin on the seamline. Baste across the left front end and along each side. (Leave the opposite end open for turning the cummerbund to the right side.) Stitch the basted edges, taking a ½-inch seam; however, at the lower edge leave an opening of ¾ inch at the closed end and

at the marking for the right side seam, and ¾ inch plus ½-inch seam allowance at the open end as illustrated. Reinforce each seam end with backstitching. (These three openings are necessary for the stays, which you will insert between the two layers of fabric.)

**4.** Trim lining seam edges to ⅛ inch, top fabric seam edges to ¼ inch, and trim both seam edges across the openings to ¼ inch. Press. Turn the cummerbund to the right side. Fold on the stitching line and baste. Press. *(Continued)*

**5.** At the open end, turn the seam edges to the inside ½ inch, and pin together. Baste and press. Stitch from the right side, close to the edge. Stitch again a scant ⅜ inch from the first row of stitching to form the casing for the stay. Pull threads to the underside and tie. Stitch the opposite end

in the same way to form the casing there.

**6.** At the right side seam, pin and baste on each side of the marking to keep the bias from stretching while stitching. Space the bastings about ½ inch apart. Stitch on each side of the marking, spacing the lines of stitching a scant ⅜ inch apart. Pull threads to the underside and tie. Press. Remove bastings.

**7.** Cut three stays of featherboning 3½ inches in length. Remove the casing on the featherbone.

At the lower edge of the cummerbund, slip a featherbone stay into each opening between the rows of stitching and work the stay up to the top edge. Stitch the featherboning in place about ⅛ inch from the top edge. Stitch very slowly, turning the hand wheel by hand. Turn the fabric on the needle and stitch again on the first line of stitching. Pull threads to the underside and tie.

Ease the fabric back on each featherbone stay until the end of the stay is at the lower edge and under the fold of the seam. Stitch across the end of the stay the same as before. Distribute the fullness evenly. Slip-stitch the open edges of the casing together. Use four hooks and eyes to fasten the ends.

# Belt Carriers

Belt carriers are used to hold a belt in position. They may be hand-worked with a blanket stitch or chain stitch, or they may be made of fabric.

### Blanket-Stitch Carriers

**1.** Pin-mark the position for the carriers at the side seams, above and below the beltline.

**2.** Use a double strand of thread and knot the ends together. On the underside of the garment, take two backstitches to tie the thread at the top marking. Bring the needle through to the top side, then take a stitch at the opposite marking, leaving enough slack in the thread to fit over the belt.

Work back and forth two or three times, always allowing the same amount of slack. Blanket-stitch over the strands of thread, drawing the stitches firmly. Fasten the thread securely on the underside with two backstitches.

### Chain-Stitch Carriers

**1.** Mark the position for the carrier the same as above.

**2.** Use a double thread and knot the ends together. On the underside, take two backstitches in the seam at the top marking. Bring the needle through to the top side, then take a small stitch and draw the thread part way through, leaving a 2-inch loop. Hold the loop open with the needle. Reach through the loop with the thumb and one

finger of the left hand and grasp the needle thread, pulling it through to form a new loop. Draw the released loop down to the fabric. Continue chaining for the length required. Pass the needle through the last loop to lock the chain. Stitch through the fabric and fasten the thread with two backstitches on the underside.

You can make chain-stitch carriers quickly by machine if you have the Chain-Stitch Accessories. Refer to the instruction book accompanying the machine and to page 63.

### Fabric Carriers

Fabric carriers add a styling note to the waist and serve a utilitarian purpose as well. They are found on the waistbands of skirts, shorts, and slacks and in side seams of dresses. Generally, four to six carriers are used around the waistline. They vary from ¼ to ½ inch in width, depending on the fabric and garment.

**1.** Cut a strip of fabric on the lengthwise grain, twice the finished width plus ½ inch for seam allowances, and more than sufficient in length for the number of carriers required.

**2.** Fold the strip lengthwise, right sides together, and stitch a scant ¼ inch from the edge. Trim the seam edges to ⅛ inch. Ease the seam to the center of the strip and press open with the fingers. Stitch across one end.

**3.** Turn the strip right side out. (Use an orange stick with a straight end.) Turn the stitched end to the inside, then ease the strip back over the orange stick. Clip off the stitched end. Ease the seam to the center and press.

**4.** Cut each carrier long enough to fit over the belt with ease plus 1 inch for seam allowances. Fold under ½ inch at each end and press.

**5.** Mark the position for the finished end of the carrier on the garment. Place the carrier right side up, with the cut end ⅛ inch inside the marking. Stitch ⅛ inch from the edge. Backstitch at each end; do not stitch beyond the edges of the carrier. Trim the end close to the stitching and press.

**6.** Fold the carrier back on the stitching line and press. Stitch ⅛ inch from the fold, using a closely spaced zig-zag stitch. Finish the opposite end in the same manner.

### Belt Attached with French Tacks

A French tack may also be used to hold a belt in place. See *French Tacks*, page 208 for instructions.

## BUTTONS AND FASTENINGS

### Positioning Buttons

Buttons are positioned *on the center line* of the garment, opposite the buttonholes.

**1.** Lap the buttonhole side of the garment over the button side, *matching center lines,* and pin together between the buttonholes.

**2.** Mark the position of the button by placing a pin straight through the outer end of a horizontal buttonhole at the center line marking, and through the center of a vertical buttonhole. Carefully lift the buttonhole over the pin. The pin marks the position for the center of the button.

# Sewing on Buttons

Buttons may be sewed on by hand or with a zig-zag sewing machine. Whether or not you make a thread shank depends on the garment and the thickness of the fabric. A shank is not necessary on skirts, blouses, washable dresses, and pajamas; it is necessary on suits, coats, and garments of heavy fabric. The shank raises the button from the surface of the garment, allowing space for the layers of fabric on the buttonhole side to fit smoothly under the button. Mercerized or cotton thread is generally used on lightweight and washable fabrics; buttonhole twist is preferred for suits, coats, garments made of suede, and the like.

### Buttons without a Shank

Use thread matching the button in color. Knot the long end of the thread. Position the button over the marking and *on the center line* of garment.

Bring the needle through the fabric from the underside and up through one eye of the button. Place a pin across the button between the eyes, then bring the needle down through the second eye and back into the fabric. Take about six stitches; then fasten the thread with two or three overcast stitches around the threads on the underside.

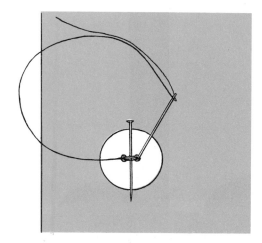

Buttons with four eyes may be sewed in various ways for decorative effects.

### Buttons with Thread Shank

For coats, suits, and garments that will be worn open, make the stitches through the garment and interfacing, but not through the facing. Knot the long end of the thread.

**1.** On the right side of the garment, take a stitch through the top layer of fabric and interfacing at the position for the button and on the center line of the garment. Bring the needle up through one eye of the button. Place a bodkin or smooth toothpick across the button between the eyes, then bring the needle down through the second eye. Take a stitch through the top layer of fabric and interfacing. Make about six stitches the same way. On the last stitch, bring the thread down through the eye.

**2.** Remove the bodkin, then pull the button away from the fabric and wind the needle thread evenly around the threads between the fabric and button to form the thread shank. Fasten the thread securely with two overcast stitches.

### Reinforced Button

On garments made of suede, leather, or heavy coating, where the underside must be as neat as the top side, sew a small button on the underside so that the stitches will be inconspicuous. This gives added strength and prevents the thread from cutting the suede or leather.

Use buttonhole twist and knot the end of the thread.

**1.** Position the top button. Bring the needle through the fabric from the underside and up through one eye of the button. Place a bodkin across the button between the eyes. Then bring the needle down through the second eye and fabric, and through the eye of the bottom button. Make about six stitches through the eyes of the top and bottom buttons at the same time. On the last stitch, bring the thread down through the eye of the top button.

**2.** Remove the bodkin, pull the top button away from the fabric and finish the thread shank between the top button and fabric as described above.

### Machine-Sewed Buttons

A zig-zag machine may be used to sew on buttons with or without a thread shank. Refer to the instruction book accompanying your machine for directions.

## Snap Fasteners

Snap fasteners are usually placed at the neckline and waistline to hold the facing edge flat when buttons are used; at the pointed end of the waistband with hooks and eyes; and at the waistline of blouses and the closing for long, closely fitted sleeves. They are seldom used alone.

Snaps are available in various sizes. Select a size that is not too heavy for the fabric. A small snap is preferred in dressmaking.

**1.** Mark the position for the snap on the overlap about ⅛ inch from the finished edge so that it is not visible when the garment is worn.

**2.** Sew the ball part of the snap to the underside of the overlap. Take about six stitches through the hole, then carry the thread under the snap to the next hole. Make the stitches through the facing and interfacing only so that they are not visible on the right side of the garment. Fasten the thread securely with two overcast stitches around the threads.

**3.** Chalk the ball and press it against the underlap to mark the position of the socket. (On some fabrics, merely pressing the ball against the underlap will mark the position.) Sew the socket to the underlap in the same manner as the ball section.

## Lingerie Strap Holder

Strap holders are used at the shoulder seam to hold lingerie straps in position.

Use straight seam binding about 1½ inches long. Fold under the ends and press, then fold through the center and press. Stitch on each side. Mark the position for each end of the strap at the shoulder seam. Hand-stitch one end to the seam allowance at the marking near the armhole.

Sew one part of the snap to the free end of the strap and the other part to the seam allowance.

## Hooks and Eyes

Hooks and eyes are placed at the waistband closing of a skirt, at the neckline when a zipper is used, at a closing where the edges meet, and at the waistline and neckline when a button is used.

Hooks and eyes are available in various sizes. Select small, fine ones for lightweight fabrics and a medium size for heavy fabrics. A straight eye is generally used when there is an overlap, and a round eye when edges meet.

### Overlap in a Waistband

**1.** Sew the hook to the underside of the overlap of the waistband, placing the end far enough from the edge so that it will not be visible when the garment is worn. Make about six stitches through each loop, then carry the thread under the hook and take several stitches through the end to hold it flat. Do not stitch through to the right side of the garment. Fasten the thread with one or two overcast stitches.

**2.** To mark the position for the eye, lap the closing and pin-mark the underlap directly opposite the end of the hook. Center the straight eye over the marking and sew through each loop.

**3.** On the underlap, sew a round eye at the end of the band. Fasten the hook in the eye, then sew it in place on the underside of the front band section.

### When Edges Meet

**1.** When edges of a closing meet, mark the position for the hook and eye on each side of the closing. Sew a round eye on one side, extending the edge slightly, or make a thread eye, following the instructions given below.

**2.** Fasten the hook in the eye, then bring the garment edges together to determine exactly where you should sew the hook on the opposite edge. Sew the hook in place. Be sure the stitches do not show through on the right side of the garment.

## Thread Eye

A thread eye is generally used at a neckline closing with a zipper and at a waistline closing with a button.

**1.** Sew the hook to the underside of the overlap, placing the end far enough for the edge so that it will not be visible when the garment is worn.

**2.** To mark the position for the eye, lap the closing and pin-mark the underlap directly opposite each side of the hook end.

**3.** *To make a thread eye,* use thread matching the fabric in color. Knot the long end of the thread. Bring the needle through from the underside at one end of the marking for the eye. Then take a stitch at the opposite end. Work back and forth two or three times, then blanket-stitch over the strands of thread, firmly drawing the stitches. Fasten the last stitch securely on the underside.

## Thread Loops

Thread loops are often used with buttons at a neckline opening in a dress or blouse.

**1.** Determine the spacing for the buttons and mark the edge of the garment. Center the button on the marking and pin-mark the position for the loop on each side of the button.

**2.** Use a single strand of matching thread and knot the long end of the thread. At the top marking, bring the needle through the fabric from the underside near the edge of the opening; then take a stitch in the edge at the bottom marking, leaving a loop large enough to slip easily over the button. Work back and forth two or three times, keeping the loops even. Blanket-stitch over the strands of thread, firmly drawing the stitches. Fasten the threads securely on the underside.

## French Tacks

French tacks are used when two fabric surfaces must be connected with a certain ease allowance —for example, linings at the lower edge in coats or draperies, or the lower edge of facings in coats. They are placed at the seams and intervals between. French tacks may also be used in attaching a belt to a garment or joining buttons to form cuff links.

**1.** Use a double strand of silk or mercerized thread or a single strand of buttonhole twist. Knot the end of the thread. Take a stitch near the top of the garment hem (through the hem and seam allowance), then a stitch directly opposite in the lining, leaving a ¼- to 1-inch slack in the thread. Work back and forth two or three times, allowing the same amount of slack.

**2.** Blanket-stitch over the strands of thread, firmly drawing the stitches. When finished, fasten stitches securely in the fabric with one or two overcast stitches.

## Eyelets

Eyelets are used in belts, in cuffs that require cuff links, and for lacings. They may be hand-worked or machine-worked with the Buttonholer.

### Hand-Worked Eyelets

**1.** Mark the position for the eyelets. Punch a hole in the fabric with a stiletto. (It may be necessary to cut out the excess fabric with sharp, pointed scissors. Do not make the hole too large.)

**2.** Use a single strand of silk or mercerized thread, or buttonhole twist. Bring the needle up through the fabric from the underside a scant ⅛ inch from the edge of the hole, leaving about 1 inch of the thread on the underside. Work around the hole and over the 1-inch thread on the underside with blanket stitches, forming the purl on the outer edge. Keep the stitches as even as possible. When finished, fasten the thread securely on the underside with one or two overcast stitches.

# Pleats and Godets

Pleats and godets are styling points that appear and disappear at intervals, depending on the whim of fashion. Both add fullness and interest to a skirt.

## FORMING PLEATS

In your sewing you will come across many kinds of pleats. This chapter deals with the four most common ones: side pleats, inverted pleats, box pleats, and pleated skirts.

### Side Pleats

Side pleats run in one direction—from right to left. They are often used to provide fullness at the lower edge of a pencil-slim skirt.

If the pattern you are using does not extend the pleat allowance the entire length of the skirt,

do so by marking the fabric with chalk before cutting.

**1.** Mark the position of the pleat and the seamline above the pleat with tailor's tacks. Pin and baste the seamline and the extension for the pleat. Then stitch close to the basting. Remove bastings and press.

Baste the fold line for the pleat and remove tailor's tacks.

**2.** Working from the wrong side, turn the pleat and seam allowance to the left side. Cut out the top layer of fabric above the pleat, leaving a ⅝-inch seam allowance. This eliminates bulk. The second layer of fabric will hold the pleat in position so that you do not need to stitch across the top of the pleat on the right side.

**3.** Press the seam open above the pleat. Turn the pleat and seam allowance to the left side and press. Press lightly in the hem area since the crease is reversed in the hem when it is folded.

## Inverted Pleat with Underlay

An inverted pleat is formed by folding two pleats toward each other. When an underlay is used on the underside of an inverted pleat, there is a seam instead of a fold on each side of the pleat that is concealed by the depth of the pleat.

If the pattern does not extend the pleat allowance the entire length of the skirt, do so by marking the fabric with chalk before cutting.

**1.** Mark the position of the pleat and the seamline above the pleat with tailor's tacks.

Pin and baste the entire length of the seam and pleat. Then stitch the seam from the waistline to the top of the pleat, reinforcing the ends with backstitching. Remove bastings along the stitching but not in the pleat area. Press. Then press the wide seam open the entire length of the seam and pleat. Press lightly in the hem area.

**2.** Place an underlay over the pleat section, right side down, extending the edge ⅝ inch above the top of the pleat. Pin and baste the underlay to each side of the pleat section. Stitch seams, and press.

**3.** To stay the top of the pleat, cut straight seam binding the width of the pleat. Fold it lengthwise through the center, and press. Turn the pleat away from the skirt. Pin the stay across the pleat with the lower edge exactly at the top of the pleat. Stitch the underlay and stay to the pleat from seam edge to center. Treat the opposite side in the same way. This eliminates the need for stitching across the top of the pleat on the right side and also prevents the seam from ripping above the pleat. Press, then remove bastings.

## Box Pleats

A box pleat is formed by folding two side pleats in opposite directions to make a panel. Transfer the markings for the pleats, following the instructions given for a *Pleated Skirt;* then lay in the pleats.

## Pleated Skirt

When the entire skirt is pleated, each pleat in the pattern is marked with two vertical lines from the waistline to the lower edge. One line designates the top fold for the pleat, the other the position of the fold that forms the pleat. Each pleat is made proportionately deeper at the waistline. The depth of the pleats conceals the seams within the skirt.

**1.** Transfer the markings to the fabric with tailor's tacks, using contrasting colors of thread to designate the two lines that form the pleat. This will simplify your work later when you begin to lay in the pleats, for you can fold one color to the other. *Be sure to use the correct marking on the pattern to form the top fold for each pleat.*

**2.** Before forming the pleats, stitch the seams within the skirt, and press. Determine the skirt length and finish the hem at the lower edge.

Three methods are suggested for forming the pleats. Use the one best suited to your fabric. Always work on a flat surface, and remember to press. See page 66 for information on pressing various types of fabric.

*Method 1:* Use this method of pleating for medium-weight fabrics with body that crease easily.

Work on the right side of the fabric. Lay in the pleats, matching markings. Place pins at right angles to the pleats. Baste near the fold, using silk thread. Press from the wrong side. Be sure to use the appropriate press cloth and moisture, and glide the iron the length of the pleat.

*Method 2:* Use this method on woolens that resist creasing and on heavy fabrics where pressing the fold of the pleat against the fabric is apt to form a ridge under the fold.

Work on the right side of the fabric. Pin, then baste the top fold for each pleat, using silk thread. Press from the underside of the fold to form a sharp crease. Since this step requires pressing on the right side of the fabric, use a wool press cloth and moist cheesecloth as protection.

Lay in the pleats, matching markings. Pin, then baste, using silk thread. Press from the wrong side, as instructed in Method 1, and crease the under fold for the pleat.

**Method 3:** Use this quick and easy method for cottons and similar fabrics.

Work on the ironing board. Turn the fabric right side up and lay in each pleat, matching markings. Pin straight through the fabric into the ironing board. Press between pins. Since the pressing is done from the right side, use the appropriate press cloth and moisture required by the fabric. Remove pins, and press again.

## Stitching Pleats

Pleats may hang freely from the waistline or may be stitched from waistline to hipline. They may be top-stitched or stitched from the underside. Do the stitching after you have applied the zipper and before you attach the waistband.

After you have basted and pressed your pleats as described in any one of the methods above, follow the instructions given here.

### Top-stitched Pleats

Pleats may be either edgestitched or stitched about ¼ inch from the edge. Since they are made proportionately deeper at the waistline, they overlap in this area.

Pin-mark the length to be stitched on each pleat. On the underside, fold back the pleat that precedes the line of stitching; then on the right side, stitch the pleat in place from the marking up to the waistline. Stitch each pleat in the same way. Pull threads to the underside and tie. Press. Attach the waistband; then remove all bastings for the pleats.

### Pleats Stitched on Underside

Remove the bastings from the waistline to about 3 inches below the hipline. Turn the skirt to the wrong side. Then turn the pleat away from the skirt and mark the length for the stitching with chalk. Pin and baste in the crease designating the top fold of the pleat. Then stitch in the crease from the marking up to the waistline. Reinforce each end with backstitching.

Turn the pleats in the direction they were pressed. Then press from the wrong side.

Apply the waistband before you remove the bastings.

## Pleated Ruffles

The small pleats required for ruffles can easily be made with the Ruffler. See page 281 for instructions.

As the Ruffler forms each pleat at the seamline, finger-press the entire length of the pleat. Then press with an iron. For fabrics that you cannot finger-press satisfactorily, use an iron after pleating the ruffle. Work on the ironing board and form the pleat from the stitching line to the outer edge; then place a pin straight through the outer edge and into the ironing board. Pin each pleat in the same way. Press.

## INSERTING GODETS

Godets may be set in a cutout of the skirt or in a seam. They should be stitched in place before you stitch the side seams since it is easier to work with a flat piece of fabric.

### Godet in a Cutout

When setting in a godet, you will be working with two curves—an outside curve, which is in the godet, and an inside curve, which is in the cutout of the skirt.

1. Stay-stitch a scant ⅝ inch from the seam edge of the cutout for the godet. Press. Slash the seam allowance on the curve almost to the stitching.

2. On the underside, pin the center of the godet to the center of the cutout, right sides together. Then, on each side, pin from the center to the lower edge. Carefully shape the inside curve of the cutout around the outside curve of the godet and ease the godet slightly around the curve, keeping seam edges even. Hand-baste on each side from center to lower edge, using a fine stitch. Check the right side to be certain that the curve is maintained on both pieces of fabric. Hang the garment overnight to allow for any stretching in the godet.

3. Place the godet next to the feed and stitch slowly in a continuous line from one edge to the other. Finish seam edges as required by the fabric. Press the seam, then press it away from the opening.

## Godet in a Seam

Stitch the seam above the opening for the godet and reinforce each end with backstitching. Finish the seam edges. Clip into the seam allowances at the top of the opening, almost to the stitching. Press; then press the seam open.

**1.** Position the godet in the opening, right sides together, matching the marking at the point with the end of the seam above the opening; pin at the point. Pin and baste one side from the point to the lower edge; keep seam edges even. Do not stretch the bias seam in the godet.

**2.** Stitch on the garment side, from the lower edge to the point, joining the stitching in the seamline above the godet. Pin, baste, and stitch the opposite side in the same way.

At the point of the godet, pull all threads to the underside and tie them together in a single knot. Remove bastings and press. Finish seam edges.

**3.** To stay the seam at the point, cut straight seam binding the width of the open seam edges. Fold the binding lengthwise through the center and press. Pin the stay across the godet and garment seam allowances, keeping the lower edge of the stay exactly at the top of the stitched point. Turn the seam allowances away from the garment and stitch from seam edge to seamline; treat the opposite side in the same manner. Clip off seam allowances at the point ¼ inch from the stitching.

# Fabrics
# that Require
# Special Handling

THERE IS A WIDE ARRAY OF FABRICS that demand special attention in sewing. To mention a few—knits, silks, soft leather and suede, and stretch. Techniques used in stitching and handling vary with the fabric. Although these fabrics require a little more time and patience, if you follow the suggestions given here as well as the usual methods of good dressmaking, your finished garment is certain to become one of your favorites.

Instructions for the various sewing techniques referred to in this chapter can be found in other parts of this book. Check the alphabetical index.

## SILK FABRICS

Silk can go anywhere. Ranging in weight from sheer chiffon to heavy tweed, it is suitable for all types of garments. "Light and gentle" describes the hand for working with silk.

### Preparing to Sew

*Pattern.* You can select almost any pattern for silk provided you also select the correct weight of silk for the garment. Heavy silks are suitable for tailored dresses, suits, and coats; soft silks for blouses and dresses; and sheer silks, such as chiffon or lace, for softly draped styles and full skirts. Unless completely underlined, however, sheer silks will not be pleasing to the eye if neckline and sleeve facings are used or if styling seams and darts are obvious.

*Cutting.* Do not try to cut silk on a highly polished surface and certainly not on the carpet or floor. A cork or felt surface is preferred, but sheeting pinned tightly over your usual cutting table or board will make a good substitute.

Use fine pins or, better still, needles, when pinning the pattern to the fabric. Place them close together and within the seam or dart allowance.

Use sharp scissors of medium length. Your careful cutting will be reflected in the accuracy of seam width and garment proportions. On sheer silk, cut notches outward so that they will not interfere with the seam construction or final finishing.

*Markings.* Use tailor's tacks only.

*Underlining and lining.* For the custom-made look you desire, you should either underline or line silk fabric. The chapter on underlining and lining contains comprehensive instructions. See page 95. Select such fabrics as China silk, silk organza, silk crepe, or silk taffeta.

*Interfacing.* Select the interfacing the same way as you would for any fabric of similar weight. If the silk is sheer, use self-fabric or silk organza; match the fabric color exactly.

### Stitching and Handling

*Basting.* Hand-baste seams and darts. Avoid temporary machine stitching that must later be removed since many silks will show needle marks. Baste with silk or soft mercerized thread contrasting in color, and use a size 8 or 9 hand-sewing needle of appropriate length.

**Thread and needle.** Machine-stitch silk fabric with silk thread as the expert always does. Use a size 11 machine needle in lightweight silks and a size 14 on heavy or rough-surfaced silks. In most cases, the needle thread tension must be lessened one to two points or until the stitching looks the same on the top and underside and does not pucker.

**Stitch length and pressure.** Use a 15 to 20 stitch length for sheer and soft silks and a 12 stitch length for medium and heavy silks.

The pressure exerted by the presser foot on the fabric should be light, no heavier than needed to carry the fabric gently and evenly under the foot.

**Stitching.** Medium and heavy silks require guiding only in front of the needle during the machine stitching. Crepe weaves and chiffon require gentle support; when stitching them, hold the seam in back of the presser foot as well as in front of the needle. Do not pull the fabric under the foot; merely place it under slight tension. When stitching with a zig-zag machine, use the straight-stitch throat plate and presser foot for best results.

**Darts.** If the silk is underlined, construct the darts in the silk and underlining separately unless the fabric is sheer. On sheer fabrics, make the darts through both layers at once so that they will not be distracting. Unstitched darts, gathers, and shirring are generally more pleasing in a sheer fabric than the conventional stitched dart.

**Seams and seam finishes.** Select a finish that will give the seam as little bulk as possible. Some closely woven silks require no seam finish; others you may prefer to pink. Finish rough, open weaves that tend to ravel with either the blindstitch zig-zag or the multiple-stitch zig-zag.

Sheer silks, such as chiffon, require narrow French seams. The hairline seam is a neat finish for enclosed seams in facings and collars, and fine double-fold bias binding makes a more pleasing neckline and sleeve finish than a shaped facing.

**Zipper closing.** Follow the conventional method of inserting the zipper until the final step. Then, instead of top-stitching, hand-sew, using a fine, short backstitch, or machine-stitch using the blindstitch zig-zag. The method you choose is more a matter of preference than of necessity.

**Buttonholes.** Machine-worked, hand-worked, or bound buttonholes are appropriate for all silks except sheers, where buttonholes should be avoided. Always use an underlay of a firmly woven lawn or muslin to reinforce the stitching around the buttonholes.

**Hems.** Seam tape is acceptable for the hem edge finish, but a pinked edge with a line of machine stitching ¼ inch from the edge is preferred. Rough, open weaves that tend to ravel may be finished with the blindstitch zig-zag or multiple-stitch zig-zag.

Always hand-sew the hem with silk thread, using the French method, which places the stitches between the hem and garment and not over the hem edge.

If the silk is sheer and the lining is joined only at the waistline, hem the silk and lining separately. A double-fold hem is a favorite. It adds weight to the bottom edge, improves the hang of the skirt, and eliminates the turned, raw edge that would normally show through. However, it can be used only if the hemline is straight, not flared. Double the hem allowance; if you want a 4-inch hem, allow 8 inches. Turn a 4-inch hem and press, then turn 4 inches again. Slip-stitch the hem in place, catching only one thread of the skirt in each stitch and slipping the needle inside the fold between the stitches to conceal the thread. When the hemline is circular or flared, make a narrow machine-stitched or hand-rolled hem, or use horsehair braid. Hem the sheer silk and underlining separately to avoid sagging and to prevent the sheer from blousing over the underlining.

**Pressing.** Follow the instructions given for pressing silk on page 66.

**Lining.** Coats and jackets should be lined in the usual way. Always select a lining of crepe or taffeta.

Knit fabrics have as many different faces and characteristics as woven fabrics, and for that reason no single set of sewing guidelines can be applied to all knits. *The Many Faces of Knits*, page 417, describes the construction of knit fabrics and the uses and characteristics of the various types of knits. It includes guidelines for stitching and suggestions for many different seams and constructions appropriate for the fabrics in each knit group.

Firm, stable knits — such as double knits and warp knits of polyester, wool, or blends of polyester and wool or cotton — are the most popular fashion knits. They are the easiest to sew, and they react more like woven fabrics than any of the other knits. For a capsule review of how to sew them, read the suggestions below.

## Preparing to Sew

*Pattern.* Many styles of suits, dresses, and coats make up well in firm knits. In selecting your pattern, pick one with simple, uncluttered lines. Some patterns are designated "suitable for knits"; other patterns include firm knits or double knits in the list of suitable fabrics on the pattern envelope. Do not choose a pattern designated "stretchable knits only" if you are working with a firm, stable knit. Smart ways to accent double knits and firm warp knits include matching fabric, braid, or satin binding; topstitching; and welt seams.

*Shrinking.* Washable knits, such as polyester and polyester-and-cotton blends, should be laundered before cutting to remove the excess finishing solution, which imparts permanent-press qualities. Wool double knits should be sent to the tailor/dry cleaner for shrinking unless labeled washable. Prepare them for shrinking by folding on a lengthwise rib, right side out, squaring the ends with a table, and basting the ends and edges. (Knits that are finished out-of-square can seldom be straightened by pulling diagonally.)

*Cutting.* Lay out the pattern following a "with nap" pattern layout. Knits have an up-and-down direction because of their loop construction and will reflect light differently in the crosswise and lengthwise directions. If the fabric has a deep center crease, it seldom can be pressed out, so avoid including the crease in a prominent part of the garment. If the crosswise courses of the knit do not run perpendicular to the lengthwise rib, or if a design in one direction is not perpendicular to one in the other direction, expand all half pattern sections with tissue paper into whole pattern sections; cut the fabric singly, using the most prominent direction of a fabric as the "grain line."

Use ball-point pins, preferably within dart and seam allowances. To avoid stretching, do not let the fabric hang over the edge of the cutting table. Cut with sharp, heavy-blade shears. Cut extended notches.

*Markings.* Use hand basting for center lines and tailor's tacks for internal markings. Tracing paper and a tracing wheel do not perform well on most firm knits.

*Underlining and lining.* Both are optional and impart different characteristics to a garment. Underlining and lining cancel the comfort of a knit fabric. They increase the stability of the fabric and cause the garment to hang free of the figure just like a woven fabric. Select a thin, soft, supple fabric for a softly draped look or a thin, crisp fabric for a mounted look. Suit jackets may be lined with either a color-matching single knit or a tricot to preserve the give of knit.

*Interfacing.* Collars, cuffs, pocket flaps, and front facing areas should be interfaced in firm knits. Select a thin, supple woven interfacing or an all-polyester nonwoven interfacing for minimum support; a lightweight hair canvas for tailored shaping; or time-saving press-on interfacing (fused to the underside of the outside section) for a crisp effect.

## Stitching and Handling

*Basting.* Hand basting ensures a smooth seam and enables you to test the fit of the garment before machine-stitching the seams. Machine basting with the Even Feed machine foot, or speed basting (if your sewing machine has this feature), will give you the same advantages as hand basting.

*Thread and needle.* Select strong thread for machine stitching. Silk, nylon, spun polyester, and polyester-core threads are suitable. They provide both stretch and strength. Use a size 14 ball-point needle (Singer No. 2021 or 2045). Regulate tensions to produce a balanced stitch.

*Kind of stitch.* For plain seams in firm knits, a 12 length straight stitch made with a strong thread is suitable. For seams that will be subjected to strain, the straight stretch stitch is recommended. Use one of the overedge stitches for finishing hem and facing edges.

**Presser-foot pressure.** Use medium or normal presser-foot pressure.

**Stitching.** For straight stitching, use the straight-stitch presser foot and throat plate. Guide and support the fabric while stitching by holding the seam under tension in back of the presser foot and in front of the needle. Or use the Even Feed foot instead to ensure that the seam ends come out even without basting or guiding and supporting the seam.

Stabilize seams that must not stretch, such as shoulder, neckline, and waistline seams, with woven-edge seam binding.

Armhole seams for set-in sleeves should be double-stitched, first on the seamline with a straight or straight stretch stitch, then ¼ inch outside the seamline with a straight stitch or a zig-zag overedge stitch. Trim seam allowance outside second stitching.

Topstitching with buttonhole twist is a fashion accent recommended for firm knits. Use a size 16 or 18 needle to carry the buttonhole twist, and thread the bobbin with either silk or mercerized thread. Increase the needle-thread tension slightly to set the stitch firmly. The Even Feed foot will improve the feeding of the fabric layers for all topstitched detail. Topstitching may also be done

with the same thread used for constructing the garment.

**Darts.** To eliminate bulk in small darts, slash through center and press open. Trim the inside layer of slanted bustline darts to ½ inch and press downward.

**Seam blending.** Blend, grade, or bevel seam allowances inside collars, cuffs, and similar constructions in the same way as on woven fabrics.

**Seam finishes.** Press plain seams open. Edges do not ravel and do not require a seam finish.

**Buttonholes.** Bound or machine-worked buttonholes are appropriate. Always make buttonholes through firm woven or all-polyester non-woven interfacing or stay.

**Hems.** To ensure an even and accurate hemline, allow knit garment to hang at least 24 hours before hemming. Mark, fold, and baste the hem in the same way as on woven fabrics. Finish the hem edge with a zig-zag overedge stitch or a straight stitch ¼ inch from edge. Blindstitch hem by hand. For deep hems, place the first row of blind hemming stitches at the center of the hem width and the second row ¼ inch from the hem edge.

**Pressing.** Always use a thin press cloth between the iron and the fabric. A slightly dampened cheesecloth will produce sufficient steam with the iron on the silk setting. Steam-press polyester thoroughly as you sew. Little or no pressing is required after laundering if thorough pressing is done during the construction of the garment.

# STRETCH FABRICS

Since the stretch characteristic has been added to fabrics primarily for comfort in action plus neatness of fit, the direction in which the stretch is used in a garment is important. Stretch should run across the shoulders in blouses, shirts, dresses, and jackets; from waistline to ankle in pants or slacks; and from side to side in skirts and shorts. Examine the fabric carefully *to be sure that the stretch goes in the right direction* for your garment.

Some fabrics are woven to look the same lengthwise as crosswise even though they stretch in only one direction. They can be used for any garment, but you must cut the fabric with the stretch running in the proper direction, as stated above. For a description of stretch fabrics, see page 11.

## Preparing to Sew

**Pattern.** Select a pattern in your usual size, with slim, simple styling. In adjusting the pattern to your fitting requirements, remember that you may not need quite so much ease allowance for body action as you do when using a firm fabric.

**Shrinking.** It is advisable to shrink the fabric before cutting since laundering may cause it to shrink more in the stretch direction than a firm fabric.

**Cutting.** Lay the pattern pieces on the fabric in the direction of the desired stretch. Use fine pins with sharp points, and place them perpendicular to the direction of the stretch. Cut, following the same procedure you use for regular fabrics. A 1-inch seam allowance is recommended for lightweight or medium-weight twill weaves and heavy stretch fabrics. Simply cut 1 inch from the seamline marking on the pattern.

*Markings.* Use either tailor's tacks or tracing wheel and dressmaker's tracing paper. Tailor's tacks are recommended for heavy fabrics since the tracing wheel may not mark the bottom layer of fabric.

*Interfacing.* Interface the garment in the same way as one made of regular fabric.

## Stitching and Handling

*Basting.* Hand basting is recommended for stretch fabrics. It saves time in the long run because it enables you to test the fit of the garment before machine stitching; also, it ensures an even seam width when stitching. Baste darts from the wide end toward the point, leaving a 4-inch thread end at the point. After fitting the garment, clip the seamline bastings at 4-inch intervals to allow for stretching the fabric during the machine stitching.

*Thread and needle.* Select strong thread for machine stitching. Nylex, Nymo, and Dacron are all excellent because they provide strength plus give to seams. Silk thread may also be used. Select size 14 machine needle.

Regulate the tension to produce a balanced stitch, otherwise strength is sacrificed.

*Stitch length and pressure.* Use a 12 stitch length. The pressure exerted by the presser foot on the fabric should be medium.

*Stitching.* Seams on the stretch grain require special handling. Make a test sample on your fabric before actually stitching on the garment. Do not forget to clip seamline bastings at 4-inch intervals. As you sew, stretch the fabric by holding it in front and in back of the presser foot; in other words, keep the fabric under tension while stitching. If you are using Nymo, Nylex, or Dacron thread, all of which have a certain amount of elasticity, stretch the fabric slightly during the stitching. If you are using silk thread, stretch the fabric the full amount of the built-in stretch. Use medium to slow speed. Backstitch at each end of the seam for reinforcement. After stitching a seam, stretch it the full amount to be sure that the thread

will not break under strain. If you have a slant-needle zig-zag machine, you can use the Overedge Foot and *Fashion* disc, which will produce a flexible stitch that will stretch with the fabric.

In some seams stretch is undesirable, such as those at the neckline, waistline, and shoulders. Stay them with straight seam binding.

*Seam finishes.* Press the seam open and finish the edges with a plain zig-zag stitch, wide stitch width, and 12 stitch length; or with a multiple-stitch zig-zag, wide stitch width, and "fine" stitch length. Pink the seam edges if the fabric is firmly woven. Blend seams inside collars, cuffs, facings, and similar construction in the usual way.

*Waistband on skirt and pants.* Cut the band on the lengthwise grain of the fabric and interface it with grosgrain ribbon. If you want stretch in the band, cut the band on the stretch grain and interface it with elastic that has been fitted for the desired snugness. (Remember, the waistline of the garment must also be on the stretch grain.) Stretch both the elastic and fabric as you sew, using a medium width zig-zag stitch.

*Zipper closing.* Insert the zipper in the conventional way. Do not stretch the fabric since the zipper tape will not stretch. A side closing or fly front is preferred for skirts, shorts, slacks, or pants.

*Buttonholes.* Machine-worked or bound buttonholes are suitable. Always stay buttonholes with a backing of a firmly woven fabric.

*Hems.* Finish the hem edge the same way as the seam edges. Then blindstitch the hem in place, using the machine. If the hem is along the stretch grain, use a plain zig-zag stitch, medium stitch width, and 12 stitch length instead of the blindstitch.

*Pressing.* Press carefully to avoid stretching the fabric. Use the regular steam setting on the iron. Place the iron lightly over the section to be pressed and allow the steam to enter; lift the iron and move to another section. Do not glide the iron in the direction of the stretch grain. To avoid the imprint of the seam edge on the fabric, slip a strip of brown paper under the seam allowance.

*Lining.* Select a stretch fabric for the lining, if you are using one; otherwise you will lose the "stretch" advantage of your garment.

# BONDED FABRICS

In bonded fabrics (see description on page 12), the face fabric and lining are bonded together. This means that you can make a garment in less time than with other fabrics because only a single cutting and sewing operation is required.

## Preparing to Sew

**Pattern.** Bonded fabrics are appropriate for dresses, suits, and coats with tailored lines. Avoid circular skirts and softly draped styles. Top stitching is a smart way to accentuate the lines of the garment.

**Cutting.** A fabric that has an "up" and "down" to the design should be treated the same way as any floral fabric. If the face fabric is knit, treat the rib as the true lengthwise grain and follow the directions for knit fabric. When you are unable to straighten the fabric because of the bonded lining, square off the crosswise grain with a ruler and use only the lengthwise grain as a guide in cutting. See page 15. These fabrics are quite satisfactory because the bonded lining retains the shape of the fabric.

Always fold the fabric wrong sides together, and lay the pattern on the right side. Use plenty of fine pins.

**Markings.** Mark with tailor's tacks or chalk pencil.

**Interfacing.** Preshrunk muslin and batiste are preferred for tailored dresses. Hair canvas may be used for suits and coats.

## Stitching and Handling

**Basting.** Pin or hand-baste all seams, darts, and the hem to ensure an even seam. Basting will also permit you to test the fit of the garment before stitching.

**Needle and thread.** Silk, mercerized, or synthetic thread may be used for the machine stitching. A size 14 needle is required. Regulate the tension to produce a balanced stitch.

**Stitch length and pressure.** Select a 12 stitch length. The fabric requires medium pressure.

**Stitching.** Guide and support the fabric in front and in back of the foot. Do not pull the fabric as it passes under the foot; merely place it under slight tension. This will allow give in the seam and prevent puckering. Where sleeve and bodice are cut-in-one, stitch underarm seams with a narrow, open zig-zag stitch to allow for greater ease in the seam.

To emphasize the seamline, make slotted seams or press seams open and top-stitch on each side ½ inch from the seamline. Stabilize seams at shoulders, neckline, and waistline with straight seam binding to prevent stretching. If set-in sleeves are chosen, stabilize the armhole seams also; preshape the binding by steam pressing and pin it over the seamline. After setting the sleeve into the armhole, finish the seam allowance with zig-zag stitching as described on page 323. Corners should be blunt. Either round the corners slightly, or take two or three stitches across the point to allow sufficient width for turning.

**Darts.** Slash through the center of darts and press them open to eliminate bulk.

**Seam blending.** Blend seams inside collars, facings, and similar construction, in the usual way to eliminate bulk.

**Seam finishes.** Seam edges require no finish since the cut edges will not ravel.

**Finishing the edges.** Tailored binding or braid is a fashionable finish for the neckline, sleeves, and all outside edges of dresses, jackets, and coats.

**Waistline joining.** Follow the procedure for knit fabrics, page 218.

**Buttonholes.** You may use machine-worked or bound buttonholes. Always use an underlay such as batiste or muslin to reinforce the stitching around the buttonholes.

**Hemming.** Finish the free edge of the hem with pinking, then stitch close to the edge, using a 20 stitch length. Make a French hem—that is, a catch stitch below the hem edge and between the hem and garment.

**Pressing.** Use the regular steam setting on the iron. Cover the fabric with a lightweight press cloth, and press from the wrong side. For extra moisture on seams, use a moist cheesecloth over the press cloth. Faced edges may be tapped gently with a wooden pounding block to flatten them. Press the hem lightly so that the fold will not be sharply creased.

# LAMINATED FABRICS

Laminates are relatively easy for the home sewer to handle. For a description of them, see page 12.

## Preparing to Sew

*Pattern.* Choose a simple, bulkless style with a minimum of darts and seam details. Styles with center front and back seams or openings are preferred. Adjust the pattern to your individual requirements. Cut off the pattern margin on the cutting line before placing the pattern on the fabric.

*Cutting.* Lay the pattern pieces on the right side of the fabric so that the fabric grain line is always visible. For accuracy in cutting, cut only a single layer of fabric at a time. When the fabric is folded with wrong sides together, the foam sticks together. (A lightweight fabric, however, can be cut double.) Place pins parallel to the seamline. Follow the same cutting procedure used for regular fabrics. Large, bent-handle cutting shears give a cleaner edge to seams than smaller scissors. Cut all notches outward.

*Markings.* Use tailor's tacks only.

*Interfacing.* Laminated fabrics do not require interfacing.

## Stitching and Handling

*Basting.* Seams, darts, and hems should be hand-basted to prevent the fabric from slipping during machine stitching. Basting also allows you to test the fit of the garment before stitching.

*Thread and needle.* You may use silk or mercerized thread for machine stitching. Dacron, Nymo, and Nylex threads are also satisfactory and stronger than mercerized thread. Usually, a size 14 machine needle produces the best results. Regulate the tension to produce a balanced stitch.

*Stitch length and pressure.* Select 10 to 12 stitch length. The pressure on the fabric should be medium.

*Stitching.* Before machine stitching, baste straight seam binding or a strip of crisp lawn about ⅝ inch wide over the foam sides so that both the presser foot and feed dog are in contact with the lawn or seam binding and not with the foam.

This prevents the foam from sticking to the presser foot and feed and produces a smooth seam. After the stitching is completed, trim lawn to ¼ inch to eliminate bulk yet strengthen the seam.

Corners must be blunt, not pointed. Either round corners slightly, or place two or three stitches across the point to allow sufficient width at the point for a smooth turning.

*Darts.* Slash through the center of darts, and press them open to eliminate bulk.

*Seams.* Press the seam open. Top-stitch on each side of, and about ¼ inch from, the seamline. Trim the seam allowance on the underside to ¼ inch. This will produce a neat, tailored finish as well as strengthen the seam. A welt seam is also appropriate. See pages 335 and 88.

If the fabric is heavy, stitch the top collar and facing to the undercollar and garment with the foam sides together. Trim the seam allowance to ½ inch, and bind the edges with a bias strip or braid. See *Tailored Binding*, page 334.

*Seam blending.* Blend seams inside collars, cuffs, facings, and similar construction in the usual way to eliminate bulk.

*Buttonholes.* Always stay buttonholes with a backing of a firmly woven muslin or lawn. Machine-worked or bound buttonholes are suitable.

*Hems.* You may sew the hem in place by machine or by hand. Fold and baste the hem in the conventional manner. Place several parallel rows of top stitching in the hemline, spacing them about ¼ inch apart.

If a hand finish is desirable, finish the hem edge by stitching seam binding over the cut edge. Then finish by hand, using a blind hemming stitch. Make the stitches through the entire fabric, catching only one thread on the right side of the fabric. Stitches made through foam alone will not hold.

*Pressing.* Laminates require little pressing. Finger pressing is effective. Light steam pressing, with a press cloth between the fabric and iron, helps to sharpen seams.

*Lining.* Garments made of laminated fabrics should be lined to protect the foam backing. Follow the method used in lining a jacket or coat.

# WASH-AND-WEAR FABRICS

The term "wash-and-wear" as used here means any fabric that is washable and requires little or no ironing after washing. It can be of cotton, nylon, Dacron, Orlon, Acrilan, Arnel, and other fibers, or a blend of synthetic and natural fibers.

When selecting a wash-and-wear fabric, bear this in mind: The fabric must be finished *straight of grain*—that is, the crosswise threads must be at right angles with the lengthwise threads (or selvage edge). If they are not, it means that the fabric has been finished off grain and cannot be straightened; therefore, they must be squared off with a ruler and cut with only the lengthwise grain as a guide. See page 15. Obviously, this fabric fault impairs the quality of the garment.

## Preparing to Sew

*Pattern.* A wide variety of styles are appropriate for wash-and-wear fabrics. Avoid those with seam details; select a design that calls for single seam construction rather than multiple thickness.

*Cutting.* If the manufacturer folded the fabric through the center, press out the crease before cutting. If the crease cannot be pressed out, arrange the pattern pieces to avoid the crease so that it does not appear in the finished garment. Pin the pattern to the fabric with fine, sharp-pointed pins. (Blunt pins may mar some fabrics permanently.) Cut with sharp scissors.

*Markings.* Use either tailor's tacks or a tracing wheel and dressmaker's tracing paper. Do not use a wax chalk since the marking cannot be removed from wash-and-wear fabrics.

*Interfacing.* Always select fabric of the wash-and-wear type or of nylon taffeta or marquisette.

## Stitching and Handling

*Thread and needle.* On cotton fabrics having a wash-and-wear finish, mercerized thread is most acceptable. Wash-and-wear blends of natural and synthetic fibers may be stitched with mercerized, Nylex, Nymo, or Dacron thread, depending on the fiber make-up of the blend. (Check the fabric label for fiber content.) The size of the needle is determined by the thread: size 14 for mercerized thread; size 11 for Nylex, Nymo, and Dacron.

*Stitch length and pressure.* As a rule a 12 stitch length is preferred. Pressure should be heavy enough to carry the fabric without showing the print of the feed.

*Stitching.* Since many wash-and-wear fabrics are blends of two or more fibers, it is wise to test your stitching on a swatch of your fabric. If the seams pucker after being stitched with one of the synthetic threads, you must adjust the tension. Begin by changing the upper tension to a lower number; then if the stitch is not locked in the center of the fabric, it may be necessary to loosen the lower tension slightly. (A dense or tightly woven fabric usually requires a heavier upper tension.)

Stitch slowly. Check seams immediately after stitching and then a few hours later. Synthetic threads have a "recovery" factor. Although the seam may appear to be smooth and without pucker immediately following stitching, a few hours later the thread may recover its set dimension and cause a pucker. Seams that are smooth after stitching and before pressing will remain smooth through many washings. This is the secret of sewing wash-and-wear.

# VELVET, VELVETEEN, AND CORDUROY

Velveteen is fashionable for daytime, sports, and formal wear; velvet is used primarily for formal wear. Corduroy, which is generally less expensive than the other two, is practical for sportswear and children's clothes. These pile fabrics are also used in robes, bedspreads, curtains, and slipcovers.

Pile fabrics have an "up" and "down." To determine the direction of the pile, follow the instructions on page 55.

## Preparing to Sew

*Pattern.* Many pattern designs are appropriate for velvet, velveteen, and corduroy. The most effective, however, are those with simple lines that show off the rich tone of the fabric. Avoid too many styling seams within the garment. Unpressed pleats are suitable. Always cut off the pattern margin on the cutting line before placing the pattern on the fabric.

**Fitting.** It is important to fit and adjust the pattern exactly to your requirements before you cut pile fabrics. Any alterations after cutting affect the pile and are noticeable. If your pattern design is intricate, cut, stitch, and fit a muslin shell on which you can make all corrective adjustments before cutting the fabric.

**Cutting.** Lay the fabric on a smooth, flat surface with the pile side (right side) up. For sections where you must lay the pattern on a fold, be sure to fold the fabric lengthwise with the pile side on the outside. You must lay all pattern pieces in one direction with the pile running up. To avoid marring the pile, pin the pattern to the fabric with long, fine needles instead of pins.

**Markings.** Make tailor's tacks only, with silk thread.

**Interfacing.** Use preshrunk muslin, batiste, or a similar fabric for interfacing; silk organza is excellent for a soft velvet. Interface suits and coats with a fine grade of hair canvas, following *Method 1*, on page 136.

**Underlining and lining.** You may underline or line the entire garment or just a portion of it. Cut the underlining or lining by the same pattern pieces and on the same grain as the garment. Select such fabrics as silk crepe or China silk and match the fabric exactly in color.

## Stitching and Handling

**Basting.** Always baste with silk thread. Fit the garment and make all necessary adjustments before machine stitching. Avoid temporary machine stitching that must later be removed; it will mar the pile.

**Thread and needle.** Stitch velvet with silk thread and velveteen and corduroy with silk or mercerized thread. Use mercerized thread on washable velveteen and corduroy that are made into children's clothes. Most pile fabrics require size 14 needle; however, a size 11 is frequently used to stitch velvet. When stitching with silk thread, decrease the needle thread tension one or two points, or until the stitching looks the same on the top and underside.

**Stitch length and pressure.** A 12 stitch length is correct. The pressure exerted by the presser foot should be somewhat lighter for pile than for a flat woven fabric of the same thickness—just heavy enough to carry the fabric without showing the print of the feed.

**Stitching.** The rule is to stitch with the pile. Since the pile runs up, this means that seams are stitched from the bottom to the top. A plain seam, pressed open, is preferred.

**Seam finishes.** Several methods of finishing the seam edges are appropriate. They are: pinking; binding with nylon net; overcasting by hand; or overedging by machine, using the blindstitch zig-zag. Do not allow edges of the fabric to pucker.

**Darts.** Slash through the center of darts and press them open to eliminate bulk.

**Underlining and lining.** A pencil-slim skirt should be completely lined to retain its shape. Page 95 describes how to use underlining and lining. Use the method where underlining and skirt are joined only at the waistline.

To eliminate bulk in velvet, velveteen, and corduroy, omit the facing at the neckline and at the lower edge of short sleeves and let the lining serve in its place.

Line the bodice from the neckline to about two inches below the armhole. First stitch and press the shoulder seams separately in the velveteen and lining. Place velveteen and underlining sections right sides together. Pin, baste, and stitch around the neckline, following the seamline. Blend the seams and press. Turn the underlining to the underside and ease it under slightly at the seamline; baste flat against the velveteen. Press. Handle as one fabric in the balance of construction.

To line short sleeves, stitch underarm seams separately in the velveteen and lining; then, at the lower edge of the sleeve, stitch the velveteen to the lining, right sides together. Blend seams and press. Turn the sleeve to the right side, with the lining on the underside. Ease the lining under slightly at the seamline; baste and press. Baste the two fabrics together at the sleeve cap and handle as one in the balance of construction.

**Zipper closing.** Hand-sew the final step of the zipper to give your dress the couturier touch. Follow the conventional method of inserting the zipper up to the final step. Then, finish by hand, using a short backstitch. See page 178.

**Hems.** The free edge of the hem may be finished with silk seam binding or bound with nylon net. Always hand-stitch the hem with silk thread. Place the stitches between the hem and garment and not over the hem edge. On a circular skirt, where a narrow hem is essential, use a hand-rolled hem.

**Pressing.** Follow the instructions given on page 66.

Lace fabrics may be made of cotton, rayon, wool, linen, silk, or other fibers. They may be expensive or inexpensive, depending on what fibers they contain and whether they are made by hand or by machine.

Fashion dictates the uses of lace. It may advocate lace fabrics for wedding, late afternoon, and evening dresses; for daytime dresses, blouses, stoles, jackets, and evening coats; for tailored garments and beach coats. The lace must, of course, be appropriate for the occasion. Silk laces are used primarily for formal wear; most of the other lace fabrics may be used for other occasions as well as for formal wear.

## Preparing to Sew

**Pattern.** To emphasize the design of the lace, choose simple style lines. The pattern should have a minimum of darts and seam details; too many break the continuity of the design of the lace. Styles with bodice and sleeve cut-in-one are excellent. Avoid neckline and sleeve facings unless you plan to underline the lace with an opaque fabric; cut the facings of matching fine net or tulle to eliminate bulk. Do not use styles requiring faced front and back openings unless the facing and bodice are cut-in-one, which will eliminate the seam. Avoid shoulder pads or shapes, even when in fashion, if you are using a sheer underlining.

**Cutting.** The design of the lace must be matched. Some laces have an "up" and "down" to the design and must be cut with all pattern pieces laid in the same direction. See the directions for *Florals, Prints and Jacquards,* page 55. Always fold the lace wrong sides together. Use sharp pins. (Some sewers prefer needles to avoid snagging or marring the lace.) As a further precaution, pin within the seam allowances and gathered areas. Cut all notches outward so that they will not interfere with seam construction or final finishing. Shears should be sharp and not excessively large.

**Markings.** Use tailor's tacks only.

**Underlining and lining.** Underlining is necessary to support the delicate network of threads in lace fabrics. Lining, however, is sometimes used in full skirts if there is little openwork in the lace and the texture is firm. Select a smooth, firm fabric. Opaque fabrics such as taffeta, satin, peau de soie, polished cotton, or wool crepe will place the lace in the category of a heavy fabric. If you wish to maintain the sheerness of the lace, underline with silk organza, fine net, marquisette, or chiffon, and make a special slip of opaque fabric to wear with the dress. In a dress-and-jacket ensemble, the dress may be underlined with an opaque fabric and the jacket with fine net or organza. Wool crepe is an appropriate underlining for wool lace.

Generally the underlining should match the lace exactly in color, although a subtle contrast may occasionally be used effectively—for example, off-white with white, écru with white, or a shade darker than the color.

*Underlining and Lining* beginning on page 95, describes the techniques you should follow.

## Stitching and Handling

**Basting.** Use a size 8 or 9 hand sewing needle and baste all seams to prevent the lace from slipping during machine stitching. If there is a design to be matched at the seamline, slip-baste.

**Thread and needle.** Select silk thread for the machine stitching on silk, wool, or synthetic lace, and mercerized thread for cotton and linen. These threads require a size 14 needle; however, use a size 11 if you can do so without thread breakage. Stitching synthetic laces with synthetic thread will permit you to use a size 11 needle.

**Stitch length and pressure.** In stitching the fine openwork of lace, use a 15 stitch length and light pressure—no heavier than needed to carry the fabric evenly under the presser foot without marring the lace.

**Stitching.** Medium-weight laces require guiding only in front of the needle during machine stitching; soft and silk laces require a little more support. Gently control the fabric both in front and in back of the foot, taking care not to pull or stretch the lace.

**Darts.** Use darts only if your underlining is opaque; it will conceal the darts in the finished garment. If your underlining is sheer, change darts to soft gathers.

**Seams and seam finishes.** An opaque underlining will prevent the seam allowances from showing through the lace, so you may use a plain seam in your dress. Pink the seam edges and press the seam open. If you are using a sheer underlining, however, or are attaching the skirt and underlining at the waistline only, you must use a fine, narrow seam and conceal the seam edges. Use a French seam or, to eliminate bulk, a double-stitched seam.

**Seam blending.** Blend curved seams in the usual way to eliminate bulk.

**Finishing the edges.** A fine double-fold bias binding makes a pleasing finish for the neckline, sleeves, and front or back opening. Use it rather than shaped facings. Satin, taffeta, and organza, matching the lace exactly in color, are all excellent fabrics for the binding.

**Zipper closing.** Insert the zipper by hand to give the couturier touch. Buy a fine zipper and follow the conventional method of applying it up to the final step. Then, instead of top stitching, hand-sew, using a short backstitch. To vary from the conventional zipper application, use the slot seam method. Center the zipper under the machine-basted seam; hand-sew ¼ inch from the center seam.

**Fastenings.** Do not make buttonholes in lace; thread loops are better suited to the fabric. Choose small buttons; large buttons are inappropriate and too heavy for lace.

**Hems.** If the lace has a border or scalloped edge, use that as the finish. In circular skirts, where a lining is used, hem the two fabrics separately. A narrow hem is essential; either make a hand-rolled hem or use horsehair braid. If the lace is underlined with an opaque fabric, form a hem of average width. Finish the free edge with a multiple-stitch zig-zag, or pink it and stitch ¼ inch from the edge, using a 20 stitch length. Then make a French hem by catch-stitching below the hem edge and between the hem and the garment.

**Pressing.** Use the regular steam setting on the iron. Place a wool-faced pressing pad on the ironing board with the wool-facing side up. Lay the lace, right side down, on the pad. (A turkish towel may be substituted for a pressing pad.) Cover the lace with a thin press cloth; if additional moisture is required for seams, place a moist cheesecloth over the thin press cloth before pressing. If you follow these suggestions, you will not flatten the raised design of the lace during the pressing.

# SOFT LEATHER AND SUEDE

Acquaint yourself with the approximate size and shape of the skins you contemplate using. Remember that many skins have thin areas and you must avoid placing them in garment sections subject to strain. Unless you are experienced in selecting and handling skins, limit your sewing to small apparel items and trims. It takes a knowing eye and sound judgment to select skins of the correct weight and regularity for large garments.

## Preparing to Sew

**Pattern.** Select a design with seams that will accommodate the size and dimension limitations of your skins. Other seaming, unless it contributes to styling, is not attractive.

**Fitting.** You must do all fitting *before* you cut the suede or leather. Adjust the pattern; cut, stitch, and fit a muslin shell; then make all corrective fitting adjustments *in the shell.* Trim all seam allowances to ⅜ inch for economy in cutting the leather *unless* you plan to place top stitching more than ¼ inch from the edge, or to use a welt seam. The narrow seam allowance will also eliminate bulk in the finished garment.

**Cutting.** Lay the muslin pattern pieces on the wrong side of a *single layer* of suede or leather. Do not fold the skins or cut two pieces at one time. Be sure to turn the pattern pieces over to cut the second half so that you will have a right and left side. Since leather has no grain, the pattern pieces may be laid either lengthwise or crosswise on the skins, depending on which direction gives you the most even distribution of thickness. Note, however, that *all pieces must be laid in the same direction.* Since suede has an up and down, you must lay all pattern pieces lengthwise on the skins and in one direction with the nap running down. To determine the direction of the nap, brush the suede with your fingers as you would velvet and napped fabrics. See pages 55 and 56. Do not pin into the body of the garment since punctures will permanently mar the leather. Either pin within the seam allowance or use cellophane tape to hold the muslin pattern in position. Use sharp scissors. Cut all notches outward or mark them with chalk on the underside of the leather.

**Markings.** Mark darts, buttonholes, center lines, and styling points with chalk on the wrong side of the skin. Do not use a tracing wheel; it will mar the leather. To transfer markings, turn back a portion of the pattern and fold along the line of the dart, buttonhole, or other marking; chalk-mark the skin along the line of the fold. Use a ruler to keep lines straight. Reinforce thin spots with "press-on" mending tape on the wrong side of the skin.

**Underlining and lining.** Suede and leather garments should be lined. Synthetic linings such as SiBonne, UnderCurrent, Veriform, rayon taffeta, and acetate sheath lining are appropriate.

**Interfacing.** Interface collars, cuffs, and front facing areas with hair canvas or a nonwoven interfacing. Follow directions given for *Method 1* on page 136. For additional shape retention, extend the front section of the interfacing to the armhole.

## Stitching and Handling

**Basting.** Although seams may be pinned or basted, be careful to make the pin or needle punctures within the seam allowance. Paper clips are a safe substitute. Or, you may find that you can handle the seaming without pinning or basting, depending on your sewing skill.

**Thread and needle.** Use either silk or heavy-duty mercerized thread for machine stitching. Select size 14 machine needle for medium-weight skins, size 11 needle for fine leather and thread, and size 16 for heavier leather and thread. A wedge-point needle, designed expressly for stitching leather, is available at your Singer Center in the sizes mentioned. The narrow wedge point pierces the leather cleanly, ensuring a neat, uniform stitch.

Regulate the tension to produce a balanced stitch. In most cases the upper tension should be slightly higher for leather than for medium-weight woven fabrics.

**Stitch length and pressure.** Regulate the stitch length to 12 for lightweight and medium-weight leathers, and to 10 for heavier weights. The pressure should fall within the medium range and carry the leather without showing the print of the feed.

**Stitching.** Preshrink straight seam binding and use it for staying seams and points of strain. Hold the tape gently against the upper side of the leather and against the presser foot as you sew the seam. The tape will strengthen the seam and prevent the leather from sticking to the presser foot. Stitch slowly and handle the leather lightly. Do not pull the leather as it passes under the presser foot, for this may stretch it. After the seams are stitched, slash the edges of the tape at even intervals to prevent them from pulling. Be sure your garment fits correctly before you begin stitching because ripped seams have needle holes that will permanently mar the skins.

Corners must be blunt, not pointed. Either round the corners slightly or place two or three stitches across the point to allow sufficient width for turning.

**Seams and seam blending.** To enhance center front and back seams and yoke seams, use welt seams, or press the seam open and top-stitch on each side an equal distance from the seamline.

Blend seams inside collars, cuffs, facings, and similar construction in the usual way. To prevent facings and seams from rolling out of place, glue the seam allowances in place. Use rubber cement, "Sobo" glue, or a similar liquid adhesive suitable for leather, fabric, or a combination of two materials. Spread the glue on the underside of the seam allowance; then finger-press the seam allowance against the garment.

**Darts.** Slash through the center of darts, and press them open to eliminate bulk.

**Lining.** Line the skirt, following the method given on page 98 where lining and skirt are joined only at the waistline.

Avoid facings and hems in a waistcoat or vest. The lining can serve as facing as well as support the suede. See *One-Piece Neckline and Armhole Facing*, page 141. Before joining shoulder and underarm seams, place the suede and lining sections right sides together. Stitch around the neckline, front opening, lower edge, and armholes following the seamline. Blend seams, turn to right side, ease underlining under slightly at the stitching line, and press. Join shoulder and underarm seams of suede with machine stitching, and press seams open. Then, on the lining, fold under the seam allowance on one side and lap it over the opposite seam allowance, and pin. Slip-stitch in place. Top-stitch around the neckline, front opening, lower edge, and armholes, gauging the stitching from ¼ to ⅝ inch from the finished edge.

**Buttonholes.** Machine-worked, hand-worked, or bound buttonholes are suitable. Stay them with a backing of firmly woven muslin or lawn between the facing and top fabric.

If you are making bound buttonholes, follow the *One-Piece Method*. See page 112. Instead of basting the buttonhole strip in place, place cellophane tape across the ends, and use a 12 stitch length in the stitching.

The facing treatment is different from the method used for woven fabrics. Stitch the facing in place in the usual way. Then, from the right side of the garment, machine-stitch around the button-hole just inside the seam on the buttonhole strip and across the ends through the facing. Slash the facing and trim away the suede or leather inside the stitching line.

*Hems.* The depth of the hem should be no greater than 1½ or 2 inches, and the hem must conform exactly to the body of the skirt. Use chalk to mark the hemline on the wrong side of the leather. For an invisible finish, glue the hem in place. See *Seams and Seam Blending* above. Lay the skirt right side down on a flat surface and work from the hem side. Spread glue along the under-side of the hem as far as the fold line. Turn the hem; then finger-press it against the skirt. Begin at the center front or back and work toward the side seams, matching seams and center lines.

*Pressing.* Seams in leather and suede should be pressed with a warm, not hot, iron (do not use steam). Cover the area with brown paper, and press on the wrong side. Seams may also be tapped lightly with a wooden pounding block to compress them.

*Lining.* Suede and leather jackets must be lined. Crepe, faille, and China silk are suggested fabrics.

# FIBERGLASS

Fiberglass is a synthetic fabric that is ideal for curtains, draperies, and bedspreads. It is available in a variety of weaves, either translucent or opaque. It will not shrink, stretch, or sag, and needs no ironing. There is no problem in stitching it when a few simple rules are followed.

Instructions for constructing home furnishings begin on page 338 of this book.

## Preparing to Sew

*Cutting.* To cut a plain fabric, always draw a thread from the fabric to indicate the cutting line. Cut printed designs on the patterns. If the fabric is cut off grain, curtains and draperies will not hang well.

*Lining.* Fiberglass draperies are seldom lined. The translucent beauty of the unlined fabric is preferred by many decorators. If a lining is used, however, it should also be of fiberglass so that it will not shrink, stretch, or sag. When extra opaqueness is desired, make an underdrapery instead of a lining, and hang it from a separate rod so that it can be opened and closed independently.

Be sure to use washable, preshrunk stiffening in the heading.

## Stitching and Handling

*Thread and needle.* Select mercerized, Dacron, Nymo, or Nylex thread for the machine stitching. Use a new, sharp machine needle, size 11 for translucent fiberglass and size 14 for heavy or rough-surfaced fiberglass.

Regulate tensions to produce a balanced stitch.

If the seam puckers, it may be necessary to loosen the upper tension.

*Stitch length and pressure.* A 10 to 12 stitch length is satisfactory for sheer as well as opaque fiberglass. The pressure must be light—no heavier than required to carry the fabric gently and evenly under the presser foot. If the pressure is too heavy, the print of the feed shows on the fabric and the feed may cut the threads of the fiberglass.

*Stitching.* Pin the seam edges together. Stitch slowly and guide the fabric gently behind the presser foot and in front of the needle. Let the machine do the work. When using a straight stitch on a zig-zag machine, use the straight stitch throat plate and presser foot for best results.

To prevent the edges from raveling and to achieve a finished underside, make French seams on all fiberglass fabrics.

It is wise to experiment with stitch length, tension, and pressure, and with guiding the fabric on a swatch of fiberglass before you begin your work. You will find that with a little practice you can handle the fabric expertly.

*Seam finishes.* Seam edges in glass curtains and draperies should be enclosed and do not require finishing. Finish the seam edges of bedspreads with the blindstitch zig-zag.

*Hems.* Make a double-fold hem in sheer fabrics to eliminate the turned raw edge that would normally show through. Pin hems in place before stitching. Stitch hems in sheer fabrics with a straight stitch and hems in heavier and rough-surfaced fabrics with either a straight stitch or the blindstitch zig-zag.

# Hand Sewing—
# Plain and Fancy

HAND SEWING IS STILL AN ESSENTIAL PART of dressmaking. In professional, well-made wearing apparel, hems are finished by hand. In children's clothes and table linens, decorative fashion details are added by hand to provide an attractive accent. To achieve the custom-made look in home decoration, hand sewing is preferred in many areas.

This chapter tells you how to make many of the basic hand stitches. If any of them are unfamiliar to you, practice making them on a swatch of fabric before you attempt to use them in your work. All the decorative or embroidery stitches described here may be used individually or in various combinations to produce a design; they may be worked in matching or contrasting thread, or in two or more colors of thread.

## A Word about Thread

Hems should be finished with mercerized, silk, or synthetic thread, depending on the fabric; the thread should match the fabric exactly in color.

Hand embroidery stitches may be made with single or multiple strands of sewing thread, six-strand floss, synthetic or silk floss, pearl cotton, buttonhole twist, and wool or synthetic yarn. The selection depends on the fabric, the size of the stitch, and the effect desired. Choose colorfast threads to trim children's clothes and household linens that will be laundered.

## Slip Stitch

The slip stitch is almost invisible. It is used when one edge is turned under as in hems, bias binding, curved seams, top facings, coat or suit linings, and similar places.

Baste the folded edge in position. For stitching, use mercerized, silk, or synthetic thread matching the fabric exactly in color. Knot the long end of the thread.

Work toward you, or from right to left, with the hem fold between the thumb and index finger of the left hand. Bring the needle up through the fold. Directly opposite and barely outside the fold, take a stitch, catching only one thread of the fabric; then slip the needle through the fold a stitch length. Continue making the stitches, spacing them from ¼ to ⅜ inch apart. In seams that may be subject to excessive strain, space the stitches a scant ⅛ inch apart. Do not pull the threads taut. When completed, fasten the thread with two tiny backstitches in the hem edge or seam.

## Blind Hemming Stitch

This is the stitch most frequently used for hemming. The edge may be finished with seam binding or edgestitching.

Baste the hem in place. For stitching, use mercerized, silk, or synthetic thread matching the fabric exactly in color. Knot the long end of the thread.

Work toward you, or from right to left, with the hem fold between the thumb and index finger of the left hand. Bring the needle up through the hem edge. Directly opposite and barely outside the hem, take a stitch, catching only one thread of the fabric; then direct the needle diagonally up through the hem edge. Continue making the stitches, spacing them from ¼ to ⅜ inch apart, depending on the fabric. Do not pull the thread taut. When completed, fasten the thread with two tiny backstitches in the hem edge. The stitches are invisible on the right side.

## Hemming or Whipping Stitch

The hemming or whipping stitch is another popular stitch for hemming. The edge may be finished with bias seam binding, edgestitching, or straight seam binding.

Baste the hem in place. For stitching, use mercerized, silk, or synthetic thread matching the fabric exactly in color. Knot the long end of the thread.

Work toward you, or from right to left, with the hem edge between the thumb and index finger of the left hand. Bring the needle up through the edge of the hem and take a stitch in the fabric over the hem edge, catching only a single thread of the fabric; then bring the needle out through

the hem edge. When completed, fasten the thread with two tiny backstitches in the hem edge. The stitch is invisible on the right side and long slanting stitches are visible on the wrong side.

## Overhand Stitch

The overhand stitch is a tiny stitch used to join lace, insertion, and grosgrain ribbon.

For stitching, use a short, fine needle and fine

thread. Knot the long end of the thread.

Place the lace or ribbon right sides together. Pin or baste the edges to prevent them from slipping. Make small over-and-over stitches along the edge of the seam. Space the stitches about 1/16 inch apart.

## Catch Stitch

The catch stitch is used in hemming, in seaming lapped joinings on the underside, in attaching interfacings to garments, and in hand-sewing darts and tucks in suit and coat linings.

Baste the hem, facing, tuck, dart, or edge in place. For stitching, use mercerized, silk, or synthetic thread. Knot the long end of the thread.

Work from left to right, with the needle pointed to the left. Hold the hem edge between the thumb and index finger of the left hand. Make a stitch in the hem or facing, catching one or two threads in the top layer of fabric; then make a stitch barely outside the hem edge, catching only a single thread of the under layer of fabric. Alternate the stitches along the edge in a zig-zag fashion. The threads will cross between the stitches. When finished, fasten the thread with tiny backstitches in the hem.

When using a catch stitch to sew darts and tucks in coat and suit linings, work on the right side of the fabric and make the stitches through all thicknesses of fabric, near the top fold for the tuck or dart.

## Backstitch

The backstitch is a small stitch that is used when top stitching by machine would be too harsh—for example, in the final stitching of the zipper in sheer, delicate fabrics or fine woolens. It is also used in other areas of dress construction where machine stitching would be difficult (for example, in lapped seams in interfacings) and in the repairing of ripped seams.

For stitching, use the same kind of thread you used for the machine stitching. Fasten the thread with two backstitches on the underside. Work toward you, or from right to left. Bring the needle up through the fabric to the right side. Insert it one or two fabric threads behind the place where the thread came out, and bring the needle forward and out a scant ⅛ inch from the backstitch. Begin each additional stitch just outside the preceding stitch. (The stitches on the underside will be twice as long as those on the top side.) Make the stitches through all layers of fabric. When completed, fasten the thread on the underside with two tiny backstitches.

## Running Stitch

The running stitch is used for seaming, tucking, mending, gathering, and other kinds of delicate sewing.

For stitching, use a long, slender needle, size 7 or 8, and mercerized, synthetic, or silk thread matching the fabric exactly in color. Knot the long end of the thread.

Work from right to left, with the fabric edge between the thumb and index finger of the left

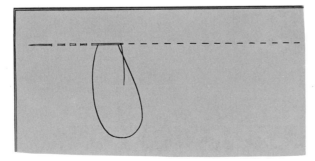

hand. Weave the point of the needle in and out of the fabric five or six times before pulling the thread through. Make small, even stitches. When finished, fasten the thread with one or two tiny backstitches.

## Handpicked Stitch

Handpicked stitching adds a smart touch to collars, cuffs, lapels, pockets, and fashion seams of coats, suits, and tailored dresses. The garment should be completed before you add this fashion detail.

On the right side, baste the line for the stitches ⅜ to 1 inch from the finished edge, depending on the fabric, the design of the garment, and personal preference. Use a gauge to measure the distance as you baste.

For stitching, use buttonhole twist matching the fabric exactly in color. Knot the long end of the thread.

Work toward you with the needle pointed in the same direction. Bring the needle up through the interfacing and top layer of fabric. Insert it 1/16 inch behind the place where the thread came out, through the top layer of fabric and interfacing; then bring it out a generous ⅜ inch from the backstitch. (With this spacing, the finished stitches should be about ¼ inch apart.) Do not draw the threads taut; the backstitch should lie beadlike on the fabric surface. Remove the bastings as you work. When completed, fasten the thread between the layers of fabric with two tiny backstitches. The stitches are not visible on the underside.

**If your costume has lapels,** you must transfer the stitches to the opposite side of the seam at the

## Buttonhole Stitch

The buttonhole stitch is used for a decorative finish on edges as well as for hand-worked buttonholes. As a decorative finish, the stitches may be almost any depth; in buttonholes, however, they should be from 1/16 inch to 1/8 inch in depth and closely spaced.

For the stitching, see *A Word about Thread*, page 228. Work from right to left. Hold fabric, needle, and thread in the position shown in the illustration.

With the right side of the fabric up, bring the edge over the first finger of the left hand. Take two backstitches at the edge to fasten the thread. Bring the thread to the left and then to the right to form a loop around the edge where the stitch will be made. Insert the point of the needle from the underside up through the fabric, keeping the thread behind both the point and the eye of the needle. Hold the loop with the left thumb and pull the needle up through the fabric, then away from you to place the purl of the stitch on the edge of the fabric. Keep the stitches as even as possible.

turn of the lapel. At this point, and on the backstitch, bring the needle through all layers of fabric to the opposite side of the seamline and continue making the same stitches.

## Padding Stitch

The padding stitch is used primarily in tailoring to hold two layers of fabric together to prevent slipping—for example, to hold the interfacing in place along the roll line of lapels and collars.

Baste the interfacing in place. Work toward you and on the wrong side, with the needle pointed to the left. For stitching, use thread matching the fabric exactly in color. Hold the work between the thumb and fingers of the left hand and take a short stitch from right to left through the interfacing

## Blanket Stitch

The blanket stitch is often used to decorate children's clothes, lingerie, and household linens. It is an excellent edge finish for babies' receiving blankets, sacques, and kimonos. It is also used for hand appliqué.

Fold and baste the hem.

For stitching, select thread appropriate for the

and fabric, catching only one thread in the fabric. Space the stitches about ⅜ inch apart. The long slanting stitches on the wrong side are visible but the short crosswise stitches on the right side are not.

fabric. Take two backstitches on the underside in the hem fold to fasten the thread. Work from left to right, with the right side of the edge toward you. Hold the thread down with the thumb and insert the needle from the right side, barely catching the top edge of the hem; then bring it out from under the edge and over the thread. Draw the thread through by pulling it toward you, forming the blanket stitch. Do not pull the thread taut. When completed, fasten the thread on the underside with two tiny backstitches in the lower edge of the hem. The stitches may be evenly spaced, closely spaced in groups of three, or varied in length to form a pattern or a fan-shaped design.

## Chain Stitch

The chain stitch is an outline stitch used in children's and babies' clothes as well as in linens and lingerie.

Knot the long end of the thread. Work from right to left. Bring the needle up through the fabric to the right side. Hold the thread against the fabric with the left thumb. Insert the needle close to the point where the thread came out and bring it out over the thread just a stitch length to form a loop. Keep the thread to the left of the needle. Begin each successive stitch inside the loop to form a chain. The length of the stitch will depend on the fabric. Do not pull the thread taut. When finished, fasten the thread on the underside with two tiny backstitches.

## Cross-Stitch

The cross-stitch is one of the oldest decorative stitches. It may be used on household linens, blouses, children's clothes, and collar and cuff sets as well as on canvas in needle-tapestry work.

The cross-stitch is usually made over a stamped transfer design; however, if the design of the fabric is a small ¼-inch check, you may use it as a pattern. If you are working with hopsacking or a

similar coarse weave, you can make even cross-stitches by counting the fabric threads for each stitch.

Work from left to right with the needle pointed toward you. Bring the needle up through the fabric to the right side of the lower left corner of the cross, leaving a thread about ½ inch long; catch that thread under the stitches as they are made to fasten it. Carry the thread diagonally to the right, insert the needle in the upper right corner, and bring it out at the lower left corner of the next cross. A diagonal stitch will appear on the right side and a straight stitch on the underside. Continue making the same stitches across the work. Then work back over the stitches in the opposite direction to form the crosses. Be sure that the crosses touch. The stitches should be firm so that the threads lie smooth on the surface.

## Featherstitch

The featherstitch, also known as the "brier" stitch, is appropriate for decorating household linens, children's and babies' clothes, and is used in stitching darts and tucks in suit and coat linings.

Baste or chalk the line of the stitch on the right side of the fabric. Work toward you and bring the needle up through the fabric to the right side where the stitch is to begin. Hold the thread down with the thumb and take a small stitch on the right side of the line, slanting the needle toward the line and passing the thread under the needle. Make the same kind of stitch on the left side of the line, slanting the needle toward the line. Continue alternating the stitches on the right and left, keeping the stitch length, spacing, and slant of the needle the same in each stitch. Draw the thread firmly enough to keep it flat, yet loosely enough to curve it slightly. When completed, fasten the thread on the underside with two tiny backstitches.

## French Knot

The French knot is a familiar embroidery stitch in the center of flowers. Groups of knots are also used to form designs. They are generally placed close together and combined with other stitches.

Knot the long end of the thread. Bring the needle up through the fabric at the point where the knot is to be made. Hold the needle close to the fabric and wind the thread two or three times around the point. Hold the thread taut around the needle and insert the needle through the fabric close to the point where the thread came

out. Place your thumb over the knot to hold the twist in place and pull the thread through to the underside, bringing the knot snugly against the fabric. Then bring the needle up through the fabric for the next French knot. When the work is finished, fasten the thread on the underside with two tiny backstitches.

## Lazy Daisy

The lazy daisy is a loop stitch used to form a daisy petal.

For stitching, select a thread size that is appropriate for the size of the petal.

Bring the needle up through the fabric at the center end of the petal. Loop the thread to the left. Insert the needle close to the point where the thread came out, and then bring it out over the thread at the opposite end of the petal. Insert the needle barely outside the petal loop and bring it out again at the center where the next petal begins. Do not draw the thread taut. When the lazy daisy is finished, fasten the thread on the underside with two tiny backstitches. French knots placed in the center enhance the design.

## Outline Stitch

The outline stitch may be used to form a border, to make flower stems and leaf veins, or to outline a design.

Lightly mark or transfer the design to the fabric. Knot the long end of the thread.

Work from left to right with the needle pointed to the left. Bring the needle up through the fabric from the underside. Make small backstitches, lapping each stitch slightly by bringing the needle out about 1/16 inch behind the previous stitch. Hold the thread down with the thumb as you pull the threads through. Keep the thread above the needle; insert the needle and bring it out on the line of the design. When completed, fasten the thread on the underside with two backstitches.

## Hand Hemstitching

Hemstitching is used in table linens, lingerie, and babies' clothes.

Measure the hem allowance and draw about three or four threads from the fabric parallel to the hem. The number of threads drawn will depend on the weave of the fabric and the width desired for the hemstitching. Fold the fabric edge under ¼ inch; then fold and baste the hem, keeping the folded edge barely below the drawn work.

For stitching, use a fine mercerized thread. Knot the long end of the thread. Work from right to left on the wrong side. Bring the needle up through the hem edge so that the knot will be between the hem and top fabric. Slide the needle under several threads of the fabric; loop the thread to the left under the point of the needle. Pull the thread through and draw up the stitch tightly by

pulling the thread toward you. Then take a stitch in the edge of the hem fold, catching only a single thread of the fabric. Repeat the stitch until one edge is finished. Keep the same number of fabric threads in each group.

**For double hemstitching,** turn the work and make the same kinds of stitches on the opposite edge, picking up the same threads in the fabric to form a bar. Fasten the thread on the underside with two small fastening stitches.

## Fagoting

Fagoting is a decorative stitch used to join sections in blouses, dresses, lingerie, collars, and cuffs.

Fold under the seam allowance on the cut edges, and press. Hand-baste the folded edges to heavy paper for support. The distance between the edges is the width of the fagoting.

For stitching, use pearl cotton, buttonhole twist, or a similar thread. Knot the long end of the thread. Bring the needle up through the fabric fold. Carry the thread diagonally across the opening, and insert the needle up through the fabric fold on the opposite side; pull the thread through. Pass the needle under the thread, diagonally across the opening, and up through the fabric on the opposite side. Continue alternating the stitches across the opening. Evenly spaced stitches are essential. When finished, fasten the thread on the underside. Remove the basted paper, and press.

# Decorative Touches

A DECORATIVE TOUCH THAT ADDS INTEREST and femininity to your costume marks you as a competent, creative seamstress. It transforms a simple dress into a special dress, a plain-looking blouse into a lovely one, and much more.

The many fashion "extras" you can apply in sewing are described in this chapter. They include tucks, ruffles, shirring, cording, appliqué, smocking, quilting, beads and sequins, lace edging and insertion, and braid. Some of them can be used in home decorating as well as in wearing apparel.

## TUCKS

Tucks are always in fashion in dresses, blouses, neckwear, children's clothes, and lingerie. They are equally at home in sheer and heavy fabrics. They may be very narrow, as a dainty "pin tuck," or an inch or more wide. They may be machine-stitched or hand-stitched.

Since the beauty of a tuck depends on its absolute accuracy, you must stitch exactly along the woven thread of the fabric. The Tucker and Edge Stitcher are two accessories that will help you. The Tucker makes tucks from ⅛ to 1 inch in width and ensures tucks of equal width and spacing from start to finish; the Edge Stitcher guides the width for tucks from "pin" width to ¼ inch. See pages 286 and 284. Both are timesavers and contribute a great deal to the attractiveness of your work.

### To Estimate Fabric Width Requirements

If the pattern calls for tucks, it will allow sufficient width for the size of the tuck specified. If you decide to add tucks to the dress as a point of interest, you will need extra fabric as follows:

When the tucks and spaces are equal, fabric twice the finished width is required. When the fold of the tuck touches the stitching of the previous tuck, as in a blind tuck, three times the finished width is required.

If an entire section such as a pocket, yoke, or collar, is to be pin-tucked, you should *tuck the fabric first and then cut out the section according to the pattern.*

### To Mark the Position of Tucks

Tucks are usually made on the lengthwise grain of the fabric since it is always firmer than the crosswise grain and lends itself well to tucking. Occasionally, however, a design calls for crosswise tucking to emphasize style lines.

Draw a single thread from the fabric to mark the position for each tuck. Fold and press the fabric on the drawn thread the entire length of the tuck. If tucks are ¼ inch or wider, hand-baste along the line of each tuck to prevent the layers of fabric from shifting during the stitching.

### To Stitch Tucks

#### Rules to Remember

Always stitch tucks so that the stitching uppermost under the needle is visible when the garment is worn (unless you are applying lace in the tucking operation as on page 237). When tucks are used on both sides of the garment section, they are turned in opposite directions from the center, and you must alternate the direction of the stitching on the right and left sides.

Be sure that tensions are balanced. Since tucks are top stitched, they require a shorter stitch than that used for inside, straight seams. See the *Fabric, Thread, Needle, and Stitch Length Chart*, page 24. The thread should either blend perfectly with the fabric in color and texture or be a decided contrast.

Always make a few practice tucks in a swatch of your fabric to be certain that the stitch length, tuck size, and spacing are satisfactory.

### Pin Tucks

Pin tucks, as their name implies, are only as wide as a pin. They are generally spaced about 3/16 inch apart in groups of three or five, with a wider space between each group. Lace is often inserted between the groups.

Mark the position for each tuck, following the instructions given above. Adjust the Edge Stitcher, see page 285, so that the stitching falls very close to the folded edge of the fabric. Stitch slowly, guiding the fabric. Press.

When the tucks extend only a few inches into the garment section, as in the yoke of a baby's dress or shoulder of a blouse or dress, pull the threads through to the underside and tie the two threads together at the end of each tuck.

### Hand-Stitched Tucks

Hand-stitched tucks are found in babies' clothes and sheer blouses.

Mark the position for each tuck, following the instructions given on page 235. Hand-stitch, using a long, slender needle, fine thread, and a very small running stitch. When finished, fasten the thread on the underside of the fabric. Press.

### Tucks and Space of Equal Width

When spacing and tucks are equal, you will need twice the finished width in the fabric. The space between the markings for each tuck is four times the width of the finished tuck, or 1 inch for a ¼-inch tuck.

Mark the position for the tucks, following the instructions on page 235. Stitch, using either the *Edge Stitcher* or *Tucker*. See pages 285 and 286. Press.

### Blind Tucks

In blind tucking, the fold for the tuck touches the stitching of the previous tuck. The tucks may be of almost any width; the 1-inch tuck is illustrated. The space between the markings for each tuck is three times the width of the finished tuck.

Mark the position for the first tuck, following the instructions given on page 235.

On most fabrics, the space scale on the Tucker will mark the position of the second and succeeding tucks as the present one is being stitched. If the fabric is one that the scale will not mark, you must mark the position for all the tucks before you begin to stitch. See *Tucker* page 286. Use the Tucker and adjust it for the desired width of tuck and spacing. Stitch slowly, guiding the fabric. Press.

### Decorative Tucks

Decorative tucks are made by using the Tucker on a zig-zag machine.

Mark the position for the first tuck, following the instructions given on page 235. Adjust the Tucker for the desired width of the tuck and spacing. Select a stitch pattern appropriate for tucks and stitch slowly, guiding the fabric. Press.

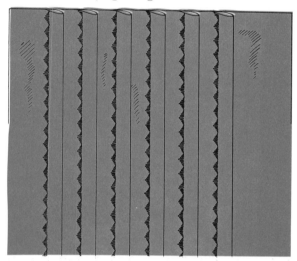

### Tucks with Lace

You can make ¼-inch tucks and apply lace underneath with a single line of stitching when you use the Edge Stitcher. *(Continued)*

Select lace wide enough to extend beyond the tuck but not dwarf it. Mark the position for each tuck, following the instructions on page 235.

Use the Edge Stitcher with the lug adjusted far enough to the left to place the stitching on the selvage of the lace. Insert the folded edge from the right in slot 5, and the lace edge from the left in slot 1. Stitch slowly, guiding the fabric and the lace. Press the tuck over the lace.

### Smocked Tucking

Smocked tucking, a variation of straight tucking, provides a texture contrast on the yoke or pockets of a dress or blouse made of plain fabric.

Tuck the fabric on the lengthwise grain, making ⅛- or ¼-inch tucks spaced ¼ inch apart, using the Edge Stitcher. See page 284.

For the crosswise stitching, use the Edge Stitcher. Adjust it so that each side is the same distance from the needle. Alternate the direction of each row of stitching, keeping the rows the same distance apart. The Edge Stitcher turns the tucks in the same direction of the stitching, creating a smocked effect.

When the stitching is completed, press. Cut the tucked section by the plain pattern piece.

### Shell Tucks

Shell tucks are an attractive treatment for babies' dresses and blouses. Usually ⅛ to ¼ inch in width, they can be stitched by hand or by machine. Use silk, batiste or a similar soft fabric.

*Hand Stitched.* Mark the position for the tucks as instructed on page 235. Machine-stitch the tucks, using a line of straight stitching and either the Tucker or Edge Stitcher to keep the stitching an even distance from the edge.

Lightly mark the size of each shell or scallop at equal intervals—generally ¼ to ⅜ inch apart. Use a fine needle and knot the end of the thread. Bring the needle up through the tuck at the first marking; take two stitches across the tuck, drawing the thread tightly to form a scallop. Slip the needle between the two layers of fabric in the tuck and bring it out at the marking for the next stitch. When finished, fasten the thread on the underside of the fabric. Press.

*Machine Stitched.* Mark the position for each tuck as instructed on page 235. Baste if necessary. Set selectors on the machine for the blindstitch zig-zag. Make a test on a sample of your fabric to find the right needle thread tension, stitch length, and stitch width.

Place the prefolded tuck under the presser foot, with the fold toward the left. Stitch slowly, guiding the fabric by hand so that the sideward stitches do not pierce the folded edge. Press.

### Scalloped Tucks

Dainty, scalloped tucks are used extensively as self-trimming on blouses, dresses, lingerie, and children's clothes.

In your planning, allow sufficient width in the fabric for the tucks, as instructed on page 235, plus an additional ½ inch for seam allowances on the edge of the scallops.

Fold and crease the fabric on the line for the tuck, with right sides together. Trace the scallop on the fabric, placing the edge of the scallop ¼ inch from the fold to allow for seaming.

Use a short stitch and the Quilter if you have one. (The open construction and short toe of the Quilter greatly facilitate the stitching of small scallops.)

Stitch around the scallops exactly on the traced line, taking one stitch across the point between each scallop. This extra stitch gives you width when cutting and prevents pulling at the point between the scallops in the finished work.

On small scallops, blend the seam allowances to a scant ⅛ inch; on large scallops, blend them a generous ⅛ inch, and blend one edge shorter than the other. Slash at the point almost to the stitch-ing. Cut notches in the seam edges at evenly spaced intervals. Press.

Turn the scallops to the right side. Gently work the seam edges between the thumb and finger to bring the stitching to the very edge. Baste the edges with silk thread to retain the shape of the scallop until after pressing.

Using the desired width, stitch the tucks an even distance from the edge with a line of straight stitching. Press.

You can also stitch small scallops easily on the zig-zag machine. Set the selectors for the scallop pattern. The stitch length and stitch width vary the length and depth of the scallop; select the length and width you want. As you stitch, the fabric passes straight under the presser foot, and the needle follows a scallop pattern. Always start each row of stitching at the beginning of a scallop unit. See page 266 for instructions. Press, blend seams, and turn the scallops as instructed above.

## To Press Tucks

To imbed the stitching, press the underside of each tuck in the same position as it was stitched. Then on the wrong side, press the tucks to one side, flat against the fabric. (Normally, tucks are turned away from the center of the garment.) Cover the fabric with the appropriate press cloth and use the amount of moisture required.

Ruffles add a feminine touch to blouses and dresses. They are also a pleasing trimming on lingerie and children's clothes, and on curtains and bedspreads.

## To Prepare the Fabric

Ruffles on garments are usually cut on the crosswise grain or true bias. Ruffles on sheer curtains are cut on the lengthwise grain to keep seaming to a minimum. The texture of the fabric makes a difference in the fullness—soft and medium-weight fabrics are more adaptable to ruffles than firm fabrics.

Double or triple fullness may be required for the ruffle depending on the width of the ruffle as well as the texture of the fabric. Wide ruffles require more fullness than narrow ruffles. It is always wise to cut and ruffle a little more length than the estimated requirement.

Cut the fabric two to three times longer than the length of the finished ruffle.

Before gathering the ruffle, finish the outer edge either by machine, using the Hemmer Foot; by hand; or by one of the pattern stitches on the zig-zag machine that is suitable for an edge finish. You may apply lace at the same time you machine-stitch the hem.

## To Gather the Ruffle

The Ruffler enables you to gather the fabric quickly, easily, and evenly. See *Ruffler*, page 280, for instructions.

After you have adjusted the setting of the Ruffler, test the fullness on a swatch of the same fabric you are working with.

To ruffle organdy or chintz, dampen the fabric along the seamline with a small, moist sponge and gather while damp.

## To Apply the Ruffle

### To an Edge

Pin the ruffle to the edge, right sides together, extending the straight edge a scant ½ inch beyond the gathering stitches of the ruffle. Pin at close intervals. Baste if necessary. Stitch with the ruffle side up, just beyond the gathering stitches.

Trim the seam allowance on the ruffle to ⅛ inch. Fold the straight edge under ⅛ inch, then fold it over the seam edges to the stitching line on the underside, enclosing the cut edge. Pin. Stitch near the first fold. Press. Turn the ruffle away from the garment and press the seam toward the garment.

The fabric may be gathered and stitched to a straight edge in one operation. See page 281.

### For a Lingerie Edge

Pin the ruffle to the edge, right sides together, keeping the edges even. Stitch with the ruffle uppermost under the needle.

Trim the seam allowance to ¼ inch. Overcast the cut edges together, using the blindstitch zigzag. Use a fine stitch length and medium stitch width.

### In a Straight Seam

Pin the ruffle to the seam edge, right sides together, extending the straight edge a scant ½ inch beyond the gathering stitches of the ruffle. Stitch from the ruffle side on the gathering stitches. Press the seam.

Place the attached ruffle over the second seam edge, right sides together. Pin at close intervals. Baste if necessary.

Place the work under the needle with the first line of stitching uppermost so that you can use it as a guide. Stitch barely beyond the previous line of stitching. Press. The stitching is not visible on the right side.

### To a Faced Edge

When a ruffle is added as a decorative trim to the edge of a collar or cuff, it is set between two layers of fabric and often must be eased around a corner.

Pin the ruffle to the outer edge of the top collar or cuff, right sides together. About ½ inch on each side of the corner, ease the gathers closer together with the thumb as you pin. This will give the extra fullness needed around the corner. Baste if necessary. With the ruffle side up, stitch on the gathering stitches. Press the seam.    *(Continued)*

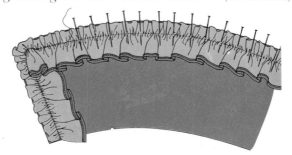

241

Place the edge of the attached ruffle over the undercollar or cuff, right sides together, matching markings. Pin and baste, leaving the neckline edge, or lower edge of the cuff, open. Smooth out the ruffle so that only the seam allowance is caught in the stitching.

Place the first line of stitching uppermost under the needle; stitch barely beyond it. Press the seam.

Trim the seam allowances on the undercollar and ruffle to ⅛ inch and the seam allowance on the top collar to ¼ inch. Clip off the corners and notch into the seam allowances on the outside curve. Turn the collar to the right side, and press.

## To Attach Pinafore Ruffles

Shoulder ruffles in the bodice of a pinafore are shaped at each end; that is, they are wider through the center and taper almost to a point at the ends.

Therefore, they must be gathered to fit the bodice length. You will often find it necessary to adjust the fullness of the ruffle after you have gathered it.

Loosen the upper tension slightly on your machine and use the Ruffler to gather the fabric. See page 280 for instructions on using the Ruffler. Leave long threads at each end of the seam. (Do not forget to return the tension to its previous setting.)

Pin the ruffle to the pinafore, matching markings. Work from the center to the outer edges, and adjust the ruffle to fit the pinafore by easing the fabric back on the bobbin thread.

Stitch and blend the seam allowances as instructed above for a ruffle applied to a faced edge.

## To Attach Ruffle with Heading

Finish both edges before gathering the ruffle. See *Ruffle with Heading,* page 281 for instructions.

Turn the straight edge of the garment to the underside and make a ⅛-inch double fold. Press. Pin the ruffle to the right side of the edge at closely spaced intervals, centering the gathering stitches over the double fold. Stitch from the ruffle side on the previous line of stitching. The folded edge and ruffle are held in place with one line of stitching.

# SHIRRING

Rows of shirring often appear as a styling point at the shoulder line, waistline, and lower edge of sleeves. Sometimes an entire section, such as a yoke or pocket, may be shirred for a decorative effect.

Soft fabrics—batiste, voile, silk, net, and fabrics of similar textures—lend themselves better to shirring than firm fabrics. Crisp sheers, however, can be shirred if they are steam-pressed to soften the finish and stitched while damp. The true bias or crosswise grain of the fabric is more easily shirred than the lengthwise grain. Shirring by machine is quick and produces strong, even stitches.

## Shirring with the Gathering Foot

You can achieve many lovely effects with simple rows of evenly spaced shirring made with the Gathering Foot. For instructions on how to use foot and the stitch length required, see page 285.

Draw a single thread or crease the fabric on the crosswise grain at selected intervals for the spacing desired. Stitch on each of these lines, using the Gathering Foot. If you are spacing your rows ½ inch apart, you can gauge the distance by the edge of the foot.

When you are shirring an entire section such as a yoke or pocket, shirr the fabric, then cut the section according to the pattern. Always test the fullness on a swatch of your fabric before working on the garment.

### Waffle Shirring

Waffle shirring gives texture interest to smooth-surfaced fabrics. It has a broad application on cottons, silks, woolens, and rayons, and is particularly interesting for details on children's dresses, blouses, and lingerie.

With the Gathering Foot, stitch on the crosswise grain of the fabric and then on the length-wise grain. Use a stitch length short enough to produce only a slight fullness.

## Controlled Shirring

When a section of a seam is to be shirred and stitched to a straight seam, the shirring must be "controlled" so that the seams, when joined, are of the same length. See *Gathering to Control Fullness*, page 105.

Use a stay of the same fabric to prevent strain on the shirring. Cut the stay ½ inch deeper than the rows of shirring and wide enough to fit across the entire garment section when shirred.

Place the stay over the wrong side of the shirred section, keeping the seam edges even. Pin and baste in position. Stitch the stay into the seam when the garment sections are joined.

## Shirring with Elastic Thread

Elastic shirring is appropriate for lingerie, children's clothes, and washable skirts. It requires no special machine accessory.

Wind the bobbin with elastic thread, using the bobbin winder on the machine. The elastic thread will stretch slightly as it is wound on the bobbin. If you have a *Touch & Sew* machine, wind the bobbin by hand, stretching the elastic thread slightly. For a heavy fabric where greater strength is required, wind double strands of elastic thread on the bobbin. Use mercerized thread for the top threading of the machine.

Select a 10 to 12 stitch length, depending on the fabric. Always test the fullness on a swatch of the same fabric used in the garment. In stitching the second and subsequent rows, stretch the elastic in the previous rows as you sew so that the shirring will be even. Rows spaced ¼ inch apart may be gauged by the edge of the presser foot.

At each end of the stitching, tie the elastic and needle threads together by forming a single knot in the two strands of thread; use a pin to set the knot tightly against the fabric.

## CORDING

Cording is a versatile and handsome detail in dressmaking and an excellent finish for slipcovers, bedspreads, and decorative pillows. It is made by covering a length of cord with a bias strip of either the same color as your work at hand or a contrasting color.

Corded seams may be either delicate or bold,

depending on the size of the cord. If you are going to use corded seams, make a corded "welting," which can be stitched into the seam or onto an edge. If you are going to use the cording for button loops, trimming, or frogs, you will make what is called "tubular" cording. Instructions for both are given here. But first you must cut and join your bias strips.

## Cutting Bias Strips

The true bias is the diagonal line of a square of fabric. Fold the crosswise grain of the fabric to the lengthwise grain; this forms a true bias. Cut along the fold.

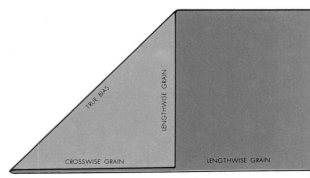

How wide to make your bias strips depends on the size of the filler cord. Cut the strips 1¼ inches plus three times the width of the cord. Use a ruler and measure the required width from the true bias edge of the fabric. Mark the line with tailor's chalk. Measure and mark as many strips as you will need, then cut on the markings.

## Joining Bias Strips

If you need only a short length of cording, avoid piecing it; however, if you need a long, continuous length, you will have to join bias strips.

All bias strips are joined on the lengthwise grain so that the seams will be less noticeable. If one end of your bias strip is on the crosswise grain, fold this fabric end on the lengthwise grain and cut.

Join the lengthwise ends; offset the width of the joining seam and stitch, taking a ¼-inch seam. Be careful to match any prominent weave, stripe, or design of the fabric. Press the seams open.

## Corded Seams

### Covering the Cord

Replace the presser foot with the Zipper Foot and adjust it to the left of the needle.

Bring the bias strip around the cord, right side

out, keeping the seam edges even. Use a slightly longer stitch than that ordinarily used for seaming the fabric. Stitch close to the cord, but do not crowd the stitching against the cord. You have now formed a "welt." Press the stitching.

A chain stitch is an ideal stitch for fabrics that are cut on the bias since the loop formation of the stitches makes them less taut than regular straight stitches. If your machine has Chain Stitch Accessories, refer to the instruction book accompanying the machine and to page 63.

**If sheer fabric is used** to cover the cord, underline the bias strip with an opaque fabric, such as taffeta or polished cotton, that matches the sheer fabric in color. Cut bias strips of the underlining. Place the sheer bias strip, right side up, over the right side of the underlining and handle the two as one in covering the cord. Follow the above procedure.

### Applying the Cording to a Straight Seam

Pin the cording to the right side of the single seam edge, keeping the previous line of stitching over the seamline. Adjust the Zipper Foot to the right of the needle. Stitch with the same stitch length used when covering the cord. Press the stitching.

Pin and baste the second seam edge over the cording, right sides together. Place the work under the needle with the first stitching uppermost so that you can use it as a guide. Stitch, *crowding the stitching between the cord and the previous line of stitching.* Press. All stitching is on the underside of the finished garment.

### Applying the Cording to Curves
**Inside curves.** See *Corded Neckline,* page 146.

**Outside curves.** Pin the cording to the right side of the garment, keeping the previous line of stitching on the seamline. Clip into the corded seam allowance almost to the stitching so that the cord will lie smooth around the curve. Baste, if necessary. Adjust the Zipper Foot to the right of the needle. Stitch, using a stitch shorter than that for straight seams. Press.

Pin and baste the facing over the cording, right sides together. Place the work under the needle with the first line of stitching uppermost so that you can use it as a guide. Stitch, crowding the stitching between the cord and the previous line of stitching. Press.

Trim the corded seam allowance to ⅛ inch and the garment and facing seam allowances to ¼ inch. Notch the seam allowance on the curve at regular intervals. Press. Turn the facing to the underside. Fold on the seamline and press. Finish the free edge of the facing. All stitching is on the underside of the finished garment.

### Applying the Cording to Square Corners
Pin the cording to the right side of a single seam edge, keeping the previous line of stitching on the seamline. At the corner, slash the bias edges almost to the stitching. Stitch the seam as instructed for a straight seam; take one stitch diagonally across the corner for a smooth turning. Press.

Lay the facing over the cording with the right sides together, and pin. Place the work under the

Use a filler cord twice the length of the bias strip. Machine-stitch the center of the cord to the wrong side of the pointed end. Stitch from the point to about ⅜ inch from it.

Turn about ⅜ inch of the pointed end and the filler cord to the right side of the bias, then fold the bias in half around the cord. The remaining half of the cord extends from the point.

Adjust the Zipper Foot to the right of the needle. Use a short stitch. To avoid stitching the turned-under point, form a funnel at the point and taper it for about 1 inch; then crowd the stitching against the cord and, at the same time, stretch the bias slightly. One half of the filler cord is covered and one half extends beyond the funneled end. Press, then trim the seam allowances to ⅛ inch.

(If your machine has Chain Stitch Accessories, use them for stitching fabrics that are cut on the bias. See page 63.)

Work the bias back over the extended cord while pulling the encased cord. *Do not twist.* The

the stitching between the cord and the previous line of stitching. Press.

Cut diagonally across the corner close to the stitching. Trim the corded seam allowance to ⅛ inch and the garment and facing seam allowances to ¼ inch. Press, then turn to the right side and press.

## TUBULAR CORDING

### To Make Tubular Cording

Cut a true bias strip 1 inch wide plus three times the width of the filler cord. Cut one end to a point.

stitches will not break if you have used a short stitch and have stretched the bias in the stitching.

## Button Loops

Button loops are in and out of fashion. When they are "in," they may be found at openings in the neckline, sleeves, and front bodice; in jackets and in lingerie. Ball and half-ball buttons are appropriate for this type of closing.

Always make a test button loop in a swatch of your fabric before working on the garment.

### Length and Spacing of Button Loops

To determine the length and spacing of button loops, make a paper diagram. Draw a straight line ⅝ inch from the edge to represent the seamline. Draw a second line in the seam allowance, ¼ inch from the first line and parallel to it to represent the position of the loop ends.

Place the exact center of the button on the seamline. Bring the tubular cording around the top edge of the button *with the seam to the inside of the loop.* Pin the end of the cording on the marking you made ¼ inch from the seamline. Form the loop to the left, around the button and back to the seam ¼-inch line. Pin. Mark the tubular cording at the ¼-inch line as illustrated. *This is the length for each button loop.*

Mark the position for the outer edge of the loop at the seamline, above and below the button. *This is the spacing between each loop.*

Measure the space and mark the fabric at these intervals. Measure the determined amount for each loop and mark the tubular cording at these intervals. Clip through the seam allowance and into the cord at each marking, but not far enough to separate the loops.

### Stitching of Button Loops

Turn the garment to the right side. Baste or draw a line in the seam allowance, ¼ inch from the seamline (⅜ inch from seam edge). Lightly mark the spacing for the button loop as determined on the paper diagram. Be sure to make your marks within the seam allowance so that you do not mar the garment. If interfacing is used, baste it to the wrong side of the garment.

Form the button loops between the markings, extending the ends to the guideline in the seam allowance, ¼ inch from the seamline. (The loops are formed away from the opening.) Pin the loops in place at the seamline with fine needles. The outer edges of the loops should touch. Tack the loops together so that they hold their shape until the stitching is completed. Stitch the loops to the garment 1/16 inch outside the seamline. This stitching is not visible in the finished work.

Pin and baste the facing over the garment, right side together. Place the work under the needle with the previous stitching uppermost so that you can use it as a guide. Stitch on the ⅝-inch seamline to conceal the previous line of stitching.

Trim the facing seam allowance to ⅛ inch and the garment seam allowance to ¼ inch. Press.

Turn the facing to the underside. Fold on the seamline, and press. When the facing is turned, the loops will extend beyond the opening edge.

## Frogs

Tubular cording may be looped into many interesting designs to form frogs.

Loop tubular cording into the desired design, keeping the seam on the underside. Determine the length needed for each loop and pin-mark the cord-

ing at these intervals. Do not cut. Allow a ¼-inch seam allowance at each end. Pull out the cord at the ends and clip off ¼ inch.

Form the first loop and insert a pin up from the underside to hold the loop in place. Then slip each consecutive loop over the end of the pin as illustrated. Leave the last loop free to slip over the button.

Tack the loops together at the crossing on the underside, concealing the end. Make the tack through the first two loops and catch only the underside of the third loop. Determine the length required to slip over the button, then form the last loop and tack it to the underside, concealing the end.

Make a frog for each side of the opening. Pin them on the right side of the garment, then tack them in place on the underside. Use half-ball, full-ball, and shank buttons with frogs.

## Buttons

To make buttons of tubular cording, fold under the end, then wind the cording into a circle the desired size, keeping the seam on the underside. Pin through the side to hold the cording in place and hand-stitch it on the underside. Bring the outer end to the underside and tack. Sew the buttons on the garment with a thread shank.

## Other Tubular Trimming

You can make tubular scrolls. Follow the instructions above for the button; however, allow enough tubular cording for two buttons. Begin at the center of the cording; at one end wind the cording clockwise and at the other end wind it counterclockwise.

You can loop tubular cording into a graceful design and apply it to your dress as you would braid. You can also use it for spaghetti trimming in belts and bows.

Shoulder straps made of tubular cording are practical and attractive on sunback dresses and evening gowns. The straps may be looped together as illustrated or used as a single or double strand.

## APPLIQUÉ

Appliqué is the loving touch in sewing. It offers an unlimited opportunity for self-expression and adds beauty and interest to wearing apparel, linens, and fabric furnishings.

You can create your own design or buy pattern motifs and appliqué transfers ready for tracing. Fabrics of like textures or of different textures and weaves combine equally well.

Printed linen handkerchiefs or drapery fabric, chintz, and other fabrics with a definite design, make interesting appliqués.

Appliqué may be done by machine or by hand. Machine appliqué, however, is preferred since the work may be accomplished with greater ease and accuracy. The zig-zag machine ensures close evenly spaced stitches and enables you to stitch many intricate designs, too difficult for hand work.

## Transferring the Design

Transfer the design on a swatch of fabric slightly larger than the design, using one of the methods given below:

1. If you are using a hot-iron transfer, carefully follow the instructions on the back of the pattern envelope.

2. If you are not using the hot-iron method, trace the design on heavy paper or lightweight cardboard, and cut it out. Position the cutout on a swatch of fabric slightly larger than the design. Mark lightly around it with pencil or chalk.

3. If the fabric is not too heavy, place the pattern for the design over a windowpane and secure it with cellophane tape. Hold the fabric swatch over the design and trace lightly around it.

4. On heavy fabrics, place dressmaker's tracing paper between the design and the fabric. Then trace lightly around the design.

5. Place sheer fabrics such as organdy over the design, then lightly trace the design on the fabric with pencil or chalk.

*Do not cut out the fabric after tracing the design.*

## Machine Appliqué

A closely spaced zig-zag stitch is the most versatile in appliqué work. Although you may vary the width of this stitch to accommodate fabric weaves and textures, never allow the stitch to be too wide.

### Preparation *(Lower left)*

Carefully position the fabric design on the article to be decorated and pin it in place. Hand-baste near the design outline.

Outline the design with straight stitching; use a short stitch. Stitch any lines shown within the design. Remove bastings, and press.

Replace the presser foot on the machine with the Special Purpose Foot designed for use in appliqué work. Set the selectors for a narrow zig-zag stitch and shorten the stitch length for satin stitching. See *Satin Stitching*, page 266.

Before starting the work, study the design to determine which section you should complete first. Avoid crossing the lines of stitching whenever possible since this may break the continuity of the design.

### Simple Appliqué

Two methods may be used in the appliqué stitching. Choose the one appropriate for your fabric. Remember a test sample is always advisable.

**Method 1:** Use a closely spaced zig-zag stitch. Stitch over the straight stitch outline. Stitch any lines shown within the design first. Pull the threads to the underside and tie. Press. Cut away the fabric on the outer edge close to the stitching, using embroidery scissors.

**Method 2:** Trim the outside edge of the fabric close to the straight stitching. For added body, baste an underlay of lawn on the wrong side of the fabric, under the design.

Overedge the design with a closely spaced zig-zag stitch. A smooth, lustrous finish results, which requires no additional trimming. Pull the threads through to the underside and tie. Press. Trim the underlay on the wrong side close to the stitching, using embroidery scissors.

**To make smooth, rounded corners,** stop the machine with the needle in the outside edge of the fabric; lift the foot, turn the fabric slightly, and take two stitches, turning the hand wheel by hand. Repeat several times. To make square, open corners, pivot the fabric on the needle when the needle is on the inside edge.

### Corded Appliqué

Corded appliqué is an ideal finish for a motif of lace. Use gimp, fine crochet thread, buttonhole twist, or heavy-duty thread for the filler cord.

Select wide lace edging with a definite floral design. If you are applying the lace to an edge, extend the fabric edge at least 1 inch beyond the line of the appliqué stitch. Choose a motif from the lace and position it separately above the edging; hand-baste in place.

Either *Method 1 or 2* described above may be used for corded appliqué. *Method 1* is recommended for intricate lace designs. The only change in procedure is the introduction of the filler cord, over which appliqué stitching is formed. Insert the filler cord into the eyelet on the Special Purpose Foot. See *Hairline Seam,* page 88 for threading instructions. This stitching technique gives a raised, three-dimensional effect.

When the work is finished, removed the bastings. From the right side, cut away the excess lace close to the stitching; from the wrong side, trim the excess fabric ¼ inch from the stitching, using embroidery scissors. Press.

### Appliqué Monograms

Appliqué monograms add a luxurious touch to bath towels, shower curtains, and bedspreads. Heavy fabrics such as slipper satin, chintz, Glosheen, and taffetta are excellent for this purpose.

Use *Method 1* for monogramming bath towels and either method for bedspreads and shower curtains. Corded appliqué is also an effective finish.

## Shadow Appliqué

Shadow hems and designs are lovely for table linens and children's clothes of crisp organdy or fine linen.

Baste the hem the full depth of the design and miter all corners. Lightly trace the design for the hem and motif on the right side of the article to be appliquéd. See page 251.

Cut a swatch of the same fabric slightly larger than the motif. Pin it over the wrong side of the motif. Hand-baste about ¼ inch from the lines of the motif and the hem.

Follow the instructions for *Corded Appliqué* and stitch around the design, using a fine filler cord; remove bastings and press.

Cut away the outer edges of the fabric on the underside close to the stitching, using embroidery scissors. Press.

## Hand Appliqué

The cut edges of the design are folded to the underside in hand appliqué.

Trace the design to be appliquéd on a swatch of fabric slightly larger than the motif. See page 251.

Cut out the design ¼ inch from the marking. Fold the cut edges to the underside ¼ inch and hand-baste. Miter the corners; notch the seam edges on outside curves, and clip into them on inside curves so that the seams will lie flat. Steam-press.

For stitching, use one or two strands of six-strand floss and a fine needle, and blanket-stitch over the edge of the design. Uneven as well as even stitches may be used. Fasten the threads on the underside. Remove bastings, and press. Stems and lines within the design may be embroidered.

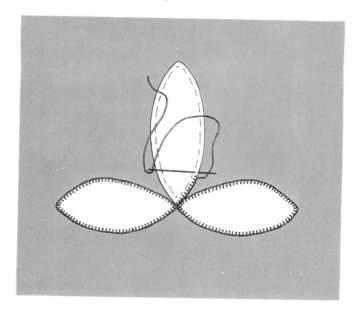

Carefully position the fabric design on the article to be decorated and pin. Hand-baste about ¼ inch from the edge. Remove the first bastings on the folded edge.

If you prefer an invisible finish, slip-stitch the design in place instead of using the blanket stitch.

# SMOCKING

Smocking is always in fashion. It is a youthful detail—at home on children's clothes as well as women's lingerie and soft cotton and silk. A smocked band at the yoke of a dress or at the hipline of a gathered skirt lends charm to both the costume and the wearer.

Smocking may be done by hand or by machine. Almost any type or design of fabric can be used but it must be smocked before the garment is assembled.

## Hand Smocking

You can buy patterns that show the several types of stitches used in smocking. The honeycomb stitch is illustrated here.

Transfer the design on the right side of the fabric. If you are working with a small check or plaid, you may use it as a guide.

Six-strand floss is suitable for both cotton and silk fabrics; on silk, however, you may prefer a silk floss. Use two or three strands in the needle and knot the long end of the threads. Choose a thread color that matches your fabric or, for a pleasant change, one that contrasts with it.

Work from left to right with the needle pointed to the left. Bring the needle up through the fabric between the first two dots of the second row. Take a small stitch through the second dot and a small stitch through the first dot in the same row; then draw the dots together. Insert the needle to the right of the stitch just finished and bring it out between the second and third dots of the first row so that the thread is under the fold. Take a small stitch through the third dot, then the second dot in the first row; draw the dots together. Repeat the procedure over the third and fourth dots of the second row; then over the fourth and fifth dots of the first row. Continue working in this way, alternating between the first and second rows, to the end of the row; make the last stitch in the second row. Turn the work in the opposite direction and bring the needle out in the third row to

the right of the last stitch. Work over the dots in the third and fourth rows; then the fifth and sixth rows, as illustrated. Continue until the smocking is completed.

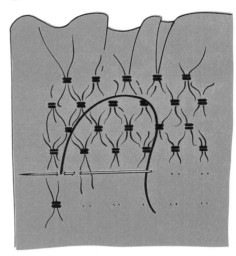

When drawing the stitches together, always pull the threads either up or down at right angles to the stitches to form even pleats or folds. When each row is finished, gently pull the fabric lengthwise to straighten the pleats.

*To press with a steam iron*, pin the top row of the smocking securely to the ironing board; place a pin above each stitch. Hold the iron about 1 inch above the smocking and allow the steam to penetrate the fabric while you gently pull the smocking from the bottom.

*To press with a dry iron*, follow the instructions for velvet, page 66.

## Machine Smocking

Machine smocking resembles hand smocking when the rows are accurately stitched. It is quick and easy and any one of the three methods given below may be used.

**Method 1:** Use matching thread and loosen the upper tension slightly so that the bobbin thread may be drawn later to gather the fabric.

From the right side of the fabric, place a row of stitching in the seam allowance, ½ inch from the edge. This stitching is not visible in the finished work. Place a second row of stitching barely beyond the ⅝-inch seam allowance, and a third row ⅛ inch from the second row. Place additional rows in groups of two, spaced ⅛ inch apart, and allow ½ inch between groupings.

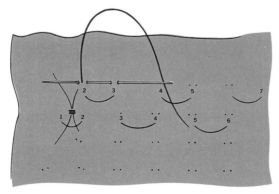

Gather the fabric to the desired width. See *Gathering to Control Fullness*, page 105.

Cut an underlay of lawn or organdy the length and width of the shirring. Position it on the underside, over the shirring. Pin it in place from the right side.

Select one of the zig-zag stitch patterns and stitch between the rows that you spaced ⅛ inch apart, using thread contrasting in color. For an interesting effect, select two stitch patterns and alternate them in stitching the rows.

**Method 2:** Use the Gathering Foot and heavy-duty thread for both the bobbin and the upper threading. Stitch following a design. See *Gathering Foot*, page 285 for instructions on its use.

**Method 3:** Use heavy-duty thread for both the bobbin and the upper threading and about 10 stitch length. Stitch from the right side, following a design similar to the one illustrated. You may use different colors of thread in stitching alternate rows. (If you are using a heavy thread only on the bobbin, stitch from the wrong side of the fabric.)

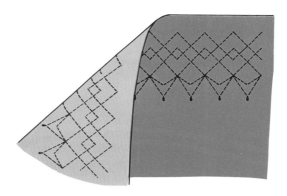

After you have stitched the design, wind the bobbin with elastic thread and place several rows of stitching across the work, spacing them in harmony with the design. See *Shirring with Elastic Thread*, page 244.

Quilting is the art of stitching two or more thicknesses of fabric together in a planned design. A light padding is stitched to the underside of the fabric to produce a soft, puffed effect that is becoming to some wearing apparel and to many fabric furnishings.

Your sewing machine enables you to quilt quickly and easily and to achieve a variety of effects. The Quilter Foot, which has an open construction and short toe, simplifies the stitching of padded fabrics. Its adjustable and removable space guide may be placed to the right or left of the needle. This makes it especially adaptable to diagonal quilting.

Select the thread, needle, and stitch length appropriate for your fabric. (Do not use a long stitch.) The pressure should be slightly heavier than that for medium-weight fabrics.

## Diagonal Quilting

Outing flannel, canton flannel, sheet wadding, or lightweight interlining makes a practical padding. If you choose sheet wadding, back it with voile or soft batiste for greater durability.

Place the padding over the wrong side of the fabric. Baste the layers of fabric together on both the lengthwise and the crosswise grains to prevent the layers from shifting as you sew. Space the basting rows about 2 inches apart.

Draw a diagonal line on the padding to mark the first line of stitching in each direction.

Replace the presser foot with the Quilter and adjust the space guide for the width desired between the rows of stitching. Place the work under the needle with the padded side up, and stitch on the drawn line. Space each successive row of

stitching by guiding the edge of the space guide along the previous row, as illustrated.

If you are quilting a large piece, work from the center to the edge of the fabric. After you have completed the stitching in one direction, stitch the lines in the opposite direction to form squares or triangles.

Guide the work with both hands placed on the fabric so that the lengthwise grain forms a straight line between the hands. This ensures even quilting, with a characteristic soft puff.

## Pattern Quilting

Floral and scroll designs may also be stitched with the Quilter. The space guide is removed, however.

Prepare the fabric following the instructions for diagonal quilting, but transfer the design to the padding before basting the two layers of fabric together. Then stitch around the outline for the design as instructed for trapunto quilting below.

If the fabric has a floral or scroll design, the pattern in the fabric can be your quilting design. Stitch it from the top side, using either straight stitching or zig-zag stitching.

## Trapunto Quilting *(Illustrated on next page)*

Trapunto quilting is a form of quilting in which small designs are made to stand out in relief. The fabric is backed with soft batiste, voile, silk organza, or organdy. Trace the motif on a swatch of the backing. Carefully plan the position of each motif so that the design is attractively spaced. Baste the backing on which the design has been traced to the wrong side of the fabric.

Raise the space guide of the Quilter or remove it entirely. The short open toe permits you to follow the curved lines easily and accurately. Choose thread that matches the fabric in color, and use a short stitch.

After stitching each portion of the design from the wrong side, pull the threads to the underside and tie. If the design has large leaves, flowers, or scrolls, place a second row of stitching inside the design, about ⅛ inch from the first row.

When the stitching is completed, pad the design with strands of wool yarn carried by a tapestry needle or darning needle. (Wool yarn should be used because of its resiliency.) Pass the needle through the backing from one stitching line to the other. It often is necessary to use several strands of yarn to fill a section of the motif.

Clip both ends of the yarn close to the stitching. Gently stretch each portion of the design on the bias to conceal the ends of the yarn on the inside of the backing.

*Lace and other transparent fabrics* are often backed with satin or taffeta and the design padded with silk yarn to produce a delicately tinted pattern.

# BEADS AND SEQUINS

Beads and sequins are glamorous accents on cocktail and evening dresses, sweaters, blouses, scarves, and evening bags. They may be used alone or combined with decorative zig-zag stitching as illustrated on page 276. A variety of fabrics may be used for this work.

## Beading by Machine

Small beads may be sewed in place by machine. Use a medium-width, open-spaced zig-zag stitch and the Zipper Foot. Stitch the beads in place before you assemble the garment sections so that you have only a small section to deal with.

The spaces between the sections within the design must be far enough apart for the Zipper Foot to work between them. In straight or block designs, however, several rows may be stitched close together. (For small, intricate designs, bead by hand.)

Transfer the motif for the beading to a backing of organdy, voile, or lawn. If the garment is underlined, transfer the design to the underlining. Carefully position the backing on the wrong side of the fabric and pin near the design. Use matching thread and machine-stitch on the lines of the design to transfer it to the right side of the fabric.

String bulk beads on a double strand of matching mercerized or silk thread, using a fine needle. Knot the ends together. Pass the needle through the first bead, then between the two strands of thread near the knot. This will prevent the beads from slipping beyond the knot. After you have strung the beads, arrange them smoothly; then pass the needle through the last bead a second time to prevent the beads from slipping on the thread.

Adjust the machine for a medium-width zig-zag stitch in central needle position and 15 stitch length. Use either silk or mercerized thread matching the fabric exactly in color.

Place the beads directly over the line of the design and adjust the Zipper Foot far enough to the left or right to ride against the beads. This adjustment enables you to position the zig-zag stitching over the beading thread. As you sew, hold the beads in place with the index finger, close to the needle. The threads are drawn between the beads, making the stitching invisible.

On scroll designs, start the stitching on the inside curve with the Zipper Foot adjusted to work inside the design; stitch to the beginning of the outside curve. Stop the machine *with the needle in the fabric*, adjust the Zipper Foot to the opposite side, then work outside the design, as illustrated. (It is necessary to remove the foot to make this adjustment since the needle is in the fabric.) In the illustration, dotted lines and arrows indicate the direction of the stitching and the position of the Zipper Foot in relation to the beads.

After stitching each portion of the design, draw the thread ends to the underside and tie them together in a single knot set close to the fabric. Clip the bead threads about 4 inches from the design and remove all beads on them except one to cover the knot. With a needle, bring the thread ends through the first bead at the beginning for a smooth joining; then bring the needle through to the underside of the fabric and fasten the threads with several backstitches.

## Beading by Hand

Round beads, pearls, and bugle beads can be sewed in place by hand. Baste or lightly trace the design on the right side of the fabric, then follow one of the methods described below.

***Method 1.*** Use a needle fine enough to slide through the beads without splitting them and select thread matching the fabric in color.

Fasten the thread on the underside of the fabric with two tiny backstitches. Bring the needle up through the fabric. Pass the needle through a bead; take a backstitch and bring the needle out exactly a bead length from where the thread came out. Start each successive backstitch against the previous bead to place the beads close together. Draw up the thread tightly enough for the beads to lie flat against the fabric. When completed, fasten the thread on the underside with tiny backstitches.

***Method 2:*** String the beads on mercerized or nylon thread, leaving a 4-inch thread end to fasten on the underside.

Use a second thread, matching the fabric exactly in color, and a fine, short needle to couch on the beads. Fasten the thread on the underside of the fabric with two tiny backstitches. Hold the beads in position and bring the needle up through the fabric on the left side of the beading thread. Bring the thread to the right, between the beads, and take a slanting stitch over the beading thread, bringing the needle out on the left side of the beading thread at the end of the next bead.

When completed, fasten the needle thread on the underside with tiny backstitches. Clip the beading thread about 4 inches from the design and remove the excess beads. Use a needle to bring the end threads to the underside. Tie them in a single knot set close to the fabric.

## Sewing on Sequins

Outline the design first, then fill in the center. Use a fine needle and a thread matching the sequins exactly in color.

Fasten the thread on the underside of the fabric with tiny backstitches. Bring the needle up through the fabric and through a sequin. Hold the sequin flat against the fabric, right side up, and take a stitch in front of it. Pass the needle through a sequin from the right side and take a backstitch as illustrated. Draw up the thread and at the same time turn the sequin right side up. The sequins will overlap and the stitches will be hidden. The stitch length on the underside must be the same size as the sequin. When finished, fasten the threads on the underside with tiny backstitches.

*To add a bead to the center of a sequin,* bring the needle up through the fabric and through a sequin. Pass the needle through a bead, then down through the sequin and fabric. Draw up the thread and take a tiny backstitch to fasten it. (The bead acts as an anchor, holding the sequin in place.) Bring the needle up through the fabric at the point where the next sequin will be sewed. This method is excellent when sequins are not sewed close together.

# LACE EDGING AND INSERTION

Lace adds a delicate trimming to blouses, women's and children's dresses, babies' clothes, lingerie, and household linens.

You may apply lace to the edge of the fabric or set it into the fabric. Lace edging and insertion of cotton, silk, linen, rayon, nylon, wool, and other fibers are available in a variety of widths, patterns, and types.

The delicate network of threads in lace requires special sewing techniques. Whether you stitch the lace by hand or by machine depends on your fabric, the position of the lace on the garment, and personal preference. In all cases, use a short stitch and fine needle and thread. In handwork, the needle should be short as well as fine. *Always press the lace before applying it to the fabric.*

## Gathering Lace

To gather lace, gently draw the top thread of the selvage and ease the lace back on the thread to the desired fullness. Be careful to distribute the fullness evenly.

## Applying Lace Edging

### Lace over Rolled Edge

**Straight lace.** Baste the lace over the seam allowance of the fabric; both lace and fabric should be right side up. Trim the seam allowances under the lace to a scant ¼ inch. On the underside, roll the edge of the fabric and make small stitches through the rolled hem and lace. On the right side, the lace is over the hem.

**Gathered lace.** Baste the gathered lace on the seamline of the fabric, right sides together. Trim the fabric seam allowance to a scant ¼ inch. Roll the fabric edge over the stitching line, and make small stitches through the rolled hem and lace. When finished, turn the lace over the rolled hem.

If you want the rolled hem on the top side in the finished work, baste the gathered lace on the seamline of the fabric, *wrong sides together* instead of right.

### Gathered Lace under Rolled Edge

Place a line of stitching ⅛ inch from the seamline, using a short stitch. Press. Trim off the edge close to the stitching.

Roll the fabric to the underside as you sew the lace in place. Place the gathered lace over the rolled hem, right side down, and make small stitches through the lace and rolled hem. On the right side, the lace is under the hem.

### Lace on Finished Edge

**By hand.** The fabric edge may be finished with a hem or facing. Lay the lace over the finished edge, right sides together, keeping the edges even. Pin. Working from the lace side, make very small

**Plate 5**

**The bride wears satin**

*Above:* Twin-needle stitching on satin gives raised look to diamond outlines; diamond stitch patterns in centers carry out the motif.

*Right:* Satin leaves appliquéd on fine tulle make a delicate veil.

*Below:* Velvet leaf appliqué points up Empire waistline on bridesmaid's peau de soie gown.

**Plates 6 and 7**

**Sheer elegance in hems and a border**

*Top:* Three rows of twin-needle stitching
produce raised design on silk organza hem.

*Bottom left:* Border of delicate rows of zig-zag stitching
is enhanced by edge-stitched scallops.

*Bottom right:* Shadow hem. The edge of organza
on the underside is cut away,
above design, after stitching.

**Bonnet promenade**

1) Pique with Irish
lace attached by a band
of yellow zig-zag stitching.

2) Flannel tam with corded edge, ribbon
trimmed with decorative stitch patterns.

3) Pique cap with flag appliqué,
satin-stitched flagstaffs.

4) Organdy costume features lace appliquéd to dress hem, lace cutouts appliquéd to pin-tucked yoke. Scalloped bonnet under-faced with edge of lace.

5) Pique cap with contrasting corded seams, appliquéd kite; decorative stitch patterns form kite tail.

6) Lace ruffle adds charm to an embroidered organdy "dust cap."

7) Lace trim applied with narrow plain zig-zag satin stitching.

8) Lace insertion and pin tucking form brim; shirred crown with cutout design outlined in plain zig-zag satin stitching.

## Plate 8

### Night-blooming flowers

*Left:*
Appliquéd lace cutouts
form a delicate tracery
on a taffeta
evening gown.

*Below:*
Midnight black
zig-zag stitching
on stark white satin
becomes exotic
with the addition
of hand-sewn bugle
and round beads.

overhand stitches over the edge. The stitches should be loose enough so that the seam may be spread open when it is finished.

**By machine.** Lace edging and a narrow hem may be sewed in place with one line of machine stitching when the Hemmer Foot is used. The lace may be stitched over or under the fold for the hem. See *Hemmer Foot*, page 283.

## Joining Lace Edging and Lace Insertion

**By hand.** The lace edging may be straight or gathered. Match the lace patterns when cutting the lace into lengths. Lay the right sides of the lace together, keeping the edges even, and pin. Work from the gathered side and make small overhand stitches over the edge. The stitches should be loose enough so that the lace and insertion may be spread open when the stitching is finished. Two rows of insertion may be joined in the same way.

**By machine.** Match the lace patterns when cutting the lace into lengths. Replace the presser foot

with the Edge Stitcher. Place one piece of lace in slot 1 and the other in slot 4. (The edges will barely overlap.) Adjust the lug to position the stitching close to the lace edge, and guide the lace against the slots as you sew. See *Edge Stitcher*, page 284.

## Joining Lace Insertion and Fabric Bands

Fold the edge of the fabric under ½ inch, and press. Replace the presser foot with the Edge Stitcher. Place the fabric band in slot 1. Adjust the lug to position the stitching close to the folded edge. Insert the lace in slot 4 with the fabric band overlapping it slightly. Stitch, guiding the band and lace against the edges of the slots as instructed above. See *Edge Stitcher*, page 284.

## Inserting Lace

Pin each edge of the lace insertion in place; both lace and fabric must be right side up. Machine-stitch on each side of the insertion close to the edge. Press. If the fabric is to remain under the

261

lace, the work is finished. If a lace insert is desired, trim the fabric under the lace to within ⅛ inch of the stitching. Turn the fabric edges away from the lace, and press.

inch from the edge; baste the insertion where it is to fall in the garment. Select one of the decorative zig-zag stitches and set the stitch length for satin stitching. Position the work under the needle so that when the needle is on the extreme right stroke, it catches the selvage of the lace edging. Stitch. Then stitch down one edge of the insertion in the same way. Turn the fabric and stitch the other edge of the insertion from the opposite end. This procedure places the points of the design in opposite directions. Press. Trim the fabric under the lace close to the stitching.

## Applying Lace to Curved Area

Mark the line on the right side of the fabric for the position of the lace. Draw the thread on the top edge of the lace and shape it to fit the curve. With both fabric and lace right side up, pin and baste in position. The lace may be stitched in place by hand, using a short overhand stitch or by machine. A narrow open-spaced zig-zag stitch or one of the decorative zig-zag stitches may be used instead of straight stitching.

## Using Decorative Stitching with Lace

Many of the decorative zig-zag stitch patterns can be used effectively as both a finished and a trimming for lace edging and insertion.

Baste the lace edging over the fabric about ½

## Applying Lace to Square Corner

Miter the lace insertion at the corner and press. Join with overhand stitches across the miter. On the underside, cut away the excess at the corner.

Stitch the lace edging and insertion together. The lace edging is generally gathered around the corner. About ½ inch from the corner, draw the top thread of the lace edging and gather it just enough so that it will lie flat when turned down. Catch the loop of the drawn thread under the overhand stitches as the lace and insertion are joined.

If lace edging is used alone, you may miter it at the corner instead of gathering it.

## ENTREDEUX AND BRAID

### Entredeux

Extredeux, sometimes called veining or beading, is a narrow insertion of open embroidered design. It is used between fabric edges in blouses, lingerie, and babies' and children's clothes. The wider width can be laced with ribbon.

Place the entredeux over the fabric, right sides together, with the embroidered edge on the seamline. Stitch close to the embroidery. Press; then press the seam edge away from the entredeux. On the underside, trim seam edges to ⅛ inch, and overcast them together.

*(Continued on next page)*

If top stitching is desired, fold the seam allowance to the underside and press. Lap the fabric over the entredeux, keeping the fold close to the embroidered edge. Stitch close to the fold. Trim, then overcast the seam edges on the underside the same as above.

## Braid

Braid is used to edge collars, cuffs, lapels, and pockets and to accent other parts of a dress.

Finish the edges in the usual way before applying the braid. Carefully pin the braid over the finished edge; shape it to conform to curved edges, and miter square corners. Baste. Slip-stitch each edge of the braid in place.

# Zig-Zag Sewing

Zig-zag sewing has found a solid place in dress construction and home and family maintenance sewing. That is not the end of the story, however. To stimulate your creative imagination, this chapter explains how you can also use your zig-zag machine for decorative sewing and fashion detailing. The opportunities for self-expression and originality are almost unlimited. You can enhance the appearance of clothing, household linens, and fabric furnishings without adding to their cost; you can achieve lovely effects in a formal evening dress or a simple apron or cottage curtain.

Like most women you are probably more creative than you realize. Learn to look for suggestions in ready-to-wear and in newspaper and magazine fashions; learn to use as design sources such unlikely material as wallpaper, children's coloring books, and printed fabrics. Decorative zig-zag sewing is easy, but do not make the mistake of overdecorating. Plan your placement of stitch patterns carefully, considering the fabric and the age of the person for whom the garment is intended or the type of household article you are making. If you do, your results will be pleasing and rewarding.

Many of the machine accessories may be used in zig-zag sewing. Check the instructions for accessories, beginning on page 280. For guides on how to use the zig-zag stitch in dress construction and family maintenance sewing, consult the alphabetical listing under *Zig-Zag Sewing* in the index.

## Planning Preliminaries

The decision to use decorative zig-zag stitching must be made when the garment or article is in the planning stage. Often the stitching will extend through a seam allowance and must, therefore, be applied before the seam is stitched. Or the decorative stitching may be confined to a small section of the garment as for a motif or monogram; then it is easier to handle the small section under the needle than the finished garment.

Mercerized or silk sewing thread may be used in decorative stitching. It may blend with the fabric in color or be a decided contrast in shade or color. Subtle color contrasts are more tasteful and are usually preferred to bold contrasts, which tend to cheapen the appearance of a garment. Do not hesitate to experiment, however. Even the experts find that they can always learn something new about color combinations.

## To Prepare the Work for Stitching

You can do decorative zig-zag stitching on almost any fabric. On soft fabrics you must add a backing to ensure firm satin stitching, and on many other fabrics you will achieve better results when a backing is used. Crisp lawn, organdy, or organza is suitable for this purpose. When the work is completed, the backing is cut away close to the stitching with small, sharp scissors.

To prepare your work for stitching, take these steps:

1. Steam-press the fabric so that it will be wrinkle-free.

2. Transfer the design to the fabric.

3. Cut the backing on the same grain as the fabric and at least 4 inches wider than the decorative stitching that will be applied.

4. Press the backing and position it carefully on the wrong side of the fabric, where the stitching will be applied. Pin, then baste in place.

5. After you complete each line of decorative stitching, press the work on the wrong side before proceeding with any additional stitching.

## To Prepare the Machine

Some zig-zag machines have built-in discs and one or two selectors that may be set for any stitch pattern you want. Others have an assortment of discs (or cams), and you insert one for each stitch pattern.

The *stitch length selector* regulates the space between the stitches. The *stitch width selector* regulates the width of some stitch patterns and completely changes the pattern of others. The instruction book accompanying the machine explains how to select the stitch patterns as well as how to adjust the stitch length, stitch width, and tension.

### Satin Stitching

For decorative zig-zag stitching the stitch length should be very short so that the zig-zag stitches are placed close together. A series of closely spaced zig-zag stitches that form a smooth, satinlike surface is known as "satin stitching." It is used for almost all the decorative work described in this chapter.

**A Special Purpose Foot,** designed for use in satin stitching, is generally provided with the machine. The foot has a raised center section that allows mounds of satin stitches to move freely under it. It also has an eyelet through which a filler cord or decorative thread may be inserted. Use this foot in your decorative stitching.

***To adjust the stitch length for satin stitching.*** Move the stitch length selector to the "fine" area. Then run the machine at slow speed and gradually tighten the thumb nut until the stitches are closely spaced and form a smooth surface on your fabric.

***To adjust the tension for satin stitching.*** Satin stitching requires a lighter needle-thread tension than straight stitching or open-spaced designs. The wider the satin stitch, the lighter the tension required. A properly balanced satin stitch should lie flat across the fabric. Any tightness or

puckering usually indicates too high a needle thread tension.

**Test stitching.** To be sure that you have the correct tension setting, stitch length, and stitch width, test your stitching on a swatch of the same fabric you are using in your work. Use a backing if your fabric requires one.

On the same swatch, make a stitching test to determine which stitch pattern you wish to use. If you are planning to use two or more patterns, decide which ones may be combined attractively and how they should be spaced.

## To Find the Beginning of a Pattern Unit

When you use a decorative stitch pattern in a motif or monogram, you must always start stitching at the beginning of a pattern unit. To do this, stitch on a scrap of fabric until you come to the end of a complete pattern unit—that is, to the end of the diamond, arrowhead, or whatever pattern you are using. Now you are ready to start stitching

at the beginning of the next unit. Remove the scrap of fabric from under the presser foot and position the motif or monogram under the needle, aligning the marking with the center of the presser foot. Lower the foot, and stitch. After you have stitched one portion of the design, pull the threads through to the underside and tie them. This sequence is recommended for all precise design placement.

# DECORATIVE ZIG-ZAG STITCHING

The stitch patterns may be applied in a simple or an elaborate way. Either is attractive. It would be impossible to illustrate all of the many interesting, pleasing, and practical applications you can devise. The suggestions that follow give you an idea of what you can do. They also present instructions that are basic to the placement of *all* stitch patterns.

## Applying a Trimming

### Braid, Ribbon, and Rickrack

Metallic braid or narrow velvet ribbon adds an unusual and dramatic touch when combined with one of the decorative stitch patterns as either finish or trim. If a backing is required, baste it to the wrong side of the fabric. Then baste the braid or ribbon in position. Select one of the decorative stitch patterns, and set the stitch length selector for satin stitching. Stitch down one side of the braid or ribbon; then turn the fabric and stitch down the other side from the opposite end. This procedure places the points of the stitch pattern in opposite directions. In the illustrations, only the points of the stitching catch into the metallic braid, and the satin stitches are on the edge of the velvet ribbon with the points extending into the fabric. When finished, remove bastings and press. Trim the backing close to each side of the stitching.

Braid and decorative stitching are an effective trimming on hand towels, pillows, and other household articles. For a stitch pattern such as the one illustrated, position the work under the needle with the edge of the braid aligned with the center of the presser foot. Stitch as instructed above. Press.

For a simple treatment on children's clothes, aprons, and cottage curtains, add rickrack—either a single row or two colors braided together. Baste the rickrack in position. Align the center of the rickrack with the center of the presser foot, and sew in place using a decorative stitch pattern or an open zig-zag stitch. Press.

### Bias Strip with Lace or Rickrack

Decorative stitching combined with bias tape and lace or bias tape and rickrack is an interesting treatment for little girls' dresses, blouses, and lingerie. *(Illustrated on next page)*

Open up the binding and stitch the rickrack or lace to each side of the cut edge. Extend the edge of the rickrack about ⅛ inch beyond the binding edge; keep the edges of the binding and lace even, and match the patterns in the lace. Fold the binding edge back in place; the lace or rickrack will extend beyond it. Press.

Baste the binding in position on the garment. Select a stitch pattern, and set the stitch length selector for satin stitching. To place the stitching on each edge of the binding, as illustrated with rickrack, position the work under the needle so that when the needle is on the extreme left stroke it catches the left edge of the binding; then turn the work and stitch down the other side of the binding from the opposite end.

### Bias Binding with Net Ruffles

Bias binding applied with decorative stitching adds a dainty touch to net ruffles on petticoats.

Replace the presser foot with the Binder and insert in it either silk or rayon bias binding. Carefully select a stitch pattern that complements the binding. Set the stitch length selector for satin stitching, and bind the edge. Press. See page 282 for instructions on using the *Binder*.

To place one row of stitching through the center, as illustrated with lace, align the center of the binding with the center of the presser foot, and stitch. Remove bastings, and press.

### Lace with Decorative Stitching

Baste two strips of lace in position on the garment with the inside edges of the lace touching. Match the patterns in the lace. Baste a backing of crisp lawn to the underside. Select the stitch pattern, and set the stitch length selector for satin stitching. Align the center of lace with the center of the presser foot, and stitch. Remove bastings and press. Trim the backing close to the stitching. *(Illustrated at top of next column)*.

## Stitching Designs

### Geometric Design

A geometric design with an interlaced effect will enhance the appearance of a full-skirted dress made of organdy, organza, or linen. It is also appropriate for such household articles as place mats and hand towels.

Trace the design lightly on the right side of the fabric. See page 251. Baste a backing of crisp organdy or lawn on the underside of the design for added body. Study the design to determine which sections you should stitch first. Select a narrow, plain zig-zag stitch, and set the stitch length selector for satin stitching. Align the markings of the design with the center of the presser foot, and stitch around each edge. Press.

Next, select an open-spaced stitch pattern, and stitch midway between the two previous lines of stitching. Pull the threads through to the underside and tie. Remove bastings; press. Trim the backing close to the stitching. To add glitter to glamour on a cocktail dress, sew on a few sequins or beads by hand.

### Outline Design

An outline design may be used in the same places as the geometric one. Prepare the work as described above. Select one of the open-spaced stitch patterns, and set the stitch length selector for satin stitching. Align the marking for the design with the center of the presser foot, and stitch. Guide the fabric with both hands, turning it as you sew. At the corners, stop with the needle in the fabric, raise the presser bar, and turn the fabric, pivoting on the needle. Lower the presser bar and continue the stitching. (On sharp curves, you may need to raise the presser bar slightly when the needle is in the fabric, and ease the fabric to the right or left.) When completed, pull the threads through to the underside and tie. Press. Either stitch the lines within the design, using a narrow, plain zig-zag stitch, or sew on beads. Trim the backing on the underside close to the stitching.

### Scalloped Hems

Scalloped hems add interest to babies' and children's clothes, cotton dresses for adults, and household linens.

Fold and press the hem. Mark a 2-inch scallop about 1 inch below the top of the hem. Baste close to the marking to prevent the two layers of fabric from slipping.

Select an open-spaced stitch pattern, and set the stitch length selector for satin stitching. Position the work under the needle with the scallops to the right, and align the marking with the center of the presser foot. Stitch around the scallops, using both hands to guide the work and turning the fabric gradually as you sew. At the point of the scallop, and on the left swing of the needle, stop with the needle in the fabric. Raise the presser bar and turn the fabric, pivoting on the needle, then lower the presser bar and stitch the next scallop. (On sharp curves, it is sometimes necessary to raise the presser bar slightly when the needle is in the fabric and ease the fabric slightly to the right or left.) When completed, press. Trim the upper edge of the hem on the underside, close to the stitching.

Many of the decorative stitch patterns are adaptable to scallops that have a curve instead of a point between the scallops.

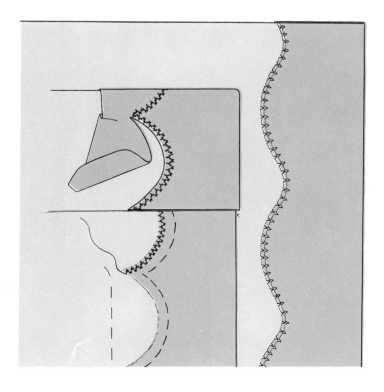

### Pin Tucks, Lace, and Stitch Patterns

Groups of pin tucks combined with pattern stitching add a fashionable and delicate touch to blouses, babies' clothes, and children's dresses made of soft fabrics.

Pin-tuck the fabric as instructed on page 236. Then lightly mark the position for the decorative stitching midway between the groups of tucks. Select one of the open-spaced stitch patterns, and set the stitch length selector for satin stitching. Align the marking for the pattern with the center of the presser foot and stitch. Press.

**Lace insertion** may also be combined with decorative stitching to give the same delicate touch.

### Individual Motifs

You can give individuality to blouses, summer dresses, children's clothes, and place mats by grouping small designs made of such stitch patterns as the solid scallop or pyramid. The designs may form a border or they may be placed asymmetrically on the garment.

Dot the fabric with chalk to mark the position of the design. Prepare the work as described under *Geometric Design,* page 268. Select the stitch pattern, and set the stitch length selector for satin stitching. Start at the beginning of the pattern unit as instructed on page 266. Stitch, completing only one pattern. With the needle in the fabric, pivot, turning the fabric left 90 degrees. Stitch, completing

another stitch pattern, then pivot again. Continue in the same manner until the four sides are finished. Pull threads through to the underside and tie. Press.

### Arrowheads as a Finish

The arrowhead provides a decorative and secure finish on fashion seams or darts that end within the garment, at the top of pleats, and at the ends of pockets in tailored clothes.

Start at the beginning of the arrowhead pattern. See page 266. Begin the stitching at the very end of the seam, dart, or pocket. When finished, pull threads to the underside and tie. Press.

### Flowerlike Design

Bar tacks may be placed in sequence to form flowerlike points—an exquisite touch in babies' and children's clothes, blouses, and summer dresses. The design may be used around the neckline, in a yoke, above the hem, or along each side of a front closing.

Dot the fabric with a pencil to mark the position of each flower. When the design borders a curved edge, such as a neckline, mark the cutting line instead of cutting the fabric. By not cutting the edge, you can prevent it from stretching as you stitch and guide the fabric.

Adjust the machine for a wide zig-zag stitch. Make the feed inoperative so that it will not move the fabric as you sew. (This is done by either raising the throat plate or lowering the feed. Check the instruction book accompanying your machine.)

When the needle is on the left stroke, position it in the fabric at the marking for the design. Lower

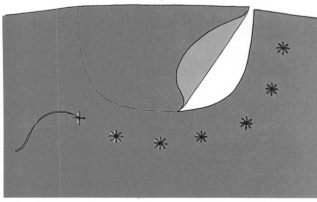

the presser foot and make four stitches, stopping with the left stroke of the needle in the fabric (center of the design). Raise the presser foot and turn the fabric left 180 degrees, pivoting on the needle. Lower the presser foot and make four stitches, again stopping with the needle in the fabric on the left stroke (center). Pivot again, turn the fabric left 90 degrees, and make four more stitches; then pivot, turn the fabric left 180 degrees, and make four stitches. You have now finished the first four points.

To make the remaining four points, pivot and turn the fabric on the needle far enough each time to place stitches midway between each of the four finished points. Take four stitches each time, stopping with the needle in the center of the design. When finished, use a needle to bring the thread through to the underside; then tie it with the bobbin thread. Press.

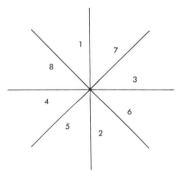

### "Twin-Needle" Scallops

Scallops stitched with a twin needle add a delicate touch to dresses, blouses, and children's clothes.

Select the scallop pattern. The stitch length and stitch width vary the length and depth of the scallop; make the appropriate selection. If you are making several rows, start each row at the beginning of a scallop unit. See page 266. Press.

### Appliquéd Designs

Interesting block designs lend distinction to curtains, place mats, and dresses. For a vivid note you can combine blocks contrasting in color with the fabric. Or you may appliqué a striped fabric to a solid-colored fabric for a simple, bright trim on blouses, dresses, and informal table linens. See *Appliqué*, page 250.

For the block design, first appliqué the blocks in position. Then lightly mark the lines for the crossbar stitching. Align the marking with the center of the presser foot and stitch, using a narrow, closely spaced zig-zag stitch. Press.

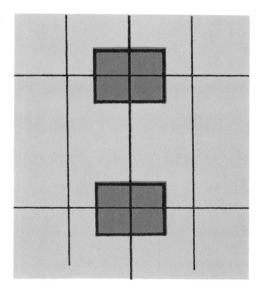

To appliqué a stripe to a solid color, mark a geometric or irregular design on the striped fabric and appliqué the striped fabric in place.

### Border Designs

Border designs of unlimited variety can be created by combining several stitch patterns. Simple or elaborate, delicate or bold, they can be varied to suit the application. And they have many applications on dresses, blouses, children's clothes, men's or boys' sport shirts, curtains or linens. Use a border design as you would a braid—at the top of a hem, through the bodice and sleeve sections, in a yoke, and on collars, cuffs, belts, and pockets. The stitching may be placed on the horizontal, vertical, or bias line.

***Preparation.*** Mark the center line for the first row of stitching with a light brush of pencil or chalk, using a ruler to keep the line straight. If the spacing between rows is no greater than ½ inch, you can gauge additional rows with the presser foot. If the spacing is wider, mark each line for the stitching. Use a backing of crisp lawn, organdy, or organza. See page 265. Make a test sample on a swatch of your fabric before proceeding with the actual work.

***Stitching.*** Select the stitch pattern and set the stitch length selector for satin stitching. Stitch the center row, aligning the marking with the center of the presser foot. Select the pattern for the next row and stitch down one side of the center row; then turn the fabric and stitch down the other side from the opposite end. This procedure places the points of the stitching in opposite directions. Repeat it for each additional row of stitching used in the border.

Borders may be made more glamorous by couching metallic thread or bouclé yarn with one of the open-spaced stitch patterns or by using the twin needle, as illustrated below. When finished, press. Trim the backing on the underside close to the stitching.

### Fagoting

Seam edges joined with fagoting are a delicate addition to blouses, dresses, lingerie, and children's clothes. Two strips of bias binding joined with fagoting make an unusual yoke treatment.

Fold under the seam allowance and press. Baste the folded edges to onionskin paper or art tracing paper, allowing ⅛ inch between the edges.

Select either the multiple-stitch zig-zag or the fagoting stitch pattern. Use the widest stitch width and "fine" stitch length. Align the center of the work with the center of the presser foot. As you sew, the stitches will catch into the fabric fold on alternate sides.

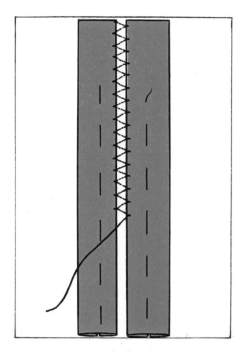

When completed, remove the bastings and gently pull the paper away from one side of the stitching, then from the other. Press.

### Buttonholes for Lacing

Buttonholes, accented with decorative stitching, can be used to produce interesting lacing on clothing for children and teen-age girls as well as for adults.

Mark the position of each buttonhole. Use a backing of crisp lawn or organdy. Refer to the instruction book accompanying the machine, and work the buttonholes. Press. Add a row of decorative stitching above and below the buttonholes. Velvet ribbon, grosgrain ribbon, or braid may be laced through the buttonholes.

### Drawn Work

Fabrics with a balanced weave are suitable for this decorative treatment, which may be used on informal table linens and scarves.

Draw a thread from the fabric to indicate each edge of the drawn work. Select the blindstitch zig-zag pattern, a "fine" stitch length, and medium stitch width. Stitch down the left side of the drawn work, then turn the fabric and stitch down the other side from the opposite end. This procedure places the point of the stitching in the solid fabric. Draw the remaining threads from the fabric to form the openwork between the rows of stitching.

To fringe the edge, draw a thread from the fabric to mark the depth of the fringe. Stitch with this edge to the right. Draw the threads below the stitching to make the fringe. Press.

### Shadow Design

A shadow effect is an interesting finish for collars and cuffs, facings, and yokes. It can be created easily on a double thickness of sheer fabric such as organdy, organza, voile, and sheer crisp nylon *when a closely spaced stitch pattern is used. Open-spaced stitch patterns are not suitable for this work.*

Cut the garment section by the pattern and construct it, using a hairline seam. See page 88 for instructions. Turn the section to the right side and press it, forming a sharp crease on the stitching line. Baste the two layers of fabric together just outside the line for the decorative stitching.

Select a closely spaced stitch pattern, such as the scallop in the illustration, and set the stitch length selector for satin stitching. Place two rows of stitches on the right side of the fabric—the first row about ⅜ inch from the edge, the second about ⅜ inch from the first. Carefully guide the fabric with both hands, turning it as you sew. Remove bastings and press. Cut away the undersection of fabric between the two rows of stitching to create a shadow effect. Use small, sharp-pointed scissors and trim close to the stitching.

reverse the ruler and draw the scallops facing the opposite direction, overlapping the first scallops about ¾ inch.

Prepare the work as described above. Stitch around the design. When completed, cut away the fabric on the underside between the rows of stitching.

### Edgestitched Finish

Edgestitching is a delicate finish for babies' clothes, children's dresses, ruffles, and lingerie *when a closely spaced zig-zag stitch pattern is used. Open-spaced patterns are not suitable for this work.* Edgestitching may be used on many types of fabrics.

Mark the seamline, but instead of cutting on the seam edge, cut at least 1 inch from the seamline. When curved edges are not cut, the fabric is easier to guide and will not stretch during the stitching. If edgestitching is used on a single thickness of fabric, baste a backing of crisp lawn to the wrong side of the fabric for added body.

Select a closely spaced stitch pattern, and set the stitch length for satin stitching. Place the work under the needle so that the outer edge of the stitching will fall barely inside the seamline. Carefully guide the fabric with both hands, turning it as you sew. Remove bastings and press.

A narrow plain zig-zag stitch may also be used to obtain shadow effects. Set the stitch length selector for satin stitching. For the design illustrated, lightly draw the scallops on the fabric, using a 2-inch scallop ruler as a guide. Then

Trim the outer edge of fabric and backing close to the stitching, using embroidery scissors. Then trim the backing close to the inside edge of the stitching.

**Ruffles.** Edgestitching is a pleasing finish for ruffles. If the ruffle has a heading, finish each edge. After stitching the first edge, turn the fabric and stitch down the other side from the opposite end.

**Large scallops.** An edge of large scallops is appropriate for wearing apparel and linens when it is made with a narrow, plain, zig-zag stitch.

Lightly mark the scallops 2 inches from the edge of the fabric, using a 2-inch scallop ruler as a guide. *Do not cut.* For added body, baste a backing of crisp lawn on the underside of the scallops.

Select the plain zig-zag stitch, narrow stitch width; set the stitch length selector for satin stitching. Use a filler cord to prevent the scallops from stretching. Replace the presser foot with the Special Purpose Foot, and insert the filler cord into the eyelet. See *Hairline Seam,* page 88 for threading instructions. Position the work under the needle with the scallops to the right; align the marking with the center of the presser foot. Guide the fabric with both hands as you sew, turning it gradually, following the scallops. At the point of the scallop, and when the needle is in left position,

raise the presser bar and turn the fabric, pivoting on the needle. Then lower the presser bar and stitch the next scallop. When finished, press. Trim surplus border and backing close to the stitching. Then trim the backing close to the inside of the scallops.

### Couching

You can achieve novel effects by couching gimp, yarn, or braid with zig-zag stitch patterns. Spaced patterns, such as the blindstitch zig-zag or narrow, open-spaced zig-zag, are most appropriate since they allow the decorative cord to show as part of the work. You may use either a single or twin needle in the machine.

Lightly mark the position for the couching. Place the cord over the marking, and align it with the center of the presser foot. Stitch, allowing the stitches to form over the cord. Press.

## MOTIFS AND MONOGRAMS

Many of the decorative stitch patterns lend themselves perfectly to the creation of attractive and unusual motifs or monograms. Select a simple design from the many transfer patterns available, or sketch one to suit your purpose.

### Motifs

#### Simulated Appliqué

A design for children's clothes similar to the one illustrated is a special decorative touch that looks like appliqué.

Trace the design lightly on the right side of the fabric. See page 251 for instructions. Baste a

backing of crisp organdy or lawn on the underside for added body. Set the stitch length selector for satin stitching and use the following stitches: (1) A narrow, plain zig-zag stitch to outline the design; (2) the scallop stitch pattern for the eyebrows, hair, and lines within; (3) the ball stitch pattern for the eye and nose; and (4) the arrowhead for the bow at the neckline. Pull the threads through to the underside and tie them after stitching each section. When finished, trim the backing close to the stitching. Press.

### Floral and Leaf Motifs

The floral motif illustrated is an excellent example of how you can combine several different stitch patterns and achieve pleasing results.

Prepare the work as described under *Simulated Appliqué*. Select the stitch pattern, and set the stitch length selector for satin stitching. Align the

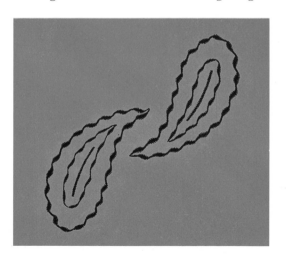

marking with the center of the presser foot, and stitch. To bring a stitch pattern to a point, as in the ends of the stems, flowers, and leaves, gradually move the stitch width selector to the narrowest width as you sew.

The leaflike motif is appropriate for dresses and table linens where a small design is required for the accent desired. Prepare the work and stitch as instructed in *Simulated Appliqué*.

### Beads with Stitch Patterns

Beads combined with decorative stitches are an elegant way of enhancing cocktail and evening dresses, jackets, and stoles.

Prepare the work as described under *Simulated Appliqué* above. Set the stitch length selector for satin stitching. Select a closely spaced and an open-spaced stitch pattern to use within each leaf and a narrow, plain zig-zag stitch to outline the leaf. Pull the threads through to the underside and tie them after stitching each section. When completed, trim the backing close to the stitching. Press. To add a touch of glamour, arrange a few beads asymmetrically on the designs and hand-sew them in place.

## Monograms

To monogram the "K" shown here, prepare the work as described under *Simulated Appliqué*, page 275. The first stitching is within the monogram. Select the stitch pattern, set the stitch length selector for satin stitching, and stitch. Then select a narrow, plain zig-zag stitch. Align the marking

**Plate 9**

ding adds glitter
ala evenings

ht: Peau de soie leaves
bands in warm golden tones
liquéd on peau de soie obi.
d-sewn bugle beads.

w left:
ding applied with open-spaced
zag stitching in a design
explodes with the gaity
sparkling fountain.
sters of round beads
n by hand.

w right: Muted glimmer
short evening dress.
n band is decorated
zig-zag stitching,
liqué, and hand-
n beads;
slip-stitched
ress
edged
beading.

## Plate 10

### Appliqué for all seasons

*Above:* Appliqué of gold
synthetic leather (easier to
handle than the real thing)
forms an elegant jewel on deep blue velvet.

*Left:* Airy silk organza shadow-appliquéd with
three colors. Different layers are cut away
to obtain various shades.

*Below:* Gold synthetic leather appliqué highlights
decorative stitching on taffeta.

for the monogram with the center of the presser foot, and stitch, outlining the outer edges. Pull the threads to the underside and tie them after stitching each section. When finished, trim the backing close to the stitching. Press.

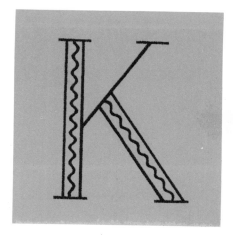

For the "G W" monogram, prepare the work as described under *Simulated Appliqué,* page 275. Set the stitch length selector for satin stitching. First, work the individual flower petals, using the ball stitch pattern. To start stitching at the begin-

ning of the pattern unit see page 266. Then outline the monogram with a narrow, plain zig-zag stitch. Align the marking for the design with the center of the presser foot. Begin stitching at the point near the finished petals; gradually turn the fabric with both hands as you sew. When completed, pull the threads through to the underside and tie them. Trim the backing close to the stitching. Press.

# EMBROIDERY

Script monograms and satin-stitched scallops that look like hand embroidery can be made with zig-zag stitching when you use the "free-motion" method.

In free-motion stitching, you sew without a presser foot and control the fabric movement (and hence, stitch length) yourself by means of embroidery hoop. Because you can move the hoop in any direction—forward or backward, from side to side, and even diagonally—free-motion stitching is well adapted to intricate embroidery designs.

## To Prepare the Machine

Adjust the machine for a plain zig-zag stitch and either a medium or wide stitch width. Generally, a lighter needle thread tension is required. See page 266. Raise the stitch length selector to a short stitch. Remove the presser foot. Make the

feed inoperative so that it will not move the fabric. (This is done by either raising the throat plate or lowering the feed. Refer to the instruction book accompanying your machine.)

## Monograms

Always make a test sample first to determine the correct stitch width, spacing, tension, and hoop movement.

Trace or mark the monogram on the right side of the fabric. See page 251. If the fabric is soft or loosely woven, add an underlay of crisp lawn or organdy slightly larger than the hoop used. Carefully baste the backing to the wrong side under the area where the stitching will be applied.

Center the work, right side up, in embroidery hoop large enough to encompass the entire design. Be sure that the fabric is held taut in the hoop.

277

Position the work under the needle. Lower the presser bar to activate the tension. Turn the hand wheel toward you and bring the bobbin thread up through the fabric to start the design.

Lower the needle into the fabric, hold both thread ends, and start stitching. Move the hoop slowly, following the outline of the design. To maintain parallel stitches, follow the monogram without turning; the work should remain straight in line with the feed at all times. The shading of stitches from wide to narrow is controlled by slowly moving the hoop to the right or left and at a slight angle. Where lines cross, make the first line of stitching less dense and the second line more prominent. This takes practice.

Run the machine at an even rate of speed so that the stitches are uniformly spaced. A slow motion of the hoop produces a close satin stitch; a more rapid movement produces an open stitch.

When finished, bring the threads through to the underside by means of a needle, and tie them. Cut away the backing close to the stitching. Press.

### Monograms on Terry Cloth (Above right)

Monograms can easily be applied to bath and hand towels, beach robes, and other articles made of terry cloth.

Trace the monogram on a firm fabric, such as crisp lawn or organdy, slightly larger than the hoop used. Carefully position the lawn *on the right side of the terry cloth* and baste it in place. Then stitch, following the directions given above. When finished, cut away the lawn close to the stitching, using small, sharp scissors. Steam from the wrong side.

## Satin-Stitched Scallops

Satin-stitched scallops provide a beautiful and durable finish for household linens as well as wearing apparel.

Trace the scallops on the *right side* of the fabric; *do not cut*. See page 251 for instructions. When scalloping is used as an edge finish, allow at least a 1-inch margin beyond the tracing. Machine-baste a strip of fabric to the cut edge so that the work is wide enough to fit in hoop.

If the fabric requires a backing, use crisp lawn or organdy cut slightly wider than the hoop. Machine-baste the marked scalloped edge over the center of the backing. The lawn or organdy serves as an extension on the edge as well as a backing.

Center the work in embroidery hoop and position it under the needle the same as for monograms.

To maintain parallel stitches, follow the scallops without turning; the work remains straight in line with the feed at all times. Stitch slowly, moving the hoop to the right or left, so that the needle on its left swing follows the marking for the scallops. This produces the effect of a narrow stitch at the point between the scallops; the stitch widens to its full depth at the arc. Maintain an even rate of speed so that the stitches are uniformly spaced.

**To cord scallops.** A fine corded edge is used as an edge finish to complete satin-stitched scallops. Use the Special Purpose Foot on the machine,

and insert the filler cord into the right eyelet. See *Hairline Seam,* page 88 for threading instructions.

Position the needle close to the scalloped edge; lower the foot and stitch close to the scallops, covering the filler cord with narrow, closely spaced, plain zig-zag stitches. Crowd the stitches against the scallops all the way. Press.

If scallops border a hem, cut away the surplus of hem on the wrong side, close to the inside of the scallops. If scallops form an edge, cut away the surplus border and backing close to the cording stitches on the outside of the scallops. Then cut away the backing close to the inside of the scallops.

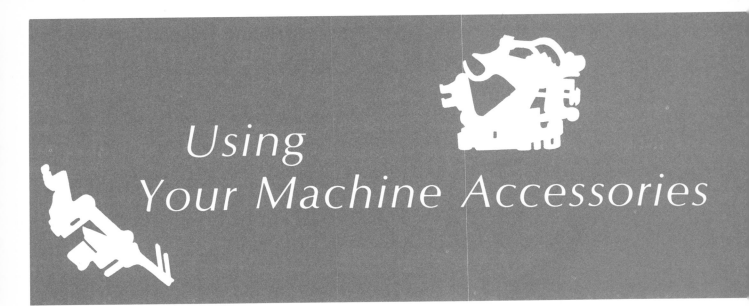

# Using Your Machine Accessories

ACCESSORIES ADD NEW DIMENSIONS to machine sewing. They enable you to accomplish quickly and expertly many finishing details that would be laborious and time consuming by hand.

Accessories are available for almost every phase of sewing. Many are standard and come with the machine; others can be purchased separately. This chapter explains how to use them all.

## To Attach an Accessory

*The accessories replace the regular presser foot on the machine.* Refer to the instruction book accompanying the machine or accessory for complete information on how to place each one on your machine. If the accessory has a needle hole, be sure to draw the needle thread through it by taking a stitch in a swatch of fabric before starting to sew.

## Zipper Foot, Seam Guide, and Quilter

These three accessories are illustrated elsewhere in the book. For pages giving instructions on their use, consult the alphabetical index.

The *Zipper Foot* simplifies zipper application and cording. It can be adjusted to the right or left of the needle and enables you to stitch close to the chain portion of a zipper or the bulk of a filler cord. It is a boon in dressmaking as well as in making home decorations.

The *Seam Guide* ensures accurate seam width and parallel lines of stitching for accent. It is in-

valuable to the beginner and even to the experienced sewer.

The *Quilter,* with its short, open foot and adjustable and removable space guide, is especially adapted to stitching lightly padded fabrics.

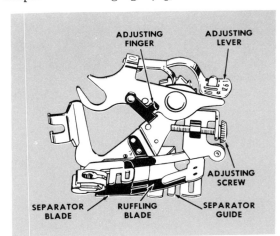

## Ruffler

The Ruffler makes uniform gathered or pleated ruffles on light or medium-weight fabrics. The simple settings belie the variety of work possible.

For instructions on fabric requirements and cutting of ruffles, and for additional information, see *Ruffles,* page 240.

*Gathering.* Adjust the Ruffler for gathering. For maximum fullness, turn the adjusting screw clockwise; for less fullness, turn it counterclockwise. The stitch length also affects the fullness; a short stitch produces more fullness, a long stitch less.

Insert the fabric to be ruffled between the two blue blades. Bring the edge under the first guide to keep the seamline even. Stitch, guiding the fabric.

Correct Position for Fabric to be Ruffled

**Ruffle with heading.** Insert the fabric to be ruffled between the two blades, extending the right edge beyond the needle the width of the heading. As you sew, guide the fabric to keep the heading width even.

Correct Position for Fabric to be Ruffled

**To form and attach a ruffle in one operation.** Insert the ruffle strip, wrong side up, the same as for plain gathering. Place the fabric to which the ruffle is to be joined, right side up, between the

Ruffler and feed of the machine. Bring the fabric edge under the first guide. Stitch.

Correct Positions for Fabrics

**Pleating.** Adjust the Ruffler for pleats, either six or twelve stitches apart. Turn the adjusting screw clockwise as far as it will go. A short stitch places the pleats close together; a long stitch places them farther apart. Insert the fabric to be pleated between the two blue blades as you did for gathering. Stitch; as each pleat is formed, finger-press it the full depth of the ruffle.

Correct Position for Fabric

when you apply the binding, see *Zig-Zag Sewing* page 268.

**Inside curves** are straightened as they are fed into the Binder. If the fabric is soft and has a tendency to stretch, reinforce the edge with a single row of stitching before binding.

## Binder

The Binder is used to apply commercial binding or self-fabric bias to an unfinished edge. Binding is a suitable finish for seam and hem edges that fray easily and a pretty trimming for ruffles, aprons, children's wear, curtains, and novelty items. Straight or zig-zag stitching may be used with the Binder.

Cut the binding diagonally to form a long point at the end. Insert the point in the slot in the Binder and pull it through the scroll until the evenly folded binding is under the needle. Stitch just far enough to place the stitching close to the edge. To do this, move the scroll to the right or left. Do not pull the binding as it feeds through the scroll. Do not raise the presser bar after the stitching is in the correct position.

**Outside curves** tend to lead away from the scroll. Guide the fabric to the left in line with the needle so that the full seam width is taken. Do not attempt to pull or straighten the fabric into the full length of the scroll.

**When rickrack braid** is applied to an edge as it is bound, insert the edge and rickrack into the Binder at the same time, keeping the edges flush.

Insert the edge to be bound as far to the right as it will go in the center scroll, and stitch.

To use decorative or plain zig-zag stitching

## Hemmer Foot

With the Hemmer Foot you can turn and stitch narrow hems without basting or pressing. A time-saving accessory, it is especially suited to hemming ruffles, sashes, or any long edge where a narrow, machine-stitched hem is appropriate. Many yards may be finished as quickly as stitching a straight seam. Either straight or decorative stitching may be used. See *Narrow Hem Finishes*, page 195 for additional information.

**Hemming.** Form a ⅛-inch double fold at the very edge of the fabric and crease it for a distance of about 2 inches. Place the fabric under the foot and stitch through the creased fold for several stitches. Hold the thread ends in the left hand and

evenly guide the raw edge in front of the Hemmer into the scroll. Soft fabrics will enter the scroll best with the foot down; firm, crisp fabrics, with

the foot raised. Even feeding is essential. As you sew, keep the same width of fabric in the scroll at all times.

**Hemming with lace.** You can form a hem and stitch lace edging in place with one line of stitching.

*To apply lace over the hem,* fold and start the hem in the usual way. Start about 1 inch down from the end of the lace and place the selvage under the needle; lower the needle to hold the lace firmly. Raise the foot slightly and slip the lace under the back portion of it. Stitch, guiding the hem with the right hand and the lace with the left.

*To apply lace under the hem,* place the selvage of the lace ⅛ inch from the fabric edge; then fold and start the hem in the usual way. As you stitch, keep the lace ⅛ inch from the fabric edge, and form the hem over the lace selvage.

**Hemmed seam.** See page 85 for instructions.

## Edge Stitcher

The Edge Stitcher enables you to accurately place stitching on the extreme edge of a fabric. Using the numbered slots as your guide, you can join lace edges, fabric bands, and lace insertion; make French seams of uniform width; stitch tucks from pin width to ¼ inch; and edgestitch hems, facings, and seams.

The distance from the line of stitching to the edge of the fabric is regulated by the lug, which can be moved to the right or left. Test the adjustment on a swatch of fabric before working on the garment.

***To edgestitch.*** Pink the edge of the seam allowance, facing, or hem. Fold the edge under from ⅛ to ¼ inch, and place it in slot 1. Adjust the lug to the left, far enough to position the stitching near the edge of the fold. Stitch, guiding the edge against the edge of the slot.

***To join lace insertion and fabric bands.*** See page 261 for instructions.

***To make a fine French seam.*** Trim the seam allowance to ¼ inch. See *French Seam*, page 86 for instructions on forming the seam. For the first

row of stitching, place the seam in slot 1 with the lug adjusted to the left for a ⅛-inch seam.

For the second row of stitching, use slot 1 with the lug adjusted to its extreme right. For a wider French seam, use slot 5 and move the lug to its extreme left for the second row of stitching.

**To make tucks from pin width to ¼ inch.**
See *Tucks,* page 235 for instructions on marking the position of the tucks on the fabric and for other information. Fold and press the fabric on the drawn thread the entire length of each tuck. The Edge Stitcher keeps the tucks uniform in width.

*To make pin tucks,* insert the creased fold in slot 1, and adjust the lug far enough to the left to position the stitching *just a few threads from the folded edge.* Guide the fold against the edge of the slot as you sew.

*To make ¼-inch tucks,* insert the. creased fold in slot 5 and move the lug to its extreme left position.

**To make tucks with lace.** See page 237 for instructions.

See *Shirring,* page 242 for instructions on marking the fabric, suggestions on fabrics that are appropriate for shirring, and additional information.

Rows of shirring spaced ¼ inch apart may be gauged by the edge of the foot. The center of the Gathering Foot is your stitching guide. Align it with the marking for the shirring.

## Gathering Foot

The Gathering Foot enables you to place single or multiple rows of shirring quickly and expertly. Since the foot is designed to lock fullness into every stitch, it ensures evenly spaced shirring.

The stitch length on the sewing machine regulates the fullness of the shirring; a long stitch produces more fullness than a short one. Tension also affects fullness; your shirring will be fuller with heavy tensions than with light. Matching thread is generally used, but thread contrasting in color is quite acceptable for variety.

## Tucker

The beauty of a tuck depends on absolutely accurate stitching. The Tucker enables you to achieve that for tucks from ⅛ to 1 inch in width. It carries two adjustable scales—a tuck guide and a space scale. *The tuck guide* is numbered from 0 to 8 at 1/8-inch intervals, with markings between the numbers spaced at 1/16-inch intervals; it ensures tucks of equal width from start to finish. *The space scale* is numbered from 0 to 8 at ¼-inch intervals, with marks between the numbers at ⅛-inch intervals; it ensures equal spacing between the tucks. The grooved blade and spur blade on the space scale mark the fabric for the fold of the next tuck while the present tuck is being stitched. Each scale is locked in position by means of an adjusting screw.

Before you begin, carefully study the material under *Tucks*, beginning on page 235. It will give you guides on fabric width required, marking the first tuck, proper stitch length, and additional information.

Adjust the tuck guide to the left or right for the desired width; move the space scale to the left or right for the desired space.

Fold and crease the fabric for the first tuck. Insert the creased fold between the grooved blade and spur blade on the space scale and between the two blades on the tuck scale. Place it far enough to the right to feed against the tuck guide. As you sew, the space scale marks the position for the next tuck.

**Tucks and spaces may be equal, or the fold of the tuck may touch the previous tuck as in a blind tuck.** Follow the suggested settings for tucking when adjusting the scales.

## Suggested Settings for Tucking

|  | Tuck Guide | Space Scale |
|---|---|---|
| ⅛″ tucks with no space | 1 | 1 |
| ⅛″ tucks with ⅛″ space | 1 | 1½ |
| ¼″ tucks with no space | 2 | 2 |
| ¼″ tucks with ¼″ space | 2 | 3 |
| ½″ tucks with no space | 4 | 4 |
| ½″ tucks with ½″ space | 4 | 6 |
| 1″ tucks with no space | 8 | 8 |

Straight or decorative stitching may be used with the Tucker. See page 237.

## Buttonholer

The Buttonholer makes neat worked buttonholes in a variety of fabrics in a fraction of the time required by hand. The buttonholes are firmer and more durable than those made by hand—and also more regular. In addition, they are all the same length because a template controls the buttonhole length as well as style. The Buttonholer controls the stitch width and cutting space, which can be adjusted to accommodate fabric from sheer to heavy coating.

Five templates of varying lengths come with the Buttonholer—four for straight buttonholes and one for eyelet-end buttonholes for suits and coats. Five additional templates are available—three for straight buttonholes, one for an eyelet-end buttonhole, and one for eyelets for belts, studs, and lacings.

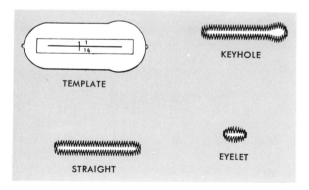

TEMPLATE    KEYHOLE

STRAIGHT    EYELET

Determine the buttonhole length and position as described under *Worked Buttonhole*, page 116. Carefully mark the length and line of the buttonhole with chalk or hand basting along the thread of the fabric.

Place the fabric under the cloth clamp on the Buttonholer. (The cloth clamp will hold the fabric in position when the presser bar is lowered.) Align the buttonhole marking with the center front and back lines of the cloth clamp, and align the center line of the garment with the horizontal lines that are second from the back on both sides of the clamp. This alignment will accurately position the starting point of the buttonhole ⅛ inch beyond

the center-line marking of the garment. Follow this procedure for all succeeding buttonholes so that they are the same distance from the garment edge.

For guides on stitching the buttonholes, refer to the instruction book accompanying the Buttonholer. It gives you complete information.

Always make a test buttonhole on a swatch of your fabric to determine the correct settings of the stitch width and cutting space as well as the buttonhole length. Duplicate the number of fabric layers you will be using in the garment and include the same type of interfacing.

# Sewing for Children

SOME OF THE GREATEST JOYS in sewing come from making well-fitting and becoming clothes for children and delicate dresses and articles for babies. Aside from your own satisfaction are other rewards, equally important: the individuality you can give your child's wardrobe and the money you can save. If your clothing budget is limited, you will find that you can outfit your children handsomely, in better fabrics, and at a fraction of the cost of ready-made clothes in expensive children's shops.

## MAKING CLOTHES FOR BOYS AND GIRLS

Fashion is important to children. Little girls and boys know when they are smartly dressed and when a garment fits well. They begin at an early age to develop good taste and good grooming habits.

Sewing for little girls is a mother's delight—a pastime that may develop into a truly creative hobby as the girls grow older. Sewing for little boys generally continues until the boys reach the age where their shirts and pants require tailoring techniques.

Children's patterns are available in a variety of styles. Mother and daughter dresses and brother and sister outfits can be attractive and are often in the fashion picture. A word of caution here: Never make children's clothes too large, thinking they can be worn for a longer time. Both fit and fashion are lost along the way and generally the garment is worn out and discarded before the child grows to fit it. However, skirts may be made with deep hems so that they can be lengthened and worn a second year; the same is true of coats, including the sleeves.

### Fabrics

Fabrics most suited for children's dresses, suits, and coats are gingham, broadcloth, chambray, poplin, percale, batiste, linen, dotted Swiss, organdy, organza, denim, sailcloth, piqué, seersucker, madras, flannel, lightweight wool, tweed, velveteen, corduroy, synthetic fabrics such as dacron and nylon, and bonded fabrics. Wash-and-wear and a blend of two fibers are practical and popular since they are easy to launder and require little ironing.

Always select a fabric that will withstand the wear and laundering necessary for children's clothes. Also, be certain that the fabric is tubfast and sunfast. If it is not preshrunk or Sanforized, shrink it before cutting. See page 15.

### Color and Design

When sewing for children, you have an almost unlimited selection of colors from which to choose. Dark as well as pastel shades may be used. Let common sense be your guide. Select colors that are becoming to the child and practical for the outfit you are making.

As for design, solids, small plaids and prints, narrow stripes, little dots, and tiny checks all look charming on children.

### Measurements

Measure the child accurately and record the measurements on the charts; girls' opposite, boys' on page 290. If the child is very young, it is advisable to measure a garment that fits the child correctly and record those measurements on the chart. To measure the crotch for slacks and shorts, see page 49.

Here are some rules to observe in measuring:

Sleeve seams should be at the shoulder line, not dropping over the shoulder.

A round neckline and collar should hug the neckline closely; a square or V neckline should fit the neckline closely over the shoulder line.

The waistline should be midway between the hip bone and the end of the ribs and should fit with a slight ease.

Short sleeves should end halfway between the shoulder and elbow; puffed sleeves should be shorter. Full-length sleeves extend to the wrist. Three-quarter length sleeves extend halfway between the elbow and wrist.

The skirt length must be correct for the dress to be fashionable. For a small girl, the skirt is short, usually midway between the knee and hip-line. As a girl grows older, the skirt should generally be longer.

# GIRL'S MEASUREMENTS

The illustrations below show you where to place the measuring tape when taking each measurement. **Measurements are taken from right side.**

*(Consider seam allowance in checking with pattern)*

| | CHILD'S MEASUREMENT | ALLOWANCE FOR EASE | PATTERN MEASUREMENT |
|---|---|---|---|
| **1. CHEST** . . . . . . . . . . . . . . . . . . . . . . . . . . . | _____ | 1½" to 2" | _____ |
| **2. BREAST** . . . . . . . . . . . . . . . . . . . . . . . . . . | _____ | 1½" to 2½" | _____ |
| **3. WAIST** . . . . . . . . . . . . . . . . . . . . . . . . . . . . | _____ | _____ | _____ |
| **4. HIP: 3" below waist** . . . . . . . . . . . . . . . . . | _____ | _____ | _____ |
| **5. NECK CIRCUMFERENCE** . . . . . . . . . . . . . | _____ | _____ | _____ |
| **6. SHOULDER LENGTH:** Right . . . . . . . . . . . | _____ | _____ | _____ |
| Left . . . . . . . . . . . | _____ | _____ | _____ |
| **7. SHOULDER TO SHOULDER** . . . . . . . . . . . | _____ | ½" to 1" | _____ |
| **8. WAIST LENGTH: a—**Front . . . . . . . . . . . . | _____ | ½" to 1" | _____ |
| **b—**Back . . . . . . . . . . . . | _____ | ½" to 1" | _____ |
| **9. SLEEVE LENGTH:** | | | |
| **a—**Shoulder to elbow . . . . . . . . . . . . . . | _____ | _____ | _____ |
| **b—**Elbow to wrist . . . . . . . . . . . . . . . . . | _____ | _____ | _____ |
| **c—**Inside from underarm seam to wrist . . . . . . . | _____ | _____ | _____ |
| **10. SKIRT FINISHED LENGTH:** | | | |
| **a—**Front . . . . . . . . . . . . . . . . . . . . . . . . . | _____ | _____ | _____ |
| **b—**Back . . . . . . . . . . . . . . . . . . . . . . . . . | _____ | _____ | _____ |
| Plus allowance for hem (3" to 5") . . . . . . . . . | _____ | _____ | _____ |
| Plus allowance for "let-out tuck" . . . . . . . . . . . . | | | |
| (2" if desired) . . . . . . . . . . . . . . . . . . . . . . | _____ | _____ | _____ |

# BOY'S MEASUREMENTS

The illustrations below show you where to place the measuring tape when taking each measurement. **Measurements are taken from right side.**
*(Consider seam allowance in checking with pattern)*

| | CHILD'S MEASUREMENT | ALLOWANCE FOR EASE | PATTERN MEASUREMENT |
|---|---|---|---|
| 1. **CHEST** . . . . . . . . . . . . . . . . . . . . . . . . | _____ | 5" to 7" | _____ |
| 2. **WAIST** . . . . . . . . . . . . . . . . . . . . . . . | _____ | _____ | _____ |
| 3. **HIP** . . . . . . . . . . . . . . . . . . . . . . . . . | _____ | _____ | _____ |
| 4. **HEIGHT:** Neckline to Floor . . . . . . . . . . | _____ | _____ | _____ |
| 5. **BACK LENGTH OF SHIRT** Neck to waistline plus "tuck-in" . . . . . . . . . | _____ | 1½" to 2" | _____ |
| 6. **SHOULDER TO SHOULDER** . . . . . . . . . . | _____ | ½" to 1" | _____ |
| 7. **FINISHED LENGTH OF TROUSERS** . . . . . | _____ | _____ | _____ |
| 8. **FINISHED LENGTH OF SHORTS** . . . . . . . | _____ | _____ | _____ |
| 9. **FINISHED LENGTH OF JACKET:** **a**—Front . . . . . . . . . . . . . . . . . | _____ | _____ | _____ |
| **b**—Back . . . . . . . . . . . . . . . . . . | _____ | _____ | _____ |
| 10. **NECK CIRCUMFERENCE** . . . . . . . . . . . . | _____ | _____ | _____ |
| 11. **SLEEVE LENGTH** . . . . . . . . . . . . . . . . . | _____ | _____ | _____ |

# Patterns

### Selecting Pattern Size

Before selecting the pattern, study the measurements on the back of the pattern envelope. For girls, select the pattern according to the breast measurement; for boys, chest measurement. *Never select a pattern by age.*

The size designated on the pattern will give the approximate age for which the pattern was designed. But children of the same age often differ in height, weight, and contour. A three-year-old child, for example, may require a size 4 or size 2 pattern. By using the breast and chest measurement as a guide, you will have to make very few, if any, adjustments in the pattern for a good fit.

The pattern allows sufficient ease for action; however, the ease may vary with the style and make of pattern. Buy the same size coat pattern as dress or shirt pattern since the necessary ease is included.

### Checking the Pattern

Always measure the pattern and make any necessary adjustments. See *Checking the Pattern against Your Measurements,* page 37.

Pin the pattern pieces together and try the pattern on the right side of the figure if the child is not too young.

### Adjusting the Pattern

The adjustments for children's patterns are essentially the same as for adults'. See *Adjusting the Pattern,* page 39. Shown here are adjustments for the *chubby child.*

**To add width across the chest, waistline, and sleeves.** Slash the front and back bodice and sleeve from lower edge .to armhole as illustrated. Place a piece of tissue paper underneath and spread the pattern to add one-fourth the width required. Pin the pattern to the tissue. Adjust the skirt in the same manner. Remember that only one-half the pattern is given; therefore, an adjustment of ½ inch in both the front and the back bodice sections will add 2 inches to the chest and waist measurement.

**To add width across the shoulders, chest, and waistline.** Slash the front and back bodice from the center of the dart at the lower edge to the shoulder line. Place a piece of tissue paper underneath and spread the pattern to add one-fourth the width required. Pin the pattern to the tissue. Adjust the skirt in the same manner. The shoulder width will be increased the amount of the adjustment; the chest and waistline will be increased four times the amount of the adjustment.

Decrease the darts the amount of the adjustment, as indicated by the dotted line. The darts should be in the correct position when the adjustment is made through their center.

## Construction Tips

Good workmanship is essential. The construction tips listed below will guide you in your sewing for children. For specific instructions on each one, consult the alphabetical index.

**Seams.** Make sturdy seams that will withstand the many washings and rough wear to which the garment may be subjected. For little girls' dresses of washable cottons, wash-and-wear, and sheer fabrics, use French seams. For velveteen, corduroy, and linen, use plain seams pressed open, and finish the seam edges with overcasting.

Boys' shirts should be constructed with either a flat felled seam or a French seam. For shorts and pants, use a flat felled seam for play clothes and a plain seam pressed open for better clothes. Finish seam edges with binding, edgestitching, or overcasting.

Blend seams the same as you would in clothing for adults. See page 89.

**Interfacings.** Use a washable interfacing such as muslin, batiste, or lawn in boys' shirts, girls' dresses and blouses, and collars and cuffs. Always interface the waistband on shorts.

**Plackets.** The continuous bound placket is appropriate for the skirts of dresses and for boys' shirt sleeves with cuffs.

**Hems.** Always allow 3 or 4 inches for hems in full, gathered skirts and about 2 inches for hems in gored skirts. Hem finishes should be durable. Edgestitching is excellent for most fabrics. Finish velveteen, corduroy, and linen with seam binding. Hems blindstitched by machine are satisfactory for everyday dresses and shorts; for better clothes, finish hems by hand.

**Closings.** Buttons and worked buttonholes are used for most closings. On pajamas, coveralls, and boys' shirts, dot snappers may be substituted.

**Decorative touches.** To vary the look of often-used patterns, add something new. Dresses, for example, may be changed with the application of tucks, lace, ruffles, appliqué, lacing, rickrack, braid, bias folds, pockets, smocking, cording, or decorative zig-zag stitching. The neckline, waistline, and sleeve edge of little girls' dresses may be finished with a double-fold bias or covered cord; such details are found only in the better ready-made dresses. An organdy pinafore may be added for charm. Your machine accessories will simplify the stitching of many decorative details. (Refer to the alphabetical index for the listing of these finishes.)

**Petticoats.** When a dress has a full skirt, sew the petticoat to the waistline. Make the petticoat of net and cut it by the skirt pattern. Use a French seam to join the skirt sections. Gather the petticoat and skirt fabric separately, then join them to the bodice in a single seam. For instructions on gathering the skirt, see page 106.

After hemming the skirt, trim the petticoat to the same length and finish the edge with silk seam binding. Use decorative zig-zag stitching or straight stitching to sew the binding in place.

## Special Features in Children's Clothes

### Growth and Shrinkage Tucks

A tuck is frequently put into children's clothes to allow for growth or fabric shrinkage. The tuck *must be on the true grain of the fabric* and may be placed in the following sections, among others: (1) in the hem so that it is not visible on the right side; (2) on the right side just above the hem; (3) in the bodice near the waistline; and (4) vertically over the shoulder. Although you may use a regular

straight stitch, a chain stitch is ideal, for it makes "letting out" a simple task—you merely unlock the last loop of the chain formed on the underside of the tuck and pull out the stitching. (If your machine has Chain Stitch accessories, see page 63.)

### Sash

The sash on a child's dress is often cut in two pieces and joined to the garment at each side seam.

**To make the sash.** Hem each side of the two pieces, using the Hemmer Foot. Hem one end of each piece by making a ⅝-inch double fold. Press, then stitch near the edge of the first fold.

292

## Plate 11

### A girl's garden of roses

*Above:*
Roses cut out of a printed linen handkerchief,
appliquéd to sheer fabric.

*Below:*
Flowered ribbon laced through two rows
of buttonholes, as described on page 273.

*Above:*
Folded sheer fabric
forms rosebuds,
which are held in place
by appliquéd leaves.

**Cheery bibs**

*Below:* Terry cloth bibs with bias-bound edges. All motifs are appliquéd with plain zig-zag or decorative zig-satin stitch. Fish scales are scallop-stitched by machine.

*Below, left to right:*

1) Plain zig-zag satin stitching used to appliqué clown and outline his features.

2) Pique "paper dolls" appliquéd on gingham.

*Below, left to right:*

1) Shadow appliqué.
After the two layers are stitched together
in squares, top layer of each square is cut away.

2) Polished-cotton pelican with fish, appliquéd with
plain zig-zag satin stitch. Scallop stitch pattern forms
backbone of fish, and ball pattern makes flower and eye.

**Plate 14**

**Fragile femininity**

*Above:*
Rows of lace edging
applied with
scallop stitch pattern
form the yoke
of an organdy
party dress.

*Above right:*
Tissue gingham trimmed
with bias strips and lace edging,
applied with
scallop stitch pattern.

*Left:*
On organdy, open-spaced
plain zig-zag stitching
forms floral outline
with lace flower
tacked in center.
Rows of decorative
stitching trim
double-fold hem.

Another method is to form a point at the sash ends. Fold the end, right sides together, and stitch ¼ inch from the cut edge. Backstitch at each end. Clip off the corner at the folded edge, and press the seam open. Turn to the right side, forming a tie point.

**To join the sash to the bodice.** Fold the unfinished ends of the sash into pleats and join them to the bodice, following one of the methods given below:

**Method 1: *Before stitching the side seams of the bodice.*** Pin the sash, right side up, to the right side of the back bodice, keeping the cut edges even at the side seam and the lower edge of the sash even with the waistline seamline. Stitch in place as the front and back bodice sections are seamed together.

**Method 2: *After the dress is finished.*** On the right side, position the sash, right side up, at the side seam, keeping the cut edges to the front, the sash to the back, and the lower edge even with the waistline. Pin, then stitch ¼ inch from the cut edge; backstitch at each end. Trim the cut edge to ⅛ inch. Fold the sash to the front and stitch in place on the side seam. Backstitch at each end. This encases the cut edges and forms a finish similar to a French seam.

### Fly Closing

For boys past the age of three, a fly closing should be used on shorts and pants. A trouser zipper is available in an 11-inch length only; it must be cut off at the top after it is stitched in place. A neckline zipper can be used for small boys' shorts and pants.

Cut the shorts or pants by the pattern. Transfer the notches and markings to the fabric. The fly closing is the first construction work.

Pin the facing for the opening over the left front, right sides together. Stitch from the waistline to the marking for the crotch. Trim the seam allowance to ¼ inch and clip into it on the curve. Press. Clip into the seam allowance ⅜ inch at the lower end of the opening. Turn the facing to the underside, fold on the stitching line, and press.

Turn the facing and seam allowance away from the garment. Place the closed zipper, face down, over the right side of the facing, with the edge of the tape even with the seamline and the bottom stop ¼ inch above the crotch seamline. Curve the tape to fit the lower end of the opening. Pin in place.

Adjust the Zipper Foot to the right of the needle and place two rows of stitching from the bottom to the waistline. Place the first row close to the chain portion of the zipper and the second row near the edge of the tape.

On the right front, clip into the seam allowance ⅜ inch at the lower end of the opening. Fold the edge of the opening under ¼ inch from the seamline. Open the zipper and pin the folded edge to the right side of the tape, with the bottom stop ¼ inch above the crotch seam and matching the left front at the end of the opening and at the waistline. Construct the fly shield, then pin it in place under the zipper, with the seam edges even. Baste through all thicknesses. Stitch in place from the bottom of the zipper to the waistline, close to the fold. Remove bastings.

Pin the crotch seams together with the cut edges even. Stitch, joining the stitching of the left front facing seam. Backstitch at each end.

Turn the left front facing to the underside and pin. Baste in place, following the markings on the right side. Stitch on the right side, close to the basting, from the lower end to the waistline. (Do not catch the fly shield in the stitching.)

At the lower end, pull the threads through to the underside and tie. Make a bar tack through all thicknesses at the end of the opening. See page 337. This prevents ripping. Press the stitching, but do not press over the zipper.

Interface the waistband with muslin, following the instructions under *Method 1*, page 154. Open the zipper and pin the waistband to the waistline, right sides together, extending the band ends ½ inch beyond the opening. Stitch. Trim the seam edges to ¼ inch and cut off the ends of the zipper if they extend beyond the waistline seam edge. Press. Turn the band away from the garment and press the seam allowance toward the band. Turn the ends of the band under ½ inch and press.

Turn under the free edge of the band and pin it in place on the underside, enclosing the seam allowances. Top-stitch around the band. Work buttonholes and sew on buttons.

### Elastic Band on Boxer Shorts

To apply elastic to the waistline of boxer shorts you may use zig-zag stitching or straight stitching. Use conventional elastic or a woven elastic made especially for boxer shorts, pajamas, and underwear.

Fit the elastic band at the waistline for the desired snugness, allowing 1 inch for joining the ends. Lap the ends 1 inch, then fold one end under ¼ inch and join with two rows of narrow zig-zag stitching.

To attach the elastic to the waistline, use one of the methods described here—*Method 1* if the elastic is visible on the underside, and *Method 2* if the elastic is concealed between the hem and garment.

**Method 1:** Fold under the waistline seam allowance on the garment and press. Divide both the elastic circle and the garment waistline into quarters and pin-mark the garment and each edge of the elastic at these intervals.

Place the elastic circle over the wrong side of the garment, extending the fold for the seam ⅛ inch beyond the elastic. Pin each edge of the elastic to the garment at the quartered intervals.

Join the two with a row of stitching placed near each edge of the elastic. Sew with the elastic up; as you stitch, stretch the elastic between the pins so that it will remain stretchable after the stitching is completed. Use a medium-width zig-zag stitch and a 10 stitch length. If you want a third row of stitching, space it evenly between the first two rows. Pull threads to the underside; tie and clip.

**Method 2:** Finish the cut edge of the waistline hem with the blindstitch zig-zag, or fold it under ¼ inch and edgestitch. Fold the waistline hem to the underside of the garment and press. Divide both the elastic circle and the garment waistline into quarters and pin-mark the garment and each edge of the elastic at these intervals.

Turn the hem away from the garment and, on the underside, align the elastic edge with the crease for the hem. Pin each edge of the elastic to the hem at the quartered intervals. Then, with the elastic up, stitch near the top edge of the elastic. Stretch the elastic between the pins as you stitch so that it will remain stretchable after the stitching is finished. Use a medium-width zig-zag stitch and a 10 stitch length.

Fold the elastic and hem to the underside and pin to the garment at the quartered intervals. On the right side, place a row of zig-zag stitching close to each edge of the elastic, stretching the elastic between the pins as you sew. If you add the third row of stitching, space it evenly between the first two rows. Pull threads to the underside; tie and clip.

### Shirt-Sleeve Opening

**The opening.** Finish the opening before stitching the sleeve seams. Slash the opening as marked on the pattern. Cut the pieces for the overlapping and the underlapping edges of the slash.

Bind the back edge of the slash with the narrow piece, taking a ¼-inch seam. Pin the overlap

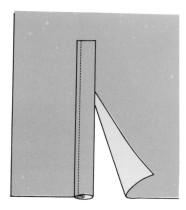

piece to the front edge of the slash with the right side next to the wrong side of the sleeve. Stitch, making a ¼-inch seam. Press, then press the seam edges toward the sleeve.

Turn the overlap to the right side of the sleeve. Turn under the cut edge and adjust the piece so

that it will overlap the back edge. Press. Top-stitch around the overlap and stitch twice across the point to hold the underlap in position.

Stitch the sleeve seam, using a flat felled seam. Gather the lower edge. Turn the sleeve to the right side.

**The cuff.** Use a muslin interfacing. Make the cuff following the instructions on page 172, leaving the top edge open. Trim one seam edge and the interfacing to ⅛ inch and the other edge to ¼ inch. Press. Turn the cuff to the right side, and press. Pin the underside of the cuff and interfacing to the sleeve, matching markings. Adjust the gathers to fit the cuff, and stitch. Trim the seam allowance to ¼ inch, then press. Turn the cuff away from the sleeve and press the seam allowances toward the cuff. Turn the cut edge under on the top side of the cuff and pin it to the sleeve at the stitching line, enclosing the gathered seam allowance inside the cuff. Top-stitch as illustrated. Press. Work buttonholes and sew on buttons.

Sewing for babies brings you into a world of soft fabrics, fine seams, and dainty trimming. Choose soft cotton, silk, or woolen fabrics that will withstand frequent laundering. Kimono sleeves are practical in most infants' wear except dresses. They are simple to construct and their loose fit makes them comfortable for the baby and simplifies dressing for the mother.

A fine French seam, machine or hand-stitched, is preferred in garment construction. Your first stitching of the seam may be by machine and the second by hand. Since the fabric is delicate, the stitches should be short.

Trimming should be dainty. Narrow Val lace edging and insertion, entredeux, tiny pin tucks, dainty hand stitches, small appliquéd motifs, narrow hemstitching, smocking, scallops, and small zig-zag stitches that are lacy in design are all appropriate, decorative finishes for infant apparel.

## Needle and Thread

The sewing thread should blend with the fabric in fiber, color, and size. In selecting a needle, consider both the fabric and the thread. Silk and woolen fabrics are stitched with silk thread and size 11 needle. Cottons, such as batiste, outing flannel, flannelette, piqué, pin wale corduroy, and cotton knits, are stitched with size 50 mercerized thread and size 14 needle. Threads used for embroidery stitches should be fine enough for you to make dainty stitches on the soft fabrics you will be working with.

## Fastenings

Use tiny buttons and hand-made buttonholes or thread loops in dresses, slips, and diaper shirts; use string ties in sacques and kimonos. The hammer-on snap fastener is practical for the crotch opening of sleepers and crawlers. A narrow, ¼-inch, continuous bound placket or a hemmed placket is appropriate below the yoke of a garment. If the garment does not have a yoke, a hemmed placket is preferred.

## Patterns

Basic layette patterns can be purchased at pattern counters. It is wise to select two or three and adapt them to your needs.

The seam allowance in layette patterns varies from ¼ to ½ inch, depending on the location of the seam and the make of the pattern. Observe the allowance indicated.

## Pinning and Receiving Blankets

Pinning and receiving blankets are made of outing flannel and flannelette. Each blanket requires 1 yard of 36-inch fabric. Remove the selvages and finish the edges following one of the methods given here.

*Method 1:* Turn the cut edge under ¼ inch and press. Then fold a ¼- or ⅜-inch hem and baste. Finish the edge with a blanket stitch or buttonhole stitch. See page 231.

*Method 2:* For a wider hem, which is frequently used, turn the hem to the underside 2¼ inches and press. Fold the cut edge under ¼ inch; miter the corners as instructed on page 195. Baste the hem in place and finish on the top side, using a featherstitch near the inside edge of the hem. A group of French knots or a small lazy daisy stitch placed in each of the corners adds a touch of daintiness.

## Gowns

Gowns are made of batiste, cotton crepe, nainsook, outing flannel, flannelette, and fine cotton jersey.

For sturdy seams that will withstand many washings, use a fine French seam throughout the construction. Finish the neckline and sleeves with a narrow hand-rolled hem, or face the edges with ⅝-inch lace insertion. Gather the lace and hand-sew it around the neckline and sleeves. If the fabric is white or a solid color, consider adding French knots near the neckline and sleeve edge. A small design, such as a duck, bunny, or kitten may be outlined with a cable stitch or small buttonhole stitch; use a pastel color and a single strand of six-strand floss.

Hem the lower edge by turning the cut edge under ¼ inch; then fold and baste the hem. Finish with a slip stitch.

If a drawstring is used at the bottom, leave one underarm seam open about ⅜ inch in the hem area. Turn the casing in the same manner as the hem and machine-stitch in place. Insert 1½ yards of ¼-inch twill tape in the casing.

## Sacques

Sacques are made of crepe de chine, challis, albatross, fine soft woolen, pin wale corduroy, outing flannel, and flannelette. Whites and pastel colors are appropriate; kimono sleeves are customary. Line silk and wool with China silk or crepe de chine; line cottons with batiste.

### Lined Sacque

Cut the sacque and lining by the same pattern. Stitch the underarm seams separately in each. Clip

into the seam allowance at the underarm curve. Press the seams open and stay them at the curve of the underarm seam. See page 162.

Apply decorative detail around the neckline, front opening, lower edge, and sleeve—for example the featherstitch, French knots, lazy daisy stitch, or one of the lacy zig-zag machine stitches. A tiny appliqué may be placed near one side of the neckline or a very small pocket may be added as a finishing touch.

Turn the sacque to the wrong side. Place the lining inside, right sides together, matching seams and cut edges. Pin, then baste along the neckline, fronts, and lower edge. Stitch in a continuous line; make one stitch diagonally across the corners and overlap a few stitches at the starting point. Leave the sleeve edges open for turning the sacque to the right side. Trim the lining seam allowance to ⅛ inch and the sacque seam allowance to ¼ inch. Clip diagonally across the corners, close to the stitching, and clip into the seam allowance on the neckline curve. Notch the seam allowance of outside curves that may occur. Press.

*(Continued)*

Turn the sacque through the sleeve opening to the right side. Fold on the seamline and baste. Press. To finish the sleeve edges, turn the seam allowance of the sacque to the underside and pin. Press. Turn the edge of the lining to the underside and pin it to the sacque. Slip-stitch the folded edges together.

Narrow lace edging may be gathered and hand-stitched to the outer edges.

Cut two 9-inch lengths of narrow ribbon for the ties. Fold one end to the right side ⅛ inch and pin to the underside of the neckline opening, overlapping the edges ⅛ inch. Hand-sew in place.

***Zig-zag finished edge.*** The sacque in the illustration is made of albatross lined with China silk. The neckline is finished with a single bias fold that extends about 8 inches beyond each side of the opening for ties.

Stitch the underarm seams separately in the sacque and lining, following the instructions given above. Place the lining inside the sacque, wrong sides together, matching seams and keeping the cut edges even. Baste near all edges. Select the small scalloped zig-zag stitch on the machine and set the stitch length for satin stitching. See *Edge-stitched Finish*, page 274. From the right side, stitch down the front, around the lower edge, and up the opposite front. Stitch around the sleeve edges. Press. Trim the fabric close to the stitching.

center of the back neckline. Then pin around the neckline to the center fronts. When the neckline is finished, fold the tie ends under ¼ inch and press. Turn the long cut edges of the tie to the center and finger-press. Bring the folded edges together and pin; then slip-stitch. Do not draw the threads taut.

### Unlined Sacque

Unlined sacques are made of cotton crepe, crepe de chine, and soft rayon. Ideal for summer wear, they are constructed in the same manner as unlined kimonos.

## Kimonos

Kimonos are made of outing flannel, flannelette, pin wale corduroy, challis, cotton crepe, cotton jersey, and sheer cotton print. They may be lined or unlined. Batiste and fine terry cloth are appropriate fabrics for linings.

### Lined Kimono with Raglan Sleeves

Cut the kimono and lining by the same pattern. Sew in the raglan sleeves and stitch the underarm seams separately in the kimono and in the lining. Press the seams open. Finish the lower edge of the kimono sleeve with a rolled hem and lace. See page 260. Gather the lower edge of the sleeve leaving a ½-inch heading, and gather the lining sleeve ½ inch from the edge.

Finish the neckline with a single-fold bias binding with ends long enough to tie. Cut off the seam allowance if binding is not specified on the pattern. Pin the neckline edges of the sacque and lining together and stitch a scant ⅛ inch from the edge.

Refer to *Single-Fold Bias Binding*, page 146, for instructions on finishing the neckline. Cut the true bias strip ¾ inch wide and 26 inches long. Begin by pinning the center of the binding to the

Turn the kimono to the wrong side. Place the lining inside, right sides together, matching seams and cut edges. Pin, baste, stitch, and blend the seams, following the instructions for the lined sacque; however, leave the lower edge open enough for turning the kimono to the right side.

Turn the kimono through the opening to the right side. Fold on the seamline and press. Slip-stitch the open edges together.

Trim the edge of the sleeve lining to within ¼ inch of the gathering stitches. Turn it under, barely beyond the stitching, and pin it to the gathering stitches of the kimono sleeve. Slip-stitch in place.

Gather the lace edging. See page 259. Hand-sew the lace to the edges of the neckline and front. Make buttonholes and sew on buttons.

### Unlined Kimono

Cotton crepe, outing flannel, batiste, and sheer cotton print are appropriate fabrics for summer wear.

French-seam the underarm seams. Finish the neckline, fronts, lower edge, and sleeve edges with a single-fold bias binding (see page 146) or with a ⅛-inch rolled hem, hand-stitched in place. Gather narrow lace edging and sew it to the rolled hem, or use a blanket stitch in place of the lace. Appliqué a small design near the neckline, or use a fine featherstitch close to the hem. Use tiny buttons and thread loops for the closing.

## Diaper Shirts

Diaper shirts are made of batiste, nainsook, outing flannel, flannelette, and cotton jersey.

Use a fine French seam at the shoulder and underarm. Finish the edge of the neckline, fronts, and sleeves with one of the decorative zig-zag stitch patterns (see *Edgestitched Finish*, page 274), with binding, or with the blanket stitch applied

over a ⅛-inch hem. Finish the lower edge with a ⅛-inch hem, hand-stitched in place. Place a dainty appliqué near one side of the neckline. Close with buttons and buttonholes.

## Dresses

Dresses are made of batiste, organdy, and silk organza. A fine French seam is used throughout the construction. If the dress has a set-in sleeve, sew in the sleeve before stitching the underarm seam whenever possible. It is much easier to work with a flat surface than with a dress that is joined at these seams, especially when it is so small. Also, complete the placket before stitching the underarm and inside seams. Use tiny buttons and hand-worked buttonholes in the back opening.

Babies' clothes can be finished in so many beautiful ways that it is impossible to list them all; a few of the prettiest finishes are illustrated here.

### Tucked Yoke Dress

Tiny pin tucks spaced 3/16 inch apart in groups of four, six, or eight, add a delicate beauty to the dress. Tucks may be hand- or machine-stitched. Fold, press, and stitch tucks in the front and back sections. See *Tucks*, page 235. At the lower end of the tucks, pull the threads to the underside and tie them together in a single knot.

**Placket.** Make a hemmed placket in the back of the dress. Slash down the center back to the end of the opening. At the end, clip diagonally into each side ⅛ inch. On one side, turn the hem on the marking and press. Then turn the cut edge under ⅛ inch and pin it to the dress. Slip-stitch

**Seaming and pleating.** Join dress front and back at the shoulder line and underarm, using a fine French seam.

Many patterns show an inverted pleat at the underarm. Lay in the pleat and press. Stitch in place at the armhole, barely outside the seamline.

in place. Finish the opposite side in the same way. Lap the right hem over the left, and hand-stitch the lower ends together. This forms a soft pleat in the dress below the opening.

**Neckline finish.** Draw up the thread at the top edge of narrow lace edging and gather it to fit the neckline seam. Distribute the fullness evenly. Finish one end of the lace with a narrow hem. Baste the gathered lace, right side up, to the wrong side of the neckline seam. Finish the opposite end of the lace. Trim the neckline seam allowance to a scant ¼ inch. Roll the fabric edge over the seamline, and make small overhand stitches through the lace and rolled hem. Remove bastings. Turn the lace up over the edge, and press.

**Sleeves.** Finish the lower edge of the sleeves with narrow lace edging and a rolled hem the same as the neckline. Gather the lower edge of the

sleeve, leaving a ⅜-inch heading. Pin narrow lace insertion over the gathers and hand-sew each edge of the insertion, using a hemming stitch. Use a French seam to stitch the underarm seams.

Stitch the sleeve in the armhole. See *Set-In Sleeve*, page 158. Trim the seam allowance on the sleeve side to ⅛ inch, and on the armhole side to ¼ inch. Turn the edge of the armhole seam allowance under ⅛ inch; fold this seam allowance over the sleeve seam allowance to the stitching line, enclosing the cut edge. Pin. Slip-stitch in place.

**Hem.** A plain hem is generally used. Make it about 3 inches deep. Turn the hem to the underside and baste ¼ inch from the fold. Press. Turn the free edge under ⅛ inch and baste to the dress. Slip-stitch in place. On the top side, finish the hem with fine featherstitches or French knots.

Work buttonholes in the placket and sew on buttons.

### Round Yoke Dress

The dainty, simple design of the yoke dress is traditionally favored for babies.

**Yoke.** Join the yoke sections at the shoulder line, using a fine French seam. Fold and hand-stitch the hems in the back opening. See *Placket*, page 302. Finish the neckline with gathered lace applied to a ⅛-inch rolled hem, as instructed on page 260.

Draw the thread at the top edge of lace insertion and shape it to fit around the seamline of the outer edge of the yoke. Press. Finish one end of the insertion with a hem the same width

as the yoke opening. On the right side of the yoke, baste the insertion, right side up, with the edge on the seamline. Finish the opposite end of the insertion. Trim the seam allowance under the lace to a scant ¼ inch. Roll the fabric edge and make small hand stitches through the rolled edge and lace.

**Joining yoke and dress.** Join the shoulder seams of the dress, using a fine French seam; hem the placket, following the instructions for the tucked yoke dress. Gather the dress to fit the yoke. Pin, then baste the lace insertion on the yoke over the seam allowance of the dress. Trim the seam allowance under the lace to a scant ¼ inch. Roll the fabric edge and make small hand stitches through the lace and rolled edge. In the gathered section of the dress, sew the insertion in place from the top side, using small hand stitches over the lace edge; then overcast the fabric edges on the underside.

*Sleeves.* Stitch the sleeve seam, using a fine French seam. Sew gathered lace to the lower edge. See *Puffed Sleeve,* page 161. After you have stitched the sleeve in the armhole, finish the seam as instructed for the sleeve, page 303.

*Hem.* The scalloped hem is a dainty finishing touch. Transfer the scallop pattern to the lower edge of the dress, as illustrated. (The scallops will be reversed when the hem is turned.) Cut on the scalloped line. Turn the hem to the underside and baste ¼ inch from the fold. Press. On the free edge, clip ⅛ inch into the curve of the scallops at even intervals. Turn the edge under ⅛ inch, retaining the shape of the scallops, and baste. Baste

the scalloped edge to the dress. On the right side, finish the hem with a featherstitch or place French knots around the scallops. Gathered lace edging, hand-sewed on the right side of the scalloped edge, is also a lovely finish.

### Christening Dress

Christening dresses may vary in length from 21 to 30 inches or longer. For this special occasion, the dress should be elaborate, yet dainty and delicate enough to belong to a baby.

## Additional Dress Finishes

Make a tiny collar of a single thickness of fabric. Either roll the collar edge and hand-sew gathered lace around it as instructed on page 260, or use

a small decorative zig-zag scallop on the edge. See *Edgestitched Finish,* page 274. Join the collar to the garment with a ½-inch bias facing, following the instructions on page 148. Or use narrow lace insertion instead of a bias strip—especially if you are hand-sewing the collar. Steam-press the lace and shape it to fit the curve of the neckline; pin it in place and finish by hand.

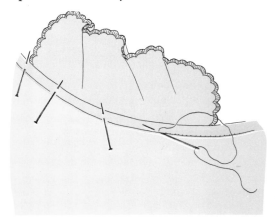

Instead of a hem, finish the lower edge of the baby's dress with edgestitching as you did the collar above.

## Bassinet Cover and Skirt

The bassinet skirt illustrated has seven visible rows of shirring at the top and is finished with a tiny cord on the edge. Two 6-inch ruffles are sewed to the lower edge of the skirt. The skirt is held in place with dot-snap tape and can easily be removed for cleaning and storing.

A bassinet skirt may be made in any number of ways. The construction of the one illustrated is basic to all skirts.

There should be an *overskirt* and an *underskirt.* The overskirt may be of a sheer fabric, such as nylon net, organdy, eyelet embroidery, point d'esprit, or dotted Swiss. Taffeta, Glosheen, cotton satin, or chintz are suitable opaque fabrics for the underskirt. The overskirt may be white and the underskirt a pastel pink or blue, or both skirts may be white.

The inside of the basket should be lined with the same fabric used for the underskirt. The lining is quilted with a small cross-bar design.

The bassinet in the illustration is 90 inches in circumference and 27 inches from the top edge to the floor. The basket is 12 inches deep.

### Fabric Requirements

The skirts should be gathered. Use triple fullness in the sheer overskirt and double fullness in the opaque underskirt. Fabric width may vary from 36 inches to 42 inches, and net may be 72 inches wide. In figuring your yardage requirements, therefore, consider the width of the fabric. In the bassinet illustrated, 40-inch fabric was used. Two inches were allowed for selvage and a French seam on each side, leaving a finished width of 38 inches.

Fabric requirements are determined as follows:

**Overskirt.** For the **width,** measure the circumference of the bassinet and multiply this figure by the amount of fullness required. *Example:* 90 inches (circumference) x 3 (fullness) = 270 inches after seaming. (Multiply the circumference by 2 when twice the fullness is required.)

For the **number of lengths** of fabric, divide the circumference plus fullness by the width of the fabric after seaming. *Example:* 270 inches (circumference plus fullness) ÷ 38 inches (width of fabric) = 7 lengths of fabric. (If the division results in a fraction of a length, buy another entire length.)

For the **skirt length,** measure from the top edge of the bassinet to the floor. (When the skirt is hemmed at the bottom and seamed at the top, it will be a scant 1 inch from the floor.) *Example:* 27 inches (length of skirt) x 7 (number of lengths) = 189 inches or 5¼ yards. Allow an additional ¾ yard for covering the cord and straightening the ends of the fabric; purchase 6 yards.

If the fabric has a design, remember to allow extra yardage for matching. See page 367.

The **two 6-inch ruffles** are twice as full as the overskirt. *Example:* 270 inches (fullness of skirt) x 2 (ruffle fullness) × 2 (number of ruffles) = 1080 inches, or 30 yards of ruffling. Six 6-inch widths, each 38 inches long, can be cut from 1 yard of fabric; therefore, buy an additional 5 yards of fabric for the ruffles.

**Underskirt and bassinet lining.** The fullness of the underskirt is twice the circumference of the bassinet. Multiply the circumference by 2 instead of 3, then figure the fabric requirements the same as you did for the overskirt. Five 27-inch lengths of 40-inch fabric, or 4 yards are required for the skirt in the example.

Line the inside of the bassinet with the same fabric as the underskirt. One and a half yards will be needed. Purchase an equal amount of outing flannel or sheet wadding to back the fabric for quilting.

### The Lining

For the bassinet in the illustration, the lining must be 15 inches deep and 93 inches in circumference (including seams).

Straighten the ends of the fabric as described on page 14. Then cut strips of fabric on the lengthwise grain 15 inches long; cut as many strips as you will need for the 93 inches (about 2½ strips of 40-inch fabric). Join the strips with a ½-inch seam allowance; do not join the last ends together for the circle yet.

Cut the backing of outing flannel or sheet wadding the same size as the lining, and quilt the two pieces together. See *Diagonal Quilting*, page 256. When the quilting is finished, join the open ends with a ½-inch seam allowance.

Place the quilted lining inside the basket, wrong side out, with a seam at one corner, and extend the edge over the top rim of the bassinet about 2 inches. Shape the lining to fit smoothly by pinning a dart at each of the corners. Stitch the darts; then trim the dart width to within ½ inch of the stitching. Press the darts open. Sew ½-inch twill tape to the lower edge of the lining. Separate the dot-snap tape and stitch one half to the right side of the upper edge.

Place the lining smoothly inside the basket, right side out, and tack the twill tape to the bottom of the basket. Turn the upper edge over the top rim of the basket.

### The Overskirt

Straighten the fabric. See page 14. Cut the required number of fabric lengths for the overskirt. Measure accurately and draw a thread from the fabric to indicate the cutting line and to ensure cutting on the true grain (see page 14).

Remove selvages and join the fabric on the lengthwise grain with a fine French seam. Press. Finish the lower edge with a narrow hem, using the Hemmer Foot. Press. If net is used, you need not hem it.

Cut 6-inch strips on the crosswise grain of the fabric for the ruffles. Draw a thread from the fabric for the cutting line. Join the strips; then hem each edge, using the Hemmer Foot. (Net need not be hemmed.) Gather the ruffles with a ½-inch heading. Pin them to the skirt, keeping the lower edge of the first ruffle even with the lower edge of the skirt, and the lower edge of the second ruffle barely above the heading of the first ruffle. Stitch on the gathering stitches of the ruffles.

Gather the top edge of the skirt. Use heavy-duty mercerized or nylon thread on the bobbin because it will not break while you are easing the fullness across the width of the skirt. Follow the instructions for *Gathering to Control Fullness* on page 105. (Omit the pin tuck across the threads in this application.)

First divide the skirt into two sections and pin-mark. Then gather each section separately. After you have placed the first two rows of stitching in the seam allowance, place seven additional rows below the first, spacing them ¼ inch apart. Use the presser foot as a guide. To gather each skirt section, pull the bobbin thread at each end of the section and ease the fullness toward the center. Distribute the fullness evenly. Try the skirt on the bassinet to be sure it fits correctly. Pull the threads to the underside and join the broken lines of stitching by tying the four threads together in a single knot close to the stitching.

### The Underskirt

Cut the required number of fabric lengths for the underskirt. Make them the same length as the overskirt and on the same grain. Remove the selvages, and join the fabric on the lengthwise grain, with a narrow French seam. Finish the lower edge with a narrow hem, using the Hemmer Foot.

Gather the underskirt in the same way as the overskirt. However, place only three rows of stitches below the first row; space them ½ inch apart.

### Joining the Skirts

For the corded welting around the top edge, cut a true bias of the sheer overskirt fabric and one of the opaque underskirt fabric. Cut enough lengths for the circumference of the gathered skirt plus seam allowances. Cover the cord, following the directions for sheer fabric on page 245.

Follow the instructions for cording a straight seam on page 245. Pin and stitch the cording to the right side of the overskirt. Join the ends of the cording as described on page 397. Then join the two skirt sections with the right side of the overskirt next to the wrong side of the underskirt.

Trim the corded seam allowance to ⅛ inch, and trim the seam allowance on both skirts to ¼ inch. Press. Turn the overskirt to the right side over the underskirt. The right sides of both skirts should face in the same direction. Fold on the seamline, and press.

Turn the underskirt and seam allowance away from the overskirt and pin the remaining side of the dot-snap tape to the underskirt, barely below the cording. Stitch on each side of the tape. Turn the underskirt back in place. Place the skirt around the bassinet, and fasten the dot-snap tape to hold the skirt in position.

## CHILDREN CAN SEW TOO

While you are busy making dresses for your child or outfitting the nursery, there may be a pair of young eyes that enjoys watching you work and a pair of young hands that wants to stitch a seam too. This is the moment to lay your own sewing aside and to teach your child some simple sewing skills.

As an activity for children, sewing has much to recommend it. It brings out and stimulates children's innate creative talent, builds self-confidence, and gives them a sense of accomplishment.

Also not to be overlooked is the value of sewing in developing dexterity and coordination.

Sewing is an activity in which both boys and girls can express themselves easily and fluently. But keep it simple at first. The best beginning for small hands is hand sewing. Teach the child to make an X or sew on sequins and buttons, using a coarse needle and thread and following no particular pattern. A little later show the child how to thread a needle, to knot the end of the thread, and to baste two pieces of fabric together.

As you go along, teach the child that safety and care of her sewing equipment are two good friends. Needles, for example, belong in a pin cushion when not in use. Get her a pin cushion of her own and a small sewing box fitted with other supplies—a pair of small scissors, a small thimble, two or three needles with large eyes, several spools of colored thread, one lead pencil and one white pencil, and a ruler.

When your young beginner is old enough to sit at the sewing machine, teach her first how to stitch straight on lined tablet paper with the needle unthreaded, how to raise and lower the presser foot, how to control the speed of the machine, and how to keep her fingers a safe distance from the needle. When you are satisfied that the child can control the machine safely, teach her to thread it and to make a plain seam and hem. A sewer visualizes an idea, and the moving needle gives it shape and form. Thus real creativity is likely to manifest itself in each sewing project.

## Sewing Machines for Children

If you have an eager young seamstress, you might consider the Little *Touch & Sew* sewing machine by Singer. Designed for the age level five to nine, it bridges the transition between hand sewing and real sewing.

The machine has a bobbin and bobbin winder, and it makes a lockstitch on real fabric. The presser foot has a guard that keeps little fingers out of the path of the needle.

Although the machine comes with batteries, you can remove them if your daughter is very young and let her begin sewing by using the hand crank. Later on, if you wish, you can buy an electrical adapter that converts the machine from battery or hand power to regular electric power.

## Sewing Projects for Children

When children do begin to sew, they should start with simple projects—things they can make quickly and without much trouble. Nothing is more discouraging to a child than to undertake a project with excitement and anticipation and then find the

details beyond her skill. But if the child is taught the details gradually and systematically, she will soon master them and enjoy the thrill of seeing real results.

Doll clothes are the first thought of many little girls. Save scraps of fabric for doll dresses and sequins, old buttons, and short lengths of lace, braid, and rickrack for trimmings. As your child progresses, she may want to try a real pattern for her doll's outfit. Pattern companies have created patterns for an entire wardrobe for dolls of all sizes.

To encourage individuality, let children be their own designers if they choose, cutting patterns when they need them. They may design items for gifts as well as for their own use.

Felt, flannel, and terry cloth are three fabrics that are easy for children to handle and that lend themselves to many gift articles. Some of the possibilities are listed below. They can all be made without patterns but do require accurate measuring and the drawing of straight lines or circles:

| | |
|---|---|
| Apron | Mat for dog dish |
| Baby bib | Needle case |
| Bath mitt | Pencil and pad |
| Beanbag | holder |
| Bird cage cover | Pencil case |
| Book cover | Placemat |
| Bookmark | Potholder |
| Collar | Puppet |
| Dog's coat | Record tote bag |
| Doorknob cover | Scarf |
| Eyeglass case | Shoe bag |
| Marble bag | Tool case |

When children reach the age of nine, they become more ambitious and adventuresome in their sewing projects. They are able to do neat finishing, and many are capable of making a simple dress, skirt, or blouse for themselves. They should be taught how to use a thimble and how to press. This may be the time when a young girl will wish to increase her sewing skills by studying sewing in school or taking a sewing course at the Singer Center during her summer vacation.

**Plate 15**

**The animal kingdom at play**

A part of each of these felt motifs was made with a PROFESSIONAL* buttonholer (note the owl's beak, the fish's scales, and the bulldog's nose.) Eyes are eyelets stitched with a buttonholer.

Other facial features are stitched with zig-zag patterns.

Children's clothes, tote bags and decorative cushions are just three of the many articles that would be brightened by these whimsical motifs.

**Plate 16**

**A flight of fancy butterflies**
Imaginative ways to combine
machine-worked buttonholes and eyelets
with decorative stitch patterns.

Any of these
gay butterflies
would add a delightful touch
to a gift wrapping,
could later serve
as a charming
button-on decoration
—on an apron, for example.

# Tips on Mending

THE MENDING BASKET, like the ironing basket, is seldom empty. Just when you think you've reached the bottom, it disappears beneath an armful of socks and blue jeans and sheets.

Although mending is an unending task, it need not be an onerous one.

Mending is the term used to cover all types of fabric repairs—restitching ripped seams; darning socks; patching children's clothes; mending sheets and wearing apparel; replacing elastic in the waistline of lingerie, pajamas, and boxer shorts; repairing girdles; and replacing blanket binding. All the small jobs that prolong the life of worn but still usable articles can easily be taken care of by hand or by machine. Whenever possible, *mend by machine*. It is quicker, easier, and more durable than hand mending.

For machine mending, you may use the zig-zag machine with the presser foot or free-motion stitching. In free-motion stitching, the presser foot is removed, the feed is made inoperable, and the fabric to be mended is placed in embroidery hoop under the needle and moved manually in any direction you desire. Free-motion mending is usually best suited to a straight stitch machine.

## Needle and Thread

Use a fine needle for both machine mending and hand mending. The thread should match the fabric in color and texture. You can use the warp threads of the fabric to darn small holes by hand, especially in woolens. When darning socks, separate the strands of darning thread and use only one or two in a fine darning needle.

## Machine Darning with Embroidery Hoop

Free-motion darning is easier to do when the machine is designed with a throat plate that can be raised above the feed or with a feed that can be lowered below the throat plate.

Remove the presser foot and raise the throat plate or lower the feed. Set the stitch length lever in the "fine" area (above 20).

### Darning an Open Area

Trim away any ragged edges from the area to be darned. Center the worn section, right side up, in embroidery hoop to hold it taut.

Position the work under the needle and lower the presser bar to activate the tension. Hold the needle thread loosely with the left hand, turn the hand wheel toward you, and draw the bobbin thread up through the fabric. Hold both thread ends and lower the needle into the fabric.

For reinforcement, outline the area to be darned with a line of stitching ⅛ to ¼ inch from the open edge. Stitch across the opening, moving the hoop backward and forward under the needle at a slight angle. Overlap the outline stitching at each end of the area; keep the lines of stitching closely spaced and even in length.

Run the machine at a moderate speed and control the hoop with a steady, continuous movement.

When the opening is filled, turn the work and cover the area with crosswise lines of stitching. Pull threads to the underside; tie and clip. Press.

### *Darning Rents or Tears*

A straight tear may follow either the lengthwise or crosswise grain of the fabric. A three-cornered tear follows both grains.

Press the area around the tear. Cut an underlay, of the same fabric if possible, for reinforcement. Bring the edges of the tear together, and pin the underlay to the wrong side. Baste.

Center the worn section, right side up, in embroidery hoop. Position the work under the needle and pull up the bobbin thread as instructed above. Move the hoop backward and forward under the needle, making about six stitches across the tear until the work is finished. In a three-cornered tear, cross the stitches at the corner for extra strength. Pull the threads through to the underside; tie and clip. Trim away the underlay close to the stitching. Press.

## Machine Darning without Embroidery Hoop

With a little practice, you can darn worn or torn spots effortlessly and quickly without the aid of embroidery hoop.

Turn the pressure dial to D, which releases pressure and permits darning with the presser foot on the machine. See page 25. Set the selectors on the

machine for straight stitching and 10 to 15 stitch length.

If the worn area is open, baste an underlay in place on the underside.

Place the area to be darned under the presser foot. Lower the presser foot and start stitching, alternately drawing the fabric gently away from you and pulling it gently toward you. Continue this forward and backward motion until the area is filled with parallel lines of stitching. For additional strength, turn the work and cover the area with crosswise lines of stitching.

## Darning by Hand

Use a darning ball to darn socks and small embroidery hoop for flat work. Use a fine needle and do not knot the end of the thread.

Darn the sock over the darning ball, or place the flat work in the hoop. Make small running stitches, beginning about ¼ inch beyond the edge of the hole; work across to the opposite side, extending the stitches ¼ inch beyond the hole. Work back and forth, keeping the lines of stitching and the threads across the hole parallel and evenly spaced until the hole is covered. Then turn and work across the threads, weaving alternately over and under in parallel lines until the repair is completed. Be careful not to draw the threads taut; this will cause the work to pucker. Fasten the threads on the underside. Press.

## Zig-Zag Mending without Embroidery Hoop

Zig-zag stitches are just as useful for mending as they are for creative sewing. The multiple-stitch zig-zag and plain zig-zag stitch provide a firm, flexible bond for repairing rents and tears, replacing elastic and blanket binding, and mending lingerie. Select the stitch length and stitch width suitable for the work. Use the presser foot on the machine.

### Repairing Rents or Tears

Trim away the ragged edges. Cut an underlay, of the same fabric if possible, for reinforcement. Bring the edges of the tear together and pin the underlay to the wrong side. Baste.

Place the work under the presser foot with the needle directly over one end of the tear. Use the multiple-stitch zig-zag, and stitch along the line of the tear. Shorten the stitch length at the ends and cross the stitches at the corners for added strength.

Pull threads to the underside; tie and clip. Trim away the underlay close to the stitching. Press.

### Applying Elastic

Elastic is easily applied to the waistline of lingerie, pajamas, and boxer shorts with zig-zag stitching. The elasticity of the stitch prevents the stitches from breaking when the elastic is stretched.

*Lingerie.* Fit the elastic for the desired snugness at the waistline, allowing 1 inch for joining the ends. Lap the ends 1 inch, then fold one end under ¼ inch and join the two, using two rows of narrow zig-zag stitching.

Remove the worn elastic, and press the garment. Divide the elastic circle and the garment

waistline into quarters. From the right side, pin the two together at these intervals, lapping the elastic over the seam allowance of the garment. Join the layers with two rows of the multiple-stitch zig-zag or a narrow, plain zig-zag stitch; stretch the elastic between the pins as you stitch so that it will remain stretchable when the stitching is completed. Pull threads to the underside; tie and clip.

*Boxer shorts.* Remove the worn elastic and press the garment. To apply the new elastic, follow the instructions for *Elastic Band on Boxer Shorts*, page 295.

*Girdle repairs.* Either the multiple-stitch zig-zag or the plain zig-zag is appropriate for mending girdles. Both produce an elastic stitch that will not break when the girdle is stretched. If the repair requires elasticity in two directions—that is lengthwise and crosswise—the multiple-stitch zig-zag should be used, however.

Regulate the stitch length and stitch width according to the need. If you are sewing through several layers of elastic and fabric—for example, repairing the seams, garters, or waistband on foundation garments—use a needle slightly larger in size than that used for regular stitching.

### Replacing Blanket Binding

Remove the worn binding and press the edges of the blanket. Fold under the cut ends of the new binding ½ inch, and pin and baste it securely in place. Stitch, using the multiple-stitch zig-zag. Adjust the pressure, if necessary, to accommodate the thickness of the blanket. Remove basting.

## Patching

If a hole is large, a patch is preferred to darning. The fabric for the patch should be the same as the garment; if no scraps are available, cut the patch from the facing or pocket, or from the undercollar or cuff. If the fabric is a print, plaid, or stripe, match the design of the pattern.

### Patching with Embroidery Hoop

Press the area around the hole. Cut the hole into a square or rectangle, following the thread of the fabric.

Cut the patch 1 inch larger than the hole and center it over the wrong side of the hole, matching the fabric grain and design. Baste.

Center the patch, right side up, in the embroidery hoop.

Prepare the machine and work as instructed in *Machine Darning with Embroidery Hoop,* page 309. .

Work around the patch; move the hoop back and forth under the needle at a slight angle, making about six or eight small stitches across the cut edge. Turn the work at the corners, crossing the stitches for added reinforcement. Press. Trim the edges on the underside close to the stitching.

### Tailored Patch

Press the area around the hole. Cut the hole into a square or rectangle, following the thread of the fabric. Clip diagonally into the corners about ¼ inch. Fold the cut edges under ¼ inch and baste. Press.

Cut the patch 1 inch larger than the hole and

center it over the wrong side of the hole, carefully matching the fabric grain and design. Pin.

From the right side, slip-baste the folded edge to the patch. See *Slip Basting,* page 62.

Remove the pins and the first line of basting that was used to retain the fold.

On the wrong side, turn both the seam allowances away from the garment and stitch through the center of the short basting stitch in the fold. Stitch around the patch, pivoting the fabric on the needle at the corners; overlap a few stitches at the starting point. Pull threads to the underside; tie and clip. Press.

Stitch diagonally across the corners for reinforcement. Remove slip basting and press.

Catch-stitch the wide seam allowance to the garment as illustrated. Be sure that the stitches do not show on the right side. Press.

### Top-Stitched Patch

Top stitching is often used to hold a patch in place.

Cut the fabric for the patch and baste it in place, following the instructions for the *Tailored Patch;* use regular basting instead of slip basting.

On the right side, stitch the patch in place near the folded edge. On the wrong side, fold under the cut edges of the patch and baste in place. Stitch again near the folded edge of the patch. Pull threads to the underside; tie and clip. Press.

## Reinforcing Worn Areas

You can add months of wear to a garment by reinforcing areas that are worn thin. Such areas occur most often at the elbow and underarm of a dress and at the knee and seat of boys' pants. Use a piece of the same fabric or a lightweight fabric such as chiffon, nylon net, or batiste. To reinforce the elbow and knee, select a fabric with some "give."

### To Reinforce the Elbow or Underarm

Cut the reinforcement 1 inch larger than the worn spot. Center it over the wrong side of the worn section, and baste.

Use matching thread and a fine needle. Make small stitches by hand through the two layers of fabric, catching only a single thread of the fabric on the right side. Keep the rows of stitching parallel to the grain of the fabric and extend them slightly beyond the worn area. If extra body is needed, make several rows of stitches in the opposite direction. Fasten the threads on the underside; tie and clip. Press.

If the worn area is in the underarm of the garment, shape the upper edge of the reinforcement to fit the armhole and stitch it to the seam allowance.

### To Reinforce Boys' Pants

Boys' pants last longer if the knees and seat are reinforced with zig-zag stitching when they are worn thin. The thread must match the fabric exactly in color.

Cut the reinforcement 1 inch larger than the worn area. Center it over the wrong side of the worn section, and baste.

Select the multiple-stitch zig-zag, medium stitch width, and short stitch length. Begin and end the work with backstitching. Stitch on the right side. To do this, turn the pants to the wrong side and work on the inside. If the reinforcement is to be placed at the knee, roll up the pants' leg to the stitching. Place several rows of stitching parallel to the grain of the fabric, extending them slightly beyond the worn area but not beyond the reinforcement. At the end of each row of stitching, stop with the needle in the fabric, raise the presser foot, and turn the fabric, pivoting on the needle. Lower presser foot and continue stitching.

# Graduate to Tailoring

TAILORING IS AT THE POST-GRADUATE END of sewing. To it you should bring a thorough knowledge of sewing techniques, flawless workmanship, and actual sewing experience. You must be able to sew with care, know how to handle fabric, respect tailor's tacks and bastings, and exercise care in fitting, seam blending, pressing, and hand finishing. In addition, tailoring requires that you be experienced in the use of underlining and interfacing, which are important in the molding and shaping of the garment. When you use fine fabrics, follow proper sewing techniques, and observe the rules of good workmanship, professional results will not be hard to achieve.

This chapter explains and illustrates the details of suit and coat construction. The principles given here are basic to tailoring and apply equally to other types of tailored apparel.

## PRELIMINARIES

### Pattern

Select the pattern with care. Choose one that is suitable for the fabric and classic enough to be fashionable for several years. Think of the pattern in relation to yourself and your needs and, above all, your figure proportions. Buy the same size suit and coat patterns as dress patterns since the necessary ease is included in the pattern.

### Fabric

Firmly woven wool, tweed, flannel, wool broadcloth, knit fabric, raw silk, heavy cotton, linen, heavy silk, velveteen, corduroy, faille, rayon, a blend of natural and synthetic fibers, and many others are appropriate fabrics for suits. Coats are made of coating, flannel, cashmere, vicuna, wool broadcloth, and faille, to name a few. Although the fabric may be any one of a variety of weaves and weights, it must be heavy enough to prevent the interfacing, and the stitching securing it, from showing through, and sturdy enough to withstand several years of wear and many trips to the cleaners. See *Fabric,* page 7 for additional information.

As for color, select one that is becoming to you. Avoid plaids if you have not worked with them previously. Unless plaids are matched exactly at the seams, they destroy the harmony of the costume.

## Lining and Interlining

To avoid bulk in suits, choose a lightweight fabric for the lining—for example, silk crepe, rayon crepe, or China silk—which matches the jacket fabric in color. Or, as a fashion note, choose a print or contrasting color for the lining and make a matching blouse.

Line coats with heavy silk or rayon crepe, satin, taffeta, Sunbak,[1] or Milium.[2] For warmth and added body, coats are generally interlined with wool or cotton interlining, lamb's wool or with cotton flannel. If Sunbak or Milium is used for the lining, interlining is not necessary. Sunbak lining has a rayon face and an acrylic back that has a fairly deep nap. Milium lining is an aluminum insulating treatment that increases warmth without increasing weight.

## Interfacing and Underlining

Interfacing fabrics are available in many weights and textures. The weight of the garment fabric, the effect desired, and personal preference determine the choice. See *Interfacings,* page 16. For most coats and suits, hair canvas is appropriate. Lightweight suits may also be interfaced with Formite, Siri, or a similar fabric.

Underline jackets and coats designed to stand away from the figure. Hair canvas and pellon are two excellent fabrics that give the added body required for this effect. Loosely woven fabrics may be underlined with China silk, batiste, or voile to support the fabric and give added weight. Shrink batiste and voile before using them. See *Underlining and Lining,* page 20, for additional information.

## Shrinking

Most quality fabrics are preshrunk and ready for cutting. They are usually labeled to that effect on the selvage or tag. If there is any doubt, shrink the fabric as instructed on page 15. Shrink interfacing fabrics except those that are nonwoven.

## Pattern Adjustments

Select the pattern pieces for the version you have chosen. Measure and adjust the pattern to fit correctly. See *Fitting the Pattern to Your Figure,* page 37, and *Adjusting the Pattern,* page 39.

## Pressing

Press out any wrinkles in the fabric before starting the construction work. See *Pressing as You Sew,* pages 66 and 67, for instructions on how to press the fabric you are using and how to press each construction detail. Before attaching the lining, press the jacket carefully on the wrong side; use the proper press cloth and the moisture the fabric requires. Do not press dry. Place the jacket on a hanger; lap and pin fronts and allow the jacket to dry completely before inserting the lining.

## Muslin Shell

If you are a beginner in tailoring, or even an experienced sewer, it is a good idea to construct the suit jacket of muslin before cutting into the suit fabric. The muslin shell will ensure a perfect fit.

Use a good quality of unbleached muslin. After making the necessary pattern adjustments, cut the jacket of muslin. Transfer all notches and markings and mark the center lines on the front and back sections. (Use a tracing wheel and dressmaker's tracing paper to speed up the marking; on the jacket fabric, however, use tailor's tacks and bastings.) Mark the balance lines on the muslin. See page 77.

Stitch and press the darts, seams within the jacket, and shoulder and side seams. Apply the facings and undercollar. Blend all seams properly and press them open. Seam the sleeves and baste them into the armholes. Fold, baste, and press the hems at the lower edge of the jacket and sleeves.

A chain stitch is ideal for stitching the muslin shell for a fitting because the stitching can be ripped out in seconds if adjustments are necessary. If your machine has Chain Stitch Accessories, refer to the instruction book accompanying the machine, and to page 63.

Try on the jacket. For the muslin fitting, wear the blouse, lingerie and shoes you expect to wear with the finished jacket. Also wear a skirt made of a fabric similar in weight. If shoulder shapes or pads are used, slip them between the jacket and blouse. Lap the front opening, matching center

[1] Sunbak. Trademark of Wm. Skinner.
[2] Milium. Trademark of Deering Milliken & Co., Inc.

lines, and pin together at the buttonhole markings.

Check the position of the darts, buttonholes, and pockets; the length of shoulder and waist; the fit across the bustline, shoulder line, and hipline, allowing for the lining. Be sure that the waistline curve is in the correct position. The seams should hang straight from underarm. Check the position of the balance lines. See page 77. Check the fit, the "hang," and the length of the sleeves. The jacket length is important too; it may be necessary to lengthen or shorten the jacket, depending on your figure proportions. Pin-mark any adjustments.

Stitch the adjustments in the muslin shell and try it on again to prove them. Make the same adjustments in the tissue pattern before cutting the fabric.

## Layout and Cutting

Straighten the ends of the fabric as instructed on page 14.

Study the instruction sheet accompanying the pattern and select the layout suited for the fabric width you are using. Lay all the pattern pieces on the fabric in the same direction so that the sheen and color will be uniform throughout the garment. Be sure to place the pieces on the correct grain, then pin them in place. Carefully cut out the garment, using dressmaker's shears.

Cut the notches and use tailor's tacks to mark the position of the buttonholes, pockets, darts, pleats, and any other joinings, such as slashes, gussets, and collars. Use different colored threads to designate each type of marking. Baste the center lines of the collar, skirt, and jacket, both front and back. See *Transferring Notches and Markings*, page 56.

Cut the interfacing, lining, and underlining and transfer the notches, markings, and center lines the same as above.

## The Skirt

Make the skirt first and wear it each time you try on the jacket. Stitch the darts and underline or line the skirt, using the method appropriate for the fabric and style. See *Underlining and Lining*, page 95.

Baste the seams, then try on the skirt to check the fit. If you are satisfied, stitch and press the seams. Finish the seam edges according to the fabric. Use a hand finish for the final stitching of the zipper. See *Skirt Placket Zipper in Lapped Seam*, page 179.

Interface the skirt band; Method 2 on page 156 is excellent. Sew on hooks and eyes at the belt closing.

Try on the skirt, and mark the length. Finish the hem as required by the fabric. See *Hems and Hem Finishes*, page 187.

# CONSTRUCTING THE JACKET

Pin, baste, and stitch the seams within the front and back sections, then press them open. It is not necessary to finish the jacket seams since the lining will cover them.

Baste all darts. Baste the front and back sections together at the shoulder and underarm seams. Baste the sleeve seams. If the sleeve has a center seam, stitch and press it open. Place a line of stitching around the sleeve cap between the notches for ease. Baste the sleeves in the armhole. Stitch the center seam of the undercollar. Pin the collar to the neckline in an overlapped seam, matching seamlines.

## The Jacket Fitting

Try on the jacket with the finished skirt and the blouse and shoes that will be worn with the suit. If shoulder shapes or pads are used, slip them between the jacket and blouse. Lap the fronts so that the center lines coincide, and pin at the buttonhole markings.

Check the position of darts, buttonholes, and pockets; length of shoulder and waist; the fit across the bustline, shoulder line, and hipline, allowing for the lining. Check the fit and "hang" of the sleeve. Be sure that the waistline curve is in the correct position. Check the position of the balance lines. Seams should hang straight from the underarm. Turn the jacket and sleeve hems to be certain of their length. Pin-mark any necessary adjustments, then pin-mark the roll line of the lapels and collar.

Remove the jacket and mark the adjustments with bastings. Try on the jacket again to prove the adjustments. If you are satisfied, continue with the other construction steps in the sequence given below.

## Buttonholes

Bound buttonholes are preferred in better made suits. Place an underlay over the wrong side of the right front section where the buttonholes will be made. Then follow the instructions given under *Bound and Corded Buttonholes*, on page 108.

## Darts

Stitch all darts. Underarm, shoulder, elbow, diagonal, and contour darts are used in making jackets. When they are made on the right side of the jacket, they become a styling point and the "continuous-thread" method should be used in

the stitching. If the fabric is heavy and the dart wide, slash through the center of the dart and press it open. See *Darts*, page 100.

## Back Underlining

Cut an underlining of preshrunk muslin, batiste, cotton broadcloth, or a similar fabric for the back section of the jacket. Use the jacket pattern as a guide. If the back has a center seam, pin the pattern pieces together with the seamlines meeting in the center. Cut the underlining in one piece about 10 inches deep at the center and shaped to fit around the armholes. Slash through the center of the shoulder darts. Lap one cut edge over the other with the seamline meeting in the center; stitch, using the multiple-stitch zig-zag. Backstitch at each end. Press.

Place the underlining over the wrong side of the back section, matching center lines and seam edges. Pin, then baste in place about 1 inch from the edges.

## Front Interfacing

Use *Method 1*, page 136, to treat the seam edge of the interfacing. It ensures a thin seam since the organza instead of the interfacing is included in the seam. If the interfacing has darts, read the instructions under *Interfacing Darts*, page 104.

Pin the interfacing over the wrong side of each front jacket section, keeping the organza strip and garment edges even.

Determine the roll line of the lapels from the neckline to the top button. Place a ruler between these points, and mark the interfacing with chalk. Pin the interfacing in place along this line. Stay it to the lapels with padding stitches, catching only one thread of the fabric under the interfacing. Use thread that matches the fabric. Begin each line of stitches at the top of the lapel and end at the seamline, working from roll line to seamline. As you work, roll the lapel over the first finger, and hold it firmly with the thumb. This will shape the lapels as they will be worn.

Baste the interfacing in place along the seamline; then make a few lines of long diagonal bastings within the interfacing to hold it in position as you work. Press the lapels over a tailor's ham or press mitt.

## Shoulder Seams

Join the front and back sections at the shoulder line; make the seam through the garment fabric only. Clip off the corners of the dart in the seam allowance. Press, then press the seam open. Join the back underlining and front interfacing at the shoulder seam using either Method 1 or 2 below.

**Method 1:** Lap the back underlining and front interfacing over the shoulder seam and pin. Place the shoulder seam, right side up, over the hand to be certain that the interfacing and underlining fit smoothly on the underside. On the wrong side, catch-stitch the lapped seam from the neckline to within ¾ inch of the armhole, catching only the seam allowance of the garment.

**Method 2:** Trim off the seam allowance on the back underlining and front interfacing, and slip the edges under the seam allowance of the jacket. Pin, then catch-stitch the seam edges to the back underlining and front interfacing.

## The Undercollar

### Interfacing the Undercollar

Stitch the center seam of the undercollar and press it open. Lap the center seam of the interfacing, matching the seamlines, and stitch, using the multiple-stitch zig-zag. Mark the interfacing a measured ¾ inch from the edges. Place the markings close together to retain the shape of the collar. Trim on the marked line.

Cut a collar of organza, using the undercollar pattern and omitting the center seam. Center the interfacing over the organza and pin. (The organza should extend ¾ inch beyond all edges of the interfacing.) Clip off the corners of the interfacing to eliminate bulk when the collar is turned. Stitch, using the multiple-stitch zig-zag. Trim the organza under the interfacing ¼ inch from the stitching. Press.

Pin the interfacing over the wrong side of the undercollar, keeping the organza and collar edges even. Baste along the roll line. Use thread matching the fabric. Stay the interfacing to the undercollar with padding stitches from the roll line to the neckline. Then stay the interfacing to the balance of the collar with rows of padding stitches as far as the seamline. As you work, roll the collar to shape it as you did the lapels. Baste the interfacing in place along the seamline. Press over a tailor's ham or press mitt.

### *Attaching the Undercollar to the Jacket*

Pin the undercollar to the jacket, right sides together, matching markings. Work from the garment side. Pin at the center, shoulder, and front markings, then pin at intervals between, easing the collar between the markings. Baste. Try on the jacket to be sure that the collar fits properly.

Stitch the undercollar to the jacket, beginning ⅝ inch from one collar edge and stitching to within ⅝ inch of the opposite edge. Backstitch at each end of the seam. (The open seam allowance at the ends prevents drawing when the facing is stitched and turned.) Remove bastings. Trim the seam allowance of the back underlining to ¼ inch and clip off corners where seams cross at the shoulder and center back. Press. Slash into the seam allowances at evenly spaced intervals so that they will lie flat when pressed. Press the seam open.

## Buttonholes in Interfacing

Baste the interfacing smoothly around each buttonhole. Follow the instructions on page 110 and cut out the interfacing around the buttonholes.

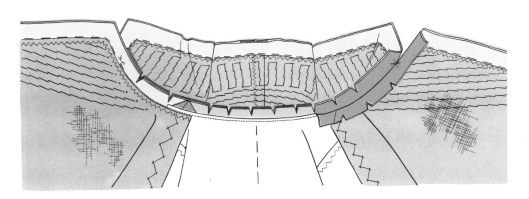

## Facings and Top Collar

If a back neckline facing is not given with the pattern, cut one about 3½ inches deep, using the jacket tissue pattern to shape the neckline and shoulders.

### Joining Facing to Top Collar

Join the front and back sections of the facing at the shoulder seams. Press the seams open.

Pin the top collar to the facing, right sides together, matching markings. Work from the collar side and pin at the center, shoulder, and front markings, then at intervals between, easing the collar between the markings. Baste. Stitch, beginning ⅝ inch from one collar edge and stitching to within ⅝ of the opposite edge. Pull threads through to the underside and tie. Clip off corners where seams cross at the shoulder. Remove bastings and press. Clip into the seam allowances at evenly spaced intervals so that the seam will lie flat. Press the seam open.

### Attaching Facing and Top Collar to Jacket

Place the top collar and facing over the jacket, right sides together. Work from the top collar side and keep the seam edges even. Pin the collars together, first at the center, points, and notches. Match seams where the undercollar joins the jacket and the top collar joins the front facing. Then pin at intervals between, easing the top collar between the markings.

Pin the front facing in place, first at the lapel point, notches, and lower edge. Then pin at intervals between, easing the facing from the top button to the lapel point. Baste with silk thread but do not baste through the seam allowances of the crossing seams where the collars join.

*To stitch the collar seam,* turn the seam allowance on both the top side and the underside away from the collar. Carefully position the needle in the seamline, exactly at the end of the stitching that joins the collar and facing. Lower the presser foot and stitch around the collar to the same point on the opposite side. Make one or two stitches diagonally across the points to avoid bulk when the collar is turned.

*To stitch the facing seam* so that it will join the collar stitching perfectly, place a needle through the seam from the collar side to the facing side. The needle should come out at the end of the stitching that joins the collar and facing. Turn the seam allowance on both the top side and the underside away from the facing. Carefully lower the machine needle in the seamline at the needle marking and stitch. Make one or two stitches diagonally across the point. Stitch the opposite side in the same manner. Check the right side to be sure of an exact seam joining.

Pull the threads on the collar through to the underside and tie. Repeat the same procedure on the facing side, then use a needle to carry the threads through the seam to the collar side and fasten them in the interfacing with two backstitches. This gives added strength at the notch of the collar.

top of the lapel to the top button, trim the garment seam allowance to ⅛ inch and the facing seam allowance and organza strip to ¼ inch. Reverse the blending below the top button by trimming the facing seam allowance to ⅛ inch and the garment seam allowance and organza strip to ¼ inch. Cut diagonally across the points, close to the stitching, and clip off corners where seams cross at the outer edges. Press, then press the seams open.

Trim the seam allowances joining the undercollar and jacket to ⅜ inch from the outer edge to the shoulder line. Catch-stitch the open seam edges to the interfacing on each side.

Turn the facing to the underside. Ease out the corners of the collar and lapels. Baste, using diagonal basting and silk thread. As you work, ease the garment under slightly at the seamline along the lapels and collar, and ease the facing under slightly from the top button to the lower edge. Do not remove these bastings until the jacket is finished. Press, then press lapels and collar over a tailor's ham or press mitt.

Remove the bastings and press. Trim the undercollar seam allowance to ⅛ inch and the top collar seam edge and organza strip to ¼ inch. Notch the seam allowances on the outside curve. From the

Roll the lapels and collar as they will be worn, allowing sufficient ease in the top collar and facing

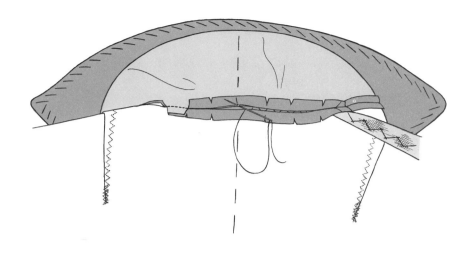

for them to fit smoothly over the roll. Pin the facing and top collar in place along the roll line, then near the neckline seam. Where the collars join the neckline across the back, stay the open seams together between the shoulders with loose hand stitches. (You will complete the work on the front facings after you have set in the sleeves.)

## Sleeves

Before you sew in the sleeves, pin and baste the underarm seams of the jacket; include the back underlining in the seam. Try on the jacket to be sure that it fits correctly. Stitch the seams. Slash the seam allowances at the waistline just far enough so that they will lie flat. Press, then press the seam open.

Construct the sleeves. Refer to *Set-in-Sleeve,* page 158 for instructions on pinning and basting the sleeve in the armhole. Include the back underlining, but not the front interfacing in the seam.

Try on the jacket. Check the "hang" of the sleeve. Turn the hems in the sleeve and jacket and check their length. Pin-mark any adjustments.

Remove the jacket and adjust the sleeve if necessary. Baste the marking for the hemline of the sleeves and jacket.

Stitch the sleeve in the armhole, overlapping the stitching at the underarm seam. Remove bastings, clip off corners where seams cross at the underarm and shoulder. Trim the back underlining seam allowance to ¼ inch. Press. Turn the seam into the sleeve.

If the fabric is heavy and the armhole snug, trim the seam allowance on the sleeve side to ⅜ inch over the cap between the notches, then baste it to the garment side of the seam, using easy stitches. At the underarm, between the notches, trim the armhole seam allowance to ⅜ inch, then sew the edges together, using either the multiple-stitch zig-zag or the blindstitch zig-zag. Place the stitching between the seamline and seam edge. Hand-sew the front interfacing to the sleeve seam, barely outside the previous line of stitching, using matching thread. Trim the interfacing to within ¼ inch of the hand stitching.

*To maintain the roll of the sleeve cap,* cut sheet wadding on the true bias 1¼ inches wide. Fold it through the center, then pin it to the sleeve side of the seam allowance over the cap between the notches, keeping the fold even with the stitching line. Hand-stitch the sheet wadding to the sleeve seam.

## Shoulder Pads or Shapes

Suits with set-in sleeves require support at the shoulder line. If shoulder pads are not in fashion, use two layers of heavy felt or hair canvas to make shoulder shapes.

Use the jacket tissue pattern as a guide. Fold and pin the shoulder darts in the front and back bodice sections of the pattern. Cut a double thickness of felt the shape of the shoulder line and armhole as far as the notches. Remove the tissue pattern. On the back section, begin 1 inch from the neckline and cut the felt diagonally to the armhole notches. On the front section, begin 1 inch from the neckline and cut the felt straight down to the lower edge, then across to the armhole notches. Four front and back sections are required to make a pair of shoulder shapes.

Join the front and back sections at the shoulder line by lapping one edge over the other, with seamlines meeting in the center; pin. Stitch, using the multiple-stitch zig-zag. Join the two layers of

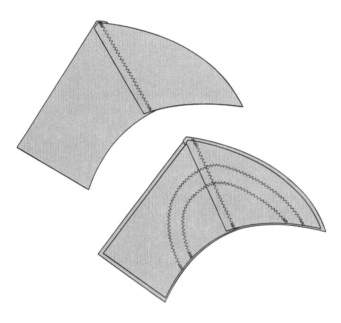

shapes with two lines of multiple-stitch zig-zag, as illustrated. Cut off the bottom layer of felt ¼ inch from the outer edge; remember to trim one shape for the right shoulder and one for the left.

Turn the jacket to the right side. Position the shoulder pads or shapes on the underside and pin them in place from the top side of the jacket. On the underside, tack the pads or shapes to the sleeve seam allowances between the notches and to the shoulder seam allowance at the neckline edge.

## The Front Facings

Roll the lapels as they will be worn, allowing sufficient ease in the facing for it to fit smoothly over the roll. Carefully pin the free edge of the facing smoothly in place. Catch-stitch the facing to the interfacing from the shoulder to the point where the interfacing extends across the front; then baste it to the jacket down as far as the hemline.

## Jacket Hem

Compare the front edges of the jacket to be sure that they are the same length. Remove enough diagonal basting to fold the hem. Turn the facing away from the jacket. Fold the hem in the jacket and facing, and pin. Ease the hem down slightly at the seams to allow for the fold over the seam allowances. (The front interfacing should extend to the hem fold.) Baste with silk thread ¼ inch from the hem fold. Press. Trim the hem to an even width. Trim the hem across the facing and joining seam to ½ inch; trim all seam allowances to one-half their width from hem fold to edge. Press, shrinking out any fullness.

*Interface the lower edge of the jacket* with preshrunk muslin to give extra body and weight at the hem. Cut the interfacing on the true bias 1 inch wider than the hem and the length of the lower edge of the jacket plus 1 inch for seam allowances. Remove the bastings at the lower edge of the hem after pressing, and turn the hem away from the jacket. Place the interfacing between the hem and jacket; align the lower edge of the interfacing with the crease for the hem and extend the ends ½ inch over the front interfacing. Pin, baste, then catch-stitch the interfacing to the jacket along each edge, catching only one thread of the fabric outside the interfacing and only the interfacing on the opposite side. Use thread to match the fabric. Press.

Turn the hem over the interfacing and pin the free edge in place, matching seams. Hand-baste. Catch-stitch the hem to the interfacing as far as the facing seam. Make a stitch in the hem, then a stitch in the interfacing over the hem edge. Continue, alternating the stitches.

Turn the front facing to the underside; ease it under slightly at the lower edge and pin it to the hem. Slip-stitch in place, then catch-stitch over the cut edge the depth of the hem. (A soft hemline is described on page 194.)

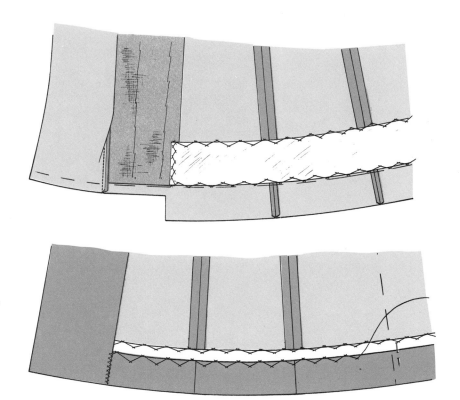

## Sleeve Hem

Turn the sleeve hem and baste ¼ inch from the fold, using silk thread. Trim the seam allowances to one-half their width from the fold to the hem edge. Interface the hem of the sleeve the same as the jacket. Cut the interfacing ends on the lengthwise grain and join them, overlapping about ½ inch. Catch-stitch the interfacing in place, then hem the sleeve in the same way you hemmed the jacket.

## Buttonholes in Facing

Finish the back of the buttonholes, following the instructions on page 111.

## Lining

Any adjustments you made in fitting the jacket must also be made in the lining.

Stay-stitch the back neckline of the lining ½ inch from the edge and stitch the shoulder darts. Fold and baste the release pleats and waistline darts in the front and back lining. Press.

Use a fine catch stitch to hold the release pleats and darts in position. Make the stitches through the three thicknesses, near the fold, on the right side of the lining. On the fronts, catch-stitch the release pleats from the shoulder to about 3 inches down, and the waistline darts about 1 inch above and below the waistline. On the back, catch-stitch the release pleat from the neckline down about 2 inches, across the pleat at the waistline, and just above the hem.

Stitch the underarm seams. Clip into the seam allowances at the waistline. Press, then press the seams open. Stitch the sleeve lining seams and press them open. Press the lining thoroughly.

### Joining Lining to Jacket

Place the lining inside the jacket, wrong sides together, matching all seams and center backs. Pin at the center back, underarm and around the armhole. Fold back the lining front and pin the lining and jacket seam allowances together at the underarm, matching markings. Sew with long basting stitches, starting below the armhole and ending 3 inches above the hem.

Turn under the seam allowance on the front edge of the lining and pin it over the free edge of the facing. Slip-stitch in place.

Pin and hand-sew the front lining over the shoulder seam. Turn under the back shoulder seam allowance, then lap it over the front lining and pin. Baste the lining to the seam allowance around the armhole. Clip into the lining seam allowance at the back neckline. Turn it under just beyond the stay stitching, and pin it to the neckline facing. Slip-stitch the lining in place from the outer edge of one shoulder to the other.

Place the jacket on a hanger, right side out. Smooth out the lining and pin it to the jacket 3 inches above the hem.

*(Continued)*

Allow ½ inch for ease in the lining length. Turn under the edge of the lining so that it overlaps the jacket hem 1 inch. Press. Pin the lining to the jacket hem, matching seams and darts, then baste it in place ½ inch above the fold. Turn back the lining on the basting line and slip-stitch it to the jacket hem, catching only the under layer of the lining.

### Lining the Sleeves

Place a line of stitching around the sleeve cap of the lining between the notches, ½ inch from the edge. Turn the sleeve to the wrong side.

Turn the jacket sleeve to the wrong side. Pin the lining and sleeve seam allowances together at the underarm seams, matching markings in the seams and armhole. Sew with long basting stitches, beginning about 3 inches below the armhole and ending 3 inches above the hem. If the sleeve is a two-piece one, hand-sew the back seams together.

Turn the lining sleeve to the right side over the jacket sleeve. Draw the bobbin thread around the sleeve cap and ease the lining to fit over the armhole seam allowance. Turn the seam edge under just beyond the stitching; overlap the armhole seam allowance and pin the sleeve lining in place at the shoulder, notches, and underarm seam, then at intervals between. Slip-stitch in place.

Allow ¼ inch for ease in the length of the sleeve lining. Turn under the lower edge and slip-stitch it to sleeve hem, following the instructions for the lower edge of the lining as described at the beginning of this page.

### Chain Weight

To add weight at the hem and preserve the line of a jacket, hand-sew a chain weight to the jacket after you have sewed in the lining. The chain, made of flat links, is available for lightweight and heavyweight fabrics. If one chain is too long for your purpose, remove any links not required. If you need a longer weight, use two chains together.

*(Continued)*

Place the chain weight on the inside along the hem of the jacket, about 1½ inches above the hem fold. Extend the ends to the facings, or place the weight across the back between the side seams. Overcast the chain flat against the fabric at the ends, center, and about every 2 inches between. Make the hand stitches through the hem and interfacing only so that they will not be visible on the topside. The chain is exposed and can easily be removed when the garment is cleaned.

## Fitted Jacket

In addition to front and collar interfacings, fitted jackets generally have an interfacing from the waistline to the hemline.

To shape interfacing darts and eliminate bulk, see the instructions under *Interfacing Darts,* page 104. Join the interfacing side seams with a lapped seam. See page 83.

Pin the interfacing in place over the wrong side of the jacket, with the lower edge aligned with the crease for the hem. Catch-stitch it in

place along the lower edge. Turn the hem over the interfacing and catch-stitch it in place, following the instructions for the jacket hem on page 324. If the hem is full, control the fullness with a line of stitching ¼ inch from the free edge before hemming.

### Waistline Stay

To prevent stretching, stay the waistline of fitted and semifitted jackets and princessline coats with straight seam binding or ½-inch grosgrain ribbon. Work with the jacket in the shape it will be worn.

On the underside, pin the tape around the waistline, extending the ends ¾ inch beyond the front facings. Turn the ends of the tape under ¼ inch, and pin them to the front facings and interfacings. Tack the tape in place at the ends and at all seams and darts. When interfacing is used below the waistline, tack it in place with the tape.

# CONSTRUCTING A COAT

## Basic Construction

Coat construction follows the same procedures and sequence as jacket construction up to the point of making the hem. Remember always to fit a coat over the type of dress or suit you will wear under it.

Sleeve styles vary. One comfortable and popular style is a sleeve that has a center seam with the back (or front) section cut-in-one with the bodice and the other section set into the armhole. Gussets are frequently used, so are raglan and regular set-in sleeves. Instructions on making the several types of sleeves are given under *Sleeve Styles and Finishes,* page 158.

Before you hem the coat, interface the sleeve

hem and finish it, following the directions for the jacket, page 325.

## Coat Hem

Mark the coat length. Refer to *Hems and Hem Finishes,* page 187, and follow the first three steps in forming the hem. Turn the facing away from the coat and form the hem across it. The front interfacing should extend to the hem fold.

### Hem Finishes

Finish the free edge as required by the fabric. The finishes most frequently used are the *Pinked Hem* for firmly woven fabrics and the *Bound Hem* for loosely woven fabrics that fray easily. See page 188. Baste the hem in place and finish it by hand, using a blind catch stitch. If the fabric is heavy or the hem wide, double-stitch the hem. See page 193.

### Interfaced Hem

For added body and weight, interface the hem with a true bias strip of unbleached muslin or tailor's linen, cut the width of the hem.

Press the fold for the hem, shrinking out any fullness. Finish the free edge of the hem. Remove all bastings. Place the interfacing over the underside of the hem, extending the ends ½ inch beyond the front interfacings. Shape the interfacing to the hem and catch-stitch it to the hem near the fold and top edge. Press.

Hand-baste the free edge of the hem to the coat, and blind catch-stitch it in place. Press.

## Lining and Interlining

Cut the lining and interlining by the same pattern; however, cut the interlining to extend to the turn of the lining hem at the bottom of the coat and sleeves. Be sure to make the same adjustments in the lining and interlining that you made in the coat after fitting it.

Place the interlining pieces over the wrong side of the lining pieces, matching markings; baste together along the edges. Place several rows of diagonal basting within the sections to hold the layers together. Handle as one in constructing the lining. See *Underlining a Dress*, page 95.

Stay-stitch ½ inch from the neckline edge. Stitch any seams within the lining; also stitch shoulder, underarm, and sleeve seams. Press, then press the seams open. Sew in the sleeves. Treat the darts and release pleats the same as in the jacket lining, page 325.

### To Join the Lining to the Coat

Place the lining inside the coat, wrong sides together. Pin it in place at the center back, shoulders, sleeves, and underarm, matching seams and markings. Sew the lining and coat seam allowances together at the underarm and sleeve seams, following the instructions given for the jacket, page 326. Remove any pins necessary to sew the seam allowances together in the sleeves.

Clip into the lining seam allowance at the back neckline. Turn the edge under just beyond the stay stitching and pin it to the coat. Turn under the seam allowance on the front edge of the lining and pin it over the free edge of the facing. Slip-stitch in position.

Allow ½ inch for ease in the length of the sleeve lining. Turn under the lower edge and slip-stitch it to the sleeve hem, following the instructions for the jacket lining, page 327.

### To Hem the Lining

Turn the hem in the lining so that it overlaps the coat hem 1 inch. (The interlining extends to the hem fold.) Press. Turn the free edge of the lining hem under ½ inch and pin it in place. Finish by hand, using a blind hemming stitch.

French-tack the lining to the coat at the seams, just above the hem; make the tacks about 1 inch in length. French-tack the free edge of the facing to the coat hem with a ¼-inch tack.

### To Handle the Interlining Separately

The interlining and lining may be treated separately. Construct the interlining with lapped seams. See *Lapped Seam*, page 83. Sew in the sleeves, using a plain seam.

Slip the interlining into the coat. Match the seams and pin. Hand-sew the coat and interlining seam edges together at the underarm and sleeve, following the jacket lining instructions on page 326. Hand-sew the interlining to the facing edge.

Slip the lining into the coat and finish, following the lining instructions above.

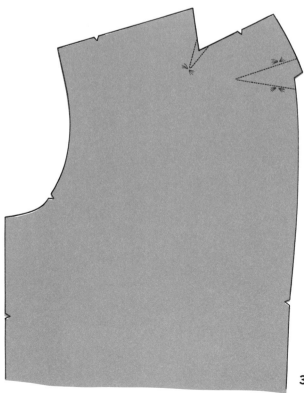

### To Make a Notched Shawl Collar

In a shawl collar, the top collar and facing are cut-in-one with a center back seam. The tailoring technique is about the same as that for the jacket collar on page 321, except for the treatment of the notches.

Tailor-tack the position of the notches in the garment, facing, and interfacing. To retain the shape of the notches, do not cut them out until after the final stitching is completed.

Stay-stitch around the notched area of the garment and facing, barely outside the seamline. Use a 20 stitch length; take one or two stitches across the point. Press. (This stitching is not visible in the finished work.) Stay-stitch the slash in the neck-

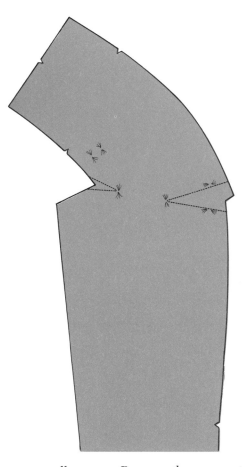

Cut a strip of organza wide enough to cover the notch; use the pattern to shape the neckline and front edges. Pin the organza strip over the interfacing, extending the edge ¾ inch beyond the interfacing. Cut out the notches in the interfacing only, ⅛ inch beyond·the seamline. Clip off the corners of the interfacing to eliminate bulk when turned. Stitch, using the multiple-stitch zigzag. Press.

Position the interfacing on the wrong side of the jacket or coat, keeping the organza strip and garment edge even. Be sure that the uncut notches in the garment coincide with those in the interfacing. Finish, following the instructions under *Front Interfacing*, on page 318. Join the shoulder seams, and interface the undercollar. See page 319.

Pin the undercollar to the neckline, matching markings, and slash the neckline seam at the inside corner. Baste, then stitch. Clip off the corners where seams cross, and slash into the seam allowances at evenly spaced intervals so that they will lie flat when pressed open. Remove the bastings and press the seam open. Trim the seam edges to ⅜ inch from the outer edge to the corner, then catch-stitch the open seam edges to the interfacing on each side. Press.

line seam allowance. Prepare the garment for a fitting as instructed on page 316.

Mark the neckline and front edges of the interfacing a measured ¾ inch from the edge (⅝ inch seam allowance plus ⅛ inch). Trim off along the marked line, *but do not cut out the notches.*

Stitch the center back seam of the top collar and facing, then press the seam open. Attach the back neckline facing in the same manner as the undercollar. Press the seam open.

Place the facing over the jacket, or coat, right sides together. Pin together at center, points, and notches. Match seamlines of the uncut notches in the garment, interfacing, and facing, and pin together. Then pin at close intervals between, easing the top collar and lapel section of the facing between the markings. Baste. Stitch in one continuous line from one hem edge to the other. Take one or two stitches diagonally across the corners; stitch the notched area barely beyond the stay stitching, taking one or two stitches across the point. The width at the point provides space for cutting and prevents pulling at the point in the finished work. Remove bastings.

Trim the undercollar seam allowance to ⅛ inch and the top collar seam allowance and organza strip to ¼ inch. From the top of the lapel to the top button, trim the garment seam allowance to ⅛ inch and facing seam allowance and organza strip to ¼ inch. Reverse the blending below the top button by trimming the facing seam allowance to ⅛ inch and the garment seam allowance and organza to ¼ inch. Cut between the lines of stitching in the notch, almost to the point; then trim the garment seam allowance to ⅛ inch and the facing seam allowance and organza to ¼ inch. Clip diagonally across the corners at the lapel points and where seams cross. Press, then press the seams open.

Turn facing to the underside and finish, following the instructions on page 322.

## To Interface

You will probably prefer interfacing suits and coats according to the instructions given in the construction of the jacket. However, you may catch-stitch the interfacing in place as instructed under *Method 2*, on page 136. Or you may use the method explained here, which is appropriate for loosely woven fabrics such as tweed and heavy coating.

Mark the neckline and front edges of the interfacing a measured ¾ inch from the edge (⅝-inch seam allowance plus ¼ inch). Trim off on the markings. Clip off corners.

Place the interfacing over the wrong side of the garment front section with the fabric extending ¾ inch beyond the interfacing edge. Pin. Stay the interfacing to the lapels with padding stitches; then baste the interfacing in place, following the instructions on page 318.

Tape the front opening, lapel, and front edge of the collar with ¼-inch twill tape. Shrink and shape the tape with steam pressing. Position the tape so that it overlaps the interfacing and the outer edge is 1/16 inch from the fabric seamline. Miter the tape at the corners. Sew the outer edge of the tape to the fabric, using a hemming stitch. Then sew the opposite edge in place, making the stitches through the interfacing and tape edge only. Press.

Apply the facing and top collar, following instructions on page 321.

## To Stay Neckline Seam

To prevent the back neckline seam from stretching, stay it with ¼-inch twill tape or straight seam binding folded and creased through the center. Steam-press the tape, shrinking and shaping it to fit the neckline. After the undercollar is stitched in place and the seam pressed open, pin the tape over the open seam between the shoulders; then catch-stitch it to the seam allowance on each side.

## To Stay Armhole Seam at Underarm

The armhole seam at the underarm of coats and suits is subject to extra strain. For added strength in tweed and loosely woven fabrics, tape the seam with ¼-inch twill tape (narrower, if possible) or straight seam binding folded through the center. Steam-press the tape, shrinking and shaping it to fit the armhole at the underarm.

Pin the tape over the right side of the seam allowance of the armhole, between the notches, with the lower edge barely above the seamline. Stitch it in place about 1/16 inch from the lower edge of the tape, using a 15 stitch length.

The seamline is just below the tape; therefore, when the sleeve is stitched in the armhole, the tape between the seam edges will carry the strain, not the seamline. Trim the armhole seam allowance at the underarm to ⅜ inch.

## Tailored Binding

Suits, coats, and dresses occasionally carry a tailored binding as a finished edge on front openings, necklines, collars and cuffs, and pocket flaps. The binding is not difficult to apply if you follow the procedure given here.

A good quality of slipper satin is an excellent fabric for binding since it will not wear along the folded edge as quickly as other fabrics. Self-fabric may also be used if it is not too heavy. The finished width of the binding is generally ½ inch although it may be as wide as 1 inch. Buy enough fabric to cut long bias strips so that your binding will have a minimum of joinings.

Before applying the binding, finish the garment up to the point of attaching the interfacing. If the pattern does not specify binding, mark the edges to be bound ⅝ inch (seam allowance) from the edge and trim on the marked line. Treat the facing and interfacing the same. Baste the interfacing in place on the wrong side. Place the facing on the underside of the garment, wrong sides together, with the cut edges even; pin. Baste the layers of fabric together ⅝ inch from the edge. On a heavy fabric, it may be necessary to baste again ¼ inch from the edge.

Cut the binding on the true bias, four times the finished width. See *Cutting Bias Strips*, page 244. Fold the bias strip through the center, wrong

sides together, and press lightly. Since this means pressing on the right side of the fabric, be sure to place a press cloth between the fabric and iron. Do not glide the iron, but merely lift it from one section to the other. Open the bias and fold the cut edges to the center, leaving a ⅛-inch space between the edges. Press. This spacing allows for folding the bias over the edge of the garment.

### To Bind a Straight Edge or Curve

Open the binding and carefully pin it to the edge, right sides together, keeping the cut edges even. Extend the end of the binding ¼ inch beyond each end of the seam to allow for turning and finishing. Do not stretch the binding on straight edges; ease it slightly on outside curves and stretch it slightly on inside curves.

Carefully stitch in the folded crease of the binding. Trim the interfacing in the seam allowance close to the stitching. Press to the stitching, but not beyond.

Fold the ends of the binding under ¼ inch, then fold the binding over the seam edge to the stitching on the underside; pin. Finish by hand, using a slip stitch. Slip-stitch the folded ends of binding together.

### To Bind a Square Corner

Open the binding and pin it along *one* side, following the instructions above. Stitch in the folded crease from the outer edge to the intersecting seamline at the corner. Pull the threads to the underside and tie them together in a single knot.

Fold the bias over the edge and miter the corner from the seamline to the center fold of the binding, as illustrated; pin. Turn the binding back over the garment, right sides together, and finish pinning the edge in place along the adjoining side. Carefully stitch in the folded crease of the binding. Press only the stitching.

Finish, following the instructions for the straight edge. On the underside, miter the binding at the corner, folding it in the same direction as on the top side. Slip-stitch the folds of the miter together.

## Top Stitching

Top stitching is a smart and practical way to accent the lines of a garment and at the same time add firmness. A single line of stitching on a heavy fabric, such as coating or a laminate, produces a welt effect. Single or multiple rows of parallel stitching on a lighter weight fabric lend importance to finished edges such as lapels, facing edges, collars, and pockets, as well as to style seams and hemlines.

For top stitching you may use either regular thread or buttonhole twist. Buttonhole twist is frequently preferred for medium-weight and heavy-weight fabrics. Use it for the needle thread and the regular thread for the bobbin. Select a size 18 needle and a slightly longer stitch than for the regular seaming. It is generally necessary to increase the needle thread tension when stitching with buttonhole twist. To determine the best stitch length and tension, make a stitching test on a swatch of your fabric; fold the fabric, duplicating the seam allowance, and include the same type of interfacing or underlining you are using in the garment.

Before applying top stitching to an edge, attach the interfacing and facing to the garment, blend the seams, and turn the facing and press as instructed on pages 318 and 321. Baste the layers of fabric together to prevent them from slipping during the stitching. Use diagonal basting and silk thread. One line of basting is sufficient if the top stitching will be close to the edge. Baste again just outside the stitching line if the stitching will be ½ inch or more from the edge.

Mark the stitching line with basting on the right side and use it as a guide in your machine stitching. Use a gauge to measure accurately, and take tiny stitches through all thicknesses of fabric. Space the stitches about 1 inch apart; keep the slack out of the thread between them. On curved edges and seams, place the basting stitches closer together, with the short thread on the top side and the long one on the underside.

On the right side of your garment, top-stitch very close to the basting but not on it. Stitch slowly, using the appropriate stitch length for the fabric. Additional rows of stitching may be gauged with the presser foot if the spacing is less than ¼ inch. For wider spacing, mark each stitching line the same as the first one. At corners, pivot and turn the fabric on the needle, following the directions on page 28.

When the stitching ends at a finished edge, leave thread ends about 4 inches long. Then use a hand sewing needle to fasten them in the seam allowance between the facing and garment.

The Quilter and the Seam Guide are two aids in top stitching. The Quilter helps you gauge the stitching line and keep it straight and parallel to the edge or seam depression. See *Welt Seam*, page 88, for instructions on its use. As you sew, guide the finished edge or seam depression against the space guide of the Quilter. With the Seam Guide you can stitch parallel to the edge of the fabric at any distance from ⅛ inch to 1¼ inch from the edge.

The interesting use of top stitching in the style seams illustrated is simple to achieve. After stitching the seams, press them open. Then top-stitch on each side an equal distance from the seamline. The seam allowance on the underside must be wider than the distance between the top stitching and seamline.

## Arrowhead

The arrowhead is used in tailored costumes as a decorative and secure finish at the ends of pockets and top of pleats and on fashion seams that end within the garment.

Mark the triangular shape of the arrowhead with chalk or thread. Use buttonhole twist in the needle.

Make two small stitches, bringing the needle out at the lower left corner. At the upper corner, take a stitch from right to left. Insert the needle at the right corner and bring it out at the left corner, barely inside of the previous thread. Repeat the procedure, placing the threads side by side until the triangle is completely filled in. Fasten the thread on the underside with two tiny backstitches.

## Crow's Foot

The crow's foot is used in the same places as the arrowhead. With thread or chalk, mark a triangle that is slightly curved on the sides. Use buttonhole twist in the needle.

Make two small stitches, bringing the needle out at the lower left corner. At the upper corner, take a horizontal stitch from right to left. At the lower right corner, take a diagonal stitch from left to right. Then at the lower left corner, make a diagonal stitch from left to right. Continue making stitches in the same sequence, placing them side by side until the center is filled in. Fasten the thread on the underside with two small backstitches.

## Bar Tack

Bar tacks are used to prevent ripping at the end of a fly opening and at the ends of pockets in shorts and slacks. They are also used to hold belt carriers in place. Make them by hand or by machine. Use mercerized, silk, or synthetic thread.

### By Hand

Make two or three long stitches the length of the bar tack. Then make small overhand stitches across the threads and through the fabric. When the bar is finished, make tiny bar stitches across each end.

### By Machine

Use a fine, closely spaced zig-zag stitch. Stitch the length of the bar tack. Pull the threads through to the underside and tie.

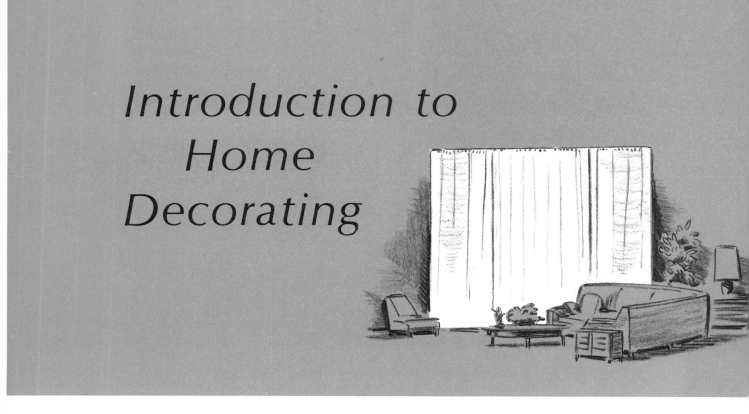

# Introduction to Home Decorating

HOME DECORATING IS, IN MANY WAYS, the most rewarding adventure in sewing. It offers you a perfect opportunity to express yourself—your sensitivity to design and proportion, your flair for color. In short, it brings out you—your personality and your creative talent.

Since the home you decorate is an intimate part of the life you share with your family, you want it to reflect as well as contribute to the charm and beauty of that life. Before you plunge into decorating, therefore, consult the several magazines available on the subject. They will give you many excellent ideas on style, color, and fabric. Consider fashion trends but do not let novelties or fads influence your judgment. Strive for harmony and unity, for beauty and comfort, and you will give your family a home they can enjoy for many years to come.

In making your decorating decisions, remember that fabric furnishings, should be planned in relation to the size and shape of the room, the height of the ceiling, the number and placement of windows, and the effect you wish to achieve. Fabric, color, and style, as well as construction, determine the end results.

This section of the book will guide you in choosing styles and fabrics and in planning color schemes. Its most valuable contribution, however, is the techniques it explains, through words and pictures, on construction. In custom-made fabric furnishings, it is not the price of the fabric that makes the greatest difference—it is the construction, the fit of a slipcover, or the fullness and "hang" of curtains and draperies.

## PLANNING A COLOR SCHEME

The success of your entire decorating project may depend on how wisely you use color. But do not let this statement intimidate you. If you follow a few basic rules, you will find that it is not difficult to assemble colors harmoniously.

### The Color System

To use color skillfully, you should have some knowledge of the color system. See color wheel, Plate 17 opposite page 340. The primary colors are red, yellow, and blue. They are pure colors and cannot be produced by mixing other colors. The secondary colors—orange, green, and violet—are produced by mixing equal amounts of two primary colors, as illustrated in the color wheel. The primary and secondary colors together comprise the six standard colors.

Intermediate colors or hues are produced by combining a primary color with the secondary color that flanks it in the color wheel. The six intermediate hues and the six standard colors are known as the twelve "true" colors because they are not diluted with white, black, or grey.

When true colors are diluted, a shade or tint results. A shade is produced by adding varying degrees of grey or black to the true color to give a color value darker than the true color. A tint is produced by adding varying degrees of white to the true color to give a color value lighter than the true color. Each true color has numerous shades and tints. A slight degree of color value is illustrated in the color wheel.

## Warm and Cool Colors

The warm colors are red, orange, and yellow. All the hues in the color wheel containing these colors share in their warmth. The cool colors are blue and all the hues grouped around it in the color wheel. Green, which contains equal amounts of blue and yellow, and violet, which contains equal amounts of blue and red, are neither warm nor cool. As greater percentages of the warm colors are added to them, however, they gain in warmth; as the percentage of blue is increased, they grow cool.

Warm colors make the size of an object seem larger and the size of a room smaller. Cool colors behave in the opposite way, diminishing the apparent size of an object and giving an illusion of spaciousness in a room.

Neutral colors—white, grey, and beige—are frequently used in home decorating. Neutral walls, ceilings, windows, and floors provide an effective background for the bold, bright colors so often found in fabric furnishings. Colors appear darker than they actually are when placed against a light background, lighter against a dark background. Middle tones are less forceful than extreme light or dark tones.

## Color Harmony

Color harmony is the art of grouping colors pleasingly in a room. Many ideas on color combinations can be gleaned from the beauty of nature. Study a sunset or a rainbow; notice how subtly each color blends with and accents the other. Study color proportion, keeping in mind the colors nature used for the redbird and the elephant. In short, be aware of color!

Shades and tints are mainstays in home decorating. They make it possible for you to repeat a color, but to alter it slightly to retain interest without sacrificing unity and harmony. Strong contrasts may also be welcome in your decorating scheme. For example, red, blue, and yellow can produce a striking and still harmonious effect, provided the tints or shades are compatible.

Here are some suggestions for you in planning color schemes:

Think not only of the color value but also of color balance—that is, the placement and quantity of the colors you are using. Concentrating dark colors on one side of the room and light colors on the other upsets the balance of a room and prevents you from achieving the harmony you seek.

Prints or florals in fabric, rug, or wallpaper can add interest to the decorating scheme. However, do not mix two different figured or patterned fabrics; this creates a feeling of confusion. A wide assortment of coordinated colors is available to you. It is also possible to buy fabric in the identical pattern or color found in the wallpaper.

In decorating, the focal point of a room may be the window treatment or a picture, chair, or sofa. Plan your color scheme around one dominant color and use shades or tints of this color in moderate amounts to give interest. Select a third color for accent and contrast.

Slavish repetition of a color is monotonous, but judicious repetition is generally welcome. Draperies and walls of the same color or tone-on-tone are pleasing to the eye. White and gold produce a rich accent. Or, if you are using a print in the draperies, repeat one of the colors in the sofa, another in a chair. Keep the texture and weave of the fabrics compatible.

Consider the exposure of the room as well as the effect you wish to achieve. Some decorators advocate warm colors for north and east exposures and cool colors for south and west. Rooms that are distinctly feminine in character stress pale, pastel tints and shades; those that are masculine tend toward deep, strong colors. Family rooms and dens seem to require brighter colors. In planning color schemes for them, however, consider the family's living habits as well as the style and purpose of the room.

When your decorating project is confined to a

window treatment, a bedspread, or a chair or sofa covering, consider the colors and fabric textures now in the room.

Experiment with color. Drape swatches of various colors together to see whether they combine felicitously. If you wish to use red, choose shades or tints that harmonize with and complement the colors already selected.

# SELECTING FABRICS

Fabrics today are interesting and exciting. Study them carefully when you are planning your room, for the variety at your disposal is bound to influence your decorating decisions. You can choose from the traditional natural fibers, man-made fibers, or a blend of natural and man-made fibers—each is offered in a variety of textures and weaves as well as colors. Often a metallic thread that will not tarnish is interwoven in a fabric for decorative effect.

The variation of weave may be the means of introducing pattern into the room. The weave may also determine where the fabric can be used—whether it will hang gracefully in draperies or be durable in slipcovers. (The tighter the weave, the more durable the fabric.) Both texture and weave should meet your functional needs as well as produce the decorative effect you desire. For more information on fabrics, see page 7.

In selecting a fabric, consider these facts about the room: its size and exposure; its purpose—whether formal or informal, whether for the entire family or only one of its members; its furniture—whether modern or traditional; and the effect you wish to achieve. Above all, be sure that the fabric is in keeping with family living as well as family likes and dislikes. Each style has its own way of achieving beauty.

*For formal rooms,* select antique satin, damask, etruscan, brocade, brocatelle, faille, antique taffeta, slipper satin, mohair, velvet, or velveteen. These fabrics may be of silk or man-made fibers, or a blend of two fibers.

*For informal rooms,* the selection is much greater—chintz, polished cotton, antique satin, gingham, sailcloth, burlap, denim, Indian Head†, hand-blocked linen, frisé, corduroy, poplin, and many synthetic fabrics such as fiberglass, nylon, and Dacron.

*Curtains.* Glass curtains are generally made of a soft, sheer fabric that softens and diffuses light without impeding it—for example, ninon, fiber-
†Indian Head

glass, Dacron, sheer nylon, theatrical gauze, marquisette, Orlon, and pongee. Ruffled tieback curtains should be made of crisp organdy, lawn, dotted Swiss, net, nylon, Dacron, unbleached muslin, marquisette, or gauze. Café curtains are made of gingham, Indian Head†, muslin, chintz, polished cotton, dotted Swiss, corduroy, and nylon, to name just a few.

*Draperies* are constructed of medium-weight and heavyweight fabrics, and the selection is unlimited. Some of the fabrics listed for glass curtains are also suitable for draw draperies.

*Slipcovers* should be made of a medium-weight or heavyweight, closely woven fabric so that they will retain their shape.

*Lining.* Draperies are frequently lined. A sateen lining is available in widths of 36 and 50 inches. Generally, white, light beige, eggshell, or soft grey is used to blend with the neutral color of the glass curtain.

When you contemplate changing only the window treatment, bedspread, or slipcover, carefully consider the function and existing design of the room before you choose a fabric. Harmony in texture as well as color must be maintained. Fabrics may be comparable in weight but may differ in light reflection.

If the entire room is to be redecorated, study it carefully before visiting the decorator's shop. Begin with your focal point of interest—a window, chair, sofa, picture, or lamp. For example, if windows are the focal point, select fabrics for the curtains and draperies, then blend and harmonize all other fabrics with this selection. Drape the fabrics together while you are still at the decorator's shop to be certain that the textures, weaves, and colors are compatible. Then try the fabrics in the room where they will be used. If swatches large enough for this purpose are not available on loan, it is advisable to buy yard lengths of the fabrics you are considering. In view of the ultimate investment, such a small expense is worthwhile.

To determine the yardage you will need, take the measurements of each project you are planning before you visit the decorator's shop. In making your purchase, be sure to consider the width of the fabric as well as the length.

Last, but not least, consider how the fabric will be cleaned. Must it be dry-cleaned? If washable, is it tubfast and colorfast? Will it shrink? Examine the labels for information on the properties of the fibers which will predict the performance of the fabric. Some fabrics are now chemically treated to resist soiling.

**Plate 17**

**Color Wheel**

The twelve true colors shown in the center (widest) ring,
can be varied to shades (inside ring) by adding black,
or to tints (outside ring) by adding white.
For an explanation of the color system, see pages 338 and 339.

From The American Home © 1964, The Curtis Publishing Co

### Plate 18

#### Color brings the outdoors in

Brilliant floral linen slipcovers
reflect the garden atmosphere of the
patio. For privacy and convenience,
Roman shades, taped in red to echo
the red-beamed ceiling, solve the
drapery problem for the patio doors.

#### Romantic dining corner

Scalloped valance lends
an air of formality
to flowered cotton-satin draperies
in print to match wallpaper.
Pink ball fringe with tiny green
tassels adds finishing touches
to draperies, valance and tiebacks.

Courtesy of McCall's magazine

The selection of the thread depends on the fabric to be stitched. The thread should blend with the fabric in color, fiber, and size. Needle selection depends on both the thread and the fabric. The weight and texture of the fabric determine the stitch length.

Silk and wool fabrics are stitched with silk thread; cottons, linens, and some blended fabrics, with mercerized thread (however, fine linens may be stitched with silk thread). Synthetic fabrics and blends of natural and man-made fibers may be stitched with silk, mercerized, or synthetic thread. Use a size 14 needle with mercerized or silk thread and a size 11 needle for finer threads such as nylon.

Organdy, voile, dotted Swiss, marquisette, batiste, and similar fabrics used for glass curtains should be stitched with mercerized thread, size 14 needle, and 12 to 15 stitch length, depending on their weight. Nylon, Dacron, and similar synthetic fabrics may be stitched with either nylon or mercerized thread.

Damask, brocade, taffeta, satin, and similar fabrics appropriate for draperies and bedspreads should be stitched with silk or mercerized thread, size 14 needle, and 12 stitch length.

For lightweight or medium-weight fabrics like chintz, polished cotton, linen, percale, antique satin, corduroy, and faille, use mercerized thread, size 14 needle, and 12 stitch length.

Heavyweight fabric used in slipcovers—linen, cotton damask, sailcloth, ticking, denim, and the like—should be stitched with heavy-duty thread, size 16 needle, and 12 stitch length.

If the fabric you are working with is not listed above, check the chart on page 24.

# A Look at Your Windows

WINDOWS BRING LIGHT AND AIR into your home. When you look at them with a homemaker's eye, your first thoughts are to ensure privacy without obstructing the sunlight or the view if it is a pleasing one. When you look at them with a decorator's eye, your concern is to create a window treatment that is in harmony with the other furnishings of the room and still captures the light and the view. The window treatment you decide on depends mainly on your plans for the room. True, the style of the window may suggest or even dictate the treatment, but even that can be changed by clever use of curtains and draperies or by simple carpentry tricks that alter inside window proportions.

The term "curtain" as used here refers to glass curtains and tieback curtains, which have a casing that fits around a rod, and to café curtains, which may have a casing, hooks, or clip-on rings. The term "drapery" designates hangings with pleated headings. Draperies may be of sheer or heavy fabric, lined or unlined. They are attached to rods by hooks.

**Adjustable double rod**

**Extender plate
for increasing height**

**Traverse rod extension**

## Changing Window Proportions

Window proportions can be changed to make them appear higher or wider or to create the illusion of an entire wall of windows.

*To increase height.* A window may be increased in height just a few inches or all the way to the ceiling by using either a board or an extender plate.

The board should be as thick as the window frame, at least 4 to 6 inches wide, and cut to the same length as the window width. Use the recommended method (opposite page) to attach the board to the wall above the frame. Then paint or finish the board to match the finish on either the frame or the wall, whichever will look better. When dry, mount the fixtures on the extreme ends of the board, 1 inch below the top.

Extender plates, available in three sizes, are mounted vertically on the window frame, and do not touch the wall or mar the paint.

*To increase width.* Narrow windows can be widened to bring them into proportion to the size of the room and to admit as much light as possible. Either boards or extender plates may be used to extend the top portion of the frame on each side.

Cut the boards, one for each side, to the desired increase in width. Use the recommended method (opposite page) to attach the boards to the wall on each side. Then paint or finish the boards to match either the finish on the frame or the wall, whichever will look better. When dry, mount the fixtures on the extreme ends of the boards, 1 inch below the top.

If the extender plates suggested above are to be used, mount them horizontally on the frame.

**Extension rod and bracket**

**Extender plate
for increasing width**

*To increase both height and width.* Often, a better proportion can be obtained by increasing both the height and the width. A board, cut to the required dimensions, can be mounted above the window frame using the method recommended on the opposite page. Mount the fixtures at the extreme ends of the board, 1 inch below the top.

**Two-way traverse rod**

342

A **cornice board** may also be used to change window proportions. Mount it above the board you used to lengthen or widen the window. The cornice covers the top of the draperies.

Two-way traverse rod

## Rods and Fixtures

The type of rod and fixture you select depends on the style and weight of the curtains or draperies. The rod should be sturdy enough to prevent the curtains from sagging; it may be decorative or utilitarian. There is a rod available for every window treatment, and you can generally find the kind you need in shops that specialize in curtains and draperies.

Most rods have a return at each end. "Return" is the term used for the distance the rod projects from the wall. In the adjustable rod for glass curtains, the return is the distance from the curve of the rod to the wall. In the traverse rod, it is the depth of the bracket. Always measure the return, for its depth may vary from 3 to 4 inches, or more. Curtains and draperies extend around the returns.

The fixtures holding the rod in place should be mounted on the extreme ends of the window frame, 1 inch below the top, so that the curtains cover the entire window frame. Café curtains, however, may be recessed within the window frame and casement curtains are mounted on the window sash.

Since the measurements for your curtains and draperies are based on the position of the rod, the rod and fixtures should be fastened in place before you take any window measurements. In this way you will be sure of measuring accurately to determine the yardage required and the length and width of your curtains and draperies.

## Installing Fixtures on a Wall

A moderate degree of skill with tools and some previous experience in mounting fixtures on walls are necessary if you expect to get a satisfactory result. If you do not have the skill or the experience, have the job done by a professional.

For the purpose of mounting drapery hardware or cornice boards on every type of wall construction, a **plastic anchor** used with a matching sheet-metal screw is the easiest to install. These anchors are available in many lengths and sizes, and your choice of the correct size will depend on the weight of your draperies. The heavier the drapery, the larger the anchor and screw should be.

Plastic anchor

Use the mounting bracket as a template, and mark the wall for the holes. Cover the mark with transparent tape (about an inch square) to prevent cracking the plaster. Use a drill bit of the size specified for the anchor with either an electric drill (750 revolutions per minute) or a hand drill (eggbeater type) and drill a hole in the plaster wall. Be sure to hold the drill steady at a right angle to the wall so as not to drill too large a hole. After the holes are drilled, tap the anchors into the holes, insert the matching sheet metal screws through the holes in the bracket, and turn in the screws with a screwdriver.

If the wall is hollow, the plastic anchor must be long enough to extend well into the hollow space so that it will expand when the screw is turned in.

The same procedure is followed for drilling holes in concrete or other masonry except that the bit must be tipped with tungsten carbide, and greater pressure must be exerted against the wall while drilling.

*Caution:* Do not touch the masonry bit when removing it from the hole. It will be hot enough to cause a burn on the skin.

This section explains how to measure different kinds of windows and how much to add for hems, headings, casings, seams, and shrinkage tucks. In all cases, the amount you should allow depends on the style of the window treatment. You will need these measurements later to estimate the yardage and to cut and construct your curtains and draperies.

## Sash Windows

The curtain and drapery treatment possible for sash windows is practically unlimited. Any of the

styles described in the chapters that follow can be used. When two or three windows are grouped together, they are treated as a single unit.

Living room and dining room curtains and draperies may be sill, apron, or floor length, depending on the style of the room and on whether there is an air conditioner in the window or a radiator below the window. Bedroom curtains and tiebacks may also be sill, apron, or floor length although here you will want to consider not only the effect desired but also the age and sex of the person occupying the room. Kitchen, bathroom, and breakfast room curtains generally extend to the sill or the lower edge of the apron.

To measure windows, use a steel tape or folding ruler if possible.

**Length:** Measure from the bottom of the rod to the sill, the lower edge of the apron, or the floor. (The finished length should be about ½ inch above the floor. The turning of the hems will take up the fabric slightly.)

**Width:** Measure from edge to edge of the window frame. To this width, add the depth of the return on each side. (The measurement for the return will be used later for positioning the end pleat in the drapery heading.)

This gives you your basic window measurements. To them you must add the allowances given below. Café curtains are an exception. For them, see page 358.

### For Glass Curtains

Two panels are required for each window.

**Length:** To the measured length of your window, add 2 inches for casing, 2 inches for heading, ¼ inch for turning, 2 inches for shrinkage tuck

(1 inch per yard), and 3¼ inches for bottom hem and turning. If double bottom hems are used, and they are desirable for sheer fabrics, allow 6 inches for the bottom hem instead of 3¼ inches.

**Width:** Multiply the measured width of your window by 2½ or 3 for fullness. To this figure, add 8 inches for hems (1-inch double hem on each side of the two panels).

### For Panel Draperies

A pair of drapery panels is required for each window or group of windows.

**Length for lined draperies:** To the measured length of your window, add 1 inch for rod, 2 inches for heading, 4 inches for top hem, and 3½ inches for bottom hem and turning.

**Length for unlined draperies:** Add an extra ½ inch for turning on the top hem.

**Width:** Determine how wide you want your finished drapery panel to be. To this measurement, add 4 inches for the depth of the return at one end, plus 5 inches for hems (2-inch hem and ½-inch seam allowance on each side), plus the amount required for pleats. See page 367.

### For Draw Draperies

A pair of drapery panels is required for each window or group of windows. Use a two-way traverse rod. Measure the length as described above; however, since draw draperies cover the entire window, measure the width as instructed below for picture windows.

## Picture Windows

Draw draperies are an attractive and practical treatment for picture windows. Use a two-way traverse rod. Install the brackets for the rods on the extreme ends of the window frame, 1 inch below the top of the frame or ceiling. (Use the ceiling-mounted track if feasible.)

**Length for lined draperies:** Measure from the bottom of the rod to the floor. To this measurement, add 1 inch for rod, 2 inches for heading, 4 inches for top hem, 3½ inches for bottom hem and turning.

**Length for unlined draperies:** Add an extra ½ inch for turning on the top hem. If double hems are used, and they are recommended for sheer fabrics, allow 8 inches for the top hem and 6 inches for the bottom hem.

If draperies extend from the ceiling, measure from the ceiling to the floor and add only the amounts stated for top and bottom hems.

**Width:** Measure across the window from one end of the rod to the other. To this measurement, add the depth of the return on each side, 10 inches for hems (2-inch hems and ½-inch seam allowance on each side of the two panels), 2½ inches for overlap, plus the amount required for pleats and seams within the drapery. See page 368.

Two-way traverse rod

**Cord extension pulley**

## Sliding Windows or Doors

Sliding windows or doors should be treated as a single unit. Draw draperies are an effective way to do this. Use either a two-way or one-way traverse rod, depending on the position of the window. Mount the brackets for the rod on the extreme ends of the window frame, 1 inch below the top of the frame or ceiling. Measure the length as instructed for the picture window and make the same allowances for top and bottom hems.

**Cord extension pulley**

**Two-way traverse rod**

## Corner Windows

Corner windows are treated as a single unit; however, the draperies for each window should be an independent unit. Use two one-way traverse rods (a one-way left and a one-way right) and position them so that you draw each side drapery *away from the corner* when opening it. The rods may meet at the corner, or one rod may be fully in the corner and the second rod almost against the first, as illustrated. If the second installation is used, be sure to allow enough room for the drapery on the first rod to pass by the end of the second rod.

If a wall space intervenes between two windows that are near a corner, the windows may be treated separately or the wall and windows may be treated

**One-way traverse rod (right)**      **One-way traverse rod (left)**

as a single unit as illustrated here. Install two one-way traverse rods the same as for the corner windows above, but reverse the rods so that you draw each side drapery *toward the corner* when you open it. With this positioning of the rods, the draperies cover the wall space at the corner whether they are opened or closed. Install one bracket for the rod on the wall in the corner and the other bracket on the extreme end of the window frame; position both brackets 1 inch below the top of the frame or ceiling.

Measure the length and width the same as instructed for picture windows on page 345; however, the length may be to the sill, the lower edge of the apron, or the floor.

One-way traverse rod
(left)

One-way traverse rod
(right)

## Casement Windows

If casement windows open inward, sheer casement curtains must be mounted on the window sash so that they will swing in with the window. The curtains have a heading and casing at the top and bottom and require two rods. They are stretched tightly over the glass.

Use the elbow bracket and rod. Place the brackets so that the curtain will cover the glass portion of the window.

*Length:* Measure from the bottom of the upper rod to the top of the lower rod. To this measurement add, to top and bottom, 1½ inches for heading, 1½ inches for easing, and ½ inch for turning, or 7 inches in all. Either shrink the fabric before cutting, or allow an additional 2 inches for a shrinkage tuck at the top.

*Width:* Measure across the window from one bracket edge to the other. Allow for double or triple fullness. To this figure, add 2 inches for hems (½-inch double-fold hem on each side).

If the windows open outward, the rods are mounted on the window frame so that the windows will swing free of the curtain or drapery. Draw draperies are an appropriate window treatment. They may be sill or floor length, depending on the style of the room and personal choice.

Elbow bracket

Elbow bracket and rod

## French Windows and Doors

French windows may swing either in or out. The window treatment is the same as for casement windows.

French doors open inward. Use the casement curtain and follow the instructions for the casement window opening inward.

**Elbow bracket and rod**

## Projected Windows

Projected windows swing out and are generally placed high in a wall. Draw draperies are a customary treatment. A decorative two-way traverse rod with rings is shown in the illustration. Make the draperies in two panels that meet in the center of the window, and line them since the projected window usually has no venetian blind or window shade.

Install the brackets for the rod on the wall, 1 or 2 inches above the window and a few inches beyond each side of the window.

*Length:* Measure from the lower circle of the ring to about 2 inches below the window. To this measurement, add 5 inches for top and bottom hems (2-inch hem and ½ inch for turning).

*Width:* Measure from the edge of one bracket to the other. Multiply this measurement by 2 for fullness. To this figure, add 10 inches for hems (2-inch hem and ½ inch for turning on each side of the two panels).

**One-screw bracket**

**Clip-on ring**

**Rod with one-screw bracket**

## Awning Windows

Café curtains are a pleasant informal treatment for awning windows. Draw draperies are also appropriate. In the illustration, café curtains are used and the tiers are uneven in length. They do not overlap and decorative rods and rings are visible above each tier. Two brass rods with sew-on or clip-on rings are required for this style of café.

Mount the brackets for the top rod on the wall, 1 or 2 inches above the window and a few inches beyond each side of the window. Mount the brackets for the second rod at the point where the top and second window sections meet; extend them the same distance beyond the window as the top brackets.

*Length, top tier:* Measure from the lower circle of the ring to the top of the second rod.

*Bottom tier:* Measure from the lower circle of the ring to 2 inches below the window. To these measurements, add 5 inches to each tier for top and bottom hems (2-inch hems plus ½ inch for turning).

*Width:* Follow the instructions for the projected window.

Clip-on ring

**Two-screw bracket and rod**

**Two-screw bracket**

## Hopper Windows

Draw draperies and a two-way traverse rod should be selected for these windows so that the draperies can easily be drawn to the sides when you open or close the window. Position the bracket and measure the same way as for a projected window.

**Two-way traverse rod**

**Curved traverse rod**

## Bay or Bow Windows

A group of three or more windows placed at angles to each other and projecting outward, forming a recess or alcove in the wall, is known as a "bay window." If the window or windows are curved, they are call a "bow window." Many pleasing treatments are possible; however, the bay or bow should always be treated as a single unit.

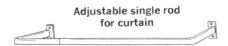
**Adjustable single rod
for curtain**

## Dormers

The dormer is a window in a gable rising from a sloping roof. Simple ruffled tiebacks, full sheer curtains hanging straight from a rod, or casement curtains, are all suitable.

# Success with Curtains

**Adjustable single rod
for curtain**

YOUR SUCCESS WITH CURTAINS depends on your accuracy in measuring your windows, in adding the allowances necessary for your curtain style, in estimating fabric requirements, in cutting your fabric, and in sewing. This chapter will guide you through those steps for four basic curtain styles: glass curtains, casement curtains, tieback curtains, and café curtains.

## GLASS CURTAINS

Full, sheer curtains that hang straight from a rod against the glass are called "glass" curtains. They have a casing and heading at the top and are made in two panels, which are gathered on the curtain rod. Their purpose is to ensure privacy, to soften the interior, and to diffuse light. They also create a uniform appearance from the outside. Glass curtains may be used with panel or draw draperies. The curtains and draperies should be the same length and hung on separate rods.

Use an **adjustable curtain rod.** Secure the fixtures for the rod on the extreme ends of the window frame, 1 inch below the top.

Marquisette, ninon, fiberglass, theatrical gauze, Dacron, and other gossamer, or semi-sheer synthetics and blends are all appropriate fabrics for glass curtains. Neutral colors are generally used—beige, eggshell, white, or grey; however, pastels are seen occasionally.

## Adding Allowances to Measurements

Glass curtains should hang in graceful, soft folds. To get the fullness necessary, you must allow from 2½ to 3 times the width of the window. Ready-made curtains are often skimpy and two pairs may be required for the desired fullness. If your budget is limited, choose less expensive fabric but *do not skimp on yardage.*

*Length:* To the measured length of the window (see page 344), add 2 inches for casing, 2 inches for heading, ¼ inch for turning, 2 inches for shrinkage tuck (1 inch per yard), plus 3¼ inches for the bottom hem and turning. *Example:* 72 inches (measured length) plus 9½ inches = 81½ inches. If double-fold bottom hems are used, and they are desirable in sheer fabrics to eliminate the turned raw edge that would normally show through, allow 6 inches for the bottom hem instead of 3¼ inches. 72 inches (measured length) plus 12¼ inches = 84¼ inches.

*Width:* Multiply the measured width (page 344) by 2½ or 3 for fullness. To this figure, add 8 inches for hems (1-inch double-fold hem on each side of the two panels). *Example:* 42 inches (measured width and returns) x 2½ (fullness) = 105 inches plus 8 inches (hems) = 113 inches. Each of the two panels is 56½ inches wide.

## Estimating Yardage

To estimate yardage for each window, you must consider the fabric width. *Example:* Three lengths of 40-inch fabric are required for the 113-inch width in the example above. (Remember, lengths cannot be pieced. If your figures result in a fraction of a length, such as 2½, buy 3 full lengths.) 84¼ inches (length required for curtain with double bottom hem) x 3 (lengths of fabric) = 252¾ inches, or 7 yards and ¾ inch for each window. It is advisable to buy an extra 9 inches to allow for straightening the ends of the fabric.

## Cutting the Curtains

Curtains must be cut on the true lengthwise and crosswise grains of the fabric so that they hang in straight, smooth lines.

Straighten the end of the fabric by drawing a single thread on the crosswise grain to indicate the cutting line. See page 14. Press the fabric and remove selvages.

Work on a flat surface and use a tape measure to measure the lengths for your curtain. Draw a thread on the crosswise grain to mark the cutting line of each length. Cut, do not tear, the fabric. Straighten the fabric grain, following the instructions on page 14.

## Constructing the Curtains

### Seams

If it is necessary to seam the fabric to gain the width you need, use a fine French seam. See page 86.

### Suggestions for Folding and Pressing Hems

For convenience in folding and pressing hems and casings of your curtains, work on the ironing board. Reverse the direction of the board and place the iron on the small end so that you have a wider working area. If the height of the board is adjust-able, lower it so that you can work in a sitting position. Use a small gauge to measure each turn of the fabric; accuracy is extremely important. As you make each fold for the hem, pin straight through the fabric into the ironing board. Place the pins far enough from the fold so that they do not interfere with your pressing.

### Side Hems

Finish the side hems first. Use a 1-inch double-fold hem on the side and center hems; then the panels will be interchangeable. (A 2-inch hem may be used if you prefer, but be sure to make the extra allowance when cutting the curtains.)

Turn a scant 1 inch to the underside and pin along the cut edge. Press the fold. Then make a second 1-inch turn and pin in place. Press the fold. Stitch as close to the first fold as possible. Backstitch at each end. Press.

### Casing and Heading

In the measurements, 4¼ inches were allowed for the casing, heading, and turning. At the top edge, turn ¼ inch to the underside and finger-press. Turn 2 inches to the underside and pin the free edge in place. Press along the top fold. Stitch close to the first fold. Backstitch at each end. Press.

Divide the hem for the casing and heading by placing a row of pins midway between the stitching and top edge. Stitch along this line. Backstitch at each end. Press.

### Shrinkage Tuck

On the right side (or wrong side, if you prefer), barely below the casing, fold and pin in a 1-inch tuck. Press. Stitch close to the previous line of stitching, using a long stitch. Backstitch at each end. If the curtain shrinks when laundered, let out the tuck the required length.

Note: If your machine is one with Chain Stitch Accessories, chain-stitch the shrinkage tuck. Then you can easily let out the tuck when necessary—merely unlock the last loop of the chain and pull out the stitching. Refer to the instruction book accompanying the machine, and to page 63.

### Bottom Hem

Compare the panels to be sure that they are the same length. Place them wrong sides together, and check the length at the center and outside hems.

In the measurements, 6 inches were allowed for a 3-inch double-fold hem. Turn under a scant 3 inches and pin along the fold. Make a second 3-inch turn and pin the first fold to the curtain.

Before pressing and stitching the hem, hang the curtain on the rod. Adjust the fullness and check the length; the curtain should be about ½ inch above the floor. If your measurements were accurate, the length should be correct; however, if there is a slight difference in length, adjust the hem width accordingly.

Press the hem, then stitch it in place close to the fold. Backstitch at each end. Press.

### Weights

Weight the bottom hems so that the curtains will hang evenly. A round-bead weighted tape is most suitable. Draw the weighted tape through the hem in back of the double turn and secure it on the underside with diagonal hand stitches. Make the stitches about ¼ or ⅜ inch apart, through a single thickness of the hem and the weights. Fasten each end of the thread with tiny backstitches. Remove the weights when laundering the curtains.

**Elbow bracket**

**Elbow bracket and rod**

## CASEMENT CURTAINS

Casement curtains should be used on casement windows that open inward and on French windows and doors. They are tightly stretched over the glass portion of the window. Use the same types of fabrics suggested for glass curtains.

Mount elbow brackets and rods, then measure the window as instructed on page 347.

### Adding Allowance to Measurements

*Length:* To the measured length (bottom of upper rod to top of lower rod), add to top and bottom, 1½ inches for heading, 1½ inches for casing, and ½ inch for turning. *Example:* 68 inches (measured length) plus 7 inches = 75 inches. Either

shrink the fabric before cutting, or allow an additional 2 inches for a shrinkage tuck at the top.

*Width:* Measure from bracket to bracket. Allow for double or triple fullness. To this figure, add 2 inches for hems (½-inch double hem on each side). *Example:* 26 inches (measured width) x 2 (fullness) = 52 inches plus 2 inches (hems) = 54 inches.

To estimate the yardage you will need, follow the guides given under *Glass Curtains*, page 352.

### Cutting and Constructing the Curtains

Straighten and cut the fabric as instructed on page 352.

*Side Hems.*

Fold and press a ½-inch double-fold hem on each side, following the instructions for glass curtains on page 352.

*Casing and Heading.*

In the measurements, 7 inches (3½ inches for each end) were allowed for casing, heading, and turning. Turn under ½ inch at each end and press; then turn 1½ inches to the underside and press. Pin and stitch the casing and heading as instructed for glass curtains. See page 353.

## TIEBACK CURTAINS

Informal, refreshing tieback curtains with ruffles brighten bedroom, breakfast room, kitchen, and bath, and may even be used in the living room. They are made in two panels that meet in the center or, in the case of crisscross curtains, overlap the width of the window as shown in illustration at top of opposite page.

Organdy, lawn, ninon, dotted Swiss, unbleached muslin, and similar fabrics are appropriate.

For crisscross curtains, use the adjustable crisscross or double rod. For tieback panels that meet in the center, use an adjustable curtain rod. Mount

the fixtures for the rod on the extreme ends of the window frame, 1 inch below the top.

### Adding Allowances to Measurements

Measure from the bottom of the rod to the floor. See page 344. (Remember to consider the width of the finished ruffle in the measurement and when cutting the curtains.) To this measurement, add 2 inches for casing, 2 inches for heading, and ¼ inch for turning.

Allow 2½ to 3 times the width of the window

Adjustable double rod
for curtain

Crisscross rod

for fullness. If you are making crisscross curtains, double this figure since each gathered panel covers the entire window.

The width of the ruffle may be from 4 to 8 inches, depending on the texture of the fabric. Double or triple fullness may be required, depending on the width of the ruffle and the texture and weight of the fabric. Sheer fabrics require triple fullness; unbleached muslin may require only double fullness.

To estimate the yardage you will need, follow the guides given under *Glass Curtains,* page 352. Be sure to include the yardage for the ruffles.

## Cutting the Curtains

Straighten and cut the fabric lengths as instructed on page 352. Generally, fabric for ruffling is cut on the crosswise grain. For curtains, however, cut the fabric on the lengthwise grain since you will need a great deal of yardage. Ruffles cut on the lengthwise grain require fewer seam joinings than those cut on the crosswise grain and will remain fluffy much longer when exposed to atmospheric conditions. It is always wise to cut and ruffle a little more length than your estimated requirement. If you are planning to make ruffled tiebacks, allow sufficient length for each pair.

## Constructing the Curtains

### Seams

Use a fine French seam if it is necessary to seam the fabric to gain the required width. See page 86. Join strips for the ruffles with a hemmed seam, using the Hemmer Foot.

### Making the Ruffle

Finish the edges of the ruffle with a narrow hem, using the Hemmer Foot. Hem each edge if there is a heading on the ruffle. One of the decorative zig-zag patterns may be used in the hemming.

If crisp organdy or lawn is used, finished the edges with a decorative zig-zag stitch rather than a hem. See *Edgestitched Finish,* page 274.

Use the Ruffler to gather the fabric. Always adjust the setting of the Ruffler and test the fullness of the ruffle on a swatch of your fabric. To ruffle organdy or chintz, dampen the fabric along the seamline with a small, moist sponge, and gather the fabric while it is still damp. Press when finished.

### Joining Ruffle to Curtain
**Ruffle with heading.** First finish the center and lower edges of the curtain with a narrow hem. Use the Hemmer Foot or turn a ⅛-inch double hem to the underside and stitch. Press. Pin the ruffle, right side up, over the right side of the hemmed edge. Ease in extra fullness at the corners, beginning and ending about 1 inch from each side of the intersecting edge. Pin at close intervals. Stitch on the gathering stitches, with the ruffle side up.

**Ruffle without heading.** Pin the ruffle to the curtain, right sides together, extending the curtain edge a scant ½ inch beyond the gathering stitches. Ease in extra fullness at the corners. Stitch with the ruffle side up. Trim the seam allowance on the ruffle to a scant ¼ inch. Fold the curtain edge under ⅛ inch, then fold it over the seam to the stitching line, enclosing the raw edge; pin it in place. Stitch near the first fold. Press. Turn the ruffle away from the curtain and press the seam toward the curtain.

### Side Hem
Finish the hem on the outer edge of the curtain and ruffle with a ½-inch double-fold hem. To do this, turn the cut edge under a scant ½ inch and press. Make a second ½-inch turn for the hem, and press. Pin the hem in place, then stitch. Backstitch at each end. Press.

### Casing and Heading
In the measurements, 4¼ inches were allowed for casing, heading, and turning. Turn, press and stitch the casing and heading now, following the instructions for glass curtains on page 353. However, extend the hem through the ruffle, making

sure that you keep it straight with the grain line of the ruffle.

### Ruffled Valance

Finish the ends of the ruffled valance with narrow hems to match those on the ruffle. Pin and stitch the ruffle to the curtain over the top line of stitching that forms the heading.

### Casing and Cord for Draping

To ensure a consistently even drape in the curtains, you may use a cord with a casing on the underside of each panel.

Hang the curtains; then drape each side back, using a tape measure as a tieback. (At the same time, take the measurement for the length of the tiebacks.) Pin-mark each side of the curtain for the diagonal line of the drape.

*To make the casing.* Cut a strip of the curtain fabric on the lengthwise grain the length of the diagonal line plus ½ inch for turning, and 1 inch wide. Fold under all edges ¼ inch and press. On the wrong side of the curtain, pin the strip on the diagonal line, from the ruffle to the outer edge. Stitch on each side of the strip to form a casing. Do not catch the ruffle heading in your stitching. Backstitch at each end. Press.

*To add the cord.* Insert a small cable cord (size 9) through the casing. Knot the end of the cord at the center edge of the curtain. Then stitch across the end of the cord and casing two or three times; do not catch the ruffled heading in the stitching. Tie the threads on the underside. Cut the opposite end of the cord to within ¼ inch of the curtain; then wind thread around the cord to keep it from raveling.

Hang the curtains. Draw the cord to gather the curtain the required amount. Tie a loop in the end of the cord so that the gathers may be released when the curtain is laundered. The tieback covers the casing.

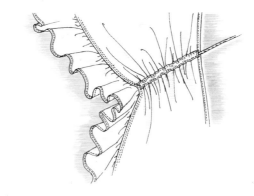

Instead of making a casing, you can purchase a shirring tape that has a woven-in cord. It is stitched in place the same way as the casing described above.

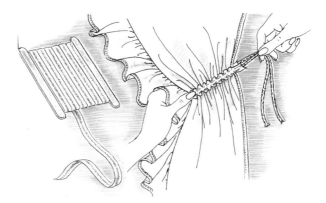

### Tiebacks

A pair of tiebacks is used to hold the drape of the curtain in place. The position of the tieback depends on fashion as well as personal choice. Generally, however, it is at the center sash or below it.

The length of the tieback depends on the amount of fullness in the drape. For an average-sized window, the tiebacks are about 20 inches long; for a wide window, they may be 36 inches long. To determine the length necessary, hang the curtains, bring a tape measure around each curtain, and secure it with a thumbtack in the edge of the window frame. Drape the curtain, and adjust the tape measure for the length desired. Make one pair of tiebacks for each window.

**Tieback with one ruffle.** Cut the band for the tieback on the lengthwise grain the required length plus ½ inch for seam allowances, and 2½ inches wide. Crease the band through the center, wrong sides together. Cut the ruffle the same width as

the curtain ruffle and the same length as the band. Finish each end of the ruffle with a ⅛-inch hem. Pin the wrong side of the ruffle to the right side of the band, extending the ends of the band ¼ inch beyond the ruffle. Stitch in place and backstitch at each end. Press the seam allowances toward the band. Turn under ¼ inch on the free side of the band and press. Turn the band, right

sides together, and stitch across each end, taking a ¼-inch seam. Clip diagonally across the corners. Turn the band to the right side and pin the folded edge in place at the stitching line, enclosing the seam allowance inside the band. Top-stitch close to the edge. Press.

Sew a small ring near each end of the tieback. Place a hook in the side edge of the window frame at the position for the tieback.

**Tieback with ruffle on both edges.** If the ruffle is no more than 3 inches wide and the fabric is crisp, you can stitch a ruffle on each side of the band. Cut two bands on the lengthwise grain the required length plus ½ inch for seam allowance, and 1½ inches wide. Cut two ruffles the length of the band and finish each end with a ⅛-inch hem. Lay the bands right sides together, and pin one ruffle between the two strips, extending the ends of the band ¼ inch beyond the ruffle at each end. Turn the ends of the band to the wrong side ¼ inch and press. Stitch, backstitching at each end. Pin the second ruffle to the

opposite edge of one band section, right sides together. Be sure the right sides of both ruffles face in the same direction. Stitch. Press the seam allowances toward the band. Turn the free edge of the band under ¼ inch and pin it in place at the stitching line, enclosing the seam allowances. Stitch around the band from the top side.

# CAFÉ CURTAINS

Cafés are never full-length curtains. They may start at the center of the window or midway down on the upper half of the window, or they may be made in tiers that start from the top of the window. The tiers may be even or uneven in length. The bottom tier can be sill, apron, or floor length. Each tier must hang on a separate rod.

Café curtains are generally made in two panels. If the curtains begin at the center or upper half of the window, they are often used with a one-piece valance. *(Illustrated on left at top of opposite* 

*page.)* The heading may be styled in several ways. Cafés may also be used in combination with draperies or tieback curtains.

Select such fabrics as chintz, sailcloth, Indian Head, gingham, dotted Swiss, organdy, muslin, nylon, corduroy, and polished cotton. Solid colors, plaids, prints, or stripes may be chosen for informal curtains, and antique satin, fiberglass, sheer silk, or taffeta for formal treatments.

Café curtains usually are not lined. They should be lined, however, when expensive fabric is chosen or when no venetian blind or shade is used; the lining prevents the fabric from fading and ensures privacy. It also gives the window a uniform appearance from the outside.

## Rods and Fixtures

Before taking measurements and purchasing fabric, you must decide what style and heading you are going to use for the curtains and what type of rod, fixture, and hooks you will need. Several types of rods and fixtures are illustrated. Also shown are two types of clip-on rings; they are ideal for hanging the curtains because they can be removed quickly when laundering is necessary.

*(Continued on following page)*

One screw bracket

Two screw bracket

Adjustable rod

Rod for valance

Clip-on rings

Decorative rod

Slip-in hook

Slip-on ring and pin-on hook

Pleater pin with ring

End pin with ring

If the curtains are to be pleated to control the fullness, they are constructed the same way as draperies and require both rings and drapery hooks.

Always position your rod (or rods) even with any horizontal strips between the glass panes or even with the center sash of the window.

Secure the brackets and rods before taking measurements. If you have chosen a valance for the top of your café curtains, mount the brackets for the first rod on the extreme ends of the window frame as close to the top as possible. (If you have recessed windows, see page 365.)

**One-tier cafés.** Place the brackets for the rod on the extreme ends of the window frame and at the center of the window (**C** in the illustration) or midway down on the upper half of the window (**B**).

**Two-tier cafés.** Place the brackets for the first rod on the extreme ends of the window frame as close to the top as possible. Position the rod for the second tier halfway between the first rod and sill, or lower edge of the apron (**A** in the illustration).

A. **Two-tier curtain —**
   **To sill or lower edge of apron**

B. **One-tier —**
   **Midway upper half of window to sill**

C. **Center of window—To sill**

D. **Three-tier curtain—To sill**

**Three-tier cafés.** Measure from the top of the first rod to the sill or lower edge of the apron. Divide the measurement by 3. Position the second and third rods at one-third intervals as shown in **D**.

## Adding Allowances to Measurements

You must measure your windows and add allowances for hems, seams, and fullness. Make a note of your measurement and the allowances added and use them when you figure the yardage required and when you cut and make your curtains.

### Measure each tier of the café as follows:

**Length:** Measure from the lower circle of the ring to the top of the next rod. To this measurement, add 5 inches for top and bottom hems (2-inch hems, plus ½ inch for turning). *Example:* 30 inches (measured length) plus 5 inches (hems) = 35 inches.

**Width:** Measure from the inside edge of one bracket to the other. Multiply this measurement by 2 for fullness. To this figure, add 10 inches for hems (2-inch hem and ½ inch for turning on each side of the two panels). *Example:* 36 inches (measured width) x 2 (fullness) = 72 inches plus 10 inches (for hems) = 82 inches. Each of the two panels is 41 inches wide.

The **valance** is one piece and the finished length may vary from 6 to 18 inches. Measure as follows:

**Length:** Decide on the length you wish. To this measurement, add 5 inches for top and botton hems (the same as for the tiers). *Example:* 12 inches (length of valance) plus 5 inches (hems) = 17 inches.

**Width:** Measure from one edge of the bracket to the other. Multiply this measurement by 2 for fullness. To this figure, add 5 inches for hems (2-inch hem and ½ inch for turning on each side of the valance). *Example:* 36 inches (measured width) x 2 (fullness) = 72 inches, plus 5 inches (hems) = 77 inches.

## Estimating Yardage

The examples above are for a one-tier café. If your curtains will have more than one tier, multiply your measurements by the number of tiers in each curtain you are making. Then estimate your yardage, following the directions given under *Glass Curtains,* page 352.

## Simple Café Curtains

Straighten and cut the fabric as instructed on page 352.

### Side Hems.

Turn the edge under ½ inch and press. Turn under a 2-inch hem and press. Pin the hem in place. You may slip-stitch the hem by hand or machine-stitch it, using either straight stitching or blind-stitching. If hems are blindstitched, baste them in place, ¼ inch from the edge. With the wrong side

of the curtain up, turn the hem under on the basting line, forming a soft fold and exposing the ¼-inch hem edge. Select the blindstitch zig-zag, a medium stitch width, and 12 to 15 stitch length. Stitch so that the straight stitches are in the hem edge and the sideward stitches pierce only a few threads of the soft fold. Press.

### Top and Bottom Hems.

Turn the edge under ½ inch and press. Turn under a 2-inch hem and press. Pin the hem in place and miter the corners. Finish the same way

as the side hems. If you machine-stitch the hem, begin and end the stitching at the side hems using either straight stitching or blindstitching. Miter the corners and slip-stitch them in place. Press.

Clip rings to the top ends of each panel, then place additional rings between them at 4- or 5-inch intervals. Slip the rod through the rings and hang the curtains

## Cafes with Decorative Trim

Bands of decorative zig-zag stitching glamorize the café curtains illustrated here. The bands extend above the finished heading, forming loops that slip over the rod.

Turn, press, and stitch the hems along the sides and top, following the instructions above. Cut 10 bands (5 for each panel) the length of the curtain plus 2½ inches for loops, and about 3 inches wide. Refer to *Border Designs,* page 272 for instructions on decorative stitching. When the stitching is completed, turn under each edge of the bands close to the stitching, and press.

Pin the bands to the right side of the curtain, extending the ends 2½ inches above the top hem, following this sequence: place the first band 1 inch from the outside edge; place the second band in the same position on the opposite edge; place the third band in the center; then place one band on each side, between the center band and the outside band. Space all bands an equal distance apart.

Stitch close to the folds, carrying the stitching to the end of each band.

To form the loops, fold under ¼ inch at the top of each band extension and hand-sew it to the curtain, ¼ inch below the finished edge.

Finish the bottom hem, following the instructions, on page 361.

*Ruffles* are also an attractive addition to café curtains. For a decorative touch, finish the ruffles with zig-zag stitching. See *Edgestitched Finish,* page 274.

362

## Cafés with Scalloped Heading and Pleats

The cafés in the illustration here alternate scallops and pleats in the heading. Select and position a decorative café rod and bracket with a return.

*Length:* Measure the length of the tier as instructed on page 360; however, allow 4½ inches instead of 2½ inches for the top hem and turning.

*Width:* Measure from the outside edge of one bracket to the other. Divide this measurement by 2 to determine the space each panel will cover. If the measurement is 36 inches, then 18 inches of the window will be covered by one panel. This width allows space for four scallops 4 inches wide, beginning 2 inches from the inside edge.

### Adding Allowances to Measurements

For fullness, allow 4¾ inches for each pleat. Each panel in the illustration has five pleats. Place the first end pleat 2 inches from the inside edge and the second end pleat at the return, which is usually about 3 inches from the outside edge; then place three pleats between the four scallops. Five (pleats) x 4¾ inches (for each pleat) = 23¾ inch (required for pleats).

To one-half the measured width, add depth of return, 5 inches for hems (2-inch hem and ½ inch for turning on each side), plus the fullness required for pleats. *Example:* 18 inches (one-half window width) plus 3 inches (for return) plus 5 inches (for hems) plus 23¾ inches (for 5 pleats) = 49¾ inches. This is the width of one panel; you will need two panels for the window.

### Cutting and Constructing the Curtains

Straighten the ends of the fabric and cut the length for the curtains as instructed on page 352.

Turn under the top edge of the curtain ½ inch and stitch close to the fold. Turn and press the side hems, following the instructions on page 361.

Cut 4-inch crinoline the length of the panel width. Mark the crinoline for the position of the return, pleats, and scallops, beginning 2 inches

Decorative rod

Slip-in hook

Sew-on ring

End pin with ring

from the inside edge as illustrated. Draw an outline for the scallops. See the example for pleats under *Adding Allowance to Measurements* above. Mark one strip of crinoline for the right panel and one for the left. Position the crinoline on the underside of the fabric, 4⅛ inches from the top edge and pin it in place.

Turn the top hem to the right side 4 inches, *(Continued on following page)*

and pin. The fabric fold should be barely above the straight edge of the crinoline. Stitch the scallops, using a shorter stitch than that used in stitching the fabric. Backstitch at each end. Cut away the crinoline close to the stitching. Cut out the scallops ¼ inch from the stitching. Clip into the seam allowances at evenly spaced intervals for a smooth turning. Press. Slip the ends of the crinoline under the side hems. Turn the top hem to the underside, over the crinoline, and turn the scallops

smoothly on the stitching line; press.

Finish the side hems and the bottom hem by hand. Pin-mark the position for the pleats, allowing the same fullness and spacing as in your planning above. See *Adding Allowances to Measurements,* page 363. Make French pleats, following the instructions on page 380. Sew a drapery hook to the back of each pleat and at each end of the curtain. Fasten the hooks in the curtain rings of the rod.

**A *ready-made scalloped pleater tape with woven-in pockets*** for pleater pins is available by the yard. To use it, follow these steps: Eliminate the allowance for the 4-inch top hem but allow ½ inch for turning. Arrange the cutout scallops

and space for pleats as instructed above. Pin the pleater tape to the right side of the curtain, ¼ inch from the edge. Stitch in place ¼ inch from the edge of the pleater tape. Cut out the scallops and turn the tape to the underside. Press. Stitch the lower edge of the tape to the curtain. Finish the side hems and bottom hem. Insert the prongs of the pleater pin into the woven pockets to form the pleat. Insert the end pins into woven pockets at each edge of the curtain.

**Pleater pin
with ring**

## Café Curtains for Recessed Windows

Curtains for a recessed window may hang flush with the wall. The illustration here shows where the rods are placed for a three-tier café in which the tiers overlap.

### Rod and Fixtures

Select the spring-tension socket and round rigid rod, which must be cut to measurement. (In having this done, remember to allow for the spring in the socket.) A rod is required for each tier and is recessed between the sides of the window.

Measure the length inside the window recess. Divide the measurement by 3. Position the first rod in the recess close to the top; the middle rod at the one-third line; and the bottom rod at the two-thirds line. *Example:* If the window is 60 inches long, place the first rod at the top, the middle rod 20 inches from the top, and the bottom rod 20 inches above the sill.

### Adding Allowances to Measurements

In a three-tier café with overlapping tiers, the visible lengths of all tiers should be the same. To achieve that, you must allow an extra 2 or 3 inches on the middle and bottom tiers for an overlap.

### Measure the Window as Follows:

**Length:** Measure the top and middle tiers from the lower circle of the ring to the bottom of the next rod, and the bottom tier from the lower circle of the ring to the sill. To the measurement of each tier, add 5 inches for top and bottom hems (2-inch hems plus ½ inch for turning), and to the middle and bottom tiers, add an extra 2 inches for overlap. *Example:* Top tier, 20 inches (measured length) plus 5 inches (hems) = 25 inches. Middle and bottom tiers, each 20 inches (measured length) plus 5 inches (hems) plus 2 inches (overlap) = 27 inches.

**Width:** Measure the width inside the window recess. Multiply the measured width by 2 for fullness. To this figure, add 10 inches for hems (2-inch hem and ½ inch for turning on each side of the two panels). *Example:* 35 inches (measured width) x 2 inches (for fullness) = 70 inches plus 10 inches (for hems) = 80 inches. Each of the two panels is 40 inches wide.

Make a note of your measurements and the allowances added. Use them when you figure the yardage required and when you cut and make your café curtains.

**Round rigid rod**

**Oval spring-tension socket**

**Round spring-tension socket**

### Constructing the Curtains

Construct the curtains, following the instructions beginning on page 361.

### Hanging the Curtains

Mark the position of the rods and remove them. It is simple to reposition them since spring-tension sockets are used.

Clip rings to the top ends of each panel, then place additional rings between them at 4- or 5-inch intervals. Slip the rod through the rings. Position the first rod at the top of the window flush with the wall, the middle rod 2 inches above the marking and into the window recess 1 inch from the wall, and the bottom rod 2 inches above the marking and into the window recess 2 inches from the wall.

# Set the Stage
## with Draperies

MAKING DRAPERIES LURES MANY WOMEN into sewing. The reason is not hard to find. Ready-made draperies are expensive and seldom completely satisfactory; often you have to compromise a little on color or fabric because you cannot find exactly what you want. Custom-made draperies from a decorator's shop may be absolutely lovely to the eye—but absolutely devastating to the purse. The solution: Make your own.

This chapter charts the course you should follow for panel draperies and draw draperies. As you embark on drapery construction, however, remember that your best ally is accuracy—accuracy in measuring, in estimating yardage, in cutting and in sewing.

## PANEL DRAPERIES— PREPARATION

Draperies that hang on each side a window and do not cover the full window are known as "panel draperies." They are generally used with glass curtains and both must be identical in length. A pair of draperies is required for each window or group of windows. When the drapery panels hang at either side of a group of windows, they should be connected across the top with a cornice board or valance unless a decorative rod is used.

The draperies should be full and hang in balanced, graceful folds. Their fullness is controlled by a pleated heading. The hem at the lower edge should be at least 3 inches deep; many decorators prefer one even wider. The deep hem gives added weight to the draperies and allows for lengthening them if the fabric shrinks.

Secure the fixture for the rod on the extreme ends of the window frame, 1 inch below the top. See page 343.

**Adjustable double rod**

## Adding Allowances to Measurements

*Length for lined draperies:* To the measured length, as described on page 344, add 1 inch for rod, 2 inches for heading, 4 inches for top hem, and 3½ inches for bottom hem and turning. *Example:* 87 inches (measured length) plus 10½ inches = 97½ inches. **For unlined draperies** add an extra ½ inch for turning on the top hem. *Example:* 87 inches (measured length) plus 11 inches = 98 inches.

**Width:** For a single window 36 to 50 inches in width, the finished drapery heading after pleating should cover 12 to 15 inches of the window; however, this is a matter of choice. If you are changing the proportion of the window to make it appear wider, you will need wider panels, see page 342.

Determine how wide you want your finished drapery panels to be. To this measurement, add 4 inches for the depth of the return at one end plus 5 inches for hems (2-inch hem and ½-inch seam allowance on each side) plus the amount required for pleats.

At this point it is wise to decide what kind of pleat you intend to make. For cartridge and box pleats, the allowance for each pleat and the spacing are different from those given in the example below. See page 380.

An uneven number of pleats—5, 7, or 9 in each panel—is recommended. It is more pleasing to the eye than an even number, which tends to distract the observer and make him count the pleats in pairs. *Allow 5 to 6 inches for fullness in each pleat* and space the pleats about 4 inches apart. *Example:* 19 inches (measured width and 4-inch return at one end) plus 5 inches (hems) plus 25 inches (for 5 pleats) = 49 inches. This is the width of fabric required for each panel.

To determine the exact spacing between pleats, proceed as follows: Always locate one end pleat the depth of the return (4 inches) from the outside edge of each panel, and the other end pleat 2 inches from the inside edge; use the distance between these two pleats to figure the space between additional pleats. Since two end pleats are predetermined in each panel, the number of spaces is always one less than the number of pleats. *Example:* 19 inches (finished width) less 6 inches (depth of return and distance from inside edge) = 13 inches to be divided into spaces for additional pleats. For 5 pleats: 13 inches divided by 4 (spaces) = 3¼ inches (space between pleats). Page 379 describes how to measure and make pleats in the drapery heading.

## Estimating Yardage

Most drapery fabric is 50 to 60 inches wide, and generally two widths are sufficient for each pair of draperies. *Example:* For two panels, 97½ inches (length of drapery) x 2 (lengths) = 195 inches, or 5 yards and 15 inches. Buy an additional 9 inches to allow for straightening the ends of the fabric.

If the fabric is only 36 inches wide, allow 1 inch for each seam within the drapery (½-inch seam allowance on each edge). Each pair of panels in the example above will require four lengths of fabric, or 10 yards and 30 inches.

These are yardage estimates for one window. Multiply them by the number of windows to arrive at your total requirements.

If you are treating a group of two or three windows, your draperies should be wider than those in the example and will require more fabric. Follow the directions for the example and add the amount required for each additional space (3¼ inches) and each additional pleat (5 inches). A pair of panels may require three lengths (one and one-half for each panel) or four lengths (two for each panel) of 50-inch fabric.

### Matching the Design

If your fabric has a design, you will need extra yardage for matching since the design must fall in the same place in each panel. A full design should begin at the turn for the bottom hem. Measure from the center of one design to the center of the next one and allow this amount in each panel length for matching.

### Estimating the Lining

The lining is 10 inches shorter and 8 inches narrower than the drapery fabric. In the example above, the lining for each panel is 87½ inches long, and 4 yards and 31 inches are required for each pair. Buy an extra 9 inches to allow for straightening the ends of the lining.

Turn to page 370 for cutting and construction.

# DRAW DRAPERIES—
PREPARATION

Draperies that can be drawn closed to cover the entire window are known as "draw draperies." They may be used on almost any type of window and are the preferred treatment for sliding windows or doors, picture windows, and casement windows that open out. They are also a handsome treatment for draping walls.

Draw draperies may be made of heavy or sheer fabric. Like panel draperies they should hang in balanced, graceful folds. Pleats are the most effective means of controlling their fullness.

**Two-way traverse rod**

## Rods and Fixtures

You will need a traverse rod for draw draperies. Select a two-way traverse rod if the draperies are made in two panels that overlap at the center.

See *Picture Windows,* page 345. Select a one-way traverse rod for corner windows and sliding doors, page 346, and other windows where the drapery is drawn to one side.

Install the brackets for the rods on the extreme ends of the window frame, 1 inch below the top of the window frame. If the draperies are to hang from the ceiling, use the ceiling-mounted track.

### Adding Allowances to Measurements

*Length:* To the measured length (as described on page 345), add 1 inch for rod, 2 inches for heading, 4 inches for top hem, and 3½ inches for bottom hem and turning. *Example:* For lined draperies, 87 inches (measured length) plus 10½ inches = 97½ inches. For unlined draperies, add an extra ½ inch for turning on the top hem.

If double-fold hems are used, and they are preferred in sheer fabric, allow 8 inches for the top hem and 6 inches for the bottom hem. 87 inches (measured length) plus 17 inches (rod, heading, and double-fold hems) = 104 inches.

If draperies extend from the ceiling, measure from the ceiling to the floor and add only the amounts stated for top and bottom hems.

*Width:* Measure across the window from one end of the rod to the other. To this measurement, add the depth of the return on each side. *Example:* 92 inches (measured width) plus 8 inches (two 4-inch returns) = 100 inches. This is the width the draw draperies must cover; each finished panel must be one-half this width plus one-half the overlap.

To the measured width you must add the allowances for hems, overlap, seams, and pleats. But first you must determine the number of pleats and the space between the pleats.

Pleats in draw draperies must always be even in number although the number in each panel may be even or uneven. Allow 5 or 6 inches for fullness in each pleat, and space the pleats about 4 inches apart. (You may have to estimate the number of pleats several times before arriving at the exact spacing. The paper pattern suggested below will help you here.)

To determine the exact spacing between pleats, proceed as follows: Always locate an end pleat the depth of the return from the outside edge of each drapery panel; use the distance between these two pleats to figure the space between additional pleats. *Examples:* 100 inches (measured width and returns) less 8 inches (returns) = 92 inches (to be divided into space for additional pleats). Since two end pleats are predetermined, the number of spaces is one less than the number of pleats. For 24 pleats: 92 inches divided by 23 spaces = 4 inches (spaces between pleats). 24 (pleats) x 5 inches ( for each pleat) = 120 inches (required for pleats). Page 379 describes how to measure and make pleats in the drapery heading.

The diagram here shows the 2½-inch overlap and the position of the first end pleat at the center edge of each panel. When the spacing of the pleats is figured before making the allowance for the overlap, the distance between pleats at the center overlap will be the same as that between all other pleats when the draperies are closed.

### Making a Paper Pattern

You may feel more confident about your decisions if you make a pattern to fit your window and mark your spacings on that. Cut two strips of stiff paper about 6 inches wide and a few inches longer than the width of the window and return at each end. Lap the center edges the amount of the overlap—usually 2½ inches. Pin. Then mark paper 1¼ inches from one edge of the overlap to indicate the center line. Measure the window width and return at each end and cut the paper an equal distance from center line. *Example:* For the 100-inch width used above, the center is 50 inches from each edge of the pattern. Fit the pattern across the rod and around the return at each end to be certain that the width is correct. Mark the position of the returns and the spacing for pleats. Remember that the allowance for side hems, seams, and fullness for pleats has not been added to the pattern.

*Now you are ready to determine the width required for the draperies.* To do this, add your allowances to the window width plus the return at each end. *Example:* 92 inches (measured width) plus 8 inches (two 4-inch returns) plus 10 inches (2-inch hem and ½-inch seam allowance on each side of the two panels), 120 inches (pleats), and 2½ inches (overlap) = 232½ inches (width required). Each of the two panels is 116¼ inches wide plus seam allowances. For each seam within the drapery, allow 1 inch (½-inch seam allowance on each edge).

## Estimating Yardage

In estimating yardage, consider first the width of the fabric. If 50-inch fabric is used, it will be 48 inches wide after you have removed the selvages and allowed for seaming. In the example, 232½ inches (width required) divided by 48 inches (fabric width) = 4 5/6 lengths. Buy 5 lengths. Remember, lengths cannot be pieced. If your figures result in a fraction, always buy the next full length.

*Example:* 97½ inches (length of drapery) x 5 (lengths) = 487½ inches or 13 yards 19½ inches. Buy an additional 9 inches to allow for straightening the ends of the fabric. If the fabric has a design, allow for matching. See page 367. If the draperies are sheer, add the allowances for double-fold hems. See page 368.

If you plan to place seams barely outside pleats, you will need extra width. This is explained below in *Making Seams.* How much extra depends on the width of your drapery panels.

**Lining.** The lining is 10 inches shorter and 8 inches narrower than the drapery fabric. For the example above, the lining is 87½ inches long, and 5 lengths of 50-inch lining, or 12 yards and 5½ inches, are required. Buy an additional 9 inches to allow for straightening the ends of the lining. Information on suitable lining fabric is given on page 340.

## CUTTING THE DRAPERIES

Draperies must be cut on the true lengthwise and crosswise grains of the fabric so that they will hang straight, fall smoothly and gracefully, and clean satisfactorily.

Straighten the ends of the fabric by drawing a thread on the crosswise grain to indicate the cutting line. Steam-press the fabric, then remove the selvages.

For accuracy in cutting the draperies, work on a flat surface such as the dining room table, ping-pong table, or bedboard. *Use a tape measure to measure the lengths.* Draw a thread on the crosswise grain to mark the cutting line for each length; then cut the length. If the fabric has a design, match the pattern in each panel. See page 367.

Straighten the fabric grain as instructed on page 14.

## CONSTRUCTING THE DRAPERIES

### Making Seams

Seaming is your first construction step if you are making draw draperies or wide panel draperies. Seams are placed barely outside pleats, where they are less noticeable than they would be if placed within a pleat or between pleats. To do this, measure and pin-mark the width of the center hem and turning, the distance of the first pleat from the hem edge, and then the amounts for as many pleats and spaces as the fabric width will allow, plus seam allowance. Draw a thread on the lengthwise grain to indicate the cutting line. Cut on the drawn thread. Use a French seam in unlined draperies so that the cut edges will be enclosed, and

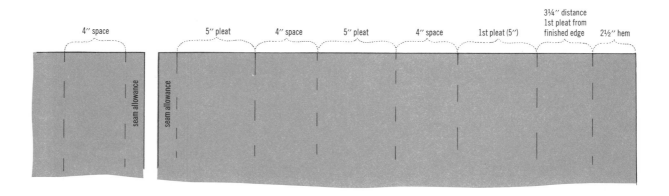

4″ space     5″ pleat   4″ space   5″ pleat   4″ space   1st pleat (5″)   3¼″ distance 1st pleat from finished edge   2½″ hem

seam allowance   seam allowance

a plain seam pressed open in lined draperies. Be sure to match designs at the seamline.

*For convenience in folding and pressing hems in draperies, work on the ironing board during the construction steps that follow, as suggested for glass curtains, page 352.*

## Making Unlined Draperies

The informal mode of today's living has increased the popularity of unlined draperies. Many of the beautiful wonder fabrics do not require lining. The color and design of the fabric are visible from the outside.

The allowances for heading, side, and bottom hems referred to below are described on page 366 (for panel draperies) and page 368 (for draw draperies).

### Heading Hem

To support the pleated heading, use crinoline of the same width as the hem at the top. In the measurements, 4½ inches were allowed for a top hem and turning. Turn 4½ inches to the underside and press.

Cut 4-inch crinoline 5 inches shorter than the width of the drapery. Place the crinoline over the underside of the hem, aligning one edge with the crease and extending the ends to within 2½ inches of the fabric edges. (This is the turn for the side hems.) Stitch the crinoline in place, ¼ inch from the crease for the hem. Turn the cut edge of fabric over the opposite edge of the crinoline and stitch. Press. Turn the hem to the underside and press again. Pin, then baste the hem in place. *Do not stitch the hem;* when the pleats are stitched, they will hold it in place. But be sure to leave the basting in until you have stitched the pleats.

CRINOLINE

2½" BOTH SIDES FOR HEMS

### Side Hems

To remove bulk, cut out the corner of the top hem edge. Begin 2½ inches from the outer edge (turn for the side hem) and cut upward to within ½ inch of the top fold; then cut diagonally to the top hem fold, and on the hem fold to the outer edge.

Turn ½ inch to the underside, and press. Turn a 2-inch hem and pin in place. Miter the corner at the top edge. Press.

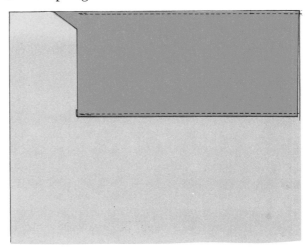

Hems may be slip-stitched by hand or machine-stitched, using either straight stitching or blind-stitching. If you finish the hem by hand, catch only a few threads of the fabric in the stitches so that they are invisible on the top side. If you machine-stitch the hem using straight stitching, place the stitching as close to the folded edge as possible.

*(Continued on following page)*

If you blindstitch the hem, first baste it in place, ¼ inch from the folded edge. With the wrong side of the drapery up, turn the hem to the right side on the basting line, creating a soft fold and exposing the ¼-inch hem edge. Select the blindstitch zig-zag, a medium stitch width, and about 15 stitch length. Stitch so that the straight stitches fall in the hem edge and the sideward stitches pierce only a few threads of the soft fold. Turn the hem down and press.

### Bottom Hem

Compare the drapery panels, wrong sides together, and check the length at the center and outer side hems to be sure they are identical.

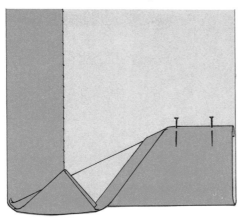

In the measurements, 3½ inches were allowed for the bottom hem and turning. Turn under ½ inch and press. Turn a 3-inch hem and pin in place. Miter the corners and ease the hem down slightly at this point to allow for the thicknesses of fabric and to square the corners. Baste the hem in place.

Before finishing the bottom hem, pleat the heading and attach the drapery hooks. See pages 379 and 381. Hang the draperies and check the length. The draperies should be ½ inch above the floor. If your measurements were accurate, the length should be correct and the change in hem, if any, will be slight.

The hem may be slip-stitched by hand or blindstitched by machine. If finished by hand, the work may be done after draperies are hung. If the hem is blindstitched, begin and end the stitching at the side hems. Then miter the corners and slip-stitch them in place, making the stitches through the hems only.

## Making Draperies with Pleat Tape Heading

Ready-made pleat tape with woven-in pockets for pleater pins is available by the yard. If you use it instead of crinoline at the top, eliminate the allowance for the 4-inch top hem; however, allow ½ inch for turning. Consider the drapery return at each end and position the woven-in pockets so that a pleat falls at the turn of the rod.

Cut the pleat tape 5 inches shorter than the width of the drapery. Pin the tape across the top

## Plate 19

### Quilting for luxury

*Right:* A quilted print screen gives this bedroom a charming touch of distinction. The quilting outlines the handsome floral motif, giving the fabric an extra dimension of luxury. The fabric design is precisely matched in the pleated flounce. The simple coverlet can be varied for a quick change of color scheme or for laundering convenience.

*Below:* The smartly tailored bedspread's diamond-pattern quilting could be stitched by machine or bought by the yard. Luxurious blue draperies, hung on bright brass rods and held with braid and tassel tiebacks, create a Victorian feeling, which is softened by sheer, white glass-curtains.

**Illustration above and below**
from The American Home © 1964, The Curtis Publishing Company

American Home © 1964, The Curtis Publishing Company

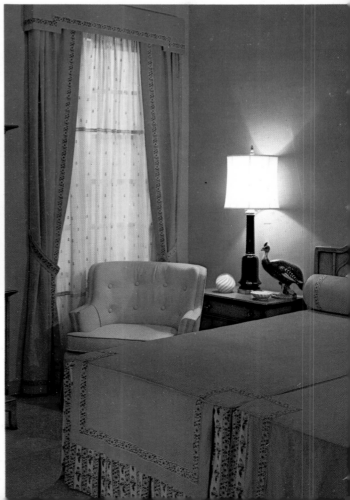

### Bands for elegance

Bands of fabric, cut from the striped pattern used for the flounce on the bed, add elegance to the brilliant orange and red tones of this room. Draperies, valance, coverlet and bolsters are all outlined with striking effect.

### Plate 20      Pretty, practical and young

*Above:* In an attic room, the sloping ceiling provides a built-in base for a ruffled canopy of provincial print. Matching café curtain, placed low on the window, and gathered valance and draperies give a pleasing balance to the room.

*Above:* Sunny yellow brightens a small room. Semi-sheer patterned café curtains ensure privacy while letting in light. The same fabric is repeated in the flounce on the bed, which is topped with a quilted box coverlet.

*Left:* An Alice in Wonderland theme is created with printed fabric for draperies, bed flounce and headboard trim and is emphasized by cutouts from the fabric on the wall. Ball fringe makes a gay finish. The solid pink of the quilted coverlet blends perfectly with the print.

## Plate 21

### Light and airy

*Right:* Sheer, white draperies that let in lots of light while softening its glare are dramatically outlined in emerald green velvet ribbon, which also bands the white shades. Café curtains of the same sheer fabric cover the lower half of the window.

Quilted solid green bedspread and boldly patterned wallpaper provide an effective contrast to the delicate window treatment.

### Cool and calm

*Below:* A wall-to-wall drapery provides a restful, unbroken wall treatment. Its refreshing blue roses are repeated in the quilted bedspread, on which corner underlays make a neat, tailored finish.

of Pictorial Living magazine

**Plate 22**

**Twin-needle stitching**
adds an expensive-looking
custom touch to
ruffled curtains.
Ruffle and heading
are both edged
with scallop stitching.

**Appliqué adds decorative inte**

*Above:* Solid on solid, leaves
and flower delineated with ope
and closed zig-zag stitching.

*Left:* The simplest of all
appliqué methods, a cutout fr
printed fabric appliquéd on a

Either of these treatments wo
enhance a pillow or draperies.

of the drapery, right sides together, 5/16 inch from the fabric edge; extend the ends to within 2½ inches of the drapery edge. (This is the turn for the side hems.) Stitch the tape in place ½ inch from the fabric edge. Press.

Turn the pleat tape to the underside, fold the fabric on the stitching line, and press. Pin the lower edge of the pleat tape to the drapery and stitch ¼ inch from the edge. Press.

Form the side and bottom hems as instructed above. Then insert hooks into the woven-in pockets to form the pleats.

**Pleater pin**

## Making Draperies of Sheer Fabric

Draw draperies of sheer fabric may be used alone or with glass curtains that are hung on a separate rod. The sheer over sheer imparts a cool, crisp look.

Refer to *Draw Draperies—Preparation*, page 368, for instructions on adding allowances to your measurements and estimating yardage. Remember that you should make double-fold hems in sheer fabrics.

### Side Hems

The side hems are stitched first. In the measurements, 16 inches were allowed for a 2-inch double-fold hem on each side of the two panels. Fold, press, and stitch the double-fold hems, following instructions on page 352.

### Heading Hem

Crinoline is used to support the pleated heading. It must be the same width as the heading hem. In the measurements, 8 inches were allowed for a 4-inch double-fold hem.

Cut 4-inch crinoline the exact length of the drapery width. Position the crinoline on the underside of the drapery hem, keeping the edges even, and pin. Stitch along the lower edge of the crinoline. Backstitch at each end. Press.

Turn the hem to the underside; fold along the edge of crinoline and press. Then turn again for a double-fold hem. Pin, press, and baste. Do not stitch the hem; the pleats will hold it in place when they are stitched. Do not remove this basting until you have stitched the pleats.

### Bottom Hem

Compare the drapery panels, wrong sides together, and check the length at the center and outer side hems to be sure they are identical.

In the measurements, 6 inches were allowed for a 3-inch double-fold hem. Fold and pin the 3-inch double hem, following instructions on page 353. Before stitching the hem, pleat the heading and attach the drapery hooks as described on pages 379 and 381. Hang the draperies and check the length; it should be about ½ inch above the floor. If your measurements were accurate, the length should be correct and the hem width will require only a slight adjustment if any.

Machine-stitch the hem, then add weights. See page 353.

## Making Lined Draperies

Draperies are lined to protect the drapery fabric. The lining also adds weight, ensures soft, graceful folds, and creates a uniform appearance from the outside. Sunfast sateen of light beige, eggshell, soft gray, or white is generally used as the lining fabric.

The allowances for heading, side, and bottom hems referred to below are described on page 366 (for panel draperies) and page 368 (for draw draperies).

### The Lining

The lining fabric must be cut on the true lengthwise and crosswise grains the same as the drapery fabric. Straighten the ends by drawing a thread on the crosswise grain to indicate the cutting line. Remove selvages.

Cut the lining 10 inches shorter and 8 inches narrower than the drapery fabric. This allows ½

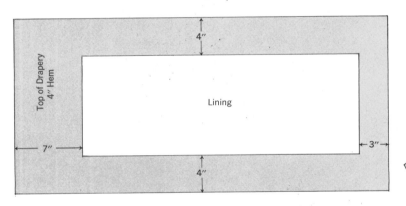

inch for seam allowance on each side, ½ inch for turning at the top, and 2 inches for the bottom hem plus ½ inch for turning. When the draperies are finished, the lining hem will overlap the drapery hem 1 inch.

Draw a thread on the crosswise grain to indicate the cutting line of each length. See page 370.

Bolts of sateen are often rolled tighter at one end of the board than the other, with the result that the fabric threads are drawn off grain. Straighten the fabric grain as described on page 14. Steam-press.

### Heading Hem

In the measurements, 4 inches were allowed for the top hem of the drapery. Turn the 4-inch hem to the underside and press.

Cut 4-inch crinoline 5 inches shorter than the width of the drapery. Position the crinoline over

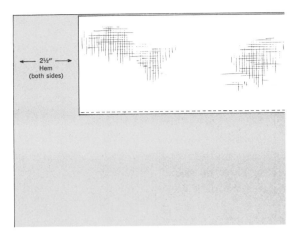

the underside of the hem, aligning one edge with the crease for the hem and extending the ends to within 2½ inches of the fabric edges. (This is the turn for the side hems.) Stitch the crinoline in place ¼ inch from the crease. Press.

Now make the side hems. You will finish the heading hem later: If you are stitching the lining to the sides of the draperies by machine, finish the heading hem *after* that step (see page 376); if you are sewing the lining in by hand, finish the heading hem *before* the hand sewing (see page 377).

### Side Hems

In the measurements, 5 inches were allowed for a 2-inch hem and ½-inch seam allowance on each side. Turn the side hems to the underside 2½ inches, and press. Pin the hem in place about 1½ inches from the fold. Place the pins parallel to the hem and leave them until you have sewed the lining in place. Turn the hem edge back on the pin line and stay the hem to the drapery. Make a stitch in the drapery about 8 inches below the top; loop the thread to the left; then, directly opposite the first stitch, make a stitch in the hem fold, bringing the needle out over the thread. Continue making the stitches, spacing them about 2 inches apart. Do not draw the threads too tight.

The next step is joining the lining to the drapery.

### Methods of
### Joining Lining to Drapery

The lining may be sewed to the drapery by machine as illustrated here or by hand as illustrated on page 377.

### Method 1, Machine-Stitched:

Hem the lower edge of the lining as follows: Turn the edge under ½ inch and press; then turn the hem to the underside 2 inches, and press. Pin the hem in place, and stitch close to the top fold. Press.

At the top of the lining, turn the ½-inch seam allowance to the underside and finger-press. Pin the lining to the drapery side hem, right sides together, keeping the top fold of the lining 7½ inches below the top edge of the drapery, and the bottom hem 5½ inches above the lower edge. Turn the seam allowance away from the drapery and stitch from the lining side, making a ½-inch seam.

Backstitch at each end. Stitch the lining to the hem on the opposite side of the drapery in the same way. Press, then press both seam edges toward the lining. Slash the seam allowances at 6-inch intervals. Turn to the right side. If measurements and seaming are accurate, the lining should fit smoothly over the drapery.

**To complete the heading hem of the drapery.** Turn the heading hem to the underside and press. To remove bulk, cut out the corner of the top hem edge. Begin 2½ inches from the outer edges (turn for the side hem) and cut upward to within ½ inch of the hem fold, then cut diagonally to the hem fold, and on the fold

to the outer edge. Miter the corners; turn under the side seam allowance on the drapery as far as the lining, and pin.

Lap the lining over the top hem edge ½ inch, and pin. Slip-stitch the mitered corners and lining in place, making the stitches through the hems and lining only. Press.

Finish the bottom hem in the drapery, following the instructions on page 378.

**Method 2, Hand-Sewed:** For draw draperies and wide panel draperies, it is advisable to hand-sew the lining to the drapery. This makes it possible to stay the lining to the drapery at even intervals, which prevents it from sagging below the drapery. Before you join the lining to the drapery, you must first finish the heading.

**To complete the heading hem of the drapery.** After you have cut and stitched the 4-inch crinoline to the heading as described under *Heading Hem* on page 374, turn the heading hem to the underside and press. To remove bulk, cut out the corner of the top hem edge. Begin 2½ inches from the outer edge (the turn for the side hem) and cut upward to within ½ inch of the hem fold; then cut diagonally to the hem fold, and on the fold to the outer edge. Miter the corners and turn under the seam allowance on the drapery as far as the lining; pin in place.

**To sew the lining to the drapery.** Fold, press, and slip-stitch the bottom hem of the lining. Along the top and side edges, turn the seam allowance to the underside ½ inch, and finger-press.

Lay the drapery, wrong side up, on a flat surface and smooth out the fabric. Place the lining over the drapery, wrong sides together, with the folded edges overlapping the heading and side

hems of the drapery ½ inch. The lining hem should extend to within 5½ inches of the lower edge of the drapery.

Now you must stay the lining to the drapery at about 24-inch intervals. Begin at the center. Pin the lining to the drapery on a vertical line, then turn the lining back on the pin line. Make a stitch in the drapery about 4 inches below the top hem, loop the thread to the left, then directly opposite the first stitch, make a stitch in the lining fold, bringing the needle out over the thread. Catch only one or two threads in the fabric so that the stitches will be invisible on the top side. Continue, spacing the stitches about 6 inches apart. Do not draw the thread taut. About 6 inches above the hem, fasten the thread in the lining with a tiny backstitch and leave a 4-inch thread end. Then pin and stitch additional vertical lines, working from the center toward each edge and spacing the rows about 24 inches apart.

Pin the lining to the drapery hems across the top and along each side, with the folded edges overlapping the drapery hems ½ inch. Slip-stitch the lining in place, making the stitches through the lining and drapery hems only so that the stitches will be invisible on the top side. Do not draw the thread tight.

### Bottom Hem

Compare the drapery panels, wrong sides together, and check the length at the center and outer side hems to be sure they are identical.

Turn the bottom edge of the drapery under ½ inch, and press. Stitch near the fold. (The lining will cover the stitching.) Turn a 3-inch hem to the underside, and pin in place. Miter the corners so that they fit smoothly under the lining. Ease the hem down slightly at this point to allow for the thicknesses of fabric and to square the corners. Sew weights at each side seam allowance to prevent drawing.

Before finishing the hem, pleat the heading and attach the drapery hooks. See pages 379 and 381. Hang the draperies and check the length, which should be about ½ inch above the floor. Let the draperies hang for two or three days before you sew the hem because some fabrics will shrink or stretch slightly. If your measurements are accurate, the length should be correct and the change in the hem width will be slight, if any.

The bottom hem may be finished after the draperies are hung. Slip-stitch the hem and mitered corners in place. Catch only one or two threads in the drapery and make the stitches through hems only at the mitered corners. The stitches should be invisible on the top side. Do not press this hem. If it is necessary to lengthen the draperies slightly after six months or so, there will be no crease to mar the fabric.

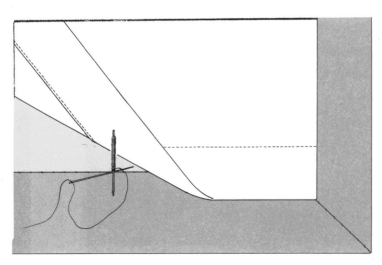

The lining hangs free of the drapery. To hold it in position, use French tacks spaced about 12 inches apart. See page 208.

## Making the Pleated Heading

The most popular styles of pleats for draperies are the pinch pleat, box pleat, French pleat, and cartridge pleat.

### Measuring for Pleats

Panel draperies should have an uneven number of pleats in each panel; draw draperies may have either an even or an uneven number in each, resulting in an even number in each pair. The number of pleats, the allowance for each pleat, and the spacing between pleats are matters you should decide before cutting the fabric for the drapery. See pages 367 and 369 for this information.

Always measure and pin-mark position of *all pleats and spaces* before you begin any stitching.

**In panel draperies,** measure 2 inches from the center edge of the drapery and pin-mark. Then measure and pin-mark the width of the **first** end pleat. At the opposite edge, measure and pin-mark the depth of the return. Then measure and pin-mark the width of the **second** end pleat. Place the **third** pleat at the exact center between the **first** and **second** end pleats. Space the **remaining pleats** evenly between the first and third pleats and the second and third pleats. Compare the two panels, wrong sides together, to be sure the pin-marks correspond.

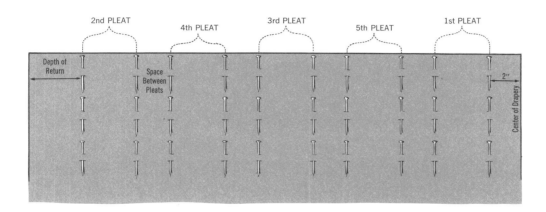

**In draw draperies,** the center edges overlap 2½ inches when a two-way traverse rod is used; therefore, the **first** end pleat must be farther from the center edge than in panel draperies. Using the measurements in the example on page 369, measure 3¼ inches from the center edge of the drapery and pin-mark. Then measure and pin-mark the width of the **first** end pleat. At the opposite end, measure and pin-mark the depth of the return. Then measure and pin-mark the width of the **second** end pleat. Continue measuring and marking the space, then the width of each pleat. All spaces between the last and first pleats must be the same; and the width of all pleats must be the same. Compare the two panels, wrong sides together, to be sure the pin-marks correspond.

### Forming the Pleats

Bring the pin-marks for each pleat together and pin. Stitch from the top edge to ½ inch below the heading hem, placing the stitching into the pleat about 1/16 inch from the pins (this allows for the width that is taken up by the layers of fabric). Backstitch at each end.

**Pinch pleat.** Divide the pleat evenly into three smaller pleats and crease the length of the pleat. At the lower edge, either hand-tack the three pleats together or machine-stitch across them. If they are hand-tacked, you can insert the shank of the drapery hook into the pleat.

**Box pleat.** Slip two fingers inside the pleat and finger-press it open. Then press flat, keeping the folds an equal distance from the stitching line. Tack the top and bottom corners of the pleat to the drapery, placing the stitches under the pleat. Box pleats should be about 2 inches wide and require 4 inches of additional fabric for each pleat; the space between pleats is 4 inches. Make this allowance in the planning stage.

**French pleat.** At the lower edge of the heading, divide the pleat into three smaller pleats; then hand-sew through them several times before drawing tightly on the threads. Fasten the threads on the underside.

**Cartridge pleat.** This small, round pleat is filled with rolled stiff paper or crinoline, which holds its cartridge shape. In the planning stage, allow about 2 inches for each pleat and about 2 inches for each space. Cartridge pleats are frequently placed in groups of three.

## Selecting Drapery Hooks and Pins

Draperies are attached to the rod by hooks or pins, which are placed in the back of each pleat and at each end of the drapery. Most draperies hooks are available in several sizes. When buying them, be sure to consider the position of the hook part on the shank and the length of the prong. Examine them closely and get the type best suited for your purpose.

A few of the more popular hooks are illustrated.

Hook **A.** This popular and practical *slip-in hook* has a long two-piece prong that holds the heading erect. It requires no sewing. The long prong slips between the heading hem and drapery and around the pleat. Select hooks with the hook part near the bottom of the shank if the draperies hang from a traverse rod and the heading extends above the rod. Select hooks with the hook part at the top of the shank if draperies hang from a decorative rod with rings or a traverse rod mounted on the ceiling.

Hook **B.** The *pin-on hook* requires no sewing. It is available with a hook shaped to fit either over the adjustable curtain rod or in the traverse rod. The long prong pin holds the heading erect. If a different type of hook is used in the pleats, use this long prong pin at each end of the drapery where there are no pleats.

Hook **C.** The *sew-on hook* has a long prong to hold the heading erect. The position of the hook part on the shank is the same as hook A.

Hook **D.** The *slip-in hook* has a long two-piece prong that holds the heading erect. It requires no sewing. The hook part on the flat shaft can be adjusted for various headings. Insert it the same as hook A. This type of hook is popular with professional decorators.

Hook **E.** The *pleater pin* with *hook* or *ring* is used with ready-made pleat tape. Slip each prong into a woven-in pocket in the tape and fasten the

hook to pinch the pleat in shape. Select the position of the hook part on the shank the same as hook A. Use hooks with rings when a decorative rod is visible above the drapery.

Whatever style of drapery hook you select, be sure to position the hook part correctly. If the drapery heading extends above the rod, measure the distance from the position of the hook part on the rod to 1 inch above the rod. Position the top edge of the hook (not the shank) this distance from the top of the draperies.

If draperies hang from a decorative rod that is visible or from a rod mounted on the ceiling, place the hook part at the top of the draperies.

## Anchoring Draperies

The outside edges of the draperies should hang against the wall in a straight, taut line. Sew small plastic rings to the heading hem in line with the rod, and to the bottom hem. Place cup hooks in the wall or baseboard in line with the rings. Fasten the rings over the hooks.

# Top It Off
# with a Valance
# or Cornice

VALANCES AND CORNICES are decorative extras at the top of your draperies or curtains which put the stamp of individuality on your windows. They can also serve the more practical functions of connecting a group of windows, increasing window dimensions, and concealing the rods and fixtures on which draperies are hung. Good taste requires that the style of the valance or cornice conform to the decorative scheme of the room. Both have a tendency to make ceilings appear lower; use them with care in small rooms.

Although decoratively and functionally similar, valances and cornices differ in this way: Valances are made of fabric and tacked to a wood "shelf" or hung from a rod; the valances may be straight, shaped, pleated, or gathered. Cornices are made of wood that may be either covered with fabric or painted to match the draperies or walls, or used as the support for swags and cascades. Whichever you plan to use, you must first construct draperies with a finished heading and hang them as instructed in the previous chapter, beginning on page 366.

Next, determine how long the valance or cornice should be. Although the length of the valance is generally one-sixth the length of the drapery, that may not give the correct proportion to your window. Cut patterns of muslin or stiff paper the exact width of the window but of different lengths. Hold them up to the window to see which looks best.

## The Valance Shelf and Cornice Board

The ends and top board of the valance shelf and cornice board should be made of ¾-inch pine, and the face board of the cornice of ¼-inch plywood. Before taking measurements for either, be sure the drapery rod is in position. See page 343. The width of the valance shelf or cornice board should be 4½ inches greater than the rod. After the ¾-inch wood is secured at the ends of the top board, there will be a space of 1½ inches between the rod and board at each end. The depth of the end sections should be 1½ inches greater than the distance from the wall to the rod (depth of the return). This allows space between the rod and the board for the draperies to hang freely and for draw draperies to be opened and closed easily.

**Cornice board**

RETURN

*To make the valance shelf,* join the end sections to the top board with finishing nails and a thin line of white glue. Keep the outer edges even. *To make the cornice board,* add a face board of ¼ inch plywood to the shelf with finishing nails and a thin line of white glue along both sides and top.

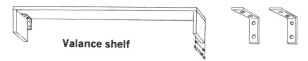

**Valance shelf**

Mount angle-iron brackets, top end extending forward, on the wall (see page 343) or frame at each end of the board. If the board is more than 40 inches across, mount extra brackets to give added support.

Although the valance shelf or cornice board merely rests on the brackets and is not fastened to them, it is advisable to hammer small finishing nails through one of the screw holes at each end to prevent the board from sliding forward. The covered board can then be lifted easily off the brackets for cleaning.

## Straight and Shaped Valances

Straight and shaped valances are made over a stiff foundation such as buckram and are interlined and lined. If the fabric is quilted, you may omit the interlining.

### Measuring the Valance Shelf

Place a tape measure across the return at one end, across the front, then across the return at the opposite end. This is the finished width of the valance.

### Making a Paper Pattern

Cut a paper pattern this exact width and the length desired. If the lower edge is shaped, mark the depth of the return at each end; shape the valance between these markings, then at the returns. Fit the pattern to the valance shelf to be sure your measurements are correct.

### Making the Valance

Cut buckram the exact measurements of the paper pattern. Press all fabrics before cutting. Cut cotton flannel interlining and drapery fabric 1 inch wider than the pattern on all edges to allow for seams. Cut the width on the crosswise grain and length on the lengthwise grain. Cut lining ¼ inch wider than the pattern on all sides for the seam allowances.

Lay the fabric on the table, wrong side up. Place the flannel interlining over the fabric and pin together along the edges. Center the buckram over the interlining. Turn the fabric and interlining

BUCKRAM

over the buckram edge 1 inch, and pin. Clip into the seam allowances at inside curves and notch them on outside curves. With a heavy needle and heavy-duty thread, catch-stitch the edges of the fabric to the buckram. Turn the lining edge under ½ inch and pin to the back of valance, ¼ inch from the edge. Slip-stitch in place. Hand-sew the top edge of ¾-inch twill tape near the top edge of the valance.

At the top and bottom edges of the valance, measure and pin-mark the depth of the return at each end. Fold the valance, wrong sides together, and crease the line of the return at each end.

Place the valance across the front and returns of the valance shelf with the twill tape over the top. Tack the tape to the shelf with upholsterer's tacks.

## Pleated Valance

A pleated valance is made the same way as draperies except that it is in one piece. Also, it requires a separate rod. If the window treatment includes glass curtains as well as draperies and valance, triple rods are needed for the hangings.

Position the rod. The depth of the return on the top rod is greater than on the other rod or rods.

Measure the length of the rod plus the depth of the return at each end. This is the finished width of the valance. To the measured width and depth of two returns, add the amount required for side hems, seam allowances, and pleats. This is the width required to make the valance. Always locate an end pleat at the depth of the return at each end. To determine the number of spaces between pleats and the amount to allow for the pleats, follow the instructions for *Draw Draperies—Preparation,* page 369, but omit the overlap.

To the length selected for your valance, add 7 inches (4 inches for top hem and 3 inches for bottom hem and turning). Cut the fabric by these measurements. Cut the lining 8½ inches shorter and 8 inches narrower than the top fabric and make a 2-inch bottom hem with a ½-inch turn.

To make the valance, see page 374, which describes how to make lined draperies, and page 379, which describes how to measure and make pleats in the heading. Select the proper hooks or pins for the heading. See page 381. Anchor the valance at the top the same as the drapery.

## Fabric-Covered Cornice Board

A cornice may be covered with a fabric identical to that used in the drapery or, if the drapery is a print, the cornice board may be covered with a solid color that picks up one of the colors in the print. For an interesting contrast, the fabric may be quilted. The cornice board should be padded and interlining should be placed between the padding and drapery fabric.

### Measuring the Cornice Board

Place a tape measure across the return at one end, across the front, and across the return at the opposite end. To this measurement, add 3 inches for turn-under. Measure the width at the widest and add 3 inches for turn-under.

Cut the drapery fabric and cotton flannel interlining by the measurements. Cut the width on the crosswise grain and the length on the lengthwise grain. If the fabric has a design, center it lengthwise and crosswise.

### Making a Paper Pattern

The cornice illustrated has a scalloped edge with corded trimming. Before you cover it or something similar, you must first make a paper pattern.

Spread the paper flat and place the cornice board over it; then bring the paper around the returns and cut it the exact width of the cornice board. Draw the shape of the scallops on the paper; cut on the marking.

Place the pattern over the right side of the fabric, 1½ inches from the edge at the deepest point of the scallops and 1½ inches in from each end. Lightly mark the scallops on the fabric. *Do not cut.*

### Covering the Cornice Board

Before you cover the cornice board, cover the cord and stitch it to the lower edge of the fabric as follows: Cut the bias strips as directed on page 244, but make the strips 2 inches wide plus three times the width of the filler cord. Bring the bias strip around the cord, right side out, with one edge 1 inch shorter than the other. Adjust the Zipper Foot to the left of the needle and stitch, following instructions on page 245. Press the seam.

Pin the corded welting on the right side of the fabric, with the stitching on the welting over the scalloped marking. Stitch with the cording up, and crowd the stitching between the cord and previous line of stitching. Press. Trim the cornice fabric to within 1½ inches of the scallops.

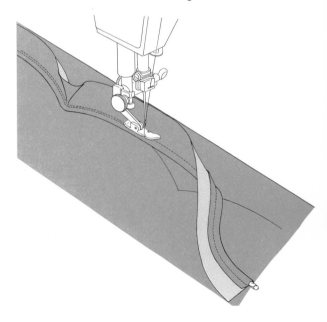

For the padding, place a layer of cotton batting, 1 inch thick, over the front and end sections of the cornice board. Trim the padding to within ¼ inch of the cornice edges. Lay the interlining and drapery fabric over the padding, right side up, extending all edges 1½ inch beyond the cornice board. Smooth out the fabric and thumb-tack it along all edges to hold it in place. (Do not push the tacks in too far since you will remove them when the cornice is finished.)

At the deepest point of the scallops, turn the fabric edges over the edge of the board and tack them to the underside with upholsterer's tacks. Be sure the cording follows the edge of the scallops. Clip into the seam allowances at the point of the scallops and finish tacking the edges to the underside of the board. Turn the fabric over the top edge of the board and tack it in place. Miter the corners. Across the returns, or end sections, turn the fabric over the edges of the board and tack it to the underside. Miter the corners. To finish the top of the board, tack ¾-inch twill tape over the fabric edges.

### Lining the Cornice

Line the inside of the cornice so that it will have a finished look when viewed from the outside.

Use sateen lining. Cut the lining by the pattern you made for the top fabric and allow ½ inch

A. Layer of cotton batting
B. Cover edge of fabric with twill tape

on all edges for seam allowances.

Lay the cornice right side down. Place the lining over the inside of the cornice and use a few thumb tacks to hold the lining in place. (Do not push the tacks in too far because you will remove them after you have finished the edges.) Turn under the seam allowance and place the folded edge about ¼ inch in from the edge of the cornice; tack it in place with small upholsterer's tacks. First tack the lower edge in place, then the upper edge, and finally the ends. Place a few tacks along each corner to hold the lining securely in this area.

## SWAGS AND CASCADES

Swags and cascades generally match the drapery fabric; the cascades may be faced with a contrasting fabric or self fabric. The edges are often adorned with decorative fringe. This touch is particularly attractive on swags and cascades made of a single thickness of sheer fabric.

A cornice board rather than a valance shelf should be used for the mounting. The shelf does not offer enough support to the swags and cascades and they tend to cup after hanging a short while. The finished swag and cascade are lapped over the top edge of the cornice board and tacked in place with carpet or upholsterer's tacks. Make the cornice board before you begin the swag. See page 382.

**Cornice board**

RETURN

## Single Swag

For a single window of average width, one swag extending the width of the window is sufficient. For an oversized window, you will need two smaller swags overlapping at the center; and for a group of windows, three or more overlapping swags. The single swag is explained first.

### Making a Muslin Pattern

Straighten the ends and cut the muslin 36 inches long on the lengthwise grain. Mark the center line along the entire length. Measure the width of the cornice. Subtract 10 inches from this measurement (5 inches from each end) and use this measurement to mark the top edge of the muslin. *Example:* 36 inches (width of cornice) less 10 inches = 26 inches. Center this measurement at the center line so that you have the same distance (13 inches) on each side of center. Then mark the muslin 1 inch from the top to indicate the lap over the top edge of the cornice. At the bottom edge, mark each side 8 inches wider than the top measurement; keep the markings an equal distance from the center line. On each side, draw a diagonal line between the top and bottom edges. Beginning 1 inch from the top, divide the diagonal lines into eight equal parts for seven folds and mark the muslin. (If five folds are used, divide the lines into six equal parts.)

Mark the center line on the top of the cornice board. Lap the straight top edge of the muslin 1 inch over the top of the cornice board, matching center lines; thumb-tack in place. Then tack the muslin at the **A** markings, which are 5 inches from the ends, and at intervals between. Fold the muslin at the first marking on the diagonal line and tack it to the top of the cornice at **A** on each side. Shape the fold smoothly from the center to each side and match the center line. Use pins

for tacking the folds; place them at an angle and drive them slightly into the wood with a hammer. Now make a fold at the second marking on the diagonal line and tack it to the board, ¼ inch from the previous fold. The fabric to the left and right of the diagonal lines lies in folds on top of the cornice board. Continue to follow the diagonal lines and tack each fold to the board, ¼ inch from the previous fold. When all folds are tacked in place, the muslin swag extends the entire width of the cornice board.

Cut off one end of the excess muslin across the top 1 inch above your pin tacks. Trim off the excess muslin along the lower curved edge 4 inches beyond the last fold, tapering gradually toward the center.

Remove the muslin swag from the cornice board. The trimmed edges have large notches along the diagonal line, and the lower edge curves toward the center. Fold the swag lengthwise on the center marking and pin. Lay it flat, with the notched edges on top, and shape the other half, using the cut side as a guide. The inside edge of each notch marks the fold of the fabric.

### Making the Swag

Cut the drapery fabric by the muslin pattern, placing the center marking on the lengthwise grain of the fabric. If the fabric has a design, center it under the pattern. Baste the center line on the fabric. Cut a sateen lining by the same pattern but ¼ inch shorter.

Turn the lower edge of the top fabric under ½ inch and press. Lay the lining over the fabric, wrong sides together; keep the top and notched edges even; pin. Turn the lower edge of the lining under ½ inch and pin it to the fabric ¼ inch from the edge. Slip-stitch in place. Sew the lining and fabric together along the notched edges and top, using the multiple-stitch zig-zag. Press.

Tack the swag to the top of the cornice board in the same way as the muslin pattern, matching center lines and markings. Fold the fabric at the inside cut of each notch on the diagonal lines, and tack it to the top of the board. As you tack each fold in place, shape it smoothly from the center to each side and match the center basting. Use upholsterer's tacks or webbing tacks that are long enough to go through the multiple layers of fabric and into the board far enough to hold the swag securely.

## Two or Three Swags

When two or three swags are needed for a large window or group of windows, overlap the swags. In the diagrams, **A** indicates the placement for the first fold at the top edges of the swags; the curved lines marked **B** indicate the space covered when the folds are tacked in place and show the overlap, which is twice the 5 inches allowed at each end of the cornice board.

*For two swags to a window.* Measure and mark the cornice board at the center and 5 inches in from each end **A**. Measure from the 5-inch marking to the center; this is the top width of each swag. Proceed as instructed above for a single swag.

*For three swags to a group of windows.* Measure and mark the cornice board at the center and 5 inches in from each end **A**. Measure the distance between the 5-inch marking at each end and divide by three. Mark the top of the cornice board at the one-third intervals; this is the top width of each swag. Proceed as instructed above for a single swag.

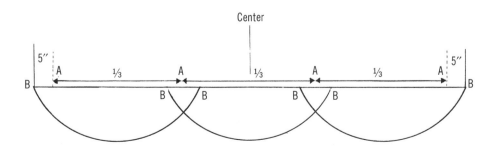

# Cascades

Cascades extend around the returns of the cornice board and overlap the swag in front about 6 inches. The longest length is the outside edge, which is generally between 27 inches and 36 inches, depending on the height of the window; however, there is no set rule. The inside edge of the cascade matches the depth of the finished swag.

### Making a Muslin Pattern

Straighten the ends and cut the muslin a few inches longer than the outside edge of the cascade. Measure the depth of the return across the end and add ½ inch for a seam allowance. Mark the top edge of the muslin this distance from the outer edge. Lay in the first pleat, bringing the fold to the inside edge of the return. Make the pleat 4 inches deep (8 inches of fabric). Form two more pleats of the same depth, overlapping the previous pleat about 3 inches. *Example:* 4½ inches (4-inch return and ½-inch seam allowance) plus 24 inches (3 pleats) plus 2 inches (1-inch space between two pleats) plus 4½ inches (from last fold to inside edge and seam) = 35 inches. If pleats are placed one on top of the other, make them at least 5 inches deep. Notch the folds at the top to mark the position of the folds for each pleat.

At the outside edge, 27 to 36 inches from the top, cut straight across the depth of the return and seam allowance. Mark the inside edge approximately 15 inches from the top, or the depth of the swag. Then draw a diagonal line between these two points. Cut on the drawn line.

### Making the Cascade

Cut the drapery fabric by the muslin pattern, placing the top edge on the crosswise grain and the outside and inside edges on the lengthwise grain. Allow 1 inch on the top edge for the overlap on the cornice board and ½ inch on the lower edge for a seam allowance. Be sure to cut one cascade for the right side and one for the left. If your fabric has a design, it must fall in the same place on each cascade. Cut the facing the same size as the fabric.

Pin the facing to the fabric, right sides together. Stitch ½ inch from the edge, leaving the top edge open. Clip diagonally across the corners, ⅛ inch from the stitching. Press. Turn the fabric to the right side. Pull out the corners, fold on the seamline, and press. Lay in the pleats and pin them in place across the top edge. Lap the straight top edge over the top of the cornice board 1 inch, and tack it in place. The pleated section must overlap the swag across the front.

### Finishing the Top

To finish the top of the cornice, cut self fabric 1 inch longer and 3 inches wider than the top of the cornice board. Spread the fabric over the top of the cornice. Turn the edges under ½ inch along the front and ends, overlap the cut edges of the swags and cascades 1 inch, and tack the cover to the board. Use steel furniture nails that are long enough to go through the multiple layers of fabric and into the board. Across the back, bring the fabric over the edge of the board and tack it to the underside.

# Brighten Your Room
# with
# Slipcovers

SLIPCOVERS ARE AN EFFECTIVE WAY of bringing new life into a room. They enable you to introduce new colors and seasonal moods in your decor, to cover worn or faded upholstery inexpensively, and to protect permanent coverings.

Slipcovers must fit snugly. If you follow the instructions in this chapter and are careful and accurate in measuring, cutting, and fitting, you will be able to achieve professional results.

## Fabric and Color

Fabric selection is almost unlimited. But *choose closely woven fabric so that the slipcover will hold its shape.* Linen, chintz, velveteen, and many of the lovely cotton and synthetic fabrics are appropriate. Consider the texture, weave, color, and design of the fabric. Remember that massive designs belong in large rooms.

Solid colors are the easiest to work with because there is no design to match. Florals require a little extra care in cutting since they must be centered on each chair section, with the design running toward the top. Stripes must be matched on the lengthwise grain and plaids on both the lengthwise and the crosswise grains. Select even stripes and plaids because they are easier to match at the seamlines. See *Plaids,* page 53.

## Measuring Your Chair

Record the measurements of your chair on the chart on page 392. Measure accurately, following the exact lines of the chair, and add seam allowances as indicated on the measurement chart. Always measure the lengths of the outside back, outside arms, and front section from seamline to floor; then deduct from these measurements the amount not required for finishing.

## Estimating Yardage

After you have recorded the measurements of your chair on the chart, estimate the yardage required.

To estimate the yardage, add the *lengthwise* measurements of the sections and divide by 36 inches. If the fabric has a design that must be centered or matched, add an extra yard for matching. If you are cording the seams, add one yard of fabric to cover the cord. If you are going to make a flounce for the chair, add the yardage required. See page 400.

## Preparing to Work

Conveniently arrange your sewing equipment. You will need a box of sharp pins, tape measure, colored pencil or chalk, hand sewing needles, heavy-duty thread, ironing board, iron, and of course your sewing machine. Place the chair to be covered on a card table or low table.

## Pin-Fitting a Muslin Pattern or the Slipcover Fabric

Your first step is to pin-fit the chair. If you are a beginner or if the chair has an unusual shape, it is advisable to make a muslin pattern. If you have made slipcovers before and feel confident about your ability, you can begin with the slipcover fabric. The sequence of steps is the same in either case.

Cut all length measurements on the lengthwise grain of the fabric and all width measurements on the crosswise grain. Block the muslin or slipcover fabric to correspond with the measurements for each section of the chair, following the sequence in which the measurements were taken. Tear the muslin; however, if you are working with the slipcover fabric in this initial blocking, draw a thread on the lengthwise or crosswise grain to indicate

the cutting line, and cut the fabric along the drawn thread. As each section is cut, mark the center on the lengthwise grain with a small notch at each end. Pin-mark the center of the chair at the top and lower edges. Then pin the section in its proper place, using one or two pins to hold it to the chair.

*To pin-fit the muslin pattern.* Pin each section to the chair, following the sequence in which the measurements were taken. The dotted lines in the illustration indicate the lengthwise and crosswise grains of the fabric; these may be marked on the muslin but not on the fabric. Center the section on the chair and pin on the lengthwise grain and crosswise grain, then pin near the outer edges. Keep the crosswise grain parallel to the floor. At the widest points, the muslin extends 1 inch beyond the seamline on each side of the chair; at narrower points, however, the extension is greater. At rounded edges, place the pins crosswise and distribute the fullness evenly between them.

Pin the sections together at the seamline, following the lines of the chair. Begin at the center of the seams and work to the outer edges, placing

*(Continued on page 394)*

FOR YARDAGE

OUTSIDE BACK LENGTH (floor to top) — **A** to **B** plus
1″ seam allowance _____ inches _____ inches

OUTSIDE BACK WIDTH — **R** to **S** plus 2″ seam allowances _____ inches

INSIDE BACK LENGTH — **B** to **C** plus 2″ seam allowances
plus 3″ tuck-in allowance _____ inches _____ inches

INSIDE BACK WIDTH — **N** to **O** plus 2″ seam allowances _____ inches

SEAT LENGTH — **C** to **D** plus 2″ seam allowances
plus 3″ tuck-in allowance _____ inches _____ inches

SEAT WIDTH — **J** to **K** plus 2″ seam allowances
plus 6″ tuck-in allowances _____ inches

SEAT WIDTH — **T** to **U** plus 2″ seam allowances _____ inches

FRONT LENGTH — **D** to **E** plus 1″ seam allowance _____ inches _____ inches

FRONT WIDTH — **P** to **Q** plus 2″ seam allowances _____ inches

OUTSIDE ARM LENGTH (arm to floor) — **F** to **G** plus
1″ seam allowance _____ inches X 2 = _____ inches

OUTSIDE ARM WIDTH — **H** to **I** plus 2″ seam allowances _____ inches

INSIDE ARM LENGTH — **F** to **J** plus 2″ seam allowances
plus 3″ tuck-in allowance _____ inches X 2 = _____ inches

INSIDE ARM WIDTH — **L** to **M** plus 2″ seam allowances
plus 3″ tuck-in allowance _____ inches

CUSHION —
    Length — **1** to **2** plus 2″ seam allowances _____ inches X 2 = _____ inches
    Width — **4** to **5** plus 2″ seam allowances _____ inches
    Depth of boxing — **2** to **3** plus 2″ seam allowances _____ inches _____ inches

# Additional Measurements for Wing Chair

FOR YARDAGE

INSIDE WING LENGTH — **A-1** to **B-1** plus 2″ seam allowances _____ inches X 2 = _____ inches

INSIDE WING WIDTH — **C-1** to **D-1** plus 2″ seam allowances
plus 3″ tuck-in allowance _____ inches

OUTSIDE WING LENGTH — **A-1** to **B-2** plus 2″ seam allowances _____ inches X 2 = _____ inches

OUTSIDE WING WIDTH — **C-1** to **D-2** plus 2″ seam allowances _____ inches

FRONT ARM LENGTH — **E-1** to **F-1** plus 2″ seam allowances _____ inches X 2 = _____ inches

FRONT ARM WIDTH — **G-1** to **H-1** plus 2″ seam allowances _____ inches

## Measurements for Chair with Wide Rounded Arm and Front Section

(Take these measurements instead of arm measurements on preceding page.)

FOR YARDAGE

INSIDE ARM LENGTH — **I-1** to **J-1** plus 2″ seam allowances
plus 3″ tuck-in allowance _____ inches X 2 = _____ inches

INSIDE ARM WIDTH — **K-1** to **L-1** plus 2″ seam allowances _____ inches

OUTSIDE ARM LENGTH — **M-1** to **N-1** plus 1″ seam allowance _____ inches X 2 = _____ inches

OUTSIDE ARM WIDTH — **O-1** to **P-1** plus 2″ seam allowances _____ inches

FRONT ARM LENGTH — **S-1** to **T-1** plus 2″ seam allowances _____ inches X 2 = _____ inches

FRONT ARM WIDTH — **Q-1** to **R-1** plus 2″ seam allowances _____ inches

SIDE-BACK LENGTH — **U-1** to **V-1** plus 2″ seam allowances _____ inches X 2 = _____ inches

SIDE-BACK WIDTH — **W-1** to **X-1** plus 2″ seam allowances _____ inches pins parallel to the seamline at close intervals. Observe the following sequence and fit the chair snugly but do not stretch the fabric:

**A** Pin the inside back and inside arm sections together with the seam fitting snugly over the round part of the arm and tapering to the full tuck-in allowance at the seat. Slash into the seam allowance on the curve for a smooth fit, then trim the seam allowance to 1 inch.

**B** Pin the inside and outside arm sections together, easing the fabric over the round part of the arm.

**C** Pin the front section to the seat.

**D** Pin the seat to the inside arm, fitting snugly at the outer edge and tapering to the full tuck-in allowance at the seat. Trim the seam allowance to 1 inch and slash into it for a smooth fit.

**E** Pin the outside arm to the front section.

**F** Join the seat to the inside arm and inside back sections, allowing for the full tuck-in allowance.

**G** Begin at the center and pin the outside back to the inside back and outside arm sections.

*A wing chair* or a *chair with front arm sections* requires additional seams:

**H** A tuck-in allowance should be made between the wing and the back, tapering from the 1-inch seam allowance at the top to the tuck-in at the seat.

**I** Pin small muslin or fabric pieces to the front of each arm section. As the seams are joined, ease the arm section slightly at the seamline.

*Block the muslin for the cushion sections* the same way as for the chair sections. Cut one continuous strip for the boxing, and place the seam in the center back. Pin the muslin or slipcover fabric sections in place, following the lines of the cushion.

When the pin-fitting is completed, examine the chair carefully to be sure that the slipcover fits snugly and that the seams are in the correct position. Make any necessary adjustments. Trim all seam allowances to 1 inch.

You can follow the above procedure for all types of chairs and sofas. The method of fitting and assembling the cover is the same regardless of the number of sections to be covered.

Before removing the pin-fitted cover from the chair, mark the seamlines and label each section.

### Marking the Seamline

Cut small notches in the seam allowances at center points and on each side of the eased sections. Open the seams with the fingers and, with colored chalk, mark the seamline on the wrong side of the fabric over the parallel pins. Be sure to mark both sides of the seam allowance. Match these markings in seaming the slipcover fabric.

*Label the muslin* so that you can identify each section—for example, "inside back," "left inside arm," "right inside arm," and so on. If the slipcover fabric is pinned to the chair, write the identifications on pieces of paper and pin them to the fabric.

Leave all seam pins in place. Remove the pins holding the muslin or fabric to the upholstered chair. Mark the length of the opening at one back seam where inside and outside backs join, then remove the seamline pins in this area. Carefully remove the muslin pattern from the chair.

## Cutting the Fabric

If you blocked and pin-fitted the slipcover fabric instead of the muslin, you are ready to proceed with the construction. If you made a muslin pattern, you are now ready to cut the fabric.

Remove the seamline pins. Lay the muslin pattern, right side up, on the right side of the slipcover fabric. Be sure the lengths of all sections are on the lengthwise grain. *Center floral designs and match strips on the lengthwise grain, and match plaids on both the lengthwise and the crosswise grains.* Pin the pattern in place along the edges, then cut. Notch the seam allowances to correspond with the pattern.

## Pin-Fitting the Fabric

It is important to pin-fit the slipcover fabric even though you pin-fitted the muslin pattern. The texture and weight of the muslin differ from those of the fabric, and pin-fitting now may save time and trouble later.

Follow the same sequence of steps as for the muslin pattern. Pin-fit the cutout sections to the chair *right side out* to ensure proper matching of the design and a good fit. One arm of a chair or sofa may be slightly lower or fuller than the other. Match notches and place pins at close intervals, parallel to the 1-inch seams. Fit snugly, but do not stretch the fabric. Very few adjustments should be necessary.

Mark the seamlines as instructed above. Remove pins controlling the ease. With a needle and double strand of heavy-duty thread, place small running stitches on the seamline between the notches, and gather the fabric to fit the joining section. Fasten the thread ends.

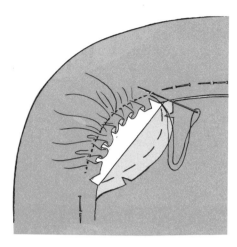

If darts are used instead of gathers to control the fullness, pin the darts to conform with the curve or corner of the chair. A word of caution: Darts may break the continuity of a striped or plaid design; avoid using them, therefore, if you can ease in the fullness.

Before removing the pin-fitted cover from the chair, measure the seams to be decorated with cording or fringe to determine the yardage required. All seams should be decorated except those joining the seat and those with a tuck-in allowance. An arm chair or wing chair may require 12 to 14 yards; a sofa with three cushions, approximately 25 yards. Remember that the cushion has two decorated seams—those that join the top and bottom sections to the boxing; so double the measurement around the cushion. If cording is used at the top of the flounce, measure the circumference of the chair.

When you have completed the seam measurements, remove the pins holding the fabric to the upholstered chair; then remove the seamline pins in the zipper area only. Carefully remove the slipcover.

## Accenting Seams

Seams in slipcovers are accented to emphasize the lines of the chair, to give added strength to the seam itself, and to ensure a professional finish.

### Corded Seam

The most popular seam in slipcovers is the corded seam. Either self or contrasting fabric may be used. The size of the filler cord used depends on the size of the chair or sofa and the weight of the fabric covering the cord.

Cut the bias strips, cover the cord, and form the seams, following the instructions beginning on page 244. The width of the bias strips must be 2 inches plus three times the width of the filler cord. Straight and curved seams as well as square corners are used in slipcovers. Do not trim the seam allowances after stitching the corded welting in place but do slash them on inside curves and square corners and notch them on outside curves so that the cord will lie smoothly.

***To join ends of cording in a seam.*** Overlap the ends of the corded welting 1 inch as you pin the cording to the single seamline. Cut the cord and bias fabric even at the first end. Pull out the cord at the second end and clip off 1 inch so that the ends of cord will just meet. Smooth the bias fabric back over the cord, then rip the stitching as far as the end of the cord. Turn the end of the bias fabric under ⅜ inch and lap it around the first end, with the ends of cord meeting; pin. Stitch the cording in place.

***To match stripes and plaids.*** Join the seams from the right side of the fabric as follows: Stitch the corded welting to the seamline of one section; then turn the seam allowance of the second section to the underside, and pin. Lay both sections right side up, and lap the folded edge over the second seam allowance to the cording; pin in place. Slip-baste from the right side. See page 62. Stitch the seam from the wrong side, following the

center of the short basting stitch. (Many women slip-baste the seams in *all* fabrics so that they can fit each section to the chair before stitching.)

### Fringe Seam

Fringe may be used on almost any type of slipcover to lend interest and color. If the slipcover is casual, select fringe that is simple in style. Pin the fringe to the single seam allowance, right sides together, extending the heading slightly over the seamline. Stitch barely outside the seamline. Pin the second seam edge over the fringe with the fabric right sides together. Place the work under the needle with the first line of stitching up so that you can use it as a guide. Stitch on the seamline, barely beyond the previous stitching.

### Bound Seam

This seam is an attractive finish for simple slipcovers where lightweight fabrics are used and where there is little stress or strain on the seam. Pin and stitch the seam, right sides together. Press. Then follow the instructions for *Plain Bound Seam,* page 93.

### Seam Finish

After the seams of loosely woven fabrics are stitched, the edges should be finished to prevent

raveling. Use the blindstitch zig-zag on the machine, or overcast by hand. See page 93 and 94. Although seam edges are turned in the same direction, finish each edge separately.

## Constructing the Slipcover

Before you begin, be sure identifying labels are securely pinned to each section, as suggested on page 395.

### Darts

If darts are used, mark the line on the wrong side of the fabric over the pins; then remove the pins. Fold the dart, right sides together, matching markings; pin and stitch, following the instructions on page 100.

### Basic Rules for Seams

—Seams that will be crossed by other seams are stitched first.

—Always pin and stitch the corded welting or fringe to a single seam allowance; then pin and stitch to the joining section. Place the pins at right angles to the seamline with the heads toward the cut edge. Do not attempt to join sections and trimming in one operation.

—If striped or plaid fabric is used, slip-baste the sections together from the right side; then stitch from the wrong side. See page 397.

### Sequence of Seams

Remove seamline pins and join the sections, right sides together, in the following sequence:

**A** Join the inside arm to the inside back, right sides together. Backstitch at each end. This seam fits snugly over the arm, then tapers to the full tuck-in allowance. Press.

**B** Where the seat joins the front, pin the corded welting to the right side of the seat seam, keeping the line of stitching on the cording over the marking (on the wrong side of the fabric) for the seamline. Adjust the Zipper Foot to the right of needle and stitch. Pin the front section to the seat, right sides together, matching notches. Stitch, crowding the stitching between the previous line of stitching and the cord. Backstitch at each end. Press the seam. Fit this section on the chair.

**C** Join seat to inside arm, as instructed in "A" on opposite page.

**D** Pin; then stitch cording to the seamline of the inside arm and front sections, as instructed in "B" above. Join outside arm to inside arm and front sections, right sides together, matching notches.

Backstitch at each end. Press. Try the assembled sections on the chair; make any necessary adjustments.

**E** Pin, then stitch seat to inside arms and back sections, right sides together. Press.

**F** Pin cording to inside back and outside arms in a continuous line, as instructed in "B" above. Stitch, leaving the cording free in the zipper opening. Try assembled sections on the chair; make any necessary adjustments. Press.

**G** Pin outside back to inside back and outside arm sections, right sides together. Stitch from the top of the zipper opening to the lower edge on the opposite side, as instructed in "B" above. Remove the pins holding the cording to the outside arm and inside back sections in the zipper opening; then pin and stitch the cording to the outside back section. Press. Try the slipcover on the chair for inspection.

## Adding a Skirt or Flounce

### Preparatory Steps

Leave the slipcover on the chair until you are ready to stitch the flounce in place. Pin-mark the position of the flounce an even distance from the floor, using a 12-inch ruler. After the flounce has been stitched in place, cut off the excess fabric 1 inch below the marking for the flounce, and press the seam allowances of both the slipcover and the flounce toward the top of the slipcover to eliminate bulk. (Be sure to keep these seam allowances turned toward the top when the finished slipcover is placed on the chair.)

The flounce on the average chair is 7 or 8 inches deep and should clear the floor by approximately 1 inch. For a 7-inch flounce, pin-mark the slipcover 8 inches from the floor. To the depth of the flounce, add 1½ inches for hem and turning plus 1 inch for a top seam allowance. If you are planning to make a heading (as for spaced box pleats, described below), add an extra inch.

To determine the length required for the flounce, measure around the chair, over the pin line. To this measurement, add the amount for pleats or gathers, plus 6 to 8 inches for seaming of strips, ease, and hems at the opening. *Example:* If the circumference of the chair is 3 yards, twice this measurement, or 6 yards, plus 6 or 8 inches is required for evenly spaced box pleats; three times this measurement, or 9 yards, plus 6 or 8 inches is required for closed box pleats or side pleats.

Cut the flounce on the crosswise grain of the fabric. Draw a thread from the fabric to indicate the cutting line. Before you begin, study the instructions for the flounce you have selected so that you can determine where to place the seams. They should not be noticeable in the finished flounce.

### Flounce with Spaced Box Pleats

The heading illustrated requires an extra inch in the depth of the flounce. Turn the top edge under 1 inch, and press.

In the illustration, the pleats and the spacing between pleats are identical in width. The back folds of each pleat meet at the center. Plan the flounce so that the center of a pleat falls at the center of the chair front and the spacing between pleats is centered at the corner, over each front leg. With this positioning, the number of pleats and spaces will be the same when you figure the pleat width and spacing.

The number of pleats across the front should be uneven. Decide on the number of pleats, then measure across the front of the chair. Divide this measurement by the number of pleats and spaces. *Example:* 28 inches (front measurement) divided by 14 (7 pleats, 7 spaces) = 2 inches (width of each finished pleat and width of spacing).

Pin-mark the top edge of the flounce at 2-inch intervals, beginning at the center. Lay in the box pleats, following diagram **A** on the opposite page. As seams are required, place them at the back folds of the pleat; use a plain ⅝-inch seam. Before stitching the seams, turn the top fold away from the flounce. Remove the pins holding the pleats, but not those at the 2-inch intervals.

Hem the flounce—either slip-stitch it by hand or machine-stitch it, using either straight stitching or blindstitching. See *Side Hems,* page 371.

Lay in the box pleats, following diagram **A**. Work on the ironing board and use *Method 3,* page 212. Hand-baste across the top of the pleats, a scant ½ inch from the edge. Pin the flounce to the right side of the slipcover, extending the heading ½ inch above the marking. Begin at the center

**Diagram A for Box Pleats**

**Diagram B for Side Pleats**

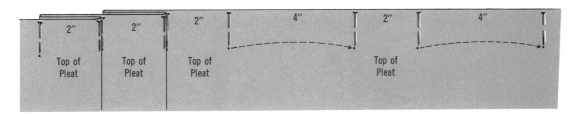

front and align the center of the pleat with the center of the slipcover. Ease the flounce slightly and extend the ends at least 2 inches beyond the sides of the opening. Stitch the flounce in place, ½ inch below the top edge of the flounce. Finish the seam edge on the slipcover.

### Flounce with Side Pleats

The flounce illustrated here has no spacing between pleats. In the 28-inch measurement in the example for spaced box pleats, 14 pleats, 2 inches deep, will fit across the front of the chair. Pin-mark the top and bottom edges of the flounce alternately at 2- and 4-inch intervals. Lay in the pleats, following diagram **B** above. Work on the ironing board and use *Method 3*, page 212. Place the seams at the back fold of the pleats.

Sew corded welting to the right side of the flounce. Pin the flounce to the slipcover, right sides together, keeping the line of cording stitching on the marking that designates the position of the flounce. Ease the flounce slightly and extend the ends about 2 inches beyond the sides of the opening. Place the work under the needle with the flounce and previous stitching uppermost so you can use the stitching as a guide. Stitch, crowding the stitching between the cord and previous line of stitching. Trim the seam allowance on the slipcover to 1 inch. Press the seam toward the top of the slipcover. Although seam edges are turned in the same direction, finish each edge separately.

### Gathered Flounce

A gathered flounce is generally used for an informal effect in Early American rooms, summer cottages, or a family room. Allow one and one-half to two times the circumference of the chair for fullness, plus 6 or 8 inches for seaming of strips, ease, and a hem at the opening. Hem and gather the flounce. Stitch the flounce to the slipcover, following the instructions above.

### Skirt with Open Inverted Pleat

A straight skirt, with an open inverted pleat at each corner over the legs of the chair, is a neat, tailored finish. An underlay forms the underside of the open pleat. This means that each pleat has openings instead of back folds, and bulk is thus

eliminated. The skirt is lined with matching sateen or batiste and needs no bottom hem.

Decide on the depth of the skirt. See page 400. To this measurement, add 1½ inches for top and bottom seams. For the length, take separate measurements for the front, sides, and back of the chair across the marking for the skirt. To each of these measurements, add 10 inches for pleat, seams, and ease. Cut the skirt in four sections, using these measurements. Pin a label to the right side of each section for identification; that is, front, back, and sides. Cut four underlays for the underside of the pleats, the depth of the flounce and 10 inches wide. Cut the lining the same as each skirt section and each underlay, but ¼ inch less in depth. Press the fabric.

Place the lining over the skirt sections and over the underlays, right sides together, and pin along the lower edge. Stitch, taking a ½-inch seam. Trim the seam allowance to ¼ inch. Press; then press the seam allowances toward the lining. Turn the right sides together again, fold the skirt and underlay fabric ¼ inch from the stitching line, and pin the lining in place across the ends. Stitch; then backstitch at each end. Trim the seam allowances to ¼ inch and clip diagonally across the corners. Turn to the right side and pull out the corners to square them. Fold the skirt and underlay fabric across the bottom ¼ inch from the stitching line and press. Fold the ends on the seamline and press.

Fold the ends of each skirt section under 4 inches to form the top folds of the pleats; pin. Do not press the folds at this time. Place the skirt

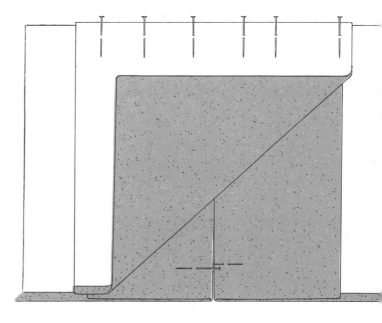

sections wrong side up. Bring the folded edges together in the following sequence: join sides to front skirt, and back to sides. Center the underlays over the joining folds, wrong side up, and pin in place across the top. The underlays should extend about ½ inch beyond the outer edges of the pleats.

Try the skirt on the chair, over the pin marking, to be sure it fits correctly. The inverted pleats should be centered over the legs and there should be a slight ease in the skirt to allow for the thicknesses of fabric. Make any necessary adjustments in the pleat folds. Press the pleats; then stitch the underlays in place a scant 1 inch from the top edge. At the side of the closing, stitch the underlay to the side skirt only.

Cut off the excess slipcover fabric 1 inch below the marking for the skirt. Before stitching the skirt in place, apply the zipper following the directions below; however, extend the open end of the zipper only to the seamline of the skirt.

Pin the skirt to the slipcover, right sides together, keeping the seam edge 1 inch below the marking on the slipcover. At each side of the zipper closing, the pleat folds extend to the seamline and the underlay on the side skirt extends beyond the seamline. Stitch with the skirt uppermost, taking a 1-inch seam. Backstitch at each end. Press the seam; then press the seam allowances toward the top of the slipcover. Although seam edges are turned in the same direction, finish each edge separately. Use snaps to hold the underlay in position under the back skirt.

## Applying the Zipper

For an average chair, one closing on the left side is sufficient; for a sofa, two closings, one at each side, are necessary. Select either an 18-, 20- or 24-inch zipper, depending on the length of the closing required.

### Side Closing

The following instructions explain how to apply the zipper when the closing is on the left side of the slipcover. When the closing is on the right side, reverse the right and left sides in the instructions as well as the adjustment of the Zipper Foot.

Trim the flounce even with the seam edge on the left side of the opening. If corded welting is used in the seam that joins the flounce to the slipcover, pull out the end of the cord and clip off 1 inch (width of the seam allowance). Turn the seam allowances toward the top of the slipcover.

On the left side of the opening, fold the seam

allowance under 3/16 inch from the seamline; carry the fold to the bottom of the flounce. Close the zipper. Pin; then baste the folded edge to the right side of the zipper tape, ⅛ inch from the chain; keep the pull-tab about 2 inches above the bottom of flounce. Adjust the Zipper Foot to the left of the needle and stitch near the fold from the top of the opening to the bottom of the flounce.
*(Continued)*

On the right side of the opening, fold the seam allowance under on the seamline; carry the fold to the bottom of the flounce. Press. In the flounce area, turn the cut edge under ½ inch and pin it to the flounce. Lap the folded edge over the zipper to the seamline on the opposite side, and pin. (The right side will overlap the left 5/16 inch beyond the zipper chain; the cording with extend beyond the seamline.) Baste through all thicknesses a measured ⅝ inch from the fold. Adjust the Zipper Foot to the right of the needle; stitch across the top end and down the side to the bottom of the flounce, following the even line of basting. Tie the threads on the underside.

Blindstitching the final step of the zipper application gives a finish that is almost invisible. Follow the instructions on page 178.

Bar-tack across the top of the closing to prevent ripping. See page 337.

## Center Back Closing

A closing at the center back of the slipcover is frequently used in sofas and chairs that are placed against a wall or in a corner.

In a sofa the outside back section generally has one or two seams in which a zipper may be

inserted. In a chair the outside back is usually in one section and it is necessary to make a center back seam. Refer to the chart on page 392. Measure the *Outside Back Width—R to S*, and add 4 inches instead of 2 inches for seam allowances. The additional 2 inches are for the center seam allowances. Block the muslin or fabric as instructed on page 391. Fold the outside back lengthwise through the center, right sides together, then cut on the fold. Pin these edges together. Stitch from the top edge to the top of the zipper opening, making a 1-inch seam. Reinforce with backstitching. Machine-baste the seam in the opening. Press the seam; then press it open.

Construct the slipcover up to the point of applying the zipper; then follow the instructions given under *Neckline or Sleeve Zipper in Slot Seam,* page 181. However, place the open end of the zipper about ½ inch above the bottom of the flounce, and place the basting and stitching ½ inch from the center basted seam.

## Plate 23

### Two handsome monogram styles

*Above:* Modern block letters formed with decorative stitch patterns.

*Below:* A graceful satin monogram appliquéd on terry cloth. Cutout work.

*Below left:* Diamond-shaped cutouts, combined with decorative stitch pattern, make an attractive pillowcase border.

**Plate 24**

**Slipcovers can remake a room**

*Above:*
Spirited red-white-and-blue
printed linen carries out
the Early American theme of this room
while contributing a contemporary glow.
Slipcovers made without skirt
show off the clean lines
of the wing chair and sofa.

*Left:*
The cheerful chintz chosen here for
slipcover and draperies is a lively addition
to this simple, restful room.
The love seat is covered in a fabric
much like the wall in color
and character, to blend
unobtrusively into the background,
yet add some textural
interest of its own.

## Finishing a Slipcover without a Flounce

If you do not add a flounce or skirt to your slipcover, allow 3 or 4 inches on the bottom edge for a turn-under. Mark the seamline across the legs, following the contour of the chair frame. Cut out the fabric over the legs to within ½ inch of the seam marking. Stitch cording on the ½-inch seamline around the cutout, as illustrated. Slash into

the corners, almost to the stitching. Press. Turn the seam allowance to the underside. Turn the cut edges of the slipcover under ½ inch and stitch near the fold.

Place the slipcover on the chair. Be sure the cover fits smoothly and the seams are straight. Close the zipper. Turn the bottom edge of the cover over the chair frame to the underside and tack it to the frame.

## Holding the Slipcover Securely

Here are two suggestions:

—Sew ½-inch twill tape to the slipcover seams next to the chair legs. Cut the tape long enough to lap twice around the legs. Tie securely.

—Push a heavy cotton cord, ¾ to 1 inch in diameter, into the tuck-in to hold it in place. Or use a roll of cotton batting, 1½ to 2 inches in size, covered with muslin, or a roll of brown paper. Any one of these will help prevent the slipcover from sliding.

## Covering the Cushion

Cushions should be reversible. Center floral designs on both sides of the cushion. Match stripes and plaids, on both sides of the cushion, with the inside back and front sections of the chair. Plaids must also match the inside arms. Match stripes and plaids across the front of the boxing with those on both sides of the cushion.

### Constructing the Cover

Pin-fit the fabric to the cushion, right side out, following the instructions for the muslin pattern, page 391. Corners may be round or square; follow the exact contour of the cushion. Trim seam allowances to 1 inch; mark the seamline and stitch cording or fringe to the top and bottom sections, as in slipcovers. Pin the boxing to the top and bottom sections. Join the ends of boxing at the

back of the cushion. Stitch the boxing in place, but leave the seam open across the back and around the corners of the bottom section the entire length of the zipper. Backstitch at each end. Clip into the seam allowances on inside curves and notch them on outside curves. Press, then turn to the right side.

### Applying the Zipper

Two methods of zipper application are explained here.

**Method 1:** Fold the boxing on the seamline of the opening and press. Open the zipper. Pin the corded seam to the zipper tape, right sides together, keeping the seamline about ⅛ inch from the chain or coil of the zipper. Stitch on the seamline. Close the zipper and turn it away from the seam. Lap the folded edge of the boxing over the zipper to the corded seam, and pin through all thicknesses. Open the zipper and baste a measured ⅝ inch from the fold. Stitch across the end, along the side, following the basting, and across the opposite end.

**Method 2:** Make a separate back section of the boxing and insert the zipper before joining the boxing to the top and bottom sections. To do this, cut the back section the length of the zipper, plus 2 inches for seam allowances and the same width as the boxing plus 2 inches for center seam

allowances. Fold lengthwise through the center, right sides together; then cut on the fold. Machine-baste the cut edges together, making a 1-inch seam. Press the seam, then press it open. Center the closed zipper over the wrong side of the basted seam, right side down, and pin through all thicknesses. Turn right side up and hand-baste, on each side, a measured ⅜ inch from the center seam. Adjust the Zipper Foot to the left of the needle and

stitch around the zipper, following the basted line. Join the ends of this separate back section to the rest of the boxing with a 1-inch seam. Stitch the boxing in place as instructed above.

Slipcovers for a studio bed or couch may be styled to obtain almost any effect you want. A tailored cover is illustrated here.

In covering the mattress, treat it as the cushion for a chair or sofa—in other words, make it reversible. Make a separate fitted cover for the box spring. Center floral designs on both sides of the mattress. Match stripes or plaids on the boxing with those on both sides of the mattress; also match the stripes or plaids on the boxing and on the flounce for the box spring with those of the mattress. Cut each section on the true lengthwise and crosswise grains of the fabric. Draw a thread from the fabric to indicate the cutting line.

## Covering the Mattress

Measure the length and width of the mattress and add 2 inches to each measurement for seam allowances. Cut two sections (one for each side of the mattress) by these measurements.

Measure the depth of the mattress and add 2 inches for seam allowances. Then measure around the mattress (both sides and ends) and add at least 8 inches for seam allowances. Cut the boxing on the lengthwise grain by these measurements; place seams at the back corners. If the fabric has a floral or one-way design, cut the boxing on the crosswise grain.

### To Round the Corners

The corners of both top and bottom sections must be rounded to fit the mattress. Here is a simple and easy method:

Place a piece of cardboard (about 8 inches by 11 inches) between the mattress and box spring, with the edges extending about 1 inch beyond the side and end of the mattress. Hold the cardboard securely, and mark it to indicate the curve of the mattress corner as well as the straight line of the

side and end. Then cut off the cardboard edge along the marking.

Place the cardboard over the corners of the fabric (one at a time) with the fabric extending 1 inch (seam allowance) beyond the straight side and end of the cardboard. Hold the cardboard firmly in position and chalk-mark the shape of the corner on the fabric. *Do not cut.* This is the seamline in construction.

### To Construct the Cover

Carefully study *Constructing the Slipcovers*, beginning on page 398; and *Covering the Cushion*, page 405. Then proceed with the construction of the mattress cover.

Stitch cording or fringe to the 1-inch seamline

of both the top and buttom sections of the cover. Join the ends of the cording at the center back, following the instructions on page 397. Try the sections over the mattress to be sure they fit correctly. Press. Join the boxing to the top and bottom sections, leaving the bottom seam open across the entire back and about 4 inches around the corners.

Trim the corner seam allowances to 1 inch. Press; then press the seam allowances toward the boxing. Use two zippers in the opening and place them so that the pull-tabs meet in the center back. Insert the zippers in the seam, following the instructions on page 406. Place the cover on the mattress and turn the seam allowances toward the boxing.

If you are not using zippers, turn under the 1-inch seam allowance on the boxing the length of the opening, and press. Place the cover on the mattress and turn the seam allowances toward the boxing. Lap the folded edge of the boxing over the second seam allowance to the cording, and pin at about 4-inch intervals. Slip-stitch in place, using a curved needle and heavy thread.

## Covering the Box Spring

Measure the length and width of the box spring and add 2 inches to each measurement for seam allowances. Cut the fabric; then *round the corners* as instructed for the mattress. Stitch cording or fringe to the seamline.

Measure the depth of the box spring and add 2 inches for seam allowances. Then measure around the box spring (both sides and ends) and add about 8 inches for seam allowances. Cut the boxing by

these measurements. Join the boxing to the top section and try it over the box spring to be sure the fit is correct. Stitch cording or fringe to the free edge of the boxing.

Measure the depth of the flounce from the bottom of the box spring to the floor and add 1 inch for seam allowance plus 1½ inches for the bottom hem and turning. Measure the length around the box spring and add 12 inches for seam allowances plus the amount required for inverted pleats (16 inches for each) at the four corners and at the center front and back. Cut the flounce by these measurements; place the seams in the back fold of the pleats. Hem the lower edge. Join the flounce to the boxing, right sides together; lay in the inverted pleats, making each fold 4 inches deep.

## Covering the Pillows

You can choose from several pillow styles—box or wedge pillows, or round or square bolsters. You may need two or three pillows of the same style. To cover the pillows, follow the instructions for the cushion, page 405. Decorative throw pillows may be added for color contrast.

## Constructing a One-Piece Fitted Cover

Take measurements for the spread over sheets and blankets. Measure the top section of the mattress and boxing as instructed above; cut one section to cover the mattress top. Round the corners; then stitch cording or fringe to the seamline. See *Covering the Mattress*, page 407. Join the boxing to the top section. Stitch cording or fringe to the lower edge of the boxing.

Measure the depth of the flounce from the bottom of the mattress to the floor and add 1 inch for seam allowance plus 1½ inches for the bottom hem and turning. Measure the length around the mattress and add the amount required for pleats. Cut the flounce by these measurements. Construct the flounce; then join it to the boxing, right sides together.

Cover the pillows, following the instructions for the cushion, page 405.

# Make
# Your
# Own
# Bedspreads

WHETHER AUSTERELY TAILORED or frivolously feminine, bedspreads are an essential element in your decorating scheme. The style of course depends on the other fabric furnishings in the bedroom. Bedspreads may match draperies or slipcovers, or they may introduce a new color note. Since bedspreads cover an article of furniture not easily overlooked, the texture and design of the fabric, as well as the styling and color, should all be harmoniously related.

## BEDSPREAD PRELIMINARIES

### What to Know before You Start

Many fabrics are appropriate for bedspreads. To name a few: rayon or silk taffeta, chintz, velveteen, polished cotton, antique satin, faille, sailcloth, handblocked linen, corduroy, fiberglass, gingham, and organdy. The fabric may consist of natural or synthetic fibers or a blend of two fibers such as Dacron and silk.

Bedspread are often underlined with taffeta, polished cotton, chintz, batiste, muslin, or the like. The selection depends on the fabric used in the bedpsread. If you are planning to use an underlining, select one that is as wide as the bedspread fabric so that the seams will fall in the same places. If lightweight or medium-weight fabric is used in the bedspread, only the center section covering the mattress may require underlining. If sheer fabric is used, the entire bedspread must be underlined. A style with a gathered ruffle is preferred in this case. The sheer fabric and underlining are hemmed and ruffled separately and then both ruffles are attached to the center section with one line of stitching.

A full width of fabric is always placed down the center of the bed, and the seams joining it to the other sections must fall in the same places on each side. When the bedspread has a flounce, the joining strips extend to the edge of the mattress, and the flounce extends from the top edge of the mattress to the floor; when the bedspread is plain, the strips joining the center section extend over the edge of the mattress to the floor. Whatever the style of the spread, most of the seams are straight lines of stitching, and a ⅝-inch seam allowance is adequate. The seams should be emphasized with cording, fringe, binding, or decorative bands of zig-zag stitching. See *Accenting Seams,* page 396.

## To Measure the Bed

Before you take any measurements, be sure the bed is made up with sheets, blankets, and pillows. Decide on the style of bedspread, then measure accurately and add the amounts specified below. Pin-mark each edge of the mattress (**A, C,** and **D**

in the illustration) to indicate the points of the measurements. Since the tape measure may not extend the entire length or width of the mattress, pin-mark the mattress at the point where the tape measure ends; then move the tape and continue your measurements.

## BEDSPREAD

LENGTH — **A** to **B.** Measure from the foot end, along the length of the mattress, over the pillow, and down well under the pillow. ADD 15″ for pillow tuck-in allowance plus ⅝″ for seam allowance plus 1″ for hem and turning at the headboard. . . . . . . . .   _____ inches

WIDTH — **C** to **D.** Measure from one side of the mattress to the other. Add 3¾″ for seam allowances. . . . . . . . . . . . . . . . . . .   _____ inches

## FLOUNCE

DEPTH — **C** to **E.** Measure the side overhang from the top edge of the mattress to the floor. Add ⅝″ for seam allowance plus 1½″ for hem and turning. . . . . . . . . . . . . . . . . . . . . . . . . . . .   _____ inches

LENGTH — **A** to **B.** Measure as for the bedspread length above. ADD 15″ for pillow tuck-in x 2 (sides) plus **C** to **D** (width across foot) plus allowances for pleats or gathers.

For Box Flounce—ADD depth of 2 inverted pleats (16″ each) plus 2½″ for seam allowances plus 2″ for hems and turnings at the headboard end. . . . . . . . . . . . . . . . . . . . . . . . . . . .   _____ inches

For Gathered Flounce — Multiply the measured length by 2½ or 3 for fullness. ADD to this figure at least 8″ for seam allowances plus 2″ for hems and turnings at the headboard end. . . . . . . . . . . . . . . . . . . . . . . . . . . .   _____ inches

# COVERLET

LENGTH — **A** to **B.** Measure from the foot end, along the length of the mattress, over the pillow, and down well under the pillow. ADD 15″ for pillow tuck-in allowance plus 10″ for foot over-hang (indicated by **F**) plus ⅝″ for seam allowance plus 1″ for hem and turning at the headboard end. . . . . . . . . . . . . . . .   _____inches

WIDTH — **C** to **D.** Measure from one side of the mattress to the other. ADD 20″ (10″ overhang on each side, indicated by **G**) plus 6¼″ for seam allowances. . . . . . . . . . . . . . . . . . . . . . .   _____inches

## DUST RUFFLE COVERING FOR BOX SPRING
This is a covering that is placed between the mattress and box spring. Remove the mattress and measure the box spring.

LENGTH — **H** to **I.** Measure from one end of the box spring to the other. ADD ⅝″ for seam allowance at the foot end plus 1″ for hem and turning at the headboard end. . . . . . . . . . . . . . . .   _____inches

WIDTH — **J** to **K.** Measure from one side of the box spring to the other. ADD 1¼″ for seam allowances. . . . . . . . . . . . . . . . . .   _____inches

## DUST RUFFLE

DEPTH — **J** to **L.** Measure the overhang from the top edge of the box spring to the floor. ADD ⅝″ for seam allowance plus 1½″ for hem and turning. . . . . . . . . . . . . . . . . . . . . . . . . . . .   _____inches

LENGTH — **H** to **I.** Multiply the length measurement by 2 (sides) plus **J** to **K** (width across foot). ADD  12″ (6″ on each side) for returns at the headboard end; then multiply by 2½ or 3 for fullness. ADD to this figure at least 8″ for seam allowances plus 2″ for hems and turning at the headboard end. . . . . . . . .   _____inches

The average measurements of finished bedspreads are:

**Full-size: 97 by 120 inches**

**Twin-size: 82 by 120 inches**

**Dual or King-size: 115 by 122 inches**

*Remember,* the necessary allowances for seams and hems must be added to these finished measurements.

The average height of a bed (from top of mattress to floor) is 21 inches; however, it may vary from 19 to 22½ inches.

# YARDAGE ESTIMATES FOR BEDSPREADS

|  | 36" Fabric | 50" Fabric |
|---|---|---|

**FULL-SIZE BED — 54" x 75" (or 78" to 80")**

| | | |
|---|---|---|
| Plain . . . . . . . . . . . . . . . . . . . . . . . . . . . . . . . . . . . . . . . . | 10⅓ yards . . . . . . | 7 yards |
| Box Sides with Inverted Pleats at Corner . . . . . . . . . . | 10¼ yards . . . . . . | 8½ yards |
| Gathered Flounce (2½ times length for fullness) . . . . . | 20½ yards . . . . . . | 13½ yards |

**TWIN-SIZE BED — 39" x 75" (or 78")**

| | | |
|---|---|---|
| Plain . . . . . . . . . . . . . . . . . . . . . . . . . . . . . . . . . . . . . . . . | 10⅓ yards . . . . . . | 7 yards |
| Box Sides with Inverted Pleats at Corner . . . . . . . . . . | 10¼ yards . . . . . . | 7½ yards |
| Gathered Flounce (2½ times length for fullness) . . . . . | 19½ yards . . . . . . | 12½ yards |

**DUAL AND KING-SIZE BEDS — 78" x 84" (or 80")**
                                  **or 72" x 84" (or 80")**

| | |
|---|---|
| Plain . . . . . . . . . . . . . . . . . . . . . . . . . . . . . . . . . . . . . . . . . . . . . . . . | 10½ yards |
| Box Sides with Inverted Pleats at Corner . . . . . . . . . . . . . . . . . . . . . . | 10¼ yards |
| Gathered Flounce (2½ times length for fullness) . . . . . . . . . . . . . . . . . . | 15⅓ yards |

**QUEEN-SIZE BED—60" x 80"** . . . . . . . . . . . . . . . . . . . . . . . . Same yardage as King-Size Bed.

If you are planning to use corded seams, add an extra yard. If the fabric has a large floral design or plaid, allow one full length of the motif for each additional length required after cutting the center length.

The above figures are the approximate requirements. To be on the safe side, measure your own bed carefully. Remember it is better to have extra fabric than not enough.

412

# MAKING THE BEDSPREAD

## Box Bedspread

Refer to the *Bedspread Measurements* chart, page 410, and measurements **A** to **B, C** to **D,** and **C** to **E.** Check your measurements to be sure that they are accurate and that you have added the correct allowances for seams, hems, and pillow tuck-in.

### The Center Section

Cut one length of fabric for the center section, using the full width. Remove selvages. Since the full width of the fabric is seldom as wide as the bed, cut two additional strips (one for each side) the length of the center section and wide enough to give the amount required to cover the top of the mattress plus 3¾ inches for seam allowances. If you have 50-inch fabric, cut both of these strips from one length, and use the remaining width for the end section of the flounce. If you have 36-inch fabric, cut the strips from two lengths of fabric so that sufficient width remains in each length for the flounce. If you are going to underline the bedspread, cut the underlining fabric the same length and width as each section. Pin the underlining to the top fabric, wrong sides together. Baste ½ inch from the edges if necessary.

Join a strip to each side of the center section, right sides together. Accent the seams with corded welting. See page 396. Try the section on the bed to be sure it fits properly. The ⅝-inch seam allowance should extend beyond the foot and each side of the mattress. Round the corners at the foot, following instructions on page 407. Pin corded welting, in a continuous line, to the right side of the ⅝-inch seamline: Begin at the headboard end and pin the cording in place along the side, across the end, and along the opposite side to the headboard. Stitch.

### The Flounce

Cut the flounce in three sections: Cut two side sections (on the lengthwise grain) the length of the center section plus 12⅝ inches for pleat and seam allowances, and the depth of measurement **C** to **E** plus 2⅛ inches for seam allowances and hem; cut one end section (on the crosswise grain) the length of measurement **C** to **D** plus 9¼ inches for pleats and seam allowances, and the same depth as the side sections. This allows for two seams, one at the back fold of each corner pleat. If 50-inch fabric is used, cut both side lengths from one length of fabric; if 36-inch fabric is used, cut the side lengths from the fabric left from the strips that join the center section (see above).

Join the three sections of the flounce with a

⅝-inch seam. Hem the bottom edge: Turn the edge to the underside ½ inch and press; then turn a 1-inch hem and press. The hem may be slip-stitched by hand or machine-stitched, using either straight stitching or blindstitching. See *Side Hems,* page 371.

### To Join the Flounce and Center Section

Pin-mark the center of each of the following: the foot of the center section, the rounded corners, and the end section of the flounce. Pin the flounce to the center section, right sides together, matching the center pin marks. Lay in the inverted pleats at the corners, making each fold 4 inches deep. (Seams joining the sides of the flounce to the end section should fall at the back fold of the pleats.) Then pin each side of the flounce in place. Stitch, following the directions for *Corded Seams,* page 245. Finish the headboard end with a ½-inch double-fold hem.

If the bed has a footboard, make an opening in the back seam of each corner pleat so that the flounce will fit over the frame joining the footboard.

## Plain Bedspread with Decorative Bands

For a plain bedspread, the entire length of the spread—that is from the floor to the headboard end (including tuck-in allowance)—is cut in one section. Refer to the *Bedspread Measurements* chart and illustration, page 410. Measure from **E** to **B**. Add 17 inches for a 15-inch pillow tuck-in and a 1-inch hem at each end. Measure the width from the floor, up and over the mattress, and down to the floor on the opposite side. Add 5 inches for seam allowances plus 2 inches for a 1-inch hem on each side.

Cut the center section the length required, using the full width of the fabric. Remove selvages.

### The Decorative Bands

Cut two strips of fabric the length of the center section and about 3½ inches wide. Place the decorative stitching as explained in *Border Designs*, page 272. Allow ¾ inch on each side of the decorative stitching for a border.

Pin a band to each side of the center section, right sides together. Stitch, taking a ⅝-inch seam. Press the seams open.

### The Side Sections

Cut two side sections the length of the center section and wide enough to complete the overhang on each side of the bedspread plus 2¼ inches for seam allowances and a hem at the bottom edge. (If you are adding a ruffle, make the allowance for its width.) Pin a side section to the band on each side of the center section, right sides together. Stitch, taking a ⅝-inch seam.

Place the spread on the bed; keep the edges even with the floor. *To round the corners* of the spread, pin-mark them in line with the floor. Remove the spread and check the evenness of the pin marks to be sure the curves are identical. Finish the lower edges with a narrow hem.

### The Ruffle

The spread in the illustration has a ruffle at the bottom. Cut the ruffle on the lengthwise grain of the fabric, allowing for double or triple fullness. Finish each edge of the ruffle with decorative zig-zag. See *Edgestitched Finish*, page 274. Gather the ruffle with a ½-inch heading; then stitch it in place. See *Ruffle with Heading*, page 281. Finish the headboard end with a ½-inch double-fold hem.

## Bedspread with Appliqué Monogram

A monogram is an individual and distinctive touch on a plain or tailored bedspread.

The center of the monogram should measure about 12 or 18 inches. Center the monogram in the center section of the bedspread and complete the appliqué before joining the flounce or overhang. See *Appliqué Monograms*, page 252.

## Coverlet and Dust Ruffle

The overhang on a coverlet extends only a little below the mattress, not to the floor. The coverlet is used with a dust ruffle, which covers the box spring and extends to the floor.

For a pleasing contrast, the coverlet may be of a quilted or floral fabric and the dust ruffle of a solid color that matches the quilting or the background of the floral design. For instructions on quilting, see page 256.

### The Coverlet

Refer to measurements **A** to **B** and **C** to **D** on the measurement chart on page 411. Be sure that your measurements are accurate and that you have added the correct allowances for seams, hems, and pillow tuck-in.

Cut and construct the center section of the coverlet, following the instructions for the box bedspread on page 413. Use corded seams, and stitch the cording to the outer edges. Try the section on the bed to check the fit. The ⅝-inch seam allowance should extend beyond the foot end and sides of the mattress.

The overhang in the coverlet illustrated is lined and has an open inverted pleat at each corner of the footboard end. An underlay forms the underside of the open pleat. This means that each pleat has openings instead of back folds so that bulkiness is eliminated. The edges of the overhang are finished with tailored binding.

Cut the overhang in three sections: Cut two side sections (on the lengthwise grain) the length of the center section and 10 inches deep (or more) plus ⅝ inch for seam allowances; cut one end section (on the crosswise grain) long enough to extend across the width of the center section and the same depth as the side sections. Cut two underlays 10 inches wide and 10 inches deep plus seam allowance. Cut a sateen lining the same length and depth as each section of the overhang and underlap; then pin the lining to the fabric sections, wrong sides together. Finish these edges with tailored binding: the lower edge of the underlays; the lower edge and both ends of the end section; and the lower edge and end at foot end of each side section. Be sure to finish one section of the overhang for the right side and one for the left. For instructions on applying the binding, see *Tailored Binding*, page 334. Overcast the side edges of the underlays.

Pin the end section, then the side sections, of the overhang to the center section, right sides together, with the bound edges meeting at the corners. (Keep the ends the same depth.) Center an underlay, right side down, over each joining; pin. Refer to *Corded Seams*, page 245 and stitch. Finish the headboard end with a ½-inch double-fold hem.

### Dust Ruffle Covering for Box Spring

Refer to measurements **H** to **I, J** to **K,** and **J** to **L,** page 411. Measure accurately and add allowances for seams, hems, and returns at the headboard end.

The section covering the box spring, **H** to **I** and **J** to **K,** may be cut of good-quality muslin; it is placed between the box spring and mattress, and the coverlet overlaps the edges joining the dust ruffle. Round the four corners of the muslin, following the contours of the mattress. See the instructions on page 407. Pin-mark the center of the rounded corners.

Cut the dust ruffle on the crosswise grain the length and depth required. See *Dust Ruffle* on the chart, page 411. Seam the strips for the ruffle, using a French seam. Press. Hem the lower edge; then gather the ruffle. See page 280.

Pin the ruffle to the center section, right sides together, placing the gathering stitches on the seamline. Begin at the headboard end and extend the ruffle 7 inches around the corner (the return); pin along the side, across the end, along the opposite side, and 7 inches around the corner at the headboard end. (The returns at the headboard prevent the cover from slipping out of place.) Finish the ends of the ruffle with a ½-inch double-fold

hem. Stitch the ruffle in place, with the ruffle side up, barely beyond the gathering stitches. Hem the end of the muslin center section between the returns.

***If the bed has a footboard,*** you must make an opening in the ruffle at each corner so that the ruffle will fit over the frame joining the footboard. Cut the ruffle as instructed above but add 20 inches to the length for the underlap and turn-under at the corners of the foot end.

Join the strips for the ruffle. Hem, then gather, the ruffle as instructed above.

Pin the gathered ruffle to one side of the center section, right sides together, extending it 7 inches around the corner (the return) at the headboard end. At the footboard end, extend the ruffle 5 inches beyond the corner; then cut it off at this point. Turn the end of the ruffle to the underside 5 inches. (The turn-under is not gathered.) Finish the cut end with a ½-inch double-fold hem. Pin the ruffle to the opposite side in the same manner. Pin the ruffle across the foot end, extending it 5 inches around each corner for the underlap. Finish the cut edges. Stitch the ruffle in place, and finish the headboard end between the returns with a ½-inch double-fold hem.

416

# The Many Faces
# of Knits

## The Many Faces of Knits

Flattering, comfortable, and easy to care for, knits are an increasingly important part of the fashion scene. Indeed, they play a larger role than most people realize. In addition to the familiar types of knits used in dressmaking, an ever-growing variety is available for lingerie, clothes for active sports, and even fake fur and leather coats.

The great variety of knit fabrics presents the home sewer with an equally great variety of sewing challenges. No single set of sewing guidelines can be applied to all knits. It is possible, however, to classify knits into groups, each of which calls for a specific set of sewing procedures.

This section first presents a comprehensive picture of knits and what they mean to the home sewer, and then deals with the specific guidelines for sewing each of nine groups of knits.

# Table of Contents

# About Knits

## WHAT IS A KNIT?

KNITTED FABRICS FUNCTION DIFFERENTLY from woven fabrics. Woven fabrics are rigid; they resist stress. Knitted fabrics are mobile and "give" with stress. Good knitted fabrics are truly elastic in the sense that they can be stretched and will return to their original form.

Knitted and woven fabrics function differently because they are of two *different structures*. Woven fabrics are structured from two systems of yarns that cross each other and are interlaced. See page 10.

Knitted fabrics are structured from only one system of yarns. The single system of yarns is looped either in the lengthwise direction of the fabric (warp knitting) or across the width of the fabric (weft or circular knitting).

than weft knits. In warp knitting, multiple yarns (but all part of a single system of yarns) run vertically and parallel to each other. The fabric is constructed by manipulating all these warp yarns at the same time into interconnected loops.

The two most familiar types of warp knits are *tricot* and *raschel*. Until a few years ago, tricot was used mainly as a lingerie fabric or as backing for bonded fabrics, and raschel as lace for curtains. But today, so many advances have been made in both tricot and raschel knitting machines that the fashion fabric potential in warp knits is beyond simple classification.

Tricot: A system of vertical yarns interlocks loops vertically and horizontally, producing a smooth-surfaced fabric, resistant to runs, and with little lengthwise but considerable crosswise stretch.

Tricot: Warp knitting — yarns run up and down.

Raschel: Rows of plain knit resembling chainstitch run vertically, interlocking crossing insertion yarns, to form lace-like or looped surface patterns.

Plain Knit: Weft or circular knitting — yarns run across fabric.

**Warp Knits,** which are made on flat-bed machines, are generally tighter, flatter, and less elastic

**Weft Knits,** which are made on either circular or flat-bed knitting machines, are constructed in much the same way as hand knits. In weft knitting, the fabric is constructed with one yarn at a time running in a horizontal direction, with the needles forming loops in horizontal courses, building one on top of the other.

The most familiar types of weft knits are jersey, rib knits, double knits and jacquards. Double knits appear to have been knitted twice; the effect is produced by two-needle construction, which interlocks two fabrics into one. Double-knit fabrics have become familiar to most women who sew because they have become available in volume and have performed well in sewing and wearing.

**The differences in knit fabrics** come from many things, such as: the capabilities of the knitting machine; the design of the needle; the number of sets of needles; the gauge or number of needles per inch; the stitch formation or pattern; the type of yarn (filament, textured filament, or spun); the kind of fiber the yarn is made of; the size of yarn; and the finishing processes applied to the fabric.

**To sew knitted fabrics successfully,** you need to recognize that they have just as many different faces, textures, and characteristics as woven fabrics.

Jersey: A plain knit with a face of flat, smooth, vertical ribs and a back of horizontal loop segments.

Rib Knit: A combination of sets of knit and purl stitches, which form prominent vertical ribs separated by receding spaces. The back of the fabric shows a reverse of the face ribs and spaces.

Double Knit: A smooth-surfaced face and back produced by interlocking stitches from two sets of both yarns and needles.

Jacquard: A figured surface produced by two or more sets of both yarns and needles working periodically together and separately to produce designed fabric.

Yarn strands are made of long filaments; textured filaments; or short, spun fibers.

Long Filaments    Textured Filaments    Short, Spun Fibers

Textured filaments may be coiled, crimped, or looped.

Coil    Crimp    Loop

Yarns are made from one or more of the same or different strands

3-ply novelty yarn

Plain yarn

Knits place a greater demand on your sewing machine than wovens. Knowing more about your sewing machine and how it reacts to knits will help you to sew knits easily and well.

## Machine Care

Because knits contain more yarn than wovens, they tend to drop more lint, fibers, and finishing granules into the machine; so frequent cleaning and light oiling are important. Your cleaning tools are: a lint brush; a piece of clean cheesecloth or any soft cloth; and a tube of SINGER* sewing machine oil. Disconnect the electric cord for safety and then brush out lint, wipe off residue or film, and oil lightly.

The upper threading points collect sticky film and fine lint because friction from the flow of thread creates heat and static electricity. To ensure an even flow of the needle thread, brush and wipe these threading points with a cloth, but do not oil them.

The *feed and bobbin-case area* collects a surprising amount of lint, fibers, and granules. A clean bobbin case is essential. Remove the throat plate and open the slide plate to expose the working

**Feed and bobbin-case area**

parts. Brush out all of the lint you can see. Then turn the hand wheel slowly, stop, and brush out additional lint as it appears. Remove the bobbin case and repeat the brushing procedure. Then, with a soft cloth, wipe the bobbin case and the surfaces it touches. If the metal parts feel sticky, put a little oil on the cloth to enable you to rub off the residue. Place a drop of oil at each point indicated in the instruction book for your machine. Replace the bobbin case and throat plate carefully when finished.

*Open the face plate* and brush out the small amount of lint that may have accumulated. Lightly oil the points indicated in the machine instruction book. Turn the hand wheel slowly to reveal the oiling points. Give special attention to the presser bar. Raise and lower the presser foot so that you can see which parts move. A freely moving presser bar improves the feeding of seam layers.

**Inside face plate**

When you have finished, close the face plate and wipe again around the lower part of the presser bar and needle bar to remove any excess oil. Then run the machine slowly to distribute the oil around the parts as they move.

## The Needle

The importance of the sewing machine needle takes on a new dimension when one is sewing knits.

The correct **needle size** depends on the fabric thickness (consider both plain and crossing seams) and on the diameter of the needle thread. The needle should be large enough, and therefore strong enough, to penetrate seam layers without being deflected; also, it should have an eye large enough to allow the thread to pass through it freely.

**Needle sizes 9, 11, 14, 16, 18**

Loosely constructed knits present no unusual problems; but closely constructed knits of nylon or polyester fibers, or those with a heat-set or fused surface, resist the needle's penetration. As a result, the needle forces the fabric downward, loosening it under the foot, before it penetrates; and this loosening of fabric may cause skipped stitches. Closely constructed fabrics also cling to the needle, choking off the flow of needle thread and causing skipped stitches. To overcome skipping from these causes, change to a finer needle and a finer but strong thread.

The **needle point** must be of a shape that will not damage the fabric. Sharp-pointed needles tend to pierce the yarns and sometimes cut them, whereas ball-point needles tend to separate the yarns when penetrating the fabric.

Regular 15 x 1, No. 2020, SINGER* needles have a modified point and thus are appropriate for all-purpose use on wovens and loosely constructed knits. SINGER needle No. 2021 has a ball point and thus is appropriate for many knits.

Regular (2020)    Ball Point (2021)    Side View   Back View   Leather (2032)

Knit (2045)

A **special needle for knits** is the SINGER ball-point needle No. 2045. In addition to the ball shape of the point, it has other features that make it stitch knits more dependably. It has a deeply cut flat side at the top, which brings the needle close to the point of the sewing hook and thus prevents skipped stitches; and it has a slanted crosswise groove just above the needle eye to let the hook pass without striking the needle as the stitch is being formed. The long groove on the opposite side of the needle is wider and deeper than on other needles to prevent the needle-thread supply from being choked off as the knitted fabric hugs the needle. These No. 2045 needles can be used only on SINGER sewing machine Models 750, 758, 737, 717, 719, 640 series, 413, 416, 418 and 252. On other models they are likely to strike the needle guard of the sewing hook.

Knit-backed vinyl, synthetic leather, or thermoplastic-coated fabrics should be sewn with a special **wedge-point needle,** style 15 x 2, No. 2032. These needles make a small, clean slash in the fabric. This kind of penetration is appropriate for leather and leather-like coated fabrics but not for other knits.

**Blunt, bent, or out-of-set needles** can cause stitching problems on knits. A needle is blunt when its point has been flattened or burred. Tightly constructed polyester or nylon knits wear off the needle point amazingly fast. A blunt needle will cause snagged or broken yarns and will make a thumping sound as you stitch.

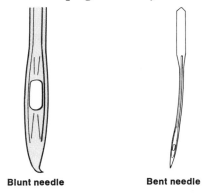

**Blunt needle**      **Bent needle**

A **bent needle** is usually caused by striking a pin, the presser foot, or a nonyielding crossing seam. Or it may be caused if fabric is removed from the machine by pulling it when the needle thread is above the presser foot. A needle can also be bent by changing from a straight-stitch to a zig-zag setting while the needle is in the fabric. A bent needle will cause skipped stitches and it may cause the seam to pull to the side as you stitch.

An **out-of-set needle** is one in which the lower part is angled in a different direction from the top part. To test for correct set, remove the needle from the machine and place it flat side down on the slide plate, holding it at the top. You should be able to see an even space between the needle and the plate for the full length of the needle blade. If the space is uneven, the needle will cause skipped stitches and should be replaced.

**Out-of-set needle**

A **sticky or coated needle** can cause skipped stitches after several seams have been stitched. The solutions used to stabilize the stretch in knits, or to impart permanent-press qualities, often remain in fabrics and rub off. (Excess finishing solutions can be removed by laundering before the fabric is cut.) Sometimes, the synthetic fibers themselves cause the needle to be coated. This coating results from the heat generated by the friction of the needle penetrating the fabric at a fast and constant speed.

Regardless of cause, the resulting skipped stitches can be corrected by cleaning or replacing the needle. To clean the needle, pass it repeatedly through an emery-filled cushion or wipe it with a cloth moistened with SINGER oil. Clean the long groove carefully and thoroughly.

## The Thread

Knit sewing demands the correct size and kind of thread. Because of the overriding importance of thread size, however, you cannot always match the fiber of the thread with that of the fabric. The most reliable rule to follow is to use the strongest fine thread available so that you can use a fine needle for stitching. This rule is especially important when you sew firm, tightly constructed knits. The following comments on thread types will help you to make a wise choice.

**Size A silk** is often the best available thread for nylon and polyester knits; it is fine and strong, and it allows you to use a size 11, fine needle.

**Size A nylon** 3-cord thread is also fine and strong but not as widely available as silk.

**Fine spun polyester,** marked for lingerie sewing, is a little more wiry and harsh than silk or nylon, but it allows you to use a size 11, fine needle.

**General-purpose spun polyester,** which is suitable for heavier knits, must be used with a size 14 needle.

**Polyester core** that has a mercerized-cotton wrap is a general-purpose thread with stretch and strength, but it must be used with a size 14, medium needle.

**Mercerized cotton,** size 50, is generally available in all colors and should be used in a size 14,
medium needle. (Occasionally, you can break the rule and use mercerized thread in a size 11, fine needle, but the thread may fray or break.) Mercerized cotton lacks strength and stretch for knits. It is satisfactory only for seams that are stayed with tape or woven underlining, or seams that are stitched with the straight stretch stitch.

**Size D silk,** known also as buttonhole twist, should be used with a size 16 or 18 needle for top-stitching seams, collars, and faced edges where a heavy thread accent is desired.

## The Stitch

A balanced straight stitch will produce a smooth, strong seam that will elongate slightly as the fabric stretches; when this stitch is made with silk or synthetic thread, it will stretch a little more.

By regulating the needle-thread tension, you can achieve a balanced straight stitch on almost every kind of fabric. A straight stitch is balanced if it looks the same on both sides.

**Both tensions correct**

Before making any change in your tension setting, however, make a test stitching on two layers of the fabric, using the thread and needle you have selected for stitching the garment. Start with a 12 stitch length and a straight-stitch setting. Inspect the stitching. Both sides should look the same If the seam is puckered, shorten the stitch and test again. Seam pucker caused by too long a stitch should then disappear.

**To correct an unbalanced stitch** when the thread on the *upper* side of the fabric looks straight and tight, loosen the needle-thread tension by turning the dial to a lower number and test again.

**Tight upper tension**

**To correct an unbalanced stitch** when the thread on the *under* side looks straight and tight, tighten the needle-thread tension by turning the dial to a higher number and test again.

**Loose lower tension**

*If thread loops* appear on the underside, the needle-thread tension is too loose; tighten it and test again.

**Very loose upper tension**

Some nylon knits require a higher needle-thread tension than you would ordinarily choose for thin supple fabrics. The reason is that nylon hugs the needle and retards the flow of thread.

Once the bobbin-thread tension is set at a normal and versatile setting, you should seldom need to change it on most machines, and never on *Touch & Sew\** machines.

**There are some things you should not do.** One is to attempt to test the bobbin-thread tension by pulling and feeling it. This test is invalid because every machine has a bobbin-thread pull-off device that supplies an increment of thread for each stitch; thus, what you feel is not the same tension as when the stitch is being formed. Neither should you set the needle-thread tension so low that there is no tension on it at all. With little or no tension on the needle thread, the take-up lever will pull thread from the spool instead of retrieving the thread loop from the bobbin case. The result, at best, is short thread loops on the underside of the seam and, at worst, a thread jam in the bobbin case.

Do not assume that seam pucker is caused by tensions balanced at too high a level. Seam pucker on knits is more often caused by too long a stitch, or too heavy a thread, or too coarse a needle.

## Starting to Stitch

Many home sewers have formed careless habits for starting a seam. The combination of soft, tightly constructed knit fabric and strong synthetic thread makes it necessary to start seams carefully if you are to avoid having the machine stall from tangled threads on the underside of the seam or in the bobbin case. In extreme cases, threads will jam tightly under the bobbin case and pull the soft fabric down into the throat-plate needle hole.

When sewing on knits with strong synthetic threads, always place both bobbin thread and needle thread under the presser foot, across the feed diagonally to the right and back. Position the

fabric and lower the needle into it *before* lower-the presser foot. The needle should enter the fabric at least ½ inch from the end of the seam. Before

starting to stitch, grasp both the needle and bobbin threads; hold them securely in a position to the right and back of the presser foot; and then begin to stitch forward slowly for one or two stitches. When backstitching, stitch only to within ¼ inch of the end of the seam and then stitch forward.

## Handling the Fabric

"Fabric handling" refers to the way the seam layers pass under the presser foot. Three elements affect fabric handling: the selection of sewing machine accessories, the degree of presser-foot pressure, and the way you control the seam layers by hand when stitching.

**Machine accessories.** Select proper machine accessories for the work you are doing. (For the various types of stitches suitable for knits, see page 427.) Plain and stretch straight stitching on knits should be done with the straight-stitch presser foot and throat plate. These accessories hold the fabric very close to the needle; the small opening in the throat plate supports the fabric upon penetration of the needle; and the presser foot strips the fabric from the needle as it is withdrawn.

**Straight-stitch accessories**

Zig-zag stitching must be done with the zig-zag throat plate and the general-purpose presser foot or one of the special feet that accommodate the stitch width.

**Zig-zag accessories**

Loosely constructed knits—such as sweater, chenille, raschel, and novelty-yarn knits—sometimes catch over the toes of the general-purpose presser foot. To overcome this, simply cut a short strip of plastic transparent tape to ¼-inch width and wrap it around the foot, encasing both toes. Remove the tape after the project has been completed.

**¼"**

**Tape**

The **overedge foot** is designed for finishing edges or narrow seam allowances. (Available in the attachment set of many SINGER* sewing machines, the overedge foot is also available for separate purchase for both straight-needle and SINGER slant-needle zig-zag machines.) This foot may be used for a plain zig-zag stitch, an overedge stitch (use Disc 22 on slant-needle machines), or an overedge stretch stitch (available on SINGER sewing machine Models 750, 758, 737, 717, 719, 413, 416, and 418). The overedge foot is narrow and has a wire-like pin that extends from the front to beyond the needle. The stitch is

formed over the pin, which prevents the seam edge from curling or crushing. The pin also holds the fabric down when the needle is being withdrawn and helps to prevent skipped stitches on tightly constructed knits. The overedge foot should be used with the zig-zag throat plate, and the needle should be set at "right" position to ensure that the needle straddles the pin.

**Overedge foot**

The **Even Feed sewing machine foot** is a very important accessory that solves many of the stitching problems presented by knits. By providing top feeding action, which works with the feed of the machine, it ensures that all seam layers feed evenly, with no puckers. At the same time, it prevents skipped stitches by providing a perfectly timed "hold" and "lift" action: the frame of the foot holds the fabric firmly when the needle is down and lifts on the feeding stroke. Finally, this foot eliminates the need to hold the fabric under tension during stitching.

The Even Feed foot can be used for straight and zig-zag stitching, as well as for forward and reverse stitching. Use it for stay stitching, machine basting, stitching seams, and topstitching through several layers of fabric. Use it also whenever instructions suggest a roller presser foot, because the Even Feed foot performs the same functions better.

**Even Feed foot**

**Presser-foot pressure** is the force that the presser foot exerts against the seam layers. It is regulated by a dial inside the face plate or a dial or screw at the top of the presser bar. Presser-foot pressure holds the fabric in place while the stitch is being formed. When the pressure is correct, the top and bottom layers of fabric move as one layer under the presser foot.

When the pressure is too heavy, the top layer will lag behind the bottom layer, the bottom layer will pucker, and the seam will be uneven. Also, the presser foot or feed may make a permanent impression on the fabric. Pressure that is too light causes other problems. On heavy, spongy knits, the stitch length will be shorter than the setting indicates; the seam will not feel firm when you guide it; and crossing seams will stall under the foot. On firm, tightly constructed knits, the fabric will loosen under the foot, causing skipped stitches.

Guiding the seam

Pressure dial

Decrease

Increase

Most knits should be stitched at a normal or medium pressure setting, even those that appear soft and supple but are tightly constructed.

To arrive at the best pressure setting for a specific fabric, cut two 12-inch strips and "stitch" a seam without thread. If the two seam layers come out evenly at the ends, the pressure setting is correct for the feeding stroke. Then thread the machine and stitch with thread. If the stitch length is uniform, with no skipped stitches, the pressure setting is correct. However, if the seam ends come out unevenly in the first test, try decreasing the pressure a little at a time. If, on the second test with thread, there are skipped stitches, increase the pressure to see if skipping can be eliminated. If this does not work, check the other possible causes of skipping discussed earlier.

**_Manual control of the seam layers_** is sometimes necessary to improve stitching if you are not using the Even Feed sewing machine foot. Such control is called "guiding and supporting" the seam. The

illustration indicates the hand position for guiding the seam and applying tension to the fabric while you stitch. This control does three things: 1) It prevents the fabric from loosening under the foot as the needle penetrates and is withdrawn from the fabric, thus preventing skips. 2) It stretches the seam while the stitch is being formed and puts more stretch into the seam when it is relaxed to its normal length. 3) It enables you to put ease in one seam layer and not the other when the construction calls for it. The recovery characteristic of most knits makes this method of handling ease possible; on woven fabrics, it is not appropriate.

Guiding and supporting the seam

## The Nine Knit Groups

The following chapter gives sewing guidelines for four of the nine basic groups of knits; these four are the types traditionally thought of as knits, such as single and double knits, raschel knits, and sweater knits.

Guidelines for the five special groups —tricot, spandex, terry, fake leather, and fake fur—begin on page 455.

# TYPES OF STITCHES

Today's sewing machines offer a wide variety of stitches that are appropriate for sewing knits. Take advantage of this variety for the special purposes described below.

**Straight** stitch. Use with strong thread for stitching plain, pressed-open and double-stitched seams.

**Straight stretch** † stitch. Use for stitching plain, plain, pressed-open and double-stitched seams.

**Narrow zig-zag,** 1 to 2 stitch width. Use for stitch-pressed-open and double-stitched seams.

**Wide, open zig-zag,** 3 to 5 stitch width. Use for finishing seam, facing, and hem edges.

**Chainstitch.** Use double row, made from opposite directions, for double-stitching seams in thin knits. Use single row for stay stitching where some give is desired.

**Overedge** †† stitch. Use for finishing seam, hem, and facing edges and for seams stitched and finished with one row of stitching.

**Overedge stretch** † stitch. Use for finishing seam, hem, and facing edges and for seams stitched and finished with one row of stitching.

**Slant overedge** ††† stitch. Use for finishing seam, hem, and facing edges and for seams stitched and finished with one row of stitching.

**Blindstitch.** Use a 5 stitch width for finishing seam, hem, and facing edges; a 2 to 3 stitch width for blindstitching hems. When guided with seam allowance to left, the blindstitch duplicates the overedge stitch.

**Multi-stretch** † stitch. Use for finishing and flattening seam, hem, and facing edges and for top-stitching seams in spandex power net for girdles and swimwear.

**Multi-stitch zig-zag** stitch. Use for finishing and flattening seam, hem, and facing edges and for top-stitching seams in spandex power net for girdles and swimwear.

**Featherstitch** † for topstitching spandex power net for girdles and swimwear.

†Made with a *Flexi-Stitch*\* disc, built in or inserted.
††Can be obtained with disc 22 or 32, available separately for all SINGER slant- and straight-needle zig-zag machines with interchangeable *Fashion*\* discs.
†††Available on SINGER sewing machine Models 413 and 416.

# Knits for Dressmaking

## IDENTIFYING YOUR KNIT

Both the kind of garment and the characteristics of the knit fabric must be considered when selecting a pattern and a sewing procedure. It is important to consider the amount of stretch, recovery ability, thickness, loft, and surface texture of the fabric. The following four groups of fashion knits have both similarities and differences, and some fashion knits will fall on the borderline between groups. However, by treating knits in groups, instructions can be simplified and made easier to understand.

- Firm Dress- and Costume-Weight Knits and Bonded Knits
- Raschel and Rough-Textured, Medium-Firm Knits
- Sweater and Loose, Lofty, Stretchable Knits
- Single and Thin, Supple Knits

**Determine the degree of stretch** in your fabric so that you can identify the group into which it falls. Measure and mark exactly 8 inches on the width of your fabric. Do this at least 6 inches from all edges. Mark each point with a thread marking, made with a single stitch, and tie the thread ends together. Hold the fabric at one width mark between the thumb and fingers of your left hand, and at the other width mark between the thumb and fingers of your right hand. Then gently stretch the fabric against a ruler, stretching the fabric only as far as it will go without distortion. Take a reading for the amount of stretch in the width. With the fabric relaxed, measure it again and take another reading; this will indicate the recovery ability in the width.

In another area of your fabric, mark 8 inches on the length, and follow the same procedure to determine the degree of stretch and recovery in the length.

Using the reading for the amount of stretch in the crosswise direction (width), classify your fabric according to the scale below.

If an 8-inch portion stretches in the crosswise direction:

—to 9¼ inches or less, it is a firm, stable knit;

—to more than 9¼ inches but less than 10½ inches, it has medium or moderate stretch;

—to 10½ inches or more, it is a stretchable knit.

428

*The amount of crosswise stretch* is the primary factor in determining the suitable pattern classification, the amount of fitting ease needed, and the sewing methods to use.

*Knowing the amount of lengthwise stretch* will give you a clue as to how much lengthwise ease you may need to allow in the bodice of a garment with a waistline joining, or in the crotch length of pants. It will help you decide the kind of stitch, thread, and seam construction needed to prevent lengthwise seams from breaking, and it will guide you in deciding whether to tape seams.

*Knowing the degree of recovery,* or the ability of your fabric to return to its original length or width after being stretched, will tell you how well your fabric will hold its shape when you wear it. It will help you decide whether to line or underline it to prevent bagginess.

With respect to knits, *patterns* made by the four major companies may be classified in three categories:

*Those that are designed primarily for woven fabrics* but that list specific firm, stable knits that are also suitable. These patterns include standard basic ease allowances beyond actual body measurements and design ease allowances appropriate for the specific style.

*Those designated as "Recommended for Knits" or "Suitable for Knits."* These patterns have standard basic ease plus appropriate design ease allowances. They differ from the first group only in that the styling elements and lines are especially good for knits. They, too, will indicate specific knit fabrics on the pattern envelope.

*Those designated for "Stretchable Knits Only."* These patterns are smaller in comparison with other patterns of the same type and size. Less total ease, both basic and design, has been incorporated into the pattern; and shaping, normally achieved by seams and darts, is minimal. They are designed to utilize the stretchability of the fabric for both shaping and ease. These patterns should not be used for woven fabrics or firm and medium-firm knits. And they are suitable only for those with attractive body proportions.

## PREPARING, CUTTING, AND PRESSING KNITS

### Preparing Knits

Double knits and warp knits made of **polyester** or polyester and cotton have a permanent-press finish; therefore, they cannot be straightened by diagonal pulling. Simply fold, right side out, on a lengthwise rib. Place fold along table edge and cut crosswise ends square with the end of the

table. Baste crosswise ends together and lengthwise edges together. To shrink and to remove excess finish, launder the basted fabric in the same way you plan to launder the garment. Set your washing machine for gentle motion and warm water, and use a mild soap or detergent. An anti-static fabric softener is also recommended. After laundering, put the fabric and a dry Turkish towel in a dryer set for low temperature. (The towel will help to remove moisture from the fabric.)

Remove fabric from dryer before completely dry. If you do not have a washer with a gentle-motion cycle, wash fabric by hand. If you do not have a dryer, roll fabric in towels to take off most of the moisture and dry over a shower rod. Pressing before cutting is seldom necessary.

*Wool* jersey and double-knit fabrics can usually be straightened by pulling them diagonally. Fold, right side out, on a lengthwise rib. Lengthwise edges may not match exactly because tubular knits are sometimes cut crookedly. Single knits are more likely to be crooked than double knits. If the fabric is extremely crooked, there is no way to straighten it perfectly. Merely square the ends by placing the lengthwise fold along a table edge, and cut the crosswise ends square with the table end. Baste crosswise ends and lengthwise edges. Have the dry cleaner shrink the fabric.

If a knit that cannot be straightened has a **prominent crosswise** stripe or pattern, shrink it without squaring or basting the ends and edges.

*Raschel knits* with a soft finish are often made of acrylic fiber, which is washable. With right sides together, fold at center along a lengthwise chain. Lengthwise edges will be straight because they are knit on flat-bed machines. The crosswise yarns are very prominent and can be followed when cutting the ends straight.

Raschel knits with a sheen are usually polyester and can be treated the same way as acrylics.

Lace-patterned raschel knits should be handled in accordance with the fabric-label instructions. Some are washable; others must be dry-cleaned. Washable lace-patterned raschel knits should be shrunk before cutting; dry-cleanable ones should not.

Soft, loosely constructed raschel knits should be machine-stitched singly along crosswise edges before laundering to prevent raveling. Fold in center, baste ends and edges together, and launder.

*Bonded knits* should be straightened according to the rules for the face fabric. They are usually not labeled washable and usually do not need to be shrunk. Cut bonded knits folded right side out to make it easier to match designs.

*Sweater knits* labeled washable can be hand-laundered before cutting but they should be dried on a flat surface to prevent stretching out of shape. Wool sweater knits should not be laundered before cutting unless labeled otherwise. Machine-stitch along crosswise edges in a single layer to prevent raveling. If fabric is tubular, do not cut on lengthwise rib before shrinking or when laying out the pattern unless the layout calls for it.

*Single knits* that are labeled hand washable should be shrunk in warm water. Those labeled machine washable can be machine-washed. It is a good idea to test-launder a 6-inch square of the fabric to find out whether it shrinks and whether the colors run or fade. If there is no shrinkage, skip the shrinking step; if there is color fading, plan to dry-clean the garment rather than launder it.

## Cutting

There are seven rules that apply to cutting all knits.

**1.** If knit fabric has a prominent lengthwise rib, fold the fabric right side out along a lengthwise rib.

**2.** If knit fabric has a prominent crosswise stripe, yarn, or pattern, treat it as you would a woven fabric with a crosswise stripe, matching stripes at corresponding notches.

**3.** Do not let fabric hang over the table edge because it will stretch out of shape.

**4.** Follow "with nap" pattern layout diagram. Because of their loop construction, knits have an up-and-down direction.

**5.** When pinning pattern to fabric, use ball-point pins. Pin sparingly and only within seam and dart allowances.

**6.** Use heavy, sharp shears and long cutting strokes.

**7.** Cut extended notches on firm knits and mark notches on loosely constructed knits with tailor's tacks.

If a **knit with a prominent crosswise stripe** or pattern cannot be straightened, cut it in a single layer, giving the crosswise detail precedence over the lengthwise rib. To reproduce the needed additional half of the pattern, cut duplicate pattern sections in plain tissue paper. Mark a crosswise grain line perpendicular to the lengthwise grain line on all pattern pieces and place the crosswise grain line parallel to the crosswise stripe. Match crosswise details at corresponding seam lines. To produce right and left sleeves, lay the sleeve pattern on the fabric twice, once face down and once face up.

**Knits with a sharply pressed fold** should be cut to avoid letting the fold fall within a pattern section. A sharply pressed fold can seldom be entirely removed with pressing. When parts of the pattern must be placed on a fold, create a new fold and place pattern edges on it.

## Pressing

Pressing during construction is essential with all knits.

Iron temperature must be regulated according to the fiber content. When pressing blends, do not exceed the iron-temperature setting for the fiber that has the lowest heat tolerance. Always test-press a fabric scrap in which you have made a dart and a seam. Test for heat setting and amount of steam needed.

Never use the iron directly on the fabric. Protect the fabric with a dampened press cloth of thin cotton or cheesecloth; or use an attachment that covers the bottom of the iron and allows steam to escape through its perforated surface.

A softly padded ironing board is better for knits than a firmly padded one. Final pressing on the right side of the garment, and with the fabric protected from direct contact with the iron, will give a smoothly pressed surface because the impressions of seams, darts, and hems will be made in the soft surface of the ironing board rather than in the garment.

Trimming excess bulk from seam allowances and darts on knits is just as important as careful pressing. Slash narrow darts and press them open; then trim seam allowances diagonally within the crossing seam allowance. Press bustline darts

downward and trim the layer next to the garment to ½ inch; trim the other layer on the fold line. This method of trimming will hold the seam allowances of the dart in position and reduce bulk.

Square-cut the dart seam allowances at the crossing seam.

In hems, trim the seam allowances to half width from hem fold to hem edge.

On loose, lofty knits, use a blocking, rather than a conventional, pressing technique. "Blocking" means creating steam without iron pressure on the fabric. Cover the fabric with a moist cloth. Apply the iron to produce steam but do not allow the full weight of the iron to rest on the fabric. Move the iron from one position to another by lifting it rather than sliding it. Remove press cloth. Use a pounding block to flatten seams and eliminate steam. Do not move the garment section until it is dry.

**Yarn-pulls** may show up as you press. To repair a yarn-pull, grasp the fabric and stretch it along the pull to work as much yarn back in place as possible. Then insert the wire of a wire-loop needle threader through the fabric at the yarn-pull from the wrong side of the fabric. Pass the pulled yarn through the wire loop and draw it to the inside of the fabric.

Conventional sewing and sweater construction methods, either singly or in combination, are used to sew knits. The method you select will depend on both the characteristics of your fabric and the type of garment you are making. This section will acquaint you with the various types of seams and construction methods called for in later instructions on various types of knits.

## Plain and Double-Stitched Seams

Seam allowances in knits should be wide enough to support the structure of the garment, but they should not be too wide or they will roll and have excessive bulk. Seams should stretch and not break with the motion of the body. The strength and stretch of a seam are determined by the strength of the thread, the type of stitch, and the way the seam is handled. In the following instructions, wherever strong thread is indicated, use silk or synthetic thread.

### Plain seam—straight stitch

• Straight stitch, 12 to 15 stitch length; or straight stretch stitch.
• Straight-stitch presser foot or Even Feed foot; straight-stitch throat plate.
• Strong thread; ball-point needle of appropriate size.

• Prepare seam with hand basting when necessary.
• Stitch seam under tension by guiding and supporting, except when using the Even Feed foot.

• Press seam as stitched, then press open; cut off notches and leave edges unfinished.

### Plain seam—narrow zig-zag stitch

• Narrow zig-zag stitch, 1 to 2 width, 15 to 20 stitch length.
• General-purpose presser foot, overedge foot†, or Even Feed foot; zig-zag throat plate.
• Strong thread, ball-point needle of appropriate size.
• Prepare seam with hand basting if necessary.
• Stitch seam under tension by guiding and supporting, except when using the Even Feed foot.
• Press seam as stitched, then press open; cut off notches and leave edges unfinished.

†Use left needle position setting when using overedge foot. Test placement of zig-zag stitch over pin at left of foot before stitching.

### Double-stitched seam

• Stitch on seam line with straight, straight stretch, or narrow zig-zag stitch.
• Stitch again ⅛, ¼, or ⅜ inch outside seam line. Width depends on fabric weight, kind of garment, and desired width of finished seam allowance.

- Trim seam allowances near second stitching.
- Press seam as stitched, then toward the front on side and shoulder seams, and toward the sleeve on armhole seams.

## Double-stitched seam, mock-overedged

- Stitch on seam line with straight, straight stretch, or narrow zig-zag stitch.
- Stitch again ⅛, ¼, or ⅜ inch outside seam line. Width depends on fabric weight, kind of garment, and the desired width of the finished seam allowance.

- Use blindstitch (illustrated) or one of the following stitches:

| | |
|---|---|
| Overedge† | Multi-stretch zig-zag†† |
| Overedge stretch† | Slant overedge ††† |
| Multi-stitch zig-zag†† | Plain zig-zag† |

- Use zig-zag throat plate and general-purpose presser foot, overedge foot†, or Even Feed foot.
- Trim seam allowances near stitching and press.

†Use a stitch width less than 5 for seam-allowance widths less than ¼ inch and use left needle position with overedge foot.
††Use to finish and flatten seam allowances in bulky knits.
†††Available on **SINGER** sewing machine Models 413 and 416.

## Double-stitched seam, overedged (Above)

- Stitch on seam line with straight, straight stretch, or narrow zig-zag stitch.
- Trim seam allowance to ⅛†, ¼, or ⅜ inch, depending on fabric weight and kind of garment.
- Use zig-zag throat plate and general-purpose or overedge foot.
- Stitch over the trimmed edges with overedge, slant overedge, or overedge stretch stitch.

†Use a stitch width less than 5 for seam widths less than ¼ inch and use left needle position with overedge foot.

## Seams stitched and finished with one stitching

- Use only for seam allowances ¼ inch or less† in width.
- Hand-baste on seam line if necessary.
- Trim seam allowances to ¼ inch or less.††
- Use general-purpose throat plate and overedge foot.
- Stitch over seam-allowance edges, placing straight edge of overedge, slant overedge, or overedge stretch stitch on seam line.

†Use a stitch width less than 5 for seam-allowance widths less than ¼ inch and use left needle position with overedge foot. Seam-allowance widths less than ¼ inch are suitable for sheer nylon tricot only.
††Place seam allowance to left when stitching.

## Stayed Seams

Neckline, shoulder, and waistline seams usually need to be stayed to prevent stretching and to support the shape of the garment. Other seams may also need to be stayed, depending on garment styling. Woven-edge seam binding and ¼-inch-wide twill tape are firm and do not stretch. Bias seam binding of rayon is pliable and allows for some stretch, and it prevents seam slippage on open knits of medium firmness. Shrink woven-edge seam binding and twill tape and, if seam line is curved, press it to shape before applying it.

*Front shoulder seam.* Baste seam line, center the stay tape, and stitch through stay and seam at the same time. Press seam as stitched, then press open.

*Neckline.* Baste neckline including interfacing, garment facing, and stay tape (pressed to shape and centered on seam line). Stitch on seam line. Press. Then trim seam allowances to uneven widths. Press seam open, then turn and understitch facing to seam allowances.

*Waistline.* Baste and stitch waistline seam. Position edge of stay tape near seam line and stitch along edge. Trim seam allowances even with out-side edge of tape. Finish tape and seam allowances together with multi-stitch zig-zag.

*Bias stay for flexible seam.* Cut rayon bias seam binding through center. Open fold, place it along the seam line, and stitch.

The seam may be a plain seam pressed open; and the edges may be finished or unfinished, depending on the fabric and construction. Or the seam edges may be trimmed even with the stay. Turn all edges toward seam edge and form a double-stitched seam with a blindstitch edge finish. This treatment is recommended for raschel knits and other open knits that tend to show seam slippage under strain.

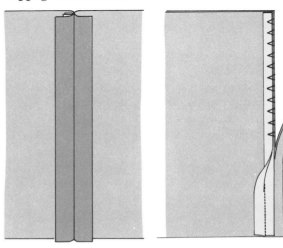

Interfacing in collars and facings is just as important for firm and medium-firm knits that are constructed like conventional garments as it is for woven fabrics. You should omit interfacing only when you use sweater-knit construction methods. The interfacing fabric may be a soft woven fabric when you need only to increase the stability of the interfaced section. It may be a nonwoven fabric, such as all-bias, polyester nonwoven interfacing, when you need to increase the stability and add loft to the section. Or, it may be tailor's canvas or hair canvas when you want a crisp, tailored look in a lapel or collar detail. Handling the interfacing so as to eliminate seam bulk is especially important with knits.

## Soft woven and nonwoven interfacing

• Baste interfacing (soft woven or all-bias polyester nonwoven) to wrong side of under collar.†

• Baste upper collar to under collar unit, right sides together, and ease upper collar slightly along seam line.

• Stitch on seam line, forming blunt corners by making one or two stitches diagonally across corners.

• Trim seam allowances to uneven widths, keeping the upper collar seam allowance widest. Notch seam allowances along outside curves.

• Press seam, then steam-press seam allowances open over a seam board.

• Turn seam allowances toward under collar and understitch from facing side through facing, interfacing, and all seam allowances.

## Tailor's canvas or hair canvas interfacing

Where a firm, crisp texture is desired—as in faced-front and open-neckline styles, collars, pockets, pocket flaps, and cuffs—either of the canvas interfacings can be handled in three different ways:

### Method 1—organza strip

• Measure, mark, and cut the seam allowance from the interfacing.

• Attach canvas to a shaped section of organza (or crisp, thin underlining fabric), 1½ inches wide, with multi-stitch zig-zag stitching.

• Baste interfacing unit to wrong side of garment section and facing to right side with right sides together.

• Stitch on seam line near the edge of the interfacing.

---

† To reduce collar thickness, under collar may be made of color-matched taffeta or another crisp, woven fabric.

### Method 2—catch stitch

• Measure, mark, and cut the seam allowance from the interfacing.

• Baste interfacing to garment with the edge along the seam line.

• Catch-stitch interfacing to seam line.

• Baste and stitch facing as described in Method 1.

### Method 3—fusibles

• Cut iron-on interfacing or interfacing and fusible web from pattern and carefully cut off all seam allowances.

• Fuse interfacing to the upper collar; to the upper side of cuff, pocket, or pocket flap; and to the facing of a neckline, lapel, or garment-front, depending on the design. Follow the instructions for the fusible material being used.

• Stitch facing and garment section on seam line near edge of fused interfacing.

## BOUND BUTTONHOLES

Bound, piped, or corded buttonholes are suitable for firm knits. Make them according to your favorite method. Finish them through the facing in a way that reduces the seam layers to a minimum. Baste the facing securely with a lengthwise basting along the inner edge. Make crosswise bastings above and below each buttonhole. Using a 20 stitch length and the straight-stitch presser foot, stitch around the buttonhole from the right side, letting the needle enter the crevice of the buttonhole stitching. Slash through the facing at the center of the buttonhole from the right side. Then turn the garment and trim the facing close to the stitching line on each side of the buttonhole. The result will be a smooth, sturdy finish on the facing side and almost invisible stitching on the right side.

# BANDS AND BINDINGS

Fabric bands, shaped facings, and edge bindings are especially suited to knit fashions. They eliminate the bulk of conventional facings and add a special interest. Knowing how to apply them will enable you to vary simple patterns in ways that add a professional touch to your clothes.

## Shaped bands

- Appropriate for firm, stable knits.
- Cut shaped band by pattern, 1½ to 2½ inches wide plus seam allowance.
- Cut interfacing for band from crisp, thin, color-matched fabric.
- Stitch and trim edge as illustrated. *(Below left)*

- Position band on wrong side of garment with right side of band facing the garment.
- Pin, baste, stitch, and trim neckline and front seam allowances. Press and turn band to right side of garment.
- Diagonally baste neckline and front edge.
- Baste free edge to garment and slip-stitch invisibly.
- Remove all basting and press.

- Press and turn to place seam on inside of band. Then hold edge, favoring right side, with diagonal basting.
- Baste 1 inch from neckline and front edges through band and interfacing to keep edges in place.
- Trim seam allowance plus ⅛ inch from interfacing near 1-inch basting line.

## Straight bands

For firm and medium-firm knits, straight-cut bands form practical finishes for V necklines and sleeve ends. They can also substitute for a hem at the bottom edge of the garment. Cut the fabric lengthwise twice the width of the finished band plus two ½-inch seam allowances.

### V necklines

Three methods for completing the band at the point of a V neckline are: seamed and opened, hidden seam, and crossed. Regardless of method, the preparations are the same and start with cutting. Do not cut the front of a neckline on the seam line, but cut as a high round neckline.

Using a piece of pulpy paper, such as newspaper or practice-weight typing paper, mark the outline of the V, both the seam line and the cutting line,

providing a ½-inch seam allowance. Pin the marked paper to the wrong side of the front section and stitch with a straight stitch, 15 stitch length, on both the seam line and the cutting line; pivot and blunt the point by making one stitch across it. Tear away the paper and slash the center

front as far as the cutting line, leaving the extra fabric beyond the seam line until the entire band is completed. Stay-stitch the back neckline exactly on the seam line and trim seam allowance to ½ inch. Then stitch and press shoulder seams. Be sure the V neckline is deep enough to allow the finished neckline to slip over your head without strain, or use a center-back zipper.

### Seamed and opened

- Fold strip in center, right side out, to form band; press.
- Pin-mark center back of band.
- Starting at center of both back and band, with right sides together, pin together along seam

• Turn garment to wrong side and fold on center-front basting, carrying fold through the band matching the pin marks. The line should be straight from pin marks through point of V and along center-front fold. Baste band ends together along this line to form a miter.

• To stitch miter, lower needle $\frac{1}{8}$ inch from point where band folds meet. Carefully backstitch two stitches, then forward only far enough to meet the seam-line stitching that joins the band at the V. Backstitch two stitches. Tie the thread ends at both ends of this stitching.

line. Slash back neckline seam allowance in several places almost to stay stitching. Do not ease or stretch. Continue pinning one side to V point. Baste if necessary.

• Stitch, garment side up, from center back to V just inside the seam-line stay stitching, stopping exactly at the end of the V. Carefully backstitch three stitches and tie threads.

• Slash V to stitching line.

• Repeat for second side.

• Place the front of garment right side up over the end of the ironing board. Extend folded edges of band toward neck opening and extend seam allowances toward garment. Let the ends of the band fold under, adjusting the fold to form a center line above the V point. Pin-mark the band at the edges where the centered folds meet.

• Press band ends open along mitered seam and pin ends to seam allowances. Trim excess length from bands.

• Working with garment wrong side up, extend seam allowances and stitch 1/16 inch outside seam line through all layers including end of band. Do this on both sides of V. See detail in circle on opposite page.

• Trim seam allowances to uneven widths and finish with an overedge stitch.

• Press from right side over a padded surface to give a soft seam, being careful not to bring up the impression of the seam allowances. Do not press with iron directly on fabric; use a press cloth and light steam.

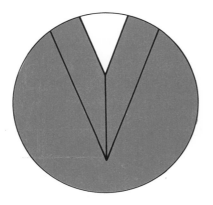

### Miter, hidden seam

• Cut strip for band, but do not fold. Mark center back of band with basting.

• With right sides together, start at center back to pin one edge of band to garment along seam line. Slash seam allowance almost to stay stitching in several places at back neckline curve. Do not ease or stretch. Continue pinning one side to V point. Baste if necessary.

• With garment side up, stitch from center back to V barely inside seam-line stay stitching, stopping exactly at the end of the V. Carefully

backstitch three stitches and tie threads.

• Slash V to stitching line.

• Repeat for second side.

• Turn garment wrong side out, fold entire front on center basting, and pin. Extend band, letting seam allowances extend toward the garment. Cut off ends of band straight and even, ¼ inch beyond end of V. Pin seam lines of band together along V and pin unstitched edges of band together for 4 inches. Pin along exact center of band.

• To form a stitching line for the V miter, baste through the band in a straight line following the center-front fold, from point of V to center of band. Turn and continue basting from the center of band in a straight line to the seam line of the band (½ inch from outer edge, ¼ inch from end), forming a V.

• Stitch along basting, blunting V miter point by taking 1 stitch across point. Backstitch at both ends of this stitching.

• Trim seam allowance to ¼ inch and press seam open.

• Unpin and unfold garment.

• Pin bottom ends of band together with miter seams matching, and continue pinning the seam allowances of the band together along the entire neckline. Baste.

• Stitch through seam allowances of neckline and band, from wrong side of garment 1/16 inch outside neckline stitching.

• To reduce bulk, trim seam allowances to uneven widths—garment to ¼ inch, inside band seam edge to ⅛ inch, and outside band to ⅜ or ½ inch. Overedge seam allowances.

• Place garment right side up over a soft surface; cover with a press cloth and lightly steampress the neckline.

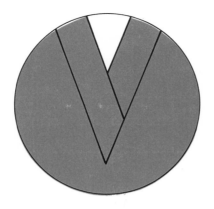

### Crossed bands

- To form band, fold strip in center, right side out; press.
- Pin-mark center back of band.
- With right sides together, start at center back (on the right-hand side of a garment for a woman and the left-hand side of a garment for a man). Pin together along seam line. Slash seam allowance almost to stay stitching in several places at back neckline curve. Do not ease or stretch. Continue pinning one side to V point. Baste if necessary.
- With garment side up, stitch from center back to V barely inside the seam-line stay stitching. Stop exactly at the end of the V, carefully backstitch three stitches, and tie threads.
- Slash V to stitching line.
- Repeat for second side, but end the stitching about 1½ inches above point of the V.

- Turn the garment right side out and slip it over the end of the ironing board; let the band extend toward the neckline and the seam allowances toward the garment. Cross the ends of the band at the V point by letting the end of the band on the stitched side pass over the band on the unstitched side and into the unstitched seam.

Arrange the garment front so that it is smooth and the V is not distorted. Place a pin through both layers of the band at the V. Using a press cloth and steam, press lightly along the stitched seam line, but avoid pressing over the pin and unstitched seam.

- Turn the garment inside out and stitch the open portion of the seam barely inside the stay stitching from the garment side to the point of the V. On second side, stitch 1/16 inch outside the seam line through all seam layers, including the extended portion of the crossed band.

- Trim seam allowances to uneven widths, leaving the bottom seam allowance widest.
- Finish with machine overedging. See detail of underside of neckline, in circle on opposite page.

## Open-front, sleeve, or hem edge finish

- Estimate length needed for band and add 1 inch. Width of finished band may be from ½ to 3 inches, depending on styling. To determine cutting width, add 1 inch to twice the finished width. Cut a continuous strip or plan locations of seams

to match cross seams. Leave ends unstitched until later. Band may be interfaced if desired.

- Fold band in center, right side out, and press lightly.

- Open band and, with right sides facing, pin one edge to the garment, starting with the center of the band. Do not ease or stretch. With garment side up, stitch to within 2 inches of the end of the band.
- Repeat for second side.
- Determine the exact location for seaming the ends of the band together (or the exact location for finishing each end of an open band). Stitch, trim seam allowances to ¼ inch, and press seam open.
- Stitch open portion of band, overlapping stitching lines.
- Press seam open and trim seam allowance of band to ¼ inch for bands wider than ½ inch. Do not trim seam allowance on ½-inch bands.
- Fold band along center crease, match the seam edges of the band and the garment, and pin them together. Baste through seam allowances only. Steam-press from right side, using a press cloth.
- Extend seam allowances and stitch from the wrong side, garment side up, through the seam allowances only, 1/16 inch outside the previous stitching.
- Machine-overedge the seam edges together or trim garment seam allowance to ¼ inch and overedge one edge only.

## Stretched Bands

Stretched bands, sold as "ribbing," are usually made of rib knit or a knit made of textured yarn that has a great deal of stretch and a strong recovery. Stretched bands are used: 1) at sleeve ends to ease or gather a wider sleeve end into a smaller band that fits snugly; 2) at or below the waistline of a sweater, overblouse, or jacket to shape the edge to the figure; 3) at the neckline to form a crew neck, mock turtleneck, or turtleneck finish; and 4) at the armhole of a sleeveless shell for a snug fit.

In all cases, the length of the band is determined by: 1) the body measurement at the location it is to fit or pass over and 2) the amount of tension that you want on the band as it is worn. The seam allowances for both band and garment are ¼ inch. Cut the band so that the direction of greater stretch is on the length of the band.

If the band is to form a closed circle (which would be the case except for the waistline of a cardigan), seam the band ends together with a narrow double-stitched seam. Then, fold the band right side out and pin the seam allowances together.

To ensure even distribution of fullness or ease, pin-mark both the band and the garment in four equal parts. Locate the joining where it will be noticed least and pin the band to the right side of garment, all seam edges even, matching pin locations of the equal parts.

Place garment under presser foot, band up, eased side toward feed. Set machine for a straight stretch stitch or an overedge stretch stitch, which seams and finishes at the same time. Stretch and stitch simultaneously; keep the work under tension by holding the seam both in back and in front of the presser foot, but allow the feed to carry the fabric. Stretch the band until the edge it is being applied to lies flat but is not stretched. Steam the seam by holding the iron above the fabric to assist the seam and band to recover to an unstretched length.

*For a crew neck,* cut the band 3 inches wide and, if you are working with a basic pattern with a round neckline, cut the crew neckline below the normal seam line, ¾ inch lower at center front tapered to ¼ inch lower at shoulder. This new cutting line allows for a ¼-inch seam allowance.

*For a turtleneck,* which turns back on itself, cut the band or ribbing about 9 inches wide and use a basic round neckline, but trim the seam allowance to ¼ inch.

**For a mock turtleneck,** which does not turn back, cut the band or ribbing 4 to 4½ inches wide and use a basic round neckline, but trim the seam allowance to ¼ inch.

## Blocked-to-shape Bands

Double knits of polyester, wool, or blends of these fibers, as well as some warp knits and single knits of these fibers, can be steam-pressed or blocked into shapes such as those used for accenting rounded pocket flaps, U necklines, rounded yokes, and patch pockets.

· Trace the outline of the finished edge on a large piece of laundered muslin or sheeting. Pin this to your ironing board cover to use as a shaping guide.

· Cut the strip for the shaped band twice the finished width plus two ½-inch seam allowances.

Cut either lengthwise or crosswise, after testing a short length to determine the best choice for shaping.

· Hand-baste edges of strip together, leaving one end of basting long and unknotted. Press lightly to form crease.

· Pin-mark band at center and position center of band at center of the marked shaping guide. Baste band to guide across center.

· Plan to use the surface of the band that is up as the underside in the garment in case some shine develops from pressing.

· Using a dampened cheesecloth over the band and working from the center basting, apply steam, stretch the band, and pin it along the cut edges, keeping the fold edge even with the marked line. Working with only a few inches of the band at a time, slightly ease the fold edge and stretch the cut edge. Place pins along the outside edge into the padding of the ironing board so that you can press over them without marring the band. When the entire band has been shaped and pinned, steam-press again to give a permanent set to the detail. Polyester knits will retain this shaping after laundering, as will wool after dry cleaning.

· Apply as described on page 443, Open-Front, Sleeve, or Hem-Edge Finish.

## Bound, Piped, and Corded Edges

Bound, piped, and corded-edge finishes on knits differ from those on woven fabrics: on knits, the free edge may be finished with an overedge stitch; on wovens, the free edge is turned to the inside or covered with a facing. Fabric strips, which may be cut lengthwise, crosswise, or bias, are perfect for knits because they eliminate facings that often show an impression on the right side. These strips can be applied to an unstitched edge, to an edge that has been stay-stitched on the seam line for moderate control, or to an edge stayed with woven seam binding for firm control.

### Bound Edge

For a ¼-inch-wide bound edge, cut a strip 1¼ inches wide and overedge one edge. Trim garment on seam line. Place bias strip over garment, edges even and right sides facing. Stitch ¼ inch from edges, as at **A**. Press seam allowances open. Turn strip over one seam allowance and hand-baste through center of binding, as in **B**. Turn garment wrong side up; extend both the seam allowance and the finished edge of strip. Stitch 1/16 inch outside first stitching line, as at **C**.

Remove basting and steam-press to shape binding and free edge, as in **D**. Tack edge at crossing seams.

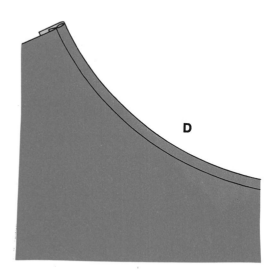

## Piped Edge

For a piped edge, cut a strip 1½ inches wide and finish one edge with the overedge stitch. Fold back the unfinished edge ½ inch and steam-press, as in **E.** Trim garment on seam line. Place prepared strip right side down and garment edge over it, also right side down. Pin garment edge to strip, matching edges as at **F.** With general-purpose presser foot on machine, straight-stitch, 15 length, ¼ inch from edges, using edge of foot as a guide. See **G.** Remove pins before stitching over them. Fold strip to underside, letting piping extend from stitching line. See **H.** Steam-press to shape the piping and the free edge of strip. Tack edge at crossing seams.

## Corded Edge

For a corded edge, cut strip 1½ to 2 inches wide, depending on diameter of cord. Fold strip over cord, right side out, near one edge of strip; allow ¼ inch to extend beyond the stitching line at the cord on one side and ¾ inch on the other. Machine-baste, using the cording foot, as in **I.** Finish the wider edge of the strip with machine overedging. Trim garment edge on seam line. Place prepared strip right side down with garment edge over it also right side down, edges matching as in **J.** Pin; then stitch, using the cording foot adjusted to the left of the needle and very

close to the cord as shown. Remove pins as you stitch. Fold strip to underside, letting the cording extend, as in **K.** Steam-press to shape the cording and the free edge of the strip. Tack edge at crossing seams.

## Soft-Roll Edge Finish

A bound edge with a bold, soft roll is an attractive finish for the neckline and armholes of tank tops and jumpers. Trim the garment edges to allow for a ½-inch seam allowance. Cut the strip for binding 2¾ inches wide on the crosswise direction of the knit. Set your sewing machine for a 15 stitch length and attach the straight-stitch presser foot. Then, with right sides together, stitch the binding strip to the garment ½ inch from edge; stretch the strip slightly at the curves, as in **A**.

Press seam allowances and stitching to remove any ripples along the curve. Then roll the binding over both seam allowances and place pins perpendicular to the edge along the crevice of the seam, catching the unfinished side of the binding, as in **B**.

Stitch in the crevice of the seam from the right side, using the zipper foot adjusted to the left side of the needle, and a 15 to 20 stitch length, as at **C**. When stitching is completed, trim the seam allowance of the binding close to the stitching.

## Elastic Waistbands

In most knit skirts and pants, you may omit the placket unless you have a larger-than-average difference between your waist and hip measurements. Test the knit fabric for suitability by making a test waistband. In the direction of the greatest stretch, cut a strip of fabric 3 inches wide and long enough to go around your waistline. Machine-baste the ends together, making the band the same measurement as your waistline. Fold the band right side out and hand-baste edges together, leaving ends of basting free. Step into the waistband and bring it up over your hips to the waistline. If it does not stretch enough to go over your hips without undue strain, you should use a zipper placket.

If the waistband does slip over your hips easily, you may go ahead with the construction of the elastic waistband.

There are two basic types of elastic waistbands: 1) those in which the elastic is enclosed in a separate band, which is then applied as a unit to the garment; and 2) those in which the garment fabric is cut to provide an allowance for a hem or casing through which the elastic will run.

Even though an elastic waistband is used, pants and skirts are generally more flattering if darts are used for shaping at the waistline; however, sweater knits and knits that stretch freely look better without darts.

### Elastic enclosed in separate band

• Cut waistband twice the width of the elastic plus two ⅝-inch seam allowances and the length of your waistline measurement plus two seam allowances.

• Stitch the ends of the strip together, press seam open, and fold strip right side out to form a band. Press.

• Cut ¾- to 1-inch-wide elastic long enough to go around your waistline under slightly more tension than you need for a snug fit, since some tension on the elastic will be lost in the construction.

Add 1 inch to the length for an overlapped joining and then hand-whip the joining.

• Divide and pin-mark both the waistband and the garment into four equal portions.

• Place elastic inside band and pin seam allowances of band together at 2-inch intervals.

• Pin waistband unit to garment waistline, right sides together, matching the four points that divide the two edges into equal portions. Place waistband joining seam at center back or at a side seam.

• Equip machine with the zipper foot or the overedge foot, and set the machine for a narrow zig-zag or a straight stretch stitch. Test-stitch to see that machine settings are correct and that the needle does not strike the foot.

• Place garment under foot, right side down, with open edge of foot against the elastic.

• Stitch slowly, stretching the band if necessary and easing the garment seam to the band.

• Trim the center seam allowance to ¼ inch and machine-overedge the remaining seam allowances together. See illustration at bottom of previous column.

• Tack seam allowances to crossing seams.

### Elastic enclosed in hem or casing

• Measure waistband elastic to fit snugly around your waistline and add 1 inch for overlapping ends. Hand-whip overlap of elastic together.

• Machine-overedge waistline seam allowance of garment.

• Turn garment hem over the elastic and pin at lower edge of elastic at 2-inch intervals. Hand-baste if necessary. Stitch with garment right side up, open side of zipper foot against elastic, and use a straight stretch stitch.

• To prevent elastic from turning, distribute ease evenly over the elastic, pinning through casing and elastic at crossing seams. Stitch in the crevice of each crossing seam through the casing and the elastic from the right side. Tie thread ends.

### Elastic stitched to casing

• Measure and cut ¾-inch waistband elastic 1 inch less than your waist measurement.

• Overlap ends ½ inch and stitch joining.

• Divide elastic and waistline into 4 equal parts and mark with pins.

• Place top edge of the elastic ⅛ inch from edge on inside of the garment.

• Using the general-purpose presser foot and the straight stretch stitch, stitch near the lower edge of the elastic while holding the garment and elastic under enough tension to stretch the elastic to fit the fabric.

• Turn the elastic and fabric once to the inside. The elastic will then be covered.

• While holding the fabric and elastic under tension, stitch near the edge of the elastic through the turned fabric, the elastic, and the garment. Again, use the general-purpose presser foot and the straight stretch stitch.

## SLEEVES

Always set sleeves in firm and medium-firm knits by the conventional method for woven fabrics and finish the seam allowances, ⅜ inch wide, together.

On stretchable knits, follow the sweater method. Stitch the open sleeve to an open armhole and stitch the underarm and sleeve seams later as one continuous seam. Patterns that are designed for stretchable knits and recommend this method have a sleeve with less cap width and less ease than regular patterns. Work with ⅜-inch seam allowances on both the armhole and the sleeve cap.

• Pin sleeve to armhole, matching symbols at top of sleeve cap, at front and back notches, and at the underarm seams.

• Using the straight stretch stitch, straight-stitch presser foot and throat plate, and with garment side up, stitch from top of sleeve cap to underarm seam. Stretch the seam as you stitch.

• Overlap the stitching at the top of the sleeve cap and stitch the second side of the sleeve.

• Apply an overedge finish. On thin knits, where a narrower than ⅜-inch seam allowance is appropriate, trim seam, then overedge.

• Stitch underarm and sleeve seam the same way, matching crossing seams at the underarm.

• Apply steam to assist recovery of shape.

## HEMS

Follow the same preparatory steps for hemming as for hemming woven fabrics. Select a hem-edge finish that has the least bulk for your knit. Always use either the blind hemming stitch or the blind catch stitch, both of which go between the hem edge and the garment and not over the edge. For most firm or heavy knits, use the double-stitched hem in which two rows of blind hemming stitches support the weight of the hem.

## FABRICS

**Characteristics.** These knits are stable and have the hand of woven fabrics, minimum lengthwise stretch, and crosswise stretch of less than $1\frac{1}{4}$ inches in 8 inches.

**Types.** Double knits; bonded knits; firm, untextured warp knits; jacquard knits.

**Fiber Content:** All polyester, all wool, fiber blends and yarn mixtures of wool/nylon, wool/polyester, cotton/polyester, nylon/acrylic, etc.

## PATTERN CHOICE

**Dresses**—look for simple style lines; darted or seamed shaping; pocket details; topstitched seams; soft pleats; collars, cuffs, facings; eased fullness; A-line, fitted one-piece styling; waistline joinings.

**Also**—separates, pants costumes, jackets, soft suits, children's wear, light- or medium-weight coats, some slacks and jackets for men.

## PREPARATIONS

- Fold on lengthwise wale or rib, square ends, baste ends and edges for shrinking (unless fabric is labeled "preshrunk").
- Woolens—have shrunk by tailor or dry cleaner.
- Polyesters—launder to remove excess finishing solution.
- All other washables—launder by hand or machine according to label.
- Bonded knits—straighten according to face fabric; shrinking is usually not necessary.

## PATTERN FITTING

- Purchase your regular pattern type and size.
- Allow no less than basic ease allowances.
- Fit pattern accurately to reduce garment fittings during construction.

## CUTTING AND MARKING

- Fold fabric right side out on lengthwise rib.
- Follow "with nap" layout.
- Pin with ball-point or smooth, new pins.
- Cut with sharp shears.
- Cut notches outward.
- Mark center front and back lines with hand basting.
- Mark internal details with tailor's tacks.

## STAY STITCHING

- Stay neckline and waistline seams with regular straight stitching (12 stitch length) or chain-stitching.
- Use Even Feed foot to avoid easing or stretching seam line.

## STITCHING

- These fabrics are generally easy to stitch.
- Use size 14 regular or ball-point needle with polyester-core or spun-polyester thread.
- Use size 11 regular or ball-point needle with silk or nylon thread.
- Balance tensions.
- Use normal or regular presser-foot pressure.
- Set stitch length at 12 for straight seams, at 15 for curves.
- Kinds of stitches: regular straight stitch with strong thread; straight stretch stitch; narrow zig-zag ($1$-$1\frac{1}{2}$ stitch width).
- Guide and gently support seam while stitching, holding it under tension with both hands, or
- Use the Even Feed foot.

## SEAMS AND SEAM FINISHES

- For general use: Use plain seams pressed open, no seam finish.
- For unlined jackets, coats, pants, armhole of set-in sleeves: Use straight-stitched seam, pressed in one direction, cut to $\frac{3}{8}$ inch or half-width, and edges finished together with machine overedge.
- To accent style lines: Topstitch seams with buttonhole twist or heavy thread. Use the Even Feed foot to reduce need for basting.
- For seams that must not stretch, such as shoulder and waistline seams: Use stayed seams.

## FACINGS, INTERFACINGS, LININGS, UNDERLININGS

- Finish shaped facings with machine overedge stitch. Always understitch facing to seam allowances.
- Use lightweight woven or nonwoven interfacing for dresses.
- Use lightweight tailor's canvas in the conventional way to interface jackets or coats.
- For quick method, apply interfacing to facing with thermoplastic adhesive, but cut off seam allowances.
- Underlining or lining is optional for dresses, but recommended for tailored jackets or coats.

## PRESSING

- Limit iron temperature to that for fiber with lowest heat requirement.
- Use damp cheesecloth to produce steam.
- Press at each construction step.
- Place heavy paper under seams and darts to keep them from marking the right side when pressed.

## HEMS AND EDGE FINISHES

- For fashion garments—use blind hemming methods; consider also the double-stitched hem.
- For pants, sleeves, children's dresses and straight hems in fashion garments, use machine blind stitch.
- Edge finishes, such as folded straight-cut bands and cross- and diagonal-cut bindings, may be used instead of conventional hems.

## FABRICS

**Characteristics.** These knits have:
—firmness without rigidity
—loft without cumbersome bulk
—soft, supple hand
—parallel rows of chainstitching on back of fabric, which hold filling yarns together.

**Types.** Raschel (often with embroidery-like surface) and other nubby knits that have medium stretch in both directions.

**Fiber Content:** Wool, polyester, acrylic cotton blend. Yarn may be smooth, looped, or chenille type.

## PATTERN CHOICE

**Dresses**—look for simple lines, ease for shaping (gathers disappear as ease), soft unpressed pleats, set-in or raglan sleeves.

**Pants**—long and graceful or short.

**Vests**—long, sleeveless.

**Skirts**—wrap-around, gathered, or softly pleated.

**Also**—scarves, stoles, coats, hooded capes.

## PREPARATIONS

- Fold lengthwise on chainstitch visible on back of fabric, right sides together.
- Cut ends crosswise along single filling yarn.
- Pull diagonally to square ends.
- Baste ends and edges for shrinking when necessary.
- Polyesters—launder to remove finishing solution.
- Woolens—have shrunk by tailor or dry cleaner.
- Acrylics—usually need no shrinking.
- Cottons—refer to label; should be easy-care and ready-to-sew.

## PATTERN FITTING

- Purchase your regular pattern type and size.
- Allow no less than basic ease allowances. (Remember, these fabrics have minimum-to-medium stretch.)
- Fit pattern accurately, to reduce garment fittings during construction.

## CUTTING AND MARKING

- Fold right sides together on lengthwise chain.
- Match patterns or designs.
- Determine which end of chain will unchain and use that end for tops of all pattern pieces.
- Lay out pattern according to "with nap" direction.
- Place pins close together; do not allow fabric to hang over table edge.
- Cut with long, even strokes, using sharp shears. Do not cut notches.
- Mark with basting lines and tailor's tacks.

## STAY STITCHING

- Do **not** use conventional stay stitching.
- Through a single layer of fabric, stitch ¼ inch from seam edges to prevent raveling, using straight stitch, 15 stitch length.
- Do this on all edges except bottom edges of sections before you begin any construction.

## STITCHING

- These fabrics are generally easy to stitch.
- Use size 14 regular or ball-point needle with polyester-core or all-polyester thread.
- Use size 11 regular or ball-point needle with silk or nylon thread.
- Balance tensions.
- Set stitch length at 12 for straight seams, at 15 for curves.
- Use normal or regular presser-foot pressure.
- Encircle presser-foot toes with a ¼-inch width of transparent tape to prevent loops of fabric yarn from catching on presser foot.

## SEAMS AND SEAM FINISHES

- You do not need to stay seams that are stitched with the straight stretch stitch.
- Stay seams that are stitched with regular straight stitch to prevent pulling or "slipping." Use woven-edge or rayon bias seam binding, or twill tape. Shrink before using.
- Trim seam edges to eliminate frays.
- Finish seam edges separately when open, or together when pressed in one direction, with a zig-zag seam finish:
  1) overedge (Disc 22) and overedge foot.
  2) multi-stitch zig-zag.
  3) multi-stretch (Disc 55).
  4) blindstitch pattern.
  5) overedge stretch (Disc 59).

## FACINGS, INTERFACINGS, LININGS, UNDERLININGS

- Facings—standard shaped facings for less bulky varieties; color-matched taffeta or soft-surfaced woven fabric for bulky knits. Understitching is appropriate. Optional: instead of using facings, finish edges with braid, bindings, or self-fabric bands.
- Interfacing—nonwoven or woven, soft or crisp, depending on styling. Test see-through effect and color-match interfacing to knit or underlined interfaced portion.
- Lining—optional, depending on styling.
- Underlining—optional, depending on styling. If you use underlining, preserve soft, supple hand of combined fabrics and color-match.

## PRESSING

- Limit iron temperature to that for fiber with lowest heat requirement.
- Use damp cheesecloth to produce moisture.
- When pressing soft-surfaced raschels: stop pressing before fabric is dry; brush surface with soft brush or piece of same fabric; do not move fabric until dry.
- Press at each construction step.

## HEMS AND EDGE FINISHES

- For fashion garments—use blind hemming methods; consider also the double-stitched hem.
- For casual garments—straight-stitch hem by machine, but hem edge should be machine-finished rather than turned.

## FABRICS

**Characteristics.** These knits look and act like hand knits; stretch freely in both directions; shape to the body; and have a loose, lofty look.

**Types.** Patterned, plain, or rib knits.

**Fiber Content.** Wool, polyester, or acrylic fibers or blends of these fibers.

## PATTERN CHOICE

Choose patterns marked "for knits only" or with close-to-the-body styling.

**Dresses**—straight and slim with few or no darts, set-in or raglan sleeves, scoop or high neckline.

**Vests**—long, sleeveless.

**Sweaters**—cardigan or turtleneck.

**Pants outfits**—with sweater overblouse.

**Scarves, ponchos.**

**Note:** Sweater knits can also be used for couturier two-piece, tailored outfits if they are mounted over a firm, layered base of underlining, thin hair canvas, and lining. In this case, construction methods are the same as for woven fabrics.

## PREPARATIONS

- Relax fabric by allowing it to lie flat on floor or table overnight.
- Cut ends along crosswise courses.
- Fold on lengthwise rib, right side out.
- Pull diagonally to straighten crosswise ends.
- Square ends with table edges.

## PATTERN FITTING

- Pattern should accommodate body measurements only. All ease can come from the fabric itself for both length and girth measurements.
- Often, one size smaller than you normally wear is adequate.

## CUTTING AND MARKING

- Observe grain-line principles.
- Pin sparingly.
- Do not let fabric hang over table edge.
- Lay out pattern according to "with nap" directions.
- Cut with strong, sharp shears.
- Do not cut notches.
- Mark with basting lines and tailor's tacks.

## STAY STITCHING

- Do **not** use conventional stay stitching.
- Through a single layer of fabric, stitch $1/4$ inch from seam edges to prevent raveling, using straight or chainstitch, 12 stitch length. Stitch slowly and neither ease nor stretch edges. The Even Feed foot helps with this stitching.
- Mount very loosely knit fabrics on tissue or pulpy paper for this stitching. Tear away paper after stitching.

## STITCHING

- Requirements: 1) a stitch that will elongate, such as a straight stretch stitch, plain zig-zag ($1/2$-1 stitch width, 20 stitch length), or a plain straight stitch (15 stitch length) done under tension. 2) strong thread, such as polyester core or spun polyester with size 14 needle; or nylon or silk with size 11 needle.
- Use normal or regular presser-foot pressure.
- Balance tensions.
- Use ball-point needle to prevent snags.

## SEAMS AND SEAM FINISHES

- Usually, seam edges are pressed and finished together. Pressed-open seam edges tend to roll.
- Most seams should **not** be stayed so that they will stretch with body movement.
- To prevent drawn seams, hand-baste. Leave bottom thread end long and free. Allow garment sections to hang overnight. Then stitch.
- Seams that should not stretch, such as some shoulder, back-of-neck, or waistline-joining seams, should be stayed with woven-edge seam binding or narrow twill tape (both shrunk).
- Seams that should stretch but need some support can be stayed with $1/4$-inch "light soft" elastic.
- Select a seam-finishing stitch that will stretch, flatten, and retain the yarn ends but will not be harsh.
- Apply the seam-finishing stitch first, then trim seam allowance to $1/2$-to-$1/4$-inch width. Heavy fabrics usually have wider seam allowances than medium-weight fabrics.

## FACINGS, INTERFACINGS, LININGS, UNDERLININGS

- Not used, except for unusual styling; e.g., couturier 2-piece outfits are mounted over color-matched underlining, lightweight canvas interfacing, and a soft lining.

## PRESSING

- Limit iron temperature to that for fiber with lowest heat requirement.
- Block rather than press. Steam, holding iron above the pressing surface, and allow fabric to dry before moving it with both hands.

## HEMS AND EDGE FINISHES

- For dress hems—use a machine seam finish for edge and blind hemming for stitching hem; consider also the double-stitched hem.
- For sweater hems—use seam finish for edge and machine blindstitch for hemming.
- Apply finishing bands or folds of knit fabric, cut for greatest stretch, to finish neckline, sleeve ends, armhole, or bottom edge. These bands may be applied with or without being stretched, depending on styling.

## FABRICS

**Characteristics.** Knits in this group are thin and supple; have moderate to maximum crosswise stretch and moderate lengthwise stretch; and tend to cling to the figure.

**Types.** Solid-color, printed, or knitted with a design. Surface may be brushed, dull or lustrous. Yarns may be filament, textured or crimped.

**Fiber Content.** Cotton, wool, triacetate, polyester, acrylic, or nylon.

## PATTERN CHOICE

Fashion uses these fabrics for three distinctive "looks"—skinny and covered, elegantly draped, and comfortably supple.

**Dresses**—sportive, casual, dressy, or high-fashion.

**Leisure Wear**—turtleneck tops, gathered and scoop-neckline tops, shirts, draped jumpsuits. Children's dresses and fitted tops and men's shirts.

## PREPARATIONS

- If fabric is tubular, cut on lengthwise rib.
- Plan not to use fold, which seldom will press out.
- Refold on lengthwise rib for cutting.
- Square and cut ends of fabric with table edges.
- Launder to shrink washable fabrics.
- Have dry cleaner shrink wool.
- Before cutting out pattern, relax fabric by allowing it to lie flat on table or floor overnight.

## PATTERN FITTING

- Purchase your regular pattern type and size for supple or draped styling.
- Purchase patterns labeled "For stretchable knits only" for the skinny and covered look.
- Fit and alter pattern carefully before cutting to reduce number of fittings during construction.
- Handle design ease in accordance with the fashion look you intend to interpret.

## CUTTING AND MARKING

- Cut on soft surface.
- Do not let fabric hang over table edge.
- Pin difficult-to-control fabrics to tissue for cutting.
- Use ball-point or fine, smooth pins, placed within seam allowances.
- Cut notches outward.
- Mark internal details with tailor's tacks.
- Use a whole pattern piece, rather than a half, for cutting crosswise stripes that cannot be squared.

## STAY STITCHING

- Stay-stitch only neckline and waistline-joining seams.
- Use chainstitch or regular straight stitch, 15 stitch length. Even Feed foot eliminates the need for easing or stretching.

## STITCHING

- For lightweight wool jersey, use silk thread, size 11 needle, regular straight stitch, 12 to 15 stitch length.
- For cotton knits, use fine spun polyester or polyester-core thread, size 11 needle, and regular straight stitch; or ball-point needle, straight stretch stitch and mercerized thread.
- For shiny-surfaced synthetics, use silk or nylon thread, ball-point needle or regular size 9 or 11 needle, and straight stretch stitch or regular straight stitch, 12 stitch length.
- Stitch all seams under tension by holding them in back and front of presser foot, or use the Even Feed foot.
- Normal or above-normal presser-foot pressure.
- Use straight-stitch presser foot and throat plate for all straight stitching.
- If you encounter stitching problems, remember: **Skips** result from too coarse needle, too heavy thread, too little tension on the fabric while stitching, or bent needle. **Fabric pulls** result from too heavy needle and thread or blunt needle. **Puckered seams** result from not supporting fabric while stitching, unbalanced tensions, too tight tensions, too long stitches. **Stitching through paper** next to feed helps to eliminate some puckering and skipping.

## SEAMS AND SEAM FINISHES

- Kind of seaming depends on kind of garment.
- Fashion garments are made with plain, pressed-open seams with no seam finish.
- Casual garments are made with seam edges pressed in one direction, trimmed to 1/4-to-3/8-inch width and finished together.
- The overedge stretch stitch (Flexi-Stitch Disc 59) is preferred for seam finishing.
- Alternatives are: blindstitch, multi-stitch zig-zag, regular overedge (Disc 22), plain zig-zag (3 to 5 stitch width).

## FACINGS, INTERFACINGS, LININGS, UNDERLININGS

- Skinny-look garments need none.
- Slim, straight-line dresses need none in body of garment but require soft interfacing in cuffs, collars, or faced necklines.
- Softly draped fashions usually require soft, firm underlining as a shape-builder.
- Loft is achieved with nonwoven all-polyester, all-bias interfacing.

## PRESSING

- Limit iron temperature to that for fiber with lowest heat requirement.
- Pressing should be gentle and of a blocking nature.
- Use moist cheesecloth to produce steam.
- Do not over-press.

## HEMS AND EDGE FINISHES

- For fashion garments—finish hem edge with straight stitching, 15 stitch length, placed 1/4 inch from straight cut edge, and use blind hemming stitch.
- For casual garments—machine-blindstitch hems.
- Folded bands may be substituted for hems.
- Narrow self bindings are suitable for necklines and armholes.

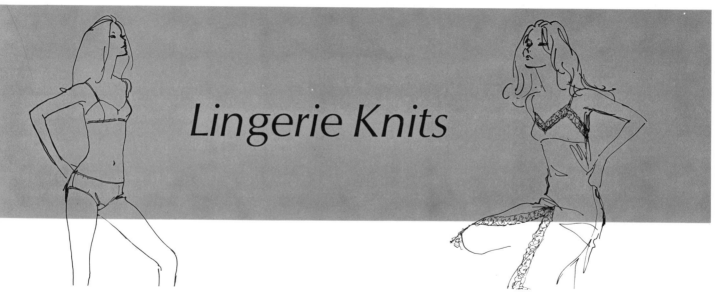

# Lingerie Knits

NOW THAT NYLON TRICOT CAN BE PURCHASED by the yard, many women are finding that sewing lingerie can be both fun and economical.

Lingerie can be made amazingly fast because it requires little if any hand basting, pressing, or hand finishing. Most garments have very few seams, and the elastic and lace finishes are simple to apply with a zig-zag sewing machine.

The very simplicity of lingerie sewing may seem a little strange to you at first. You may have a tendency to overdo each step. But, once you relax, develop a light touch, and realize that a cut edge is acceptable (because tricot does not ravel), you will quickly learn to stitch seams and finishes on your machine without hand basting.

## TRICOT FABRICS

Tricot is a two-thread warp knit that will not run or ravel because of its interlocking yarns. It has fine vertical ribs, or wales, on the right side and crosswise courses on the wrong side; the direction of greatest stretch is crosswise. The fabric is usually 108 inches wide although you may find it sold in narrower widths if the yardage has been split for easier handling.

The fiber content can be all nylon, a blend of nylon and acetate, or triacetate. Some stretch tricot fabrics contain spandex yarns to give light figure control. The surface may be smooth, satin-like, crepe-like, or napped, depending on the texture of the yarn used in knitting.

**Tricot**

Tricot comes in different weights, ranging from very sheer to heavy, depending on the size of the yarn and how closely it is knitted. Heavy tricots are used for robes, pajamas, and opaque slips. Medium tricots are used for panties, slips, night-gowns, pajamas, chemises, and the underlayer of nightgowns and peignoirs designed for two-layer construction. Sheer tricot resembles chiffon and is used for the outer layer of nightgowns and peignoirs, for underlining lace sections and insertions, and for edge trims. Brushed nylon, which has a napped surface, is suitable for warm robes and pajamas.

Stabilized nylon tricot has a special finish that limits its stretch and the amount of static it generates. Thus it is suitable for slips that are to be worn under knit dresses where noncling characteristics are essential.

Stretch tricot is usually made of nylon and spandex yarns and is used for light figure control in panties, briefs, bras, sections of bra-slips, and body suits.

455

# PATTERNS

You can look to three sources for lingerie patterns: the four major pattern brands, special lingerie pattern brands, and your own favorite garments.

Patterns for full slips, half slips, panties, nightgowns, robes, dusters, peignoirs, and body suits are available in your favorite pattern brand and in the usual size ranges. Patterns that are marked "for stretchable knits only" are close fitting and rely on the stretch of the knit for comfort. Patterns that are marked "suitable for knits" have enough ease for woven fabrics, but their style lines are also appropriate for knits.

There are also patterns available from sources that make patterns for lingerie, girdles, and swimwear only. These are usually multi-size patterns that can be used for any size within a range of sizes, depending on which cutting line you use. Because these patterns usually have seam allowances other than the standard ⅝-inch width, it is wise to read the pattern instructions carefully.

The most challenging type of pattern is the one you cut yourself from a favorite garment. There are two ways to proceed.

*Method 1.* Cut apart a discarded garment. Cut on the seam lines and carefully lay each section on paper, keeping lengthwise and crosswise lines true. Mark the edges and then mark a ¼-, ½-, or ⅝-inch seam allowance, whichever is most appropriate for the garment, and cut out the pattern on the cutting lines. Check corresponding seam lengths and cut notches to identify the seam lines that join.

*Method 2.* Transfer the shape of each garment section to paper without destroying the garment. Make either a half or a whole pattern for each major section and a whole pattern for small sections. Work on a padded surface such as an ironing board or table. Fold the garment at the center front. For a half pattern, pin the fold to the straight edge of the paper; for a whole pattern, pin the garment fold to the folded edge of the paper. Keeping lengthwise and crosswise lines straight, plunge pins through the garment seam lines into the paper and padded surface at short intervals (every ½ inch on straight seams; every ⅛ inch on curved seams). Remove the garment and draw the seam lines, following the pinholes in the paper. Add seam allowances and mark cutting lines. Follow the same procedure for each large section, and mark all edges for small sections.

Because tricot is so wide, you will usually be cutting two or more garments at one time; you will find this easier if you lay out whole, rather than half, patterns.

# NOTIONS AND TRIMMINGS

**Needles and thread** must be fine; thread must also be strong. Nylon twist, silk, and fine spun polyester labeled "for lingerie" are the best threads for stitching tricot because they can be used with fine needles. Choose size 11 ball-point needles, Singer number 2021 or 2045. Size 11 regular needles will also work satisfactorily in many cases, but ball-point needles are recommended because they are especially designed for stitching knits.

**Lace** is an important edge finish for tricot garments and for decorative sections and insertions. Choose nylon or polyester lace because it requires no ironing and wears well. Lace comes in three forms. Lace for edging has one selvage edge and one decorative edge; it comes in widths from ½ inch to more than 3 inches. Lace for insertions

Edging     Insertion     Galloon

has two selvage edges and comes in widths from ½ inch to more than 3 inches. A third form, galloon lace, has two decorative edges and comes in a variety of widths.

**Elastic** in lingerie is primarily functional but it can also be decorative. The following descriptions of the different kinds of elastic and their uses will enable you to select the one that is best for your purpose.

**Elastic braid** (also called tunneling elastic) is the most familiar type. It looks the same on both sides and on both edges. It has lengthwise ridges of rubber or spandex. When stretched, elastic braid narrows. It comes in widths of ¼, ⅜, ⅓, ¾ and 1 inch. The yarn may be rayon, nylon, mercerized cotton or a blend. Rayon elastic braid relaxes when wet and should not be used for swimwear. Elastic braid is usually drawn through a hem or casing rather than stitched to an edge. Stitching should always be done between the lengthwise ridges; when stitching penetrates the lengthwise ridges, the rubber or spandex is damaged or broken and the elasticity is weakened.

**Elastic braid**

¼″    ⅜″    ½″    ¾″    1″

**Elastic edging** for lingerie can be of either braid or web construction. Braid narrows when stretched; webbing does not. Edging always has one decorative edge that resembles a frill or picot. Widths of ⅝ or ½ inch are suitable for waist-bands of half-slips and panties; widths of ⅜ or ¼ inch, for legbands of panties and briefs. Elastic edging is not enclosed in a casing; it is applied to either the outside or the inside edge of the garment. Refer to page 465.

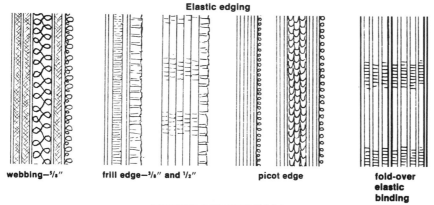

**Elastic edging**

webbing—⅝″    frill edge—⅜″ and ½″    picot edge    fold-over elastic binding

## PREPARATIONS

Launder nylon tricot before cutting the garment to prevent shrinkage later and to remove any finishing solution, which could cause stitching problems. Use an antistatic fabric softener to reduce the tendency of nylon tricot to cling to the needle during stitching. After laundering, place fabric and a dry Turkish towel in a dryer set at low temperature. (The towel will help to absorb moisture.) Remove fabric when not quite dry. If you do not have a low-heat dryer, roll the fabric in a Turkish towel to remove as much moisture as possible and finish drying by draping the fabric over a shower rod.

Pressing should not be necessary; but if there are wrinkles, press at a low temperature, moving the iron in a lengthwise direction only.

Prepare your pattern carefully. Patterns for tricot garments that fit the figure closely should measure at least as much as your figure and preferably 1 to 2 inches more at the hipline to allow ease. If you ordinarily need to increase or decrease the crotch depth on pants, apply the same alteration to lingerie pants patterns. Nightgowns should be roomy enough for comfort, and they look best with considerable ease. All fitting changes should be made at the pattern-alteration step so that construction can be completed without further fitting.

# LAYOUT AND CUTTING

The right side of tricot is the side with fine lengthwise ribs. On sheer tricot, it is sometimes difficult to see the ribs. For a quick test, stretch a crosswise edge. Tricot always rolls to the right side. Mark the wrong side with strips of magic transparent tape.

Lay out the fabric on a large table and do not let the fabric hang over the edge. Because of the 108-inch width, cutting on the floor or a bed is sometimes necessary when a large table is not available. Four layers can be cut at once if you are making a number of identical garments. A layer of tissue paper placed between fabric layers will help you to cut a smooth edge.

Tricot stretches most in the crosswise direction, always cut it with the stretch running across the figure. Cut crotch sections with the stretch running from back to front. Use ball-point pins and pin sparingly, preferably within seam allowances. Placing a square of magic transparent tape, instead of pins, at the top and bottom edge of each pattern piece is useful in holding the pattern on grain.

Cut extended notches to mark corresponding seams, and trim them off as you approach them when stitching. Cut with sharp scissors and be careful to cut all edges smoothly, especially if your pattern has narrow seam allowances.

# PREPARING TO STITCH

Begin your sewing with a lint-free, carefully oiled sewing machine. Put in a new ball-point needle and thread it with fine, strong thread. Set the presser-foot pressure at normal or medium and the stitch length between 12 and 20, depending on the kind of stitch you have chosen to use. Refer to page 427 for appropriate stitches. If you are using a plain straight stitch or a straight stretch stitch, use the straight-stitch throat plate and the presser foot recommended for the kind of stitch and seam you will use. Regulate the needle-thread tension to produce a balanced stitch that looks the same on both sides. The best tension setting is usually a point or two lower than you regularly use for other fabrics. If your sewing machine has a "fast" and "slow" speed setting, use the slow setting because you should stitch slowly enough to control the unbasted seam edges. Remember to guide and support all lengthwise seams with one hand in front and one hand in back of the presser foot to keep the seam under tension during stitching.

Test-stitch seams on fabric scraps before stitching your garment. This will enable you to get the feel of handling the fabric. Also, it will indicate whether your tension, pressure, stitch length, needle and thread sizes are correct.

Always position the needle in the fabric at the start of a seam, then lower the presser foot. Hold the thread ends until a few stitches have been made. This procedure is essential to prevent thread and fabric from jamming at the start. The softness of the fabric, coupled with the strength of the thread, makes this necessary.

If skipped stitches appear, look first at thread and needle size and remember that "fine" is the requirement. To rule out the needle as the cause, it is always a good idea to change the needle. Presser-foot pressure may not be heavy enough, so increase it slightly and also increase the tension under which you are holding the fabric while stitching. Needle-thread tension, unless it is very high, is seldom a cause of skipped stitches.

If skipped stitches appear after you have been stitching for some time, the cause may be that the needle has lost its set and has become slanted away from the sewing-hook point, which picks up the thread loop from the needle. Sometimes you can correct an out-of-set needle by drawing your

thumb down the long-groove side of the needle, exerting slight pressure to flex the needle back into its original position. *Do not* try to bend the needle; merely stroke it a few times, flexing the lower part back slightly. Before testing the stitching, turn the hand wheel by hand to make certain the needle enters the hole in the throat plate without rubbing or striking the edge. Then test-stitch on a fabric scrap.

## SEAMS AND DARTS

### Seams

The following guidelines will help you to handle seams in tricot lingerie.

• Seams in tricot lingerie are always either double-stitched or stitched and finished with a single row of machine overedge stitching.

• Always stitch seams under tension by guiding and supporting the fabric.

• Almost all seams are lengthwise on both the fabric and the garment. The few exceptions are crotch seams in briefs and the horizontal seams at or above the waistline in slips and nightgowns.

• Pin short seams at notches and ends; long seams at 12-inch intervals.

• Finish crosswise edges with elastic, lace, or decorative edge finishes.

**Double-stitched seams.** The kind of double-stitched seam you select will depend on both the abilities of your sewing machine and personal preference. In the two seams where zig-zag or overedge stitches are placed over the seam edges, the straight stitching may be done either before or after the finishing stitch. When the straight stitching is done last, the zipper foot may be substituted for the straight-stitch presser foot.

*Straight or straight stretch stitch.* Use the straight-stitch presser foot and throat plate, center needle position, and a 15 stitch length or straight stretch settings. Stitch on the seam line and again

⅛ inch outside the seam line. Trim seam allowances near second stitching.

*Straight and zig-zag stitches.* Straight-stitch on the seam line as above. Trim seam allowances to ⅛ inch. Use zig-zag throat plate and overedge foot, a zig-zag stitch, right needle position, 2½ to 3 stitch width, and 20 stitch length. Guide seam edges along the right edge of the overedge foot.

*Straight and overedge stitches.* Straight-stitch on seam line as above. Trim seam allowances to ⅛ inch. Use zig-zag throat plate and overedge foot, overedge stitch or overedge stretch stitch, right needle position, 2½ to 3 stitch width, and 20 stitch length. Guide seam edges along right edge of foot. Seams may be double-stitched before trimming if you do not have an overedge foot.

*Chainstitch.* Use chainstitch accessories and 15 stitch length. Stitch on the seam line. Stitch second row close to first row, outside the seam line and in the opposite direction from the first stitching. Stitch the third row close to the second row, outside the seam line and in the opposite direction from the second stitching.

## Seams stitched and finished with one stitching

Some sewing machines are capable of stitching and finishing in one step.

*Overedge stretch stitch.* Trim seam allowances to ¼ inch or slightly less for a seam narrower than ¼ inch. Use the overedge stretch stitch and either the overedge or the general-purpose presser foot. Set stitch width at 5 for a ¼-inch seam or between 3 and 5 for a narrower seam. Use right needle

position setting when using the overedge foot with a stitch width less than 5. Guide the edges of the seam along the right-hand edge of the overedge foot or under the general-purpose presser foot so that the needle goes over the right-hand seam edge rather than through it. The overedge foot prevents the seam from rolling.

*Overedge stitch.* Follow the same procedure as described for the overedge stretch stitch above, but use a 15 to 20 stitch length and the overedge stitch.

*Slant overedge stitch.* Some models of sewing machines make a slant overedge stitch instead of the overedge stretch stitch. Refer to your sewing machine instruction book for machine settings. Trim seam allowances to a scant ¼ inch. Place trimmed seam under general-purpose presser foot with seam edges to your left. For a slightly narrower seam, use a stitch width setting less than 5.

## Darts

In tricot lingerie, darts are usually in the bodice sections of full slips, nightgowns, pajama tops, and bras. Trim away the fold of the dart by cutting a scant ¼ inch inside the stitching lines. Treat the stitching lines as seams. Where the darted section is of more than one layer, stitch all layers as one. With a seam-finishing stitch, stitch from the widest end of the dart to the point, then pivot on the needle and turn the fabric around half circle for the second stitching. Lower the presser foot and raise the needle. Set the machine for straight or straight stretch stitching, and stitch close to the inside of the first stitching. The reason for this procedure is that threads used for lingerie seldom remain knotted and in this way you can achieve neatness.

using general purpose foot, stitch from bottom of dart to point

pivot on needle at point and straight-stitch close to zig-zag stitching

## Seams in Pants

### Crotch Seams in Briefs

Briefs are made from three pattern sections: front, back, and crotch. The crotch section is double with the lengthwise rib running across the section.

Stitch side seam first to ensure correct handling of right and wrong sides of these sections, which can easily be confused if crotch seams are made first.

Join front crotch seam, placing right sides of crotch sections next to the front section, front section in between. Stitch with straight stretch stitch and trim seam allowance to a scant ¼ inch; or trim seam allowances first and stitch with stretch overedge stitch.

Pin back seam of outside crotch section to the right side of the back.

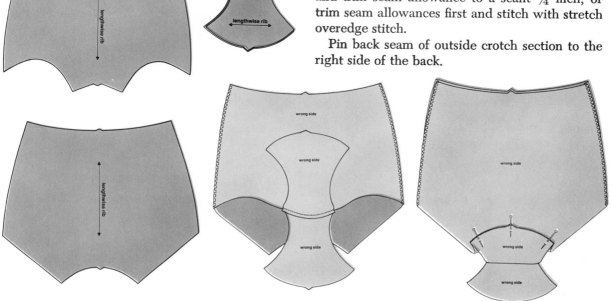

Pin back seam of inside crotch section to the wrong side of the back by bringing it entirely around the top of the briefs, crushing the fabric. Stitch in the same way as the front crotch seam.

Pull the body of the garment through one open side of the crotch section and turn it right side out. Seams will be concealed inside crotch sections.

To finish briefs, refer to *Elastic Finishes* on page 464.

## Crotch seams in flare-leg panties or petti-pants

These garments differ from briefs in that they are usually cut with center front and back seams instead of side seams. This makes the crotch section easy to insert and durable.

There are three shapes for crotch sections. One is a two-piece construction designed with a curved crotch seam from front to back. The other two shapes, the diamond and the modified diamond, are one-piece constructions. All styles have a double-layered crotch, and the sections are cut with the lengthwise rib running from side to side, placing the crosswise rib (the direction of greatest stretch) from front to back. All three crotch types are applied in the same way, but the two-piece crotch requires one preparatory step that the others do not.

To prepare the two-piece crotch, place the sections right sides together. Fold, matching the curved edges, which will form four seam layers. Stitch on the seam line, using the straight stretch stitch, and trim seam allowances to ⅛ inch or use the stretch overedge stitch. Grasp the two center layers and pull them out of one side opening; this places the seam allowances between the remaining two layers. Reverse the fold in the outside layers to flatten the seamed sections. The folds become the finished bottom edges of the inside portion of the legs. Apply lace to finish the outside leg sections of the panties before taking the next step.

To assemble the crotch section and garment, stitch one leg front seam to the corresponding side of the crotch section. Then stitch the entire front seam, continuing across the seam joining and down the other leg seam, joining the remaining side of the crotch. Repeat the same steps at the back.

## Seams in Pajama Pants

Tricot pajama pants are usually cut without side seams. If you need to lengthen or shorten a pattern above the crotch line for pants, you should do the same for pajamas, although pajamas should have at least 1 inch more ease at this point than pants. Stitch the center front and center back seams before stitching the leg seams, using one of the double-stitched seams or the overedge stretch seam. Then stitch the leg seams, starting at the crotch and stitching down one leg first and then the other. Hold the center back seam in one direction and the center front seam in the other, and overlap the stitching at least 1 inch. Finish the waistband with elastic (page 465). Finish the hem as outlined on page 470.

## Setting in Sleeves

There are two ways to set in sleeves in robes, peignoirs, and pajamas. You may follow the conventional method of stitching the sleeve seams and side seams before putting in the sleeve, and trimming and finishing the seam allowances together to ¼ inch. Or, you may use the open construction method. Trim the seam allowances on both the armhole and the sleeve to ¼ inch. Stitch and finish the seam allowances together before the side and sleeve seams are stitched. Then stitch each side seam and sleeve seam as one continuous seam.

## Elastic Braid in Casing

For children's panties, use ⅜-inch elastic for the waistline and ¼-inch elastic for the legs. For women's briefs or panties, use ⅝- or ½-inch elastic for waistline and ¼- or ⅜-inch elastic for legs. Measure elastic around waistline and legs at a comfortable degree of tension, allowing ½ inch for overlap.

**Method 1.** Overlap the elastic at the ends and hand-whip them together along the overlapped edges and ends. Fold top of garment over the

elastic to the wrong side. Let the edge extend beyond the elastic at least ¼ inch. The stitching may be done in one of two ways. Using the adjustable zipper foot and the straight stretch stitch, stitch through the tricot layers alongside the elastic. Or, using the overedge foot and a narrow zig-zag stitch (width 3, length 15, and right needle position), stitch along the elastic through the tricot layers. Trim the seam allowance close to the stitching. Finish the legs the same way.

**Method 2.** Fold waistline or leg edge to the inside, and turn again to form a hem or casing the same width as the elastic. Stitch along the turned edge with a narrow zig-zag or straight stretch stitch. Leave a 1-inch opening through which to draw the elastic into the hem. Join the ends of the elastic as above. Then stitch the 1-inch opening.

***To prevent elastic from twisting*** inside casing, distribute the fullness evenly and pin through the fabric and elastic at center front and back and at the centers between these points. Stitch, holding the fabric and elastic under tension, using plain zig-zag (5 stitch width, 12 stitch length) or multi-stitch zig-zag stitch (5 stitch width, 15 stitch length). Test this stitching on a scrap before stitching the garment because elastic braid with a heavy rib will cause stitching problems that prevent this step.

## Nylon Elastic Lace Webbing

Measure elastic around **waistline at a comfortable tension** and allow 1 inch for joining. Machine-stitch across ends, wrong sides together. Open seam and stitch ¼ inch on each side of seam. Trim ends near stitching.

Place seam at center front. Divide elastic in four equal segments and mark with pins. **Do the same to the garment.** Then pin together at corresponding points, pinning elastic over right side of **tricot,** bottom edge on seam line. Stitch, using a **15 to 20 stitch length and a narrow zig-zag stitch (2 to 3 stitch width)** that is just wide enough to **cover the elastic ridge near the edge. Trim seam allowance near stitching.**

Cover elastic joining at center front with ½-inch satin ribbon folded over the elastic and topstitched on the sides and the lower edge.

## Frill- and Picot-Edge Elastic

Apply narrow elastic to the legs of briefs as described above. Allow 1 inch for overlapping the ends at the side seams for comfort. Catch the ends into the stitching as illustrated.

For a more feminine treatment at the waistline, the elastic may be concealed except for the decorative edge. Place the elastic with frill edge on seam line of garment, right sides together, elastic covering seam allowance. Stitch over the elastic rib nearest the frill, using the general-purpose presser foot and a narrow zig-zag stitch (2 stitch width and 18 stitch length). Hold elastic and tricot under tension as you stitch, and guide the stitching uniformly over the elastic rib. Trim seam

allowance to ¼ inch. Turn elastic to the inside of the garment and, using the multistitch zig-zag stitch (5 stitch width and 15 stitch length), topstitch through the tricot and the center of the elastic while holding it under tension.

# EDGE FINISHES

## Lace Edging

**Method 1.** The easiest and quickest way to apply lace edging is to hold it on top of the tricot, lace selvage edge along the seam line. Use the general-purpose presser foot and a narrow zig-zag stitch (1½ to 2½ stitch width and 15 to 18 stitch length). Allow the starting end of the lace to extend ¼ inch beyond the starting point, which will also be the joining point for the ends of the lace. After stitching all but 2 or 3 inches of the lace edging, and without removing the work from under the needle, measure and cut the free end of the lace ½ inch beyond the starting point. Fold ¼ inch of the lace over the first end and fold both ends another ¼ inch. Whip overlapped lace seam edges together by hand. Continue the zig-zag stitching, overlapping the starting point a few stitches. Pull thread ends to underside and tie. Cut away tricot seam allowance near stitching on inside of garment.

Lace without a selvage can be applied in the same way, but let the decorative edge extend slightly above the zig-zag stitching.

**Method 2.** Place lace over tricot, right sides together, with selvage of lace on seam line and decorative edge away from the seam edge. Stitch over selvage with a narrow zig-zag stitch (1½ to 2 stitch width, 15 stitch length) or along selvage with a 15 to 20 length straight stitch. Turn lace toward the edge, seam allowance toward garment, and topstitch along tricot fold with a narrow zig-zag or straight stitch. Trim seam allowance near stitching on underside. This method is also suitable for lace insertions.

**Tricot appliqué.** Place tricot right side up over right side of lace and pin. Hand-baste, if necessary. Stitch near selvage of lace, using a decorative satin stitch ("fine" stitch length, 5 stitch width), such as the open scallop or crescent pattern. Trim tricot seam allowance outside decorative stitching and trim lace inside decorative stitching from the underside. Any width of lace with or without a selvage may be used.

## Sheer Footing or Fold Tricot Appliqué

Net footing or a fold of sheer tricot may be used for an edge finish instead of lace. Hand-baste the fold underneath the tricot edge above the seam line. Using a decorative zig-zag stitch, such as the crescent pattern, stitch on the seam line. Trim tricot along the outside edge of the stitching, and trim the underneath edges of the applied fold straight along the top edge of the decorative stitching.

## Applied Band

An applied 1- to 1½-inch band or false hem makes a sturdy, smooth, tailored finish for legbands and the hem edge of slips. Cut a lengthwise strip of tricot twice the finished width plus ⅜ inch for two seam allowances, and the length of the edge to be finished plus ⅜ inch for two seam allowances. Stitch ends of strip together with the overedge foot and the overedge stretch stitch. Fold band and place the edges even with the right side of the tricot edge. Offset seams slightly in band to reduce number of layers at a single point. Pin in at least four places to avoid stretching the garment edge and band unequally as you stitch. Stitch over the two edges of the band and one edge of the tricot, using the overedge foot and either the overedge or the stretch overedge stitch. Regulate stitch width to suit fabric weight. Turn band toward edge when completed.

## Shell Edge

The shell edge can be made with either the blind-stitch, *Flexi-Stitch** Disc 59, or Disc 22. Use the general-purpose presser foot; 5 stitch width; and 15 stitch length. Fold tricot edge to underside ½ inch. Guide edge to your right with *Flexi-Stitch* Disc 59 or Disc 22, and to the left with the blind-stitch. Stitch from the right side of the fabric, guiding it so that the needle passes over the fabric fold at the zig-zag stitch. Tighten needle-thread tension slightly if shell formation is indistinct.

Disc 22          Disc 59

## Tricot Bound Edge

For a self-fabric finish on tricot, a ¼-inch bound edge is tailored and durable and an appropriate finish on a slip, chemise, flare-leg panty, night-gown, or pajama top. Cut tricot binding 1¼ inch wide on the lengthwise direction for straight edges or on the crosswise direction for curved

right side

right side

edges. With right sides together, place binding along garment edge and straight-stitch a ½-inch seam, using a 15 to 20 stitch length. Trim both seam allowances to an even ¼ inch. Fold the binding around the seam edges snugly, and stitch near the crevice of the first seam through the garment and the single free edge of the binding strip. Trim the seam allowance of the binding strip near the stitching. This finish is practical and durable for tricot because it does not ravel.

## Simulated Rolled Edge

To finish the edge of a tricot ruffle or frill, turn the edge under ½ inch. Stitch over the turned edge from the right side, using the general-purpose presser foot, a plain zig-zag stitch, 3 stitch width, and 12 stitch length. Trim seam allowance on underside near stitching.

right side

## Double Collar with Decorative Edge

Place collar sections wrong sides together and stay-stitch ⅛ inch outside neckline seam line through both layers. If you prefer more firmness and loft than two layers of tricot give, use one layer of all-polyester, nonwoven interfacing between the layers. Hand-baste outer edges. Stitch outer edges together on seam line, using a satin stitch, 5 stitch width, and open scallop or crescent stitch pattern. Trim seam allowances near outside edge of scallop.

There are many other decorative stitch patterns that can be used in place of the crescent. A bound edge and lace edging are also suitable finishes. The conventional faced collar is not as attractive as other finishes.

## Tailored Hem

Appropriate for pajama sleeves and legs, the tailored hem is 1 to 1¼ inches wide and is formed after the sleeve and leg seams have been stitched. Turn and press the full hem width to the wrong side of the garment. Turn and press the full hem width again, keeping the edge inside the second fold. Stitch ¼ inch from the fold, hem side up, through the three thicknesses with a straight 15 length stitch and the general-purpose presser foot. Turn hem fold downward when stitching is completed.

## Machine-Blindstitched Hem

Suitable for pajama tops, robes, nightgowns and general use where a hem is required; the machine-blindstitched hem is easy to make. Measure and fold hem the width desired. Press lightly. Hand-baste ¼ inch from top edge if desired. With garment right side out, fold hem to right side, forming a soft fold ¼ inch from top edge of hem. Place under the general-purpose presser foot with machine set for the blindstitch (2½ stitch width, 15 stitch length) and with the needle entering the single edge during the straight-stitching interval and just piercing the soft fold on the zig-zag stitch. When completed, trim edge near stitching and turn hem downward.

## Buttonholes

Machine-stitched buttonholes are the most appropriate kind for tricot garments although bound buttonholes can be made in tricot. Those made by the manual method on a zig-zag machine are the most effective. The buttonhole foot or special-purpose foot will not mar the fabric surface, as sometimes happens with an attachment with a cloth clamp, and the stitch length can be set to space the stitches far enough apart to avoid stretching the buttonhole with too-dense stitching. Always use an interfacing of either nonwoven all-polyester or a crisp, fine woven fabric. Stitch width settings of 2½ and 4½ are appropriate on most machines.

wrong side

right side

# Lingerie Knits (Tricot)

## FABRICS

**Characteristics.** Crosswise is direction of greater stretch. Tricot is usually very wide, 108 inches.

**Types.** Tricot comes in different weights, depending on yarn size and number of loops per inch. 40-denier is a medium weight. 15-denier is a sheer, light weight.

**Fiber Content.** Nylon, acetate, triacetate.

## PATTERN CHOICE

Choose from the growing selection of commercial patterns.

Or, cut apart a favorite discarded garment and make a pattern of its sections.†

Or, make a pattern from a favorite garment without cutting it apart. Lay each section, one at a time, over paper on a soft surface. Mark outline by plunging pins through fabric and paper along seam lines at short intervals; then cut paper along pin marks.†

†Add seam allowances when cutting new fabric.

## PREPARATIONS

- Test-stitch a swatch before cutting to test ease of stitching. If stitches are skipped, launder yardage before cutting, using fabric softener to remove excess finish and static.
- Relax fabric by allowing it to lie flat on floor or table overnight.
- Fold, right sides together, and square and cut ends with table edge.
- To find right side, stretch a crosswise edge; tricot will roll to the right side.

## PATTERN FITTING

- Purchase your regular pattern type and size.
- Alter pattern before cutting.
- Garments are usually sewn without fitting during construction.

## CUTTING AND MARKING

- Fold fabric, right sides together.
- Since crosswise direction has greater stretch, cut with the stretch to encircle the figure and to run from front to back on crotch sections of panties or briefs.
- Use ball-point or sharp, smooth pins. Pin sparingly, within seam allowances.
- Patterns may be anchored with magic transparent tape instead of pins. (Some patterns allow only ¼-inch seam allowances; others ⅝-inch.)
- Do not let edges of fabric drape over table edge.
- Observe lengthwise grain-line markings on pattern and place on lengthwise rib.
- Cut with sharp shears and keep cut edges even and regular.
- Cut notches outward.
- Mark internal details with tailor's tacks.

## STAY STITCHING

- Usually omitted.
- Used occasionally to hold 2 layers together.

## STITCHING

- Use ball-point or size 11 needle and very fine thread (silk, nylon, or fine polyester).
- Balanced tensions.
- Normal to above-normal presser-foot pressure.
- For straight stitching, use straight-stitch (round-hole) throat plate and straight-stitch presser foot. (Rigid presser foot—not hinged—helps to prevent skipped stitches.)
- 15 stitch length for straight stitching.
- Guide and support fabric, keeping seam under tension while stitching.
- Kinds of stitches: regular straight, straight stretch, stretch overedge, plain zig-zag (narrow widths), chainstitch (2 or 3 rows in alternating directions), overedge with Disc 22 and overedge foot, or plain narrow zig-zag (right needle position with overedge foot).

## SEAMS AND SEAM FINISHES

- Narrow, machine-finished seams are generally used.
- Choose from three different procedures: 1) stitch, finish, and trim; 2) stitch, trim, and finish; or 3) trim and stitch, using the stretch overedge (*Flexi-Stitch* Disc 59).
- Pin seams at ends and center; do not hand-baste; trim off notches before stitching; stretch short side of seam where ease is indicated.

## FACINGS, INTERFACINGS, LININGS, UNDERLININGS

- Use double layer of same weight tricot for crotch.
- Underline lace inserts or sections with sheer tricot.
- Face collar with same weight tricot.
- Interfacing is often omitted.

## PRESSING

- Limit iron temperature to that for nylon.
- Press lightly with moist cheesecloth to generate steam to remove stretched portions.

## HEMS AND EDGE FINISHES

- Hems may be finished with:
  - Machine blindstitching (1- or 1½-inch hem).
  - Shell edging (½-inch hem).
  - Machine stitching with hemmer foot (⅛-inch hem).
- Hems or edges may be finished with:
  - Folded, cross-cut matching or sheer tricot.
  - Applied lace.
  - Appliquéd lace with finished selvage, sometimes underlined with sheet tricot.
  - Taffeta or satin binding cut on bias (suitable also for tubular straps or ties).
- Waistline may be finished with lingerie elastic encased or stitched and turned to underside with picot edge extending.

# Spandex Knits

KNITS THAT INCLUDE SPANDEX YARN have an elastic-like ability to stretch and recover. Thus they are appropriate for action-wear clothing and figure-control lingerie.

Spandex knits that look like regular knits are usually used for garments worn for swimming, skiing, skating, gymnastics, and other active sports. These knits are cut and stitched in much the same way as stretch knits, but special attention must be given to retaining the stretch in the seams. Unlike other knits, on which strong thread and straight stitching are often adequate, knits that contain spandex require stretch stitches, such as the straight stretch stitch, the overedge stretch stitch, and the multi-stretch stitch.

*Power net,* stretch lace, and satin-faced tricot, all containing spandex, are primarily used for figure-control lingerie. The methods for sewing them are easy but quite different from other sewing.

## Seams in Power Net

Almost all seams start with a plain seam, stitched with right sides together using the straight stretch stitch, the general-purpose presser foot or the Even Feed foot, lingerie thread of nylon or spun polyester, and a ball-point needle. If your sewing machine does not make the straight stretch stitch, you can substitute the narrow plain zig-zag stitch, 2½ stitch width and 15 stitch length. Topstitching is usually applied to hold the seam allowances in one position and to strengthen the seam. The featherstitch, *Flexi-Stitch* Disc 51, and the multi-stitch zig-zag are good choices for topstitching because they will stretch in all directions.

**Featherstitch—centered.** Finger-press plain

Straight stretch stitch

Featherstitch

seam open. Topstitch from right side of garment, centering the featherstitch over the seam line.

**Featherstitch—double row.** Finger-press plain seam open. Topstitch on each side of seam line from right side of garment through seam allowances.

**Featherstitch—welt seam.** Finger-press seam allowances in the same direction and topstitch through garment and seam layers from the right side with the featherstitch.

## Figure-Control Panels

For areas of the figure that need strong control, the degree of stretch can be decreased by using two or more layers of power net as an underlay. Power net does not ravel so a cut edge is acceptable and the application simple.

Pin panel in place on the underside of the girdle section. Set your machine for the featherstitch or the multi-stitch zig-zag, 5 stitch width, above-20 stitch length, and use the general-purpose presser foot. Stitch near the panel edge, from the right side of the garment section.

## Crotch and Leg Seams

Seams that join the crotch and leg sections of panty girdles consist of two layers of nylon tricot and one layer of power net. Stitch these three-ply seams with ¼-inch allowances, using the overedge foot and the overedge stretch stitch, Flexi-Stitch Disc 59, which seams and finishes in one stitching.

## Waistline Finishes

Soft-back elastic in a wide or narrow width can be used for the waistline finish of girdles. Apply medium and narrow widths with hidden seam allowances; apply wide widths with a shaped and topstiched edge. Do not stretch or ease the girdle or the elastic.

**Hidden-seam waistband.** Place soft-back elastic, soft back up, frill edge extended, slightly below the seam line. Stitch with the general-purpose presser foot and a narrow zig-zag stitch, 2½ stitch width, 15 stitch length, over elastic rib nearest frill. Turn elastic to underside of garment and topstitch from the outside of the garment through the elastic near the bottom edge.

**Shaped, topstitched waistband.** Shape top edge of girdle by trimming on the seam line and pin wide, soft-back waistband elastic in position right side up underneath the shaped edge. Baste if necessary and do not stretch or ease either elastic or girdle. The firm waistline control comes from the greater strength of the waistband elastic.

With a narrow plain zig-zag stitch (2½ stitch width, 15 stitch length) and the general-purpose presser foot, stitch near the shaped edge of the power net.

With the multi-stitch zig-zag (5 stitch width, above-20 stitch length) and the general-purpose presser foot, topstitch, guiding the edge of the foot along the bottom of the zig-zag stitching.

## Leg Finishes

The legs of panty girdles can be finished with soft-back elastic applied in the same manner as described for the hidden-seam waistband. Or they can be finished with stretch lace.

Stitch ends of stretch-lace leg band with the stretch overedge stitch and topstitch seam from the outside.

Pin lace to overlap bottom edge of power net ½ inch. Do not stretch or ease either edge.

With leg turned wrong side out, topstitch the stretch lace near the edge, using the general-purpose presser foot and the featherstitch, multi-stitch zig-zag stitch, or plain zig-zag stitch.

## Bra Edge Finishes

Power net is a favorite for the backs of bras and, whether you are making an entire bra or replacing the back in a worn one, the edges require a finish. The best finish is narrow soft-back elastic applied with a hidden seam as described for waistbands. An alternative finish is the bound edge of power net.

Cut a 1-inch-wide lengthwise strip of power net. With right sides together, using the straight stretch stitch and general-purpose presser foot, stitch a seam with a ¼-inch seam allowance. Turn the strip over the edge to the underside, letting the cut edge extend ¼ inch below the seam line. Stitch near the seam line below the binding with a narrow zig-zag stitch, 2½ stitch width, 15 stitch length.

## Spandex Stretch (Power Net)

### FABRICS

**Characteristics.** Spandex yarns, combined with yarns of other fibers, impart stretch and recovery to any knit fabric.

**Types.** Many look like other knits but have elastic-like stretch. These are used for action sportswear and are handled like stretchable knits.

Power net, stretch lace, and satin-faced tricot with spandex are figure-control lingerie fabrics.

### PATTERN CHOICE

- For figure-control lingerie, choose from the growing selection of commercial patterns.
- Or, cut apart a favorite discarded garment and make a pattern of its sections.†
- Or, make a pattern from a favorite garment without cutting it apart. Lay each section, one at a time, over paper on a soft surface. Mark outline by plunging pins through fabric and paper along seam lines at short intervals, then cut paper along pin marks.†

†Add seam allowances when cutting new fabric.

### CUTTING AND MARKING

- Fold fabric right sides together on lengthwise rib.
- Use few pins, within seam allowances.
- Use ball-point or fine, smooth pins; or anchor pattern with magic transparent tape. Cut with sharp shears and keep edges even.
- Cut notches outward.
- Mark internal details with tailor's tacks.

### STAY STITCHING

- Usually omitted. Used occasionally to hold 2 layers together.

### STITCHING

- Use ball-point needle; fine, strong thread (nylon, polyester, or polyester-core).
- Balanced tensions.
- Normal presser-foot pressure.
- Select stitches that stretch, preferably in both

lengthwise and crosswise directions.
- Kinds of stitches: straight stretch stitch, multi-stitch zig-zag, featherstitch, plain zig-zag, over-edge stretch, and multi-stitch stretch.

### SEAMS AND SEAM FINISHES

- Power net does not require a seam finish.
- Seams are usually made as plain seams, stitched with straight stretch stitch, opened and finger-pressed, then stitched opened from right side with plain zig-zag, featherstitch, or multi-stitch zig-zag.
- Seam edges are sometimes finger-pressed in one direction and stitched decoratively as above.
- Underlays for strengthening figure control are pinned on the underside and stitched decoratively near the edge from the right side.
- Satin-like-surface lingerie fabrics with spandex are usually seamed with straight stretch stitching, trimmed to ¼ inch, and finished with over-edge stretch stitch.
- Seams may be strengthened on the underside with a stay of woven elastic applied with zig-zag stitching.
- Seams may be stiffened with featherboning, plastic, or metal foundation-garment stays.

### FACINGS, INTERFACINGS, LININGS, UNDERLININGS

- Usually not used.

### PRESSING

- Use an iron sparingly, if at all, and at low heat setting.
- Finger pressing is usually adequate.

### HEMS AND EDGE FINISHES

**Girdle edges** — Finish with soft-back elastic. 1) Stitch elastic, soft side up, to right side of garment, using stretch stitch; 2) turn elastic to underside and stitch near unattached edge, using plain or decorative stretch stitch.

# Terry and Stretch Terry

KNIT TERRY, WITH ITS LOOPED SURFACE and stretchable back, has become a favorite for all ages, from babies to grownups. It is a companion fabric to knit velour, which has a cut rather than a looped pile surface. There is considerable range within this fabric type, and the appearance and density can vary greatly, depending on the kinds and sizes of yarns, size and number of needles used in knitting and whether the fabric also contains spandex yarn, which strengthens its recovery after being stretched.

## Preparing to Stitch

Use the general-purpose throat plate and presser foot, the overedge foot, or the Even Feed foot for most stitching. Use normal presser-foot pressure, a size 14 ball-point needle (catalogue 2021 or 2045), and strong thread such as polyester core, spun polyester, or nylon twist.

Unless you use an Even Feed foot, guide and support the seam layers by holding the seam taut in back of the presser foot with one hand and in front of the needle with the other.

If the looped surface catches over the toes of the general-purpose foot, wrap it with a ¼-inch width of magic transparent tape (see page 425).

## Seams

When seaming knit terry or stretch terry, the important points to remember are: Most seams must stretch with the fabric. Seams that should not stretch should be stayed with twill tape or woven-edge seam binding. And seams should be made in ways to keep bulkiness to a minimum because pressing will not sharpen seams appreciably.

**Stitched and finished in one stitching.** The most frequently used seam for joining garment sections is the one that uses the overedge stretch stitch and the overedge foot. Stitch on the seam line while holding the seam taut. Trim the seam allowances near the outside edge of the stitching. The stitching-then-trimming sequence retains the garment shape better than the reverse sequence.

**Stitched and finished in two steps.** Another favorite is the narrow seam that is first stitched on the seam line with the straight stretch stitch and either the general-purpose presser foot or the Even Feed foot and then finished with a flattening stitch such as the multi-stretch as illustrated.

Alternative stitches are the regular straight stitch or a narrow zig-zag stitch (2 stitch width, 15 stitch length) instead of the straight stretch stitch, and multi-stitch zig-zag or wide plain zig-zag (5 stitch width, 12 stitch length) instead of the multi-stretch zig-zag stitch.

**Mock flat-felled seam.** For men's wear and baby clothes, a flat seam is sometimes preferred. Stitch first as a plain seam on the seam line, using the straight stretch stitch and the Even Feed foot, or the regular straight stitch and the general-purpose presser foot. (Hold seam taut if you use the general-purpose presser foot.) Finger-press both seam allowances in one direction and topstitch from the right side of the fabric an even distance (¼ to ⅜ inches) from the seam line through both seam allowances. Trim both seam allowances near the stitching. The seam may appear slightly stretched when finished, but it will recover after light steam pressing or when the garment is worn.

**Plain seam, double topstitched.** Where a flat and bulkless joining is necessary, a plain seam, topstitched ⅛ inch from the seam line on both sides, is preferred. Seam allowances can be trimmed near the topstitching to further reduce bulk.

**Plain seam, double topstitched, taped.** For seams that should not stretch, such as the shoulder and back-of-neck or yoke seams, include woven-edge seam binding or twill tape on the underside when topstitching.

## Collars and Band Finishes

While garments of knit terry and velour should retain their soft, supple, stretchable characteristics, collars and finishes of some garments must have body and shape. Men's sport shirts, kimonos, V-neck pullovers, and girls' robes are a few examples. All-polyester, nonwoven featherweight interfacing will supply the shape and body needed in these areas without robbing the terry of its softness or washability.

**A firm band** suitable for a kimono, V-neck pullover, or cardigan cover-up is cut twice the width of the finished band plus two ⅝-inch seam allowances on the lengthwise direction of the fabric. Cut the interfacing the same length and width. With a plain, straight-stitch seam, join one edge of the interfaced band to the garment edge. Finger-press seam allowances open and trim the seam allowances of the band and interfacing band to ¼ inch. Pin free edges of interfaced band to the extended seam allowance of the garment. Stitch with either the Even Feed foot, or the general-purpose presser foot, using the blind stitch (5 stitch width, 15 stitch length). Place the stitching with the left edge slightly outside the seam line.

Trim the seam allowances near right-hand edge of the blind stitching.

**A tailored collar** will have shape and stay neat when interfacing is attached to both the upper and under collar sections. Cut both upper and under collar sections on the lengthwise rib from the upper-collar pattern. The fabric has adequate give for shaping. Cut also two collar sections of all-polyester nonwoven featherweight interfacing. Stitch one interfacing to the wrong side of each collar section ½ inch from all edges.

Place right sides of interfaced collar sections together; pin and stitch ⅝ inch from edges, blunting the collar points by taking 3 stitches diagonally across point.

Trim seam allowances on upper collar and interfacing to ¼ inch and on under collar and interfacing to ⅛ inch. Turn collar right side out, finger-press, and pin edges to turn sharply on seam line. Topstitch ⅜ inch from edge.

**A round collar,** interfaced with one layer of all-polyester, nonwoven interfacing and finished with a self-binding, makes a feminine finish. Cut two collar sections and one interfacing section. With collar sections right sides out, place the interfacing between them. Cut a binding strip, on crosswise direction of the fabric for greatest stretch, two times the width of the finished binding plus two seam allowances. Pin the binding to the collar unit, edges matching and binding stretched slightly. Stitch with multi-stitch zig-zag stitch (5 stitch width, 20 stitch length), inside edge of

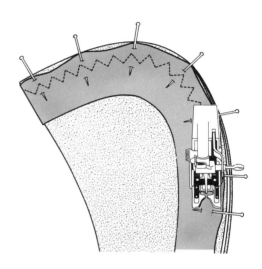

stitching on seam line. Trim all seam allowances near outside edge of stitching. Fold free edge of binding over seam allowances and pin. Topstitch with Even Feed foot and straight stitch, 15 stitch length, in the crevice of the seam line through collar layers and free edge of binding on under-

476

side. Trim binding seam allowance near the stitching.

**Soft finishes** applied as bands or bindings are appropriate for garments that should look unstructured and molded to the body. Remember that lengthwise-cut bands or bindings have greater control of an edge than crosswise-cut strips because knit terry stretches less lengthwise. Also, as on tricot, a cut edge near a line of stitching is acceptable. Many of the techniques suggested for lingerie apply to terry garments as well.

## Hems

Machine-blindstitched hems are appropriate for terry, as are multi-row topstitched hems and applied bands instead of hems.

## Buttonholes and Closures

Machine-stitched buttonholes are appropriate if made in an interfaced area and with uncrowded stitches, as in lingerie tricot. Metal snaps, which are attached with a tool, are preferred for young children.

---

## *Terry and Stretch Terry*

### FABRICS

**Characteristics.** Greater stretch in crosswise direction.

**Types.** Plain, printed, or striped. Some have a velour surface and terry back.

**Fiber Content.** All-cotton, nylon, polyester, or blends of these fibers; some include spandex yarn.

### PATTERN CHOICE

**Casual wear**—Jumpsuits, long or short pants, swimwear, hooded cover-ups, robes, dresses.

**Children's** wear.

**Men's** wear.

### PREPARATIONS

- Relax stretch terry by allowing it to lie flat on floor or table overnight.
- Pin crosswise edges of stretch terry to tissue to control, since they tend to roll.
- Cut ends on crosswise course.
- Pull diagonally to straighten.

### PATTERN FITTING

- Purchase your regular pattern type and size.
- Patterns for "Stretchable Knits Only" are suitable.
- Alter pattern before cutting.
- Stretch terry may be fitted with no ease in the stretch direction.

### CUTTING AND MARKING

- Fold most terry wrong side out.
- Cut heavy terry from single thickness.
- Stretch terry (crosswise stretch) may be cut in either direction, depending on where you want the stretch.
- Cut with sharp, rigid-blade shears.
- Mark notches with tailor's tacks.

### STAY STITCHING

- Instead of using conventional stay stitching, stitch seam allowances with chainstitch or straight stitch, 12 to 15 stitch length, $\frac{1}{4}$ inch from cut edge to keep crosswise-cut edge from raveling or rolling during construction.

### STITCHING

- Use size 14 ball-point needle. Needles may blunt quickly because of yarn density.
- Spun polyester, polyester-core, or nylon threads.
- Normal presser-foot pressure.
- Guide and support seam by holding fabric taut behind and in front of presser foot, except with Even Feed foot.
- Wrap toes of presser foot with $\frac{1}{4}$-inch strip of magic transparent tape to prevent snagging.
- Kinds of stitches: regular straight stitch, straight stretch stitch, or narrow zig-zag. For finishing: wide zig-zag, overedge stretch, multi-stretch stitch, multi-zig-zag stitch, blind stitch.
- Even Feed foot handles seam layers evenly.

### SEAMS AND SEAM FINISHES

- Stitched and overedged seams, $\frac{1}{4}$ to $\frac{3}{8}$ inch wide, are generally used.
- Plain seams, opened and topstitched, are used to reduce bulk and, when taped, to give stability.
- Mock flat-felled seams are used for some men's wear.

### FACINGS, INTERFACINGS, LININGS, UNDERLININGS

- Generally not used.
- For some garments, all-polyester, featherweight nonwoven interfacing is suitable.
- Facings are often cut as one with garment.
- Applied bands may replace facings.
- Ribbing is a popular finish.

### PRESSING

- Press sparingly.
- Finger pressing is adequate in many situations.

### HEMS AND EDGE FINISHES

- Finish hem edge with overedge stitch, turn once, and machine-stitch hem.
- Or, finish edge as above and machine-blindstitch hem.
- Or, finish edge as above and hand-whip hem.
- Or, finish edge with decorative braid or fabric binding.
- Use worked or bound buttonholes or fabric or cord button loops.

# Shiny-Faced Knits

LEATHER-LIKE FABRICS HAVE REACHED A HIGH PLACE in fashion. Those with a knit back are more supple than those with a woven back. The knit-back fake leathers consist of a plastic layer of polyurethane or vinyl over a knitted base fabric. Polyurethane produces a soft, spongy fabric; vinyl tends to be more rigid. Whether made to look like patent or grained leather or like fabric, the new plastics are handled alike.

## Preparing to Stitch

Stitch plastic-coated fabrics with spun polyester or polyester-core thread, a style 15 x 2 (catalogue 2032) needle, size 14, and a 10 stitch length.

Equip your sewing machine with the straight-stitch presser foot and throat plate for straight stitching, or the general-purpose presser foot and throat plate for zig-zag stitching, or the Even Feed machine foot for either straight or zig-zag stitching. The top feeding action of the Even Feed foot overcomes the natural tendency of plastic-coated fabrics to adhere to the underside of the presser foot and thus retard the movement of the top seam layer. When you do not use the Even Feed foot on polyurethane or vinyl fabrics for topstitching, use clear oil[†] or powder[††] as you stitch to keep the top layer from adhering to the underside of the presser foot. Test before applying to the garment for complete removal of oil or powder.

[†]—SINGER* oil or clear baby oil.
[††]—Talcum powder, cornstarch, or chalk spot remover.

Test-stitch seams. Usually, you will need to increase the needle-thread tension slightly to compensate for the lack of porosity of these materials. Medium or normal presser-foot pressure is usually adequate. However, if the stitch length appears shorter than set for, increase the pressure slightly; or if feed marks show on the underside and the machine runs hard, decrease the pressure. Use your test-stitched seams to test the new ways of treating seams that follow in the next section.

## Darts and Seams

**Preparations.** Leave the pattern on the cut-out sections and defer marking until you are ready to use the section. Mark seam widths that vary from the standard ⅝ inch, and mark notches with short, perpendicular lines.

**Darts.** Fold right sides together, matching markings. If you use pins, place them within the dart allowance because of the permanent holes they will leave, or use paper clips over the fold.

Darts, which are placed over rounded parts of the figure, should be stitched on a slight outward curve, and the last few stitches near the point should be on the edge of the fold. Tie threads at both ends. Slash through the fold as far as possible, finger-press the allowances open, and trim to ¼ inch.

**Pounding, Rolling, and Gluing.** Pounding seams open on leather-like fabrics is equivalent to pressing to embed the stitches and to pressing a seam open with the point of the iron. With the garment held over a padded and rounded hardwood surface (or a firm tailor's ham), use a wooden mallet to pound along the stitching line glue **under** the seam allowance slightly inside the seam edge. Finger-press the seam allowance against the garment. Pound lightly or roll to compress the two layers, and allow to dry.

Plan to do as much gluing at one time as possible. Be meticulous and avoid smears. A fine, stiff-point brush for applying the glue and a small glue cup will help you to do a neat job. To protect the shiny face of the fabric, work with the garment section over a Turkish towel.

with short, staccato strokes. Pound near the dart point to flatten the fold, distributing it equally on each side of the stitching.

**Plain seam.** Place garment sections right sides together. Match edges, if seam allowances are equal, or seam lines, if seam allowances are unequal. Match seam ends and notches first, and hold together with paper clips or small squares of magic transparent tape. Add clips or tape as needed.

Rolling, another substitute for pressing leatherlike fabrics, is superior to pounding. Use a small roller similar to that used for sealing the edges of wallpaper. Hold the seam allowances open and run the roller back and forth, exerting pressure along the stitching line.

Gluing is the process by which seam allowances are held in an opened position. Use a glue, such as Sobo brand, or rubber cement. Place a thin line of

If there is slight ease in one layer of the seam, stitch with that side against the feed. Stitch slowly and keep a firm hold on the seam. Remember, you cannot remove stitches without leaving holes. Tie threads at both ends, remove tape, and finger-press seam open. Pound or roll along stitching line, and glue seam allowances open.

**Taped seam.** When extra strength is required, include pre-shrunk twill tape or woven-edge seam binding in the seam as you stitch. Pound or roll along the stitching line, and glue seam allowances open the same as a plain seam.

**Double-Topstitched seam.** Straight-stitch a plain seam, pound or roll it open, but do not glue. Topstitch an equal distance from center on each side through garment and seam allowance.

**Welt seam.** Seam allowances may be equal or unequal for the welt seam. Stitch a plain seam on

the stitching line. Pound or roll seam open first. Then turn seam allowances to one side and pound or roll again. Trim the seam allowance next to the garment to 1/4 inch. Topstitch through garment and one seam layer. Use no glue.

**Slot seam.** Turn both seam allowances under along seam line. Pound or roll and glue. Cut a strip of fabric twice the seam width plus 1/2 inch. Center the strip, right side against one seam allowance, and topstitch one side. Hold the strip and abutted edges in place with strips of magic transparent tape or masking tape, as illustrated, and stitch second side. Do not stitch through the tape.

**Clipping, notching and trimming seam allowances.** Straight seam allowances present few problems in handling, but curved seam allowances must be carefully clipped or notched to form a smooth and continuous line. Clip small wedges to flatten seam allowances that ripple, and slash into seam allowances that draw too tightly and restrict the shape of the garment. Cut seam allowances diagonally at cross seams. Cut seam allowances that are inside faced edges to unequal widths, such as 1/4 and 1/8 inch.

## Pockets and Buttonholes

Pockets and bound or corded buttonholes should be completed before garment sections are interfaced and assembled; hand-worked buttonholes should be made after the garment is completed.

## FABRICS

**Characteristics.** Thermoplastic or vinyl coating gives knit-backed fabrics a shiny, water-repellent surface and makes them highly stable, with little or no give. Supple and soft, they are easy to sew.

**Types.** Surface may be smooth, crinkled, or marked with reptile-skin pattern.

**Fiber Content.**
Face—Vinyl or polyurethane.
Back—Cotton, polyester.

## PATTERN CHOICE

Select patterns with a tailored look.
- Avoid gathers, sharp pleats or tucks.
- Select styles with shaped seams rather than darts.
- Topstitching is a good fashion accent and is also functional (substitutes for pressing).
- Raglan sleeves are easiest to handle.

**All-weather** coats, capes, jackets, jumpers, pants outfits.

**Children's** wear.

**Men's** wear.

**Home furnishings**—cushions, chair covers, table-cloths, and mats.

## PREPARATIONS

- Store rolled. Do not fold or crease.
- Fold face out.
- Square and cut ends with table edges.

## PATTERN FITTING

- Purchase your regular pattern type and size.
- Fit pattern carefully, preserving standard basic ease and design ease.
- Test-fit in muslin or nonwoven interfacing fabric.
- Convert ease to darts.
- Eliminate seamed-on facings if possible.
- Remove excessive ease in sleeve cap.
- Once stitched, the garment cannot easily be refitted.

## CUTTING AND MARKING

- Lay out pattern on grain of fabric.
- Observe pattern-matching rules required by the design.
- Avoid pinning into garment areas; pin marks will show.
- Pin only within seam allowances and sparingly.
- Weights and transparent tape can substitute for pins.
- Mark fabric back with chalk or marking pencil.

## STAY STITCHING

- Do **not** stay-stitch.

## STITCHING

- Use size 14 leather-sewing needle, style 15 x 2, and polyester-core or all-polyester thread.
- Increase needle-thread tension to balance stitch.
- 10 stitch length for straight stitching.
- Normal or regular presser-foot pressure.
- When stitched from right side, the shiny surface will adhere to presser foot. To prevent sticking, dust the surface with a thirsty powder such as talcum powder, cornstarch, or one of the powders used for spot cleaning. These brush off without stain.
- The Even Feed foot will enable you to stitch without need for the above precautions.

## SEAMS AND SEAM FINISHES

- Pin only within seam allowances or hold edges together with paper clips.
- Topstitched seams and darts are best because they control and hold the seam allowances in place.
- Or, use a thin line of glue.
- No seam finish is required.
- Shoulder and neckline seams should usually be taped to prevent stretching.

## FACINGS, INTERFACINGS, LININGS, UNDERLININGS

### INTERFACING
- Hair canvas for sharp support.
- Nonwoven for soft support.
- Nonwoven fleece for loft and support.

### LINING
- Line for comfort.
- Washable fabric that does not show soil.
- Fake fur for zip-out type.
- Interline for warmth and to prevent harsh seams from abrading lining.
- Machine-stitch lining to facing.

### UNDERLINING
- Generally not used except at back across shoulders and in front to anchor interfacing.

## PRESSING

- Do **not** press with an iron.
- Instead, finger-press, weight or topstitch.
- "Press" seams open with a small roller.

## HEMS AND EDGE FINISHES

- Turn and topstitch.
- Use glue to hold hem.
- Or, stitch on a folded band for hem substitute.
- Bound or worked buttonholes and sewn-on buttons with protective, flat sew-through button on back make pleasing closures.

# Furry-Faced Knits

MANY FUR FABRICS ARE OF KNIT CONSTRUCTION. Knit-back furs are more flexible, more drapable, and more responsive to easing and thus easier to sew than woven-back furs.

## Cutting

Cut fur fabrics with sturdy shears and cut through the backing only, not the hairs. The way you cut is entirely different from the way you cut other fabrics. Cut with the tips of the shears only, taking one short snip at a time. Do not rest the shears on the table but hold them up enough to allow the underneath blade to separate the hairs. Fur fabrics can also be cut with a single-edge razor blade, an artist's knife or a regular fur-cutting knife, but most women find it far easier to cut them with shears.

## Preparing to Stitch

For most fur fabrics, select strong thread, such as spun polyester, polyester core, or 3-cord nylon in general-purpose sizes. For lightweight fur fabrics, use size A silk thread.

For all knit-back fur fabrics, use a size 14 ball-point needle, style 15 x 1, catalogue 2021 or 2045.

The Even Feed sewing machine foot gives the best results on most fur fabrics for both zig-zag and straight stitching; on very thick varieties, however, the zipper foot is superior.

The straight-stitch or general-purpose presser foot also can be used for straight stitching and the general-purpose presser foot only for zig-zag stitching.

Stitch lengths of 10 to 12 are best for straight stitching. Use the shorter length, 12, for short-pile and 10 for long-pile fur fabrics. Stitch lengths of 12 to 15 are best for zig-zag stitching. Use the shorter length, 15, for short-pile and 12 for long-pile furs.

Needle-thread tension should be regulated to produce an evenly set stitch. In most fabrics, it must be regulated at a slightly higher setting than for fabrics of similar weight without pile.

Presser-foot pressure should be tested at a regular or normal setting first and then increased slightly if the stitch length appears shorter than the setting indicates or if the fabric is not firmly held under the presser foot.

## Seams

For a lined garment, you have a choice of two basic types of seams: 1) plain, straight-stitch seams with ⅝-inch seam allowances pressed open and 2) zig-zag seams with seam allowances trimmed to narrow width before stitching. Procedures vary for making each of these basic types of seams, depending on the bulk and length of the fur pile and whether you use tape to support the seam.

For an unlined fur garment, you have a choice of straight-stitch or zig-zag seams with a decorative covering or a flat-felled seam.

Using scraps, test-stitch different kinds of seams and procedures described in this section in order to decide which ones are best for your fur. Two or more different kinds of seams may be used in a single garment because some seams function differently from others.

### Plain straight-stitch seams
(⅝-inch seam allowances)

In short-pile furs, pin, hand-baste (optional), and stitch in the same direction as the pile.

**Stitch in direction of pile**

Finger-press the seam open. Inspect the right side and, with the eye end of a heavy, long darning needle, raise hairs caught in the stitching. Then apply steam by holding the steam iron level, an inch or two above the fabric. Roll along the seam line to press. Use long, loose padding stitches to hold seam allowances open.

**Finger-press seam open**

**Raise hairs caught in stitching**

**Steam,
holding iron above fabric**

**Roll along seam line**

**Hold seam allowances
open with padding stitches**

**In medium-length-pile furs,** pin, hand-baste (optional), and stitch in the direction of the pile, working the pile away from the seam line with a long needle. Finger-press seam allowances open. Inspect both sides of the seam and raise the hairs caught in the stitching from both inside and out-

**Work pile away from seam line with long needle**

side. Shear pile from seam allowances with scissors, snipping the hairs close to the backing. Steam, holding the iron an inch or two above the fabric. Roll along the seam line to press.

Use long, loose padding stitches to hold seam allowances open.

**In long-pile furs,** shear pile from ½ inch of the seam allowances and baste on the seam line. Inspect the outside and then raise hairs caught in the basting. Stitch on the seam line in the direction of the pile and, if necessary, use the zipper foot adjusted to the right of the needle to avoid the bulk of the fur. Finger-press seam allowances

open. From the outside, raise hairs along both sides of stitching with a long needle. Press seam allowances with steam iron, allowing it to rest on the two layers of seam allowance only. Cover the seam allowances with a thin press cloth if testing indicates a fiber content that needs protection.

Open the seam allowances with your fingers and roll to hold them open temporarily. Use long, loose padding stitches to hold seam allowances open permanently.

**To tape straight-stitch seams** that should not stretch, include ¼-inch shrunk twill tape in the seam as it is being stitched. This procedure applies to furs of any pile length.

### Zig-Zag seams ( ⅛ -to- ¼ -inch seam allowances)

In sparsely covered, short-pile furs, do not use a zig-zag seam.

**In short-but-dense-pile furs,** trim seam allowances to ⅛-inch width, transferring notches to new seam-allowance edge. Pin edges together at seam ends and at notches. Use a plain zig-zag stitch, 3 stitch width, and 15 stitch length; stitch in the direction of the pile, letting the needle enter at the seam line on one side and beyond the seam edge on the other side. Backstitch at both the start and the finish of the seam. Finger-press seam allowances open. From the outside, raise hairs caught in the stitching. Steam, holding the iron above the inside of the fabric, and roll lightly.

**In medium- and long-pile furs,** trim seam allowances to ¼-inch width, taking special care to snip with the points of shears through the backing only. Do not cut off the fur. Transfer notch markings as you work. Pin seam-allowance edges together at ends and notches, and at shorter intervals if necessary. Hand-baste with thread of matching color, with an overcasting stitch. From the outside, raise hairs caught in the basting. Stitch with the plain zig-zag stitch, 5 stitch width, and 12 stitch length, back-stitching at both ends of the seam. Finger-press seam open. Raise hairs caught in stitching. Steam, holding the iron above the inside of the fabric, and roll lightly.

**To tape** zig-zag seams that should not stretch, add ¼-inch shrunk twill tape to the basting step of the above seam preparation, catching only the outside edge of the tape in the basting and allowing the greater width of the tape to extend toward the garment.

**To cross a zig-zag seam,** make sure that the stitching at the end of the seam being crossed is reinforced. Trimming the seam allowance before crossing is likely to remove the backstitching that reinforced the seam end. When this has happened, reinforce the seam end again. Position the seam under the needle ½ inch from the new seam end and stitch backward ½ inch, then forward ½ inch.

**To cover seams with tape,** use ½-inch shrunk twill tape and catch-stitch it over the seam. This taping method prevents abrasion of the lining and gives a slightly more flexible seam than the taping method described above. A covering is usually preferred for side seams and other major structural seams.

**To tape folds,** such as the fold of a soft pleat or the fold line of an in-seam pocket, catch-stitch ½-inch twill tape on the underside of the fabric, bringing the outside edge of the tape to the fold line. The purpose of taping is to prevent the fabric from stretching. For an in-seam pocket, tape both back and front sections alike for firmness, although only the front section is folded.

### Seams in unlined furs

Straight-stitch or zig-zag seams can be covered with grosgrain ribbon, leather or leather-like fabric, braid, or folded bias-cut bands of fabric. Edges can be finished with contrasting ribbon that has been pressed to shape before being applied. This kind of detail is usually applied to the fabric side of fur fabric by hand or machine. Experiment with this creative construction and adapt the method to suit the specific situation.

**Flat-fell** seams can be used for unlined garments made from fur fabrics that are boldly printed on the back and have a matted lamb's wool face. The printed side is usually used as the outside of the garment so that the lamb's-wool side becomes the lining. Often, the lamb's wool is turned to the right side for trimming bands on front, sleeve, and hem.

To make a flat-fell seam, straight-stitch the

seam first. Trim the seam edge that will be covered to ¼ inch; shear the pile from it and from ½ inch of the garment area underneath it. Also, shear the pile from the wide seam allowance for ⅛ inch so that you can turn it under and top-stitch. These fabrics are often polyester and can be steam-pressed like other fabrics, using a moist cheesecloth to protect the fabric.

**Above.** Finish turned-back facing edges with twill tape. Apply the tape with a narrow zig-zag stitch. Turn tape and stitch it to the backing with an overcasting stitch.
**Right.** Slip-stitch the finished taped edge to the garment.

### Darts

Darts can be straight-stitched in your fur fabric in the same way as the seams. However, in all except sparsely covered short-pile furs, narrow zig-zag stitching is preferred.

## FABRICS

**Characteristics.** These fabrics are highly stable, with little give in either lengthwise or crosswise direction. Some are washable; others must be dry-cleaned.

**Types.** Range is great, from thin ones that handle like corduroy to long-haired ones that require special handling. Some are printed on the back, hence reversible.

**Fiber Content.** Backing—cotton, acrylic, or polyester. Face—rayon, modacrylic, polyester, acrylic, or wool.

## PATTERN CHOICE

Look for simple lines, few seams, and raglan or set-in sleeves. Choose patterns recommended for fur fabrics, if possible. Remember, fur-lined garments must be cut generously to allow for fur on the inside. These fabrics combine well with leather, suede, tweed, or bulky wool knits.

**Coats and capes**—casual, country, or dressy; long vests.

**Children's** coats, capes, jackets.
**Men's** wear—car coats, jackets, vests.

## PREPARATIONS

- Store suspended from a hanger.
- Relax fabric by allowing it to lie flat on floor or table overnight, fur side up.
- Notice stripes, animal-like markings, shadings and any special design or pile characteristics.
- Square and cut ends with table edge.

## PATTERN FITTING

- Usually, purchase your regular pattern type and size.
- If using fur on inside, add up to ³/₄ inch to side and sleeve seams; or, use a pattern one size larger than usual; or, use a pattern designed for fur lining.
- Attach facing sections to garment sections where possible, to eliminate seams.
- Cut and fit garment of muslin.

## CUTTING AND MARKING

- Plan for one-way cutting, fur running downward, except for sheared beaver or seal types, which should run upward.
- Plan for single-layer cutting. (Purchase two patterns or cut duplicate pattern sections from tissue, or cut from fitted muslin.)
- Be sure to cut pairs, not two for same side.
- Lay fabric fur side down.
- Lay pattern on fabric side, right side down.
- On patterned furs, observe pattern-matching procedures.
- Cut fur with cutting knife, razor-type cutter, or tips of shears, through backing only and with very short strokes.
- Mark notches with chalk or thread.
- With your vacuum cleaner, pick up fall-out of fur fabric as you cut.

## STAY STITCHING

- Do **not** stay-stitch.

## STITCHING

- Fur fabrics stitch quite easily.
- Use all-polyester or polyester-core threads.
- Size 14 ball-point needle for thinner weights.
- Needle-thread tension usually must be increased one or two points above normal to balance the stitch.
- Normal to heavy presser-foot pressure.
- Use a 10 stitch length for straight stitching, 12 to 15 for zig-zag stitching.
- Use Even Feed foot for best results.

## SEAMS AND SEAM FINISHES

- For plain, pressed-open seams in lined garments, pin and stitch, using hands to put tension on seam, and withdraw pins as you stitch; or use Even Feed foot.
- On long-pile furs, stroke fur away from seam line as you stitch.
- Pull long hairs from seam on right side with coarse darning needle.
- To reduce seam-allowance bulk, shear fur.
- Stitch seam allowances to backing with padding stitches.
- For zig-zag seams, trim seam allowances to ¹/₄ or ¹/₈ inch; use plain zig-zag, 5 or 3 stitch width.
- For two-faced fur fabrics in unlined garments, use flat-felled seams and trim fur from all underlayers of the seam allowances. Hand-stitch the second stitching where stitching will not embed.

## FACINGS, INTERFACINGS, LININGS, UNDERLININGS

- Fur fabrics styled for conventional construction —Use these fabrics in the regular way, except for underlining, which is seldom required.
- Two-faced fabrics—When using reverse side for trimming, stitch, turn back, and whip twill tape to edge of fur facing used for trimming, then slip-stitch to garment.

## PRESSING

- Limit iron temperature to that for fiber with lowest heat requirement.
- Fur fabrics accept padding and inside tacking stitches without showing on outside.
- Many fur fabrics should not be pressed at all.
- Press only all-polyester lamb's-wool types with steam from moist cheesecloth and with low temperature.
- Embed stitching and shape seams with a small roller.
- Stitch sheared seam allowances to backing instead of pressing.

## HEMS AND EDGE FINISHES

- Lined garments—Turn hem only 1 inch, stitch twill tape to edge, hand-whip to garment, and face hem with 2-inch bias of lining fabric.
- Edges may be finished decoratively with suede, leather, plastic or woven binding.
- For long furs, make closures of button loops, toggles, or metal fasteners rather than buttonholes.
- Reinforce sewn buttons with a protective, flat sew-through button on back.

# GLOSSARY OF SEWING TERMS*

**abutted seam**—Two cut seam edges joined edge to edge with an underlay of a lightweight fabric. Usually used in interfacing and interlining.

**appliqué**—To sew a design of a small piece of fabric over the main fabric. The design or motif may be applied either by machine with a zig-zag stitch, or by hand with the blanket stitch.

**armhole**—The garment opening for the arm and sleeve. Formerly known as "armscye."

**backstitch**—1. The reverse stitch on the machine. Used to reinforce the stitching at the beginning and ending of seams. 2. A hand sewing stitch.

**balance lines**—The horizontal level on which the crosswise grain of the fabric falls at a right angle to the lengthwise grain in each dress section.

**basting stitch**—A long stitch made by hand or machine to hold two pieces of fabric together temporarily. Used to join garment sections before fitting and to prevent the fabric from slipping during stitching of seams.

**belting**—Stiffening used as interlining or backing in a belt and inside a waistband.

**beveling seams**—See Seam blending, beveling, or grading.

**bias**—The diagonal line of fabric that is on neither the lengthwise nor the crosswise grain. A "true bias" is the diagonal line formed when the lengthwise grain of the fabric is folded to the crosswise grain.

**binding**—A single or double bias finish used to encase raw edges. It may be applied without top stitching or with top stitching, using the Binder Foot.

**blindstitch**—1. A hand stitch used for hemming and finishing which is invisible on the right side. 2. A zig-zag machine stitch pattern. See Zig-Zag stitches.

**block**—To outline on muslin, paper, or fabric, the principle sections of a chair, sofa, or cushion before the slipcover fabric is cut. Sections of dress fabric also are often blocked to ensure a perfect matching of design.

**bodkin**—A heavy needle with a blunt point and large eye. Used to draw tape, elastic, ribbon, cord, etc., through a casing or heading; also used to help form a thread shank in button sewing.

**boning**—See Featherbone.

**cable cord**—Soft cotton cord used for cording and tubing; available in several sizes.

**canopy**—1. Fabric hung or draped over a frame attached to a four-poster. 2. A decorative treatment above a headboard.

**casing**—1. A hem or tuck through which ribbon, tape, cord, or elastic can be drawn. 2. Opening at the top of a curtain through which a rod is run.

**center line**—The vertical center of the bodice, skirt, or yoke section of a garment. It is designated on the pattern pieces and is transferred to the fabric sections with a basting thread.

**clip**—To cut a short distance into a seam allowance or selvage with the point of the scissors. Used in curved seams, square corners, buttonholes, and the like so that seams will lie flat when pressed.

**controlled fullness**—The gather-ing necessary on a long seam edge so that it can be joined to a shorter seam edge.

**crease**—1. A line or mark made by folding the fabric and pressing the fold. 2. The line or mark that may result when the manufacturer folds the fabric and rolls it on the bolt.

**crinoline**—A coarse, stiff, cotton fabric used to hold the heading erect in curtains and draperies and to give body to contour belts, and similar constructions.

**custom finish**—Perfection in fit and construction of garments, slipcovers, bedspreads, draperies, and the like.

**decorative stitching**—1. A zig-zag machine stitch that is ornamental in design. 2. Hand embroidery stitches.

**directional stitching**—Stitching of seams in the correct direction of the grain so that the fabric will not stretch during the stitching.

**drape**—1. A property many fabrics have of falling easily into graceful folds; a soft silk, for example. 2. An attractive arrangement of folds in a garment or window drapery. The folds may be controlled by means of gathers, tucks, or pleats.

**drop shoulder**—Shoulder line located below the normal line.

**ease**—The even distribution of fullness when one section of a seam is joined to a slightly shorter section without forming gathers or tucks. Used to shape set-in sleeves, the shoulder line, and other areas.

**ease allowance**—That amount added to body measurements to make garments more comfortable and allow for action.

*Many of the terms defined here are explained more fully in the text. Consult the alphabetical index.

**edgestitch**—1. To stitch close to a finished edge or seam from the right side of the fabric. 2. To stitch close to the edge of a fold after the fabric edge is turned to the underside. Used to finish the edge of hems and facings.

**emery cushion**—Small bag filled with an abrasive. Used to sharpen needles and remove rust.

**facing**—The second layer of fabric used to finish necklines, front and back openings, sleeves, and the like.

**featherbone**—A narrow strip of boning used to stiffen the seams and edges of closely fitted garment sections to prevent them from slipping or rolling; for example, the bodice of strapless dresses and cummerbunds.

**fibers**—Natural or man-made filaments from which yarns are spun.

**finishing**—The sewing techniques used in garment construction to finish seams, facings, hems, necklines, and other sections.

**fly**—A finished closing that conceals the zipper or buttons. Generally used in shorts, men's pants, and topcoats.

**footboard**—The upright board at the foot of a bed.

**grading seams**—See Seam blending, beveling, or grading.

**grain**—In woven fabrics, the lengthwise and crosswise direction of the yarn. The lengthwise yarn forms the lengthwise grain; the crosswise yarn, the crosswise grain. When these two threads or grains are at right angles, the fabric is "on the true grain."

**gusset**—A small shaped piece of matching fabric set into a slash or seam for added width and ease. Often found at the underarm when sleeve and bodice are cut-in-one.

**headboard**—The upright board at the head of a bed.

**heading**—1. A fabric tuck above the casing or at the top edge of curtains. 2. A narrow edge above a line of gathers that form a ruffle.

**hemline**—The line on which the hem is marked and turned to the underside. This line is an even distance from the floor.

**interfacing**—A third thickness of carefully selected fabric which is placed between the garment and facing fabrics for added body, shaping, and support.

**interlining**—A fabric placed between the lining and outer fabric. Used in coats, jackets, and the like to add warmth or bulk; in bedspreads to give body; in draperies to add body and to prevent light from showing through and fading the fabric.

**intersecting seams**—Seams that cross one another when garment sections are joined together at the waistline, shoulder line, set-in sleeve, and similar points.

**joinings**—The points at which one garment section is joined to another, such as skirt and bodice.

**lap**—To extend or fold one piece of fabric or garment section over another.

**lapel**—The section of a garment which is turned back between the top button and collar.

**layout**—The position in which pattern pieces are laid on the fabric for cutting.

**layering**—Another term for blending or beveling. See Seam blending, beveling, or grading.

**lining**—A carefully selected fabric that covers the underside of another fabric, adding body to the article. 1. In dress construction, the lining is cut the same as the dress fabric and constructed separately. It adds a finished look to the underside. 2. In tailoring, the lining is constructed to fit into the jacket or coat and prevents the unfinished seam allowance from showing. 3. In home decorating, the lining is used to finish the underside of draperies and protect the top fabric. It is also used in bedspreads.

**markings**—The symbols shown on the pattern for darts, buttonholes, tucks, and other construction details. They are transferred from the pattern to the fabric by means of tailor's tacks, chalk, bastings, or tracing wheel.

**mercerized**—A finish for cotton that adds strength and luster and makes the fabric more receptive of dyes.

**miter**—1. The diagonal line formed when fabric is joined at a square corner. After seaming, the excess fabric is generally cut away on the underside where the hems meet. Used where hems join at the corner as in a vent in a jacket, draperies, and linens. 2. The diagonal fold made when applying a band, lace, or the like to square or pointed shapes.

**multiple-stitch zig-zag**—See Zig-Zag stitches.

**notches**—V-shaped cutouts in the cut edge of the seam allowance that indicate which edges are to be seamed together. Matching notches are always joined.

**notions**—Small items used in sewing such as thread, needles, pins, buttons, and the like.

**overlap**—The part of the garment that extends over another part, as the opening of a blouse, jacket, coat, or waistband.

**pattern layout guide**—The instruction sheet that shows how

*(Continued)*

to arrange the pattern pieces on the fabric before cutting. It includes the most economical layout for different types and widths of fabrics and for the various pattern sizes.

**pattern stitching**—Zig-zag stitching of designs on a zig-zag machine which is made possible by setting selectors in a certain position or by inserting specific cams or discs.

**pivot**—To turn the fabric on the machine needle while the needle is still in the fabric. Used when stitching square corners such as in buttonholes, pockets, and notched sections.

**placket**—A finished opening that is generally closed by means of a zipper, snaps, or other fastening. Used in dresses, skirts, shorts, and other garments to make them easy to put on and to assure a good fit at the waistline, sleeve, etc.; also used in such fabric furnishings as slipcovers and cushions.

**preshrunk**—To shrink the fabric before cutting so that its dimensions will not be altered by laundering or dry cleaning. Many fabrics are preshrunk by the manufacturer.

**pressure**—The force the presser foot exerts on the fabric during the machine stitching. The pressure can—and should—be regulated to suit the fabric.

**ravel**—1. To separate or pull the woven threads away from the cut edges of the fabric, leaving long threads; to unweave. 2. To fray, as unfinished seam edges.

**reinforce**—To strengthen an area that will be subjected to strain. The area may be reinforced with an underlay or patch of fabric or with extra rows of stitching.

**regular stitch**—The machine stitch length best suited to the fabric being stitched;

usually applied to straight stitching.

**return**—In curtain and drapery fixtures, the distance from the curve of the rod to the wall. Curtains and draperies are constructed so that they extend around the return.

**revers**—Wide, shaped lapels on coats and suits.

**reversible**—Describing: 1. A fabric that is woven so that either side may be used for the right side—for example damask or double-faced wool. 2. A garment finished so that it may be worn with either side out.

**rip**—1. To remove machine stitching. 2. To tear, usually along the seam.

**sag**—To hang or droop below the normal line or level. A seam sags when it is stretched or pulled down from the normal position through weight of the fabric (for example, a bias seam).

**seam allowance**—The amount of fabric allowed for seams in joining sections of a garment or other article together—generally ⅝ inch.

**seam blending, beveling, or grading**—Trimming all seam allowances within a seam to different widths. Blending removes bulk so that the seam will lie flat.

**seam edge**—The cut edge of the seam allowance.

**seam finish**—The finish used on the edge of the seam allowance to prevent the fabric from raveling or fraying.

**seamline**—The line designated for stitching the seam—generally ⅝ inch from the cut edge.

**selvage**—The finished edges on all woven fabrics which parallel the lengthwise thread.

**shank**—The stem between the button and the garment to which the button is sewed. The shank can be made with thread or it can be a part of the button. It allows room for the buttonhole side of the garment to fit smoothly over the button.

**shrink**—To relax the fibers of the fabric through moisture or steam to prevent subsequent shrinking.

**sizing**—A finish applied to fabrics to add body and stiffness.

**slash**—A cut in the fabric along a straight line. A slash is longer than a clip. Examples are: a finished slit in a garment that is faced, and an opening into which a gusset is inserted.

**spanking**—Act of pounding or flattening fabric to shape a finished edge after it has been steam-pressed.

**stay**—A small piece of fabric or tape that is sewed to an area of the garment for reinforcement. Use at the point of a slash, under bound buttonholes, and at the waistline.

**stitch pattern**—See Pattern stitching.

**tack**—To attach one piece of fabric to another with tiny hand stitches—generally with several backstitches over the first stitch; for example, a facing to seam allowance.

**tailoring**—A method of sewing characterized by classic lines; encompasses suits, coats, dresses, and shorts.

**tailor's tacks**—Markings made of thread which are used to transfer symbols from the pattern to the fabric.

**tension**—The degree of looseness or tightness of the needle and bobbin threads that interlock to form the sewing machine stitch. There are two tensions

—the upper (needle thread) and the lower (bobbin thread). When the two are balanced, both the needle and the bobbin threads are drawn into the fabric to the same degree.

**thread count**—Number of threads (yarns) per inch in the warp and weft of woven fabric.

**underlap**—The edge of a garment that extends under another edge, as in the opening of a coat, jacket, or waistband.

**underlay**—1. A strip of fabric that is placed on the underside of the main fabric for reinforcement. Used in stitching buttonholes, pockets, and similar sections; in mending; in decorative zig-zag stitching. 2. A piece of fabric placed under finished shirring to prevent strain on the shirring stitches.

**underlining**—The second thickness of a carefully selected fabric which is cut by the same pattern as the garment and is stitched in place with the garment seams. Used to give added body and shape.

**up and down**—The direction of the nap, pile, or design of a fabric. On napped and pile fabrics, the shading varies depending on the angle from which the fabric is viewed. On prints, the design may run in one direction—for example, flowers with "heads up," or uneven plaids.

**vent**—A lapped opening. Used in hems of tailored jackets and sleeves and in other garment sections.

**warp**—The threads or yarns that run lengthwise in the weaving of the fabric.

**weft** (old term woof)—The threads or yarns that cross the warp. Also called "filler."

**zig-zag stitches:**

**blindstitch zig-zag**—A stitch pattern that produces four straight stitches separated by a single sideward stitch to the left. Used in finishing seam edges, in stitching hems, and in decorative stitching.

**closely spaced stitch pattern**—A decorative zig-zag stitch pattern that places all stitches close together when the stitch length selector is set for satin stitching.

**multiple-stitch zig-zag**—A stitch pattern that makes four stitches to the left, then four to the right in a zig-zag shape. Used to finish hem and seam edges, mend, stitch darts and seams in interfacing, and sew elastic and blanket binding in place; also used for decorative stitching and other sewing.

**open-spaced stitch pattern**—A decorative zig-zag stitch pattern that does not place the stitches close together although the stitch length selector is set for satin stitching.

**plain zig-zag stitch**—A regular zig-zag stitch where all stitches are of the same width and in a straight line. The stitch length and stitch width selectors may be set for various lengths and widths.

# Index

*(continued)*

*(continued)*

## index for "the many faces of knits"